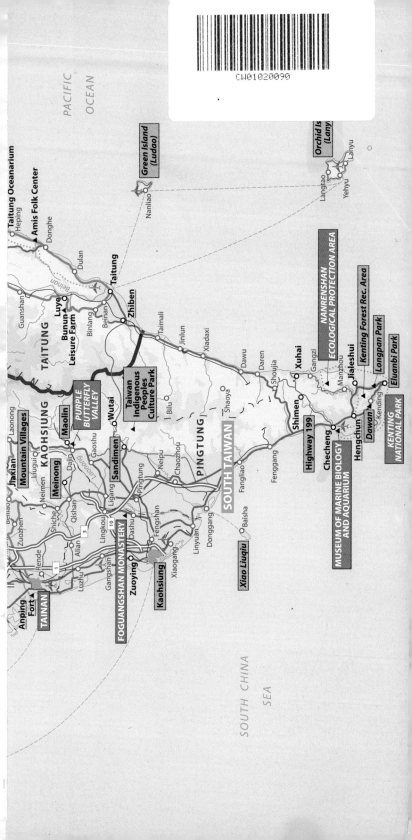

THEGREENGUIDE
Taiwan

Gate, Chiang Kai-shek Memorial Hall, Florent Bonnefoy/Michelin

General Manager   Cynthia Clayton Ochterbeck

THEGREENGUIDE **TAIWAN**

This guide has been produced with the contribution of the **Bureau de
Représentation de Taipei en France.**

Editorial Manager	Jonathan Gilbert
Project Manager	Florent Bonnefoy
Editor	Gwen Cannon
Contributing Writers	Florent Bonnefoy, Mark Caltonhill,
	Rick Charette, Brent Hannon, Linda Lee,
	Lisa Liang, Rich J. Matheson,
	Gabriel Monroe, Susannah Rosenblatt
Production Manager	Natasha G. George
Cartography	Matthew S. Tharp
Photo Editor	Yoshimi Kanazawa
Photo Researcher	Nicole D. Jordan
Proofreader	Sean Cannon
Interior Design	Chris Bell
Cover Design	Chris Bell, Christelle Le Déan
Layout	Nicole D. Jordan
Cover Layout	Michelin Apa Publications Ltd.

Contact Us	The Green Guide
	Michelin Maps and Guides
	One Parkway South, Greenville,
	SC 29615, USA
	www.michelintravel.com
	Michelin Maps and Guides
	Hannay House, 39 Clarendon Road
	Watford, Herts WD17 1JA, UK
	𝒫01923 205240. www.ViaMichelin.com
	travelpubsales@uk.michelin.com
Special Sales	For information regarding bulk sales,
	customized editions and premium sales,
	please contact our Customer Service
	Departments:
	USA 1-800-432-6277
	UK 01923 205240
	Canada 1-800-361-8236

HOW TO USE THIS GUIDE

PLANNING YOUR TRIP

The blue-tabbed PLANNING YOUR TRIP section gives you **ideas for your trip** and **practical information** to help you organize it. You'll find tours, practical information, a host of outdoor activities, a calendar of events, information on shopping, sightseeing, kids' activities and more.

INTRODUCTION

The orange-tabbed INTRODUCTION section explores Taiwan's **Nature** and geology. The **History** section spans from Prehistory through colonization up to today. The **Art and Culture and Cinema** section covers architecture, art, literature and music, while **Taiwan Today** delves into aspects of modern life.

DISCOVERING

The green-tabbed DISCOVERING section features Principal Sights by region, showcasing the most interesting local **Sights**, **Walking Tours**, nearby **Excursions**, and detailed **Driving Tours**. Admission prices shown are normally for a single adult.

ADDRESSES

We've selected the best hotels, restaurants, cafes, shops, nightlife and entertainment to fit all budgets. See the Legend on the front cover flap for an explanation of the price categories. See the back of the guide for an index of hotels and restaurants.

Sidebars

Throughout the guide you will find blue, orange and green-colored text boxes with lively anecdotes, detailed history and background information.

🌱 A Bit of Advice 🌱

Green advice boxes found in this guide contain practical tips and handy information relevant to the sight in the Discovering section.

STAR RATINGS ★★★

Michelin has given star ratings for more than 100 years. If you're pressed for time, we recommend you visit the ★★★ or ★★ sights first:

★★★	**Highly recommended**
★★	**Recommended**
★	**Interesting**

MAPS

🗺 Regional Driving Tours map, Places to Stay map and Sights map.

🗺 Region maps.

🗺 Maps for major cities and villages.

🗺 Local tour maps.

All maps in this guide are oriented north, unless otherwise indicated by a directional arrow. The term "Local Map" refers to a map within the chapter or Tourism Region. A complete list of the maps found in the guide appears at the back of this book.

© Ficent Bonnefoy/Michelin

INTRODUCTION TO TAIWAN

© Rich J. Matheson/Michelin

PLANNING YOUR TRIP

CONTENTS

DISCOVERING TAIWAN

Rich J. Matheson/Michelin

Welcome to Taiwan

Lying between Japan's southern Ryukyu Islands and the Philippines, this mountainous island nurtures a population descended from Han Chinese (partly Fujianese and Hakka) and aborigine. The Taiwanese people have put out the welcome mat for the world to discover their colorful temples, traditional festivals, lively processions, hot springs and spas, one very tall skyscraper, and shops carrying herbal medicines and high-tech gadgets.

TAIPEI AREA *(pp108-175)*

The island's political, economic and cultural heart, Taipei sits inland from Taiwan's northern coast, filling a wide basin backed by mountains. Its record-setting skyscraper Taipei 101 surveys the sprawling metropolis from an 89-floors-high observatory. Colorful Longshan Temple permits a peek into past imperial-era religion. Treasurehouse for art amassed by emperors over eons, the National Palace Museum opens its doors to all. Monuments to men and memorials to the masses neighbor roads with names like Herb Street and Snake Alley. Countless night markets entice experts and the uninitiated to taste a mind-boggling array of edible inventions. Just north, Beitou's hot springs beckon with a bounty of relaxing soaks and sophisticated cuisine. Yangming mountain's namesake national park promises trails, landscaped gardens and tourist farms. Sandy beaches along the coast lure leisure-seekers to a Pacific-ocean playground prepared for swimmers, surfers, sailors and sunbathers. City hills to the south sustain Muzha's thriving tea plantations, where rustic teahouses serve up splendid views with sips of tea.

NORTH TAIWAN *(pp176-215)*

The densely populated northern third of Taiwan is bounded by the Taiwan Strait on the west and Pacific Ocean on the east. The geographic east-west division created by the high mountains and rolling foothills of the Central Mountain Range is intensified by the ethnic diversity of aborigines, Hoklo, Hakka and recent immigrants from mainland China. This combination created distinctive characteristics of Yilan County and Keelung City to the east, Taipei City and County to the north, and Taoyuan, Hsinchu and Miaoli counties to the west. Despite being home to many of Taiwan's traditional and modern industries, as well as the cultural and economic center of Taipei, most visitors report their deepest memories are of north Taiwan's forest-clad mountains and dramatic coastlines.

CENTRAL TAIWAN *(pp216-261)*

Bordering Taiwan Strait and extending east into the mountains, Central Taiwan offers travelers a tasty banquet of touring delights. Taichung, its cultural capital, is a pleasant city known for teahouses, well-regarded museums and fine weather. Its historical capital, the coastal city

Taipei

Florent Bonnefoy/Michelin

of Lugang, is home to atmospheric temples and Qing-era architecture. In the green foothills farther east, turquoise-blue Sun Moon Lake serves up a non-stop feast of boating, bicycling, and temple touring. Tall interior mountains are threaded with tempting roads that skirt the peaks and access trails, tiny villages and tea and betelnut plantations. Farther south Alishan Recreation Area's allure is its beloved sea of clouds sunrise, while nearby Yushan National Park preserves perhaps the best piece of wilderness on the island.

Wulai, North Taiwan
Mark Caltonhill/Michelin

SOUTH TAIWAN (pp262-311)

Taiwan's southern tip hosts tropical Kenting, whose golden sand beaches and lush junglescapes rapidly give way to Mount Northern Dawu, Taiwan's southernmost peak above 3,000m/9,842ft. The Central Mountains continue northward through the villages of Sandimen, Maolin and Namasia where aboriginals dwell amid winding rivers, lofty mountains and valleys filled with exotic butterflies. In the foothills, Meinong's Hakka culture flourishes alongside golden rice fields. Farther north, magnificent Foguangshan monastery overlooks the Gaoping River basin. A string of fishing and farming villages, the fertile west coast soon recedes as Kaohsiung, Taiwan's second-largest city, bisected by the Love River, looms. Off its coast Xiao Liuqiu is an idyllic island retreat. Taiwan's oldest city, Tainan is rich in temples and tradition.

EAST COAST (pp312-353)

Far from the congested cities lining western Taiwan, the island's East Coast boasts a rugged beauty, a land of strong aboriginal heritage where mountains and valleys meet the sea. The region is home to the soaring marble cliffs of Taiwan's majestic Taroko National Park, arguably the island's premier attraction. Dramatic coastline dotted with striking rock formations connects the area's two main cities, the laid-back marble city of Hualien to the north and Taitung, home to Taiwan's first archaeological park, to the south. Just inland, the fertile East Rift Valley unfurls a dazzling patchwork of farmland supporting crops of rice, pineapple, betel nut and tea.

Offshore lie the solitary outposts of Green Island, a former political prison and now a diver's paradise, as well as Orchid Island, where the Tao people preserve their tribal traditions.

TAIWAN STRAIT ISLANDS
(pp354-373)

Three remarkable archipelagos defy the windy Taiwan Strait. Mazu, in the distant northwest near mainland China, holds high granite outcroppings, distinctive culture and military remnants, a historic vestige it shares with the Kinmen islands to the south, which are also near the Fujian Province coast. Penghu anchors the middle of the stormy strait. Here the archipelago has carved out a reputation for fresh seafood, Qing-era temples and scenic natural beauty.

Palanquin, Bao'an Temple, Taipei
© Florent Bonnefoy/Michelin

Michelin Driving Tours

Additional driving tours are described in the Discovering Taiwan section and shown on the regional maps.

1 NORTH COAST: WEST TO EAST

Map inside front cover. 132km/82mi on Highway 2, from Danshui.

This itinerary traces the northern coastline of Taiwan, showcasing its beaches, unusual rock formations and seaside towns. Overlooking the Danshui River, the colorful town of **Danshui**★★★, northwest of Taipei, initiates the tour. As the highway meets the coast, **Shalun,** a handy summer retreat for Taipei residents, appears. But a better swimming beach some 10km/6mi farther is **Baishawan Beach,** a surfer's haven where lifeguards closely monitor swimmers. The road rounds **Fugui Cape,** with its views of the Pacific, en route to **Jinshan Beach,** which also draws large summer crowds. Two well-known hot springs lie not far from the little town of **Jinshan.** Almost next door to the eerie rock shapes at **Yeliu**★★ is **Ocean World**★, where dolphin and seal shows entertain the crowds. With its busy harbor, the large port city of **Keelung**★ serves as the gateway to the scenic Northeast Coast. Jutting into the ocean, the cape at **Bitou**★ is recognizable by its 40ft lighthouse and mushroom-like outcroppings atop eroded cliffs. **Longdong** boasts the oldest exposed rock layers of the Northeast Coast National Scenic Area; its high cliffs attract avid rock climbers, **Yanliao** may have the longest of the northern beaches, but **Fulong Beach**★, just south, rates as the most popular, with its golden sands and blue waters. **Fulong** is the northern terminus of the 8.5km/5.3mi-long historic **Caoling Trail**★★, which offers spectacular views of the coastline. The trail ends in the village of **Daxi,** facing the surfers' haunt of **Honeymoon Bay**. The tour finishes in the township of **Toucheng,** whose beach attracts fewer crowds than Fulong's. Offshore the volcanic island of **Guishan**★★, once a military post, is seen.

2 CENTRAL CROSS-ISLAND HIGHWAY: WEST TO EAST

Map inside front cover. 293km/182mi on Highways 8, 21,14 and 14A, from Fengyuan on Highway 3.

Filled with scenic wonders, this hair-raising drive through the forested mountains of Central Taiwan begins in Taichung County. It cuts through fertile plains and gentle foothills before tackling the perilous route amid the fog-bound peaks of Mt. Hehuanshan and carving through magnificent Taroko Gorge to reach the East Coast. From **Fengyuan,** the county capital, Hwy. 3 turns east and parallels the Dajia River near Shigang. The road crosses the river before meeting **Dongshi**, a stronghold of the Hakka. From Dongshi, Hwy. 8 heads south as it exchanges the fertile plains for the foothills. After Chenggong, watch for Hwy. 21 and take it south through Daping. Follow Hwy. 21 as it heads east through Meizilin, then southeast to Niumian. Farther south, the town of **Puli** sits in a lovely valley within a region of mountains and

---

😊 Touring Tip 😊

Because of the crowds, summer is not the ideal time to drive along the north coast or south coast, but it is one of the best times to take the mountain routes. However, heavy seasonal rains (late May-early Sept) can result in rockslides. Taiwan's sophisticated typhoon-warning system sends out alerts two to three days in advance.

Before setting out, check the weather report and the latest road conditions by calling the Tourism Bureau's 24hr toll-free hotline in English: 0800-011765.

lakes. A center of Buddhism, it boasts several temples and the monumental **Chung Tai Chan Monastery**★★★. From Puli, Hwy. 14 leads northeast to the aboriginal community of Wushe within Renai Township. Just beyond, a spur road permits access to a resort area centered on **Lushan Hot Springs**★. From Wushe, Hwy. 14 becomes 14A. After passing Yushi, the route turns north to the popular **Cingjing Farm**★, where visitors enjoy ice cream made from sheep's milk. Hwy. 14A then climbs steeply in a northeasterly direction to elevations of 9,000ft and higher amid the grasslands of Kunyang and the slopes of fog-enshrouded **Mount Hehuanshan** (11,000ft). At **Dayuling**, Hwy. 8 begins its eastward thrust, as the road narrows into a series of stomach-churning curves above the ice-blue waters of the **Liwu River** and slices through the marble canyons of **Taroko Gorge**★★★.

③ SOUTH CROSS-ISLAND HIGHWAY

Map inside front cover. 209km/130mi via Highway 20, from Tainan. Some sights might be closed due to a 2009 typhoon; check first with the Tourism Bureau.
This west-east traverse through Taiwan's Central Mountains is a white-knuckled but thrilling ride to the East Coast, awarding those who make the challenging drive with hot springs, aboriginal villages and stunning vistas along the way. After Yongkang and Xinhua, Hwy. 20 forks at Zuozhen. The southern route leads to Nanhua, and farther east, to the village of **Jiaxian**★. At Laonong, the highway begins to parallel the scenic valley of the **Laonong River.** Near Gaozhong, the road starts an ascent that eventually reaches almost 9,000ft. A string of hot springs dot the stretch leading to the southwest edge of **Yushan National Park**★. The aboriginal settlement of **Taoyuan** boasts several natural springs. Home to another tribal community, **Meishan** serves as a park entrance, complete with a visitor

center. Then begins a windy but scenic climb of some 4,000ft to Tianchih. Just east of the **Daguanshan Tunnel**, the highest elevation of the route is reached at **Yakou**. If not obscured by fog, views from this 8,960ft height are spectacular. On the descent, the aboriginal village of **Lidao** offers visitor amenities. The prized but remote **Lisong Hot Springs** lie nearby. Passing through the dramatic Wulu Gorge, the road approaches **Wulu,** another tribal community with overnight accommodations. Hwy. 20 ends at Hwy. 9, near **Haiduan,** a sizable Bunun community.

④ EAST COAST LOOP

Map inside front cover. 119km/74mi via Hwys. 11 and 9, from Hualien.
This north-south circuit affords splendid views of the ocean and mountains along **Highway 11**★★ as the road edges Taiwan's dramatic **East Coast** from the "marble city" of **Hualien** south to **Taitung**, gateway to **Green Island**★★ and **Orchid Island**★★, before heading inland to Binlang for a northward run along **Highway 9**★ through the fertile **East Rift Valley** back to Hualien. Aboriginal farms, hot springs and white-water rafting add to the fun. *For a description of the drive, see the East Coast chapter.*

Longpan Park, Kenting Area
Rich J. Matheson/Michelin

When and Where to Go

WHEN TO GO
SEASONS

Taiwan has a **subtropical climate** in the North and a **tropical** one in the South, so travelers should be prepared to face hot and humid weather when visiting here. The island is also subject to local typhoons (July-October) and sometimes earthquakes. It is tricky to speak of spring and autumn per se, since Taiwan basically experiences a humid, or **wet**, **season** and a **dry season**. Taiwan's moody weather also brings sudden changes when temperatures can drop or rise by 10°C/50°F overnight.

Wet Season

Visiting Taiwan in the first months of the humid season (March-May) is a gamble; you will find either clear and sunny weather or gray skies and rain. May and June is the period of the year called *meiyu* (梅雨)—literally meaning "plum rain." This poetic term refers to the East Asian rainy season, what could be called **spring**. From June to September, it's the summer monsoon period. Cities become hot and sticky—partly because of air pollution—so visiting the East Coast or the mountains to find cooler weather would be advisable.

Dry Season

The dry season starts in November and ends in March. October and November are usually the best periods to visit the island. **Winters** are quite mild, especially in the South, where they are warm and dry. In Taipei the temperature rarely drops below 12°C/53°F. Northern Taiwan and the mountain areas experience a winter monsoon from October to March.

TYPHOONS

The *taifengs* (meaning "great winds" in Mandarin Chinese) regularly hit the east coast of the island. The **typhoon season** lasts from mid-July to early October. In general, no more than heavy rains and strong winds occur, but once every three or four years, the season brings "real" typhoons carrying destructive force. When they occur, sea-level cities can be flooded; coastal towns and inland cities may experience landslides and other hazards (commercial billboards and scooters can be blown away). However, be reassured: **typhoon alerts** are broadcast two or three days in advance by the Central Weather Bureau (www.cwb.gov.tw), which keeps the population updated on the latest information about the intensity, evolution and route of the typhoon.

WHAT TO PACK

No matter what time of year you travel to Taiwan, make sure to pack reliable rain gear. If you forget, inexpensive umbrellas can be found in convenience stores like 7-Eleven, which are located throughout the island. During the humid season, women and men alike would be wise to forego jeans and wear cotton or linen clothing instead, which is far more comfortable. During the dry season, warmer clothes are a must.

	AVERAGE TEMPERATURES			
City	Annual	January	July	Average annual rainfall
Taipei	22°C/71°F	16°C/61°F	29°C/84°F	2,413mm
Hualien	23°C/73°F	18°C/64°F	28°C/82°F	2,124mm
Kaohsiung	25°C/77°F	19°C/66°F	29°C/84°F	1,832mm
Hengchun	25°C/77°F	20°C/68°F	28°C/82°F	1,980mm

Source: Central Weather Bureau, Ministry of Transportation and Communications (2008)

If you plan to travel around the island, pack a pair of outdoor sneakers or hiking boots. And don't forget your swimsuit: Taiwan has lots of hot springs.

IDEAS FOR YOUR VISIT
TASTE TAIWAN: THREE-CUPS CHICKEN TO PEARL TEA

Food is a major motivating factor for travel to the island. Cuisine in Taiwan is an art, and food lovers and gourmands will find it is definitely worth the trip to taste what is considered the most refined Chinese cuisine in the world. Due to its history, Taiwan offers all the cuisines of China, such as Cantonese, Sichuanese, Beijing and Shanghainese. In Taiwan these regional dishes are cooked with a twist by adding more spices and flavors from Southeast Asia. A typical local delicacy, which originated in Jiangxi Province on mainland China, is **three-cups chicken**, chicken cooked with soy sauce, sesame oil and rice wine. In addition to Chinese cuisine, Southeast Asian and Japanese cuisines are served in restaurants all over the island. Taiwan is a culinary melting pot, offering foods that range from haute cuisine to Taiwanese snacks that are celebrated throughout Asia. Every year a competition is held to find the best **beef noodles** on the island. While strolling in the night markets, you may come across a peculiar smell, which, no doubt, will repel you: **stinky tofu** well deserves its name, but many people like it, in the same manner as malodorous French cheeses. Another common snack is the savory **oyster omelet** made of absolutely sea-fresh oysters. Snacks in **Keelung** in Northern Taiwan are known island-wide for the freshness of their sea food and the uniqueness of their taste. Gourmands will enjoy fried oysters, spearfish and shrimp chowder, as well as **braised eel** in a brown sauce. In Southern Taiwan, the city of **Tainan**★★★ offers a variety of snacks, from the **coffin-sandwich**, invented by fishermen to endure the

Maokong teahouse

Florent Bonnefoy/Michelin

slack season, to braised pork noodles. A world-famous beverage hailing from **Taichung**★ is the unrivaled **pearl milk tea**, brewed with black tea, milk and chewy sago pearls.

TEA PLANTATIONS

Taiwan's famous tea culture would make a good theme for your trip. Some of the best **oolongs** (烏龍) are grown in the area of Chiayi. On the outskirts of Taipei, **Maokong** in **Muzha**★★★ district, with its lovely teahouses, are both ideal retreats for tea lovers. Farther afield from Taipei County, **Wulai**★★ and Pingling are smaller, rural communities in the mountains that offer lots of tea farms and a strong tea culture. Tea fans can also head to the must-see city of **Lugu**★ in Nantou County in Central Taiwan. This city is surrounded by a great many farms situated within scenic mountain landscapes. The **Sun Moon Lake**★★ region is worth visiting for its black Assam tea farms as well as its lake views and aboriginal villages. World-famous tea company Ten Ren operates a pleasant tea museum in **Zhunan**, near Hsinchu on the northwest coast. Hsinchu and Miaoli counties grow one of the most famous, and most expensive, Taiwanese teas: the Oriental Beauty Oolong (also known as Baihao wulong

15

in Mandarin Chinese), a rare variety famous for its sweetness. Some of Taiwan's tea farms, such as those in Muzha and at Sun Moon Lake, welcome the public; the government tea research station at Yichih in the Sun Moon Lake region has an exhibit on tea processing.

FROM TEMPLES TO TEMPLES

Visitors will be struck by the amount of activity and liveliness that occurs at places of worship in Taiwan.
One of the most interesting temples is located in **Taipei**★★★, itself, **Longshan Temple**★★★ in Taipei City. **Zhinan Gong** in the Maokong district south of Taipei is also definitely worth a visit. Buddhist architecture fans will think they have found heaven at **Shitoushan**★, which hosts several temples, or at **Tainan**★★★, the oldest city in Taiwan; it's essential to visit at least three of Tainan's hundreds of temples.
The **temple of Confucius**★★★, the oldest and most beautiful temple on the island, enjoys a quiet and peaceful atmosphere. The **Dongyue Temple** enshrines a sobering wall painting that illustrates, in great detail, the sufferings in hell. Last but not least, the **Nankunshen Temple**★★★, north of Tainan, attracts people each year for an exuberant festival that includes exorcism.

One of Taiwan's most important religious events is the annual **Mazu Pilgrimage** during the third month of the lunar calendar. Mazu, the sea goddess of Fujian Province, migrated to Taiwan in the 17C with the Fujianese people. She has become the most revered deity in Taiwan; more than 870 temples are dedicated to her. To observe the oldest and the largest celebration, head to **Dajia** (Taichung County) to see festivities prepared to welcome the procession: puppet and theater performances, float parades, and **dragon and lion dances**. The procession moves from Dajia to Xingang (Chiayi County) and back to Dajia over a period of 9 days and 8 nights. The return journey to Dajia, when Mazu's statue is brought back on her palanquin to her shrine, isn't any less lively; devotees are heartily welcomed by their families and friends on their way back home. For more information on this celebration, access www.dajiamazu.org.tw.

HOT SPRINGS

There are more than 100 hot springs in Taiwan, the highest concentration located in Northern Taiwan. Relaxing and beneficial, they are believed to be of therapeutic value, and can be found in geographical areas throughout the island. When the Japanese occupied Taiwan, they brought with them

Rich J. Matheson /Michelin

Jiajiang troupe, Nankunshen Temple

their bath culture. In 1884 the first hot springs hotel was opened by a Japanese man in **Beitou**★★★, and since then hot spring resorts have spread all over Taiwan. Hot springs are usually found in pleasant settings, so when bathers soak, they will enjoy a calming view of nature. There's nothing better to help forget about hectic city life.

The most accessible hot springs are located in Beitou, in Taipei's most northern district. There, you'll find charming Japanese-style bathhouses along with stylish meals. Known as "beauty baths," the hot springs at **Wulai**★★ claim to smooth the skin. The water of the region is clear, odorless and thought to be health-enhancing. **Jiaoxi**★ in Yilan County is one of the few lowland hot springs sites. Rain water fills the springs, which are heated by the magma of nearby volcanic **Guishan Island**★★. In the wet season, many people prefer to head to the mountains to soak in, for example, the **Taian** hot springs resort, which is reached by a narrow, winding mountain road and surrounded by the Henglong, Niaozui and Huzi mountains. Discovered by the Atayal people and developed by the Japanese, the resort has managed to preserve a traditional atmosphere.

RAIL TOURS

A great way to tour the island is by train. Taiwan railway lines circle the coasts (West Coast Trunk Railway, East Coast Trunk Railway, North-Link Railway and South-Link Railway). Each of the routes of the four lines features distinct characteristics and scenery. Winding between mountains and rivers, they allow passengers to discover scenes invisible from the highway. Round-the-island tickets can be purchased for visitors who would like to travel extensively in Taiwan. Special tourist trains have been designed with comfortable seats as well as salons and dining cars; riders can even sing in the karaoke room. Along with the main lines, several

lesser lines like the **Jiji Branch Railway**★★ and the **Alishan Forest Railway**★★★ take passengers to bucolic settings and historic sites.

Ride the "Gaotie"

One way to get a grand overview of Taiwan's west coast within a few days is to travel by the **High Speed Rail**. Departing from **Taipei**★★★, the train runs along the shore and stops in the main coastal cities. The first stop is **Hsinchu**★★, a convenient base to visit the surrounding mountains. Next city on the route, **Taichung**★ is a nice getaway for people living in Taipei, since it has lots of cafes, teahouses and shops, and for visitors, two high quality museums. Next on the line, **Chiayi** is the gateway to the **Alishan Forest Recreation Area**★. If you don't plan to hike, you can go straight to **Tainan**★★★, the most ancient city in Taiwan, where hundreds of temples await visitors as well as an incredible array of snacks and other delicacies. The final stop on the line, **Kaohsiung**★★ is a modern metropolis—and a definite shock after the cultural treasures and slower pace of old Tainan. The second largest city on the island was totally transformed by 2009 in time to host the **World Games**. *Trains departs Taipei every 30min from 6:30am to 10pm and reach Zuoying station (north of Kaohsiung) in about 2hrs. For details, access www. thsrc.com.tw.*

BUS TOURS

Offering some 30 tours, the **Taiwan Tour Bus** will take visitors on a one-day trip to practically anywhere in Taiwan. There are tours for Taipei and other cities, as well as for outlying regions such as **Sun Moon Lake**★★. Only a few tours are available in English, but you can take the Chinese tour and still admire the scenery. Tours in English include a half-day **Taipei City**★★★ tour, a one-day tour to **Yangmingshan**★★★ and hot springs resorts, and a one-day tour to **Jiufen**★ and the Northeast Coast. For more

Shakadang Trail, Taroko National Park

Susannah Rosenblatt/Michelin

information, contact the company itself: ☏886-2-2349-1500. www.taiwantourbus.com.tw.

NATIONAL PARKS

Taiwan is a great place to hike, and the island offers a large choice of national parks for that purpose. Just a stone's throw from Taipei, **Yangmingshan National Park**★★★ is famous for its volcanic landscapes. On the East Coast, the dramatic **Taroko Gorge**★★★ consists of remarkable marble canyons, a must-see sight. Hikers will love the mountain scenery of Shei Pa National Park and **Yushan National Park**★ **(Jade Mountain**★★**)**, while beach lovers will want to head to **Kenting National Park**★★★—a small piece of Southeast Asia in Taiwan—or the Dongsha atoll, formed of coral and shells that harbor abundant marine life. Also known as Quemoy, the island of **Kinmen**★ bordering China's mainland coast has recently been opened to tourists. *For general information about the parks: http://np.cpami.gov.tw.* Contact information for each park follows:

◆ **Yangmingshan**
No. 1–20, Zhuzihu Rd., Beitou District, Yangmingshan, Taipei City
☏886-2-2861-3601
www.ymsnp.gov.tw

◆ **Taroko**
291 Fuxi Village, Xiulin Township

Hualien County
☏886-3-8621576
www.taroko.gov.tw

◆ **Shei Pa**
100 Shuiweiping, Fuxing Village, Dahu Township, Miaoli County
☏886-37-996100
www.spnp.gov.tw

◆ **Kinmen (Quemoy)**
No. 460, Sec. 2, Boyu Rd., Jinning Shiang, Kinmen
☏886-82-313100
www.kmnp.gov.tw

◆ **Yushan**
No. 515, Sec. 1, Zhongshan Rd., Shuili Township, Nantou County
☏886-49-2773121
www.ysnp.gov.tw

◆ **Kenting**
No.596, Kenting Rd., Hengchun Township, Pingtung County
☏886-8-8861321
www.ktnp.gov.tw

◆ **Dongsha Atoll**
No. 24, Demin Rd., Nanzih District, Kaohsiung City
☏886-7-3601898
http://dongsha.cpami.gov.tw

◆ **Taijiang**
No. 2, Chengping Rd., Anping District, Tainan City,
☏886-6-300-0001
www.ymsnp.gov.tw
Newly founded, this park lies in Southwest Taiwan, off the coast of Tainan. http://np.cpami.gov.tw.

What to See and Do

BEACHES

The northern and southern coasts of Taiwan are blessed with sandy beaches lying off the Pacific Ocean. Offering a variety of water sports and places to stay, these beaches are popular with the locals, especially on summer weekends. Swimming is possible from April (in the south) or May (in the north) to October, when the water temperatures average 25°C/77°F. Several beaches charge entry fees, but those that charge have on-site amenities such as changing rooms, snack bars and equipment-rental facilities.

One of the most attractive beaches in northeast Taiwan is **Fulong Beach**★; its calm waters are ideal for swimming and boating. Adjacent Yanliao, home of **Yanliao Seaside Park,** is the north's longest beach. Up the coast, the beach at **Feicui Wan** (Green Bay) appeals to fans of sailing, surfing, parasailing and even hang-gliding; equipment rental is available at the Green Bay Seashore Recreation Club *(entry fee: see below).* **Jinshan Beach**, west of Keelung City, is another favorite for weekend excursions from Taipei; it doubles as a hot-springs resort (*see Wellness,*

> ### 😊 Touring Tip 😊
>
> When swimming and playing in the ocean, beware of undertow and strong currents; weak swimmers should stay close to shore. Many of Taiwan's beaches do not have lifeguards on duty, so take extra care when swimming.

below). One of the nearest beaches to Taipei, **Baishawan**, a strip of white sand, attracts swimmers and waders. At the tip of the island, **Kenting National Park**★★★, an hour's drive south of Kaohsiung, enjoys warmer weather and is Taiwan's most extensive beach retreat. The area's bays, fronted by sandy beaches, offer opportunities for recreation (water-sports equipment rentals available on-site). You'll find snack bars, a boardwalk (at Xiao Wan), and a boisterous night market along the town of Kending's main drag. **Taitung, Hualien** and **Yilan**★★ counties, which occupy the island's sparsely populated east coast, are known for their scenery. Offshore islands like **Green Island**★★ and **Orchid Island**★★. in the Pacific Ocean, or the **Penghu archipelago**★★ (also known as the Pescadores) in the Taiwan Strait, are Taiwan's tropical beach paradises. These offshore islands require more

Shadao Beach, Kenting

Rich J. Matheson/Michelin

😊 Touring Tip 😊

A large and welcoming island, Taiwan offers a host of cultural and geographical attractions. Travel agents, visitor centers or your hotel staff can provide information and help schedule tours.

of a commitment to visit, but make up for the effort with pristine waters and beaches, a distinctive local culture and a laid-back ambience.

Feicui Wan's Green Bay Seashore Recreation Club

The beach is operated by Howard Beach Resort Green Bay. Open May–Oct. NT$500, child $300. 17 Feitsui Rd., Wanli Township, Taipei County. ☎886-2-2492-6565, http://greenbay.howard-hotels.com.

MARTIAL ARTS

Popular in Taiwan, martial arts clubs include not only traditional Chinese martial arts, but also imports like taekwondo; Japanese aikido, kendo and karate; and Brazillian ju jitsu. Many forms of kung fu, especially the deliberate breathing-focused movements of tai chi, are practiced outdoors in public parks. If you are interested in joining a group, ask them

respectfully. Most Chinese martial arts are taught in Chinese, but it's possible to find English-speaking teachers. For more information and lessons:

Lo Man Kam Wingchun Federation 盧文錦詠春總會

4Fl, No. 31, Alley 51, Lane 12, Sec. 3 Bade Rd., Taipei City. ☎886-2-2578-2405 Instructors in Taipei, Taichung and Changhua teach the martial-art system developed by Yip Man, the master who taught Bruce Lee. International instructors teach regular classes in Taipei. www.lomankam-wingchun.org.tw (Chinese only). Contact for instructors: www.lomankam-wingchun.org.tw/Declaration.htm

Yoseikan Budo

This system is a New Age mix of Japanese martial arts taught in English. No. 45-2, Lane 46, Sec. 1, Zhiyuan Rd., Beitou District, Taipei City. ☎886-2-2828-7978 or 2822-3019, www.budoasia.com

Taiwan Karate Association 中華民國台灣空手道協會

B1/F, No. 1, Lane 235, Yanji St., Daan District, Taipei City. ☎886-2-2702-9524, www.skif.org.tw (Chinese only)

Ling Yun Wuguan 嶺雲武館

This studio teaches Chinese martial arts in the tradition of Chen Pan Ling. No. 75, Zongming Rd., West District, Taichung City. ☎886-4-2316-9527 www.chenpanling.com

MUSEUMS

Taiwan offers dozens of diverse museums and cultural institutions. In Taipei more than 100 museums include the **National Palace Museum★★★**, which showcases a vast collection of Chinese art and rare books, the **Taipei Fine Arts Museum★** and the **Museum of History★**. The **Shung Ye Museum of Formosan Aborigines★★** exhibits artifacts from the island's indigenous peoples. Kaohsiung, Taiwan's second-largest city, has a **Museum**

Museum of History, Taipei

Florent Bonnefoy/Michelin

of History★ as well as a **Fine Arts Museum**★★. Taichung, the third-largest city, is home to the **Museum of Natural Science**★★. Outside these cultural centers, many other museums of merit range from the **Museum of Taiwan Literature**★★ in Tainan and the **Museum of Prehistory**★ in Taitung to the **Miniatures Museum of Taiwan**★, the **Yingge Ceramics Museum**★ and the **Sanyi Wood Sculpture Museum**★. In recent years, the government has allocated significant resources to promote Taiwan's indigenous cultures and customs, as reflected in the **Taiwan Indigenous Peoples Culture Park**★★. A must-see near Sun Moon Lake is the **Formosan Aboriginal Culture Village**★★.

OUTDOOR FUN

Despite being one of the most densely populated countries in the world, Taiwan enjoys relatively unspoiled natural beauty. Aside from Taiwan's excellent urban parks and beaches, the rugged, mountainous rural parts of the island are well worth exploring—be it by car, foot, boat or hang-glider.

BIKING

While the buzzing hordes of motorbikes discourage many from cycling in Taiwan's cities, riding a **trail bike** or **mountain bike** along the coastline or in the mountains offers great scenery and good exercise. The native brand, **Giant**, ranks among the world's top bicycle manufacturers, and bicycles are available for rent all over the island. Scenic trails snake through riverside parks in major cities, while an extensive network of mountain-biking paths weaves through the island's mountainous suburbs. The most famous scenic areas, **Sun Moon Lake**★★, **Taroko Gorge**★★★ and **Kenting National Park**★★★, are all explorable by bicycle. Taipei alone has 120km/75mi of designated bike paths, several of

Bicycle parking

Florent Bonnefoy/Michelin

them along the city's rivers. Kaohsiung has seven official paths, some with harbor or river views; more paths are under construction. For maps and more information on these and bike trails throughout the island, access www.cycletaiwan.com.

For a more challenging adventure, the three **cross-island highways** (North, Central and South) are recommended for long-distance road-bike enthusiasts. This mountainous terrain has many blind curves, is susceptible to rockslides, and is often closed to vehicular traffic during the autumn typhoon season, so check with officials well in advance before heading out (see Monsoon Driving in Getting There and Getting Around).

BIRDING

The country's lush vegetation and tropical climate constitute a haven for more than 400 species of birds, many of which are migratory. Resident species include Black-faced spoonbills, kingfishers, owls, Indian black eagles and Taiwan partridges. The best observation sites are Taiwan's national parks, many of which—like **Yangmingshan National Park**★★★—have designated bird-watching trails. **Kenting National Park**★★★ has a birding center. Books, maps and online bird-watching

Touring Tip

Before you hike, ask at the national park headquarters about weather and trail conditions. Stick to the marked route. Tell someone you know where and when you plan to hike. Take drinking water and protective rainwear; and wear sturdy, weatherproof hiking shoes or boots.

resources in English and Chinese are plentiful. For a selection of good birding places in Taipei, pick up a copy of the colorfully illustrated *Birdwatcher's Guide to the Taipei Region* by Rick Charette (Taipei City Government, 2004).

GOLF

Taiwan has dozens of golf courses— and many more driving ranges— most on the outskirts of urban centers. Most golf clubs are open to the public and require only a guest membership to play (expect high fees). Danshui's historic **Taiwan Golf and Country Club** (台灣高爾夫俱樂部), built by the Japanese in 1919, was the island's first golf course.

The Orient Golf & Country Club
東方高爾夫球場
  100, Dongfang, Quichang Rd. Guishan Xiang, Taoyuan County. ✆(03) 350 0506, http://orient.golf.net.tw

National Garden Golf Course
全國高爾夫花園球場
  1-1 Shizhen Lin, Yuanli Zhen, Miaoli County. ✆(037) 743 377, www.nggc.tw/en

Kaohsiung Golf & Country Club
高雄高爾夫球場
  270 Qiuchang Rd., Dahua Cun, Wusong Xiang, Kaohsiung County. ✆(07) 370 1101

For an extensive list of courses in English, access the following websites:

- www.golftoday.co.uk/clubhouse/coursedir/world/taiwan
- www.worldgolf.com/courses/taiwgcs.html
- www.golfworldmap.com/asia/taiwan
- http://golf.all-hotels.com/east_asia/taiwan/home.htm

HIKING

With eight National Parks, eighteen National Forest Recreation Areas and fourteen National Scenic Areas, Taiwan is a hiker's paradise. More than sixty percent of the island is mountainous and forested, and the government has dedicated large areas specifically for recreation. A multitude of trails suitable for all levels of hikers includes the famous 8km/5mi **Caoling Historic Trail**★★ along Taiwan's spectacular Northeast Coast, as well as trails at **Yangmingshan National Park**★★★, **Taroko National Park**★★★ and **Sun Moon Lake**★★. Most park headquarters have brochures, trail maps and mountain-entry permits.

WATER SPORTS

Boating/Kayaking

Kayaking, particularly sea kayaking, is popular in Taiwan, and all the recreational beaches rent kayaks. Serious kayakers can also try their hand at the island's many rivers and mountain streams.

Options for leisure cruises range from rivers like the **Danshui** and the **Keelung** in the Taipei area to **Sun Moon Lake**★★ and **Taroko Gorge**★★★.

For Diving/Snorkeling, Swimming and Windsurfing, see Beaches (above).

Water Parks

Formosa Fun Coast 八仙海岸
  1-6, Xiaguzi, 1 Lin, Xiagu Cun, Bali Xiang, Taipei County.✆(02) 2610 5200, www.fww.com.tw

Yamay Recreation World
月眉育樂世界
  115 Anmei Rd., Houli Xiang, Taichung County. ✆0800 054 080,

www.yamay.com.tw. Open
year-round Mon–Fri 9am–9pm;
Sat–Sun 8:30am–9pm. Mala Water
Park: NT$700.

WELLNESS
HOT SPRINGS

Taiwan's hot springs are soaking spots
popular with residents and visitors
who are drawn to the therapeutic
properties of the springs' minerals.
*For a sampling of hot springs in
Taiwan, see When and Where to Go.*

SPAS

From moderately priced massage
centers to expensive full-service
spas, Taiwan offers a spa experience
for everyone. Taiwan's therapeutic
mineral hot springs are a perfect
complement to any spa treatment.

Taipei

The Horizon Spa 雲天芳泉水療館
40/F, Far Eastern Hotel, 201
Dunhua S. Rd., Sec. 2, Taipei City.
℘02-2376 3165 or 02-2378 8888.
www.shangri-la.com.
This jewel in the crown of **Shangri-
La**'s downtown Taipei hotel offers a
luxury lineup of facilities, including
an outdoor pool and a salon with
aromatherapy and massage services.

Miramar Spa 美麗信花園酒店
2/F, Miramar Garden Hotel, 83
Civic Blvd., Sec. 3, Taipei City.
℘02-8772 8800, ext 2255. www.
miramargarden.com.tw.
Inventive treatments here include
an Indian energy stone massage
(NT$4,350/70min); a mud body wrap
(NT$ 6,250/70min); aromatherapy
(NT$3,950/70min) and more.

Wellspring
41 Zhongshan North Rd., Sec. 2,
Taipei City. ℘02-2523 8000.
www.regenthotels.com/hotels/
ritpe/services/1.
With a menu of massages, skin
polishings, body wraps and facials,
this hotel spa is one of the best spas
in Taiwan.

Sun Moon Lake
The Lalu Spa 涵碧樓
142 Zhongxing Lu, Shuishe Cun,
Yuchi Xiang, Nantou County.
℘(049) 285 5311.
www.thelalu.com.tw.
This luxurious spa in the resort at Sun
Moon Lake uses natural products for
its revitalizing treatments.

Tainan
**Guan-Zi-Ling Toong Mao Spa
Resort** 台南關子嶺統茂溫泉會館
28 Guanziling, Guanling Village,
Baihe Zhen, Tainan County.
℘(06) 682 3456.
http://guanzi.toongmao.com.tw.
Facilities include an outdoor mud
spa, an essential-oils pool and a
hydrotherapy room.

Hot Springs Spas/Hotels
Spring City Resort 北投春天酒店
18 Youya Rd., Beitou, Taipei City,
℘(02) 2897 2345 or 2897 5555.
www.springresort.com.tw.
This hot-springs retreat in the Beitou
hills complements natural mineral
baths with body wraps and massages.
The landscaped outdoor spa pool area
(NT$800, NT$550 child; hotel guests
free) features 9 function-specific
pools, including a flower bath, Jacuzzi
and a family pool. Private hot springs
cost from NT$600/hr.

Sweetme Hotspring Resort
水美溫泉會館
224 Guangming Rd., Beitou
District, Taipei City. ℘(02) 2898
3838. www.sweetme.com.tw.
Both public, gender-specific (NT$800)
and private bath houses (NT$1,200-
3,900) are available here.

Villa 32 三二行館
32 Zhongshan Rd., Beitou District,
Taipei City. ℘(02) 6611 8888.
www.villa32.com.
Gender-segregated public bathing is
nude at this posh hideaway in Beitou.

ACTIVITIES FOR KIDS 👥👤

Throughout this guide, sights of particular interest to children are indicated with a 👥👤 symbol.

Taiwan has abundant resources for days of family fun, like amusement and water parks (🕯️*see Water Parks*), as well as educational museums where child-friendly exhibits foster learning through play.

Of Taiwan's many beaches, **Feicui Wan's Green Bay Seashore Recreation Club** at the Howard Plaza Hotel (萬里翡翠灣福華渡假飯店, 台北縣萬里鄉翡翠路17號) has a kids' amusement park (🕯️*see Beaches*).

The **Taipei Zoo,** designed by the same team that created the world-renowned San Diego Zoo in the US, is among the largest zoological gardens in Asia. To the south, the **Shou Shan Zoo** in western Kaohsiung shows off exotic imports from Africa, Asia, America and Australia.

Window on China★ (called "Small People Land" 小人國 in Chinese) is an amusement park in Longtan (south of Taipei) with miniature scale reproductions of famous buildings throughout China and the world. Another good place for children is the **Formosan Aboriginal Culture Village**★★, an indigenous culture theme park near Sun Moon Lake (日月潭); craft demonstrations and live performances of Taiwanese music and dance are held daily.

Learning is fun at Taichung's **Museum of Natural Science**★★, Taipei's **Astronomical Museum**, and the **Science and Technology Museum** in Kaohsiung, which claims to be the largest practical science museum in Asia. The **Museum of Marine Biology and Aquarium**★★★ in the Kenting area spotlights exotic marine creatures such as whale sharks, seals and even penguins.

SHOPPING

Taiwanese people love to shop, and the island's abundant retail venues range from convenience stores to chic boutiques and massive modern malls.

NIGHT MARKETS

Taiwan's bustling night markets are filled with stalls selling a variety of inexpensive snacks and merchandise. Some are open during the daytime. Taiwan's most famous night markets are **Shilin**★★, **Shida** and **Raohe**★ (in Taipei); Danshui (north of Taipei); Fengjia (in Taichung); Liuhe (in Kaohsiung); and **Miaokou** (in Keelung). These markets are places to get a broad sampling of Taiwan's dishes at affordable prices.

Raohe Street Night Market, Taipei

Florent Bonnefoy/Michelin

Medical Tourism

Medical tourism has boomed in Asia over the past decade-plus, and Taiwan has joined the industry in organized fashion in the past few years, offering travel packages that combine adventure and accommodations with a variety of health-treatment options. These options run the gamut, encompassing Western medical procedures and traditional Chinese non-invasive practices. Taiwan's medical personnel and facilities are world-class, and most doctors who specialize in Western medicine speak sound English; many have trained in whole or in part in the West. Services cost only a fraction of what they might cost in most other advanced nations—one-fifth to one-sixth of that in the US or UK, and generally about half that in Singapore or Thailand.

Areas of Western specialization include cardiovascular surgery, liver transplants/hepatology, joint replacements, craniofacial reconstruction and cosmetic surgery, health examinations of all types, dentistry, and artificial reproduction (assisted pregnancy and fertility treatments). The main areas of traditional Chinese medicine are herbal medicine (including spa treatments and mud treatments for skin), acupuncture, acupressure, moxibustion, and *tuina*, a type of massage. Chinese-medicine practitioners are overseen by the Department of Health, and it is the general custom in Taiwan to combine Western and Chinese practices for optimal effect. Most major Taiwan hospitals have established specialized Chinese Medicine departments. The term *tuina* can be translated as "push and grasp," describing how the masseur works. By pressing, tapping, and kneading the body, the practitioner directs the flow of energy, and blood is stimulated by unblocking the meridians of the body. The principles are similar to those of acupuncture, moxibustion, and acupressure.

The official online portal for Taiwan medical travel is www.medicaltravel.org.tw (📞 02 2739 1322). Packages are personalized, meaning patients will have a personal medical team looking after them with a personal nurse to guide them through the process. Patients will be in separate facilities for preventive care, will not be placed in the general patient population if any operations are involved, and will have their privacy assured. Online instant messaging is set up before the patient arrives on the island, door-to-door service is provided from the airport, and one-to-one language translation service is available at all times.

The private medical-travel agency Formosa Medical Travel specializes in packages for knee and hip replacement surgery (toll-free 📞 866-949-9519; www.formosamedicaltravel.com).

LOCAL CRAFTS

Taiwan produces many locally made crafts—from artwork, ceramics and jewelry to rattan and bamboo to glassware, metal and marble sculpture. The town of **Sanyi**★, in Miaoli County in central Taiwan, is home to the best woodcarvers on the island. Other towns specializing in traditional crafts are: **Meinong**, known for its hand-painted paper parasols; **Yingge**★, famous for its ceramics and pottery; and **Lugang**★★, where you can purchase locally made fans and lanterns.

SHOPPING MALLS/ DEPARTMENT STORES

Many enormous malls flourish in Taiwan's cities, usually in the most affluent areas of town (i.e., Xinyi District in Taipei). The Japanese retailer **SOGO,** with eight branches in major cities, is Taiwan's most popular department store. A large mall sprawls from the lower levels of **Taipei 101,** Taiwan's landmark skyscraper, while **Core Pacific City** (aka Living Mall), also in Taipei, promotes itself as the largest ball-shaped mall on earth. Sales abound at the end of the year.

Souvenir shopping

Florent Bonnefoy/Michelin

Service Counter of the Customs Service area in the airport or seaport of departure.

To claim the refund upon your departure, present the goods purchased, the original sale invoice, the application form for VAT refund and personal identification to the Customs office for processing. If approved, the Customs office will issue a VAT Refund Assessment Certificate for you to present at a designated bank within the departure point, so you can claim the refund in New Taiwan Dollars.

STORE HOURS

With one of the highest rates of 24hr **convenience stores** per person in the world, Taiwan accommodates day and night shoppers. Most independent retailers have flexible hours. Both small retailers and large shopping centers often stay open from 9am or 10am until 9pm or later.

VAT REFUNDS

Visitors to Taiwan may claim refunds on merchandise subjected to VAT (Value Added Tax). The refund claim must be applied for on the **same day of purchase**, from the same TRS-labeled ("Tax Reporting System") store where the purchase was made. Visitors leaving Taiwan within **30 days** after their purchase (only valid for purchases exceeding **NT$3000**) are eligible for the refund. Once the VAT refund claim has been filed on the day of purchase, the refund may be collected upon exiting the country at the Foreign Passenger VAT Refund

BOOKS

Taiwan has a lively literary tradition. Here is a wide-ranging selection:

Taipei People by Pai Hsien-yung (1971).
This collection of 14 short stories, each following relocated mainlanders living in Taipei, is the defining work of Taiwan's greatest master of contemporary literature.

Elegy of Sweet Potatoes by Tsai Tehpen (1995).
This gripping read tells the story of Tsai, an innocent victim of the White Terror, and his harrowing imprisonment by the KMT.

A Thousand Moons on a Thousand Rivers by Hsiao Li-Hung (2000).
Infused with Buddhist wisdom, this tale depicts a southern Taiwanese family coping with the 1970s shift from an agricultural to an industrial economy.

Orphan of Asia by Zhuoliu Wu (2008).
This autobiographical novel was completed in 1945, at the end of Japan's colonial rule of Taiwan.

Private Prayers and Public Parades – Exploring the Religious Life of Taipei by Mark Caltonhill (2002).
A detailed look at Taiwan's fascinating religious practices, deities, festivals and temples.

Envisioning Taiwan: Fiction, Cinema, and the Nation in the Cultural Imaginary by June Yip (2004).
This overview of Taiwan's literature, cinema and arts

Taxes

Sales tax in Taiwan is included in the price of your purchase. The government taxes the reported sales directly from the vendor.

illustrates how the island's search for a global identity has affected its local culture.

Forbidden Nation: A History of Taiwan by Jonathan Manthorpe (2008). A dramatic overview of Taiwanese history, including the affect of the island's position along a lucrative trade route between the Far East and Southeast Asia.

Taiwan A to Z: The Essential Cultural Guide by Amy C. Liu (2009). This book is a practical overview of Taiwanese rituals and traditions.

Formosa Betrayed by George H. Kerr (1965). An account of the period surrounding the February 28 Incident (the violent massacre of the Taiwanese people by the Kuomintang government in 1947).

Taiwan: A Political History by Denny Roy (2003). A comprehensive, yet concise, overview of the island's political past.

Pioneering in Formosa by William Pickering (1898). This self-aggrandizing yarn of Pickering's adventures in Qing-era Taiwan captures the flavor of those lawless times when clans ruled the island.

Keeping Up With the War God by Steven Crook (2001). An Englishman's adventures in Taiwan, enlivened with personal observations and cultural oddities.

Reflections on Taipei by Rick Charette (2003). The Taiwan-based author blends his take on the island with the voices of other long-time expatriates.

Vignettes of Taiwan by Joshua Samuel Brown (2006). After moving to Taiwan as a 24-year-old with little money, expatriate Brown wrote this charming collection of witty stories, travel logs and personal meditations.

FILMS

The Taiwanese film industry has produced thoughtful movies about this dynamic island over the years.

A City of Sadness by Hou Hsiao-hsien (1989). Done by one of Taiwan's highly regarded directors, this film is set in Jiufen (northeastern Taiwan) during the Japanese occupation.

The Puppetmaster by Hou Hsiao-hsien (1993). This critically acclaimed story of a master puppeteer in war-torn China during WWII won the Jury Prize at Cannes.

The Wedding Banquet by Ang Lee (1993). This film tells the story of a gay Taiwanese immigrant to the US who marries a mainland Chinese woman for mutual practical benefit.

Eat Drink Man Woman by Ang Lee (1994) The only major film made by Ang Lee in Taiwan depicts a master chef in Taipei who watches his three daughters prepare to leave the nest.

Yi Yi: A One and a Two by Edward Yang (2000). Yang won Best Director at Cannes for this portrait of Taiwan's modern-day, urban middle-class family.

Cape No. 7 by Wei Te-sheng (2008). This unheralded, low-budget romantic comedy/musical drama, shot mostly in southern Taiwan, was a surprise hit in 2008.

No Puedo Vivir Sin Ti by Leon Dai (2009). Based on a true story, this black and white film depicts an indigent Hakka worker's struggle against Taiwanese bureaucracy to keep his daughter.

Monga by Doze Niu (2010). Set in 1980s Taipei, this film tells the story of five teenagers who enter the local mafia of Monga, one of the most vibrant neighborhoods in the city.

Calendar of Events

The following is a selection of Taiwan's most popular annual events. Many are religious observances and several are based on the lunar calendar (dates vary; check in advance). Of particular interest are the variety of aboriginal festivals held each year.

JANUARY-FEBRUARY

Foundation Day

Observed every January 1, this island-wide holiday remembers the day China became a republic. On January 1, 1912, Dr. Sun Yat-sen became the first president of the newly formed republic. Plenty of fireworks light up the night skies after daytime parades and speeches.

Lunar New Year/Chinese New Year

Officially a two-day holiday, this celebration is the longest and most significant of Chinese festivals, lasting up to 15 days. Houses, cleaned to dispel bad luck, are festooned with red strips of paper bearing blessings (*chunlian*). Families convene to light torches and feast on rice cakes called *niangao*. Most businesses close. Families exchange gifts; children receive "lucky money" in small red packets (*hong bao*).

Yanshui Fireworks Festival

This hugely attended event occurs two weeks after Chinese New Year (𝒾 *see p307*).

FEBRUARY-MARCH

Lantern Festival

The final day of the Lunar New Year celebration marks the beginning of the 7-day Lantern Festival. Elaborate lanterns, often modeled after figures from Chinese astrology, are lit throughout the island and sweet dumplings called *yuanxiao* are consumed.

Sky Lantern Festival

This festival, held in the town of Pingxi in Taipei County, is part of the Lantern Festival. Thousands of paper lanterns lit with candles and inscribed with wishes glow in the night sky. Several different carnivals are held throughout the celebration.

Guanyin's Birthday

This religious festival is held at the island's Buddhist temples, such as Longshan Temple in Taipei, to honor the goddess of mercy.

MARCH-APRIL

Dajia Mazu Pilgrimage

Thousands of people convene to view the annual pilgrimage of Mazu, the revered goddess of the Sea, as her statue is carried on a 300km/184mi

Lantern Festival, Tainan

Rich J. Matheson/Michelin

Dragon Boat Racing, Tainan

Rich J. Matheson/Michelin

journey around Central Taiwan. The 9-day religious procession—the island's most elaborate—begins and ends at Zhenlan Temple in the west coast town of Dajia.

Alishan Cherry Blossom Festival
From late March to early April, cherry blossoms are in full bloom in the Alishan Forest Recreation Area. The region boasts a variety of species, with blossoms ranging from vibrant pinks to creamy whites. Breathtaking sunrises are an added bonus of springtime here.

Flying Fish Festival
Orchid Island (Lanyu) is the setting for this annual custom of the Tao (Yami) aborigines. Arrayed in traditional costume, men launch their newly handcrafted boats on the open sea and call forth blessings at the start of the fishing season.

Spring Scream
Staged yearly in South Taiwan's Kenting National Park—known for its beautiful beaches—this festival is especially popular with young Western expatriates who throng the town of Kending, the festival's epicenter. Held over several days, the event features area and international indie bands that perform in a variety of venues.

APRIL-MAY

Tomb Sweeping Day
The Taiwanese honor their deceased ancestors on April 5 by sweeping their graves and paying respects at temples throughout the island.

Mazu's Birthday
Celebrated in the third lunar month, joyous tribute is paid at hundreds of temples around Taiwan to this popular deity with fireworks and dancing.

Bunun Festival
Based on a male coming-of-age ritual of the aboriginal Bunun tribe, this festival centers on a practice known as "ear-shooting"—marksmanship with a bow and arrow. Other competitions include wood-chopping and millet-husking, activities once central to the tribal way of life.

Sanyi Woodcarving Festival
The town of Sanyi, in Miaoli County, lauds its well-known woodcarving industry with displays, music and carving contests (see Sanyi).

Taipei Traditional Arts Festival
Extending from April through June, this city-wide event focuses on traditional Chinese music, performed largely by the Taipei Chinese Orchestra at Zhongshan Hall.

Dragon Boat Festival

Held the fifth day of the fifth lunar month, this popular race pits teams against each other, rowing to the beat of drums in decorated boats. The competition is based on the story of Qu Yuan, a 3C BC poet and government official who was loyal to his sovereign, but lost trust as he was edged out by peers. Fishermen failed to save him when he threw himself overboard after being exiled.

JUNE-JULY
Yingge Ceramics Festival

The town of Yingge, famous for its pottery and ceramics, stages this festival each year to showcase its highly varied output (&see Yingge).

JULY-AUGUST
Amis Harvest Festival

Evolved from a ceremony of gratitude to the gods for rain and a bountiful harvest, this colorful festival showcases the costumes, dances, songs and local food of the indigenous Ami people.

Ghost Month

Starting in August, the customs of burning paper money and incense mark the period when ghosts are believed to emerge from hell and visit the living. Festivals are held in cities such as Keelung to appease the spirits.

Ho-Hai-Yan Rock Festival

Attracting crowds of music lovers, this multi-day event is staged at Fulong Beach on the northeast coast. Both indie and mainstream groups, local and international, perform.

SEPTEMBER-OCTOBER
Mid-Autumn Festival/ Moon Festival

This traditional festival is celebrated with family feasting that typically includes barbecues, dancing, moon-gazing and eating mooncakes—the special pastries that symbolize the moon.

Confucius' Birthday

Also known as Teachers' Day, September 28 commemorates the birthday of the revered teacher-philosopher and honors teachers in general.

Double Tenth Day/National Day

Observed on October 10, this holiday heralds Sun Yat-sen's overthrow of the Qing dynasty in 1911, leading to the formation of the republic.

Retrocession Day

October 25, the day in 1945 when Taiwan was freed from half a century of Japanese rule, is remembered.

Festival of Austronesian Cultures

Held in Taitung, on Taiwan's dramatic East Coast, this festival presents the cultural diversity of the region's Austronesian peoples. Festival-goers will be treated to an array of traditional snacks, crafts demonstrations and musical performances.

NOVEMBER
Sun Yat-sen's Birthday

November 12 is observed in honor of the Republic of China's first president. Commemorative speeches are given in tribute to the revolutionary leader.

Taipei International Beef Noodle Festival

The subject of much rejoicing, Taiwan's favorite treat, for sale from Taipei's many vendors, is consumed in an endless variety.

DECEMBER
Constitution Day

An important historical milestone, December 25, 1946, is memorialized as the day in which the Republic of China's new constitution was adopted.

Countdown Party

On December 31, Taipei holds its massive New Year Countdown Party with pop stars and a midnight fireworks spectacle.

Know Before You Go

USEFUL WEBSITES

www.roc-taiwan.org/US
www.roc-taiwan.org/UK
The Taipei Economic and Cultural
Representative offices in the US and
UK both have a website providing
basic information (geography,
demographics, history), a news digest,
and business-related information.
Web pages are devoted to culture,
language study and travel.

www.taiwan.net.tw
The Taiwan Tourism Bureau website is
packed with practical information and
tips for traveling to Taiwan.

www.gio.gov.tw
The website of Taiwan's Government
Information Office.

www.taiwanembassy.org/US/NYC/
Taiwan news from the Taipei Economic
and Cultural Office in New York.

www.forumosa.com
A forum for Taiwan's English-speaking
community with details on visas,
places to visit and other practicalities.

www.taiwanease.com
This online magazine details Taiwan's
art and culture scenes.

www.taiwanfun.com
Reviews of restaurants, bars and
nightclubs, and places to visit.

www.taiwantoday.tw
An English news site with translations
of news stories from Taiwan-based
Chinese-language newspapers.

taiwanreview.nat.gov.tw
An English monthly providing in-depth
discussions about life in Taiwan.

TOURIST OFFICES

For information, brochures, maps and
assistance in planning a trip to Taiwan,
travelers should consult the official
Taiwan Tourism Bureau, which only
has only a few overseas offices.

UNITED STATES

Three Taiwan tourism offices are
located in the US. www.go2taiwan.net

- **New York**
  1 East 42nd Street, 9th floor,
  New York, NY 10017, USA,
  &1-212-867-1632/4
  tbrocnyc@gmail.com

- **San Francisco**
  555 Montgomery Street, #505,
  San Francisco, CA 94111, USA
  &1-415-989-8677
  info@visittaiwan.org

- **Los Angeles**
  3731 Wilshire Boulevard., Suite
  780, Los Angeles, CA 90010, USA
  &1-213-389-1158
  latva@pacbell.net

GERMANY

The only European office of the Taiwan
Tourism Bureau is in Germany:

- **Frankfurt/Main**
  Taipei Tourism Office
  Rheinstrasse 29, 60325 Frankfurt/
  Main, Federal Republic of
  Germany, &49-69-610 743
  info@taiwantourismus.de
  www.taiwantourismus.de

LOCAL AND REGIONAL
TOURIST OFFICES

Visitors may also contact local tourist
offices for more detailed information,
and to receive brochures and maps.
The addresses, telephone numbers,
and websites of local tourist offices
are listed after the symbol 🎫 in the
orient panels of Principal Sights in the
Discovering section of this guide.
Below are addresses for the Tourism
Bureau in Taiwan.

TAIWAN TOURISM BUREAU

Taiwan Tourism Bureau is located in
Taipei. The Bureau runs Travel Service
Centers in other cities; they offer free
brochures and pamphlets.

- **Headquarters**
  9F, No.290, Section 4, Zhongxiao East Road, Da'an District, Taipei City 10694, ✆(02) 2349 1500 24-hour toll-free Travel Information Hotline: 0800 011 765 http://taiwan.net.tw.

- **Taichung Travel Service Center**
  1F, No.95, Gancheng Street, Nantun District, Taichung City 408 ✆(04) 2254 0809 or 0800 422 022 Fax: (04) 2254 5485

- **Tainan Travel Service Center**
  10F, 243 Minchuan Road, Section 1, Tainan 700, ✆(06) 2260 5681 or 0800 611 011, Fax: (06) 226 4905

- **Kaohsiung Travel Service Center**
  5F-1, 235 Zhongzheng 4th Road, Kaohsiung 801, ✆(07) 281 1513 or 0800 711 765, Fax: (07) 281 4660

INTERNATIONAL VISITORS
OVERSEAS TAIPEI ECONOMIC AND CULTURAL OFFICE

There are several Taipei Economic and Cultural Offices overseas; they provide information about the procedure to enter Taiwan. Listed here are offices in capital cities.

- **Australia**
  40 Blackall Street, 3rd Floor. Unit 8, Barton, Canberra, ✆(002-61-2) 6120 2000, Fax: (002-61-2) 6273 3228, tecoaus@gmail.com

- **Canada**
  45 O'Connor Street, World Exchange Plaza, Suite 1960, Ottawa, Ontario, ✆(002-1-613) 231-5080, Fax: (002-1-613) 231-7112, teco@on.aibn.com

- **New Zealand**
  105 The Terrace, Level 21, Wellington, ✆(002-64-4) 473 6474 or 473 6475. Fax: (002-64-4) 499 1458, tecowlg@taipei.org.nz

- **South Africa**
  Taipei Liaison Office in the Republic of South Africa
  1147 Schoeman Street, Hatfield, Pretoria, ✆(002-27-12) 430 6071-3, Fax: (002-27-12) 430 5816, taipeisa@telkomsa.net

- **United Kingdom**
  Taipei Representative Office in the UK
  50 Grosvenor Gardens, London, ✆(002-44-20) 7881 2650, Fax: (002-44-20) 7730 3139, tro@taiwan-tro.uk.net

- **United States**
  Taipei Economic and Cultural Representative Office in the US
  4201 Wisconsin Avenue NW, Washington, DC, ✆(002-1) 202-895-1800, Fax: (002-1) 202-363-0999, usa@mofa.gov.tw

FOREIGN REPRESENTATIVES IN TAIWAN

Local trade offices offer services to citizens of international countries in Taiwan.

- **Australia**
  Australian Commerce and Industry Office
  The President International Tower, No. 9-11, 27th-28th floors, Songgao Road, Taipei, ✆(02) 8725 4100, Fax: (02) 8789 9599

- **Canada**
  Canadian Trade Office in Taipei (CTOT)
  365 Fuxing North Road, 13th Floor, Taipei, ✆(02) 2544 3000, Fax: (02) 2544 3592, www.canada.org.tw, tapei@international.gc.ca

- **New Zealand**
  Commerce and Industry Office - Taipei
  International Trade Building, 333 Jilong Road, Suite 2501, 25th Floor, Section 1, Taipei, ✆(02) 2757 6725, Fax: (02) 2757 6973, www.nzcio.com, nzcio.tpe@msa.hinet.net

- **South Africa**
  Liaison Office
  205, Dunhua North Road, Suite 1301, 13th Floor, Taipei, ✆(02) 2715 3251/4, Fax: (02) 2718 6615, www.southafrica.org.tw

- **UK**
  British Trade & Cultural Office
  26F, No. 9-11, Song Gao Road, Taipei, ✆(02) 8758 2088, Fax: (02) 8758 2050, info@btco.org.tw, http://ukintaiwan.fco.gov.uk

- **United States**
  American Institute in Taiwan – Taipei Office
  No.7, Lane 134, Xinyi Road, Section 3, Da'an District, Taipei, ✆(02) 2162 2000, www.ait.org.tw

For American Citizen Services questions: amcit-ait-t@state.gov

  American Institute in Taiwan – Kaohsiung Branch Office
  No.2, Zhongzheng 3rd Road, 5th Floor, Xin-Xing District, Kaohsiung, ✆(07) 238 7744

DOCUMENTS
PASSPORTS

You must be in possession of a valid national **passport** (valid 6 months after your scheduled date of departure from Taiwan). Report any loss or theft to the local trade office of your country of origin and to the local police.

VISAS

Passport holders from Australia, Canada and the USA are allowed to enter Taiwan without a visa for up to 30 days—no extensions allowed—if they have a passport valid for at least six months from the date of entry into Taiwan and have a confirmed return or forward air ticket. UK and New Zealand nationals can stay in Taiwan without a visa for 90 days. The 30- or 90-days' duration of stay starts from the day after arrival.

People between 18 and 30 years of age may apply for a Working Holiday Visa, providing they fulfill all the requirements. If you think you may need a visa, apply to your local Taipei Economic and Cultural Office.
US citizens are advised to consult www.travel.state.gov for entry requirements, security and other information including contact numbers of US representation in Taiwan. In an emergency, call Overseas Citizens Services: ✆1-888-407-4747 or ✆1-202-501-4444 from overseas.

VACCINES

Cholera inoculations are required for visitors from some countries. If you stay in Taiwan for more than 3 months, you will be required to get an HIV test. Recommended vaccines are: tetanus, Hepatitis A and sometimes Hepatitis B. If you travel to rural areas in summer, the Japanese encephalitis vaccine is recommended.

CUSTOMS REGULATIONS

In the UK, **HM Revenue & Customs** (*www.hmrc.gov.uk*) publishes *A Guide for Travellers* that cites customs regulations and duty-free allowances. US citizens should view **Tips for Traveling Abroad** online (http://travel.state.gov) for general information on visa requirements, customs regulations, medical care, etc. Visitors can bring the following into Taiwan without declaring them: up to 200 cigarettes, or 25 cigars, or 1 pound of tobacco; alcoholic beverages are restricted to 1000cc—minors are not allowed to carry these items. Foreign currency in cash above US$ 10,000 should be declared. Drug trafficking is strictly forbidden and can be punishable by the death penalty. Americans can bring home, tax-free, up to US$ 800 worth of goods (limited quantities of alcohol and tobacco products); Canadians up to CND$750; Australians up to AUS$ 900; and New Zealanders up to NZ$ 700. Persons living in a member state of the European Union are not restricted with regard to purchasing goods for private use, but there are recommended maximum allowances for alcoholic beverages and tobacco: 200 cigarettes, or 100 cigarillos, or 50 cigars, or 250g of tobacco; 2 liters of still table wine and 1 liter of spirits or strong liquors (over 22% volume); or 2 liters of fortified wine or sparkling wine. For updated information about the customs clearance for travelers' luggage in Taiwan, go to the website for **Taipei Customs**: http://etaipei.customs.gov.tw.

CURRENCY EXCHANGE
See Money in Basic Information.

HEALTH
Even if you are in good health, you should buy **health insurance** before going to Taiwan, since bills for emergency evacuation can cost a fortune. It is advised, but not compulsory, to have the recommended **inoculations** before entering Taiwan. There are no vaccinations required to enter Taiwan, except for yellow fever if you have visited a country infected by yellow fever within six days prior to your arrival in Taiwan. You will be asked to provide proof of vaccination. Mosquitoes carrying dengue fever are more and more an issue in the countryside as well as in the city. There is no vaccination for dengue fever, and the best way to prevent it is to protect yourself against mosquitoes. When going on a hike, don't forget to spray repellent on your body and on your clothes. If you feel any of the symptoms of dengue (high fever, severe headache and body ache), see a doctor. There is actually no treatment for dengue fever, only rest and aspirin. Usual hygiene rules should help you to prevent the flu. Don't forget to pack a small bottle of antibacterial hand soap—it can come in very "handy."
Tap water is not recommended for drinking, and you should avoid ice in beverages. Hotels and restaurants serve boiled water; iodine tablets are

the best chemical purifier, however they should not be used by pregnant women or people with thyroid problems. Hepathis A is present all over the island; vaccination is highly recommended.

Americans concerned about travel and health can contact the International Assn. for Medical Assistance to Travelers: ℘ (716) 754-4883; www.iamat.org.

Priority Care Center (Adventist Hospital) 臺安醫院
No.424, Bade Road, Section 2, Songshan District, Taipei.
℘ (02) 2771 8151;
www.tahsda.org.tw. Open Mon–Thu 8am–noon & 1pm–5pm; Fri–Sat 8am–noon.

This clinic, popular with expatriates, employs English-speaking staff.

Sun Yat-sen Cancer Center 和信治癌中心醫院
No.125 Lide Road, Beitou District, Taipei. ℘ (02) 2897 0011; www.kfsyscc.org.

This state-of-the-art hospital is affiliated with Duke University Medical Center and has developed a strong general medicine department. It offers outpatient services, and English is often spoken.

Taipei Veteran's General Hospital 台北榮民總醫院
No.201, Section 2, Shipai Road, Beitou District, Taipei City 112.
℘ (02) 2776 2651;
www.vghtpe.gov.tw.

Veteran's General has specialized services for snake bites and accidental poisonings.

For detailed descriptions of medical providers in Taipei, Taichung, Tainan, Hualien and Kaohsiung, refer to the website of the American Institute in Taiwan: http://acs.ait.org.tw/medical-info.html.

ACCESSIBILITY
Sights described in this guide that are easily accessible to people of reduced mobility are indicated by the symbol ♿.

Getting There and Getting Around

GETTING THERE
BY AIR

You can fly direct to Taiwan from the US, UK, Canada, Australia, the Netherlands, mainland China and most Asian countries. Most visitors enter through **Taiwan Taoyuan International Airport (TPE)** (50km/25mi west of **Taipei**), Taiwan's major international air hub. Direct buses from TPE go not only to downtown Taipei, but also direct to Taichung, Hsinchu, and the Taoyuan station for the High Speed Rail (HSR), which connects to all the major cities in southern Taiwan.

Other Taiwan airports that operate international flights are **Kaohsiung** and **Taichung**. A limited number of flights to mainland China leave from Songshan Airport in downtown Taipei. Other airports around the island, such as Hualien Airport, run flights to the mainland.

Island plane for excursions

Susannah Rosenblatt/Michelin

No.2, Zhongshan 4th Rd., Xiaogang District, Kaohsiung. &0800 090 108 (information, toll-free); &(07) 805 7630 (domestic); &(07) 805 7631 (international) www.kia.gov.tw
Lockers are located on the third floor of the International Terminal and on the first floor of the Domestic Terminal (small locker: NT$50 per 12h; large locker: NT$100 per 12h). Lockers can be rented for a maximum of 6 days. Lost & Found: &(07) 801 1060. Airport taxis can be found at the arrival area of both terminals. Fare to Taipei is usually around NT$1,100.

Taiwan Taoyuan International Airport (**TPE** 台灣桃園國際機場)
TPE handles only international traffic, except for transit flights to and from Kaohsiung. All domestic flights to and from Taipei use Songshan Airport (STA).
No. 9, Hangzhan South Rd., Dayuan Township, Taoyuan. &(03) 398 3728 www.taoyuanairport.gov.tw
Lost & Found is located at north side of T2, 1F. &(03) 398 2538. Open 9am–11:30am, 1:30pm–4:30pm.

Kaohsiung Siaogang International Airport (**KHH** 高雄小港國際機場)
This important domestic terminal also services international connections with most countries in Asia, including mainland China, Hong Kong, Japan, Korea, Thailand, Vietnam, Malaysia and the Philippines.

Taichung Cing Cyuan Gang Airport (**RMQ** 台中清泉崗機場)
Provides international flight connections with mainland China, Hong Kong, Palau, South Korea, Japan, Phuket (Thailand) and Vietnam, in addition to serving as a domestic hub.
No. 167, Xi'an St., Xitun District, Taichung City. &(04) 2701 1981 www.tca.gov.tw

Hualien Airport (**HUN** 花蓮機場)
This busy domestic airport on the east coast also makes cross-strait connections.
No. 1 Jichang, Jiali Village, Xincheng Township, Hualien County. www.hulairport.gov.tw

Songshan Airport (**TSA** 松山機場)
Operates cross-straight flights and all domestic flights for Taiwan's largest city.

No. 340-9, Dunhua North Rd.,
Songshan District, Taipei City.
www.tsa.gov.tw

International Airlines
China Airlines (中華航空)
☎(02) 2715 1212
www.china-airlines.com
Delta Airlines
☎(02) 2772 2188
www.delta.com
EVA Air (長榮航空)
☎(02) 2501 1999
www.evaair.com
KLM Royal Dutch
☎(02) 2711 4055
www.klm.com
Singapore Airlines
☎(02) 2551 6655
www.singaporeair.com
United Airlines
☎(02) 2325 8868
www.united.com

Domestic and Regional Airlines
Cathay Pacific
☎(02) 2715 2333
www.cathaypacific.com
Far Eastern Air Transport
☎(02) 4066 6789
www.fat.com.tw
Malaysia Airlines
☎(02) 2514 7888
www.malaysiaairlines.com
Thai Airways
☎(02) 2509 6800
www.thaiair.com

Vietnam Airlines
☎(02) 2517 7177
www.vietnamairlines.com

BY SEA

Since 2008, ferries have run on
the hour between both Xiamen
(8:30am–5:30pm) and Quanzhou
(major cities on the coast of Fujian
Province) and Kinmen Island
(administered by Taiwan, about
2km/1.2mi from Xiamen). There is
also a ferry connection between the
mainland city of Fuzhou and the
Taiwan-administered island of Mazu.
Regular ferry connections between
Taiwan's ports and Okinawa (Japan),
Hong Kong and Macao have been
suspended since 2008, although
Star Cruises (*www.starcruises.com*)
include these destinations in some
of their tours.

GETTING AROUND
BY AIR

Aside from the five airports listed
above that handle international
traffic, Taiwan's domestic air network
operates flights through 13 additional
airports, serving population centers
like Taitung, Kenting, Tainan and
Chiayi, as well as off-island territories
such as Kinmen, Mazu, Penghu,
Green Island and Orchid Island. Air
travel between Taipei and Kaohsiung
along the populous corridor of
western Taiwan has been significantly
undercut since the High Speed Rail
(HSR) began operating in 2007.
Flights within Taiwan are frequent,
fast and reliable. Flying is a relatively
inexpensive way to get around
the main island, and the most
time-efficient choice for visiting
the outlying islands. There are no
connecting flights from island group
to island group; travelers on an
outlying island must fly back to the
main island and then fly from there
to another island group. For example,
to Ludao and Lanyu from Taitung; to
Penghu from Tainan and Kaohsiung;
to Kinmen from Taipei and to Mazu
from Taipei.

Qijin Island ferry

Rich J. Matheson/Michelin

36

BY BOAT

There are ferry connections to Taiwan's outlying islands, but they are relatively slow. Most visitors to the outlying islands go by air from Taipei or Kaohsiung. Ferry service operates between the islands of Green and Orchid (Ludao and Lanyu).

BY BUS

Taiwan's major cities have extensive public bus transportation networks. Local buses run frequently, as a result of competition among several private bus companies.

Long-Distance Buses

Taipei, Taichung and Kaohsiung are the main transfer hubs for long-distance bus services. Private operators like Guo Guang, Aloha and U-Bus all offer frequent coach service around the island, often in considerable comfort. The ride from Taipei to Kaohsiung by coach takes about five hours, if there are no traffic tie-ups.

+ **Aloha** 阿羅哈客運
  www.aloha168.com.tw
+ **Guo Guang** 國光客運
  www.kingbus.com.tw
+ **UBus** 統聯客運
  www.ubus.com.tw

BY CAR

To drive a car in Taiwan, a visitor must have an international driver's license. The highways and road systems are good, although the Romanization of place names on signs may be inconsistent. Driving in Taipei and Taiwan's other major cities can be stressful, given the volume of traffic and the buzzing swarm of motorbikes. Traffic does build up in **rush hours** (7:30am–9am and 4pm–7:30pm in Taipei). Many local drivers tend to run red lights, so be extra cautious at intersections. The three cross-island highways (North, Central and South) traverse Taiwan's mountains; these winding roads can be narrow in places and full of blind curves.

Taipei city bus

Florent Bonnefoy/Michelin

Check in advance with authorities before driving through the mountains, as mud slides can occur after heavy rains, blocking roads entirely.

Rules of the Road

+ Cars in Taiwan drive on the right side of the road.
+ Both the passenger and the driver are legally obligated to wear seatbelts.
+ Right turn on red is not permitted.
+ Speed limits on unmarked roads are 50km/hr, and 40km/hr on roads without lane markings. Maximum speed on expressways is 110km/hr.
+ Pedestrians should be given the right of way.

Monsoon Driving

Before driving long distances, be sure to check the weather and the latest road conditions by calling the Tourism Bureau's 24hr toll-free hotline in English: 0800-011765. Monsoon rains are incredibly hazardous for all vehicles (two-wheel in particular). In the event of heavy rain or a monsoon, stop and if possible, park under a bridge or some sort of cover. Wait until the rain stops before continuing your journey. Typhoon warnings are given 2-3 days in advance; stay indoors and off the roads during a typhoon.

Gasoline (Petrol)

There are plenty of gas stations on the main roads and major highways. Stations are less frequent in the mountains and countryside, so it is best to fill up when you have the opportunity. Credit cards may not always be accepted, so carry some cash for gas purchases.

In Case of Accident

If you are involved in an automobile accident resulting in personal or property damage, you must notify the local police and remain at the scene until dismissed by a police officer. Vehicles should be moved if blocking traffic.

Car Rental Agencies:

◆ **Central Auto**
Branches in Taipei, Kaohsiung and Taichung, No. 3, Sec. 7, Chengde Rd., Peitou District, Taipei City.
℘(02) 2828 0033
www.rentalcar.com.tw

◆ **VIP Car Rental**
No. 148, Sec. 3, Minquan East Rd., Taipei City.
℘(02) 2713 1111; ℘(02) 2546 9966, www.vipcar.com.tw

Taipei Metro station
Florent Bonnefoy/Michelin

BY TAXI

Taxis in Taiwan are very common in larger cities. They charge by the meter and can be quite expensive. Most taxi drivers do not speak English, but will be able to help you find your destination from a written Chinese address.

BY METRO

Taipei MRT

⟨ *See Metro map on inside back cover.*
Taipei's Mass Rapid Transit (MRT) system has five main lines (along with several branches and extensions), which include 80 stations traversing 90km/56mi of routes connecting downtown with the suburbs. The MRT has eased Taipei's traffic and continues to expand. Hoping to encourage cycling, the government permits cyclists with bicycles to ride the MRT between certain stations for a special fare of NT$80. The base fare for taking the MRT under 5km/3mi is NT$20, and increases NT$5 every 5km/3mi traveled. By buying an **EasyCard** (悠遊卡) (which entitles the bearer to NT$400 in credit above the NT$100 refundable deposit), all fares are reduced 20 percent. Unlimited-ride EasyCard/TaipeiPass package deals are available for visitors, for one (NT$180), two (NT$310), three (NT$430) or five (NT$700) days. EasyCards can be purchased in convenience stores (where they can also be used for purchases as of April 1, 2010) and all MRT stations. www.easycard.com.tw

Taipei Rapid Transit Corp.
7, Lane 48, Sec. 2, Zhongshan North Rd., Taipei City,
℘02-2536 3001; 24hr line:
℘886 02 218 12345,
http://english.trtc.com.tw

Maokong Gondola

Part of the MRT system, this 4km/2.5mi scenic cable car runs between the Taipei Zoo in Muzha and Maokong Mountain—an entertainment district that contains many teahouses and is famous for its views of the downtown skyline.

Kaohsiung MRT

Opened in 2008, the Kaohsiung MRT has two lines, a north-south (red line) and an east-west (orange line) that converge at the Formosa Boulevard Station. Nine future lines are planned. Similar to the metro system in Taipei, Kaohsiung's MRT tickets start at NT$20, and increase incrementally based on the distance of the ride. Also paralleling the Taipei system, there are prepaid smart cards available to allow commuters to swipe their way around town, valid on both buses and the MRT. The Kaohsiung smart card costs only NT$200, but as in Taipei, NT$100 of that is the deposit base.

Kaohsiung Rapid Transit Corp.
(KRTC 高雄捷運股份有限公司)
No.1, Jung-An Rd. Kaohsiung
📞 (07) 793 9687.
www.krtco.com.tw

BY TRAIN

Taiwan High Speed Rail
(THSR 台灣高鐵)
This bullet train, opened in 2007 and constructed with Japanese technology, runs from Taipei to Kaohsiung in a brisk 90 minutes. From Taipei heading south, the train stops at: Banqiao, Taoyuan, Hsinchu, Taichung, Chiayi, Tainan and Zuoying Station (in Kaohsiung). A one-way economy ticket from Taipei to Zuoying Station costs NT$1,490.
Online booking is available at www. thsrc.com.tw 📞 (02) 6626 8000

Taiwan Railway Administration
(TRA 台灣鐵路管理局)
Taiwan's network of train connections between cities and towns is integrated seamlessly within the island's public transportation infrastructure. All over Taiwan, train stations form the central landmarks of towns large and small. Travel by traditional rail (i.e., not the bullet train) remains inexpensive, reasonably speedy and convenient. Several tiers of tickets are available; the cheaper tickets usually buy you

less comfortable seats on slower trains going shorter distances. www.railway. gov.tw

BY TWO WHEELS

Motorbikes

Motorcycles and motorbikes are a popular, speedy and relatively inexpensive way to get around Taiwan's cities. For a long-distance journey, a car is much more comfortable; but for convenient parking within a limited or especially crowded area (a city or beach), motorbikes are the way to go.
As with driving a car, an international driver's license is legally required to ride a motorbike. Be very careful when riding; Taiwan's fast-moving motorbike traffic can be heavy—and wild.

Rentals:

♦ **Bikefarm** (Taipei)
📞 (09) 2628 3300
www.bikefarm.net

♦ **F.A.S.T.** (Taichung, Tainan, Kenting) No. 115 Linsen Rd. Taichung City.
Open Mon–Sat 9am–9pm.
📞 (09) 1050 6911;
📞 (09) 2357 0711

♦ **Truman Motorcycle & Scooter Repair Shop** (Kaohsiung)
No. 129, Shiquan 2nd Rd., Kaohsiung City.
Open Mon–Sat 9am–9pm.
📞 (07) 323 1923;
📞 (09) 2123 8599

Pedal Bikes
See Biking in What to See and Do.

Rentals Taipei:

♦ **Sean's Bike**
No. 21 Chung Cheng Rd., Section 1, Tienmu. (Short walk from Chihshan MRT)
📞 02-2835 2101

♦ **Jung Ming Bicycle Co.**
No. 114, Sec. 3, Minchuan East Rd. Closed Sun.
📞 02-2545 1651

Where to Stay and Eat

WHERE TO STAY

See the Addresses in the Discovering section of this guide for a selection of lodgings. For price ranges, see the Legend on front cover flap.

Taiwan's hundreds of hotels run the gamut from humble and inexpensive to luxurious and high-cost. In the major cities, glitzy **upscale properties** abound, including international chains such as Grand Hyatt, Westin and Shangri-La. Taiwan has entered the modern era of corporate travel, as business-ready rooms with high-speed Internet connections and all the must-have modern conveniences have become the rule. Of course, the **boutique hotel** bug has bitten Taiwan too, and stylish destination retreats like The Lalu at Sun Moon Lake and Villa 32, on the outskirts of Taipei, are positioning themselves to attract the discerning traveler. On the other end of the spectrum, **homestay** lodgings are available for those seeking to immerse themselves in the local culture. Youth **hostels** can be found in large towns, while Taiwan's warm summer weather accommodates camping in many areas.

PRICES AND AMENITIES

Many of the hotels featured in this guide also have well-regarded restaurants; see the Addresses in each of the geographic sections (i.e. Taipei Area, North Taiwan, Central Taiwan, South Taiwan) for descriptions and contact details. For price ranges, see the Legend on the front cover flap.

The **Addresses** in this guide provide a selection of hotels and homestays located in various parts of Taiwan, and are classified according to the price of a standard **double room** in high season. However, as these prices often vary considerably throughout the year—especially at the major hotels—you are strongly advised to inquire in advance about the rates during the period chosen for your stay. It is also recommended that you reserve in advance as often as possible. Hotels accept major credit cards and offer air-conditioning unless otherwise indicated. There is no accommodations tax or sales tax, but some hotels add a 10-15 percent service charge to guest bills.

ONLINE RESERVATIONS

Rack rates (published rates) provided by hotels are usually higher than website deals. Some hotels may have special packages or promotional rates, but you may still find it cheaper to reserve your hotel through online reservation services *(below)*.
The Taiwan Tourism Board has an online hotel directory at http://eng. taiwan.net.tw.

RESERVATION SERVICES

You can book rooms and read guest reviews posted on the following sites:
www.asiarooms.com
www.asiatravel.com
www.expedia.com
www.ebookers.com
www.hotels.com
www.taiwan.yh.org.tw (youth hostels)
www.wotif.com

Half Moon Bay Bed and Breakfast

Susannah Rosenblatt/Michelin

WHERE TO EAT

For a selection of restaurants, see the Addresses in the Discovering section of this guide. For price ranges, see the Legend on the front cover flap.

Taiwan is a culinary paradise, where people are passionate about food and good food is available almost everywhere. It has become a culinary destination for many overseas visitors. Taiwan's restaurant scene is obsessed with diversity, authenticity and quality—one that adheres to the classic dishes of regional Chinese cooking (Cantonese, Sichuan, Beijing and others) yet nurtures innovation in both Eastern and Western fare.

You can find refined Japanese dishes, robust Italian meals and classic French cuisine on the island, but while in Taiwan, be sure to sample traditional Taiwanese cuisine (*see below*), including vegetarian dishes.

NIGHT MARKETS

The ultimate icon of the island's madness for gobbling up all manner of imaginative and bizarre street food is the **night market**. It was within these raucous assemblies of crowded stalls that many of Taiwan's distinctive treats were born, and where local snacks and edible curiosities still mingle today.

TAIWANESE CUISINE

What is Taiwanese cuisine? To a strict traditionalist, it might be hard to pin down. The island inherited a wealth of gastronomic lineages from mainland China with the Kuomintang migration in the mid-20C. As a result, many of the wonders of Taiwanese cooking trace their roots back to distant towns, villages and cities across the strait, especially to Fujian Province. But Taiwan's appreciation for diversity in its food looks not only to China for inspiration, but also to northern neighbors Korea and Japan, and even the far west (in terms of its baking and pastries). The island's lingering spiritual identity as a community of fishing folk also plays an important role in steering the menu toward fresh seafood. The result is a creative cuisine that hones in on a variety of flavors and textures.

From Taichung's **sun pastries** (太陽餅) to Tainan's unique **oyster rolls** (蚵卷) and "tombstone" toast (棺材板) topped with chicken liver pâté, to Hualien's **ox+-tongue pastries** (牛舌餅) and **mochi** (麻糬), every area of Taiwan boasts its own epicurean specialties. The island's pig's-blood pudding (豬血糕), **stinky tofu** (臭豆腐), snake soup (蛇羹), oyster omelet (蚵仔煎), and a dizzying array of jellies boldly go well beyond the comfort zone of the uninitiated. For the unadventurous, delicious takes on familiar food—teppanyaki, sashimi, 100 types of wheat and rice noodles, **cheesecake**—are always on hand to soothe an uncertain palate. Influenced by the strong presence of Buddhism in Taiwan, many vegetarian restaurants prepare food according to Buddhist dietary restrictions: no meat, no garlic, no onion.

To wash everything down, try Taiwan's refined, locally produced **teas** (*see p260*), plum wine (梅酒) and sorghum liquor *kaoliang* (高粱酒):

Hakka Food

With its rugged, folksy flavors, **Hakka food** has emerged as a sort of born-again home-style cuisine on the island. Han Chinese known as Hakka (*Hakka* 客家 means "guest people" in Chinese) migrated to Taiwan from northern China, and developed a distinctive food culture as they formed enclaves throughout southern China and Southeast Asia over the centuries. Their simple, salty and sour dishes and stir-fries have become modern-day comfort food for the Taiwanese. Hakka cuisine emphasizes slow-cooked stews, many different uses of pork, and preserved vegetables. The city and county of **Hsinchu**, southwest of Taipei, remains a cultural stronghold for the Hakka, and consequently a culinary destination for lovers of this popular cuisine.

MUST-TRY SPECIALTIES

Beef Noodles 牛肉麵

Slurping the perfect bowl of beef noodles is a national obsession. With ingredients of handmade noodles and choice cuts (incorporating some ligament for mouth texture) of beef, stewed to a perfect tenderness and sprinkled with a few toppings and garnishes—this simple dish is among Taiwan's most celebrated. Broths can be made fiery or mild, with riffs including curry, tomato, and satay varieties. In Taipei, the annual International Beef Noodles Festival recognizes the best.

Lu (Shandong-style) Meat Rice 魯肉飯

Cubed pork and onions are first stir-fried, then boiled to create this elemental staple of Shandong (northeastern China) cuisine. The meat infuses its juicy essence into the rice, creating hearty, savory comfort food.

Mango Milk Ice 芒果牛奶冰

Fresh cubed mango, drizzled with condensed milk over a bed of finely shredded ice is one of the world's great food experiences. Taiwan's numerous takes on shaved-ice—which usually feature your choice of toppings (fruit, beans, jellies and sauces)—make a refreshing treat throughout the long, hot summer.

Mochi 麻糬

A traditional dish in Japan, these sweet, versatile chewy snacks are made by pounding sticky rice into a glutinous paste, which is then shaped (usually into balls) around any one of an ever-increasing variety of fillings. The most common fillings are sweet red bean paste, peanut butter, black sesame paste and mashed sweet purple taro, but adventurous mochi makers have been known to use fresh fruit, cake and even ice cream. The Hakka method of eating mochi is to roll the rice ball in ground peanuts, rather than give it a filling.

Ox-tongue Pastries 牛舌餅

Taiwan's most famous ox-tongue pastries are made in Yilan County, on the island's northeastern coast. Whereas many ox-tongue pastries can be disappointingly diminutive, fried pastries—a favorite local breakfast treat—prepared Yilan-style have a flat, elliptical shape.

Oyster Omelet 蚵仔煎

This signature dish is said to have been invented in Tainan, the home of the island's great shellfish farms. Ubiquitous at night-market vendor stalls, the omelet consists of a batter of oysters, eggs and crown daisy chrysanthemum leaves fried up on a griddle and served in a special sweet and mildly spicy tomato-based sauce.

Papaya Milk 木瓜牛奶

A classic Taiwanese drink, the papaya and milk smoothie is basically a tropical-fruit milk shake—a standard at most street-front tea shops. Aside from papaya, the most popular flavors are watermelon, banana, strawberry and avocado.

Red Bean Soup 紅豆湯

Normally eaten at breakfast, or as dessert after a meal, warm, filling red bean soup typically consists of sweet azuki red beans, sugar, lotus seed and dried tangerine peel. Chewy sticky rice balls stuffed with black sesame paste are a common accompaniment to this Taiwanese wintertime dish. Industrious shaved-ice vendors often convert their operations into a red-bean-soup shop during the rainy winter.

Beef noodle soup

Florent Bonnefoy/Michelin

Sausage Bun Sausage 大腸包小腸

This Taiwanese street food—literally translated as "big sausage wraps small sausage"—represents the creativity and high standards of quality that Taiwan's sausage makers uphold. A salty, sticky-rice sausage, sliced open lengthwise, becomes a bun for a grilled pork sausage (a sweeter version of Cantonese sausage 臘腸). The pork sausage, also sliced open, is then garnished with the customer's condiments of choice—often garlic, chilies and fresh basil.

Soymilk 豆漿

Yonghe, a town just across the Danshui River from downtown Taipei City, is heralded for its fine breakfast soymilk. Fortunately, you don't have to go to Yonghe—one of the most densely crowded urban districts in the world—to drink some amazing soymilk in Taiwan. The milk is made fresh from soybeans in the dark early hours of the morning at breakfast shops all over the island. Traditionally, it is served warm and sipped like soup from a bowl, but the to-go option in plastic packaging is available everywhere. Also widely available, black soymilk is said to be even more healthful and delicious than white.

Stinky Tofu 臭豆腐

True to its name, this popular Chinese snack exudes a strong rotten odor that takes more than a little getting used to. Traditionally, stinky tofu is made from a brine of fermented milk, vegetables and meat. The firm tofu that results after weeks of fermentation is then marinated for several days. Taiwanese stinky tofu is usually deep-fried and served with a soy sauce and kimchi (a condiment of pickled vegetables). In recent years, the industry has branched out; now it is possible to find stinky tofu roasted, steamed, or boiled in *mala* (tongue-searing, Sichuan-style) broth.

Stinky tofu

Florent Bonnefoy/Michelin

Tapioca Pearl Milk Tea 珍珠奶茶

Purportedly invented in Taichung, this unique beverage—tea with milk and marble-sized balls of tapioca sipped through a wide straw—has become one of Taiwan's most famous cultural exports; on menus in the US, it is often called **bubble tea**. Specialty tea stands all over Taiwan offer endless variations on the formula, adding flavorings such as ginger, almond and taro, and gummy enhancements like coconut jelly, grass jelly and more.

Tropical Fruit

Aside from abundant mango, papaya, kiwi and passion fruit, Taiwan grows significant crops of more obscure tropical fruit such as fragrant guava (芭樂); purplish-red bell-shaped wax apple (蓮霧); dragon fruit (火龍果), the crunchy red-fleshed fruit from a type of cactus; and sweet, custardy Buddha fruit (釋迦). Exploring local produce stands, often open late, yields exciting finds for the adventurous.

Taiwanese Breakfast

The Taiwanese fast-food breakfast successfully fuses East and West. This simple meal is available at ubiquitous stands all over the island, which open early and often close before noon. Cheap and served in a jiffy, the breakfast has a few Cantonese dim sum-style twists. There is typically a range of modest breakfast burgers; an "egg pancake" served rolled up with a choice of toppings like meat and corn; steamed bread; chicken fingers; and a choice of tea or soy milk to go. It all spells satisfaction though such fare is not high on the healthy list.

Useful Words and Phrases

See also Language p95.

In 2009 the central government designated Hanyu Pinyin as the official system. Adopted by Taipei, it is being implemented progressively throughout the island. However, some street signs are still in Tongyong Romanization, used officially from 2002 to 2008. If you need help, show local people the Chinese characters.

SURVIVAL MANDARIN

Mandarin (Hakka and Taiwanese as well) is a tonal language, with four tones. Each syllable's tonal pitch must be correct to be understood. Yet a few words in Mandarin, even badly spoken, will often bring a smile—and help.

The four tones:

high tone	mā	(mother)
rising tone	má	(hemp)
falling-rising tone	mǎ	(horse)
falling tone	mà	(swear)

Some pronunciation hints:

- ai, as in eye
- ao, as in cow
- e, as in her
- i, as in ee
- ian, as in yen
- ie, as in yeah
- ui, as in may
- uo, as in wo
- ü, as in German
- c, as ts in cats
- ch, as in champion
- h, a guttural sound, sounding like ch in the Scottish Loch
- q, similar to ch. Like cheek, with the lips spread wide with ee.
- r, as between j and z, similar to the z in azure
- sh, as in she, very similar to marsh in American English
- x, as in ship
- z, as an unaspirated c, like ds in suds
- zh, as in j or dr in English.

Hello	nǐhǎo	你好
Goodbye	zàijiàn	再見
Please	qǐng	請
Bus	gōngchē	公車
Taxi	jìchéngchē	計程車
Motor scooter	jīchē	機車
Bicycle	jiǎotàchē	腳踏車
Rapid transit	jié yùn	捷運
Fork	chāzi	叉子
Knife	dāozi	刀子
Spoon	tāngchí	湯匙
Chopsticks	kuàizi	筷子
American	měiguórén	美國人
Canadian	jiānádàrén	加拿大人
British	yīngguórén	英國人
Australian	àodàlìyàrén	澳大利亞人
Telephone	diànhuà	電話
Toilets	xíshǒujiān	洗手間
Men's (Toilet)	nán	男
Women's (Toilet)	nǚ	女
Prohibited	jìnzhǐ	禁止
Police	jǐngchá	警察

Thank you
xièxie   謝謝

Excuse me
duìbùqǐ   對不起

You are welcome
bùkèqì   不客氣

How much does it cost?
duōshǎo qián?   多少錢

It's too expensive
tài guì le   太貴了

Wait a moment
děng yīxià   等一下

I am...
wǒ shí...   我是...

Do you speak English?
nǐ huì jiǎng yīngwén ma
你會講英文嗎?

I don't understand.
wǒ tīng bù dòng
我聽不懂

Where is...
... zài nǎlǐ?   ...在哪裡?

Basic Information

BUSINESS HOURS
BANKS

Banks are open 9am–3:30pm on weekdays and 9am–noon on Saturdays.

PHARMACIES

Many of Taiwan's pharmacies have extended daily hours, from 8 or 9am to 10 or 11pm. Some pharmacies are open 24hrs. In a medical emergency, call 119.

SHOPS

See Shopping in What to See and Do. Aside from holiday closings, the shops in Taiwan operate under flexible hours. Long hours (9am–9pm; 10am–10pm or later) are common for both the small retailers and the large shopping centers. Most convenience stores are open 24hrs.

COMMUNICATIONS
NEWSPAPERS AND MAGAZINES

Taiwan has three daily English-language newspapers: **Taiwan News, China Post,** and **The Taipei Times.** Other bilingual or English-language print and online publications include **The Taiwan Economic News** for business, and a handful of free magazines devoted to entertainment listings.

DISCOUNTS

Discounted tickets are available for students, children and the elderly. Admission prices are discounted at the ticket counter of local attractions, upon presentation of personal identification if required.

ELECTRICITY

Electric voltage is based on the US/ North American three-pin flat socket, at 110V/60 Hertz. Visitors will need an adapter for other types of plugs.

Neon pharmacy street sign

Florent Bonnefoy/Michelin

INTERNET

The Internet is widely available in major hotels, Wi-Fi hot spots and a large number of Internet cafes. Many of the hot spots are run by service providers (like Taichung's Mobitai) that charge a fee (particularly for 3G phone users), and might have affiliation agreements with your home-country wireless provider. Public areas like gas stations, coffee houses and even train stations may be hot spots.

MAIL/POST

Post offices are open Monday–Saturday 8am–5pm.

MONEY

The **New Taiwan Dollar** is decimal-based and comes in notes of NT$100, 200, 500, 1000 and 2000; coins are available in amounts of NT$1, 5, 10, 20 and 50. At press time, the NT dollar was equivalent to 3 cents US (1 US dollar = 32 New Taiwan Dollars), 2 cents EUR (1 Euro = 41 New Taiwan Dollars) and 2 cents GBP (1 British pound = 49 New Taiwan Dollars).

BANKS

See Business Hours, above.

CURRENCY EXCHANGE

Banks in Taiwan can help visitors with exchanging currency. Exchange counters are easily found upon arrival at the airport.

CREDIT CARDS

Major credit cards are widely accepted in Taiwan, especially for expensive things. Large department stores, gasoline stations and most entertainment venues in Taiwan's large cities accept credit cards. Credit cards are generally accepted at major chain restaurants and hotel restaurants, but are usually not accepted at small restaurants, independent cafes and market stalls. The contact numbers for the credit card companies are as follows:
American Express (02) 2545 9090
MasterCard 00801 10 3400
VISA 00801 10 3008

TRAVELER'S CHECKS AND ATMS

A passport is necessary for personal identification when cashing **traveler's checks** in banks. Commission charges vary; hotels usually charge more than banks to cash checks.

In Taiwan it is less expensive to get cash directly from your bank account using an **ATM.** You can also use your credit cards for cash advances at ATMs or banks, but be aware that your bank will charge you for this service.

ATMs are plentiful throughout the island; machines can be found in 24-hour convenience stores as well as at banks and within shopping centers. Convenience stores are located on nearly every block in urban areas; outside the cities, they are not as accessible. As a general rule, in highly touristed areas, convenience stores and ATMs are abundant.

PUBLIC HOLIDAYS

Taiwan's most important public holidays are Chinese Lunar New Year *(late Jan or early Feb)*, and the commemoration of the founding of the Republic of China, which coincides with the solar New Year.

PUBLIC HOLIDAYS

January 1-3 開國紀念日 – **New Year's Day** and the founding of the Republic of China

Chinese New Year 春節 – Differs each year according to the lunar calendar—usually in late January or early February.
The three-day national holiday for Chinese New Year is observed throughout Taiwan; almost all businesses are closed.

February 28 和平紀念日 – **Peace Memorial Day** commemorates the Incident of 1947.

April 5 清明節 – **Tomb-Sweeping Day**

Taipei Internet cafe

咖啡 簡餐 上網 遊戲
INTERNET CAFE

Florent Bonnefoy/Michelin

Dragon Boat Festival 端午節 – 5th
day of the fifth month of the
lunar calendar.

Mid-Autumn Festival 中秋節 – 15th
day of the eighth month of the
lunar calendar.

October 10 國慶日 – **National Day**

SMOKING

Smoking is not permitted in indoor
public places in Taiwan. Taiwan's anti-
smoking regulations are among the
strictest in the region, ensuring that
most restaurants have non-smoking
sections. By law all hotels in Taiwan
are non-smoking, but regulation is not
always enforced. Smoky rooms are
most prevalent in tourist-class hotels
that cater to large groups. Ask to see
(and smell) the room before you take it.

TAXES/TIPPING

Taiwan has no **sales tax.** Some
hotels and restaurants add a 10- or
15-percent service charge to customer
bills. **Tipping** is not usually expected
in Taiwan (although, of course, it is
appreciated).

TELEPHONES

The country code for Taiwan is 886;
the major city codes for Taiwan are:

Kaohsiung	**7**
Taichung	**4**
Tainan	**6**
Taipei	**2**

PUBLIC PHONES

Phone cards for public telephones are
available in convenience stores, as are
mobile phone accounts and credit. It is
possible to put a local SIM card in your
own mobile phone. The three primary
mobile phone operators in Taiwan
are **Chunghwa Telecom** (中華電信),
Taiwan Mobile (台灣大哥大), and
Far EasTone (遠傳電訊).

LOCAL CALLS

In Taiwan, **mobile phone** numbers
begin with 09 and are 11 digits in
length. To dial a **local number,** omit
the city code or county code and dial
only the 8 (in Taipei) or 7 digits.

Tomb Sweeping Day, Anping

Rich J. Matheson/Michelin

INTERNATIONAL CALLS

To call Taiwan from the US, dial 011
(international access code) + 886 +
area code (i.e., 2 for Taipei) + 8-digit
(or 7 digit) number. To call the US
or Canada from Taiwan, dial 002 +
country code 1 + 3-digit area code +
7-digit number.

IMPORTANT TELEPHONE NUMBERS

Emergency (fire, ambulance)	119
Police	110

24hr English assistance
0800 024 111 (toll free)

TIME

Taiwan is 8hrs ahead of Greenwich
Mean Time (GMT), 12hrs ahead of
Eastern Standard Time in the US, and
15hrs ahead of Pacific Time.

WATER

It is strongly advised that you do
not drink tap water in Taiwan. Tap
water on the island is almost always
boiled and/or filtered before drinking.
Kaohsiung is the notable exception,
where the tap water is not drinkable
even after being boiled, due to trace
levels of arsenic. Bottled water is
readily available at convenience
stores. It is best to avoid eating ice or
having ice in your beverage.

Xuantian Temple, Tainan City
© Rich J. Matheson/Michelin

Taiwan Today

The people of Taiwan are known for being hard-working, hard-playing, cheerful, hospitable to international visitors and strongly family-oriented. They have achieved an optimum balance in their approach to life, revealing a passion for the best elements of their traditional culture while at the same time seizing on all that is modern and high tech.

POPULATION

The population of Taiwan proper and its numerous offshore islands was just over 23 million in 2009. The main island is extremely rugged—literally having been hurled from the ocean bottom by Rim of Fire tectonic activity—and is more than two-thirds mountain.

Almost all of the populace lives on a limited amount of land, giving the island an overall **population density** second only to Bangladesh among places with 10 million-plus people.

This density is most pronounced in the city of Taipei, which has 2.62 million residents and a density of 9,600 per sq km/3,693 per sq mi. The **Greater Taipei** area, squeezed within the mountain-ringed Taipei Basin, has some 6.75 million people.

Over the past few decades, the authorities have been pouring money into the rest of the island to attract more residents, and since the early 1990s, Taipei's population has dipped slightly. Most of those fleeing mainland China with the Republic of China (ROC) government in the 1940s settled in Taipei. Under martial law during the Kuomintang's rule, the city was heavily favored in terms of investment, at the expense of the rest of the population. From the 1950s to the early 1990s, many younger people from the island's center and south moved to the city and its outlying areas in search of work, thus "tilting" the population. This phenomenon is, for the international visitor, most in evidence during the Chinese New Year holidays, when highways leading out of Taipei are at times bumper to bumper with vehicles heading south. The city becomes unusually quiet in the interim, and pleasant to walk around.

ETHNIC COMPOSITION

In terms of ethnicity, the permanent population is overwhelmingly Han Chinese, at about 90 percent. The remainder of the population is split between aborigines, divided into 14 officially recognized tribes, and recent immigrants. The breakdown for the **Han**

Xinyi District, Taipei

Florent Bonnefoy/Michelin

Chinese segment is roughly 70 percent Fujianese (or Hoklo), 15 percent Hakka and 12 percent "mainlander."

A **mainlander** is an individual who came in the exodus to Taiwan with the Kuomintang after the KMT lost the Chinese Civil War in mainland China—or a descendant of such a person. The mainlanders held almost all higher positions in government and big business during martial-law rule, and only with the island's democratization, after the lifting of martial law in 1987, is this imbalance being rectified.

The ancestors of the **Hakka** came to Taiwan almost exclusively from the mountainous areas of Guangdong Province in mainland China during imperial times. Though many settled on the better lands of the lower areas, they were quickly outnumbered and forced into the hills between them and the mountain aborigines by the Fujianese. Such actions were a repeat of the experience of the minority Hakka in their relations with the non-Hakka **Han Chinese** for centuries on the mainland. Once settled into the hills of Taiwan, the Hakka engaged in traditional pursuits such as mining, logging and slopeland farming.

Heavy concentrations of Hakka remain in these areas, notably Hsinchu and Miaoli counties and the Meinong area of Kaohsiung County. In fact, the handpainted oil-paper parasols made in Meinong are a Hakka creation. The Hakka have a reputation for frugality, diligence and community spirit. The first ROC president born in Taiwan, Lee Teng-hui, is a well-known example of Hakka success.

The ancestors of the **Fujianese (Hoklo)** came predominantly from the south part of Fujian Province in mainland China, or "south of the Min River" (hence, the adjective Minnan, as seen in architectural styles). The language spoken by their descendants in Taiwan today is referred to as both Taiwanese and Minnanyu, though some variation has been introduced during the 400 years since the Fujianese began settling on the island.

The **mainlanders** arrived in Taiwan with very few women, and tended to marry Hakka before marrying Fujianese. The Hakka shared a comparatively amicable relationship with the mainlanders, as opposed to the Fujianese.

Nowadays tensions generally simmer in the background, but are slowly fading as greater equality in education and socio-economic status accompany the emergence of democracy; **socioeconomic position** is becoming more important in marriage decisions than ethnic origin. However, temperatures rise in the lead-up to important elections, with the Kuomintang still generally seen as the party of the mainlanders and the Democratic Progressive Party decidedly the party of the Fujianese.

RECENT TRENDS

Since the 1990s a **new minority** has emerged that has challenged previous ways of thinking and official policies. Today the island is home to about 410,000 spouses born outside of Taiwan, or 1.7 percent of the population. Of the total about 260,000 are from mainland China, 140,000 from Southeast Asia, primarily Vietnam, and 10,000 from Hong Kong and Macao. More than 90 percent of these marriages involve Taiwanese men marrying women from overseas.

With money-earning ability and education levels rising quickly over the past few decades, and especially so among local women, many men left behind on the socioeconomic ladder have found it impossible to find local partners. Typically, a trip to Southeast Asia, for example, will involve a marriage broker and a choice of mate within a few days, usually a woman from a low-income family seeking a better life and money to help family members left behind.

The **divorce rate** is about 2.5 times higher for these couples compared to Taiwanese-only couples.

Children born to foreign spouses now account for 6.75 percent of elementary-school students. One in seven newborns in southern Taiwan is born to a foreign spouse, one in ten in Taipei.

Rotating Credit Associations

The basic model for *huzhuhui*, or private rotating credit associations, follows this pattern: an organizer brings together a group of people. Each promises to pay him NT$10,000 at the same time once a month. With each round members can bid against each other to borrow the entire amount, perhaps saying other members need give them just NT$9,000 each. That month each member thus earns NT$1,000 in "interest." If there is no bidder in a round, a forced bidder may be chosen by lot, and obliged to bid a minimum reduction. If anyone absconds with the money borrowed in a round by refusing to pay their share in later rounds, the organizer must make it up. Police and legal authorities will not get involved, so members seek to minimize risk by trying to ensure they know all other members in any new group. People will finance home purchases, small business ventures and other significant investments this way; none of the *huzhuhui* activity is reported for tax purposes. During the frenzied economic-miracle heyday, *huzhuhui* returns topped 20 percent and more, but today are considered good at 10-15 percent.

ECONOMY

The explosion that characterized the local economy from the 1960s to the early 90s is commonly described as the "Taiwan **economic miracle**." Growth rates have moderated since then, but are still the envy of Western nations. As in Asia's other "Little Tigers" (Hong Kong, Singapore and South Korea), Taiwan's political leaders realized in the 1960s that, for assured future prosperity, a transformation from churning out cheap consumer goods for export was needed, along with burial of the idea that "Made in Taiwan" meant made poorly.

GLOBAL POSITIONING

Then in the late 1970s and early 80s, prescient economic planners recognized the impact that **high-tech electronics** would soon have on the global market. It was decided to open what is today called the **Hsinchu Science Park**, concentrating talent and making it easier for business and government to work symbiotically. Results have been startling: a number of other high-tech industrial parks have been opened, and mainland China has used the Taiwan model for a string of coastal high-tech export enclaves that have driven its economy over the last two decades. Today the island is a dominant power in numerous related industries, including contract semiconductor manufacturing, TFT-LCD panels, laptops, computer peripherals, optoelectronics and smartphones. In 2008 Taiwan was the world's 18th-largest trading territory, 26th-largest economy, and fourth-largest holder of foreign-exchange reserves. Nominal **Gross Domestic Product** (GDP) per capita was just over US$17,000, and almost $31,000 in terms of Purchasing Power Parity (PPPs).

Since the late 1990s the central government has been encouraging and supporting local enterprises to switch from the production of other firms' original equipment to establishing their own brands. Acer has been the greatest success story, today number two in the world in terms of the production of **personal computers**, behind Hewlett-Packard.

The common business model has been to move manufacturing operations to nearby low-cost China; design and other forms of intellectual property are largely kept in the homeland.

Taiwan is mainland China's biggest source of **foreign investment**. At any one time, over 500,000 Taiwanese businesspeople and their dependants are living across the Taiwan Strait, primarily in Fujian Province because of physical proximity and the close linguistic and cultural ties.

Concentrations of Taiwan citizens are large enough that familiar Taiwanese educational institutions and commercial concerns have set up shop to cater to their needs.

TRADITION'S RELEVANCE

Taiwan has been a member of the **World Trade Organization** since 2002. The service sector accounts for about three-quarters of the island's economy. Nevertheless, though the driving forces in today's economy are decidedly white collar and high tech, with post-secondary education crucial, certain traditional approaches to economic activity remain key. Two of these are *guanxi* (關係), or "connections," and what are called *huzhuhui* (互助會), "mutual assistance associations," sometimes translated as rotating credit associations. In the days of old, bureaucracy was decidedly the enemy, though today it is much more responsive.

To expedite matters individuals will carefully cultivate *guanxi*, personal relationships with those who may be able to help them down the road—periodically give gifts, take them to dinner, help them with a personal situation, and so on. After you call in a favor from the person, sometime later that person has the right to call in a favor from you.

What keeps the system intact is **personal honor**—to not respond to a request is a shameful act, something others may find out about that will cause tremendous loss of face. While some *guanxi* cannot be defined as economic acts, much of it is; such services would most likely require financial compensation in the West.

The island's **per capita income** and personal savings rates are among the highest in the world. Though the banking sector is now well developed and stable, much economic activity still occurs off the books, with individuals in need of capital turning to family or *huzhuhui*.

RELIGION

The Taiwanese are an open-minded, accepting people, and this forbearance extends to religious expression. There is total **religious freedom** here, and an individual faces no persecution for practicing a non-mainstream religion.

REGISTERED GROUPS

The three **main organized religions** are Buddhism, Daoism and Confucianism, though, strictly speaking, the latter is not a religion. Age-old **folk beliefs** and practices also continue to play an intimate role in everyday life. Christianity and Islam are other formal forms of worship prominently practiced. Nearly 15,000 places of worship and as many as 26 religions are registered with the government, for tax-exempt status, including Confucianism.

Throughout Taiwan proper and its offshore islands are found just under 15,000 registered places of worship,

Palanquin and pilgrims, Beiji Temple, Tainan

Rich J. Matheson/Michelin

Fengshui

Fengshui, which literally translates as "wind and water," is a form of geomancy in which material elements in one's immediate environment, natural and manmade, are blended in harmony to allow beneficial *qi* (氣) to flow. *Qi* is "vital energy" that flows through the natural world. The visitor to modern, high-tech Taiwan will see fengshui in practice all around, if they know where to look. Restaurants, homes and other places might have an aquarium in the entrance, placed at a right angle. The square shape deflects bad energy, and the fish inside may absorb it; a fish found floating is believed to have died from it and thus protected the premises. Few banks or hotels have their counters directly facing the doors, for such placement invites profits to flow out. Rural hillsides will be covered in tombs facing every which way; each of these has been positioned individually for perfect fengshui, on advice of a geomancer.

encompassing 8,600 Daoist temples and 4,000 Buddhist temples. Because the ancestors of most people on Taiwan came from south of the Yangtze River, the main forms of worship are southern in nature, meaning Daoist and even Buddhist temples are more intricate and the pageantry more elaborate and colorful. South China religious expression is also characterized by a **laissez-faire mix** of Daoist, Buddhist and in some instances, even Confucian elements and icons within the same temple. The idea is that one worships whichever gods are most effective. If you ask a person in Taiwan what religion they follow, they will have difficulty answering any single one if they follow the main forms, for they follow them all and have never spent much time trying to understand which elements are which.

COMMON BELIEFS

Traditional **folk religion** is a kaleidoscopic combination of deities, spirits and mystical beliefs. Elements that the visitor will most likely see practiced are ancestor worship and fengshui.

Outsiders generally believe that Confucian respect for elders is the source of **ancestor worship**, but Confucius bowed to the already common tradition of honoring, and praying to, one's ancestors.

It is commonly believed that when a person passes away, he or she becomes a spirit, entering another world where there are material needs much like our own.

Many deities, in fact, serve roles similar to the officials of imperial days; the City God overseeing each urban area is a prime example.

Most families will burn paper money and offer food before a family altar that holds a tablet, considered sacred, inscribed with the names of most often three generations (sometimes more) of predecessors. The spirits partake of the essence of the food, which the family consumes later, and the smoke carries the essence of the money to the next world. In modern times, unusual items such as paper TVs, expensive cars and mansions are burned—all in miniature. If the ancestors are well taken

Taipei City Hall
Florent Bonnefoy/Michelin

care of, they protect home and hearth, but if abandoned, the family is inviting ill fortune.

GOVERNMENT

When the Kuomintang came to Taiwan in the second half of the 1940s, the structure of the government practiced by the Republic of China (ROC) continued. It is a semi-presidential system, and there are five branches of government: the Executive Yuan, Legislative Yuan, Judicial Yuan, Examination Yuan and Control Yuan.

The Examination Yuan is responsible for the civil-service system, including qualification examinations and screenings, and the Control Yuan has oversight over the conduct of public officials, possessing powers of impeachment, censure and audit. By law, its members are completely independent of party influence. The formation of the ROC government structure stems from **Sun Yat-sen**'s foundational political philosophy and constitutional theory as expressed in his Three Principles of the People. Martial law, imposed in 1949, was lifted in 1987. Elections at all government levels are today fully democratic, and there is **universal suffrage**.

Elections are vigorously contested at all levels, and for key elections, campaign rallies surpassing thousands of attendees are common.

LIFESTYLE

For most people on the island, identity is closely tied to one's career. It is de rigueur to carry **name cards**. On first meeting anyone new, whether for business or for private purposes, business cards are almost always exchanged.

SOCIAL STANDING

One's title in a company, and to a large extent the status of one's company, establishes a person's social status. People will take a card with two hands, inspect it closely, and then put it away with care, acts which indicate respect for the other individual. In business contexts a person with position will almost always be referred to by that position—Manager Li rather than Mr. Li, for example. The traveler to the island would be wise to have cards made up if he or she does not already have them; small printing firms are plentiful, and a hotel concierge will help.

STATUS OF WOMEN

Women in Taiwan enjoy a high degree of **equality**, achieving top positions in the workplace and generally controlling the purse strings at home. Key historical factors are said to have played a part in such status. One such factor was the great demand from factories when Taiwan's economic miracle took flight. Women took up these jobs, often moving away

Ximending, Taipei

Florent Bonnefoy/Michelin

Spirit money

Rich J. Matheson/Michelin

from home and seeing a bit of the world, and sometimes earning more than the men in their families. This factor helped to cause a change in the social standing of the sexes.

CONSUMERISM

The people of Taiwan have deep affection for the traditions of the past while at the same time pursuing the modern, especially the material modern. On the same day, a person may visit a temple to pray to a god for success in an exam, business venture, or some other important life event, and then go out shopping for the latest smartphone or laptop. As throughout the rest of East Asia, there is a fascination with new **high-tech gadgetry**, and it is common to purchase a mobile phone every so often to keep up with the latest looks and specifications.

With people of Chinese descent, one's self image, and one's image and social status with others, is usually measured in terms of **material success**, as in most modern countries. If one has achieved material success, one is expected to flaunt it. Universally sought-after brands will be prominently shown on apparel and accoutrements; one's Rolex must be worn so that others can see it. If a person has "made it," one says so by purchasing a Mercedes, an aspiration not unique to the Taiwanese, but common to most industrialized nations.

GENERATION GAP

Most young people will live with their parents until they get married, unless distant schooling or work forces them out. The structure of the family is slowly changing, with the **extended family** gradually being replaced by the nuclear family, though parents will still live close by. Younger people are increasingly individualistic, with those born after 1980 or so ignorant of the want and poverty known by their elders. The older generations, as is the case most everywhere, worry about the values of the younger, seeing the island's famed **work ethic** fading and self-interested individualism on the rise, a phenomenon unheard of, and frowned upon, in traditional Chinese culture. The elders sometimes refer to the young as the "strawberry generation"—pretty on the outside, but turning to mush as soon as any pressure is applied to them. They feel that young people want the rewards before they put in the work. The truth, of course, lies somewhere in between.

The older generations have some of the highest **personal savings rates** in the world, but the younger generations, highly educated, raised in small families and pampered by parents and grandparents, have a taste for spending money, rather than saving it. **Traditional values** clearly continue to predominate in social life, even in that of young people, despite their being more individualistic than their seniors. The people of the island pride themselves on their spirit of *renqingwei* (人情味), which can be defined as "human feeling," and for being *reqing* (熱情), or "warmhearted."

THE WELCOME MAT

Once a personal connection is made with a local, the ancient tradition of being *haoke* (好客) or the "good host" will kick in with the latter. The visitor will be taken out to meals, and any small favor asked for or anticipated will be handled. Confucius did not say "Do unto others…." Instead he said "Do not do unto others…."

The people of Taiwan thus think that, if it were they who were traveling or living in a land far away, they would not like it if the local people were cold and indifferent; and so they act accordingly when meeting new people at home. The visitor who makes an attempt to understand the local culture is commonly embraced warmly by Taiwan residents, and virtually any cultural faux pas is forgiven, knowing they'd have the same trouble if in another country.

Flying in the face of the spirit of *renqingwei* is the too-often-seen lack of civic-mindedness displayed by the people of Taiwan in public. Much of the Chinese ancient history has been turbulent, strangers have been perceived to mean trouble, and one takes care of only what one controls, with a fierce loyalty to family and friends, even when in public positions.

Thankfully much of this inconsideration is slowly disappearing as a result of government efforts and the attainment of a higher education level. Taiwanese people do exhibit virtues, such as discipline and patience, in public. In service for more than 15 years, the Taipei metro, for example, has remained free of graffiti, and people stand patiently in line to board the trains.

CULINARY CUSTOMS

The people of Taiwan have a fascination with food. People today still greet each other by saying *Chi bao le mei* or "Have you eaten?" as often as they will say *Ni hao* or "How are you?"

PLAYING THE HOST

The concept of *renqingwei,* or "human feeling," *(see above)* is extended to embrace that of *qingke* (請客), or playing the host. The local concept of **hospitality** is entrenched, and people love to treat others to a meal. Because homes have limited space, meals are often hosted out. Local folk know that Westerners often observe the custom of paying for one's own meal—or going Dutch, to use the old expression—but here someone will always *qingke* and pay the bill. Anthropologists describe this phenomenon in many societies: the big man redistributing wealth

Raohe Night Market, Taipei

Florent Bonnefoy/Michelin

Taiwan's Night Markets

In addition to enjoying delectable snacks or even a meal from stalls arrayed with vegetables, seafood, meats, fruits and desserts, many Taiwanese, especially the young, go to night markets for social reasons. The lively, crowded setting provides an opportunity to people-watch, exchange news or spot a long-lost friend.

among those present to maintain his social status, but to the Taiwanese the idea of going Dutch is usually seen as demeaning. The exception is a couple of friends deciding to dine together and to go Dutch, with no ill feeling.

In surveys tourists to Taiwan consistently rate the food, and notably the snacks at its **night markets**, among the island's top attractions. The view of this place as one of the world's great culinary emporiums is justified; the people of Taiwan, who love to eat out, have choices available that few other lands do.

When the Kuomintang came to the island in the late 1940s, a talented corps of chefs followed, some on the personal staffs of high civilian and military officials, others with renowned restaurants that changed their addresses across the Taiwan Strait. The best of all **regional Chinese cuisines** was added to mainland China's southeast coastal culinary traditions brought earlier by the forefathers of the extant population.

Within a few years, poorly educated common soldiers from mainland China were being demobilized in large numbers; unable to go home, they set up small shops and stalls and introduced to Taiwan the simple traditional snacks from many mainland China regions. Perhaps the most famous and beloved of these snacks is beef noodles, celebrated today with an annual festival in Taipei.

TRADITIONAL FEASTING

The **feast** is looked upon as a celebration of friendship, and the drinking of toasts is a much-loved part of this tradition. The Japanese introduced beer to the island; such refined Western alcohols as whisky and cognac are popular—especially as gifts—but at feasts the preference is for old-time Chinese favorites *Shaoxing* wine, made from rice, and *kaoliang*, a sorghum spirit. Both are Taiwan versions of iconic drinks given life in imperial China. *Shaoxing* is brownish-yellow in color; because it is bitter, it is generally taken warmed up and with a dried, salted plum in the glass. *Kaoliang* is firewater, the standard version being 58 percent alcohol.

One tradition that entertains travelers newly arrived from another culture is that of **fighting for the bill** at the end of a meal, (though this practice occurs less often these days). Though one person has clearly invited the others, the invitees will grab for the bill and insist on paying. The host loudly protests. A good-natured fight ensues, but the host rarely loses. The idea behind the fight is

Toasting Rituals

At feasts the first toast at a table is for everyone to join; all later rounds will be between individuals. Shot-type glasses are used, and there will be gentle, good-natured pressure each round to *ganbei* (乾杯) or literally, "dry glass," meaning to down the entire amount. The overseas visitor will be toasted by everyone, so pacing and discipline is needed. "Real man" drinking prowess is still much admired, but if approaching one's limit outright, good-natured refusal is accepted. Locals might become very red-faced when drinking, for many Chinese lack the enzyme to break down alcohol. A bit of drinking then a bit of eating is the answer, the food absorbing the alcohol, and a round or two of tea at the end is common, helping happy imbibers to sober up a little.

a compliment; that the host has been far too generous.

Feasting is a favorite activity in Taiwan. Companies throw grand year-end banquets, or take an overseas business guest out for a **small banquet.** Families invite friends out to celebrate happy family events. Temple associations host feasts for people in the community. The large round tables in a typical Chinese restaurant seat about 10 people. This capacity means the feast will have 10, or a few more, courses. At each table's center a Lazy Susan, or revolving tray, allows every diner easy access to all the main dishes. Newcomers to the island learn quickly to pace themselves. The price for each course goes down the more courses are ordered; this rule applies to alcohol as well, and empty bottles are often collected at tableside for counting at meal's end.

MUSIC

The people of Taiwan have a noted love of music. The musical traditions of the **aboriginal tribes** are well documented, and today continue to form a central part of their lives. The Hakka had a long tradition of singing while working in the fields. Traditional festivals are still at the core of living for all people of Han descent on the island, and music is at the core of these celebrations.

The **karaoke** phenomenon, a Japanese import, is a popular feature of everyday living. Groups of seniors belt out favorite old tunes in parks using a portable karaoke machine. The company bus trip, a much-loved part of Taiwan life, is outfitted with karaoke equipment so the passengers can sing on their way to sightseeing destinations. Karaoke parlors called **KTVs**, found in all urban areas, are multi-floor facilities where friends rent a den-like room with a television (the "TV") and karaoke equipment (the "K"); the KTV provides food and drink and a selection of favorite Chinese, Japanese and Western tunes. Preferred Western songs tend to be golden oldies.

The most popular singing stars specialize in **Canto-pop** and **Mando-pop**, meaning sweet and syrupy songs done in Cantonese by talent from Hong Kong and pop tunes done in Mandarin by talented musicians from the Chinese-speaking region. For decades, Taiwan has been the center of the Mando-pop universe.

The current Taiwan queen of the pop charts is **A-Mei** (Sherry Chang). A member of the Puyuma tribe, she sings in her own language, as well as Mandarin, Taiwanese and sometimes English. The reigning king is **Jay Chou**, who blends Chinese and Western musical elements to create an original sound with veins of R&B, rock and pop. Unlike the usual mainstream pop singer, Chou tackles meaty issues such as war, urbanization and domestic violence.

Percussion performance, Fuyuan Village, Hualien

Liao Tai-chi/Kwang Hwa Mass Communications Taipei

59

The island has a thriving live-music scene, with bars and clubs booking everything from pop to underground indie bands; a number of places in Taipei and Kaohsiung regularly bring in DJs, singers, and groups from the West.

Several large-scale **music festivals** are held around the island each year. The biggest is **Spring Scream**, held annually in Kenting National Park. A Woodstock-style multi-day event, it is a rite of spring for many young Western expatriates, featuring local and international indie bands. The **Ho-Hai-Yan Rock Festival** is a multi-day event held at Fulong Beach on the northeast coast each July and August. Both indie and mainstream groups, local and overseas, are featured.

The Taipei Traditional Arts Festival is staged April through June, with most concerts held at the historic Zhongshan Hall, home of the Taipei Chinese Orchestra. This event is a great opportunity to enjoy **traditional Chinese music** and arts from Taiwan and elsewhere. On December 31 each year, the Taipei New Year Countdown Party is held around the Taipei 101 skyscraper; the district is closed to vehicular traffic, and a spectacular midnight fireworks show envelops Taipei 101.

SPORTS

Frequent personal participation in recreational sports and the staging of commercial, mass-audience sporting events became taken-for-granted features of life in Taiwan only in the post-WWII era, when Westernization set in. Now, a wide variety of sports facilities—basketball and tennis courts, indoor badminton courts, swimming pools and baseball diamonds—can be found throughout the island. The games of professional baseball and basketball leagues are well-attended.

BASEBALL

Baseball was introduced to the island by the Japanese when they controlled the land from 1895 to 1945. A great moment in local history was the first time a Taiwan team beat a Japanese team, in a landmark exhibition in 1930. The game's popularity surged when Taiwan Little League teams began winning World Series titles in the 1960s, claiming 17 overall, though success has not come since the 1990s.

The Chinese Taipei baseball team—the representative team for Taiwan in international baseball—currently is ranked fifth in the world. In the past decade Taiwan talent has finally made it into the US professional baseball arena, with hero **Wang Chien-ming** becoming, for a time, the ace of the New York Yankees pitching staff before injuries hobbled him. The whole nation would seem to come to a halt for his outings; huge screens in public places drew thousands to watch in the early morning Taiwan time.

Pre-game warmup, Tianmu Baseball Stadium, Taipei

© Chris Stowers/Apa Publications

There is a local professional league, the Chinese Professional Baseball League (CPBL); the teams are owned by area corporations. Each team has a different city as a home base, but play many "home" games away in other cities to capture the widest possible fan base. Most talent is local, but teams will carry a number of overseas players, most from the Spanish-speaking Americas. The league was immensely popular in the 1990s, with crowds regularly topping 10,000, but repeated gambling scandals have reduced this number to a few thousand loyalists, save for playoff games.

The **game-day experience** is a world away from that in the US, with the two teams' fans decked out in their heroes' colors and dividing along the first- and third-base lines. They are thumpingly loud affairs with constant din, generated by drums and noisemakers. It would be the height of public rudeness to boo or mock the opposition; instead the group cries will the favored team on. That baseball icon, the hot dog, is not seen; vendors instead hawk *biandang* (便當), lunchboxes with a rice base and sausage. A good place for the visitor to take in a game is Tianmu Baseball Stadium in Taipei, easily accessed via MRT train.

BASKETBALL

Taiwan's basketball players have not done so well on the international stage, but passion for the game continues to be stoked by passion for the NBA, with games frequently on cable TV. Youth are seen wearing their favorite team jerseys in public. It is the most popular sport that people actually play; courts are found in every neighborhood, most often on school grounds, packed from the time classes let out until dark.

The top local league is the semi-professional Super Basketball League (SBL), founded in 2003, whose teams play "home" games around the island. There is also the Women's Super Basketball League (WSBL). Crowds for the men's league average about 1,000 per game. Players are mostly local, but with star players now starting to leave

to play in the richer mainland China league, organizers decided that with the 2010 season, all seven teams could hire import players, most from the US, rather than only the three non-playoff teams. A good place for the visitor to watch a game is the new Taipei Arena.

MEDIA

With the lifting of martial law in 1987 came an easing of media restrictions, and in the intervening 20-plus years, the number of TV channels has proliferated. The Chinese-language media in Taiwan are fiercely competitive and almost totally **free of political interference**. There is abundant choice in all areas; cable TV has more than 70 percent penetration, and newspapers are ubiquitous.

As in most developed economies, the majority of people rely on television for their news. Journalistic standards are not high, one reason being that salaries are low, with the result that journalists tend to be young and inexperienced. What is deemed "investigative" reporting is heavily focused on political and pop-star figures, and the basic facts on which stories are built are too often uncorroborated. Political investigative reporting is often highly politically biased.

English-language media resources are also widely available. **Cable TV** services offer about 100 channels, many English, with CNN, Discovery, ESPN and HBO carried by almost all services. There are three local English-language **newspapers**, *Taipei Times, Taiwan News,* and *The China Post,* the first being by far the most professional. Hotel newsstands carry the major international newspapers such as *The New York Times* and *International Herald Tribune,* as well as magazines such as *The Economist.*

The sole English-language **radio station** in Taiwan is the Taipei-based ICRT (International Community Radio Taipei). The FM channel 100.7 features Western and local pop music, news broadcasts, and other standard, popular radio fare. The daily schedule is carried in the local English papers.

History

Located just off mainland Asia, Taiwan has always been a crossroads for peoples on the move. In the days of oceangoing canoes and sailing ships, the seasonal winds along coastal China and the powerful Kuroshio Current flowing east of Taiwan swept in voyagers from many different lands, many permanently, some temporarily. Among the permanent were the ancestors of today's 14 recognized aboriginal peoples, whose geographic origins are debatable. In the era of sail, the ancestors of today's Hakka and Fujianese—all Han Chinese—came from the coastal areas of mainland China directly across the Taiwan Strait. In modern times engine-powered modes of transport—ships and planes—have brought from all mainland areas the Han Chinese, referred to simply as "mainlanders." The result is a culture of tremendous diversity whose treasures are becoming ever wider known to travelers from around the globe.

Remnants of Dutch Fort Provintia, Tainan

Rich J. Matheson/Michelin

PREHISTORY TO DUTCH ERA

Taiwan's earliest years of human settlement are shrouded in mystery. From finds at more than 500 sites, archaeologists have surmised, with carbon dating and other techniques, that the first prehistoric people arrived on the island 10,000 years ago, and perhaps earlier. The most widely accepted hypothesis is that Taiwan served as a stepping-stone for **Austronesian peoples** in a general movement from south China to the islands of Southeast Asia and the Pacific. Building on the marked heterogeneity of Austronesian languages spoken by Taiwan's many aborigine groups, linguists have concluded that the island was a center of language dispersal for the Austronesian diaspora, finding that the Taiwan variants are among the earliest in the family tree.

The earliest references in Chinese records to what some believe to be the island of Taiwan are the Land of Yangzhou. Documents from 206 BC, at the dawn of the powerful Han dynasty, mention the imperial commissioning of an expedition to find and explore this land out in the little-known seas. In AD 239 the **Kingdom of Wu**, which had arisen in China after the collapse of the Han dynasty, outfitted a 10,000-man force to occupy and, it seems, settle the island. This expedition is described in the ancient classic *Sanguoji* or *History of the Three Kingdoms*.

Early in the 15C began the remarkable saga of **Zheng He**, the great navigator whose giant dragon-eyed ships sailed all the way to the coast of Africa and so say some, well beyond. A eunuch in the Ming imperial court, Zheng was sent out—though he had no previous maritime experience—with a powerful, armed fleet supplied by his emperor. Considered a usurper, the emperor, Zhu Di, desired to proclaim his power to the wide world and to search for a rival claimant to the dragon throne who had disappeared. The **Chinese dragon**, a powerful and auspicious creature, was the symbol of the emperor, especially the five-clawed yellow dragon. It is believed that on one occasion, in

1430, a typhoon drove Zheng to the mysterious island of Taiwan, where he reprovisioned and returned to the empire claiming to have "discovered" this new land. He reported that he had made contact with the aborigines and learned of useful medicinal herbs, but he made no mention of any permanent Chinese settlements.

Despite his claimed discovery, the island was known to the Han Chinese of southern coastal China. From the 14C through the 16C, **pirates** from mainland China and Japan were a scourge, continually raiding the China coast and attacking ships in the Taiwan Strait, then racing to Taiwan, a safe haven beyond the reach of imperial military power. During this period, and perhaps as early as c.1200, Han Chinese were settled on the **Penghu Islands** in the middle of the strait; most are believed to have been Hakka escaping persecution back home. No friends of authority, the Hakka were not trusted. A Ming garrison was eventually set up here, but there was no willingness to chase pirates into their hiding place, since Taiwan was thought to be inhabited by fierce, headhunting "barbarians." So they wouldn't aid the marauders, the people of the Penghus were eventually forced to return to the mainland. An imperial ban was put on emigration to the Penghus and to Taiwan, and all maritime activity, except coastal sailing, was forbidden. The imperial court believed that any Chinese who set up a base outside the Middle Kingdom were suspect, since they could eventually align with others and return to contest the governing authority.

Portuguese traders en route to Japan called Taiwan **Ilha Formosa**, or "beautiful island," in the 1540s. The Portuguese established a trading settlement in north Taiwan in 1590, but the effort was short-lived. In 1598, under the Tokugawa Shogunate, the Japanese organized an expedition numbering several thousand strong to take the island, but fierce resistance from aboriginal warriors defeated the attempt. The various tribes rarely were successful in cooperating with each other, save when

a threat from without emerged. Japan did succeed in founding a settlement called **Takasago** on Taiwan's southwest coast, and a sporadic group of Japanese pirates and traders were resident elsewhere on the island. For a time the Japanese even secured tentative control of the northern coast. When the Tokugawa Shogunate implemented a policy of isolation, however, the Japanese in Taiwan were left stranded, without support from their homeland. After repeated clashes with the Dutch, who arrived in 1624 demanding taxes on trade and imposing other restrictions, the Japanese departed in 1628.

DUTCH PERIOD
THE HONGMAO OR "RED-HAIRED BARBARIANS"

The Dutch were intent on controlling the lucrative **maritime trade** between Japan, China and Southeast Asia. The Chinese court had rescinded restrictions on maritime activity in the late 15C, and there had been a boom in fishing and seaborne trade in the Taiwan Strait. After a failed attempt to wrest Macao from the Portuguese by force, the Dutch set up a small fort in Penghu, which had been christened the Pescadores, or Fisherman's Isles, by the Portuguese in 1622. The Ming government demanded they abandon the isles, considered Chinese territory. After learning that an overwhelming naval force was soon to move against them, the Dutch agreed; their counter-suggestion that they move beyond the pale to Taiwan was accepted.

In 1624 the **Dutch** settled on land where today's city of Tainan stands. They built an impressive fortification, Fort Zeelandia, at the end of a large sand spit that curved to form a natural harbor with just one safe entry point, called Luermen or Deer Ear Gate. The **Spanish**, in control of the Philippines and wishing to control the Japan trade, countered with forts on Heping Island in today's city of Keelung in 1626 and with another small fort at Danshui in 1628. The latter was abandoned in 1638; local natives up the Danshui River and in the Taipei Basin had been overwhelmingly hostile. The Keelung outpost surrendered to the Dutch in 1642, the Spanish garrison having been weakened by disease and transfer of a large contingent of soldiers back to the Philippines to quell an insurrection by the Chinese population.

The initial Dutch plan was simply to use Taiwan as an entrepôt for maritime trade. It was soon realized, however, that exploiting the island's natural resources for export and taxing the local population would bring even greater lucre. Systematic efforts to develop the island were made, though the Dutch never directly controlled more than small chunks of coastal land. Despite the imperial ban on migration, **Chinese peasants** were brought in to farm the land and work the mines. Most of these commoners came from the coastal province of **Fujian**—mountainous, with limited arable land, and overpopulated—where they had been exploited by officials. By the time the Dutch left Taiwan in 1662, the Chinese population had reached about 50,000; the Dutch numbered 2,000 to 3,000, the majority of them soldiers.

The Dutch introduced new crops and tools. Dried fish and deer meat were exported to China, sugarcane sugar and deerskins to Japan; there was great demand for deerskin from samurai, who covered armor, helmets and quivers with it. Chinese settlers were provided tools, shared oxen, and seed to set up farms, with 10 percent of production taken as tax. Fishing and hunting were also taxed. Commercial deer hunting was particularly lucrative, with licenses going to the highest Chinese bidders and 10 percent of hides, antlers and meat confiscated as tax. The antlers were used in Chinese medicine.

GROWING DISCONTENT

Grievances increased among both Chinese and aborigines as the levies grew ever more burdensome. Additional taxes on such items as alcohol and butter were imposed, followed by a **head tax** on all Chinese more than six years old. The Chinese could not buy the land

they worked, which was officially the property of the Dutch sovereign. It was also commonplace for Dutch soldiers to turn to intimidation and extortion, and the native inhabitants especially resented exploitation of their women (there were few Chinese women in this frontier society).

Having suffered a number of aboriginal attacks from outlying villages in the Tainan region, the Dutch, with the arrival of reinforcements, undertook a major **campaign of reprisal** in 1635-36. After expelling the Spanish from northern Taiwan in 1642, the Dutch launched another major offensive in 1644, moving south along the Danshui River into the Taipei Basin. Upon the aborigines' surrender, the Dutch selected village headmen to replace the old leaders, and undertook missionary and education initiatives. Romanized scripts were created for a number of tribes; such scripts were still in use by the 1800s for land contracts between the Chinese and aborigines, long after the Dutch had gone. There were conversions to Christianity, the majority in some villages, but animistic beliefs and practices continued.

In the areas they controlled, the Dutch sometimes tried to forcibly expel from the villages female shamans, who understandably attempted to turn their people against Christian ideas and Dutch rule, as threats to their own authority. The practice of headhunting in areas of Dutch control was suppressed, but not eliminated. There was also partial success in stopping the practice of abortion by massage among the Tainan-area Siraya people, who thought if a wife was pregnant while her husband was on a hunt—for game or human heads—ill fortune was sure to strike him.

Overall, the **aborigines** had better relations with the Dutch than they did with the Chinese. Major uprisings by the Chinese against the Dutch took place in 1640 and in 1652. During the second rebellion, many aborigine settlements in the Tainan region sided with the Dutch, their warriors and Dutch soldiers armed with muskets crushing the poorly armed peasant rebels. The Dutch in general did not allow farmers to use metal implements, fearing they could be turned into weapons. Thousands of Chinese peasants were slaughtered.

Its introduction attributed to the Portuguese, **opium** had been used in limited quantity in China for medicinal purposes. The Dutch introduced to the Chinese the mixing of opium with tobacco and smoking it in a pipe. The opium was brought in from the main Dutch East India Company base in Asia, Batavia (today's Jakarta). After the 18C, British-ruled India supplied the opium to China. The practice of smoking it for pleasure spread from Taiwan to Fujian and elsewhere in the Middle Kingdom, playing a direct role centuries later in the infamous Opium Wars and eventually, in the fall of the Qing dynasty.

ZHENG DYNASTY RULE
THE MING DYNASTY FALLS

In 1644 the **Manchu**, destined to rule China as the Qing dynasty, swept into Beijing. They were allowed through the Great Wall by defending Ming general Wu Sangui in the forlorn hope that the Manchu would drive out a rebel army that had taken the city, and somehow cooperate with the restored Ming thereafter. The Ming dynasty was crumbling, and over the next few decades, loyalists were squeezed, pressed into the Middle Kingdom's southern reaches. One such loyalist was Zheng Cheng-gong, better known in the West as **Koxinga**, Lord of the Imperial Surname, an honorific granted by the Ming court in recognition of his efforts to defend Chinese rule.

Zheng controlled a powerful navy along the southern coast, inherited from his father. Like his father, Zheng sometimes acted as merchant, sometimes as pirate. His base was in Xiamen (Amoy), in the coastal province of Fujian. However, after his army was driven back with heavy losses upon its near success in taking strategic Nanjing, he was hard-pressed along the coast by the besieging Manchu. The Manchu were horsemen, moving rapidly on land in the more open north but slowed in the rice-growing south, and without a navy.

Nevertheless, Zheng soon realized his Xiamen position was untenable and began formulating plans to take Taiwan from the Dutch, which would put him beyond Manchu reach. His plan was to regain his strength and return to the mainland. The head of the Dutch colony in Taiwan, Frederick Coyett, got wind that something was afoot, alerting his Dutch East India Company superiors in Batavia and requesting reinforcements. His warnings were dismissed as alarmist, and nothing was done. The Zheng attack came and succeeded, and as such things commonly work out, the hapless Coyett was blamed and even imprisoned for a time.

OUSTER OF THE DUTCH

The attack came in 1661, Zheng arriving off Tainan after first taking Penghu. With him were 25,000 men and 900 war junks. The Dutch numbered 2,800 (2,200 soldiers and 600 civilians). Zheng had a clear blueprint of Dutch infrastructure, provided to him by a former Chinese guide and Dutch defectors. He knew the one access point into the sheltered harbor, the guide advising him which small islands to sail between and where the Dutch had sunk hulks as obstacles. Just before the attack, it is said, he prayed to an icon of **Mazu**, the goddess of the Sea to whom all south China seafarers were devoted, and miraculously the tide rose to allow harbor entry. The fight was thus over the moment it began. After a nine-month siege of **Fort Zeelandia** the Dutch surrendered; Zheng allowed Coyett and his survivors to leave for Batavia, though without their lucre.

Zheng died just three months later, only 38 years old, possibly from malaria. Yet before his death, he had already begun the process of changing Taiwan into a semblance of a **Ming state**, though Taiwan's frontier character would remain until almost all arable land was claimed and cultivated in the mid-19C. In his entourage were more than 1,000 scholars, artists, monks and masters of almost every realm of classical Chinese culture. Chinese-style government was established, its base in **Tainan**. While the siege was still on, it was realized that local agricultural production was insufficient to feed the Zheng army, and military farms were established throughout the southwest, with soldiers rotating between field and active duty. Place names of these large-scale plantations survive today, notably Zuoying ("Left Camp") in Kaohsiung, southern terminus of the new high-speed rail line.

To prevent the Chinese from aiding or trading with Zheng, the Manchu forced all residents along the south coast to move inland. Great suffering ensued, and many managed to escape to Taiwan. By the time of the fall of the Zheng family in 1683, the island's Chinese population had jumped to 100,000.

THE ZHENGS BECOME RULERS

It is believed by historians that Zheng, realizing the Ming dynasty was doomed, was secretly planning to establish his own kingdom. Though **Prince Ningjing** (see p269), the last heir to the Ming throne, was in Tainan, Zheng gave him little time. The prince's palace is today's Grand Mazu Temple in Tainan, the first Mazu (goddess of the Sea) temple built by the government in Taiwan. Zheng sent a Spanish friar to the Philippines to relay a demand that the Spaniards pay Zheng an annual tribute, prompting a Spanish massacre of Manila's Chinese population on the correct suspicion that they would play a role in Zheng's planned invasion.

The short Zheng dynasty was characterized by intrigue and scandal. Zheng Cheng-gong's son **Zheng Jing** had an affair with his younger brother's nursemaid. His father was enraged, and ordered his own brother to travel to Xiamen to kill his son. The order was not carried out, and soon after his father's death, Zheng Jing defeated a competing faction to assume the throne. In 1681, upon Zheng Jing's own death, his eldest son Zheng Ke-zang was placed on the throne.

The intrigue seriously weakened the dynasty; soldiers and naval men were steadily defecting. The Qing became aware of the travails in Taiwan, and the court appointed a former Zheng naval commander named **Shi Lang** to organize and lead an expedition. Shi had long before had a falling out with Koxinga and had been pleading with the court ever since to attack Taiwan. In 1683 he set out with a large fleet and delivered a fatal blow to the Zheng navy in the Penghus, overcoming the relative inexperience of his forces by assigning five junks to each single Zheng junk and swarming it through encirclement. The die was cast, and the last Zheng king gave up without a struggle. Shi Lang showed surprising leniency by granting him and his inner circle a comfortable exile in Beijing. With one of the last pockets of Ming patriotism defeated, dreams of a Han Chinese renaissance were being snuffed out.

Today, in the 21C, Zheng Cheng-gong is considered a folk hero, and even revered by some, on both sides of the Taiwan Strait. In Taiwan his most honored deed was to wrest the island from the Dutch and bring it within the Chinese realm. In mainland China his most venerated feat was his push to drive out alien rule in the form of the Manchu. This desire for independence from outside influence was successfully attained later by the

Statue of Zheng Cheng-gong, Koxinga Shrine, Tainan

Rich J. Matheson/Michelin

Communists, who in 1949, were able to claim that China had at last "stood up" by defeating the Kuomintang (KMT) in the civil war (*see sidebar*) that erupted after the Japanese had been expelled from China in 1945, and at the same time, finally driving out the Western powers.

QING DYNASTY RULE

Shi Lang and his inner circle set about systematically confiscating the property of the local notables. The Shi clan, especially, came to acquire great wealth.

The Qing court at first wanted to abandon the island and ship the entire Chinese population back to the mainland, considering the island barbarian and requiring too much expense and trouble to govern. Shi Lang, however, was convincing in his arguments that the island could become self-sustaining, and had to be held to prevent its use as a **base for attack** of the mainland by an enemy force, Chinese or foreign. Most Chinese were shipped back by the Qing, for fear they would become an enemy force as they had been under the Zhengs. The court assented, and in 1684 Taiwan was made a prefecture of Fujian Province. Qing rule was always nominal, the limited number of Manchu officials on the island almost as a rule giving in to self-indulgence and corruption; an appointment to the outpost was considered a career-destroyer.

Taiwan under the Qing never became self-sustaining—it was subsidized until the moment the island was ceded by the imperial throne to the Japanese in 1895. The Qing never attained full control over the entire island, leaving much of the isolated east side to what were called "raw aborigines," in contrast to the "cooked aborigines" that had come under Chinese control. The Chinese controlled only about half the island's territory, and the **Han Chinese** did not become the majority ethnic group until the 19C.

THE WILD, WILD EAST

Official prohibitions on **immigration** from the mainland were roundly ignored, often with the connivance of officials on both sides of the strait in return for financial incentives. Minor and major **rebellions** were incessant—mainlanders commonly derided Taiwan by saying "every three years an uprising, every five years a rebellion"—often quelled only by rushing in thousands of soldiers from across the strait, at tremendous expense. Forces stationed on the island were incompetent, poorly trained (if trained at all) and almost always seriously under-strength; monies for pay, equipment and rations were given directly to superiors, who could pocket any unused funds. This practice remained the norm until the era of the Kuomintang. The nominal number was generally around 10,000; soldiers rotated back to the mainland every three years.

Serious **ethnic strife** was the norm. In the mountains and isolated flat areas of the east and south, the aborigines would still fight each other, but more often fought the encroaching Han Chinese. The Han Chinese were divided into three main groups: the Hakka from northeast Guangdong Province and two Minnan or "south Fujian" groups, one from Quanzhou Prefecture, one from Zhangzhou Prefecture. Though the Hakka were early settlers on the flatlands, attempting to escape persecution in the mainland, they were once again outnumbered by other Han and again forced up into the hills, pressing against the mountain aborigines. Though strife between Hakka and aborigine was at first serious, with time accommodations were reached.

This détente was in part possible because, for both Hakka and aborigine, the greater enemy was seen to be the flatland Fujianese group. The greatest ethnic bloodshed during the Qing era was between Hakka and Fujianese, the two sub-groups of the latter often joining forces. When not busy fighting the Hakka, the Fujianese would fight each other. Some towns were mixed, with temples becoming command posts when fighting broke out, but in rural areas the population of each small town or village tended to be from one ethnic group only, and some sort of fortification was common, generally tamped-earth enclosure walls. The government tended to exacerbate the situation by employing Hakka as fighters whenever there was unrest among the Fujianese, deepening the anger and mistrust between the two sides. The ethnic strife finally died out during the 1850s, when new **arable land** was no longer available to be contested.

True power in Taiwan lay with families who acquired a great deal of land and the loyalty of those in their region from the same ethnic group. The fortified residential complex of the **Lin family of Banqiao**, a satellite city across the Xindian River from Taipei, still stands today. In the 19C, and into the early 20C, the Lins were the most powerful clan in north Taiwan, building, among other things, the Small South Gate (still standing) in the old Taipei city walls and financing the Han expansion into Yilan County, including the opening of today's **Caoling Historic Trail**. The extensive irrigation systems that so dramatically expanded agricultural productivity and made the island a key supplier of produce to China, Japan and Southeast Asia were, for the most part, financed and built not by the government but by these clans. Taiwan was known as the **"breadbasket"**—for rice—to mountainous Fujian Province, which lacked arable land but not population. Despite a bounty of food, Taiwan could not cover the high cost of running a frontier society, and had to be subsidized.

During the period of Qing rule, there were 159 **rebellions**, including three of what were termed "great rebellions" in 1714, 1787 and 1833. The insurrection led by **Lin Shuang-wen** that started in late 1786 was the most destructive in the island's history. The Heaven and Earth Society was founded in Fujian Province in the 18C as a **secret society** devoted to "opposing the Qing, restoring the Ming." Frontier Taiwan played a key role in the incubation and spread of secret societies, also known as triads. Lin's anti-Manchu crusade was launched near present-day Taichung, and as the fighting spread, his followers engaged in wanton destruction, looting and murder. Simmering ethnic tensions quickly surged to the fore, and Lin's Zhangzhou fighters began attacking Quanzhou and Hakka villages. The fighting soon enveloped all Chinese-controlled areas, and 50,000 reinforcements from the mainland had to be brought in, aided by Hakka, Quanzhou and aborigine volunteers. Afterwards the government made serious efforts in central Taiwan to resettle the Quanzhou and Zhangzhou populations to keep them as separate as possible.

WESTERN POWERS THREATEN

With the **First Opium War** between China and the Western maritime powers in 1839-1842, the partition of the Middle Kingdom had begun. Taiwan's strategic location in the western Pacific was noticed by the imperial powers, who were looking for **military bases** from which to protect their trade interests—and noted in turn by an increasingly anxious Chinese government. The ending of the **Second Opium War** in 1858 opened treaty ports in Taiwan, gave foreigners the right to settle and gave them extraterritorial rights. William Jardine of the powerful Jardine Matheson and Company advocated the British annexation of Taiwan, among other strategic territories, at the start of the First Opium War. Commodore Matthew Perry later recommended the same to his American political leaders. In 1874 the Japanese sent a military force of 2,500 troops and 1,000 laborers to south Taiwan, officially to punish aborigines at the southern tip for killing shipwrecked Okinawans in an 1871 incident—historically referred to as the **Mudan Incident**—but understood to be a preparatory mission for much larger Japanese plans.

The Chinese government was galvanized to make Taiwan more defensible, in part by promoting some level of development and modernization, fearing it could be used as a launching pad for attacks against the motherland. **Japan** was the most immediate worry. Capable officials were sent out, starting in 1874,

Lin Mansion, Banqiao, Taipei County

Florent Bonnefoy/Michelin

to execute such plans as organizing militias, constructing gun emplacements along the coast, initiating coal mining in the Keelung region using efficient Western methods, setting up cable links between north and south and between the island and mainland, and building roads from lowland areas into the mountains. The last was undertaken to bring the mountain aborigines under control, to Sinicize them, and eliminate them as a rear-line threat during any attack from the sea.

The most talented, effective and progressive Qing official on the island, **Liu Ming-chuan** was Taiwan's first governor (1884-91) after it was declared a province. While in Taiwan he introduced the first street lighting in China, laid the first railroad, broadened and straightened streets, and carried out key tax and fiscal reforms that encouraged economic initiative. By doing so he also created many political enemies among the corrupt, risk-averse and ultra-conservative ranks of officialdom, who successfully moved against him. Liu was recalled under a cloud and retired; reform and development came to a halt. (One note of interest is that the hardware for Liu's rail line from Taipei to Keelung was first used for China's first railway, built by the British from the Yangtze River to Shanghai, but soon bought by the Qing and

ripped out as a fengshui abomination cutting up the countryside.)

The **Sino-French War** of 1884-85 was a struggle in which the French, successfully, sought to oust the Chinese from Tonkin (North Vietnam) and take control. The French took Keelung on Taiwan and set up a strong defensive position, but could not advance on Taipei. Their attack on Danshui was repulsed. Late in the conflict the French took Penghu. A stalemate ensued, and peace negotiations brought agreement on French withdrawal from Taiwan and Penghu and Chinese abandonment of Tonkin.

JAPANESE COLONIAL ERA
A MODEL COLONY

In 1894 war between China and Japan finally came. The modernizing Japanese were bent on **empire-building** in the same manner as their Western colonial models, and their efficient navy obliterated their Chinese foe, which famously went into battle with, among other deficiencies, a great portion of their shells empty of explosives.

Monies earmarked for naval modernization had instead either been stolen or used to rebuild the Summer Palace, destroyed by the West during the Second Opium War.

In 1895 the **Treaty of Shimonoseki** ended the First Sino-Japanese War,

69

which had focused on disputed hegemony over Korea. The 1895 treaty ceded Taiwan and Penghu to the victor. The people of Taiwan learned of this concession only after the fact, and prepared to resist.

The **Republic of Formosa** was declared, hoping that the Western powers would look upon this promise of democratization favorably and force the Japanese to back down. The Yellow Tiger Flag was unfurled, a tiger on a blue background (the original flag is on display today in the National Taiwan Museum in Taipei). The tiger was chosen as a complement to the Chinese imperial dragon to demonstrate to the dragon throne that though now a republic in name, the island still considered itself part of the Middle Kingdom.

From the West came no succor. The Japanese landed in force near Keelung, marched to and took Taipei, then worked their way south. But the Taiwanese put up a fight. Over 7,000 Chinese soldiers and thousands of civilians were killed over several months before the resistance collapsed.

The 50 years of **Japanese rule** can be divided into roughly three stages, the first from 1895 to 1918. The Japanese were anxious to make Taiwan a **model colony** as proof they were a legitimate colonial power. Their rule was strict, harsh and unpopular, yet many of their changes were beneficial. The aim was to build Japan into an industrial powerhouse, with Taiwan serving as an agricultural supply station, a market for Japanese finished products and a place to transfer surplus population from the then-overcrowded home islands.

Sporadic armed resistance was suppressed. The 1915 **Tapani Incident** was the largest revolt by the Taiwanese and approximately 10,000 lost their lives.

The Japanese implemented a number of island firsts: introducing strict police controls, eliminating widespread opium addiction, conducting a comprehensive land survey, collecting accurate census data, beginning a railroad and road system, standardizing measurements and currency, building hospitals, enforcing strict sanitation rules in the home and in public, and commencing systematic study of the indigenous Austronesian Malayo-Polynesian peoples.

CULTURAL ASSIMILATION

During the second period of Japanese rule, from 1918 to 1937, compulsory Japanese education and **cultural assimilation** were primary themes. The focus in terms of economic development was adjusted, with the island now seen as the future launch pad for military expansion into Southeast Asia to secure natural resources such as oil. Kaohsiung was transformed from a sleepy fishing harbor into a major shipping port. The Sun Moon Lake power-

Republic of China

The Republic of China (ROC) was founded in 1912 by Sun Yat-sen, its first president, and his revolutionary alliance. To assure the emperor's abdication, Sun had to relinquish the presidency. Over the years, Sun saw the government he worked to establish crumble. Before his death in 1925, he reorganized his party as the Kuomintang (KMT), or Nationalist Party of China, and worked for China's unification. A new national government was formed in 1927, and Sun's military-school protege, Chiang Kai-shek, succeeded in military campaigns to bring the divided country together. Communist revolutionaries had opposed the ROC government for years, but in 1945, the government and the Chinese Communist Party agreed to set up a democratic government after WWII. Fighting soon resumed, however, between government troops and Communist forces. Nonetheless a new constitution was in effect in 1947. By 1948 a National Assembly was elected, which elected Chiang as ROC president that same year.

Chiang Kai-shek, Franklin Roosevelt, and Winston Churchill at Cairo Conference in 1943

plant project was undertaken from 1931 through 1937, expanding the size of the mountain-surrounded lake and providing the great amount of power needed to develop aluminum, chemical and steel-alloy production on the plains, all of which had military applications.

After the **Marco Polo Bridge Incident** in 1937, in which Japanese and Chinese troops clashed in Wanping, southwest of Beijing, Japan and China were once again openly at war. The bridge controlled railway access from isolated Beijing to the Kuomintang-controlled south; it is believed that the Japanese forced a truce-breaking shooting incident as a prelude to their push into central China.

From 1937 to 1945, the duration of the **Second Sino-Japanese War**, there was an attempt in Taiwan to force the naturalization of the local population as Japanese. There was pressure, by legal means and through intimidation, to adopt Japanese names, wear Japanese attire, eat only Japanese food, and observe Japanese religious rites. Locals complied to protect themselves, but maintained their sense of identity through myriad means. One example: when puppet troupes performed, they had a safe Japanese version of a play when Japanese officials were present and a true Taiwanese one the troupe could instantly switch to when the officials were gone.

MODERN TAIWAN
IMPACT OF WORLD WAR II

The Japanese attack on **Pearl Harbor** in Hawaii in 1941 drew the US into World War II, which meant immersion in the ongoing Asian conflict. Riddled with military installations and heavily garrisoned, Taiwan was used as the **launch pad** for Japan's push into Southeast Asia and the south China mainland. General Douglas MacArthur's plan to invade Taiwan to use it as the base for final action against the Japanese home islands was abandoned since it was thought Allied losses would be too high. Instead, the island's military facilities were repeatedly bombed. More than 200,000 Taiwanese served in the Japanese armed forces, some 80,000 in combat. About 16,000 of the total volunteered; the rest were conscripted in 1944. The majority of volunteers served to escape limited rations and severe discrimination.

Generalissimo Chiang Kai-shek represented China at the **Cairo Conference** in November 1943 in Egypt. He, US president Franklin Roosevelt and Britain's Prime Minister Winston Churchill met to discuss the status of Asia after the end of the war. They agreed to continue using military force against Japan until it surrendered unconditionally, and to return Taiwan to China after the war.

In August 1945 the Japanese surrendered to Allied forces, ending World War II. Taiwan was returned to China.

71

China's Civil War

After Japan's defeat ended WW II, full-scale civil war erupted in 1946 as long-standing rival factions scrambled to claim Japan's former land holdings in China. Backed by the Soviet Union, the Chinese Communist Party (CCP), led by Mao Zedong, viewed the ruling Western-supported Kuomintang (KMT, or Nationalist Party of China) of Generalissimo Chiang Kai-shek as corrupt and elitist. Rallying millions of peasants to their side by promising land, the Communist forces engaged in the final push to defeat Kuomintang forces in late 1949. Chiang and a million KMT supporters fled to Taiwan, setting up the government of the Republic of China (ROC) "temporarily" in Taipei, until mainland China could be reclaimed. In Beijing Mao declared victory and newly named the country the People's Republic of China (PRC). Minor fighting continued in the Taiwan Strait archipelagos into the late 1950s. No treaty or armistice was ever signed to formally end the war.

THE NATIONALISTS TAKEOVER

After the Japanese surrender, Japanese soldiers and civilians on Taiwan were gradually repatriated. Kuomintang troops were transported by the Americans to Taiwan's shores. Before long, tensions arose between the local population and the KMT, or Nationalist Party of China. Hunger spread, and there was hyperinflation. Matters came to a head in 1947 with what is called the **February 28 Incident** —commonly referred to as "2-28." On February 27 an elderly woman selling black-market cigarettes in Taipei was accosted and wounded by police. A crowd gathered, shots were fired and one man was killed.

The next day the island exploded in anger, tensions boiling over, after protesters were fired upon and some killed. Governor Chen Yi feigned cooperation, negotiating reforms with local leaders, while awaiting reinforcements from the mainland. When they arrived a **witch-hunt** ensued, with leaders and potential leaders down to high-school level hunted down. A government investigation in 1992, instigated by the KMT leadership at the time, estimated that 18,000 lost their lives.

AN AUTHORITARIAN REGIME

After 2-28 came the period referred to as the "White Terror," several decades marked by authoritarian rule of the government, which strongly reacted to any form of political dissent. Defeated by the Communists on the mainland, ROC

president **Chiang Kai-shek** fled in 1949 to Taiwan, where he took tight control of the island. **Martial law** was declared in 1949, resulting in press censorship and restrictions on individual freedoms of speech and assembly. Firm political control would subside only in the 1980s, however, after Chiang's death in 1975. His son **Chiang Ching-kuo** succeeded as president in 1978, and responded to the prevailing winds of change by allowing reforms. Martial law, in effect since 1949, was finally lifted in 1987.

ERA OF REFORMS

In the 1950s the KMT began implementing changes that led to improvement of life on the island. The early steps of **land reform** were taken that helped pave the way for eventual economic prosperity. Throughout the decade agriculture was systematically supported. A land-to-the-tiller program obliged landlords to sell land they did not farm themselves; the land was sold at very affordable prices. **Economic power** became more equally distributed.

These changes included political ones. Beginning in 1950, **direct elections** of some offices were permitted. Dissenting voices eventually made their way onto the political stage, and in 1986 a new political party was founded, despite a ban on such formations. During Chiang Ching-kuo's presidency, private visits to mainland China were permitted, later to increase spectacularly in volume. Since 1991, articles have been added to the 1946 Constitution that allow direct elections of the office of president and legislators. Five years later, in 1996, the first direct presidential election was held; direct elections have continued to this day.

THE TAIWAN ECONOMIC MIRACLE

In the 1960s came a shift to light industry —the genesis of the "**Made in Taiwan**" phenomenon and the Taiwan "economic miracle," with the island transforming into one of the globe's richest and most advanced economies in just a few decades. Such labor-intensive exports as textiles, paper and electrical goods were emphasized. Benefiting from low labor costs and a hardworking people, Taiwan quickly emerged as a dynamic and successful exporting economy. During this period agricultural exports continued, notably rice, sugarcane sugar, pineapples and mushrooms—a key source of industrial-investment capital. Such items were in short supply for the general Taiwan population, and very expensive. Sweet potatoes were used as a rice substitute for bulk at mealtimes, a practice begun in WWII. Today some elderly citizens refuse to eat them, their memories of poverty distasteful.

With the dawn of the 1970s, **major infrastructure** projects were undertaken in support of the decision to try to move up the industrial ladder, among them the first North-South Freeway and the Chiang Kai-shek International Airport.

The road and rail networks were upgraded and expanded, as were ports, and the first nuclear power plant was built. Toward the end of the decade, rising land and labor costs had become a concern, and a move into high-tech manufacturing was decided upon.

In 1980 high-level government economic planners presciently discerned the beginnings of the age of high-tech electronics and gained permission to launch the Hsinchu Science Park. The park has been an immense success, and Taiwan has become a world leader in many related sectors.

Government research continually serves as an incubator for new sectors, such as optoelectronics, with vanguard knowledge and monies fed to new **private-sector** entrepreneurial undertakings.

QUALITY OVER QUANTITY

In the past few decades, the people of Taiwan have attained what are among the highest income and education levels in the world. Since the lifting of martial law, civil society has flowered. Modern conveniences such as the Taipei Metro (1996) and the Kaohsiung Metro (2008), as well as a **high speed rail** (2007) system, have greatly improved domestic

High Speed Rail

© Chris Stowers/Apa Publications

travel. Overseas study and travel have become common. The result is awareness of international best practice, and demand for these same levels at home. Efforts are being made to green Taiwan's cities and to improve recreation and leisure facilities. At the start of the Taiwan economic miracle, the city of Taipei was described as "the ugly duckling of Asia," an insult that could have been applied to other urban areas on the island. The Taiwan of today is light years away.

TIME LINE

Events in *italics* represent milestones in history.

PREHISTORY TO DUTCH PERIOD

c.10,000 BC– 500BC – Prehistoric sites in Taiwan, some dating back 10,000 years, indicate systematic settlement, though origins of peoples and connection to modern indigenous groups unknown.

206 BC – Oldest record of China believed to refer to Taiwan names it "Land of Yangzhou."

AD 239 – Kingdom of Wu sends unsuccessful expedition of 10,000 to Taiwan, first Chinese attempt to claim island.

c.1200 – First believed Chinese settlement, in Penghu Islands, primarily Hakka Chinese.

14C-16C – Taiwan becomes base for Chinese and Japanese pirates and traders, beyond reach of China authorities.

1540s – Portuguese navigators on way to and from Japan christen Taiwan *Ilha Formosa*, the "beautiful island."

DUTCH PERIOD

1622 – The Dutch, ejected from Macao, seize the Pescadores (Penghu Islands) and move to control all Taiwan Strait trade.

1624 – *A large Chinese naval force convinces the Dutch to abandon Pescadores; the Chinese allow them to relocate to Taiwan, beyond the Chinese pale.*

1626 – The Spanish seek to counter the Dutch, build fortifications at today's Keelung.

1628 – The Spanish seize Danshui and build Fort San Domingo at today's Danshui.

1642 – Spanish troops sent to deal with Philippines troubles; Dutch expel remainder of Spaniards from north Taiwan.

1652 – Chinese settlers, brought over by Dutch, rebel; 3,000 killed with help of aborigine warriors.

ZHENG DYNASTY RULE

1661 – Ming dynasty loyalist Koxinga (Zheng Cheng-gong) attacks Dutch.

1662 – *After a nine-month siege, Dutch surrender, survivors permitted to return to Batavia; Koxinga dies suddenly three months later.*

1683 – *The Manchu, which have ended the Ming dynasty, take Taiwan with minimal fighting; Koxinga's son and grandson have ruled since his death.*

QING DYNASTY RULE

1786 – Another major peasant rebellion against imperial authorities begins; of Taiwan it is said: "Every three years an uprising, every five years a rebellion."

1839 – China challenges the West, primarily Britain, on opium trade, leading to First Opium War (1839-1842).

1858 – After Second Opium War (1856-1860), four Taiwan ports are opened to foreign trade.

1860s – Scottish merchant John Dodd organizes Taipei-area tea growing and introduces Formosan oolong tea to the West.

1874 – Japanese stage attack on south Taiwan, avenging killing of Japanese sailors; Qing authorities are unnerved, and slowly begin fortifying island.

1884-85 – During the Sino-French War, the French occupy Keelung and Penghu and attack Danshui.

JAPANESE COLONIAL PERIOD

1894-95 – *The First Sino-Japanese War ends in China's defeat; Taiwan, not engaged in the fighting, is ceded to Japan.*

1895 – Taiwanese militia fights Japanese landing and occupation; final holdouts crushed after months of fighting.

1895-1945 – Japan rules Taiwan as a "model colony;" infrastructure, public order and hygiene are much improved.

1915 – Tapani Incident, last major Taiwanese uprising, in which about 10,000 die.

1930 – Wushe Uprising in central Taiwan, last major aboriginal uprising; put down with overwhelming force.

1932 – After learning baseball from the Japanese, a Taiwanese team defeats a Japanese team for first time in a friendly game between youth teams.

1935 – Taiwan Exposition staged, a propaganda showcase for Japan's colonial expansion in Asia.

1937 – Second Sino-Japanese War (1937-1945) erupts with Marco Polo Bridge Incident.

1941 – Pearl Harbor is attacked, drawing the US into World War II, in which the ongoing Asian conflict had become a part.

1943 – Roosevelt, Churchill and Chiang Kai-shek gather for the Cairo Conference, ending in agreement that when the global war ends, Taiwan will be returned to China.

1945 – *WW II ends. Taiwan returns to China. Japanese soldiers and civilians are repatriated.*

1946 – *Full-scale civil war erupts in China between the Communists and the ruling Kuomintang.*

MODERN TAIWAN

1947 – The February 28th Incident brings mass protests against Kuomintang rule; in the period that follows perhaps as many as 18,000 locals lose their lives. *Decades of political repression ensue.*

1949 – *Chiang Kai-shek and a million KMT supporters retreat to Taiwan. Martial law is imposed. In Beijing Mao Zedong declares Communist victory in the civil war and proclaims the establishment of the People's Republic of China (PRC).*

1951 – In signing the San Francisco Peace Treaty, Japan formally renounces sovereignty over Taiwan.

1960 – Taiwan's emergence as an exporting powerhouse begins, the start of the decades-long "Taiwan economic miracle."

1965 – The National Palace Museum opens in north Taipei.

1969 – Taiwan wins its first of 17 Little League World Series.

1975 – *Chiang Kai-shek dies;* Chiang Ching-kuo succeeds as president and allows reform.

1979 – *The US ends formal diplomatic relations with the ROC, switching them to the PRC.*

1980 – *Hsinchu Science Park is opened in Hsinchu, to become the engine behind Taiwan's high-tech exporting economy.*

1987 – *Martial law is lifted, and the ban on private visits to mainland China repealed.*

1988 – President Chiang Ching-kuo dies.

1996 – After almost 20 years of planning, the first phase of the Taipei Metro opens.

1999 – The massive 9-21 Earthquake hits central Taiwan; 2,400 are killed, thousands homeless.

World Games held in Kaohsiung in 2009

Chen Han-yuan/Kwang Hwa Mass Communications Taipei

2001 – *Crouching Tiger, Hidden Dragon,* directed by Taiwan's Ang Lee, wins four Oscars.

2002 – Taiwan enters the World Trade Organization as the "Separate Customs Territory of Taiwan, Penghu, Kinmen and Matsu." Drought reduces reservoirs to record lows; the government imposes water rationing in Taipei for first time in 22 years.

2003 – The SARS epidemic hits, deeply impacting the economy; within three months the World Health Organization declares outbreak contained.

2004 – Taipei 101, for a time the world's tallest building, is completed.
The full length of Taiwan's second North-South freeway opens; it is later named the Formosa Freeway.
Taiwan wins its first ever gold at the Olympics in taekwondo.

2005 – Taiwan Indigenous TV hits the airwaves.
A portable pension system is inaugurated.

2006 – Wang Chien-ming becomes the New York Yankees' ace pitcher, the third Taiwan native in the major leagues.

Xueshan Tunnel, the world's fifth-longest highway tunnel, begins operations.
Taiwan's men's team garners island's first-ever gold medal for baseball at Asian Games.

2007 – The Taiwan High Speed Rail system goes online, connecting Taipei, Kaohsiung and west-coast by bullet train.

2008 – Kaohsiung's MRT (mass rapid transit) system, the island's second, goes operational.

2009 – Landslides caused by Typhoon Morakot bury mountain villages.
The World Games are held in Kaohsiung, the largest international sporting event ever staged in Taiwan.

2010 – Taiwan is hit by its biggest-ever sandstorm, rolling in from North China.

2013 – Southern branch of Taipei's National Palace Museum to open in Chiayi County.

Architecture

The architecture of Taiwan, given the island's checkered history, spans a wide spectrum of influences and styles, both Eastern and Western.

ABORIGINAL TRADITIONS

A few distinct traditions can be found among the dwellings of Taiwan's aboriginal groups. Such types of shelter date back thousands of years. The Tsou people lived in **dome-shaped houses** with mud floors and thatched roofs; the Amis lived in homes made of wood, bamboo and betel palm. One of the more common types of abodes, however, which still can be found among the tribes of the Paiwan, Rukai, Bunun, Tao (or Yami), Puyuma and Atayal, is the stone-slate house.

Stone-slate houses were usually semi-subterranean, with a square or rectangular cavern first dug into the ground so that the structure was essentially partially above and partially below ground. The entrance was small, requiring people to hunch over when walking through. Walls were sometimes composed of stone shingles and slates; others consisted of a large, single slab of stone. Thinner, lighter slabs were thatched to create the roof of the house. The stones were gathered from nearby cliffs and riverbeds.

Stone-slate dwellings were usually built into the face of a mountain, with the back of the house supported by the mountain's base. Because they were partially underground, the houses were very low in appearance, but in effect, well protected against typhoons. The lack of adhesives in construction resulted in **well-ventilated** houses that were highly resilient in wind. Furthermore, the weight of the stone provided strong foundational support in the event of an earthquake, in which case the stone slabs of the roof would tend to slip off and away from the direction of the house.

Where to See:

The Rukai people of Wutai, and of Duona in South Taiwan, still live in stone-slab dwellings. The Museum of Natural Science in Taichung has replicas of aboriginal houses on permanent display. Also the Shung Ye Museum of Formosan Aborigines in Taipei permanently displays models of traditional dwellings of the Tao and Paiwan peoples.

THE DUTCH ERA

It was the Dutch who first made recorded history in Taiwan, taking to the island after the Chinese expelled them from the Pescadores. The Dutch soon discovered, however, that Taiwan had many assets as well, including plenty of sugar (which would become one of the Dutch East India Trading Company's core trading commodities). Mixed together, the sand and ground-up seashells made

Stone-slate house, Maolin

Henri Cholmet/Michelin

a fine mortar for the bricks that would form the wall of their first major base, Fort Zeelandia, near present-day Tainan.

FORT ZEELANDIA 熱蘭遮城

Allegedly, the original bricks for Fort Zeelandia were shipped over from Batavia (present-day Jakarta), where the Dutch East India Trading Company had already established a successful trading colony in the late 16C. Recent archaeological finds, however, show that the bricks have multiple origins—Penghu and mainland China, as well as Taiwan. This mix is likely due to the passage of the fort from Dutch to Chinese to Japanese hands over a period of 300 years. When the outpost was first completed in 1634, illustrations show the fort's walls reaching right up to the coastline and occupying a large chunk of what is now Tainan's **Anping District**. In fact, years of sedimentation and erosion filled in what was once a bay, which explains why the stronghold's remains are so far inland today. Another reason, which current archaeological finds are confirming, is that much of Fort Zeelandia is buried beneath the earth. What is visible today is but a small outcropping of land ringed by pyramid-like steps leading up to a platform with a 20C watchtower and a bungalow-type residence. It hardly seems imaginable that this "fort" once housed a colony of 4,000 people. However, radar excavations are now discovering that the foundations of the original fort extend much farther than previously thought, and that Zeelandia was at one point a large city outpost with both inner and outer walls.

The whitewashed observation tower was built by the **Japanese** after much of the remaining brick was carried off by the Chinese to build the neighboring Eternal Fortress. Later, after the end of Japanese occupation, the Anping site was redeveloped for tourism. The sole vestiges of the original Dutch complex are a section of wall, and a fragment located north of the fort; both have been classified as national historic monuments.

FORT PROVINTIA 赤崁樓

To get an idea of what the original terrain of Tainan looked like, bear in mind that the 4km/2.5mi of land separating Fort Zeelandia from Fort Provintia were once engulfed in water. Legend has it that **Koxinga** defeated the Dutch by blocking communication between the two Dutch strongholds.

Fort Provintia was built in 1653, about halfway through the Dutch colonization of Formosa and taking much less time than the 10 years it took to build Fort Zeelandia. Not only was Fort Provintia smaller, but its construction was undertaken in a hurry, following local uprisings that occurred the year before. The Dutch deemed it the "eternal" fort, while the colonized came to see it as "the tower of the red-haired barbarians." Like Fort Zeelandia, most of the original Dutch fort is gone, save only a few segments of **brick wall** located behind the pavilions (or towers) constructed on the fort's site beginning in 1875. Today the towers are red in appearance, after assimilation of Chinese and Japanese elements in the ensuing years, such as the upward curving eaves on the pavilions' red-tile roofs, which embody a typical Fujianese-style. In front of the first building, steles featuring Chinese and Manchu inscriptions ride on the backs of nine **stone tortoises** shipped over from the mainland during the Qing dynasty.

Unlike Zeelandia, Provintia was of service in the years that followed, housing officials of the Chentien government after the Dutch were expelled, and becoming storage space for **gunpowder** in the 1800s. Later, mismanagement under the Ming and Qing was reversed by the Japanese, who turned the site into an army hospital, as well as a place of worship for the Bodhisattva Guanyin. Following the end of Japanese occupation and multiple renamings, the site is now known as **Chihkan Tower** and remains a favorite among students, who come here to pray to the god of Literature.

CHINESE MASS MIGRATION

With their arrival in Taiwan, the Dutch unknowingly jumpstarted a mass migration of **Han Chinese** from Fujian, who not only provided manpower for the building of Fort Zeelandia, but also brought with them their own architectural traditions, namely in the form of temples. Taiwan's temples are a mixture of Buddhist, Daoist and Confucian elements, though often an amalgam of all three. One of the best places to glimpse how diverse they can be is Tainan.

CONFUCIUS TEMPLE 台南孔廟

Besides a lack of deities, Confucian temples share a universal feature: the **Dacheng Men** (大成門), or the "Great Hall of Achievement." This is the temple's main hall, where a **tablet** inscribed with Confucius' name will be found, but no images of the Master. The Dacheng Men of Confucius Temple in the city of **Tainan** is a majestic sight, once you emerge from the thicket of banyan trees in the outer courtyard, which is more often than not filled with people. The hall is enclosed within a tranquil pavilion on an elevated platform, surrounded by rooms dedicated to his scholars and guarded by eight **stone lions** (females holding cubs and males bouncing balls). Unlike the 300 or so other temples in

Tainan, the Confucius Temple is void of embellishment. What few decorations there are can be found on the Dacheng Men's central roof beam, where two elaborate, **glaze-tile dragons** sit facing each other. Between them is a seven-tiered pagoda, said to ward off evil; at the opposite ends of the beam are two chimney-like cylinders, to protect the Classics, works published by Confucius. Dragons at the ends of the double-eave roof function as drainage pipes.

Completed in 1666 Tainan's Confucius Temple was the first Confucian temple in Taiwan. It is spectacular in that, unlike the few Dutch structures that remain nearby, it has preserved its traditional appearance well, despite partial destruction due to war and natural disasters over the years. However, 30 renovations—in particular one extensive refurbishment in 1917 by the Japanese—have preserved the essence of the **Fujian-style** temple in pristine condition.

KOXINGA SHRINE 鄭成功廟

Koxinga, or **Zheng Cheng-gong** as he is known among the Chinese, is one of those historic figures who has—like many of the deities the Taiwanese revere—over time risen to the status of almost a god. After expelling the Dutch

Koxinga Shrine, Tainan

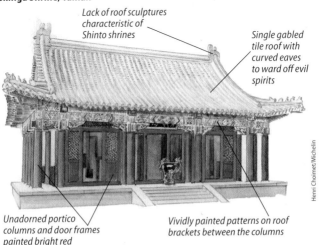

Lack of roof sculptures characteristic of Shinto shrines

Single gabled tile roof with curved eaves to ward off evil spirits

Unadorned portico columns and door frames painted bright red

Vividly painted patterns on roof brackets between the columns

Henri Choimet/Michelin

Longshan Temple, Taipei

Double gabled tile roofs topped with ornate dragon sculptures

Bronze portico columns carved with entwined dragons

Upward curved roof ridge and upward curved eaves to ward off evil spirits

Henri Choimet/Michelin

Censer (or furnace) on raised platform at entrance for lighting incense

in 1662 and reclaiming Taiwan for the Ming, Koxinga came to be regarded as a hero, and after his death, locals built a modest shrine in his honor in **Tainan** in 1663.

In 1875 the shrine was enlarged and rebuilt in the Fujianese style. Japanese elements were later added. The structure was demolished in 1961; what replaced it is the Northern China palatial-style shrine that is seen today. The **tablets** dedicated to Koxinga are also housed in a hall at the center of a spacious piazza, with stone renderings of his followers located in the piazza's encasing rooms, much like the layout of the Confucius Temple. However, unlike the tranquil gray granite of the Confucius Temple, the Koxinga Shrine gleams bright red, with a wide brick floor, and doors, pillars and walls painted an intense red. The cool teal roof tiles only slightly dampen the bright layers of blue, green and yellow paint undercoating of the surrounding ceiling beams.

The shrine is enclosed by a large courtyard, with curved walkways and artificial ponds. There are also plum trees throughout, one of which was allegedly planted by Koxinga himself. If the grounds give the impression of a Japanese garden, it is likely because the Koxinga Shrine was, for a period, also the first Japanese Shinto Shrine in Taiwan.

When compared to other temples around Tainan, this shrine is extremely clean-lined and straightforward, without the fuss of extra trimmings and overwhelming decoration.

LONGSHAN TEMPLE 龍山寺

At the other end of the spectrum is Longshan Temple in **Taipei**. The temple is indeed a carnival for the eyes: red-tile roofs, ornate rooftop sculptures of colorful dragons and other fanciful creatures, intricately carved stone columns and gilded fretwork. It is emblematic of the appearance and function of most temples in Taiwan.

Built in 1738 in one of Taipei's oldest districts, Wanhua, the temple has seen its share of natural and human destruction, in particular a devastating US bombing attack intended for the Japanese during World War II, which left the main hall and one of the side corridors completely destroyed. Still, local pride and dedication to the **Guanyin Bodhisattva**, whom this temple honors, has inspired generation after generation to rebuild and maintain what is considered the oldest and most precious temple in Taipei. Several daunting dragons sprawl across the high, concave roof of the main-gate entrance to the front hall. Red lanterns hang on opposite sides of the door; when lit in the evenings, they add a dramatic gleam to the gold-embossed walls and **ceiling underpinnings**.

The temple consists of front, main and rear halls and side rooms. Before entering the front hall, visitors light incense from a **censer** situated at the entrance and pass the two intricate bronze dragons scaling the pillars that guard the entrance. The elaborate dragons on the roofs are a signature of Longshan Temple. Upper roofs with upward soaring points at each end of the ridge are often called **swallowtail roofs**.

The first and 15th of each month of the lunar calendar are particularly good days to witness the bond between temple and community. On these days hordes of people visit to pay tribute to folk heroes and deities like Guanyin and Mazu. Though officially Buddhist, Longshan, like many temples in Taiwan, attracts worshipers of any number of other Buddhist, Daoist and folk deities.

JAPANESE TRACES

When the Japanese arrived in Taiwan in 1895, the island was in quite an unruly state, with ethnic groups constantly at odds with each other and little attention paid to them by the Qing court. And while their rule of hand could be harsh and unforgiving, the Japanese also laid the groundwork for a strong infrastructure of schools, hospitals, railways, dams and administrative buildings—many of them grandiose—throughout the island. Several of these buildings remain today, especially in Taipei City.

PRESIDENTIAL OFFICE BUILDING 總統府

The buildings in Taiwan constructed during the Japanese era are easily identifiable. They typically have, perhaps to great surprise, a distinct European exterior. In particular, the Japanese had a tendency toward **Neoclassical** features: large domes, high towers, ample use of columns and archways. The juxtaposition of red brick, the construction material of choice, against white-painted columns and arches might have been a deliberate reference to the colors of the Japanese flag.

What was deliberate is the *ri* (日) or **stacked-box shape** of the Presidential Office Building in Taipei, discernible only by an aerial view. In both Chinese and Japanese, it means "sun" and is the first character of "Japan". (The Executive Yuan, another government building erected under Japanese occupation, is also designed in this shape.) Another conscious symbolic gesture was to construct the Presidential Office Building with the main entrance facing east, towards the rising sun.

Though not completed until 1919, the Presidential Office Building began as a concept more than 10 years prior, in 1906, when the first of two contests was held to design a building to house Japan's governor-general. At the end of the second competition in 1910, the winner, **Heiji Nagano**, was selected, and his design would go on to form the tallest building at the time in Taipei.

Presidential Office Building, Taipei

Henri Choimet/Michelin

If you face the front of the building, the 11-story-high **tower,** crowned by a hollow archway and supported by a series of short ridged columns, catches your eye. The rest of the building sits uniformly at 6 stories, following linear lines that divide the grounds into two equal parts, each enclosing a spacious garden. In 1945, as World War II came to an end, air raids left multiple sections of the building destroyed; they were not repaired until 1947. Today, the Presidential Office Building is in daily use and appears in fine condition. It serves as a quintessential example of Japan's lasting impact on the island's architectural landscape.

TEAHOUSES

Though tea had been in Taiwan long before the arrival of the Japanese, it was the Japanese who brought the teahouse to Taiwan. These unimposing façades can be found all across Taiwan, particularly in **Jiufen** (九分), near the northeast coast. It is no mistake that Hayao Miyazaki modeled the town of his 2003 film, *Spirited Away*, after this mountain settlement. A gold rush in the early 1900s attracted many Japanese, bringing with them the highly refined culture of the tea ceremony.

Though the Taiwanese way of brewing tea more closely resembles the practicality of the Chinese *gongfu* **tea ceremony** (工夫茶道) and lacks the theatricality of the Japanese *chadō* (茶道), still the atmosphere of a Taiwan teahouse re-creates a Japanese ambiance, where tea is served in a small room covered in **tatami mats**; a short table is placed in the room's center, around which people sit directly on the floor. Sliding paper doors are also common, as well as a Zen-garden setting with fountains and koi-filled ponds.

Where to See:

Though largely reconstructed in the 1980s, Jiufen's narrow alleyways, wood-based structures and overhead balconies—lined by endless, hanging red lanterns—still carry strong impressions of the Japanese, who came here in the early 20C searching for gold.

ARRIVAL OF THE KUOMINTANG

The Japanese left a lasting influence on Taiwan, one that would allow the Kuomintang (KMT), when they arrived in the late 1940s, to initiate the transition from an agriculturally based economy to a commercially driven one. Concurrently, the architectural landscape began to take on the vision of Chiang Kai-shek.

THE GRAND HOTEL
圓山大飯店

One thing the Japanese didn't build in Taiwan was a high-class hotel. Although Taiwan was supposed to be only a "temporary" stop, nonetheless Chiang Kai-shek, and especially his wife Soong Mei-ling, wanted a place grand enough to house visiting foreign dignitaries.

So in 1952, it was decided that the Taiwan Hotel, constructed on the former site of the Taiwan Grand Shrine (a Shinto shrine erected by the Japanese), would be transformed into the Grand Hotel. Occupying a hill overlooking the Keelung River in northern Taipei, the monumental hotel preserves the exterior features of a traditional **Chinese temple**, such as a double-hipped roof, scarlet-colored columns embossed with gold, and brightly painted ceiling beams. However, the Grand Hotel is 12 stories high, and upon completion in 1973, it was the tallest building in Taipei. It remains the world's tallest classical Chinese-style building. That each of the 8 guest floors follows the motif of the 8 Chinese dynasties further emphasizes that it is, indeed, Chinese.

Architect **Yang Cho-cheng**—who would later conceive the design for the Chiang Kai-shek Memorial *(see below)*—had another trick up his sleeve, though it was not discovered until 1995, when a roof fire caused massive damage to the hotel's upper floors. The fire prompted a general inspection of the area that unwittingly confirmed the long-standing rumor that Chiang ordered two secret tunnels dug under the hotel, each 180m/590ft long, leading away from the hotel to nearby parks.

NATIONAL PALACE MUSEUM
國立故宮博物院

The sprawling National Palace Museum in northern Taipei is one of the most commanding buildings in Taiwan. Its mammoth interior holds one of the largest collections of **Chinese art** in the world—close to 700,000 artworks and artifacts spanning more than 8,000 years of history. To house this magnificent collection, a new museum building complex was constructed in a little over one year and opened in August 1965.

The museum's design is that of a central hall adjoined by matching wings on each side. Each wing is fronted by matching forward or protruding extensions. With its classical Chinese-style architecture featuring hipped roofs, white stone banisters and grandiose staircases, the building's exterior deliberately evokes certain aspects of its counterpart in Beijing, the Palace Museum (1925) on the grounds of the **Forbidden City**. Yet other exterior elements differ: the building is a creamy beige in color rather than vermillion red, and sports bright greenish-blue roof tiles, instead of reddish-brown, that are outlined with orange trim.

When initially completed, the 15,118sq m/27,438sq ft main exhibition building was found to be drastically short of display space. Accordingly, in 1967, the museum underwent its first **renovation**; four additional expansions have taken place since, the most recent spanning 10 years and costing over US$20 million when completed in 2007. The museum grounds now cover almost 200 acres, and include a library building and an expansive garden with picturesque pavilions, carp-filled ponds, stone bridges and tablets engraved with the verses of Chinese calligraphers.

Despite the restructuring of exhibition space and the addition of innovative displays and state-of-the-art lighting, less than one-tenth of the collection can be shown at any given time. This situation should change, however, when the National Palace Southern Branch in Chiayi, designed by **Antoine Predock**, is completed in 2013.

CHIANG KAI-SHEK MEMORIAL HALL 國立中正紀念堂

When Chiang Kai-shek died in 1975, he left behind a controversial legacy. His totalitarian rule was harsh, yet his leadership was instrumental in Taiwan's becoming one of Asia's "Four Tigers," or economic powerhouses, of the latter half of the 20C. This isolated monument in the center of Taipei was established in his honor five years after his death. Like the man himself, the hall embodies the **Chinese tradition**, but faintly alludes to American ideals—a seated statue of Chiang obliquely recalling the seated Lincoln in Washington DC, for example. Designed by **Yang Cho-cheng**, architect for the Grand Hotel, the clean, white-marble structure with double roofs of deep-blue tiles and parallel 89-step stairs (representing Chiang's age at death by Chinese count) clearly recalls the mausoleum in Nanjing of his mentor, **Sun Yat-sen**. As in Sun Yat-sen's tomb, the sun of the ROC flag is positioned in the ceiling's center. Set against plantings of red flowers, the solitary white structure with blue roofs evokes the colors of the KMT.

The ascent to the hall, which dominates a broad, open plaza, is akin to approaching the **Temple of Heaven** in Beijing. The blue-glazed tiles represent the sky. Strictly speaking, the hall's roof is octagonal, but it rises to a point to create eight "ren" ("人"), or men, symbolizing the union between heaven and earth.

POST-MODERNISM AND BEYOND

Over the past 400 years, outside forces have played key roles in shaping Taiwan's political and, consequently, architectural landscape. But the 21C is now giving rise to a new age of design, one with a bolder ambition: nothing less than to forge a unique identity. In the Taipei area, such contemporary buildings as the **Taipei Fine Arts Museum** (1983), Taipei 101 (2004) and the Dharma Drum Mountain World Center for Buddhist Education (2005) are examples of Taiwan's efforts to develop new styles befitting the times.

TAIPEI 101 (台北101)

Architects **C.Y. Lee & Partners** knew that "world's tallest building" could only be a temporary title. It was just a matter of time before Taipei 101, completed in late 2004 at a height of just over 500m/1,640ft, would be surpassed (it was, on January 4, 2010, by the Burj Khalifa in Dubai). Still, as the **world's tallest skyscraper** for 5 years, Taipei 101 made a significant mark: it was the first building to surpass half a kilometer in height, it set records for innovative technology, and it helped put Taiwan on the international map.

Described as "Neo-Regionalist Modern," the design of the stratosphere-hugging structure incorporates both old and new, borrowing from Chinese tradition while also addressing modern concerns. Curled **ruyi motifs** (a symbol of prosperity) feature prominently in the plaza, and ancient Chinese coins with square holes in the center, a traditional lucky charm, have been integrated into the design. Fengshui was used extensively: for instance, the fountain was placed strategically at the T-intersection of Songzhi (松智路) and Songlian roads (松廉路) to maintain a positive flow of *qi*.

The building's main tower is divided into 8 sections, each with 8 floors—the number 8 in Chinese culture being a symbol of fortune and prosperity. The segmentation also creates the visual effect of a pagoda or stalk of bamboo, both symbols of the earth-heaven connection and of perpetual growth. This facet of the design was not merely aesthetic; it serves a practical purpose: the 8 sections function as "mega-columns," which are designed to offer additional stability during earthquakes, to which Taiwan is highly susceptible.

The island is also prone to typhoons. To offset the force of strong winds and earthquakes, Taipei 101 has a giant, 660-ton steel pendulum—otherwise known as the world's largest tuned mass damper—which can be seen suspended between the 88th and 92nd floors. The device absorbs wind pressure and equalizes movement to prevent the building from swaying.

Taipei 101 is considered environmentally friendly: its turquoise exterior of double-paned glass offers highly efficient insulation as well as protection against UV rays. Some 20 to 30 percent of the building's water needs are supplied by recycled water. Further modifications to water, wiring and lighting systems were begun in 2009; when completed in 2011, they will make Taipei 101 the world's tallest green building (by LEED standards).

KAOHSIUNG ICONS

The **T&C Tower** in Kaohsiung was designed by the same firm as Taipei 101 (**C.Y. Lee & Partners**) and constructed in 1999. Looming high above its urban, waterside surroundings, it instantly catches one's eye. Until Taipei 101's completion, it was the tallest building (408m/1,338.5ft) in Taiwan. The tower's rather gratuitous **ogees**, the open center and other post-Modern elements are suggestive of a piece of furniture. Since the tower is in a part of town that tourists don't often visit, it's more likely that visitors will pass by Kaohsiung's striking metro stations.

Richard Rogers' linear, open-air design for the **Central Park Metro Station** tends to blend into the backdrop of a park, an effect compounded by the layered slopes of grass that enclose the

T&C Tower

Henri Choimet/Michelin

escalators of the entrance. By night, light emitted from the station and reflecting off a pure white ceiling creates a luminous glow in the darkness. The futuristic yet minimalist appearance of the Central Park station is in stark contrast to the jagged glass peak that marks the **Formosa Boulevard Station.** Its dark, almost Gothic, interior displays an altogether different kind of light show: Italian artist Narcissus Quagliata's **Dome of Light** art installation; its vivid colors and fantastical imagery evoke the stained glass of Western cathedrals.

WORLD GAMES STADIUM
世運主場

As the city with the largest population, the highest GDP and the most influential policies, Taipei often ends up stealing the show. However, the 2009 completion of the World Games Stadium in **Kaohsiung** has cast the spotlight on Taiwan's second-biggest city.

Not only is the stadium the largest in Taiwan—with a capacity of 55,000 people—it is almost completely solar-powered. Some 8,844 **solar panels** provide up to 80 percent of the building's energy needs. (On non-operation days, the power generated is fed back into the city grid.) The stadium's roof is slanted at a 15-degree angle to maximize exposure to the sun. All materials used in the construction were locally produced, from recycled or recyclable products.

At first glance, the skeletal exterior is reminiscent of **Bird's Nest Stadium** in Beijing. The two differ in great respect, however. Unlike the circular Bird's Nest, which isolates action from the outside world, the World Games Stadium is shaped like a "C," spiraling out and open-ended, allowing the spectator to feel less like being caged.

Surrounding the arena is a vast park with young trees, tropical plants, pedestrian walkways and bicycle paths. Entering the stadium from the structure's narrowest end leads to the opening of a field that drops down below the level of the main concourse. From there, white vertebrae-like concrete supports—or "saddles," as the stadium's Japanese

architect **Toyo Ito** termed them—ring the ground-level floor, supporting the upper-level seating.

From inside the stadium, the Kaohsiung skyline and nearby mountains are visible, reminding spectators that even in a stadium, they are not separated from the world. The concept of man and nature's **coexistence** epitomizes the kind of sustainable development Taiwan aims to foster in the future.

NEXT GENE 20

Next Gene 20 is the ongoing project of an impressive roster of architects from around the world, each of whom have created 20 designs for villa homes to be built along the northeast coast of Taiwan in **Aodi**, about an hour from Taipei.

In 2007 developer **Tony Lu** came up with an idea to take a picturesque plot of land, divvy it up among 20 architects, and let their imaginations go. Each of the **selected designs**—10 from Taiwan and 10 from abroad—differs drastically from the next: biomorphic (Kris Yao's "Cocoon") to fluid (Julien De Smedt's "The Twirl House") to geometric (David Chun-Tei Tseng's "Terra Vista") to mystical (Ray Chen's "Floating Courtyard"). They all present redefinitions of man's relationship to the environment, and put into question the notion "home."

In 2008 the designs were presented at the International Exhibition of Architecture at the **Venice Biennale**.

As the project picked up steam, world-renowned architects were invited to participate: Zaha Hadid (Iraq) and Ando Tabao (Japan). (Hadid and Tabao, as well as World Games Stadium architect Toyo Ito, were all advisers on Next Gene 20 from its beginning stages). As a result, the project now goes by the name Next Gene 21+1.

Construction for the housing complexes is underway, with 176 villas based on (what is now) 21 designs set for completion at the end of 2010. When finally on the market, each villa is estimated to be priced at upwards of US$3 million. *Where to See: http://www.archicentral. com/next-gene-20-taiwan-3025.*

Art

Taipei's majestic National Palace Museum, tucked into the hills north of downtown, houses close to 700,000 works of ancient **Chinese art**, including rare books, paintings, bronzes, ceramics, furniture and jades. The museum is considered one of the foremost repositories of Chinese antiquities in the world, and provides visitors with an excellent overview of traditional Chinese arts. China's wealth of artistic expression, and to a lesser extent Japan's, have undoubtedly influenced Taiwan's artists throughout the island's history, laying the groundwork for recent trajectories toward a flowering of uniquely Taiwanese works.

FINE ARTS
PAINTING

Traditional Chinese paintings were done in ink, not oils, and on silk, until paper was invented in 105 AD in imperial China. The **ink and wash** technique, created by dipping a brush into black ink, was greatly influenced by the art of calligraphy (●see below). During the Tang dynasty (618-906), the ink and wash method was used primarily to illustrate the **human figure** and the horse. Chinese artists honed the painting of landscapes during the Five Dynasties period (907-960), water and mountains being the essential components. From then until the Song dynasty (960-1279), **landscape painting** blossomed into its golden age, and is still critically considered Chinese painting's highest expression. The Song period witnessed the growing depiction of birds and flowers as the content of paintings. With the Ming dynasty (1368-1644) came the perfecting of use of **colored ink**. As artists had a wider range of colors to choose from, they filled their compositions with more elements than traditional paintings had in the past.

At the start of the 20C, Japanese colonists introduced Western artistic styles, chief among them **Impressionism**. Now-rare Taiwanese impressionist works depicting local village scenes in brightly painted colors can fetch high prices at auction.

Taiwan's short history of painting has, in recent years, jostled for a place in the contemporary art world. The 2,000-year-old tradition of Chinese ink painting has branched off into a new and vital direction on the island.

While ancient, iconic images of misty mountains topped by pagodas and gnarled trees abound at the National Palace Museum and elsewhere, contemporary ink artists have begun to use vivid color washes and **abstract compositions**.

The nascent contemporary art scene is growing steadily with the proliferation of independent galleries and art fairs showcasing the innovative work of Taiwan's artistic vanguard. Taipei's excellent Taiwan Museum of Fine Arts and Museum of Contemporary Art Taipei assemble creative exhibitions of multimedia, photography, painting, sculpture and other works by notable Taiwanese and international artists.

CALLIGRAPHY

Calligraphy is often associated with Buddhism and Daoism. Like the Chinese tea ceremony, calligraphy is thought to create an atmosphere of calm through its practice, which requires a sure hand and careful planning. The measured, **meditative painting** of Chinese characters, achieved by using a brush and black ink, is one of the most revered and ancient of Taiwan's artistic traditions. Characters can be formed in a variety of styles—from precise, geometric blocks to breezy, quickly rendered slashes of ink.

Calligraphy is found everywhere in Taiwan, from formal monuments etched in stone to Confucian temples and couplets hung above a neighborhood restaurant. Important ancient calligraphic texts are part of the National Palace Museum's vast collection. Modern calligraphic artists such as **Hsu Yung-chin** and the Ink Tide Society that he helped found are attempting to revolutionize the rule-bound art form with the use of abstract shapes and colors, at times angering traditionalists.

SCULPTURE

Taiwan's abundance of temples large and small offer colorful examples of local sculpture—from fierce-looking Daoist deities to intricately carved dragons and lions winding around columns and guarding rooftops. For most of Taiwan's history, sculpture was relegated to the realm of religious pieces and **folk art**; only in recent decades has it emerged as a fine art appreciated by critics and showcased in museums.

Contemporary sculptor **Ju Ming**'s signature series of huge, blocky bronze figures dynamically formed into tai chi poses have become quite famous. A museum in Taipei County is devoted to Ju's emotionally charged, rough-hewn works, but also includes pieces by Pablo Picasso and Joan Miró.

Ju Ming studied with another major modern sculptor, **Yang Yu-yu**, known for his highly burnished, curving abstract metal works such as *East-West Gate* on Wall Street in lower Manhattan.

Among the marquee works in the National Palace Museum's monumental holdings are historically significant sculptures. Two of them are the Qing dynasty *Jadeite Cabbage,* a surprisingly realistic bok choy cabbage carved from white and green **jadeite**, with a locust and katydid tucked into the ruffled leaves; and the *Mao Gong Ding* (1046-771 BC), a bronze tripod noted for its 500-character inscription—an outstanding example of ancient Chinese writing.

INDIGENOUS ART

Taiwan's 14 recognized **aboriginal peoples** wove textiles and baskets, carved statues, shaped pottery and made weapons for hundreds of years before settlers arrived from mainland China. A burgeoning movement that recognizes the cultural legacy of this small but vital part of Taiwan's population has helped to preserve older objects. It is also attempting to encourage younger generations of aboriginals to learn their ancestors' craft traditions. Today's Tai-

wanese artisans are producing a variety of **decorative works** that employ the native resources of the island.

ABORIGINAL HANDICRAFTS

Hailing from Taiwan's southernmost tip, the **Paiwan** are creators of distinctive, Polynesian-style carved wood statues. The **Atayal** people of northern Taiwan weave colorfully embroidered, red-patterned clothing adorned with glass beads, metal bells and shells. Pretty wooden boxes inlaid with mother of pearl are a hallmark of the **Puyuma** of southern Taiwan. The **Tao** from Orchid Island, off Taiwan's southeast coast, historically created distinctive conical helmets and armor from fish skin and rattan. This group is well-known for intricately carved wooden **fishing boats,** accented with elaborate geometric patterns in white, black and red. Taipei's Shung Ye Museum of Formosan Aborigines, across the street from the National Palace Museum, houses a wide variety of examples of indigenous handiwork and explains the origins of the Austronesian people.

TAIWANESE CRAFTS

Traditional craftsmen ply their trade around the island, turning out beautiful handmade items in shops that have operated for generations. Similar industries tend to be clustered within a single geographic area, as is the case with certain shopping districts in Taipei.

Several towns have become well known for creating specific products such as ceramics and parasols; industries have even developed around them.

Sanyi, in northern Taiwan's Miaoli County, is home to fragrant camphor trees and a bustling woodcarving industry has been the result. Hundreds of artisans in the small town's Guangsheng Village create high-quality religious and decorative works in their signature styles, some of which derive from the Fujianese style of the Ming and Qing dynasties. The community is also home to a **woodcarving museum**, the only public museum in Taiwan devoted to wood sculpture.

More celebrated than Sanyi is **Yingge**, a small town an hour's train ride south of Taipei that is the hub of Taiwan's ceramics and pottery industries. There are vendors selling both cheap, mass-produced items and finely crafted wares. Yingge also has a strikingly built, informative museum dedicated to preserving the island's ceramic industry.

The rural Hakka city of **Meinong** is famous for its beautiful but sturdy, handpainted oil paper and bamboo **parasols**. The weatherproof lacquered umbrellas feature designs of flowers or birds. The tale of the industry's arrival to Meinong is a sad one: during a visit to mainland China, a local businessman was enchanted by an umbrella maker in Guangdong Province. When the umbrella maker refused to return with the businessman to Taiwan, the entrepreneur bought out the man's business and supplies, leaving him with no choice but to move to the island.

Lantern making and decorative paper cutting are other Taiwanese crafts.

PERFORMING ARTS
CHINESE OPERA
Peking Opera

Peking Opera is a blend of music, singing, acting and acrobatics known for elaborate costumes and makeup, symbolic movements and simple stage sets. It was once heavily subsidized by the government to maintain Taiwan as a bastion of "authentic" Chinese culture. The classic opera of the 18C and 19C performed for the **Qing dynasty court** can still be found in Taiwan, where a handful of traditional and experimental troupes put on the highly stylized productions. All Peking Operas are comprised of variations on four basic character types: the female, male, painted-face male and clown. Historically, Peking Opera actors were all men. With no real props to provide contextual clues, the costumes themselves become important visual signifiers: yellow equals royalty, green means virtue and brown means old; hats and beards fill in the details. The few props there are take a little imagination to interpret as well, with an oar standing in for a boat or a whip indicating a horse.

Audiences for the complicated genre are declining, however, so troupes are attempting to find ways to update 200-year-old formulas to appeal to younger generations. The **Guo Guang Opera Company** is known for traditional staging of selections from the 1,400-work historical repertoire, while the **Fu Hsing Chinese Opera Theater** mounts more modernized productions. The experimental **Contemporary Legend Theater** has presented Western classics such as *Macbeth*, *The Oresteia* and *Waiting for Godot* in Peking-Opera style.

Performance of Rong-shin Hakka Opera Troupe

Rong-shin Hakka Opera Troupe/Kwang Hwa Mass Communications Taipei

Cloud Gate Dance Theatre of Taiwan performing "Water Stains on the Wall"

LIU Chen-hsiang/Cloud Gate Dance Theatre of Taiwan

Kun Opera

Another ancient opera form, Kun opera is gentler and more lyrical than the bombastic Peking Opera. Kun opera has been revived in Taiwan during the last decade. Dedicated Kun scholars helped prod the government into funding a program to train Taiwanese actors in Kun opera, and a few local companies have organized Kun productions in recent years, among them the *Romeo and Juliet*-like *Peony Pavilion*.

Taiwanese Opera

The island has produced its own indigenous genre. Taiwan opera, or *ge zai xi*, is a popular hybrid that combines formal Peking Opera with Taiwanese Hoklo dialect and singing styles as well as traditional *nanguan* and *beiguan* Chinese musical forms. With folk roots in turn-of-the-19C eastern Taiwan, Taiwanese opera was originally performed outdoors for religious or other festivals, and features cross-dressing female actresses portraying male characters.

The foremost practitioner of Taiwanese opera is the venerable **Ming Hwa Yuan Theater**, an ambassador of the art form, performing Taiwanese opera around the world. Ming Hwa Yuan is known for wildly creative and technically sophisticated sets and lighting as well as onstage athleticism.

DANCE

Modern Dance

Cloud Gate Dance Theatre of Taiwan, founded by **Lin Hwai-min**, is arguably Taiwan's most famous performing arts group, internationally lauded for pushing the form's boundaries and infusing it with a truly Taiwanese sensibility. Influenced by Martha Graham, yet drawing on ancient Chinese folklore and martial arts, Cloud Gate performances have interpreted Chinese legends as well as calligraphy and Taiwanese history.

In 2008 Taiwan's foremost cultural ambassadors lost their rehearsal space in a fire that destroyed three decades of props and costumes. This tragedy pushed the government to pledge additional funding and support to Taiwanese performing arts groups.

Tsai Jui-yueh was one of the first Taiwanese to study Western and modern dance technique, and in the 1950s her studio became an important center for the island's dance movement. Cultural diplomatic missions by American companies such as Alvin Ailey helped invigorate Taiwan's modern dance scene.

Liu Feng-hsueh was another pioneer in the development of Taiwan modern dance, researching and choreographing ancient Chinese movements and incorporating elements of tai chi and Peking Opera into her works. Liu was among the first to record the indigenous dances of Taiwan's aboriginal people, including the Tao, Atayal and Bunun tribes. She founded the **Neo-Classic Dance Company** in 1976 as a vehicle for her own choreography.

Aboriginal Dance

Taiwan's 14 recognized aboriginal groups have evolved unique dance traditions. Renewed interest in preserving and celebrating Taiwan's long-suppressed indigenous history and culture has led to the formation of several professional folk dance groups. The **Formosa Aboriginal Song and Dance Troupe**, founded in 1991 by young aboriginal members, recruited anthropologists to help them study and preserve the dances of their ancestors. Other important dance organizations in Taiwan include the ritualistic **Lin Legend Dance Theatre** and the Yilan-based children's folk and aboriginal dance group, the **Lan Yang Dancers**.

THEATER

In the 1970s Taiwan's theater scene began to transcend government constraints and sponsorship, producing experimental works and modern, accessible interpretations of Peking Operas. *Ho-chu's New Match,* a 1977 production by the influential but now-defunct Lanling Drama Workshop, is considered a seminal work, twisting a Peking Opera plot into commentary on Taiwan's nascent middle class. The show was restaged and updated for modern audiences in a 30th anniversary production in 2009. Director and playwright **Stan Lai** transformed Taiwanese theater in the 1980s and 90s, employing innovative improvisation techniques.

The **Godot Theater Company** adapts foreign works such as Thornton Wilder's *Our Town* and Tennessee Williams' *The Glass Menagerie* to Taiwanese settings and sensibilities. Taiwan's dynamic theater scene has attracted luminaries such as avant-garde director **Robert Wilson**, who, in 2009, helmed a Chinese version of Virginia Woolf's *Orlando,* starring Taiwan's Peking Opera diva **Wei Hai-min** in a one-woman show.

MUSIC

Chinese Classical Music

Four major professional groups perform traditional Chinese musical styles on traditional Chinese instruments. The Taipei Chinese Orchestra, National Chinese Orchestra Taiwan, Kaohsiung City Chinese Orchestra and Ensemble Orientalia of Taipei specialize in both **beiguan** and **nanguan**, the two primary traditional forms. *Nanguan,* characterized by softer, flowing melodies played on instruments such as the lute-like *pipa,* arrived on the island with waves of migrants from Fujian Province in the 17C and 18C. *Beiguan,* by contrast, came to Taiwan centuries later; it is louder and more percussive, often featuring many instruments such as gongs and drums. *Beiguan* historically accompanied traditional dramas and religious occasions.

Western Classical Music

Three prominent orchestras in Taiwan, the National Taiwan Symphony Orchestra, the Taipei Symphony Orchestra and the Kaohsiung City Symphony Orchestra, specialize in Western classical music. The Taipei Opera Theater and Taiwan Metropolitan Opera perform Western operas such as *The Magic Flute* and *Madam Butterfly.* The **National Theater** and **National Concert Hall**, a pair of handsome, red-columned classical Chinese-style buildings at the foot of the imposing Chiang Kai-shek Memorial Hall in downtown Taipei serve as Taiwan's premier performing arts venues, hosting local arts groups as well as renowned international artists.

Pop Music

The island boasts a bubbly pop music scene dominated by female artists dolled up in sexy getups and dashing boy bands singing syrupy ballads. Taiwanese pop includes catchy hooks, slick production values and entertaining videos. One innovative talent is Jay Chou, who has fused traditional Chinese sounds with hip hop and R&B; his fan base has spread across Asia. Although Taiwan dominates the Mandarin-language pop world, the Mando-pop produced in mainland China and elsewhere as well as the pop music from Japan and Korea are also big in Taiwan.

Aboriginal pop songstress **A-Mei**, known primarily for Mando-pop music, enjoys widespread success in Asia and even in the West; she appeared on the cover of *Newsweek* magazine in 2001. Death metal outfit **ChthoniC** sometimes uses traditional instruments and sings in Taiwanese or classical Chinese about Taiwanese history and folklore. Beyond the band's aggressive sound, lead vocalist **Freddy Lim** is a pro-Taiwan independence activist.

The memory of the late, beloved vocalist **Teresa Teng** lives on in her native Taiwan. Her interpretations of romantic ballads and folk songs in Mandarin, Taiwanese, Cantonese, Japanese and English, among other languages, and concerts for military personnel garnered her legions of fans across Asia. She died at age 42 from illness; her grave remains a pilgrimage site for fans.

The **indie music scene** in Taiwan has been growing since the 1980s, and now live music venues and well-known festivals such as Spring Scream showcase acts such as punk rockers **Fire Ex**, socially conscious hip hoppers **Kou Chou Ching** and indie songsters **Sodagreen**.

Pop music sung in the Taiwanese **Hoklo dialect** saw its zenith in the 1930s and 40s with local artists singing translated Japanese standards until Mandarin was enforced in 1949. These oldies are dear to many aging Taiwanese; more recent artists have interpreted Hoklo language pop for younger audiences.

Pop's dominance across the island is evident in the contagious melodies blaring from tea shops, the annual Golden Melody industry awards, and Taiwanese passion for singing karaoke versions of beloved pop tunes. Taiwan pop's high-energy style blends Western and Eastern influences to create a uniquely Taiwanese sound.

PUPPETRY

Taiwan's rich heritage of puppetry is fading in favor of faster-paced entertainment. Live shows transplanted from **Fujian Province** in the 19C used colored leather shadow puppets, marionettes or large, carved glove puppets. In the early 1900s, **traveling puppeteers** put on historical shows around the island. Japanese occupiers enlisted puppet troupes to stage propaganda plays in that language. Commonly performed for weddings, puppet shows peaked in popularity in the 1950s and 60s.

One of Taiwan's best-known puppeteers, **Li Tien-lu**, was captured in pseudo-documentary style by Taiwanese New Wave filmmaker Hou Hsiao-hsien in *The Puppetmaster* (1993). Another grandfather of the vanishing art form is **Huang Hai-tai,** who died in 2007. His grandsons run the Pili Channel, which airs televised, special effects-laden kung fu puppet adventures for modern viewers.

Puppet show, Taipei

Florent Bonnefoy/Michelin

Cinema

Taiwan's century-old film culture has reinvented itself multiple times, evolving with the island's shifting political fortunes. In recent years the government has attempted to boost the small but vibrant world of Taiwanese cinema, encouraging more high-quality local productions to entice audiences away from the Hong Kong- and Hollywood-produced fare that dominates the box office in Taiwan. In 2008 Taiwanese filmmakers made 40 local films, doubling the output of recent years, yet accounting for just 12 percent of movie ticket sales on the island.

A LOOK BACK

Japanese occupiers brought the first films to Taiwan in 1901. The earliest movies shown in Taiwan were Japanese; subsequent films of that era were greatly influenced by **Japanese cinema**, including the use of a *benshi*, or live narrator, as well as mixing film with live theater performances. The first Taiwanese-made movie, *Whose Fault Is It?*, debuted in 1925.

As the Japanese radically modernized Taiwan during their 50 years of colonial rule, they eventually moved to stamp out local culture, including use of the native Hoklo language. The tightly controlled local film industry disappeared with the start of the Second Sino-Japanese War in 1937.

It was not until 1949 that a homegrown movie industry once again sprouted—this time largely in the new official language **Mandarin**. Chiang Kai-shek's martial-law rule of Taiwan resulted primarily in the production of political propaganda.

Taiwanese cinema gathered steam amid the industrialization of the 1960s and 70s, churning out government-funded escapist **romantic dramas**, morality tales that aimed to resolve the tension between traditional agrarian life and encroaching urbanization. The era also featured the "social realist" subgenre's low-budget sex-and-violence gangster fare, in addition to popular **kung fu adventures**, such as action director **King Hu**'s well-regarded *A Touch of Zen*, filmed in Taiwan in 1969.

With the newly popular home viewing of pirated movies and the increasing sophistication of the Hong Kong film industry, tastes for Taiwanese-made melodrama waned by the early 1980s. At that time a group of filmmakers emerged intent on exploring the nuances of modern **Taiwanese identity**. Their fresh take on the realities of life in Taiwan and reflective look at the island's turbulent transformation from backwater to economic powerhouse under crumbling authoritarian rule defined Taiwan cinema's so-called New Wave.

EMERGING CINEMATIC IDENTITY

Widely considered the first New Wave Cinema work, *In Our Time* (1982) features four vignettes by four different directors about various stages of life in Taiwan from the 1950s to the 80s. Original storylines, a nonlinear narrative, long takes, documentary-style shooting, and the lack of famous actors were hallmarks of the **New Wave**.

In Our Time's director, **Edward Yang,** went on to become one of the island's most acclaimed auteurs. His films, such as *Taipei Story* (1985) and *Yi Yi: A One and a Two* (2000), explored themes of complex and painful family relationships and the loneliness and alienation of life in newly ascendant Taipei.

Taipei Story starred Yang's friend and colleague **Hou Hsiao-hsien**, considered another giant of the movement. Hou was one of three directors of *The Sandwich Man,* another omnibus film of three stories of life in Taiwan during the Cold War. Hou, who grew up on Taiwan's rugged East Coast, often returns to themes of workers' struggles and the charms of rural life versus the dislocation of cities. He also uses Japanese, Hoklo Taiwanese and Hakka dialects in addition to Mandarin. Hou's style is distinguished by exceptionally long takes, slow pacing, geometric framing techniques and long shots that create a sense of distance. *A City of Sadness* (1989) is Hou's deliberate, contemplative masterwork, which broke ground by examining the February 28, 1947 incident in which the government cracked down on Taiwanese resistance and kidnapped, tortured and killed between 18,000 to 28,000 Taiwanese. The film won a Golden Lion at the Venice Film Festival.

Heralded by critics and awarded prestigious industry prizes, Taiwan's cerebral and serious New Wave films signaled the development of a unique Taiwanese cinematic voice. Yet they were ignored by, or unavailable to, wider audiences, and were largely commercial failures.

THE SECOND WAVE

The heavy, formally constructed, politically conscious interpretations of Taiwan's tumultuous past gave way to lighter, more accessible works in the 1990s. Dubbed Taiwan cinema's Second Wave, these newer films still dealt with modern Taiwanese life, but they gained wider distribution—some garnering international honors—and subsequent commercial success.

The undisputed breakout superstar of this most recent cinematic era is director **Ang Lee**. Beginning with a trilogy of films on Taiwanese family dynamics, both *The Wedding Banquet* (1993) and *Eat Drink Man Woman* (1994) were nominated for Best Foreign Language Film Oscars. He went on to achieve major critical and commercial success in the US, tackling diverse stories such as the Jane Austen adaptation *Sense and Sensibility* (1995) and the brooding domestic drama *The Ice Storm* (1997). His martial arts blockbuster **Crouching Tiger, Hidden Dragon** won an Oscar for Best Foreign Language Film In 2000. Lee went on to win a Best Director Academy Award in 2005 for the cowboy love story *Brokeback Mountain*.

Another major contemporary talent, **Tsai Ming-liang** earned several international accolades, including the Golden Lion Award at the Venice Film Festival in 1994 for *Vive L'Amour*, a look at the lives of three strangers who converge upon a single apartment. His minimalist, metaphorical works such as *The Hole* (1998), *What Time Is It There?* (2001), and *The Wayward Cloud* (2005) use sparse dialogue, water motifs and other recurring symbols to delve into **urban isolation** and loss.

Tsai and other modern Taiwanese filmmakers continue to employ some of the stylized techniques of the New Wave pioneers.

CONTEMPORARY FILMMAKING

Taiwanese filmmakers today struggle with a lack of investment capital and apathetic local audiences who prefer to watch mainstream Hollywood and Hong Kong offerings rather than support independent Taiwanese films. As a result, compared with local film industries elsewhere, just a few dozen new Taiwanese films are made each year. *Eternal Summer,* released in 2006, was noted for its sensitive portrayal of a complex teenage love triangle.

Wei Te-sheng's *Cape No. 7*—a romance set in a small seaside town assembling a rag tag local band in preparation for a concert—made a splash in 2008 by breaking Taiwanese box office records. It also cast real-life musicians, small-town residents and diverse actors and employed a novel mix of Mandarin, Hoklo Taiwanese and Japanese tongues.

Another recent offering portraying different facets of Taiwan society was 2009's *No Puedo Vivir Sin Ti,* directed by **Leon Dai**. A fictionalized account of the true story of a poor Hakka laborer living in Kaohsiung and his fight against Taipei's bureaucracy to keep his daughter, the quiet black-and-white production earned several Taiwan's Golden Horse film awards.

In 2010 the slick 1980s gangster movie **Monga**, filmed on location in Taipei's Wanhua District, drew blockbuster Lunar New Year crowds to theaters and jammed the area around Longshan Temple with tourists eager to see sites depicted in the film.

See also Films in What to See and Do.

Literature

Although there have been Taiwanese writers for more than a century, it wasn't until two decades ago that Taiwan's literature became the subject of serious academic study. Students can earn advanced degrees in the field through newly established academic programs. Signaling this shift, the Museum of Taiwan Literature opened in 2003 in Tainan. The delayed recognition is perhaps attributable to a literary tradition historically amassed from the written works of other nations with which Taiwan was culturally, politically or economically interwoven.

EARLY WORKS

Taiwan's earliest indigenous inhabitants shared a rich oral **storytelling** practice, which has all but disappeared with the erosion of native tongues in favor of Mandarin; scholars have recently tried to translate **tribal myths**.

A small body of classical Chinese poetry was produced on the island, mostly by mainlanders such as Ming dynasty poet **Shen Kuang-wen**, who washed onto Taiwan's shores in a 1662 typhoon. Shen founded the Tung-yin Poetry Society and, like other Chinese authors of the time, wrote about nostalgia for the motherland.

OPPRESSIVE TIMES

A more distinctive local literature developed in the early 20C as Taiwanese chafed under Japanese colonial rulers. In time, a fledgling nativist genre evolved. Writers of the Taiwanese **New Literature Movement** expressed an individual Taiwanese voice, describing daily life on the island in the Hoklo language, in addition to writing works in Mandarin and Japanese. Writers of the period, notably **Lai Ho,** also used their work as a platform to speak out against the Japanese regime and call for political reform. As younger writers learned Japanese in school and were exposed to Western ideas at Japanese universities, a more multicultural, less politically strident, literary viewpoint developed.

The White Terror period of violence against Taiwan-independence advocates and intellectuals squelched much literary development. In spite of the political danger he faced, **Wu Cho-liu** and other authors dared to expose truths of the February 28 Incident that led to the government crackdown. The 1949 arrival of the exiled Nationalists and a million mainlanders ushered in an era of Cold War-influenced propaganda.

In the 1960s, Taiwan writers such as **Pai Hsien-yung** eschewed conventional 1950s thinking, embracing instead Western modernism and turning to James Joyce, Franz Kafka and Sigmund Freud as inspirations for technical experimentation and a new **humanist aesthetic**. *Tales of Taipei Characters* is one of Pai's key works, written in the same linguistic and structural mode as fellow modernist **Wang Wen-hsing**'s *Family Catastrophe*.

Throughout the mid-20C, newspaper literary supplements and writing contests played an important role in promoting and disseminating fiction of all kinds and offered new writers an invaluable launching pad. At the same time, Taiwan's **literary journals** flourished, showcasing quality work; they eventually fragmented into heated critical debate, however.

EMERGING TAIWANESE VOICES

Taiwan's rejection by the global diplomatic community in the 1970s sparked a nativist literary revival. Taiwan authors and poets shunned abstract ideals and imitations of Western forms in favor of a sharp focus on Taiwanese motifs and **social progressivism**. One representative author is **Sung Li-tsai**, known for his dark, realistic depictions of poverty and rural life. Hakka author **Lee Chiao**'s epic work of Taiwanese historical fiction, *Wintry Night Trilogy* (1979-81), tells the tale of a Hakka farming family set against the backdrop of Japanese occupation and the chaos of World War II. A loose, more diverse literary scene began to cohere as

Language

After the KMT arrived in Taiwan, Chinese Mandarin was promoted over the island's other languages. Now, in the 21C, aboriginal languages can be taught in schools. Taiwanese, a subdialect of the Hokkien language (Minnanyu) spoken in mainland China's Fujian Province, is used by the media. The Hakka language, another Chinese tongue, is being revived. Many Taiwanese born before 1940 speak Japanese.

Taiwan's Mandarin differs slightly from mainland China's in pronunciation, accent and vocabulary. Like Hong Kong, but unlike the PRC, Taiwan still uses nonsimplified (also called orthodox or traditional) characters.

Romanization, the transcription of Chinese characters into alphabetic pronunciation, is a headache for visitors. For example, the city of 基隆 is Jilóng in Hanyu Pinyin (mainland China's official romanization system), Chi-lung in Wade-Giles (a 19C British scholar's system) and Keelung in a non-systemized attempt at the Taiwanese pronunciation. *See also Useful Words and Phrases p44.*

Taiwan's authoritarian regime crumbled and martial law was lifted in 1987.

Li Ang is one of Taiwan's most famous and most divisive writers. In a career that spans the contrasting years before and after 1987, she broke ground with her shockingly honest explorations of culturally taboo subjects like feminism and female sexuality. Her best-known work, *The Butcher's Wife* (1983), was attacked in a Taiwanese newspaper, a highly unusual occurrence in Taiwan's mainstream, non-literary press. The notorious novel was translated into several languages and is now part of college curricula.

CONTEMPORARY DIVERGENCE

Modern authors have gone on to explore post-Modernism, consumerism, ethnic identity and Taiwan's chaotic history, although some literary purists lament the **commercialization** of Taiwanese letters with the emergence of a competitive market economy. Bookstore shelves are crowded with translated foreign titles; Taiwanese readers devour Western bestsellers such as the *Twilight* and *Harry Potter* series. Japanese-style *manga* comic books are also wildly popular; the Central Library in downtown Taipei opened a reading room housing 10,000 volumes of the graphic publications.

Even as Taiwan literature has grown to encompass a multitude of genres, styles and subjects, lack of English translations has remained a major obstacle to garnering a wider audience for Taiwanese writers. The vast majority of works are published in Mandarin only (some appear in Hoklo Taiwanese). Recently the government collaborated with Columbia University to produce English versions of major works such as *Notes of a Desolate Man*, **Chu Tien-wen**'s incisive novel about a gay man confronting the reality of AIDS, and *Three-Legged Horse*, short stories by **Cheng Ching-wen**. Taiwanese make reading a habit, spending hours in bookstore chains like Eslite or Kingstone; second-hand bookstores also survive. But emerging online bookstores are offering stiff competition.

Taipei bookstore

Florent Bonnefoy/Michelin

Nature

Lying in the Pacific Ocean some 200km/120mi off the coast of Asia, the island of Taiwan encompasses approximately 36,000sq km/14,400sq mi of land. To the north are the islands of Japan; to the south sits the archipelago of the Philippines. Taiwan, 395km/245mi long and 143km/89mi wide, is a big island, not only geographically (about the size of the Netherlands), but also culturally and in terms of its teeming population of 23 million (roughly equal to that of Australia). Bisected by the Tropic of Cancer, Taiwan has primarily a tropical climate, with more temperate zones at each of its narrow ends. A spine of mountains running north to south dominates two-thirds of the island; its lowlands broaden into fertile plains that stretch to the coasts.

Taiwan packs a tremendous variety of terrain into its leaf-like shape. The rugged **Central Mountain Range**, a series of steep peaks spanning most of the island's length, is the defining natural feature of Taiwan. Many of them taller than 3,500m/11,480ft, these lofty massifs capture abundant moisture from the frequent **monsoon rains** and typhoons that wash over the island. The wet climate, coupled with a warm and sunny **subtropical location** and a wide variety of climatic zones and ecosystems, supports a colorful cornucopia of plant and animal life.

LANDSCAPE
FORMATION OF THE LAND

The island has a very dynamic geology. Taiwan sits atop the world's most active geological zone: the **Pacific Rim of Fire**. Much of its northern tip is volcanic; overlooking the Taipei Basin, the brooding Datun and Yangmingshan **volcanoes** are a wooded landscape of hissing fumaroles and bubbling hot springs accompanied by the ever-present smell of sulfur.

But geologically speaking, the real action occurred farther south, where some 5 to 6 million years ago, the Philippine Sea Plate, drifting to the northwest, crashed into the giant Eurasian Plate, causing the earth to buckle and fold and give rise to the Central Mountain Range. These mountains, a series of sharply tilted blocks of sedimentary and metamorphic rock, including sandstone, shale and marble, are remarkably tall for an island as small as Taiwan: more than 200 peaks exceed 3,000m/9,800ft, and 18 peaks rise higher than 3,500m/11,480ft.

The mountains were formed from layers of seashell, coral and other sediment that was deposited hundreds of millions of years ago, when the area was under water. When the Philippine Plate

Chilai Ridge, Central Mountains

Brent Hannon/Michelin

hit Eurasia, the resulting heat and pressure melted and fused the seashells and coral, turning them to marble and other metamorphic rock. The sheer marble canyons and cliffs of **Taroko Gorge National Park** are an example. The tough, resistant marble defies erosion, and the Cingshui Cliffs, which tower above the Pacific Ocean just north of the gorge, as well as the white and black marble canyons of the gorge itself, are among the most beautiful natural sights on earth.

Such beauty comes at a price. The Philippine Plate is still surging to the northwest at a rapid rate of 8cm/3in per year. It subducts beneath the Eurasian Plate at the East Longitudinal Valley in southeastern Taiwan, while farther south, the Eurasian Plate slips beneath the Philippine Plate. This **double fault line** is highly unstable, and the ever-shifting plates are the cause of Taiwan's frequent earthquakes.

MOUNTAINS

The Central Mountain Range, which runs north and south along the southern two-thirds of the island, is one of **five ranges** in Taiwan, although it is by far the largest and most impressive. The eastern slopes are much steeper, and form a rugged, almost impenetrable landscape of fault scarps, or cliffs, of up to 1,200m/3,937 high, liberally laced with steep canyons and fast-flowing mountain streams.

Although they have slightly different geological histories, three of the remaining mountain ranges are similar in height and character. Northwest of the Central Range rises the **Xueshan Range**, which is dominated by the 3,886m/12,749ft summit of Xueshan, and the dramatic rock spire of Dabajianshan.

On the southwestern flank of the Central Range rises the **Yushan** (Jade Mountain) Range, which boasts Yushan itself, the tallest and most famous mountain in Taiwan, at 3,952m/12,966ft. The signature fan-shaped peak of Yushan is featured on logos and billboards throughout the island. Along with the Mikado Pheasant,

it adorns the back of Taiwan's NT$1000 note.

West of the Jade Mountains stands the shorter **Alishan Range**. The queen of this small cluster is 2,663m/8,737ft Datashan, the highest point on a ridge of mountains of similar height. Alishan is one of the most accessible of Taiwan's alpine regions. Alishan National Forest Recreation Area, with its iconic early morning views of the **sea of clouds**, is one of the island's most inspiring sights. The **Coastal Range**—just a series of hills compared with the other mountains—is a modest north-south extension that lies along the southern half of the east coast. This range is actually the northwestern edge of the Philippine Sea Plate. The **East Rift Valley,** which separates the Coastal Range from the Central Mountains, is the meeting point of the two tectonic giants.

PLAINS

The western slopes of the mountain ranges that dominate central Taiwan are gentler than the eastern faces, with more extensive foothills and terrain that, while still steep, is generally less forbidding. The **western foothills** are filled with small villages, and many of the slopes are dotted with tea plantations, betelnut trees, and pear and apple orchards.

Farther west the foothills subside, giving way to a broad, flat **alluvial plain** made of sand, silt, gravel and rocks that washed out of the mountains over many millennia. The process is ongoing, and every summer four or five typhoons saturate the unstable landscapes, flooding villages, washing out railroads and highways, and causing powerful landslides that permanently alter the terrain.

The **western plains** run the length of the west coast in a broad strip that extends from the Taipei basin in the north to the Pingtung plain in the south. This fertile flatland is the cradle of Taiwan's economic miracle, a heavily urbanized landscape that is filled with factories, science parks, industrial zones, and cities and towns. Home to most of the island's population, the plains are crisscrossed by roads, highways and train lines, and dotted with seaports and airports.

The western plains are also the **fruit basket** of Taiwan, yielding a remarkable abundance of mango, pineapple, papaya, pomelo, jujube, guava, litchi and other fruits that have acquired an international reputation for their juiciness and flavor. The plains also feature many small farms that grow corn, sweet potato, rice, sugar cane and other staples.

The geography of Taiwan—a rugged strip of mountain and a broad welcoming plain—has prompted most of the island's development on its western half. Taiwan is one of the most densely populated places on earth, but its mountain ranges ensure that vast tracts of wilderness remain intact.

OCEANS AND SEAS

The waters that embrace the two sides of Taiwan are quite different in character. Along the eastern seaboard lies the mild **Pacific Ocean**, a generally calm, azure blue body of water that is warmed by a tropical current flowing north from the Philippines. To the west is the **Taiwan Strait**, a gray-green sea that is choppy, windy and dangerous, especially during winter when prevailing winds, pinched by the Central Mountain Range, funnel northward up the strait. The **East China Sea** lies off Taiwan's northwest coast, the **South China Sea** to the southwest.

COASTLINES

The short coastline on the far north end of Taiwan consists of steep capes and headlands that are volcanic in origin, with small fishing harbors and a few flat sandy beaches. Facing the Pacific Ocean on the northeast side of the island is the flat, fertile Yilan Delta. South of Yilan, along the northern half of the east coast south to Hualien, a landscape of **marble and limestone cliffs** plunging straight into the Pacific Ocean, provides one of loveliest ocean views in existence.

On the southern half of the east coast, from Hualien to the southernmost tip of Taiwan, the shorelines that parallel the Coastal Mountain Range are gentler. This string of mostly rocky beaches is kissed by waves that have crossed thousands of miles of Pacific Ocean. Visible off the southeast coast is the volcanic mass of **Green Island** (also known as Ludao). Its surrounding waters, stirred by a warm tropical current, are rich in sea life. Farther southeast sits tiny **Orchid Island** (Lanyu). It, Green Island and the Coastal Range all form part of the Philippine Sea Plate that continues to subduct beneath Taiwan.

At the southernmost tip of Taiwan stretches the calm, tropical coastline of the **Hengchun Peninsula**, a landscape of raised coral blocks and azure blue seas famous for its coral reefs. This coast is home to Kenting National Park, one of the best scuba sites in Taiwan, and a magnet for swimming, fishing, whale watching, sunbathing and other warm-water activities.

Altogether different in character, the windswept west coast has wide, sandy tidal flats and relentless onshore winds. In places, the restless currents have built spits and sand bars, creating tidal ponds and broad shallow lagoons. Taiwan's best natural harbor is found in the southern city of Kaohsiung, but earlier harbors in Tainan and Lugang naturally filled with silt and sand long ago, and were abandoned. The west coast also features an abundance of wetlands that lie along its numerous **river deltas**. Many of these are now protected, and are home to birds, mangrove swamps and other wetland flora and fauna.

RIVERS AND LAKES

Wet though it is, Taiwan is too small to have many notable rivers. The wide, flat, tidal **Danshui River** that flows back and forth through Taipei is the most famous river in Taiwan, and the only one that carries any commercial traffic. On the east side of the island, the rivers are short and fierce, cascading down steep mountain flanks in a fast-flowing torrent of rapids and waterfalls, and forming tiny river deltas that support small marine populations. The exception on

Sun Moon Lake
Brent Hannon/Michelin

the east coast is the **Lanyang River**, which forms the 60km/37mi Yilan Delta, a flat, fertile area abundant with farms and villages.

A large number of rivers also flow westward from the mountains, and they too begin as fast-running mountain streams. As they emerge from the foothills onto the plains, however, they become wide, shallow and flood-prone, often bursting through their gravel banks, and forking and splitting into many small branches before emptying into the Taiwan Strait. These large, flat, boulder-strewn deltas, crossed by long bridges spanning the churning gray-brown rivers, are a common sight on the west coast.

Because the mountains of Taiwan never had widespread glacial activity, they lack the terminal moraines and deeply scoured bowls and cirques that form alpine lakes in more northerly mountain ranges. Taiwan's mountains do contain a handful of tiny mountain lakes, notably **Jiaming Lake i**n the southern Central Mountains, which was formed by a meteor crater that later filled with water.

Taiwan's largest and deepest body of fresh water is **Sun Moon Lake**, in Nantou County in central Taiwan. Vacationers like to tour the classical Chinese temples and pagodas that ring its hilly shores, and boat and swim in the cool water. **Liyu Lake** in the East Rift Valley, and Longluan Lake on the Hengchun Peninsula, a prime stopover for migra-

ting birds, are the island's other notable lakes.

OUTLYING ISLANDS

The main island of Taiwan accounts for 99 percent of the island's total landmass, but it is ringed by numerous smaller islands and archipelagoes. The biggest island chain is **Kinmen**, a cluster of 15 mostly flat islands that lie in the mouth of Xiamen Bay, a few miles from mainland China's Fujian Province. Kinmen's fertile terrain supports plentiful agriculture, and is dotted with Qing-era villages, which share the islands with extensive fortifications, army bases, pillboxes and other military features.

Far to the north of Kinmen, and also hugging the coast of mainland China, are the **Mazu Islands**, a chain of 36 rocky, hilly islands and islets made mostly of granite and other igneous rock. Like Kinmen, the Mazus are heavily fortified and have a strong military presence, but they support little agriculture and few people.

The **Penghu archipelago,** a chain of 64 widely scattered islands, of which 19 are inhabited, lies near the middle of the Taiwan Strait. Made mostly of basalt, the low-lying, windswept islands support small farming and fishing enclaves, and have a number of good natural harbors used by seafarers for centuries.

A pair of single islands, Green Island (Ludao) and south of it, Orchid Island (Lanyu), sit about 80km/50mi off the

99

southeast coast of Taiwan. Both volcanic, the islands are small, hilly and sparsely inhabited; tiny Orchid Island is famous for its Tao (Yami) aboriginal culture. Each island is surrounded by seas rich in coral reefs, fish and other marine life.

CLIMATE

Washed by warm ocean currents and bisected by the **Tropic of Cancer**, Taiwan enjoys a warm, subtropical climate with short mild winters and long, hot, humid summers. Frost is rare in the lowlands, where most people live and work, and average temperatures range from 15-20°C/59-68°F in winter, and from 25-30°C/77-86°F in summer. The mountains are much colder, with freezing temperatures in winter, and a cooler, windier climate in the summer, although the mountains seldom freeze in the summer.

Taiwan is also very wet, especially in the north, as **winter monsoons** and **summer typhoons** saturate the island year around. The wettest city is **Keelung**, which absorbs an astonishing 376cm/148in of rainfall per year, making it one of the wettest cities on the planet. Due to the presence of the central mountains, and the variable temperatures of the surrounding oceans, regional rainfall patterns vary considerably. **Taichung** receives just 172cm/68in of rain per year, and Hengchun, on the southern tip, gets 198cm/78in, with Taipei in the middle at 241cm/95in per year.

The weather follows a generally predictable seasonal pattern, with much of the rainfall related to the Asian monsoons. The winter monsoon begins in late October and brings steady rain to northern Taiwan throughout the winter until about March. The summer monsoon begins with the drizzly but short-lived **plum rains** in May and June, and tapers off during the summer. The summer monsoons, unlike the winter monsoons, bring more rain to the southern half of Taiwan. Southern Taiwan receives 90 percent of its rainfall between May and October, and is reliably warm and dry in winter.

In the summer, typhoons form in the Pacific Ocean and roar across the island from the southwest, unleashing up to 300mm/11.8in of rainfall in a 24-hour period. Three to five typhoons hit Taiwan each year, usually in mid summer, but the season can begin as early as April, and extend into November.

Taiwan's Diverse Species

Taiwan's spectrum of tropical-to-temperate climate zones has blessed the island with a rich diversity of plants and animals. It supports about 80 species of mammal, 80 species of reptile and 37 species of amphibian. In the realm of smaller creatures, it truly excels, with almost 500 species of bird, 2,700 species of fish and more than 18,000 kinds of insects, including nearly 400 types of butterfly. A high proportion of the plants and animals are unique to Taiwan due to its location in the Pacific Ocean: of 4,200 types of vascular plants, 27 percent are endemic, while more than 60 percent of the animals are endemic.

FAUNA

Despite its small size, Taiwan has a remarkable variety of **climatic zones**, including alpine meadows, upland and lowland forests, swampy estuaries, rocky seacoasts and tropical and temperate oceans, each of them home to unique ecosystems. This abundance of habitats, as well as a warm climate and plentiful rainfall, give Taiwan an impressive array of plant and animal life.

Wholesale industrialization, combined with a high population density and a century of rigorous logging and development, have taken a heavy toll on Taiwan's natural landscape. The west coast, and the western slopes of the central mountains in particular, have been heavily denuded, but pristine areas still exist in the high mountains, where the forbidding terrain protects them from development.

FISH

A wealth of sea life surrounds Taiwan, thanks in part to the warm **Kuroshio Current** that flows northward from the Philippines and brings tropical water to the south and east coasts. The nutrient-rich current supports a huge variety of corals, sponges, crustaceans and other sea life; in all nearly 300 **species of coral** live in the seas surrounding Kenting National Park, in the far south.

Farther offshore the water is colder, attracting whales and dolphins, along with swordfish, tuna, sharks, mahi-mahi and other pelagic fish.

Taiwan's most famous fish is the **Formosan Landlocked Salmon** (Oncorhynchus masou formosanus). This sleek 20cm/7.8in-long fish was cut off from the oceans when water levels dropped during the last Ice Age, but it survived in the high mountain streams of central Taiwan. A temperate fish locked in a tropical climate, it requires clear, cold water, and is found only at elevations above 1,500m/4,921ft.

MAMMALS

The island has relatively few large wild mammals, but populations of **Formosan Black Bear** (Selanarctos thibetanus formosanus) still roam the mountain forests. The strong, sturdy omnivores are Taiwan's largest mammals, and can weigh up to 200kg/440 pounds, although they are usually smaller. Solitary and shy, the bears avoid human contact, but can be dangerous when surprised or confronted.

Taiwan also has native deer populations, including the **Formosan Reeve's Muntjac** (Muntiacus reevesi micrurus), a squat little deer that weighs just 12kg/26 pounds and is common in the mountain meadows. Taiwan has two other deer species that are much rarer. The **Formosan Sambar** (Cervus unicolor swinhoei), the largest native herbivore in Taiwan, and the **Formosan Sika deer** (Cervus nippon taiouanus), notable for the white "plum blossom" spots on its back, are found mainly in captivity.

The signature carnivore of Taiwan is the **Clouded Leopard** (Neofelis nebulosa brachyurus), a beautiful, almost mythic cat that has been driven to the extreme edge of extinction and may no longer exist in Taiwan. Yet there is still a chance that these small 20kg/44-pound predators, named for their exotic, cloud-like markings, still survive in the remote mountain wilderness.

The Formosan Rock Monkey, or Formosan **Macaque** (Macaca cyclopis), is another common mammal, and groups of the loud, demonstrative monkeys can be seen at elevations up to 3,200m/10,498ft.

Henri Choimet/Michelin

Formosan Black Bear

BIRDS

Taiwan is blessed with bountiful bird life; its many habitats shelter a vast array of species, and its island location makes Taiwan a choice stopover for **migratory birds**. These factors combine to give Taiwan one of the highest densities of bird species in the world. The island has some 480 different birds, more than one-twentieth of the world's 8,600 species. By comparison, Japan has about 500 kinds of birds, the US 800, and mainland China 1,200.

This rich diversity of bird life attracts enthusiasts from around the globe. Their ultimate goal is to see all 15 of Taiwan's **endemic species**—birds found only in Taiwan. One of the most famous of these is the **Mikado Pheasant** (Syrmaticus mikado), a high-elevation forest bird that is depicted on the NT$1000 bill. The male Mikados are particularly striking, with shimmering blue-black plumage and ruby-red faces.

The **Formosan Blue Magpie** (Urocissa caerulea), the national bird of Taiwan, is another famous endemic. Also known as the Long-tailed Mountain Lady, the Blue Magpie has a bright blue body, jet-black head and blue-and-white striped tail. It is found in lowland forests, including the thickly wooded slopes of Yangmingshan National Park, on the outskirts of Taipei. Other famous endemic birds include **Swinhoe's Pheasant** (Lophura swinhoii), Taiwan Hill Partridge (Arborophila crudigularis) and **Taiwan Firecrest** (Regulus goodfellowi). Swinhoe's Pheasant is a shy and cautious bird that lives in mid-elevation broad-leaf forests, from which it emerges at dawn and dusk to search for berries, sprouts and seeds. **Taiwan Hill Partridges,** exceedingly rare, live in similar habitat, though they are active throughout the day; the island's population of hill partridges is believed to be around 5,000 birds.

The tiny **Taiwan Firecrest** is a perching bird that lives in cold, coniferous forests as high as 3,700m/12,139ft. The smallest of Taiwan's endemics, it is also one of the most colorful, with a readily recognizable flaming orange and yellow crest atop its head. Another high-altitude alpine resident is the endemic **Formosan Yellow Tit** (Parus holsti), a small, ultra-rare insect eater with yellow-green plumage.

Most of Taiwan's endemic birds live in the mountains, and to see them requires serious effort. The most famous birding site in Taiwan is **Anmashan**, in Taichung County. This wooded, remote mountainside is home to many of the prized endemics, including the two famous pheasants and the reclusive hill partridge.

One of Taiwan's must-see species is the ultra-rare **Black-faced Spoonbill** (Platalea minor). These magnificent birds winter at the mouth of the Zengwen River near Tainan each year, from

Mikado Pheasants

Henri Choimet/Michelin

Black-faced Spoonbills

The number of critically endangered Black-faced spoonbills has been on the rise in Taiwan for more than a decade, representing a victory for preservationists. Most of the global population of these migrating waterfowl spend their winters in a small area near Tainan, at the mouth of the Zengwen River. A series of rallies saved the wetland from development in the early 1990s, and the spoonbills have been coming back. At one point in the mid-1990s, Taiwan's wintering population had dropped below 300 birds, but it has since risen to almost 1,100 spoonbills.

October through the end of March, and sightings are virtually guaranteed. Another famous migrating species is the elegant Gray-faced buzzard eagle (Butastur indicus), which winters in southern Taiwan. So regular is the arrival of this magnificent soaring bird that it is nicknamed the **10-10 bird**, for its regular arrival around October 10, Taiwan's national day.

Another notable part-time resident is the rare and colorful **Fairy Pitta** (Pitta nympha), a summer migratory bird that arrives in Taiwan to escape the tropical heat of southeast Asia. The Pitta is known as the "eight-colored bird" in Taiwan because of its shimmering multi-colored feathers of red, green and blue.

REPTILES

Reptiles, including 50 species of snake, thrive in the warm, wet climate. About 10 types of snake are poisonous, including the **Hundred Pace Viper** (Deinagkistrodon acutus), a thick, 1.5m/5ft-long snake with black and yellow triangular markings that is revered by the Paiwan and Bunun aborigines, and is one of their favorite tribal motifs.

While most of Taiwan's other poisonous snakes live near sea level, such as the **Chinese green tree viper** (Trimeresurus stejnegeri), **Taiwan cobra** (Naja naja atra) and **Taiwan banded krait** (Bungarus multicinctus), the Hundred Pace Viper prefers low to medium elevations, where it lives in dense forests among rock ledges and fallen leaves.

INSECTS

Taiwan has 18,000 insect species, and many are remarkable, but the headlines belong to lepidoptera, the order that includes **butterflies**. The island is home to nearly 400 butterfly species. Glimpses of these graceful insects fluttering through the forest glades are one of the signature sights of Taiwan.

One of the more interesting examples is the **Milkweed Butterfly** (Parantica sita niphonica), a semi-translucent pale green butterfly that can fly great distances: specimens marked in Taiwan have been found in Japan, and vice versa. However, it is not clear if the Milkweed actually migrates, or if it is accidentally blown back and forth by the monsoon winds. In May and June, great flocks of Milkweeds can be seen fluttering their green wings in Yangmingshan National Park.

A genuine migratory butterfly is the **Purple Crow**, which is represented in Taiwan by four species: the Blue-branded King Crow (Euploea eunice hobsoni), Striped Blue Crow (Euploea mulciber), Two-branded Crow (Euploea sylvester swinhoei) and Dwarf Crow (Euploea tulliolous). These butterflies, all with purple spots on dark brown or blue wings, spend summers in northern and central Taiwan, but fly south beginning in September, aided by the prevailing monsoon winds, to enjoy the warmer winters there. Millions of the dazzling purple and brown insects congregate in the sheltered valleys of the Maolin area of Kaohsiung County. Along with the more famous **Monarch** (Danaus plexippus), the Purple Crow is one of only two butterfly species known to undertake a seasonal migration.

Taiwan also has a colorful selection of stay-at-home butterflies. These domestics include the **Highland Red-bellied Swallowtail** (Atrophaneura horishana Matsumura), a mountain-dwelling species known for its large size, wingspans of up to 12cm/4.7in and bright-red, almost fluorescent, belly. Visitors to the Kenting Area might see the **Hengchun Birdwing** (Troides aeacus kaguya), a lowland species with two-tone wings that are lemon-yellow on the bottom half, and blue- and black-striped on the top. Another local favorite is the **Broad-tailed Swallowtail** (Agehana maraho), a mountain dweller known for its ruby-red wingtips.

FLORA

In the plant kingdom, Taiwan is blessed with great range and variety, from the coastal shrubby reef pemphis and mangrove forests to rhododendrons and junipers that cling to life at 3,800m/12,467ft. Most visitors to Taiwan quickly notice its profusion of plant life. The dominant large tree in most cities is the **banyan** (Ficus wightiana and Ficus Machilus). Many parks and streets are lined with this tropical tree, its famous dangling vines forming tangled networks of new trunks. Banyan and acacia **forests** (Acacia confuse) once carpeted

Red Hibiscus

Susannah Rosenblatt/Michelin

the lower elevations, but like most of Taiwan's lowland forests, they no longer exist.

A once-common lowland plant is the **mangrove** (Kandelia candel), which used to cover Taiwan's deltas and sand bars of the west coast. Notable forests of mangrove still exist along the Danshui River near Taipei, forming the world's largest pure forest of the Kandelia candel species. These trees are among the northernmost mangrove forests on the earth.

Taiwan's lowland forests include Machilus-Castanopsis, an evergreen broad-leaf tree that once cloaked the island at elevations of 500m to 1,500m/1,640ft to 4,921ft. Higher still are the towering **Evergreen Oaks** (Quercus tarokoensis Hayata), and large glades of these stately trees still thrive, forming thick canopies 30m/98ft above the forest floors.

At higher elevations, where the trees are better protected by the terrain, large stands of native species still thrive. Such species include the opportunistic **Taiwan Pine** (Pinus taiwanensis), which grows thickly on forested hillsides or in fire zones.

Farther up the mountain slopes are denizens of the "cloud forests," the cool moist climate that extends from 1,800m/5,905ft to about 2,500m/8,202ft. The most eminent trees in this zone are the two celebrated **cypresses**, the Yellow (Chamaecyparis obtusa var. formosana), and the Red (Chamaecyparis formosensis, Matsum). The Yellow Cypress once dominated the western slopes of the Alishan Mountains, but because its straight-grained, oil-rich wood is so valuable, the trees were rigorously logged.

The **Red Cypress** was more fortunate. It grows with a split trunk, is prone to wood rot, and its trunks are twisted and cracked, all factors that protected some of these trees from the chainsaws. Most of the large old trees in the Alishan Forest Recreation Area are Red Cypresses, although some rare Yellow Cypresses can still be seen, soaring to stately heights.

Higher up the mountains are forests of **Taiwan Hemlock** (Tsuga chinensis var. formosana). These 50m/164ft giants are readily identified by their broad umbrella-shaped canopies, while beneath the hemlocks grow thick stands of Yushan dwarf bamboo (Yushania niitakayamensis). The impenetrable bamboo, together with the inaccessible terrain, protected many of Taiwan's hemlock forests from exploitation.

At higher altitudes, from about 3,000m/9,842ft up, the hemlocks give way to the graceful **Taiwan Fir** (Abies kawakamii), another renowned conifer with straight, erect trunks and weathered asymmetrical branches. Extensive groves of Taiwan Fir grace the higher mountainsides, making this species one of the best-preserved large native trees in Taiwan.

Higher still, clinging to life at 3,500m/11,483ft and above grows the **Fragrant Juniper** (Juniperus Sqyanata Lamb var. morrisonicola). On protected southern exposures, these trees stand tall and erect with tough, gnarled trunks and tentative shoots of greenery. On windswept ridges and higher elevations, however, they are reduced to small, wiry shrubs. They share the alpine tundra with the **Taiwan Rhododendron** (Rhododendron pseudochrysanthum), a hardy mountain-dweller that sends forth beautiful pink and white blossoms in May and June, and lives at higher elevations than any other kind of rhododendron.

CONSERVATION EFFORTS

Taiwan's economic miracle, which transformed the island into a land of wealth with a high standard of living, came at a heavy cost to the environment. From the 1950s through the 80s, toxic waste and discharge from factories, dirty exhaust from cars and scooters, comprehensive logging in the mountains and a general disregard for delicate ecosystems combined to create an environmental disaster. But by the late 1980s, the island was comfortably middle class, and conservation efforts gained momentum. Taiwan

Kenting National Park
Rich J. Matheson/Michelin

passed the **Wildlife Conservation Law** In 1989, and the Council of Agriculture began to monitor threatened species. Environmentalists won significant victories over developers, especially in areas where rare bird or butterfly species were present.

Logging and whaling were halted, and new laws set tougher standards on vehicle emissions, factory discharges, and development of sensitive environments. Meanwhile backpacking, scuba diving, bicycling, whale- and dolphin-watching, birding and other outdoor pursuits surged in popularity, lending additional weight to the environmental movement.

Creating a **national park system** was a key step in the preservation and restoration of Taiwan's ravaged landscapes. **Kenting National Park** was established in 1984 at the coral-rimmed southern tip of the island, becoming the first of an eventual eight national parks, most of them in the high mountains. The parks are not paragons of protection: development is allowed, and the battle between developers and preservationists is ongoing. Additional protections exist in the form of 16 **nature reserves** and 17 **wildlife refuges**, but here too, the protection is patchwork, and development is allowed.

Sail Rock, Kenting National Park
Rich J. Matheson/Michelin

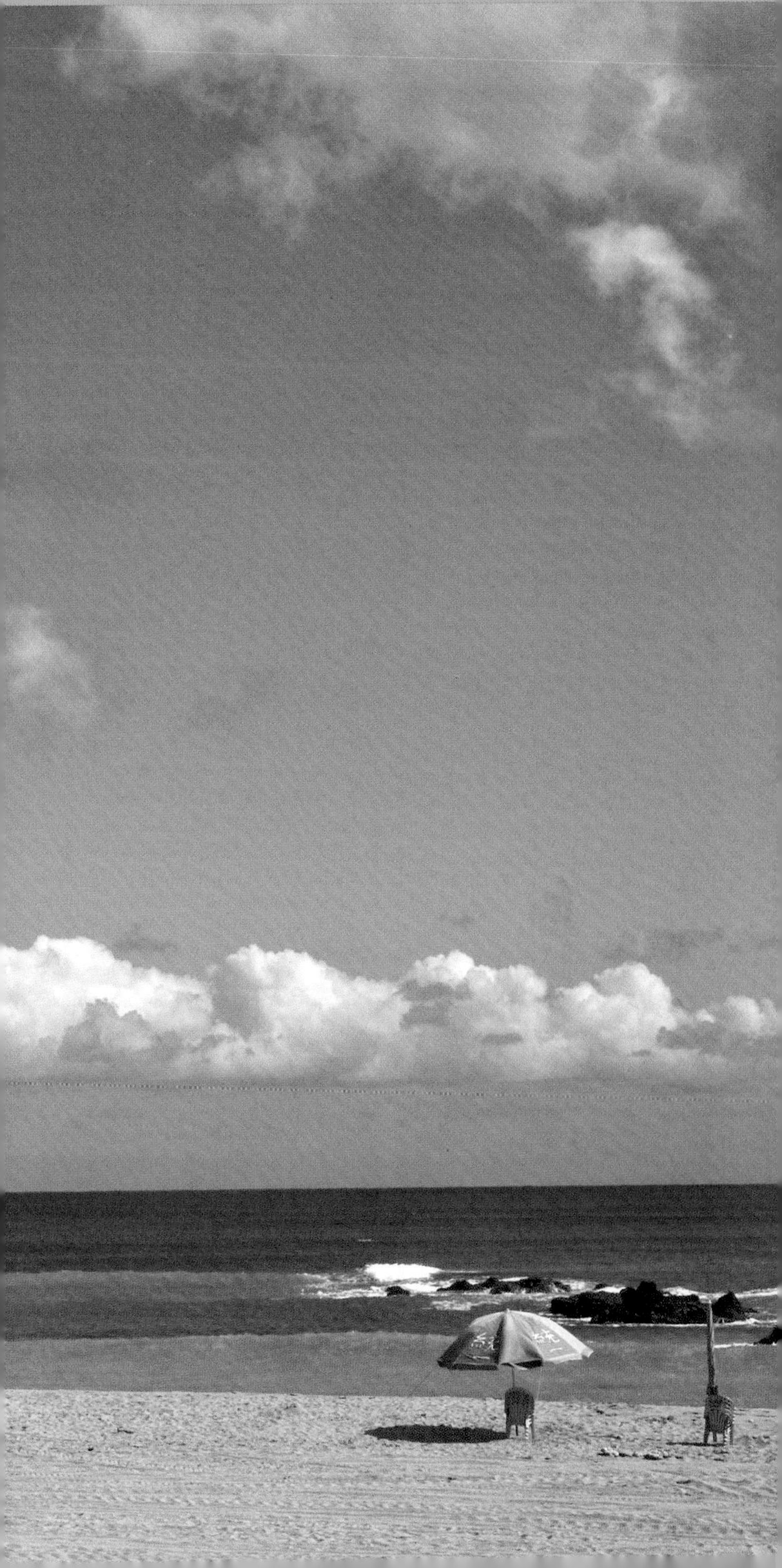

Greater Taipei encompasses both the city and part of the encircling county of Taipei—a concentration of some 6.75 million people shoehorned into the mountain-framed Taipei Basin in Taiwan's northern end. On its northeast side, the county borders Keelung City, to the southeast Yilan County and to the southwest, Taoyuan County, site of the arrival point for most international visitors: Taiwan Taoyuan International Airport. Covering 2,052sq km/792sq mi, Taipei County oversees a topography of hills, mountains, plains, valleys, and rivers such as the Keelung, Xindian and Sanxia. Other than the cultural and culinary offerings of Taipei City, it's the county's lengthy north coast off the Pacific Ocean—some 120km/75mi of it—that is its main attraction.

Highlights

1 Lively religious activity at popular **Longshan Temple** (p113)

2 The grandeur of public buildings at **Chiang Kai-shek Memorial Hall** (p126)

3 Unmissable views from high-tech high tower **Taipei 101** (p130)

4 Spectacular Chinese art in the **National Palace Museum** (p141)

5 **Muzha's** tea culture and views of Taipei's skyline (p151)

The City and Beyond

Sandy beaches stretch from Baishawan east to Fulong, home to water sports and the historic Caoling Trail.
All easily accessed from Taipei, the county's ten cities include Banqiao, site of the Qing-era Lin Family Mansion and Garden, Yonghe, Xindian and Shulin.

Among its urban townships are Yingge, Taiwan's number-one pottery town; Sanxia with its Zushi Temple; and Ruifang, starting point of the historic Pingxi Railway Line. The county's 15 rural townships include Shimen, known for delicately flavored fish caught in its namesake reservoir; Jinshan, a beach favored by novice surfers, and home to one of Taiwan's Buddhist monasteries; Wanli, reputed for its hot springs hotels; and Pingxi, heralded for its Sky Lantern Festival.

The city of Taipei is the cultural, political and economic hub of the area, offering visitors a feast of urban attractions.

Taipei County has a subtropical climate. Seasonal monsoons ensure that rain falls throughout the year.

Taipei City, in fact, is equated with rainy weather, and the skies are often over-cast. The coldest month here is January, when temperatures average 12°C/53°F; July is definitely the hottest—thermometers register an average 33°C/91°F. The dry season (Oct-Nov) is an ideal time to see the Taipei area.

Busy Taipei street

Florent Bonnefoy/Michelin

Taipei City★★★

At first sight, Taipei (臺北) is not a glamorous city. The heavy traffic, crowded streets, noisy scooters and interconnecting highways that helped make it known as Asia's "ugly duckling" remain to some extent. But a transformation is well underway: bicycle paths now ring the city, more urban parks and green spaces have been created, the metro is adding lines that should help reduce vehicular traffic, and other initiatives are in the works. Besides, Taipei grows on you. It's the kind of city one appreciates more for its atmosphere and its people. Walking around is key to discovering its captivating neighborhoods—the quiet back lanes and alleys free of motor cars and peopled with friendly shopkeepers and courteous temple attendants.

The city can also be found in its singular landmarks and museums: one museum alone makes the trip here worthwhile: the National Palace Museum—displaying imperial treasures from Beijing's Forbidden City that compose the world's premier collection of Chinese art.

A CITY OF CONTRASTS

To dive into the local popular culture, visit the old Wanhua District and its revered Longshan Temple, definitely a must-see temple. Other neighborhoods like Dadaocheng and Dalongdong reveal Taipei's vivid lifestyle. Look east, and you cannot miss Taipei 101, the second tallest skyscraper in the world, casting its shadow over glitzy Xinyi District, haunt of the young and rich.

The charm of Taipei lies in its leisurely moments. There's not a quarter where you won't find a teahouse, coffee shop or bookstore to entice you to linger a while.

▶ **Population:** 2.6 million.

Michelin Maps: p110, p114-115.

Info: Travel Information Service Center, 240 Dunhua N. Rd., Songshan District. 敦化北路240號 ☎886-2-2717-3737 or 0800-011-765. Taiwan Tourism Bureau, Taipei Office: 9th Floor, 290 Zhongxiao E. Rd., Sec. 4, Da'an District. 忠孝東路四段290號 . ☎886-2-2349-1635 or 886-2-2717-3737. http://eng.taiwan.net.tw.

Location: Six of the 12 administrative districts form the city's core, bordered on the west by the Danshui River, the north by the Keelung River, the south by the Xindian River. Taipei Main Station is the city's central hub. Major north-south thoroughfares include Zhongshan and Dunhua Rds.; main east-west streets include Zhongxiao Rd. and Civic Blvd. Wanhua is the oldest district, home to Longshan Temple. Xinyi is the major shopping district. The city is a good base to explore the North Coast, the Muzha tea plantations to the south, and the many outlying towns accessible by MRT and train from Taipei.

Kids: Taipei Storyland, Lin Liu-hsin Puppet Museum.

Timing: Plan to spend 5 days in Taipei. Avoid the wet season (Apr–early-Jun).

Don't Miss: National Palace Museum, Longshan Temple, Chiang Kai-shek Memorial Hall, Taipei 101, Lin Family Mansion and Garden, and Muzha.

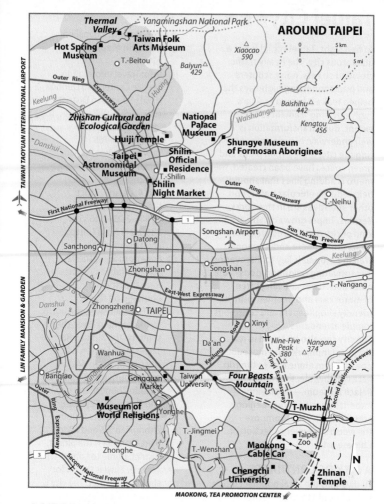

MAOKONG, TEA PROMOTION CENTER

A BIT OF HISTORY

Greater Taipei spills beyond the **Taipei Basin** that runs inland from the Pacific Ocean and the Keelung River to the surrounding mountains. To the basin's north rises **Yangmingshan**; Linkou's tableland mountains sit on the west and the Snow Mountains (**Xueshan**) loom above the southeast. Long before the arrival of Han Chinese from Fujian Province in mainland China in the late 1600s, the basin was inhabited by **Ketagalan** plains aborigines.

The 17C saw attempts at European exploitation of Taiwan. Its superb natural harbor made today's nearby coastal city of **Keelung** a target for the Span-ish, the Dutch and later the French. But foreign colonization was relatively brief in the Taipei area.

A greater influx of Han Chinese occurred here during the Qing dynasty. Early in the 18C, immigrants from Fujian Province began to farm, with imperial consent, the banks of the **Danshui River**, which borders the western edge of modern Taipei. As more Fujianese arrived, the settlement grew as **Manka**—now called Wanhua, Taipei City's oldest district. Fighting among rival clans there gave birth to **Dadaocheng**, another of Taipei's old neighborhoods.

In the year 1875 the Qing rulers created Taipei as a prefecture, for defensive

Taipei along the Danshui River

Mark Caltonhill/Michelin

purposes, in what is now the district of **Zhongzheng**. By 1879 the first walls of the foursquare city were under construction. Their completion in 1884 is considered the city's official year of founding. The following year, streets were cut, connecting the new walled city with the older settlements nearby, such as Manka and Dadaocheng, and spurring urban development. In 1886 the **provincial capital** was moved from Tainan to Taipei, and the city's growth as an amalgam of villages continued.

During the Sino-French War of 1884-85, the French took Keelung and set up a strong defensive position, but they were not able to advance on Taipei. When the Japanese took over Taiwan in 1895, they combined Taipei's existing districts into one, added infrastructure and constructed grand Western-style buildings, many of which remain today. In the early 20C, the dismantling of the **city walls** provided further impetus to integration. In 1945, with China again in control of Taiwan, the city was divided into ten districts. An incident in Taipei on February 28, 1947, sparked a massacre of thousands of people by the ruling Kuomintang government and ushered in 40 years of repressive martial law throughout the island.

The 1960s saw Taipei's growth as the island's economy blossomed. In the 1970s Taiwan's **first freeway** linked Taipei with the south, and the first international airport connected Taipei to the world. In 1996 Taipei's **metro system** was created, yet outlying areas such as Xinyi remained undeveloped scrubland until as recently as the 1990s.

Today the **Xinyi District** embodies modern Taipei, with shiny skyscrapers like **Taipei 101**. The city is home to government buildings, corporate headquarters, international hotels and respected academic institutions.

Initiatives call for a second financial center in Xinyi, a future pedestrian zone in Huayin Street, a new fashion district and a gourmet food district. To better serve the city, additional metro lines are being planned well beyond 2013.

The following city districts are ordered geographically south to north.

Touring Tip

The need for sunshine, fresh air and a change of pace is common, especially in a big city. If you want some fresh air, stroll in Da'an Forest Park, linger in the gardens of Shilin Official Residence or take the MRT south to Maokong, where tea plantations offer a change of scene and pace. Don't expect much sun in Taipei, however, a city known for rainy days. The best time to visit here is October or November, when the sun makes the city look even brighter.

GETTING THERE

BY AIR - Taipei City is served by two airports. **Taiwan Taoyuan International Airport** (IATA code: TPE) (台灣桃園國際機場) handles international flights into Taiwan. Taxi fare to Taipei (50km/31mi west) approxately NT$1200. Buses to Taipei (1hr) are cheap (NT$125) and depart from the airport every 15min (daily 5:40am–12:50am). They usually head to the Main Train Station, making interim stops at major hotels. Domestic flights are serviced by **Songshan Airport** (IATA code: TSA) (松山機場), located in the city's Songshan District (NT$200 by taxi, or metro: Songshan Airport Station).

BY TRAIN - **Conventional trains** (TRA): Taipei Main Station (台北火車站) (𝒫02-2731 3558) and Songshan Station (松山火車站), both served by metro. Travel times are at least 4hrs to Tainan (one-way on the fastest trains NT$738 up) to 4hrs 45min to Kaohsiung (one-way on the fastest trains NT$845). Points north of Taiwan are easily accessible from Songshan Station.

High Speed Rail (HSR): Trains from Taipei reach Tainan in 1hr 40min (one-way NT$1,350) and Kaohsiung in 2hrs (NT$1,490).

BY BUS - Long-distance buses link Taipei with the main cities of Taiwan. It is advisable to book your ticket in advance (ask your hotel for help).

Intercity buses depart from Taipei Bus Station (台北轉運站) (www.taipeibus.com.tw) located just north of the Taipei Main Station. Buses are a comfortable and cheap way to travel to other cities. Travel times to Tainan 4hrs (about NT$360), to Sun Moon Lake 4hrs 30mn (NT$460).

GETTING AROUND

BY METRO - Taipei's MRT serves all the main city landmarks as well as Beitou, Danshui, Taipei Zoo and other outlying points. Signs are in Chinese and English, and stations are announced in Mandarin, English,

Hakka and Taiwanese. The fare is based on the distance; the basic fare is NT$20 up to a maximum NT$65. Six lines are in service; 2 additional lines are scheduled to open at the end of 2010. http://english.trtc.com.tw.

BY BUS - Taipei's **city bus** coverage is dense; riders can get to almost any city destination. Station names are labelled in English. To check an itinerary, access www.taipeibus.taipei.gov.tw, click on the first bar on the top right and click on the English sign. A basic ride on the bus will cost NT$15. **EasyCard** (💰see p38) is valid for all of Taipei's bus companies.

BY CAR - **Car Plus** (daily 8am–9:30pm; 𝒫0800-222-568; www.car-plus.com.tw) has two outlets in the city center, one in Xinyi District, 705 Zhongxiao E. Rd., Sec. 5 and a second in Zhongshan District 71-1 Jianguo N. Rd., Sec. 1. There's a rental counter at Taoyuan airport.

HLC (www.easyrent.com.tw) has two branches downtown at 135 Zhongxiao E. Rd. Sec. 6, Nangang District (𝒫02-2651 7766) and at 557 Songjiang Rd., Zhongshan District (𝒫02-2516 3816). Rental counter at Taoyuan airport.

Taipei riverside bike path

Mark Caltonhill/Michelin

GENERAL INFORMATION

AREA CODES

The area code for Taipei is 02. It is not necessary to dial the area code when making a **local call**, but the area code has been included in telephone numbers shown in this chapter. You must dial the area code for non-local calls (for hotel reservations or advance information, for example) and calls made from mobile phones.

For **mobile phones** the prefix is 09. Some businesses' contact numbers include mobile phones; you must dial the 09 prefix from anywhere in Taiwan to reach a mobile phone.

ACCOMMODATIONS

Taiwan Tourism Bureau's official website (*http://eng.taiwan.net.tw*) has a directory of hotels in Taipei, with a link to each hotel's website. *For a selection of suggested lodgings, see ADDRESSES below.*

VISITOR INFORMATION

Taipei Main Station: 1st Floor, 3 Beiping W. Rd., Zhongzheng District. *886-2-2312-3256. http://eng.taiwan.net.tw.* Tourism Bureau: 290 Zhongxiao E. Rd., Sec. 4, 9th Floor.

LOCAL PRESS

Daily: Taipei Times, www.taipeitimes.com. **Freezines:** publications **24seven** and **Highway 11**, distributed in bars and restaurants often frequented by Western expatriates.

USEFUL NUMBERS

Police: 110 (emergency)
Police phone number 02-2556 6007 (non-emergency, English speaking)
Ambulance: 119

WANHUA DISTRICT (OLD TAIPEI)★★★

Edged by the Danshui River on the west and Zhongzheng District on the east, the oldest district in Taipei constitutes an interesting mix of decaying buildings, venerable temples and Japanese vestiges contrasted by trendy shopping centers and funky bookstores, art galleries and Internet cafes. Local culture is well preserved in the vicinity of **Longshan Temple**, where all sorts of traditional shops are found. If you want to experience Taiwanese history in a capsule, visit Wanhua, for a trip from Taipei's beginnings through Japanese rule to modern consumerist Taiwan.

WALKING TOUR 1

See map. Allow 4hrs. 2km/1.25mi. MRT: Longshan Temple.

Begin at Longshan Temple.

Longshan Temple★★★龍山寺

211 Guangzhou St. Open daily 6am–10:20pm. 02-2302 5162. www.lungshan.org.tw.
If this is your first visit to Taipei, you'll get an insight into the soul of the Taiwan-ese people at this temple. Named for **Dragon Mountain** (long shan), a sacred mountain and temple in Fujian Province, Longshan Temple is instrumental to the spiritual well-being, physical health and social life of many residents and visitors. As a Buddhist temple, it is the center of lively religious activity: it shelters the bodhisattva **Guanyin**, goddess of Mercy, as well as many other deities. It is said that a passer-by once hung an amulet of Guanyin on a tree near the present temple; it shone so brightly even in the dark that everyone knew the place was blessed. Another story tells that, during World War II, the temple was bombed by Allied raids (they claimed the Japanese were hiding armaments in it) and burst into flames so intense that the forged iron around the wooden statue of Guanyin melted. The hall burned down, but the statue survived, with only a few ashes at her feet.

People come to the temple to ask peace and prosperity of the gods. Many young people go directly to the rear hall to the **Old Man under the Moon** and ask to meet their future lover. The Old Man is so popular that even organized match-

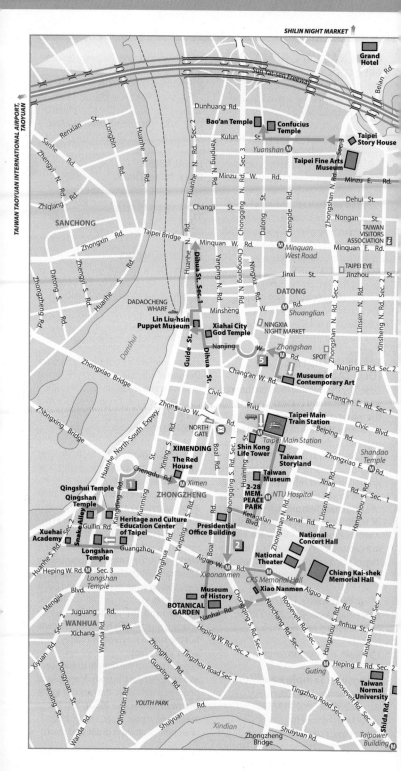

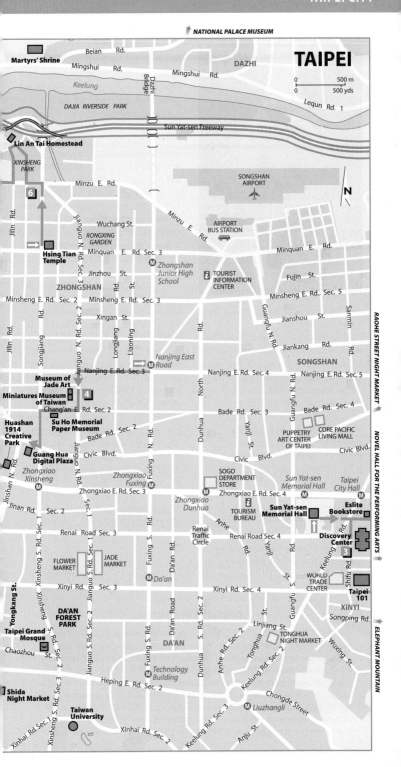

NATIONAL PALACE MUSEUM

TAIPEI

Martyrs' Shrine

Beian Rd.

Mingshui Rd.

DAZHI

Mingshui Rd.

Dazhi Bridge

Keelung

0   500 m
0   500 yds

DAJIA RIVERSIDE PARK

Lequn Rd. 1

Sun Yat-sen Freeway

Lin An Tai Homestead

XINSHENG PARK

Jilin Rd.

6

Minzu E. Rd.

SONGSHAN AIRPORT

N

Hsing Tian Temple

Wuchang St.

Minzu E. Rd.

AIRPORT BUS STATION

Jianguo N. Rd. Sec. 3

RONGXING GARDEN

Minquan E. Rd. Sec. 3

Minquan E. Rd.

Jinzhou St.

Zhongshan Junior High School

TOURIST INFORMATION CENTER

Minquan E. Rd.

ZHONGSHAN

Fujin St.

Minsheng E. Rd. Sec. 2

Minsheng E. Rd. Sec. 3

Minsheng E. Rd.. Sec. 5

Jianshou St.

Sanmin Rd.

Jilin Rd.

Songjiang Rd.

Xingan St.

Guangfu N. Rd.

SONGSHAN

Jiankang Rd.

RAOHE STREET NIGHT MARKET

Jianguo N. Rd. Sec. 2

Longjiang Rd.

Liaoning St.

Nanjing East Road

Nanjing E. Rd. Sec. 3

North Rd.

Nanjing E. Rd. Sec. 4

Nanjing E. Rd. Sec. 5

Museum of Jade Art

Miniatures Museum of Taiwan

4

Chang'an E. Rd. Sec. 2

Bade Rd. Sec. 3

Bade Rd. Sec. 4

Su Ho Memorial Paper Museum

Bade Rd. Sec. 2

Dunhua North Rd.

Yanji St.

Guangfu N. Rd.

PUPPETRY ART CENTER OF TAIPEI

CORE PACIFIC LIVING MALL

Huashan 1914 Creative Park

Jianguo N. Rd.

Civic Blvd.

Civic Blvd.

Civic Blvd.

Guang Hua Digital Plaza

Zhongxiao Xinsheng

Zhongxiao Fuxing

Fuxing N. Rd.

SOGO DEPARTMENT STORE

Sun Yat-sen Memorial Hall

Taipei City Hall

NOVEL HALL FOR THE PERFORMING ARTS

Jinshan N. Rd.

Jinan Rd.

Sec. 2

Zhongxiao E. Rd. Sec. 3

Zhongxiao E. Rd. Sec. 4

Sun Yat-sen Memorial Hall

Eslite Bookstore

Xinsheng S. Rd. Sec. 1

Jianguo S. Rd. Sec. 1

Sec. 1

Zhongxiao Dunhua

TOURISM BUREAU

Discovery Center

Keelung Rd.

3

Renai Road Sec. 3

Renai Traffic Circle

Anhe Rd.

Renai Road Sec. 4

Yanji St.

Shifu Rd.

FLOWER MARKET

JADE MARKET

Fuxing S. Rd.

Da'an Road

WORLD TRADE CENTER

Guangfu S. Rd.

Taipei 101

Yongkang St.

Xinyi Rd. Sec. 3

Da'an

Xinyi Rd. Sec. 4

Guangfu S. Rd.

XINYI

Songping Rd.

DA'AN FOREST PARK

Jianguo S. Rd. Sec. 2

Dunhua S. Rd. Sec. 2

Linjiang St.

TONGHUA NIGHT MARKET

Wuxing St.

ELEPHANT MOUNTAIN

Taipei Grand Mosque

Chaozhou St.

Xinsheng S. Rd. Sec. 2

DA'AN

Fuxing S. Rd.

Anhe Rd. Sec. 2

Tonghua St.

Keelung Rd. Sec. 2

Shida Night Market

Xinsheng S. Rd. Sec. 3

Heping E. Rd. Sec. 2

Technology Building

Dunhua S. Rd.

Chongde Street

Taiwan University

Xinhai Rd. Sec. 2

Keelung Rd. Sec. 3

Liuzhangli

Anju St.

Xinhai Rd. Sec. 3

Dizang, Longshan Temple

Florent Bonnefoy/Michelin

three **main sections**: front, middle and rear halls. It is awash in golds and reds (gold symbolizes heaven and red, happiness). Lanterns hang everywhere. When going through the **front hall**, visitors pass a pair of bronze columns decorated with dragons. Four other pairs are found in the **middle hall**. The statue of Guanyin (called Avalokiteśvara in Sanskrit) stands in this hall and is flanked by **Wenshu**, the bodhisattva of transcendent wisdom and **Puxian**, the bodhisattva of action. Wenshu is recognizable by the flame sword he wields, cutting down ignorance, whereas Puxian is holding a flower. Around them are dispatched the 18 **arhats**, enlightened disciples of the Buddha.

making tours arrive all the way from Japan to pray to him.

People burn incense and throw **bwa bwei** (擲筊) divination blocks—smooth, crescent-shaped pieces, usually of wood and red in color. Kneeling supplicants throw *(bwa)* a pair of blocks *(bwei)* onto the temple floor in front of an altar to receive an answer from a god. Expressing gratitude and repeating their question after each toss, they throw until the blocks land in the opposite position three times in a row. The up or down landing positions of the blocks indicate a yes or no answer." *see Architecture in Introduction for temple illustration.*

Visit

Erected in 1738 by Fujianese settlers— but rebuilt many times since then—the temple faces south. It's designed with

The rear hall contains a **hall of Guanyu** (on the left), where worshipers can pray to the fourth of the Four Great Bodhisattvas in Chinese Buddhism, **Dizang** (Ksitigarbha in Sanskrit), the bodhisattva of hell beings, depicted as a monk with a nimbus around his shaved head. He carries a staff to force open the gates of hell and a wish-fulfilling jewel to lighten the darkness. In the **Mazu Hall**, the goddess **Mazu** receives the prayers of people asking her to grant them a safe return when they are traveling by sea or land (air travelers should refer to Guanyin). Mazu is shielded by her two trustworthy bodyguards: **Qianli Yan** *(Thousand Mile Eyes)*, who helps her monitor the disasters of the world, and **Shunfeng Er** *(Thousand Mile Ears)*, who is in charge of listening to the complaints of the world for her.

 *Turn left as you exit the temple.*

Naming the District

The name "Wanhua (萬華)" derives from the Mandarin pronunciation of the two characters used by the Japanese to name the district. This name was based on the Japanese pronunciation of the Taiwanese name *báng-kah* (艋舺), which itself stems from an Austronesian word meaning "canoe." In early times, this spot was a gathering place for natives who came in dugout canoes to trade with the young Han Chinese settlement. Taiwanese speakers have always referred to the area as *Báng-kah*, and it is now gaining a new notoriety since the 2010 launch of the eponymous gangster movie, *Monga*, which is set in Wanhua (Monga and Manka are two transliteration attempts at the Taiwanese pronunciation).

Herb Alley 青草巷

Longshan Temple was built at a time when medical care was not widespread in Taiwan. If people got sick, they would go to the main hall and make offerings to Guanyin, and then go next door to the "herb street" *(qing cao xiang)* to buy traditional medicine at one of the pharmacopoeia stalls. People were cured, so the temple became very popular with the Taiwanese people.

While you are on Herb Street, you can grab a glass of herbal tea. Some of the teas are brewed to help people's bodies fight the heat. Just ask the shopkeeper, and add some sugar—as the Chinese saying goes: "the bitterer the medicine, the better."

 Walk east along Guangzhou St., to the right of the temple.

Heritage and Culture Education Center of Taipei
臺北市鄉土教育中心
101 Guangzhou St. Open Tues–Sun *9am–5pm.* 02-2336 1704. *http://hcec.tp.edu.tw.*

The renovated streets of the historic **Bopiliao** 剝皮寮 area host exhibits about local culture as well as cultural events. Next to the entrance, a small exhibit re-creates the setting of one scene in the 2010 Taiwan blockbuster, *Monga* (see Films), including costumes and storyboards for the movie. Buildings from the late Qing dynasty to the Japanese occupation and early post-war period are a combination of traditional shops such as old pharmacies and exhibition halls.

 Turn back in direction of the temple. At number 120 you will see a traditional pharmacy. The medicines are brewed outdoors in big pots at the side.

Xiyuan Road 西園路

Xiyuan Road runs northwest along the western flank of Longshan Temple. The temple is surrounded by medicine shops and stalls selling Buddhist paraphernalia. Some of the shops date back to the 19C and are still run by the same

Touring Tip

On each 1st and 15th day of the lunar month, worship ceremonies are held in the temple. In any case, visit the temple in the morning at 6am and 8am, or in the evening at 5pm, when worshipers gather to chant.

families. Among the explosion of reds and golds, you will find white spots that are, in fact, porcelain statues, mainly of Guanyin and the Buddha. If you want to buy Buddhist devotional items, this street is definitely the place. Other shops selling religious objects are to be found in the neighboring lanes of **Xichang Street** *(east of the temple).*

 Walk farther along the road and turn left on Huaxi St.

Xuehai Academy★ 學海書院
93 Huaxi St., Sec. 2.
Not open to the public.

The academy was housed in one of the oldest buildings in Taipei. Established in 1837, it was once the best academic institution in the Danshui-Taipei area. The school's design as an institution of learning included an outer wall, a main gate and classrooms in the left and right wings. There used to be a shrine to the early Confucian scholar Zhu Xi. Recently, the main gate was moved inward because of road expansion. During Japanese rule, the building was used as a government office and military barracks. Today it serves as the Gao Clan

Touring Tip

If you started your tour early in the morning to hear the chanting at Longshan Temple and if you seek culinary adventure, grab a typical Manka breakfast at Zhouji Rouzhou (周記肉粥, *104 Guangzhou St.*), which serves meat congee, a soup of rice with different kinds of meat like pork, chicken or beef.

Family Temple and, sadly, is closed to the public. Even if the plastic roof (meant to protect it) is not very aesthetic, you can still admire the structure's exterior, which is decorated with multicolored ceramic tiles. On the doors note the delicate paintings of guardian deities.

▷ *Return to Guangzhou St.*

Snake Alley (Huaxi Street Night Market) 華西街夜市

Huaxi St. ⏱*Open nightly 7pm–midnight.*

This market was previously a must-see for visitors to Taipei. Nowadays it looks a bit worn and neglected. Enter the market through the **Chinese-style gate** with a sign that reads "Taipei Hwahsi Tourist Night Market." In the past, shops piled with cages of hissing snakes filled the place, hence the alley's name. Only a few of these shops remain, but they still attract tourists. The blood and bile of the snakes were mixed with kaoliang liquor and herbs to be sold and drunk by men who believed the concoction strengthened their eyesight and increased their virility. The concoction is still made today. After the cobra or viper is killed and gutted, the meat is served in soup or stir-fried with vegetables in one of the several snake restaurants on the street.

A legal red-light quarter until 1997, the area still has shops that sell herbal aphrodisiacs and sex toys *(avoid foot-massage parlors that are not on the main alley)*. A good alternative to Snake Alley is **Guangzhou Street**, in the same neighborhood, where various stalls sell

---

Touring Tip

At Huaxi Market, you'll find many local trinkets like statues of small Buddhas, pearls and amulets. Among the market's food stalls, **King of Sushi** (壽司王; *157 Huaxi St.*) is one of the best sushi stalls, and **A Zhumo** (阿豬嬤; *203 Huaxi St.*) serves traditional Chinese desserts.

---

snacks, swimwear, CDs and clothes at bargain prices.

▷ *Walk to the end of Snake Alley and turn right onto Guiyang St., Sec. 2.*

Qingshan Temple★★
艋舺青山宮

218 Guiyang St., Sec 2. ⏱*Open daily 6am–10:20pm.* ☎*02-2382 2996.*

Home of the god **King of Qingshan**, this temple was built in 1854, after an effigy of the god stopped a fisherman who had brought it from mainland China to fight an epidemic. When it was carried past Old Street (today's Xiyuan Road), the statue became so heavy that the bearers couldn't move it any farther. Puzzled, the devotees had to throw *bwa bwei* to discover that the king wanted to stay here and have a temple established in his honor.

During the Three Kingdoms, Gen. **Zhang Gun** administered an area in Quanzhou, Fujian (mainland China) and was deified as the king of Qingshan. Worshiped as a god, he was believed to have the ability to dispel disease and to possess divine authority where justice was concerned. Two guardians attend him, generals **Xie Pi'An** and **Fan Wudi**; it is said that they used to patrol the neighborhood, clanging their chains and scaring away thieves and Japanese geishas who came from Kyushu, Japan, to work in Taipei.

The king's birthday is celebrated on the 22nd day of the 10th lunar month. On this occasion the king is brought out to conduct an inspection of the neighborhood. All the other temples of the area take part in this celebration, one of the most popular in the Wanhua district.

Visit

The temple is now surrounded by buildings, so be careful or you could pass it without noticing it. Laid out in a three-hall design, the temple is richly ornamented. The front hall's **octagonal ceiling**★★ reveals exquisite workmanship. The stone pillars and sculptures were built from remains of the Shinto shrine at Yuanshan (dating from the Japanese era). The wood carvings have historical value as well. The **statue** of the king is uncanny; its eyes follow you, no matter where you stand, as if it wanted to prove that none can escape justice. Climb the stairs to find myriad divinities (*first floor*), like the Sun as a red-faced man and the Moon as an empress. From the second floor, you can access a balcony with a view of the sculpted roofs of the temple.

Guiyang Street 貴陽街二段

Section 2 of this street should be seen for its **architecture**. It is lined with old shophouses, but alas, most of them have been neglected. The redbrick shops were built in the Taisho style (1912-25), when Japan administered Taiwan. The arcades, where dozens of scooters are parked and assorted fruit and snack stands attract customers, provide a good overview of Taipei's contemporary lifestyle.

▶ Walk farther on Guiyang St. At the crossroads you'll see the gate of the Qingshui Temple.

Qingshui Temple★★
艋舺清水巖

81 Kangding Rd. ⏱Open daily. MRT: Ximen. ☎02-2371 1517.

Accessed by a path lined with small eateries and local hangouts, this temple was established in 1787 by Fujianese immigrants from Anxi County, which is famous for Tieguanyin (鐵觀音) oolong tea. The temple is dedicated to Master Qingshui, who began the cultivation of this type of tea there.

A guardian god of Anxi County, Master Qingshui is also called "Master Black Face" because it is thought a ghost burned his visage while Qingshui was praying, but left his body miraculously untouched. It is also believed that, when the French attacked Danshui at the end of the Qing dynasty, Taipei remained intact because people asked for the master's protection. When fighting among rival groups over control of the Danshui River trade broke out, the temple was burned down in 1853. It was rebuilt in 1867, and used as a school during the Japanese occupation and later as a prefectural school.

Visit

Considered the best-preserved example of mid-Qing style in Taiwan, the temple was originally designed with front, main and rear halls. Outside the main entrance are exquisite **intaglio carvings**★★ on the walls. The main hall's interior features exquisite gold work, carved stone columns and elaborate wall paintings. A seated **statue** of Master Qingshui is prominently placed on an altar in the main hall. It is commonly believed that the nose of his statue will droop when a disaster is about to strike the city and thus warn citizens of impending danger. If you look closely, you will see that the nose is attached to the face. Fortunately, it appears that it won't sag any time soon.

▶ To the right is Kangding Rd.; turn left onto it, walk north and turn right into Chengdu Rd. Walk until you see the MRT Station. Next to it is the Red House.

Master Qingshui, Qingshui Temple

Florent Bonnefoy/Michelin

The Red House 紅樓劇場

10 Chengdu Rd. ○*Open Tue–Sun 11am –10pm. MRT: Ximen.* ✆*02-2311 9380. www.redhouse.org.tw.*

A landmark in the Ximending area, the Red House is a typical Japanese-era building in Taipei.

When the Ximending area was planned as a Japanese residential and entertainment section, the Japanese administration started to build facilities such as this octagonal, redbrick structure (1908) to serve as a public market. Upon its opening, the market became a preferred shopping area for Japanese settlers. After the arrival of the KMT, the Red House was converted into a Peking Opera house. Typical Beijing crosstalk performances *(xiangsheng)* were also held between these walls, bringing a little piece of the capital into Taipei. After the city started to develop eastwards, the Red House was more or less abandoned. Taipei residents rediscovered it in 2002 when it reopened after total renovation as a venue for cultural events.

Now regularly hosting vocal and visual performances, the Red House consists of the octagonal building, a cruciform-shaped building at the rear and a third, newer structure. Even if you are just passing by, it's worth visiting or sitting down for a while in its coffee shop. On weekends the square in front of the building is often used as an independent artists' market, making the area lively. The vicinity is now occupied by bars and shops. *The Red House is one of the gates to Ximending.*

Ximending★ 西門町

It is best to arrive in Ximending at dusk, when young people gather in the Harujuku of Taipei to shop and hang out with friends. Because the area jumpstarted during Japanese rule and was designed like the Asakusa quarter in Tokyo, it's no wonder that multiple boutiques here sell Japanese goods that young Taiwanese are fond of (they are called *harizu*, meaning "Japan lovers").

To glimpse the life of Taipei's youth, lose yourself in the diminutive alleys off the main intersection of Chengdu and Wuchang roads, shop in the small stores and try one of the many local eateries. Wuchang Street, known as "Movie Street" during the Japanese era, is still lined with several movie theaters.

Ximending is also the area where the so-called "red envelope clubs" or *hongbao chang* (copying Shanghai's) thrived in the 1960s. These clubs featured females dressed in gala dresses singing famous love songs from the 1950s-70s. Just a handful still remain, attended by a male audience—war veterans mostly—who come here to listen to old Mandarin songs often forgotten by the younger generation; customers reward the better performers with money in red packets.

The Red House

Florent Bonnefoy/Michelin

ZHONGZHENG DISTRICT (CENTRAL TAIPEI)★★

The political heart of the city and seat of Taiwan's government, this southern district of Taipei is named after one of Chiang Kai-shek's courtesy names, Zhongzheng (meaning "central uprightness"). As you stroll the avenues, you will pass several icons of 20C Taiwanese history. The Presidential Office Building and the Taiwan Museum are legacies of the Japanese era.

A small leap forward in time and you'll be in 1947, when Nationalist troops opened fire on city crowds: the 2-28 Memorial Peace Park was renamed in memory of this incident. Taiwan Storyland is a nostalgic capsule of daily life in Taiwan when the island served as a refuge for the Nationalists. The most compelling landmark is undoubtedly Chiang Kai-shek Memorial Hall, whose singular presence dominates a vast plaza where older people come to exercise, and young people, oblivious to the torments of the past, come to rehearse dance routines.

⭒ WALKING TOUR ②

⏱ *See map. Allow 4hrs. 3km/1.8mi.
MRT: Taipei Main Station.*

▶ *Begin at the Main Railway Station.*

Taipei Main Railway Station 臺北火車站

Zhongxiao W. Rd., Sec. 1. ⏱*Open 24hrs.*
Taipei's main train station's surroundings look rather grim. Yet this station serves as the principal hub for not only the island's entire rail network, but also the island's bus service and Taipei's metro and bus system. It is the key arrival and departure point for travelers visiting the city, a factor that accounts for its bustling activity day and night. A staffed **visitor center** on the premises helps orient newcomers.

Void of adornment and architectural interest, the multistory building is a low-rise, rectangular mass topped by a hipped roof, the fourth iteration of Taipei's station, constructed in 1989.

Ximending
Florent Bonnefoy/Michelin

The first floor is reserved for ticketing, the second floor holds shops and a food court (added in recent years for travelers' convenience), and an upper floor contains administrative offices.

Underground levels house transportation platforms as well as **Taipei City Mall**, a subterranean shopping mall that stretches to Zhongshan MRT Station. On weekends, young people gather there to rehearse dances or play music.

Shin Kong Life Tower 新光摩天大樓

Facing the station is a more interesting structure: a rose-colored tower reaching 245m/800ft in height. Its earthquake-proof construction began in 1989 and was completed in 1993, incorporating state-of-the-art Japanese seismographic technologies of the time.

Its color was chosen to symbolize both Taiwan's and Japan's national flowers (the plum blossom and cherry blossom, respectively). For four years, it was Taiwan's highest skyscraper and featured an observatory on the 49th floor.

After the opening of Taipei 101, the number of visitors declined drastically, and the observatory was eventually closed.

Exhibit, Taiwan Storyland

Florent Bonnefoy/Michelin

⚑ Taiwan Storyland★
臺灣故事館

B2, 50 Zhongxiao W. Rd, Sec. 1. ⏰*Open 10:30am–8:30pm (last admission 8pm). NT$200 (includes English brochure and headset).* ☎*02-2388 7158 or 0800 887 701. www.taiwanstoryland.com.tw.*

Located in front of the station, next to K-Mall, this museum re-creates a Taiwanese neighborhood of the 1950s to 70s. Its entrance is immediately recognizable: a massive door front adorned with colorful, sculpted fruit.

Inside the museum visitors might feel nostalgia for the "old days" as they walk along the **main street**, which is lined with decorated doorways. You may find yourself in the re-created **grocery store** with a grandfather excited to show his grandchildren the toys and sweets from his own childhood. Along the old streets and alleys, you will discover a replica police station, typical houses, an ice-cream store and more.

A small **exhibition hall** displays artifacts (mainly old toys) dating from the mid-Qing dynasty to modern times and gathered from all over the island. You can sit on a wooden folding chair at a **movie theater** and watch early Taiwanese films. End your visit with an old-time snack or a meal at one of the themed restaurants.

⏵ *Turn left and walk down Gongyuan Rd. (literally "Park Road"). When you arrive at the Peace Park, the Taiwan Museum is immediately on the right after going through the park gate.*

Taiwan Museum★
國立臺灣博物館

2 Xiangyang Rd. ⏰*Open Tue–Sun 10am –5pm. NT$20.* ☎*02-2382 2566. www.ntm.gov.tw.*

The Neoclassical architecture of the museum building, with its Greek-temple style columns and entablatures, is rather surprising in Taipei. Constructed by Japanese authorities on the site of a Mazu temple as the Kodama Goto Memorial Hall (Japan's fourth viceroy of Taiwan), the building was inaugurated in 1915 and housed the collection of a former Japanese museum in Taipei. After Japanese rule ended, the museum came under the control of Taiwan. Having undergone two major renovations, it was renamed the National Taiwan Museum in 1999. Today the focus of its holdings embraces Taiwan, southern mainland China and the South Pacific.

Upon entering the building, you'll arrive in the hall with a monumental staircase beneath the dome, features reminiscent of a London museum. The varied collections are divided among five departments (anthropology, botany, earth sciences, education and zoology) and include specimens of the island's native flora and fauna as well as historical artifacts. Some sections may look a bit dusty, but the temporary exhibits here are of good quality and scope, so check the website to see what is on view.

2-28 Memorial Peace Park★★
二二八和平公園

3 Ketagalan Bvd. ⏲*Open 24hrs.* ☎*02-2389 7228. http://english.pslo. taipei.gov.tw.*
Bordered by Ketagalan Boulevard and Gongyuan Road, this park is dedicated to the victims of the **2-28 Incident,** when protesters against the Kuomintang government were massacred on February 28, 1947 (*see History*). Today the park is a much-used green space within Taipei's concrete-heavy urbanscape, offering Japanese-style gardens, ponds, arched bridges, walking paths and an amphitheatre as places for rest and renewal.
Established in 1908 during the Japanese era, the park was the first European-style urban park in Taiwan. In 1930 Taiwan's Japanese authorities built a radio station within it to serve as headquarters for the Taipei Broadcasting Bureau, a propaganda arm. A year later, the Taiwan Broadcasting Bureau was founded, broadcasting island-wide from the park. After the Kuomintang took over the island, the park was renamed, and the broadcasting association became the Taiwan Broadcasting Company, with the same function of dispensing propa-

Touring Tip

As with all the parks in the Chinese world, it's best to visit at dawn, when tai chi, kung fu and qigong practitioners gather to exercise together. Visitors are usually welcome, but always ask permission to join the group before trying to imitate the movements of well-trained practitioners.

ganda. In 1972 the Taipei government began administering the radio station. The buddings of Taiwanese democracy prompted the government's acknowledgement of the 2-28 Incident, as well as the subsequent creation of a memorial museum within the former radio station, and the renaming of the park.
In the park's center, the **memorial** consists of a post-Modern sculpture of a needle standing on three cubes.
The **2-28 Memorial Museum** (二二八紀念博物館 ⚬⛒ *closed for renovation; scheduled reopening Jan 2011;* ☎*02-2389 7228; http://228.culture.gov.tw*), facing the memorial on the east, provides a detailed explanation of the 2-28 Incident by way of testimonies and exhibits. The current renovation will add new exhibit space to the museum.
A **wall of mementos** next to the museum is graced with spider lilies

2-28 Memorial Peace Park
Florent Bonnefoy/Michelin

(crinum asiaticum), the symbol of peace. A small hall is enclosed within glass walls on which photographs of the victims have been posted.

▶ *From the park, turn right on Ketagalan Blvd.and walk to Chongqing S. Rd.*

Presidential Office Building★ 總統府

122 Chongqing S. Rd., Sec. 1. ✆🕘*Visit by guided tour only, Mon–Fri 9am–noon. 𝄠02-2312 0760. www.president.gov.tw/en. Visitor entrance at the rear (Baoqing and Bo Ai Rds.). Photo I.D. required for entry.*

Encompassing an entire city block, the monumental Western-style building, dominated by a 60m/197ft central tower, houses the offices of Taiwan's president, vice president and various governmental authorities. It is the official venue for hosting diplomatic visits.

Long the tallest building in Taipei, the five-story Presidential Office Building was erected during the Japanese era as the governor-general's mansion (1919). Rectangular in appearance, the structure is actually two adjoining squares, resembling the Japanese kanji for "the sun" (日)—or Japan itself (the Japanese language uses some Chinese characters). The building looks toward the east, facing Sishou Mountain and the rising sun (to the Japanese, the rising sun means Japan, the "country of the rising sun") and offers an expansive view of the city. Conceived by the best Japanese architects of the time, the design is a mix of Renaissance, Gothic and Baroque styles.

The extensive brickwork is typical of this period. Bombing during WWII seriously damaged the building, but it was reconstructed in 1949, and has been used since as the presidential office.

Off the front entrance vestibule, the magnificent three-story **lobby**★ is finished in white marble; a grand central staircase leads to a landing alcove encasing a **bronze bust** of Dr. Sun Yat-sen. The corners of the building hold offices; the center is reserved for assemblies. On the first floor, an **exhibition hall** contains various displays on Taiwanese history as well as artifacts from the Japanese era. Notice the baton belonging to Chiang Kai-shek, a Bible annotated by his son, Chiang Ching-kuo, and even the bicycle Ma Ying-jeou used to tour the countryside during the presidential election campaign. An **art gallery** features rotating works of local art. The square in front of the building is a preferred gathering place for demonstrations.

▶ *Walk south along Chongqing S. Rd. Turn right into Aiguo W. Rd. Turn left into Bo'ai Rd.*

Taipei Botanical Garden 植物園

53 Nanhai Rd. 🕘Open daily 4am–10pm. 𝄠02-2303 9978. http://tpbg.tfri.gov.tw/ english.

If you feel overcome by the frenzy of Taipei, seek shelter in this beautiful oasis, just a stone's throw from the main landmarks of the Zhongzheng District. Established in 1921, the garden houses greenhouses wherein a large variety of plants thrive, gardens designed on

Releasing Animals

Among the signs displayed in the garden, one features a turtle and two hands circled and barred in red. The label in Chinese reads: "forbidden to perform the Buddhist act of releasing animals facing imminent death (in other words, animals to be eaten) in order to better one's karma." The practice is called "releasing of the life" (放生). While it's not explicitly a teaching of the historic Buddha, the act stems from Siddhartha Gautama's own actions. It is said that he once saved the life of a swan. Recently, environmental groups have protested the practice, since it can lead to the introduction of nonendemic animals that threaten the local ecology or that die slowly in an alien environment.

themes from Chinese literature or Buddhism, and a tranquil lotus pond. Surprisingly in such a big city, the park is known for bird-watching, and is one of the few places in the world where the rare Malayan Night Heron can be seen. This small migratory bird is easy to find as it hunts earthworms and utters a distinctive "bo bo" cry.

◐ *Take the Heping Rd. exit and turn left. Follow the wall to the Museum of History.*

Museum of History★★
國立歷史博物館
49 Nanhai Rd. ◐ *Open Tue–Fri 10am–6pm (Fri 8:30pm, selected floors only).* ☛*English guided tour 3pm. NT$30.* ☎*02-2361 0270. www.nmh.gov.tw. Museum staff speak English.*

Its name is misleading: this museum focuses mainly on art, not history. Housing one of the premier collections of Chinese art in Taipei, the museum boasts rare bronzes and other pieces from the Shang and Tang dynasties in particular. A large part of the collection belonged to the Henan Museum, which was relocated from mainland China to Taiwan in 1949.

Originally a Japanese-style building when the museum was established here in 1955, it was renovated in a style that combines elements of palace architecture from the Ming and Qing dynasties.

Highlights include the green-paint **pottery** of the Han dynasty, the music and dance **statues** of the Five Dynasties and sculpture of the Tang dynasty. On the first floor, **sculptures** of Tang women riding horses and playing polo (exhibit number 28) indicate that, at the time, women were free to go out in the open. The tricolor **chimeras**—tomb guardians of the Tang dynasty—are impressive; their terrifying aspects would have made them effective guardians of the dead. These beasts are direct ancestors of the sculpted lions now found at the entrance to buildings in the Chinese world. **Oracle bones** with divination inscriptions represent the earliest form

of Chinese scripture, which is seldom seen in museums. Precious Tibetan **tangkas** from various dynasties provide insight into this religious art, since their creation requires a great deal of patience and faith. The bronze **figurine** of Mañjuśrī (number 20) is another example of the prowess required by Buddhist art.

◐ *Walk east on Nanhai Rd. and turn left into Nanchang Rd., Sec.1.*

Xiao Nanmen
台北府城小南門 (重熙門)
One of the last remains of the city's walls, this small south-side **gate** (*xiao nanmen* translates as "small south gate") may help you imagine Taipei's former fortifications, where the walls were 4m/13ft thick and 5m/16ft high and extended 4km/2.5mi. According to fengshui principles, Chinese cities have four gates corresponding to the four compass points. It is said that this fifth gate was built especially for a local tycoon from Banqiao—a member of the **Lin Ben Yuan** family—who wanted to bypass the control rival groups held over the West fortified gate. Along with the West and South Gates, the gate was destroyed by the Japanese, but rebuilt in the Northern Chinese palace style after WWII. Now designated a third-grade historical relic, the foundations are the only remains of the original construction.

◐ *Walk east along Aiguo W. Rd. to Zhongshan S. Rd.*

Taipei city gate
Florent Bonnefoy/Michelin

Chiang Kai-shek Memorial Hall★★★ 中正紀念堂

21 Zhongshan S. Rd. ⏰*Open daily 9am–6:30pm.* ☎*02-2343 1100. www.cksmh.gov.tw/eng.*

The massive outline of this commemorative monument, with its blue-tile roof and white marble walls, stands as an unmistakable city landmark in a spacious, and rather empty, plaza. Add the red of the flowers in the surrounding gardens, and the whole represents the three colors of the ROC flag, symbol of the Kuomintang and its leader—the man who forged modern Taiwan with an iron hand. Despite the faded influence of the generalissimo, the monumental shrine continues to draw thousands of people to the 25ha/62acre site. As elsewhere, the changing of the guard here also attracts many visitors.

After Chiang Kai-shek died on April 5, 1975, the government established a funeral committee to build a memorial to him. Architect **Yang Cho-cheng** was chosen in a competition and designed the structure to include references to famous buildings in mainland China. The traditional Chinese architecture of the building imitates the Sun Yat-sen Mausoleum of Nanjing and recalls as well the Temple of Heaven in Beijing (⏰*see Architecture in the Introduction*). Built in the classic Chinese Palace style, the adjacent **National Theater** and **National Concert Hall** were also designed by Yang Cho-cheng. The memorial hall was opened to the public in 1976; the theater and concert hall were completed in 1987.

Visit

Three **gates** formalize the entrances to the park: the main gate, the **Gate of Great Centrality and Perfect Uprightness** (大中至正); the Gate of Great Loyalty (大忠門) on the north side; and the Gate of Great Piety (大孝門) on the south side. The octagonal, double-tiered roof of the memorial hall is symbolic of the number 8, traditionally associated with abundance and good fortune in China. The **main hall** (76m/249ft high) is accessed by 89 stairs, equaling the age of Chiang when he died. Two massive **doors**, each 16m/52ft high, open to a seated **statue** of Chiang, which evokes the Lincoln statue in Washington, DC. Unlike that statue, however, Chiang is wearing traditional Chinese dress and his statue is bronze, not marble. Inscribed on the wall behind it are the Chinese characters for Ethics (倫理), Democracy (民主) and Science (科學). Two wall inscriptions read: "The purpose of life is to improve the general life of humanity" and "The meaning of life is to create and sustain subsequent lives in the universe." Notice in the ceiling the **flag** decorated with the emblem of the Kuomintang.

On the ground level are a **library**, and a **museum** dedicated to Chiang's life. The museum displays uniforms, medals,

Chiang Kai-shek Memorial Hall.
Florent Bonnefoy/Michelin

paintings, manuscripts and the two bulletproof Cadillacs he owned.

When visiting the **gallery** of photographs and portraits, you might be surprised to see a wax figure of Chiang seated at a desk, as if he were still alive. The exact re-creation of the office (the exhibits are originals) where he used to work, including paintings of his wife, gives an uncanny feeling to the visit.

EAST TAIPEI★★

Since the late 20C, eastern Taipei—which extends west to Fuxing North/South Road and includes the original Sogo department store—has experienced a total transformation. A few years ago there was nothing but scrubland where now rise the shiny, modern buildings—most noticeably Taipei 101—of the Xinyi District, the city's ultra-chic, glamorous shopping-dining-entertainment hub.

North of Taipei's eastern district stretches the district of Songshan, dominated by Songshan Airport and the busy Sun Yat-sen Freeway. To the southwest lies the Da'an District, known for its large forested park.

Today the rich and famous come to Xinyi to shop in the most fashionable boutiques and party in the trendiest clubs and poshest restaurants in town. The eastern part of Taipei has become the playground of the young, who gather at dusk to enjoy the night—whether in Xinyi proper or the labyrinths of little streets along Zhongxiao Dunhua MRT station in Section 2 of Anhe Road.

If you hang around here in the evenings, be prepared to sleep in very late the next day.

WALKING TOUR ③

See map. Allow 4hrs. 3km/1.8mi. MRT: Sun Yat-sen Memorial Hall.

Sun Yat-sen Memorial Hall★★
國立國父紀念館

505, Sec. 4, Ren-ai Rd. Grounds open 24hrs. Exhibition hall ◔Open daily 9am–5pm. ☏02-2758 8008. www.yatsen.gov.tw.

If you are looking for a place to escape the bustle of Taipei, seek shelter in this

Touring Tip

If you take the entrance under the massive staircase of the National Concert Hall, you'll find a teahouse serving hot dishes and snacks (春水堂), as well as a shop selling design items and other nice but pricey souvenirs (Art Shop).

building and its surrounding grounds, which are much beloved by neighborhood residents. The building is mammoth, but far less overpowering than the Chiang Kai-shek Memorial Hall—and quite peaceful. As at the Chiang Kai-shek Hall, the **changing of the guard** here is meticulously executed in a solemn manner, in contrast to the demeanor of many youngsters who come to rehearse dances at dusk. During public holidays the large plaza and grassy areas around the hall are invaded by locals flying kites, chatting or listening to music. Such activities give the landmark a welcoming, relaxed atmosphere.

Chiang Kai-shek himself presided over the laying of the foundation of the building, completed in 1972, that commemorates the Father of the Republic. When Chiang died, his funeral was held in this hall as if to imply that he was the heir of Dr. Sun Yat-sen. From its beginning, the hall was devoted to the presentation of Sun Yat-sen memorabilia, such as documents and artifacts from the revolution. Today it is one of Taipei's primary art centers, hosting major shows and stage performances.

Visit

With its upwardly curved corners, the massive hipped roof of yellow-orange tiles dominates the square, temple-like structure. Unlike most Taiwanese temples, its exterior is stark and void of ornamentation.

Inside, a 6m/20ft bronze **statue** of a seated Sun Yat-sen tops a raised platform. Sun wears his signature two-piece suit, often termed a Mao suit in English. In Chinese it is called a Zhongshan suit, since Sun, also known as Sun Zhong-

Changing of the guard, Sun Yat-sen Memorial Hall

Florent Bonnefoy/Michelin

shan, helped design it. The suit is a mix of Asian and Western styles—in a gesture of opposition to the Manchu government's mandating the wearing of Manchu dress.

The four pockets were said to represent the Four Virtues of the classic Guanzi (7C BC), the five front buttons referenced the five branches of government under the constitution of the Republic of China and the three cuff-buttons stood for Sun's Three Principles (Nationalism, Democracy and Welfare of the People). After his death, the suit symbolized revolutionary ideals and patriotic feelings.

In the exhibit rooms, displays include personal items and letters handwritten by Sun Yat-sen as well as historical documents. The three-story building also holds art galleries, a library, an assembly hall and a 2,500-seat auditorium.

Planted with greenery and colorful flowers, the **grounds** are dotted with several **statues**, including a bronze of the medical doctor, casually seated and in Western business attire. From the grounds, there's a good **view** of Taipei 101.

▷ *Take the memorial's east exit and walk up Songgao Rd. Then turn right onto Shifu Rd.*

Sun Yat-sen

Sun Yat-sen (1866–1925) descended from a family of modest means in Guangdong Province. After obtaining a diploma in medicine in Hong Kong, he worked for the unity and integrity of China. He took part in uprisings in the south of the country against an imperial regime weakened by influence from the West. In 1912 he became president of the Republic of China, the first president in the history of the country. He participated in the student movement of 1919 and founded the Kuomintang. For strategic reasons, he cooperated with the Communists starting in 1924, intending to use them in the fight against Chinese warlords. Sun came to Taiwan three times, but never managed to ignite a revolution since he was closely watched by the Japanese authorities. Today Chinese people from both sides of the Strait hold him in high regard. In Taiwan he appears on the NT$100 note.

👥 Discovery Center of Taipei★ 台北探索館

At City Hall, 1 Shifu Rd. ⏰*Open Tue–Sun 9am–5pm.* ☎*02-2720 8889. www.discovery.taipei.gov.tw.*

In 2002 the Taipei City Archives, housed within the monumental City Hall building, became the Discovery Center of Taipei, an interactive educational center with the mission to promote Taipei as a modern, ecology-minded metropolis. A stop here makes a good introduction to the city.

Visitors enter the four-floor exhibition space by way of **Taipei Impressions**, where wall screens display 12 indispensable things to do in the city. The second floor houses temporary displays. **City Discovery Hall** *(3rd floor)* features highly informative, state-of-the-art presentations on Taipei's growth, transportation system, cultural attractions, environmental achievements and future goals. The most interesting section is **Dialogue with Time★** *(4th floor)*, which depicts the history of Taipei over three centuries.

Highlights include modelsa of the five city gates and the walled city. Visitors learn about the city's origins, Chinese medicines, dried foods and fabrics. Many hands-on exhibits are geared to children, who will delight in the fortune-telling machine and the glass floor over the miniature city.

▶ *Walk back to Songgao Rd. and turn right.*

Eslite Bookstore★ 誠品書店

11 Songgao Rd. ⏰*Open daily 10am–midnight (Fri–Sun until 2am).* ☎*02-8789 3388. www.eslite.com*

Pronounced *à la française*, Eslite ["ay-leet"] sounds far more chic when naming one of Taiwan's finest bookstore chains. Its first store was established on Dunhua South Road in 1989, focusing on the arts and humanities. As the needs of the marketplace evolved, Eslite gradually expanded its scope and its catalogue. Today it captures the full range of the sophistication of this international city.

This flagship store in Xinyi opened in 2006. It combines a five-floor shopping mall lined with designer boutiques and wellness shops with a giant, seven-story bookstore selling Chinese, Japanese and English titles on all manner of subjects within an arty but cozy setting. In the second-floor cafe, customers can enjoy a view of Taipei 101 while sipping a latte or an espresso. A corner *(3rd floor)* is reserved for CDs of Taiwanese music as well as classical, jazz and Western pop and rock.

Eslite's late hours have made it a favorite rendezvous for Taipei's romantic youth. Open 24/7 the Dunhua store was the setting of the 2010 movie, *Au Revoir Taipei* (一頁台北), about a young man who studies French in the bookstore in pursuit of love.

▶ *Continue along Songgao Rd. You will see Shin Kong Mitsukoshi (新光三越) shopping mall.*

Bellavita (www.bellavita.com/tw) is a huge, European-style shopping mall— a high-rise, post-Modern extravaganza with skylights, balustraded balconies and a central atrium. Among its upscale tenants is L'Atelier, the restaurant of celebrated French chef Joël Robuchon.

▶ *At Shin Kong Mitsukoshi, turn right into the pedestrian street.*

Florent Bonnefoy/Michelin

Xinyi New Life Square

Songgao and Songshou Rds. ⏰*Open daily 11am–9:30pm (Fri until 10pm)* ✆*02-8789 5599. www.skm.com.tw.*
This glass-encased multicomplex concentrates most of the international brands found elsewhere in the world within four buildings connected by sky bridges. Anchoring the square is the Japanese department store chain **Shin Kong Mitsukoshi**, which offers big-name, high-end designer labels such as Prada, Gucci and Dior, plus a food court and a staffed information center to help international visitors.

▷ *Walk to the intersection of the pedestrian street and Songshou Rd.*

Across Songshou Road, **Vieshow Cinemas** *(www.vscinemas.com.tw)* is a movie megaplex featuring 17 screens. Also just to the east on Songshou Road, the **Neo 19** complex houses restaurants and popular clubs.

▷ *Turn to your right and head to the 101 tower.*

Taipei 101★★★ 台北101

8 Songzhi Rd. Mall: ⏰*Open daily 11am –9:30pm. Observatory:* ⏰*Open daily 9am–10pm, last admission 9:15pm. NT$400. Entrance and tickets on the 5th floor of the mall. www.taipei-101.com. tw. Free shuttle bus between Taipei City Hall MRT and Taipei 101 (West Exit).*
Seen from afar, Taipei 101 maintains a high profile in a predominantly low-scale city—it would in any city. The second tallest skyscraper in the world (it was overtaken by Dubai's Burj Khalifa in 2010) rises to a height of 500m/1,640ft, including the antenna. The tower's design is an alliance of traditional architecture with the latest in 21C construction techniques. Completed at the end of 2004, it incorporates state-of-the-art anti-earthquake and anti-typhoon technology (👈 *see Architecture in the guide's Introduction*).
When you get into the elevator, take a deep breath, since you will reach the 89th floor in 37 seconds.

Taipei 101

Florent Bonnefoy/Michelin

From that floor's **indoor observatory**, the **views** ★★★ *(weather permitting)* of the city and surrounding mountains are awesome. All that you would expect from the observatory, it has: a cafe, mailboxes (to send postcards to your friends from the top of the tower), binoculars, and more.
The 88th floor provides access to the world's largest **wind damper** (it stabilizes the tower in strong winds) and the world's highest jewelry store (the tower has been the setting for countless marriage proposals). On the 91st floor, the **outdoor observatory** *(open only on certain occasions and when weather conditions are favorable)*, permits an up-close view of the antenna.
Each night the tower is bathed in colored light: Monday it is red, Tuesday orange, Wednesday yellow, Thursday green, Friday blue, Saturday indigo and Sunday violet, in accordance with the spectrum of the rainbow—another way the tower symbolizes the link between the sky and the earth.

▷ *Walk east on Xinyi Rd., turn right onto Songren Rd. when you pass the high school on your right; then turn left into the next alley and walk until you see the entrance to the path to Elephant Mountain.*

Elephant Mountain★★ 象山
15min walk southeast of Taipei 101.
Easily accessible, Elephant Mountain—which is more a hill than a mountain—is one of the four peaks that compose Taipei's **Four Beasts Mountain** (四獸山). It makes a fitting conclusion to a tour of Xinyi since you can obtain superb **views**★★ of Taipei, and especially of Taipei 101, from the summit. Stairs have been constructed to ease the climbing. The mountain has a lot of big boulders to clamber on for a better view. Avoid weekends since the area gets quite crowded with photograph-takers and walkers.

ADDITIONAL SIGHTS
Raohe Street Night Market★
饒河街觀光夜市
Raohe St. (next to Sec. 4, Bade Rd.), Songshan District. MRT: Songshan.
⏱*Open daily 5pm–2am.* ✆*02-2831 6178.*
This street market near the Keelung River in the Songshan District attracts local crowds who come here to buy their usual snacks. The queue in front of the stall selling **black pepper cakes** (胡椒餅) is usually long. Originated in Fuzhou, a city in Fujian Province in mainland China, this cake is a crispy bun filled with meat seasoned with black pepper and scallions and baked in a clay oven. It's the must-eat snack of Raohe Market. You will also find traditional street-style

beauty parlors here practicing the facial treatment *wan mian* (👆 *see p36).* At the east entrance stands the **Ciyou Temple**, dedicated to Mazu. Dozens of colorful lanterns hang on its façade, lending a festive atmosphere to the market's entrance. The temple was built during the Qianlong emperor era (1735-96). It gradually attracted more and more shops until eventually a full-fledged night market emerged, making Raohe Street Night Market one of the oldest in Taipei.

Huashan 1914 · Creative Park
華山 **1914** 創意文化園區
1 Bade Rd., Sec. 1, Zhongzheng District. MRT: Zhongxiao Xinsheng. ⏱*Open daily 9:30am–7pm.* ✆*02-2358 1914. http://web.huashan1914.com.*
Built in 1914 this former Japanese winery was Taiwan's biggest producer of sake and ginseng in the 1920s; by the 1980s it stood abandoned. In 1997 members of the **Golden Bough Theatre** renovated one of the buildings and staged theatrical performances there. Several of them were sued for trespassing, but people still kept coming, especially artists attracted by the high ceilings and natural light.
Under local pressure the government had the abandoned factory converted to an arts center. It now hosts concerts, exhibitions and plays as a dedicated urban space for artistic expression.

Food stall, Raohe Street Night Market

Florent Bonnefoy/Michelin

中山區ZHONGSHAN DISTRICT★★★

Named for Sun Yat-sen, who often identified himself as Sun Zhongshan, or "central mountain," this expansive district northeast of Taipei Main Station is bordered by the Keelung River on the north where one of Taipei's largest parks, Xinsheng Park, is located. That area has been totally refurbished for the **2010 Taipei International Flora Expo**, and makes a pleasant place for a stroll. Culture aficionados will have a heyday with the various museums found in the district, from modern art to local crafts like papermaking and puppets. On the district's west side, edged by the Danshui River, the Datong District includes **Dadaocheng**, the area where tea merchants began settling in the late 1860s; today traditional shops and the famous City God Temple help retain the neighborhood's local color. North of Dadaocheng, the once-small village of **Dalongdong** enshrines the Bao'an Temple, which should not be missed.

☙ WALKING TOUR 4

ⓘ *See map. Allow 2hrs. 1km/.7mi. MRT: Nanjing East Rd.*

▷ *From the MRT station, walk two blocks west to begin your discovery of south Zhongshan at one of the museums on Jianguo N. Rd. Turn left onto Jianguo.*

Miniatures Museum of Taiwan★ 袖珍博物館

B1, 96 Jianguo N. Rd., Sec. 1. Ⓞ*Open Tue –Sun 10am–6pm. Closed 2 days before Chinese New Year. NT$180.* ✆*02-2515 0583. www.mmot.com.tw.*

This museum features an amazing collection of the smallest items you have ever seen, but in a disappointing setting—hidden away in the basement of a nondescript high-rise building.

The remarkable collection consists of some 200 miniatures, such as **Buckingham Palace**, with several rooms and the Queen's throne—all of which took three years to complete. Requiring four years to finish, Rose Mansion is

a diminutive replica of a 19C Victorian residence in Los Angeles destroyed by urban renewal. Among the other miniatures on view are the world's smallest working TV and a treetop mine made at a ratio of 1:120.

Museum of Jade Art 瑩瑋藝術翡翠文化博物館

96 Jianguo N. Rd., Sec. 1. Ⓞ*Open Wed –Mon 10am–5pm. NT$250.* ✆*02-2509 8166. www.museumofjadeart.com.*

Reputed to be the first museum in the world devoted wholly to jade art, this museum captures the fascination the precious gem exerts on the Chinese people. Designer **Soofen Hu**, whose family is in the jade business in Myanmar, got the idea for the museum when contemplating the famous *Jadeite Cabbage with Insects* in the National Palace Museum.

Permanent exhibits include calligraphies engraved on black jade, such as **Timely Clearing after Snowfall** of Wang Xizhi (AD 303-361), whose original work is in the National Palace Museum. Among other exquisite pieces on view are a **tricolored horse** with exaggerated proportions, inspired by the Tang dynasty style, and **sandals** that seem so real you feel like trying them on.

▷ *Continue south on Jianguo N. Rd. and turn right onto Chang'an Rd., Sec. 2.*

☙ Su Ho Memorial Paper Museum★ 樹火紀念紙博物館

68 Chang'an E. Rd., Sec. 2. Ⓞ*Open Mon–Sat 9:30am–4:30pm.* Ⓞ*Closed holidays. NT$180.* ✆*02-2507 5535. www.suhopaper.org.tw.*

Founded in memory of Taiwanese papermaker **Chen Su Ho**, this interactive museum explains how paper is made by hand and promotes the culture of paper. Through several activities, visitors themselves learn how to make paper. Exhibits include the history of the invention of paper in China and materials used in the papermaking process. On the ground floor, visitors observe the fabrication of paper in the **Handmade Paper Mill** section. The second floor is dedicated to the history of paper and to the different techniques used in papermaking. The **Paper Lab** (*3rd floor*) has interactive exhibits about fireproof paper and other intriguing papers. Lastly, in **Paper Space** (*4th floor*), you can try making paper yourself. The modern museum shop has many paper products for sale, such as kites, lamps and cards; it also sells a DIY paper kit.

For some hi-tech shopping, walk farther west along Chang'an Rd., turn left onto Songjiang Rd., then right onto Civic Blvd.

Guang Hua Digital Plaza (former Guanghua Market)
光華數位新天地

8 Civic Blvd., Sec. 3. MRT: Zhongxiao Xinsheng. ⏰*Open daily 10am–9pm. www.arclink.com.tw.*

In the beginning one came to Guanghua Market to buy old books in stores that had been relocated from Guling Street. The market used to stand between Bade Road and Civic Boulevard. Once the shops diversified their offerings to jade, antiques and electronics, the market became popular. During the 1990s it was the place to go for computer equipment and electronic gadgets. In 2006 it was installed in its new location in a six-story building.

Now you can shop for most anything, from the usual electronic devices to sportswear, DVDs, CDs, books and more.

🐾 WALKING TOUR ⑤
🕰*See map. Allow 4hrs. 3.5km/2.2mi. MRT: Zhongshan Rd.*

Exit the MRT and you will see the art museum on the west side.

Museum of Contemporary Art
Taipei★ 台北當代藝術館

39 Chang'an W. Rd. ⏰*Open Tue–Sun 10am–6pm. NT$50.* ☎*02-2552 3721. www.mocataipei.org.tw.*

You cannot miss the building housing this museum. It features Japanese-era architecture in redbrick with a central

Museum of Contemporary Art
Florent Bonnefoy/Michelin

bell tower. The museum showcases cutting-edge mixed-media works, video art, photography and other forms of contemporary art, but only in temporary exhibits, usually of two months' duration or more.

Originally the two-story structure, built in 1921, was an elementary school that welcomed mostly Japanese students plus a few Taiwanese at a time when the education system separated both nationalities. After the war it served as Taipei's city hall until the Taipei government moved to a new location. After retrofitting, the building reopened as MOCA Taipei in 2001.

The building's interior, such as the central hall with its high ceiling, is suited to the space contemporary works require. Sculpture pieces, often made of unorthodox and synthetic materials, sometimes reach 15m/49ft in height. Large-scale installations, as well as video and performance art, may necessitate a large staging space. Areas outside, on the museum grounds, are sometimes used as exhibit venues.

Upon exiting the museum, turn right into lane 64 Nanjing W. Rd., and then left onto Nanjing W. Rd. Walk west

4 blocks on Nanjing W. Rd., passing the traffic circle, and turn right onto Dihua St.

You are entering **Dadaocheng**★★, one of Taipei's oldest neighborhoods. The Dihua Market pre-dates the Japanese era.

Xiahai City God Temple★★★
霞海城隍廟

61 Dihua St., Sec. 1. ⏰Open daily 6am–9pm. ☎02-2558 0346.

Lost among the modern buildings of the neighborhood, this small temple is almost invisible (only 152sq m/1,636sq ft), but make no mistake, it is said to be built on a "hen's cave"—meaning in fengshui lingo that its location will ensure prosperity and peace for the community, like a hen protects its chicks.

The highest density of statues in all Taiwan was to be found here before 1994—more than 600 deities (now reduced to some 200). Since 1856 the temple has been the home of statues of the City God *(Cheng Huang)* and his wife, as well as the Old Man under the Moon *(see p. 116)*. Every year more than 6,000 happily married couples bring "wedding cakes" *(li bing)* to the Old Man in gratitude for fulfilling their wish.

Don't forget to drink the "peace tea" offered in the temple. It is a blessed mix of dates, wolfberries (goji berries) and sugar and is said to bring protection as well as warmth.

▶ *From the temple, take Dihua St., Sec. 1 and turn right into alley 92, then turn right onto Xining N. Rd.*

Lin Liu-hsin Puppet Museum★★
林柳新紀念偶戲博物館

79 Xining N. Rd. ⏰Open Tue–Sun 10am–5pm. NT$120. MRT: Shuanglian. ☎02-2556 8909 or 02-2555 9762. www.taipeipuppet.com.

Children as well as grown-ups will enjoy this modern museum, located in a small house with brightly painted interiors and founded in 2000. Focusing mainly on the puppet tradition in Taiwan, it also mounts exhibits from Africa and other parts of Asia.

The collection is expertly presented over four floors. Of special interest are **rod puppets** from China's Guangdong Province *(1st floor)*, **glove puppets** with human hair *(2nd floor)*, ornate **puppet boxes** once carried on a pole *(2nd floor)*, and marionette (stringed) puppets *(3rd floor)*. On the third floor, visitors can actually pull the strings of a marionette puppet. In workshops you can observe costumes being made, the heads of new puppets being carved, and demonstrations by a puppet master on how to manipulate the puppets.

Xiahai City God Temple

Florent Bonnefoy/Michelin

Exhibit, Lin Liu-hsin Puppet Museum

Florent Bonnefoy/Michelin

The museum's adjoining **Nadou Theatre** hosts two puppet companies: one oriented toward traditional, northern Taiwan presentations, the other more modern in style and focused on storytelling. All shows have Chinese and English subtitles.

Walk south on Xining Rd. and turn right into lane 86. At the intersection with Guide St., you will see a small church.

Guide Street 貴德街

At number 44 the Presbyterian church was built in memory of **Lee Chun-sheng**, a tea merchant and philanthropist who is also known as Taiwan's "father of tea." The façade quite resembles a human face, with the upper windows as two round eyes, the door as the mouth and the middle window as the nose.
Walk up the street to **No. 73**, where stands the former residence (1920) of **Chen Tien-lai**, a tea merchant who founded Jinji Tea Company.

Walk back to Dihua St.

Dihua Street ★ 迪化街

This street's first section is a paradise for Chinese traditional medicine practitioners, but a horror movie for animal rights activists. All range of Chinese medications can be found here, from deer horns

and mollusks to various plants (mostly plants are used in the preparation).
The street's second section is famed for its traditional sweet shops. When the Chinese New Year approaches, Taipei people flock here to buy the necessary snacks and delicacies in the shops with Western-style façades.
At No. 309 (迪化街一段309號) at the north end of the street, **Lee Cakes** (李亭香; *open Mon–Sat 9am–8pm, Sun 9am–7pm; 02-2557 8716; www.lee-cake.com*), owned by a fourth-generation family of bakers, sells sweet as well as savory handmade cakes. The Mandarin duck cakes (this waterfowl being a symbol of love in China) and *ping xi* cakes are both traditionally bought for engagements and weddings. The latter are said to have been invented in the Tang dynasty when General Xue was

Touring Tip

Tours with a specialist are organized by the Xiahai City God Temple. Every first and third Sunday of the month at 8am visitors are guided around Dadaocheng free of charge. Ask the people at the temple to book a tour for you. It's possible to make arrangements for an English translator.

fighting warriors from the west. One of the general's camp cooks picked jack beans growing by the roadside and mixed them into a paste to make portable cakes for the soldiers. When they returned home, the soldiers remembered those cakes as the "fighting the West" *(ping xi)* cakes.

◌◌◌ WALKING TOUR 6

◌ *See map. Allow 4hrs. 3.6km/2.2mi. MRT: Hsing Tian Temple.*

◌ *Start your exploration of North Zhongshan at Minquan E. and Xinsheng Rds.*

Hsing Tian Temple★ 行天宮

109 Minquan E. Rd., Sec. 1. ◌*Open daily 4am–10:30pm. Shoujing ceremony daily 11:20am–9:30pm. MRT: Minquan W. Rd, then bus 41, 225, 63 (shuttle) or Red 32 Bus to Hsing Tian temple stop.*
℘*02-2502 7924. www.ht.org.tw.*
Welcome to the Taipei home of **Guan Yu**, one of the most revered deities in the Chinese world. Since Guan Yu is worshiped both as a war god and a god for merchants, lots of businesspeople come to this temple to pay their respects.

With just a few dragons on its roof, Hsing Tian Temple, built in 1967, is not as decorated as Taipei's other temples,

but it still attracts about 20,000 visitors a day. Another particularity is that no offerings are accepted here: no paper money for burning, no gold or food offerings, folk opera performances or donation boxes, but you will observe one unique religious service, *shoujing* (收驚), meaning "restoration after a disturbance." People who do not feel well or who seem to be having a streak of bad luck ask help from volunteer grannies, dressed in dark-blue Chinese robes, who wave incense over the body of the devotee and say prayers in order to change their fortune.

The temple is also famous for fortune telling; *bwa bwei*, the divination blocks *(see p116)*, are constantly being thrown to get an answer from the god.

Suanming Street 算命街

The pedestrian underpass outside the temple used to shelter fruit stalls. It is now nicknamed **Fortune Telling Street**, since the fruit merchants have been replaced by fortune tellers and oracles. They read faces, hands and even feet or study your *bagua*, the eight diagrams related to one's birth date. You might also catch sight of older women giving facial treatments to young women using a technique called "rolling the face" *(wan mian)* to remove facial hair. Originating with the Teochew people *(chao zhou)* from Guangdong Province on mainland China, it's a compulsory treatment for brides-to-be in Taiwan to make their skin smooth.

◌ *Walk north on Songjiang St., then turn left onto Minzu E. Rd. and enter Xinsheng Park.*

Xinsheng Park 新生公園

This park and other area parks have been markedly upgraded for the 2010 Taipei International Flora Expo, which runs from November 2010 to April 2011 *(www.2010taipeiexpo.tw)*. Spread over 92ha/227 acres, the exposition site includes well-known landmarks and encompasses Dajia Riverside Park, Yuanshan Park, and the Taipei Fine Arts Park, home to the Fine Arts Museum.

Hsing Tian Temple

Florent Bonnefoy/Michelin

Many of the 14 themed pavilions are located in Xinsheng Park. Expo Hall, which hosts cultural events, is situated next to the Fine Arts Museum.

◑ *Across the street on the park's north side, you will find Lin An-Tai.*

Lin An Tai Old Homestead★★
林安泰古厝
5 Binjiang St., in Binjiang Park. ◷*Open Tue–Sun 9am–4pm.* ⊶ *May be closed temporarily; open during Flora Expo.*
Hidden in a corner of Binjiang Park, this courtyard-style residence, Taipei's oldest, has existed for more than 200 years. Completed in 1787 in the Southern Fujian style, it was enlarged to include more than 30 rooms. Originally located on Dunhua S. Rd., it was destined to be demolished when city planners decided to enlarge the road. Fortunately, the public reacted. The remarkably well-preserved dwelling was dismantled and reassembled in 1983 on its current site. Its proximity to the Sun Yat-sen Freeway and Songshan Airport is unfortunate, however.
The complex consists of an entrance gate and an inner court, which holds the **main hall** with its symmetrical lateral wings and interior altar, as well as other structures.
Though plain in overall appearance, the buildings are decorated with a variety of fanciful **carvings**★★ such as the dragons on the front doors, as well as bats, fruit and flowers.

The ballast stones strewn about the front yard were once used to stabilize the boats that belonged to this sea-trading family. The crescent-shaped **pond** in front served practical purposes, such as supplying water and offering fire protection, as well as adding an aesthetic element. Most importantly, the body of water—a key tenet of fengshui design—acted as a mirror to deflect evil. Prepared for the Flora Expo, the mansion's Southern Fujianese-style **gardens** will become a permanent fixture, a tranquil spot where visitors can enjoy a cup of tea and take a break.

◑ *Return to the southern border of Xinsheng Park and turn right to walk west on Minzu E. Rd. Turn right on Zhongshan N. Rd. to reach the art museum.*

Taipei Fine Arts Museum★
臺北市立美術館
181 Zhongshan N. Rd., Sec. 3. ◷*Open Tue–Sun 9:30am–5:30pm, Sat 9:30am–8:30pm.* ☏*02-2595 7656. www.tfam. museum. Note: On Saturday nights the building's exterior is beautifully lit.*
This museum was the first on the island to dedicate itself solely to modern art. Exhibits concentrate on Taiwanese art from the Japanese era to the present, but spotlight international artists as well. The collection consists of more than 4,000 holdings, primarily early 20C works, but some 19C art as well as 21C works are included. Chinese and West-

Guan Yu

The god of War, Guan Yu (關羽)—also called Lord Guan (Guan Gong 關公)—ranks among the most important Chinese deities. He lived during the tumultuous period of the Three Kingdoms (AD 220-280), and his high deeds as a warrior are related in the *Romance of the Three Kingdoms* (14C), one of the Four Great Classical Novels. He is the archetype of the righteous and loyal warrior in Chinese tradition. Guan Yu is widely revered in the Chinese world, in homes and at places of business as an alternative god of wealth, hence he's believed to protect businesspeople from crooks. Surprisingly enough, he's worshiped by the police force and gangsters as well, since he was known for his sense of justice, but also of brotherhood. You will often see small statues of the god in Chinese restaurants and shops. With his long beard, red face and the long pole weapon he holds, he's easily recognized.

ern painting and sculpture dominate, but acquisitions also include antiques. All media are represented, including ink, oil, watercolor, gouache, photography, and even video art and digital sculpture. Opened in 1983 the museum is housed in a dramatic white, cube-shaped structure with stacked rectangular-tube wings. The architecture mimics the traditional layout of a Beijing courtyard (si he yuan), but makes a modern statement.

Exhibits are rotated yearly, offering an overview of the local art scene. Since 1988 the museum has been the site of the prestigious **Taipei Biennial**, a well-attended modern art extravaganza.

Taipei Story House★
台北故事館

181-1 Zhongshan N. Rd., Sec. 3. ⏰Open Tue–Sun 10am–6pm. ✆02-2587 5565. www.storyhouse.com.tw.

Next to the Fine Arts Museum, a handsome, somewhat whimsical-appearing mansion stands on busy Zhongshan North Road. This former home of a Dadaocheng tea tycoon was built in 1914, supposedly after he visited—and was inspired by—the 1900 Paris Exposition. Devoid of its former garden, the house serves today as a backdrop for musical performances as well as a museum of early 20C Taipei.

Sporting an eclectic mix of architectural styles, the gable-roof house consists of a brick ground floor, a Tudor-style second story and a Neoclassical entry with a balustraded balcony supported by four Ionic columns.

The **interior** is awash with medallion ceilings, pendant lamps, floral-patterned tiles, wainscoting of specially imported oak and fireplaces with pilaster-legged mantels. You'll also find **photographs** *(1st floor)* of the city in the early 1900s and **"memory" boxes** *(2nd floor)* relating to Taipei's history.

After your house tour, enjoy traditional English tea in the pleasant **Story Tea House** next door.

▷ *Walk west past Yuanshan MRT station and continue west on Kulun St. Entering the neighbourhood of Dalongdong, follow the red wall on your right and turn right onto the next street.*

Taipei Confucius Temple★
台北市孔廟

275 Dalong St. ⏰Open Tue–Sat 8:30am –9pm, Sun & holidays 8:30am–5pm. ✆02-2592 3934. http://english.ct.taipei. gov.tw. Video on Confucius and Shidian ceremony daily 10:30am & 3:30pm (English version available).

The temple's design and layout are based on the one in Confucius' hometown of Qufu, Shandong Province, in mainland China.

In 1907 the Japanese razed Taipei's 1884 temple to build a girls school (still standing). After a lengthy fund-raising campaign, the current temple buildings were erected here, on this new site,

Taipei Confucius Temple

Florent Bonnefoy/Michelin

beginning in 1927, in the traditional Fujian style.

Every year on Confucius' birthday (September 28), temple activity reaches its zenith. Officials, including Taipei's mayor, participate in the Shidian ceremony, children dance in yellow robes and hold pheasant's feathers, drums and flutes sound, paper money and incense are burned and a ceremonial feast is held. In the rear of the temple, a small exhibit explains the ceremony, including the costumes and instruments.

When you exit the temple, turn right and walk a short distance on Dalong St. before turning left on Hami St.

Bao'an Temple

Florent Bonnefoy/Michelin

Bao'an Temple★★★ 保安宮
61 Hami St. Open 6:30am–10pm. 02-2595 1676. www.baoan.org.tw.

The Daoist Bao'an Temple is one of the most ornate and beautiful of Taipei's temples. The original temple was built in 1742 by immigrants from Fujian Province. The current structure, lavishly decorated, was completed in 1805 and contrasts greatly with the austerity of the Confucius Temple.

Considered a healing deity, the temple god is the emperor **Baosheng**, who is supposed to protect people's health. This function is symbolized by the character meaning "human" (人), used as a recurring design on the roof beam and the external wall painting of the hall.

Visit
Prominent on the double roof are **dragons** crafted of brightly colored tile atop richly hued **reliefs** of flowers and animals along the ridge. At the entrance the **stone lions** are quite unusual in design; it is commonly believed they embody an appeal to respect the law and implement good government. Guarded by two door gods *(men shen)*, the **main doors** are painted in deep colors. Beyond them, the highly gilded **altar** is covered with flowers and offerings. The statue of Baosheng, brought from Fujian in 1805, stands in the main hall. The ceiling beams hold sculpted crabs that evoke the Taiwanese peo-

ple's link with the sea. Profusely stylized patterns on the **column brackets** are painted in bold colors. On the right wall a relief depicts two **dragons** crafted in *koji* ceramics (a kind of ceramics characterized by exuberant pastel colors that originated in Fujian Province). Behind the main hall, the **wall paintings** illustrate famous Chinese stories, such as the *Eight Immortals Cross the Sea* and *Mulan*. In the rear hall, two **pillars** are sculpted with flowers and birds, a rare design in Taiwan.

West of the Confucius Temple, on Jiuquan Street *(which follows Kulun St.)*, the bakery **Vigor Kobo** (*2586 3816; www.taiwan-vigor.com.tw*) makes the most succulent pineapple pastries in Taipei.

ADDITIONAL SIGHTS
Grand Hotel 圓山大飯店
1 Zhongshan N. Rd., Sec. 4. MRT: Yuanshan. 02-2886 8888. www.grand-hotel.org.

Since 1952 the Grand Hotel has been a landmark in Taipei. The massive 12-story main building can be seen from afar, its silhouette immediately recognizable. At 87m/285ft in height, it is reputedly the world's tallest classic-style Chinese building. It was designed by the famous

Martyrs' Shrine

Chris Stowers/Apa Publications

architect, Yang Cho-cheng (*see Architecture in the Introduction*).

After fleeing to Taiwan, Chiang Kai-shek, and especially his wife, Soong Mei-ling, wanted to build a hotel of grand stature to provide luxurious accommodations for foreign dignitaries. The setting for the hotel, on a hilltop overlooking the Keelung River, was suggested by Soong Mei-ling. The hotel opened in 1952; a year later a swimming pool and tennis courts were added. Completed in 1973, the iconic main building holds nearly 500 guest rooms. In mid-1998 the hotel reopened after suffering extensive fire damage in 1995.

Though the exterior now looks slightly dated and austere, the main building's interior is remarkably ornate; its vast **entrance hall** is centered on a wide, carpeted staircase and giant red pillars.

Martyrs' Shrine
大直忠烈祠主殿

239 Bei'an Rd. Open daily 9am–5pm. MRT: Jiantan.

East of the Grand Hotel, this shrine was built in 1969 in memory of the 390,000 soldiers of the Kuomintang who died in the war against the Japanese and the civil war between the Communists and the Nationalists. Its solemn style was inspired by the Hall of Supreme Harmony in the Forbidden City in Beijing. The bell tower and drum tower are used during official ceremonies.

People usually come here to observe the **changing of the guard** ceremony *(daily, every hour on the hour)*. In silence guards wearing blue uniforms and silver helmets and holding bayonet rifles meticulously execute their duty.

NORTH TAIPEI★★

Though somewhat removed from the bustle of districts to the south, the expansive Shilin District, which lies north of the Keelung River, holds several remarkable attractions—plus the most compelling one of all: the National Palace Museum. Indisputably, this museum possesses a collection of Chinese art unequaled in the world. Even if you have visited before, you should climb the grand entrance stairs once again, since a large part of the vast collection is rotated every three months.

The other landmark not to miss is the Shilin Night Market, the king of Taipei's night eateries. Starting at dawn, it is rapidly overrun by hordes of tourists and youngsters who go there to shop for cheap goods and good snacks.

To complete your visit of North Taipei, there are several choices, including strolling in the gardens of Shilin Official Residence, asking favors of a god at Huiji Temple in Zhishan Garden, viewing the crafts and model houses at Shung Ye Museum of Formosan Aborigines, and seeing the stars at the Taipei Astronomical Museum.

NATIONAL PALACE MUSEUM★★★
國立故宮博物館

Whether you are in Taiwan for a business trip or for leisure, you should not miss this unrivaled concentration of Chinese treasures under one roof. Although the 21C renovation plan, completed in 2006, did not result in as large an exhibition space as some expected, visitors will still find plenty of exquisite pieces on view—creations that were once hidden away in the Forbidden City of Beijing in the private holdings of successive emperors and empresses. Although a number of galleries house permanent exhibits, the majority of works on display are changed every three months, meaning a visitor could see 60,000 pieces a year. At that rate, it would take nearly 12 years to see the entire collection, which spans 8,000 years and is particularly strong in jades and bronzes as well as paintings from the Song (960-1279), Yuan (1279-1368) and Qing (1644-1911) dynasties. More of the collection can be shown when the National Palace Museum Southern Branch in Chiayi, designed by Antoine Predock, is completed in 2013.

A Bit of History

The story of the collection is an epic in itself. When **Puyi** (1906-67), the last emperor, was forced out of the Forbidden City in 1924 the imperial belongings were seized (Puyi is the subject of

Michelin Map: p110.

Location: Of the three exhibit areas, the **main building** houses the bulk of the exhibits. For a map of the grounds, see www.npm.gov.tw/en/visiting/map/museumplans.htm. For gallery layout of the main building, access www.npm.gov.tw/en/visiting/map/galleryplans.htm.

Timing: Spend at least a half day here to see not only the museum, but also the **library**, gift shops, bookstore, and the **gardens**. For an introduction to the collection, take a **guided tour**; English tours occur twice daily *(10am & 3pm)*; sign up at the Information Desk before the tour begins. Or consider renting an **audio guide** and touring on your own. For dining options: *see sidebar below.*

Don't Miss: *Jadeite Cabbage with Insects. Timely Clearing after Snowfall. Immortal in Splashed Ink.*

National Palace Museum

Bernardo Bertolucci's 1987 film extravaganza *The Last Emperor*.) The imperial collections were treasures that had never been seen by the people. Beijing's Palace Museum was founded in 1925, and after a lengthy inventory of the collections, exhibits were organized.

When Japan invaded Manchuria, the Nationalist government and the Palace Museum director decided to move the collections south for their safety. More than 10,000 crates were transported from Beijing to Shanghai in 1933. That very same year, the preparatory office of the Central Museum in Nanjing was formed and began collecting art and artifacts from all over China. The relocation of the national treasures from Beijing to Shanghai was only the first in a series of moves that would eventually take the collections to Changsha, Hankou and other places in Sichuan Province. At the end of WWII, preparatory work was undertaken to set up premises in Beijing at the Palace Museum and Nanjing at the Central Museum.

The struggle between the Communists and the Nationalists weighed heavily on the fate of the collections. The most precious artifacts were selected, as well as the rarest books from the National Library, and all were shipped to Taiwan in 1949. A total of 231,910 objects from the Palace Museum and 11,729 from the Central Museum arrived in Keelung Harbor—only a fourth of the collections that had been moved to the south of China. The objects were "temporarily" stored in Taichung for 15 years before eventually being reunited to become the core collection of Taiwan's new National Palace Museum, which opened in mid-1965. At the time, the collection totaled 608,985 objects. With new additions in the intervening years, it has reached nearly 700,000 works today.

Visit

221 Zhishan Rd., Sec. 2. MRT: Shilin Station, then Bus R30. ○*Open daily 8:30am–6:30pm (extended hours & free admission Sat 6:30pm–8:30pm). NT$160 (Garden NT$20). Guided tours (1hr) in English daily 10am & 3pm (sign up at Information Desk). Audio guide in English (small fee).* ♿✕ ☏*02-2881 2021. www.npm.gov.tw/en/home.htm.*

If you arrive by bus, you will walk through a wide corridor bordered with trees after passing a Chinese arch and two lion sculptures. The architecture of the palace is inspired by the Forbidden City in Beijing (*see Architecture in the Introduction*). Next to the east entrance, **Zhishan Garden**, modeled on a traditional Chinese garden from the Song and Ming dynasties, features a pond, a bridge and delicately carved

The Collection

Totaling 677,687 objects (Qing archives alone accounting for 386,729 pieces), the massive collection includes some 6000 paintings and works on paper (calligraphy), 57,000 antiquities and 545,800 rare books from the Beijing and Nanjing museums, as well as some 68,700 works acquired since the National Palace Museum opened. More than 6,000 bronzes, 12,000 jade objects and 25,000 ceramic pieces are part of the collection. Chinese people know many of the most famous pieces by heart, enduring treasures that parents have talked about with their children for generations: the sandalwood furniture from Qing dynasty Prince Kong Wang; the calligraphy of Su Dongpo's (1037-1101) *Cold Food Observance;* the masterpiece *Timely Clearing after Snowfall* by expert calligrapher Wang Xizhi (303-361); the *Jadeite Cabbage with Insects;* Liang Kai's (late 12C-early 13C) Zen painting *Immortal in Splashed Ink;* the white ceramic *Pillow in the Shape of a Child* (Northern Song period 960-1126)—the list is endless. Other highlights are rare books, musical instruments, inkstones, lacquered boxes, snuff bottles, fans, miniature wood and ivory carvings, as well as historical documents that include ancient maps, imperial edicts, palace memorials and a gold-leaf tribute from Siam.

wooden pavilions. One is called **Orchid Pavilion**, in honor of calligraphy master Wang Xizhi, who wrote a *Preface to the Poems Composed at the Orchid Pavilion*. Wang used to drink and chat with other literati in a similar pavilion. His piece of art is still a reference for present day calligraphers; some of the miswritten characters (probably due to the wine), reinforce the uniqueness of it.

The following is a selection of highlights in the Main Building's galleries.

Jadeite Cabbage with Insects

© Chris Stowers/Apa Publications

First Floor

Starting your visit in the **orientation room** *(102)* is highly recommended. It's in this gallery that you will see Wang Xizhi's classic calligraphy *Timely Clearing After Snowfall*. First-floor permanent exhibits include **Qing furniture** *(108)*, **Arts from the Qing Imperial Collection** *(106)* and **religious sculptural arts** *(101)*. In gallery 101, exhibit 114 is a **gilded bronze** (AD 477) of the Shakyamuni Buddha seated in the lotus position. To fully appreciate this piece, look at the back of the body halo, which is engraved with scenes from the life of the Buddha. This masterpiece of craftsmanship is a testimony to the first days of Buddhism in China.

Gallery 106 has a different atmosphere entirely since it features items that the Qing emperors collected for their amusement. **Curio boxes** were used as personal miniature museums where the imperials stored their precious possessions, such as carved stones, seals and jade pendants. Designed to be playful, they are cleverly constructed with hidden compartments as a kind of "hide-and-seek" game. In a way, they reflect the aesthetics of the lives of the privileged at the Qing court and their passion for collecting.

Second Floor

This floor houses permanent exhibits of quintessential Chinese arts: ink and brush **painting** as well as works on paper *(208, 210 and 212)*, **ceramics** *(201, 205 and 207)* and **calligraphy** *(206 and 204)*.

Paintings and calligraphies rotate every three months, but you're sure to see some of the best pieces from China's past. It might be Su Dongpo's or Wang Xizhi's calligraphies, **Liang Kai's paintings** or the works of other famous Chinese artists.

Every temporary exhibit includes some of the most precious pieces of the collections. Viewing the porcelain creations here make it apparent why the word "China" in English also means porcelain. The exhibit relates the history of various wares and the establishment of porcelain production as a state undertaking. Undoubtedly the **Ting Ware Ceramic Pillow in the Shape of a Child** is one of the highlights in this corner of the museum. The child's expression is lively, and vibrant with health; engraved on the bottom of the pillow is a poem written by Emperor Qianlong.

Be sure to see the curious **revolving vases** of the Qing dynasty that consist of two vases: the inner vase revolving within the outer vase.

Third Floor

This floor presents **ancient bronzes** *(301)* along with a special exhibit video explaining the creation of these rare pieces. Bells and other instruments, cauldrons, vases shaped in the form of mythic animals—these works date to China's early history. Look closely at the

Palace Museum Dining

In the Main Building, the **Xianjufu Café** *(East Wing, 1st floor)* serves sandwiches, snacks and beverages.

The **Sanxitang Teahouse** *(East Wing, 4th floor)* prepares hot meals and teas.

The **Fuchunju Café** *(Library Building, 1st floor)* offers light meals.

Housed in a modern glass-box building, **Silks Palace** serves Taiwanese dishes in its food court *(daily until 6pm, Sat until 8pm)* and Cantonese cuisine in its restaurant *(daily until 9pm)*.

cauldrons to see a motif that resembles a face: it's called an "animal mask."

On this floor, visitors can view curiosities of the imperial collections that are well-known in the Chinese world. Among them is the remarkable, almost translucent **Jadeite Cabbage with Insects** *(302)*, jade sculpted in the form of Chinese bok choy with two insects on the green leaves as a symbol of fertility, and dating to the Qing dynasty.

Next to it, the surprising **meat-shaped stone** looks like a popular dish from Hangzhou in mainland China called *dongpo rou* (🔍 *see sidebar*).

Often displayed on the third floor are Ming- and Qing-era **carvings** *(304)*. Supposedly used for food storage, the **ivory openwork container**, with a squared handle (Qing dynasty), looks like a piece of fine weaving, so delicately is it carved from ivory.

In the same room, a carved **olive-stone boat** (Qing dynasty), only 1.6cm/.6in high and 3.4cm/1.3in long, is meticulously detailed with eight personages, all unique in their aspect and expression. Most impressive are the **300 characters** of an ode by Su Dongpo engraved on the bottom of the miniature boat.

ADDITIONAL SIGHTS
Shung Ye Museum of Formosan Aborigines★★
順益臺灣原住民博物館

282 Zhishan Rd., Sec. 2 (walk east from the National Palace Museum). 🕐*Open Tue–Sun 9am–5pm.* 🕐*Closed Jan 20– Feb 20. NT$150.* 📞*02-2841 2611. www.museum.org.tw/SYMM_en/index. htm.Signage and audio guide in English.*

A trapezoidal concrete building fronted by a **totem pole** carved with aboriginal symbols greets visitors to this museum. Until recently, Taiwan's aborigines, who have blood ties and linguistic links to the people of Oceania, weren't given a lot of visibility. Founded in 1994, this museum embodies a renewal in interest toward the peoples who first populated the island, proving that in addition to its profuse Chinese legacy, Taiwan also has a rich indigenous heritage.

Inside, the exhibition is tastefully arranged. In the entrance hall *(ground floor)*, the first artifact you will see is a **fishing boat** from the Tao (Yami) people (🔍*see p349*). Its white hull ornately painted with red and black motifs, the vessel has become a kind of icon for the museum. A touch screen shows **videos** about the origins and history of Taiwan's aborigines.

Alongside diverse displays of pottery and hunting weapons *(1st floor)* as well

Shung Ye Museum of Formosan Aborigines

Florent Bonnefoy/Michelin

Huiji Temple

Florent Bonnefoy/Michelin

as musical instruments, costumes and personal adornment *(2nd floor)*, the museum presents belief systems, rituals and other aspects of aboriginal culture on the basement level.

If you don't have the time to visit an actual aboriginal community in Taiwan, you can view small-scale **models** of aboriginal houses.

Zhishan Cultural and Ecological Garden
芝山文化生態綠園

120 Yusheng St., about a half mile walk west of National Palace Museum or Bus 206 from Shilin MRT. Open Tue–Sun 9am–5pm. NT\$50. ℘02-8866 6258. www.zcegarden.org.tw.

The Zhishan Garden is located on a small hill (Zhishan Yan, 芝山岩) north of the Shuangxi River and west of the National Palace Museum.

Surprisingly, the garden site was the ammunition depot for the Military Intelligence Bureau until 2002. Now devoted to educational and leisure activities, the garden combines an ecological pond, a **greenhouse** and a **wild bird rehabilitation center**.

The garden also houses an archaeological **exhibition hall** that presents Taipei's history.

From the top of the hill, you can get an expansive **view** of the Shilin area.

Huiji Temple★★ 惠濟宮
In Zhishan Garden, Lane 326, 26 Zhicheng Rd., Sec. 1 Open daily 5am–7pm. ℘02-2831 6178.

Located within Zhishan Garden, this small temple combines Daoist, Buddhist and Confucian traditions. Since its first completion in 1764, the temple has been rebuilt no less than five times. The current ornate structure dates to 1968.

Stairs lead up to an old **stone gate**, through which the temple is accessed (also by a flight of stairs). Climbing the small hill, you will see many statues; one of them represents **Guanyin** pouring water into a basin to save the multitude. The statue of the temple god **Huiji**—called the Sacred Prince, Developer of Zhangzhou *(Kaizhang shengwang)*—was brought 200 years ago from Zhangzhou in Fujian Province, but he is not the sole deity of this sanctuary: the bodhisattva **Guanyin** as well as **Wen Chang**, the Daoist god of Literature, are also honored here. This latter deity is reputed to have the power to enhance one's ability to succeed in school examinations—hence the surprising offerings found in the hall dedicated to him *(1st floor, rear hall)*. **Small notes** referencing the candidate's name, date of birth and examination date are stuck to the bottom of **candles** lit in the hope of good results. Successful candidates fill in rose-tinted forms with the same information and include a monetary token of gratitude. Notice the **ink brush**: it is believed that if a visitor touches it, passing the exam successfully will be the result.

Near the temple, a **stone tablet** commemorates the massacre of many Shilin residents during a rebellion against the Qing dynasty led by a local military leader. A collection of statues depicts characters in one of the four Chinese classics, *Journey to the West*: the monkey being Sun Wukong, the **Monkey King**; the pig, the famous Zhu Bajie; and the monk Xuanzang who traveled to India to bring the Buddhist canons back to China.

Shilin Official Residence★★
士林官邸

60 Fulin Rd. about a half mile west of Zhishan Garden. MTR: Shilin. Garden 🕐 *Open Tue–Fri 8am–5pm, Sat–Sun 8am–7pm . NT$160.* ✆ *02-2881 2512.*

Once this mansion, with its sizeable park-like grounds, was the second of some 15 homes belonging to Chiang Kai-shek and his wife, Soong Mei-ling. The former **Japanese Horticulture Experiments Station** was rebuilt in 1950 to serve as a residence fit for the generalissimo and his family.

Until it opened to the public in 1996, the estate was shrouded in mystery.

Taiwan residents suddenly discovered a beautiful **garden**★★ planted with roses (a yearly Roses Festival is hosted here March to May), plum trees, palm trees, chrysanthemums, poinsettias, snapdragons, orchids and many other varieties. Colorful seasonal plantings assure that flowers bloom in profusion year-round.

The **mansion** is currently being renovated as a museum that will show the presidential couple's rooms and once lavish lifestyle; completion is scheduled for late 2011.

The .42ha/1acre garden has elements of both Western- and classical Chinese-style gardens. Large flower-filled urns, benches, and fountains with water jets and statuary dot meandering paths that lead to **rockeries** with lotus ponds, Chinese wooden bridges over streams, and temple-like gazebos with circular seating.

When strolling in the park, you might encounter a woman or two in a wedding gown. The garden is a popular place for newlyweds who come to have their wedding photographs taken in the wide variety of garden settings; the **Victoria Chapel**, where Chiang used to worship (both he and his wife were Methodist Christians), is one of the most popular backdrops for wedding photographs.

Garden, Shilin Official Residence

Florent Bonnefoy/Michelin

👤🏛 Taipei Astronomical Museum 臺北市立天文科學教育館

63 Jihe Rd. About a half mile northwest of Shilin MRT Station. 🕐*Open Tue–Fri & Sun 9am–5pm (last admission 4pm), Sat 9am–8pm (last admission 7pm). NT$40, children NT$20. 3D theater NT$100. IMAX theater NT$100.* 📞*02-2831 4551. www.tam.gov.tw. Limited English information.*

This modern museum building is identifiable by the giant gold dome of its IMAX theater. Inside, three floors present possibly everything about the universe to reinforce the museum's claim that it is the largest in the world devoted to a knowledge of space. Children and adults can explore space technology, the celestial spheres and constellations, the solar system, the stars and the galaxy.

Illustrated by models and photographs, exhibits are largely devoted to the science of astronomy from its origins to latest achievements. How a **telescope** works, for example, is explained but only in Chinese. In the basement, the **3D theater** offers visitors a life-like spatial experience with the help of polarized glasses. The **IMAX theater**, with its 25m/82ft-diameter screen and seats inclined at a 30-degree angle, allows the public to witness a starry night.

Shilin Night Market★★ 士林夜市

MRT: Jiantan. 🕐*Open daily 6am–9pm.*

Taiwan has a plethora of night markets, but few compare to Shilin's, the largest and most famous of all. The market can be divided in two sections: the **food market** per se, housed in a barracks; and the streets around the **Yangming Theater** that hold food stalls and shops. You can find almost anything here, from sportswear to trendy hats and shoes. If you feel hungry after a frenetic shopping session, just wander from stall to stall, picking up what seems the most appealing. Specialties from this Taipei "must-see" sight include **oyster omelets** (蚵仔煎), **Shanghainese fried buns** (生煎包), **lemon jelly** (檸檬愛玉), **peanut candy** (花生糖) and if you dare, braised **stinky tofu** (紅燒臭豆腐).

SOUTH TAIPEI★★

If you feel like dawdling, head to Taipei's southern parts. In the Da'an District, two prominent universities, Taiwan Normal University and Taiwan University, give the area a youthful, hip vibe, as seen in its coffeehouses, teahouses, Western-style burger and pizza joints, bars and other student hangouts. Your first choice might be Da'an Forest Park, a large public green where Taipei residents take a deep breath and a break from hectic city life. Just a few blocks away, Yongkang Street and its surroundings reveal interesting shops and pleasant places to frequent. However, if you seriously want greenery and Zen, get on the MRT and go to the "real" getaway of southern Taipei: the hills of Maokong and their tea culture. Here you can savor a cup of tea while admiring Taipei by day and by night from a distance—and a much calmer setting.

DA'AN DISTRICT 大安區
National Taiwan Normal University 國立台灣師範大學

161 Heping East Rd., Sec. 1. MRT: Taipower Building. www2.ntnu.edu.tw.

Locals call it **Shida**, an abbreviation for the university's long, formal Chinese name. The Taipei location is the main campus of this institution's three campuses in Taiwan. A total of 10 colleges and 850 full-time faculty serve 12,000 students, of which 5,000 are graduate-level; 3,000 are international students. Established as a provincial college, the university became a teacher training center in 1946. Today it provides a range of degrees, focusing on the Arts, Literature and Humanities. Founded in 1956, its **Mandarin Training Center** is one of the best such centers in Taiwan.

The peaceful, leafy Taipei **campus** is entered via an iron **gate** made of red brick typical of the Japanese era. Some of the campus buildings are a direct heritage of the Japanese period—a mix of Neoclassical and Gothic Revival styles (the Administrative Building and the Lecture, Wenhui and Puzi halls, for example).

Da'an Forest Park
大安森林公園

East of National Taiwan Normal University, at Xinsheng S. Rd., Sec. 2 and Xinyi Rd., Sec. 3.

Downtown Taipei's "green lung" covers nearly 26ha/64acres, offering many types of recreation—some as unexpected as bird-watching. After serving as a park in the Japanese era, the space was occupied by squatters during Kuomintang rule. Eventually cleared, it was opened as a public park in 1994.

Bird lovers will surely cross paths with the commonly-sighted **Black-Crowned Night Heron**, bathing in a pond or fighting voracious Florida turtles therein. Children play soccer on the greens, teenagers practice basketball, and the elderly stroll along the blooming alleys. Visitors can doff their shoes and walk barefoot to massage their feet along the **stone passageways**. The park is a good spot to glimpse Taipei 101's tower, and take photos.

Taipei Grand Mosque
台北清真寺

Southwest side of Da'an Forest Park at 62 Xinsheng South Rd., Sec. 2.

🕐 *Open to the public Mon–Fri outside of prayer times (Friday prayers are held just after noon); call in advance to confirm.* 📞 *02-2321 9475. www.taipeimosque.org.tw.*

Black-Crowned Night Heron, Da'an Forest Park

Florent Bonnefoy/Michelin

In Taipei, where Buddhist and Daoist temples flank just about every street corner, the mosque—one of the six in Taiwan—is a surprising curiosity. Sitting just outside the lower west side of Da'an Forest Park, this monumental place of worship serves as the center of Islam on the island.

The mosque's design was conceived by famous architect **Yang Cho-cheng**, who designed the Grand Hotel, the CKS Memorial Hall and other well-known Taipei landmarks. Erected at the suggestion of the island's then minister of Foreign Affairs in a friendly gesture towards Taiwan's allies in the Middle East, the building was completed in 1960.

A fence topped with small golden crescents circles the building. Blue-green domes helmet the mosque, while characteristic minarets and a 15m/49ft-tall **hall of prayer**, whose height is challenged only by the giant palm trees of the garden, point toward the sky.

Yongkang Street★ 永康街

West of Da'an park and just north of National Taiwan Normal University.

This peaceful street and surrounding streets are lined with small eateries and shops selling kitchenware, ceramics, clothes and environmentally friendly products.

After walking on the crowded avenues of Taipei, you will agree that this neighborhood is a little gem, ideal for

Yongkang Street

Florent Bonnefoy/Michelin

The Soong Sisters

Three memorable sisters mark China's 20C. Daughters of **Charlie Soong**, a Methodist missionary and businessman from Hainan Island in mainland China, they were sent to the US to get a Western education in the land where their father had spent several years as a young man. Back in China, Charlie Soong befriended **Sun Yat-sen**, both of them linked by their Hakka origin, their hatred of the Manchu rulers and their nationalistic ideals. Soong began efforts to raise funds for Sun's revolutionary movement.

Charlie's three daughters married important men of the 20C. The sisters are acknowledged for their political savvy and far-reaching influence. The eldest, Soong **Ai-ling** (1890-1973) was the wife of prominent banker **H. H. Kung**. A descendant of Confucius, Kung hailed from a rich merchant family in Shanxi Province and served as finance minister in the New Republic.

Soong Sisters meeting orphans in 1940

© Topical Press Agency/Getty Images

Against her father's wishes, Soong **Ch'ing-ling** (1893-1981) married **Sun Yat-sen**, provoking an irreparable breach between Sun and Charlie. After Sun's death, Soong Ch'ing-ling, who had taken part in her husband's movement, claimed his political heritage, but sided with the Communists against the KMT when the civil war broke out. Unlike the rest of the Soong family, she remained in the People's Republic of China after 1949, serving as its vice-president. She later became China's first female president, although the title was purely honorary. **Mei-ling** (1898-2003) followed her husband, **Chiang Kai-shek**, to Taiwan. She exerted a great influence on the politics of her time, and was the last of the three sisters to leave this world, at age 105. They had three brothers, who were also influential. A 1997 Hong Kong-made film, *The Soong Sisters*, depicts their lives from 1911 to 1949.

browsing or enjoying a cup of java in one of its cozy coffeehouses. Hidden tea shops and teahouses can be found on the south part of Yongkang Street (*near north wall of campus*). It's also a place for antiquing—there are a lot of eclectic shops that promise good finds.

Shida Night Market 帥大夜市
South of Yongkang St. along Longquan St. MRT: Taipower Building. ○*Open nightly 7pm–midnight.*

This night market has nothing to rival north Taipei's Shilin market. But it's almost as famous, and boasts a large variety of snacks sought out by students from the nearby universities.

Among the celebrated choices, the juicy *shengjian bao* (生煎包)—fried buns from Shanghai—are a must-try. Don't be concerned by the long queue in front of this small stall; the staff is efficient and service is quick.

Other popular snacks include **stinky tofu** (香酥嫩臭豆腐) and salty **crispy chicken** (鹽酥雞).

You can also find a large selection of charming cafes and teahouses, sit-down restaurants and small stores in the vicinity. Nearby **Shida Street** is lined with several popular bars, most of which cater to university students; some of these bars present live indie and rock music.

Lin Family of Banqiao

The Lin family of landholders, merchants, financiers, politicians and scholars migrated from Fujian Province to northwest Taiwan in 1784, where they flourished. They are still active in Taiwan today.

Lin Ming-cheng was ranked by *Forbes* magazine in 2008 as the 20th-richest person on the island. His ancestor **Lin Hsiung-cheng**, once an avid patron of Sun Yat-sen, was a banker and philanthropist who became the wealthiest Taiwanese in the late Qing dynasty. Their Gulangyu Shuzhuang Garden in Xiamen, Fujian, in mainland China, can also be visited.

ADDITIONAL SIGHTS
Lin Family Mansion and Garden★★★ 林本源園邸

Ximen St., in Banqiao. MRT: Fuzhong. Take Exit 3, head to arch across street; at No. 88 turn right into street market, then left at next crossroads. Grounds ○Open Tue–Sun 9am–5pm (last admission 4pm). Visit of mansion by guided tour only, Tue–Sun 9:30am–3:30pm every 30min. ✗ 02-2965 3061. www.linfamily.tpc.gov.tw. Introductory video (18min) shown in Dingjing Hall.

This mansion, with courtyards and a garden with halls and pavilions, constitutes a most interesting example of traditional Taiwanese residential architecture. The garden is undoubtedly the best preserved private garden remaining in Taiwan. Property of the Lin family (see sidebar), the estate reveals what it meant to be rich in the Qing dynasty.

Construction of the mansion began in 1851. Fengshui bases the design, but also the need for defense, since attacks by marauders were frequent at the time. Begun in 1982 the restoration work, a concerted effort by government and private institutions, was completed over a four-year period.

From the **garden**★★ you can notice that the mansion was built on a hill (the view of the river is obstructed by modern buildings). The **half-moon pond** in front of the main building was designed as a protection, but also as a well of fortune, according to fengshui principles. In fact, the whole layout of the grounds was designed to comply with the fengshui principle, "Water in front, a mirror, the hill in back, a defense." The labyrinth of passageways, smaller ponds and pavilions makes the garden a rewarding place to stroll. Wandering or sitting here while admiring the landscape and the buildings is a Zen-like experience.

The guided tour takes in the **main building**, which is now used as a family temple, and features exquisite interior decoration and woodwork.

Lin Family Garden, Banqiao

Florent Bonnefoy/Michelin

Museum of World Religions★
世界宗教博物館

1 Zhongshan Rd., in Yonghe.永和
MRT: Dingxi, then Exit 1, turn left, walk
200m/.12mi to free shuttle bus to Sogo
Department Store; the museum is next
to it. Or taxi from the metro station
(NT$150). Open Tue–Sun 10am–5pm.
Closed Chinese New Year's Eve & two
days after. 02-2361 0270. www.mwr.
org.tw/en-library/en.htm.

Laid out as a journey of faith, this museum, run by a Buddhist association, has many artifacts and exhibits that illuminate the world's major religions. Visitors enter the **Pilgrim's Way** before arriving in the **Golden Lobby** to access the museum's centerpiece, the **Great Hall of World Religions**★. In the Great Hall, each of the world's major religions has a dedicated exhibit window and digital computer screen to add to the viewer's knowledge of the featured religion through interactive games. The exhibit also describes the main houses of worship for each religion, its ceremonies and their signification, plus any missionary work in Taiwan. In the center of the hall stand **miniature reproductions**★★ of a mosque, temple, church, synagogue and other religious sanctuaries. The miniatures alone make the long trip to the museum worthwhile. The section dealing with Buddhism, Daoism and the local Taiwan folk religion provides solid insight into these faiths and should help to enhance a visit to any of Taiwan's many temples.

Muzha★★★ 木柵

MRT to Muzha, then bus to Maokong or
MRT to Taipei Zoo then Maokong cable
car to Maokong.

Just a few miles southeast of downtown Taipei, **tea plantations** flourish on the small hills of Muzha, which is easily accessible by public transportation. A combination of tea plantations, teahouses and tea shops, the actual "tea paradise" is called **Maokong** (貓空), meaning "cat hollows"—a reference to indentations eroded in stream-bed rocks that resemble cat-paw prints. These hills are famous for growing two varieties of tea, **Tieguanyin** (鐵觀音) and **Baozhong** (包種茶).

Maokong is a preferred getaway for students of **National Chengchi University** (國立政治大學) nearby, one of the most prestigious universities in Taiwan; they come here to spend the evening with friends or study in the peaceful setting. It's also a favorite place for other night-owls who love to arrive on a cloudless night and admire the lights of Taipei while sipping tea. If you visit at night, there's no need to feel rushed: many of the teahouses are open 24hrs. If you go there in late April or early May, you might see fireflies.

The **cable car** is a pleasant way to get to the top of the hills and is highly recommended, especially at night; the ride affords fine **views**★ of Taipei and its surroundings. You can get off at the interim station before the summit in order to visit **Zhinan Temple** (指南宮), built dur-

Muslims in Taiwan

Islam is known in Taiwan as *huijiao* (回教) and Muslims are referred to as Hui people (回民). The Islamic faith entered China as early as the 7C when Muslim merchants married local women. Originally from Fujian Province, the first Muslims to arrive on Taiwan followed Koxinga in the 17C. However, they became assimilated into the local Han Chinese society and abandoned their faith for the island's Daoist and Buddhist beliefs. The next wave of Muslims to arrive on the island also came from mainland China, after the Kuomintang took control of Taiwan following Japan's surrender. The Muslims established themselves in Taiwan and started to build mosques when it became apparent, despite government proclamations, that the KMT's hopes of regaining the mainland were fading. Taiwan's Muslim population is slowly growing as more Indonesians marry Taiwanese spouses and come here to settle.

ing the Qing dynasty. The temple deity is **Lü Dongbin**, one of the Eight Immortals of Daoism. It is said that unmarried couples would break up after a visit to this temple because Lü Dongbin is believed to be a ladies' man. Some whisper that, in fact, he's jealous of people romantically involved because the **Immortal Woman He**, or He Xiangu, refused him. Confucius, Mencius and even the historical Buddha are also worshiped at this golden-roofed temple, which attracts adherents of Daoism, Confucianism and Buddhism.

In Maokong there are three **tourism trails** and a lot of walking trails. For an introduction to the area's teas as well as the art of brewing tea and even tea-drinking etiquette, make your first stop the **Tea Promotion Center** (*Lane 40, 8-2 Zhinan Rd., Sec. 3* 指南路3段40巷8號之2).

Visitors are allowed to visit the tea farms, many of which are located on **Zhinan Road** (*Sec. 3*), and sample teas—and maybe enjoy a meal there.

Some of the farms are spread out on spacious grounds, and have set individual booths outdoors so that groups of friends can sit and enjoy drinks and snacks and conversation with each other. The atmosphere is often fairy-like since, at night, the staff hang dozens of glowing lanterns.

EXCURSIONS

Presented in geographical order west to east then south from downtown Taipei.

BEITOU★★★ 北投

Allow 1 day. ▷ *16km/10mi north of downtown Taipei by Hwy. 2. MRT: Xinbeitou. Bring swimsuit and towel.*

Inhabited in pre-Han times by Ketagalan aborigines, this district on the edge of the Taipei Basin (and now within Taipei City limits) was largely undeveloped until the Japanese introduced their hot-springs culture in the late 19C and early 20C. "Beitou" is a transliteration of *pataww*, meaning "witch," on account of the sulfurous fumes. Its raison d'être is still its hot springs—and its restaurants. The place is a gourmet's paradise, offering something for every palate and every wallet. Perhaps a holdover from the colonial period, the Japanese food here is one of your best dining options in Beitou.

◉ WALKING TOUR

Most attractions lie within walking distance of the metro station, so taking the MRT to Beitou is the sensible option.

▷ *From the station, walk east along Zhongshan Rd.*

The **Ketagalan Culture Center** (*凱達格蘭文化館; 3/1 Zhongshan Rd.* 中山路3-1號; ⊙ *open Tue–Sun 9am–5pm;*

Muzha's peaceful hills

Florent Bonnefoy/Michelin

Beitou Public Library

Mark Caltonhill/Michelin

$\mathscr{C}$02-2898 6500) introduces the material, social and religious lives of Taiwan's aboriginal peoples.

▷ *Continue east on Zhongshan Rd.*

Sitting within Beitou Park, the **Beitou Hot Spring Museum**★★ (北投溫泉博物館; *2 Zhongshan Rd.* 中山路2號 ; ⏲*open Tue–Sun 9am–5pm;* $\mathscr{C}$02-2893 9981) is housed in a reconstructed public bathhouse dating from 1913. Small by today's standards, the basement pool, with its Romanesque columns, displays the East-West mix beloved by Japan's colonial rulers.

▷ *Walk to the other side of the park.*

On the other side of Beitou Park, **Beitou Public Library**★ (臺北市立圖書館北投分館; *251 Guangming Rd.* 光明路251號) is commonly cited as Taipei's leading example of green architecture.

▷ *Return to Zhongshan Rd. and continue east along it.*

Beitou's **public springs** (*6 Zhongshan Rd.*中山路6號; ⏲*open daily 6am–10pm; NT$40 for 2hrs*) consist today of a series of outdoor pools (♨*see Touring Tip*). Built in the 1930s as a Japanese-style home, the **Plum Garden** (梅庭; *6 Zhong shan Rd.;* ⏲*open Tue–Sun 9am–5pm;* $\mathscr{C}$ 02-2897 8647) was later used as the summer retreat of politician and

calligrapher **Yu You-ren** (于右任). Recently renovated, it now serves as a visitor center.

▷ *Walk along Zhongshan Rd. as it continues slightly northeast.*

Thermal Valley★ (地熱谷; *Lane 30, Zhongshan Rd.* 中山路30巷; ⏲*open 24hrs daily).* Thermal Valley was, until recently, a favorite outing for Taipei schoolchildren, who were given the opportunity to cook eggs in the boiling spring water (90°C/194°F) as it emerged from the ground. Now fenced off, Thermal Valley is still worth a visit just to watch the steam rising from the rock-strewn depression. Cooked eggs are sold here for old times' sake.

▷ *Take a moderate walk east or ride the S25 minibus to the museum.*

Touring Tip

Beitou offers several commercial hot-springs options: communal bath (roughly NT$150/person); private room (2hrs at NT$500-800); overnight stay at various hotels on Wenquan Road (NT$2,500); and public bath (4hrs for NT$2,000/person). A 1.5hr soak at the top-end **Villa 32** (*32 Zhongshan Rd.;* $\mathscr{C}$02-6611 8888; www.villa32.com) will cost NT$3,000/couple.

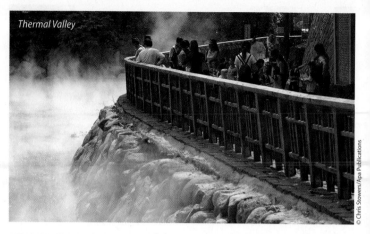

Thermal Valley

© Chris Stowers/Apa Publications

Taiwan Folk Arts Museum★★ (北投文物館; *32 Youya Rd.* 幽雅路32號; ◷*open Tue–Sun 10am–5:30pm; NT$120;* ℘*02-2891 2318; www.folkartsm.org.tw)* is housed in a Japanese-era wooden house (later used as a pre-mission club for kamikaze pilots). The museum's collection of artifacts offers insights into the daily lives of Taiwanese people in past centuries.

DANSHUI★★★ 淡水

Allow 1 day. ◗*20km/12mi northwest of downtown Taipei. MRT: Danshui.*
Though you can reach this historic riverfront town from Taipei by cycling the 18km/12mi path along the Danshui River, taking a bus, cruising along the Danshui River *(NT$300 round-trip departing from Dadaocheng Wharf in Taipei)* or driving in heavy traffic *(Chengde Rd. becomes Dadu Rd., Minquan Rd. then Zhongzheng Rd.)*, it's probably Danshui's convenient location on the Taipei MRT that accounts for its ranking among the top Taiwan tourist spots.
A bustling community, Danshui makes a great day's outing if you like history, souvenir shopping, sea air and good food. In addition to its snacks, Danshui is known for its seafood, most famously **green-lip mussels** (孔雀蛤). On the waterfront *(parallels Zhongzheng Rd.)* are stalls selling local specialties, such as marinated "iron eggs," fish-ball soup, shrimp rolls and *a-gei* (阿給; mung-bean noodles inside tofu). For more than 40 years,

the area's most famous restaurant has been the **She Family Mussels**, next to the Bali pier (佘家; *26/1 Duchuantou Rd.)* on the opposite side of the river, though it recently opened a location on the Danshui side too. From the waterfront ferries depart for Fishermen's Wharf farther up the coast and for Bali. At the southern end, past the MRT station, a piece of history tucked away beyond a stream is the slipway for Japanese seaplanes.

🐾 WALKING TOUR

Officially, the town's "old street" is **Zhongzheng Road**, but more interesting architecture is found on side streets **Chongjian** and **Qingshui**. Two historic sites lie farther along Zhongzheng Rd.

◗ *From the MRT or bus station, walk a little more than a mile northwest on Zhongzheng Rd* (中正路)*.*

Fort San Domingo★★★ (紅毛城; *Lane 28, 1 Zhongzheng Rd.* 中正路28巷1號; ◷*open Tue–Sun 9:30am–6pm;* ℘*02-2623 1001)* was the original fort built by the Spanish in 1628. In its place stands a stronghold dating to Dutch colonial (1646) and British consular (1863) times. From the fort, you'll get fine **views**★ across the river.

◗ *Take Bus 836 to Huwei Fort.*

Huwei Fort★ (滬尾砲台; *34, Lane 6 Zhongzheng Rd.* 中正路6巷34號; ◷*open*

Tue–Sun 9:30am–6pm; ℘02-2629 5390) was constructed by Taiwan's first governor in the late 1880s, after the French attempted to invade Taiwan near this point. The fort was never attacked and remains today in good condition.

▷ *Take the bus or walk back to Fort San Domingo. From the fort, turn left and walk uphill.*

Aletheia University (真理大學, *32 Zhenli St.* 真理街32號*)* was established by the town's most illustrious foreign resident, Canadian Presbyterian missionary and tooth-puller Dr. **George L. Mackay**. Buildings to note are the university's first structure, the 1882 **Oxford College** (☉*open Mon–Fri 10am–4pm)*, Mackay's Residence (1875), and residences for female missionaries (1906) and male missionaries (1909). Farther along, behind the Danshui Girls' School (*26 Zhenli St.* 真理街26號*)* are cemeteries containing the **graves**★ of Mackay and his family, as well as almost 100 other foreign residents from this period, generally divided into Catholics and Protestants, merchants and military *(free access during school hours).*

Across the road stands the **Customs Officer's Residence**★ (小白宮; *15 Zhenli St.* 真理街15號*;* ☉*open Tue–Sun 9:30am–6pm; ℘02-2628 2865)*, one of several dwellings occupied by foreign officers of the Qing customs bureau.

Danshui River

Mark Cattonhill/Michelin

▷ *Take the right fork to proceed down Mackay Street.*

You will pass the 1933 **Danshui Presbyterian Church** (*8 Mackay St.* 馬偕街8號*; open for services)* and the 1879 **Mackay Hospital** (*6 Mackay St.* 馬偕街6號*;* ☉*open Tue–Sun 11am–6pm)*, and finally back to downtown Danshui.

Chinese Temples

There are several Chinese temples (☉*open daily 5am–9pm)* that are worth visiting. They include the 1796 **Fuyou Temple**★ (福佑宮; *200 Zhongzheng Rd.* 中正路200號*;* ℘*02-2621 1731)* dedicated to the seafarers' deity Mazu; the **Qingshui Zushi Temple**★ *(*清水巖祖師

Oxford College, Danshui

Mark Cattonhill/Michelin

廟; 87 Qingshui St. 清水街87號; ℘02-
2621 2236) built in 1937 in an even
older section of town; and the **Longshan Temple**★ of 1858 (龍山寺; Lane
95, 22 Zhongshan Rd. 中山路95巷22號;
℘02-2621 4866), with its typical mix of
Buddhism and Daoism, hidden away
inside Danshui's market.

YANGMINGSHAN NATIONAL PARK★★★ 陽明山國家公園

Allow 1 day. 10km/12mi north of
downtown Taipei. **By MRT:** Jiantan,
then by bus or taxi. **By Bus:** Bus 260
(NT$30) from Taipei Main Station, then
park shuttle bus (see below). **By Car:**
Take Yangde Blvd. (仰德大道) north
from Shilin (traffic restrictions in force
on weekends and spring flower festival).
Visitor center at Zhuzihu Rd. (竹子湖
路); open daily 9am–4:30pm; closed
last Mon. of month; ℘02-2861 3601 ext.
297; www.ymsnp.gov.tw/htm1. From
the park bus station, a **shuttle bus**
(Bus 108; NT$60, unlimited stops) runs
in a circle among the park's attractions
(daily 7am–5:30pm).

Covering 11,455 ha/28,300 acres, **Yangmingshan National Park** is a natural
wonder beginning just 12km/8mi from
downtown Taipei. Based on plans begun
50 years earlier during Japanese rule,
the park finally opened in 1985. Today
this vast recreation area draws local residents to hike, bike, soak in hot springs
and soak up nature.

Rising to 1,120m/3,675ft, the park's highest peak, massive **Qixing Mountain**,
dominates the center of the park.
Throughout the park, **hot springs** crop
up; using them costs around NT$100 in
communal pools to NT$1,000 and up for
private baths in top-class resorts. The
Liu Ku (六窟溫泉; 81 Hudi Rd. 湖底路
81號; NT$150/hr for 2 people; ℘02-2861-
1728) offers an unpretentious taste
of local people's love of hot-springs
culture.

Food options at Yangmingshan range
from roadside snacks and cafes situated
around the Chinese Culture University,
through Taiwanese and Chinese restaurants in the Zhuzihu area, to fine cuisine
at the better hot-spring resorts.

Visit

The shuttle's first stop—and the best
place to start your visit—is the **Yangmingshan Visitor Center** (see address
above). Displays and films introduce the
history, ecology, agriculture and sulfur
mining of the area, and maps show the
11 recommended **hiking trails**, the
main reason most people visit.

Traveling clockwise, the shuttle will
bring you to **Yangming Shuwu** (陽明
書屋; 12 Zhongxing Rd. 中興路12號;
open daily 9am–4:30pm; closed last
Mon. of month; NT$50; ℘02-2861 1444),
Chiang Kai-shek's 1970 mansion, which
he occupied briefly before his final illness. Incidentally, it was Chiang's respect
for the Ming dynasty neo-Confucian philosopher Wang Yang-ming that brought
about the park's name change from Cao
Shan (草山; "Grass Mountain").

Next door, the **Dazhong Building** (大忠
館2F; open daily 9am–4:30pm; closed
last Mon. of month) displays copies of
maps dating back 400 years and introduces area history (no English).

Xiaoyoukeng, or "small oil pit" (小油坑;
69 Zhuzihu Rd. 竹子湖路69號; P NT$30/
hr) is a natural area, with an information
center, (5th shuttle stop) that allows visitors close access to volcanic fumaroles
and sulfurous rocks. It is also the start of
the shortest trail to Qixing Mountain.

*Silvergrass Meadow,
Yangmingshan National Park*
Brent Hannon/Michelin

Yingge's Old Street

Chris Stowers/Apa Publications

Once used for grazing cattle, the broad grasslands of **Qingtiangang** (擎天崗 ; Lane 101, 246 Jingshan Rd. 菁山路101巷246號; 🅿 NT$30/hr) are popular for their gentle slopes and **views**★.

Nearby, recreation area **Lengshuikeng**, or "cold water pit" (冷水坑; Lane 101, 170 Jingshan Rd. 菁山路101巷170號) has separate 40°C/68°F hot springs for men and women.

Finally, before heading back to Taipei, tour the **Zhongshan Building** (中山樓; 15 Yangming Blvd. Sec.2 陽明路2段 15號; free tours 8:30am, 10am, 1:30pm & 3pm; 📞02-2861 6391), formerly the site of National Assembly and Kuomintang meetings, and the **Lin Yutang House** (林語堂故居; 141 Yangde Blvd. Sec. 2. 仰德大道2段141號; 🕐 open daily 9am–5pm; closed last Mon. of month; 📞02-2861 3003; www.linyutang.org. tw; NT$30), former home of writer and translator **Lin Yu-tang** with **views** over northern Taipei and the Danshui River.

YINGGE★ 鶯歌

Allow half day. ▶23km/14mi southwest of downtown Taipei. **By Car:** No.3 Hwy. **By Train:** From Taipei Main Station (30min; NT$31). **By Bike:** Take the 24km/15mi bicycle path along the Dahan River from Huajiang Brige near Wanhua.

The small township of Yingge, on the eastern edge of Taipei County, is a top domestic day-trip destination due to its reputation as Taiwan's number-one pottery town. Yingge's confluence of clay, coal at nearby Sanxia, convenient river and later, rail transportation, made it one of the island's main ceramic producers from 1805 onward. The shops along "Old Street," **Jianshan Pu Road** 尖山埔路, are a good source for everything from cheap mainland imports and slightly imperfect Yingge-made-for-export items (NT$10 up) to works by Taiwan's best ceramic artists costing in the millions of NT$.

The **Yingge Ceramics Museum**★ (鶯歌陶瓷博物館; 200 Wenhua Rd. 文化路 200號; 🕐 open Tue–Fri 9:30am–5pm, Sat–Sun 9:30am–6pm; ✖ 📞02-8677 2727; www.ceramics.tpc.gov.tw) has permanent exhibits on the history and uses of ceramics. Among the displays are traditional aboriginal "ancestor pots," Chinese temple roof decorations, toilets and kitchenware, and futuristic high-tech products. Prize-winning contemporary pieces are on view as well.

Artists in residence have workshops at the rear, where they also assist museum staff with teaching courses to first-come-first-admitted students (Sat–Sun & holidays; NT$50 for materials, NT$150 for firing). Large works are exhibited outdoors.

For **cheap eats**, near Yingge's railway station is a 45-year established and much-imitated **A-po's Sushi** (阿婆壽司; 63 ZhongZheng Rd. 中正路63號; no English) with miso soup for NT$15, sushi for NT$35 and sliced pork for NT$35. For something more refined, **Fugui Tao Yuan** (富貴陶園; 98 Chongqing St. 重

慶街 98號), in the Old Street district, serves Chinese and Western meals for NT$380 and up.

SANXIA★★ 三峽

Allow 1 day. ◯ *26km/16mi southwest of downtown Taipei.* **MRT:** *Yongning then 916 bus.* **By Car:** *Approx. 30min drive southwest of Taipei on No.3 Hwy. to Sanying Interchange.* **By Bike:** *Cyclists are advised to stay on the north side of the river until Yingge.*

Now-sleepy Sanxia was once the largest town in the area, with an economy based on coal, tea, camphor and the dying of indigo. Although officially an "urban" township (鎮), most of Sanxia is not just rural but downright mountainous; its terrain rises to 1,700m/5,577ft in the south, hence the tea and camphor industries. The Sanxia River bisects the central part of town.

Town Center

Minchuan Street 民權街, the town's "old street," is dotted with redbrick dye stores dating from Japanese reconstruction around 1916. The street has been renovated and is popular for handicrafts and snacks. **No. 96** is worth the NT$20 entrance ticket as it shows the narrow width and full length of these "bamboo-pole" constructions.

Zushi Temple, Sanxia

Chris Stowers/Apa Publications

Photos of old Sanxia and historical artifacts can be found in the **Sanxia Historical Relic Hall** (三峽鎮歷史文物館; *18 Zhongshan Rd.* 中山路18號; ◯*open Tue–Sun 9am–5pm;* ☏*02-8674 3994*) in the old town office, which also organizes free guided tours of the town on weekends. Sanxia also hosts the county's **Hakka Museum** (台北縣客家文化園區; *239 Long'en St.* 隆恩街239號◯*open Tue–Fri, 9am–5pm, Sat–Sun 9am–6pm;* ☏*02-2672 9996; www.hakka.tpc.gov.tw*), noteworthy for its round-house architecture reminiscent of Hakka buildings in Guangdong and Fujian provinces in mainland China. The town's main attraction is the **Zushi Temple★★** (祖師廟; *1 Changfu St.* 長福街1號), whose every inch of stone and wood was exquisitely carved under the direction of locally born artist **Li Mei-shu** (1902-83). More of his work can be seen at the **Li Mei-shu Memorial Gallery** (李梅樹紀念館; *Lane 43, 10 Zhonghua Rd.* 中華路43巷10號; *Sat–Sun 10am–5pm; NT$100;* ☏*02-2673 2333; www. limeishu.org*).

Outlying Sights

Bus 1078 from Sanxia, or take Provincial Rd. 3 south out of town; after 2km/1.3mi, turn left to take County Rd. 108 as it ascends 5km/3mi to the temple.

Baiji's Xingxiu Temple 行修宮

155 Baiji Rd. 白雞路155號; ☏*02-2671 1476.*

This temple's quiet is in contrast to Zushi Temple's *renao* "heat and noise", perhaps because the temple is not Daoist, as it appears, but actually Confucian. Alternatively, 1km/.06mi farther along the No.3 road, another left turn onto County Road followed 4km/2.5mi later by a left turn onto County Road 114 takes you into **Dabao Scenic Area** (大豹), a route covered by Bus 807. The winding road follows the Dabao River, clenched between forested hills.

The **Great Roots Forestry Spa Resort** (大板根森林溫泉渡假村; *80 Chajiao Neighborhood.* 插角里插角80號; ☏*02-2674 9228; www.dabangan.com.tw*) with hot springs (*NT$350/person*), rooms

(NT\$5,000 and up), restaurant and trails sits another 3km/1.8mi along the road. Farther another 8km/5mi *(3km/1.8mi beyond the last bus stop)*, the **Man Yue Yuan Forest Recreation Area** *(滿月圓 國家森林遊樂區; 174-1 Youmu Neighborhood. 三峽鎮有木里174之1號; NT\$100; ℘02-2672 0004)* is famed for its autumnal maple trees, trails and two waterfalls.

Sanxia's mountain roads have a number of free-range **chicken restaurants** (土雞城), so travelers won't go hungry.

DAXI★★ 大溪

Allow 1 day. ▶ *37km/23mi southeast of downtown Taipei.* **By Bus:** *Buses depart for Daxi (NT\$80) from Taipei Main Station.* **By Car:** *Take Hwy. 3.*

Town Center

Lined with historical houses, Daxi's "old street," **Heping Street**★★ 和平街, rises high above a suspension bridge and the now largely dried up Dahan River. It dates to the 19C, although the famous decorative **shop façades** were added early in the 20C per Japanese regulations. Chat with store owners, who might offer you a look at the old residences behind the storefronts. The end of the street offers **views** of the river valley that accounts for the town's existence. Before construction of **Shimen Dam** (石門水壩), the river enabled boat transportation to Taipei and eventually to Danshui. To the left stands **Wude Hall** (武德殿), built in 1935 for training Japanese policemen in judo and kendo.

The town's other claims to fame are its **dried tofu** (豆腐乾), **fresh fish** (活魚), and **soy sauce**. Its reputation for tofu rests on the purity and pH level of the local water, and shops all over town sell fresh, packaged, pickled, and spiced varieties. Daxi's delicately flavored fish can be caught in the cold deep waters of nearby Shimen Reservoir, though today most is trucked in from elsewhere.

For an introduction to the manufacture of soy sauce, tour the **Kimlan Factory** (金蘭食品醬油文化博物館; *236 Jieshou Rd. 介壽路236號; ℘03-380 1226; reservations required)*, Taiwan's top soy-sauce

Daxi's Old Street

Mark Caltonhill/Michelin

producer, located just south of Daxi. Established during Japanese rule with Japanese technology, it now produces 35 million bottles per year.

Additional Sights

The countryside around Daxi apparently reminded **Chiang Kai-shek** of his hometown of Fenghua (奉化) in mainland China. He appropriated tracts of nearby land, built a resort on it in 1959, and renamed it **Cihu** (慈湖) in honor of his mother. Following his death in 1975, it became the **Cihu Mausoleum**, where it was planned that his body (and later that of his son, Chiang Ching-kuo) would remain temporarily until mainland China was reconquered.

Things remained quiet for the next 30 years, with ex-soldiers, politicians, officials and their families traveling here to pay their respects. Then Chiang was branded a dictator following the KMT's loss of power in 2000, and his statue was removed from public display at scores of locations around Taiwan. The Daxi government collected them.

At the **Cihu Sculpture Memorial Park**★ (慈湖雕塑紀念公園; *1097 Fuxing Rd., Sec 1, Daxi. 復興路1段1097號;* ⊙ *open daily 8am-5pm; ℘03-388 4437)*, next to the mausoleum, more than 100 statues, all of Chiang, stand on eerie parade.

The **Cihu Visitor Center** (慈湖遊客中心; *same address and hrs as Memorial*

Cihu Sculpture Memorial Park

Mark Caltonhill/Michelin

Park) present the **Cihu Exhibition** (慈湖特展), where Chiang's rehabilitation following the KMT electoral success of 2008 continues unabated. Key displays show **photographs** from Chiang's early life, his relocation to Taiwan and government-funded construction works in the Taoyuan area. The gift shop sells coffee mugs and T-shirts emblazoned with Chiang portrayed as Batman and his son as Robin.

Most recently opened to the public are Chiang's personal enclaves of **Back Cihu** (後慈湖; ⏱ *open 8am–5pm; NT$100; limited to 600 visitors per day, applications at http://backcihu.tycg.gov.tw/cihu)* and **Jiaobanshan Village** (角板山行館). This whole area has been renamed the **Two Chiangs Resort,** and since the access road is narrow, on weekends it can get completely blocked. There is free parking at the **Daxi Visitor Center** 2km/1.2mi away from which a riverside trail leads to the Memorial Park.

For a day trip by car, motorbike or bicycle from Daxi, keep going past the Two Chiangs Resort up to **Fuxing Township** (復興鄉), where there are the **Galahe** (嘎拉賀) and **Lala Mountain** (拉拉山) "divine forests" of ancient **cypress trees,** natural hot springs in the tributary of the Dahan River at almost 1,300 m/4,300ft above sea level, and aboriginal art and handicraft workshops run by the indigenous **Atayal** (泰雅族) group. Artifacts on sale include cloth-

ing, wicker work, embossed leather and woodcarvings.

WULAI★★ 烏來

Allow 1 day. ▶ *24km/15mi south of downtown Taipei.* **By Bus:** *1601 bus.* **By Car:** *By car, scooter or bicycle, take Xindian Rd., continue on No.9 Provincial Hwy., then turn right onto the Hwy. 9甲 for 13km/8 mi.*

Wulai derives its name from the Atayal aboriginal phrase *"kirofu ulai"* referring to the area's abundant natural hot springs, and meaning "hot and poisonous." Sitting at the confluence of the Nanshi and Tonghou rivers, the township offers cool mountain air in the summer, hot waters in the winter and interesting culture year-round.

Wulai's main attractions are outdoors, but your first stop should be the **Wulai Atayal Museum**★ (烏來泰雅民族博物館; *12 Wulai St. 烏來街12號;* ⏱ *open Tue–Fri 9:30am–5pm, Sat–Sun 9:30am–5pm;* ✆*02-2661-8162).* Chinese and English displays introduce Taiwan's aboriginal culture, the Wulai area's Atayal ethnicity, their traditional lifestyles, customs, religion and interaction with the environment. The rest of the main street is taken up with stalls and shops selling aboriginal handicrafts and food—bamboo-tube rice; boar, deer and flying squirrel meat; millet wine; and all manner of "mountain vegetables"—as well as hotels with **hot-springs rooms,** communal *(NT$250-300/person)* or private *(NT$600-800/2hr)*.

Walk south along Wulai Street, cross the bridge, turn right and head down to the **open pools** *(swimsuits required)* by the edge of **Nanshi** River. To cool off, locals swim in the river.

Better swimming, hiking and camping options can be found along the Tonghou River or farther up the Nanshi River toward Fushan 18km/11mi away, though both require registering ID for a mountain pass at a police check point.

A short walk *(about 20min)* along Road 107 toward Fushan leads to the **Wulai Waterfall**. A mini-train originally constructed to haul lumber also goes to the falls *(NT$50 one-way)*. Above the waterfall perches **Yunhsien Holiday Resort** *(*雲仙樂園*; ☏02-2661 6386; www.yunhsien.com.tw)*, which can be accessed only by cable car *(NT$220 round-trip including entry)*; hotel rooms with views of the falls start at NT$4,200 per night. Farther up the Nanshi River, **Neidong Forest Recreation Area** *(*內洞森林遊樂區*; ⏰open 8am–5pm; NT$10-80; ☏02-2661 7358)* has more waterfalls and trails.

PINGXI★★ 平溪

▶ 32km/20mi east of downtown Taipei by County Rd. 106. Buses No. 15 and 16 from opposite the Muzha MRT station (south Taipei) NT$45 one-way.

This former coal-mining town gives its name to the tourist-passenger rail line that stops here. Due to the exhaustion of Pingxi's coal resources and the town's economic stagnation, many early-to-mid-20C buildings are still standing. Today, tourism and the rail line are helping to revive the town. Pingxi's **Sky Lantern Festival** is northern Taiwan's main event during Lantern Festival, two weeks after Chinese New Year.

Pingxi Railway Line★★

Tickets (NT$54) allow passengers as many stops as they want during the day. It's advisable to bring sandwiches.

This 12.9km/8mi-long line is one of three branch lines left on the island. The scenic ride *(40min)* climbs into the forested foothills above the Taipei Plain and Kee-

lung Harbor, offering insight into northern Taiwan's industrial development.

The **old streets**★★ of Ruifang, Shifen, Pingxi and Jingtong are the main attractions—with rows of shops selling **sky lanterns** (天燈), kerosene-powered miniature hot-air balloons that ascend when ignited, bearing prayers for good fortune. Explanations for the origins of sky lanterns range from announcements of "all clear" after attacks by thieves, to a celebration of the number of baby boys born in the village each year.

The Ride

The railway starts east of Taipei at **Ruifang** (瑞芳)—named after a store that supplied mining equipment—and stops at 7 stations until the terminus at Jingtong. The first place to alight is **Shifen** (十分), where a **visitor center** (十分遊客中心; ⏰open daily 8am–5pm; ☏02-2495 8409) introduces the Pingxi Valley. A 10min film (English) explains the area's history, from the discovery of coal in the late 19C to the drying up of the seams in the 1980s. A 60min version includes oral testimonies from mine workers. Nearby **Shifen Waterfall**★ (十分瀑布), at 40m/131ft, is said to be the widest in Taiwan. The walk there is tranquil, but the land around the falls is privately owned, so a fee is charged to view them *(⏰open daily 8am–6pm; NT$80)*.

Also worth seeing is the privately-run **Shifen Coal Mine Museum**★ *(⏰open*

Wulai's riverside

Mark Caltonhill/Michelin

daily 9am–5pm; NT$200), which exhibits mining equipment.

Jingtong (菁桐) retains the original **wooden station** building (1931), period mine workers' lodgings and the **Crown Prince Chalet** built by the Taiyang Mining Co. for Japanese royalty in 1939; the prince never paid a visit, so the structure of Hinoki Cypress from Alishan became a company managers' club (closed for renovation). Adjacent to the station, the **Jingtong Coal Mining Museum** has only Chinese-language exhibits.

ADDRESSES

STAY

For price categories, see Legend on the front cover flap. All hotels in Taipei are non-smoking. Most hotels, especially the high-end properties, recommend or require reservations; to be safe, book in advance.

$ Ann's House 安的部屋 – *1st Floor, Alley 4, Lane 74, 17 Xinyi Rd., Sec. 4. 信義路四段74巷4弄17號1F. MRT: Da'an. 09 8880 0085. www.taipeiannhouse. com.tw. 2-5 rooms per property.* Ann's House encompasses a collection of converted apartments spread around the city in the Da'an, City Hall and Jingmei districts. You can book a single room or a whole apartment by the day or the week. Either way, guests enjoy use of the kitchen and laundry facilities, as well complimentary Internet access.

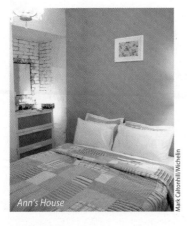
Ann's House
Mark Caltonhill/Michelin

Rooms with shared baths are less expensive.

$ Taipei Dong Wu Hotel 東吳大飯店 – *258 Yanping North Rd., Sec. 2. 延平北路二段258號. MRT: Minquan West Rd. 02-2557 1261. www. dongwu-hotel.com. 60 rooms. Breakfast included.* The decor might be a bit dated, but Dong Wu provides a quality stay at a modest price. You won't mind the hike to the nearest subway stop, when you consider that the hotel offers amenities such as safes, slippers and complimentary Wi-Fi Internet access.

$ Gwoshiuan Hotel 國宣飯店 – *10 Jinzhou St. 錦州街10號. MRT: Shuanglian. 02-2521 5205. www.gwoshiuan88.com.tw. 56 rooms. Breakfast included.* Located on the edge of the old business district, this hotel is a good option for budget travelers. Gwoshiuan is well-serviced by both bus and MRT transportation. Colorful decor fills the rooms, which come with a mini refrigerator and broadband Internet access. Breakfast is served in the on-site restaurant; for dinner, there is a good selection of eateries nearby.

$ Happy Family Hostel 快樂家庭 – *2nd Floor, Lane 56, 2 Zhongshan North Rd., Sec. 1. 中山北路一段56巷2號2樓. MRT: Taipei Main Station. 02-2581 0716 or 09 3719 5075. www.taiwan-hostel.com. 10 rooms.* This Taipei hostel has seen backpackers and expats come and go for decades, and couldn't be more convenient to the island's transportation hub. The gregarious owner keeps the spartan accommodations—single and double rooms, and dormitories that sleep six with shared baths—tidy. Multiple common areas are spread over several cheery floors; amenities include free washing machines, Wi-Fi Internet access, linens, and a small rooftop balcony.

$ Holo Family House/Taipei Traveler Hostel 阿羅住宿接待家庭 / 台北自助旅行家 – *22nd Floor-2, Taipei-K Mall, 50 Zhongxiao West Rd., Sec. 1. 忠孝西路一段50號22F之2. MRT: Taipei Main Station. 02-2311 2186. www. taiwanhostels.com/accommodation/ holo-family-house. 32 rooms.*

Breakfast included. Located inside a high-rise building overlooking Taipei Main Station, Holo Family House is decorated with photos of smiling travelers and a container of ping-pong balls scrawled with wishes. Dorm rooms with as many as eight beds share bathrooms; singles rooms and suites with private baths are also available. Relax in the common room, stocked with travel literature and computers. Coffee and tea are available all day, and soap and shampoo are provided.

$ Hotel 73 新尚旅店 – *73 XinYi Rd., Sec. 2.* 信義路二段73號. *MRT: Chiang Kai-shek Memorial Hall.* ☏02-2395 9009. www.hotel73.com. *49 rooms. Breakfast included.* This new boutique hotel just minutes from Taipei's iconic Chiang Kai-shek Memorial Hall offers stylish, centrally located budget accommodations—some designed by art students. The changing decor in the red, black and white lobby features avant-garde wooden furniture, such as an unvarnished wooden tree sprouting bare light bulbs.

$ Many Flower Business Hotel 百花商務飯店 – *55 Renai Rd., Sec.1.* 仁愛路一段55號. *MRT: Shandao Temple.* ☏02-2394 9232. http://pihua.emmm.tw. *25 rooms. Breakfast included.* Until recently, this hotel focused on the hourly trade; it has now been rebranded as a business hotel, perhaps in anticipation of the forthcoming Xinyi MRT line, which will link directly to the Taipei World Trade Center and convention halls. Though still a no-frills establishment, Many Flowers offers an excellent value for budget travelers. Internet access is complimentary.

$ Taipei Hostel – *6th Floor, Lane 5, 11 Linsen North Rd.* 林森北路5巷11號 6樓. *MRT: Shandao Temple.* ☏02-2395 2950. www.taipeihostel.com. *20 rooms.* One of Taipei's oldest (35 years and counting) hostels, Taipei Hostel offers plenty of tips for short-term travelers or newly arrived English teachers (check out the website). Well-worn but clean singles, doubles and 10-bed dorms share bathrooms. There are also three rooms with private baths and one 6-bed dorm for women only. Guests gather in the common kitchen and living areas and the pleasant rooftop garden. Wi-Fi and a coin-operated laundry are included in the room rate.

$$ Ambience Hotel 喜瑞飯店 – *64 ChangAn East Rd., Sec. 1.* 長安東路一段64號. *MRT: Shandao Temple or Zhongxiao Xingsheng.* ☏02-2541 0077. www.ambiencehotel.com.tw. *60 rooms. Breakfast included.* Part of the same group that owns Hotel 73, Ambience offers high style at a good value. Tranquil all-white rooms, conceived by noted Taiwanese interior designer Ted Su, feature Philippe Starck and Ferruccio Laviani furnishings, flat-screen TVs, DVD players, Wi-Fi, robes and music CDs to keep you chilled out. In case all that doesn't relax you, join the fashionable crowd for a cocktail in the bar, or check out one of the outdoor beer gardens nearby.

$$ Hotel Eight Zone 八方美學商旅 – *8 Jinshan South Rd., Sec. 1.* 金山南路一段8號. *MRT: Zhongxiao Xinsheng.* ☏02-2358 3500. www.hotel8zone.com. *50 rooms. Breakfast included.* With a front desk that doubles as a bar and a complimentary cocktail proffered upon check-in, Hotel Eight Zone creates a distinctly lounge-like vibe in a sophisticated setting. Light-filled rooms with spacious bathrooms, and a puff in the cigar room off the lobby will help you forget that the hotel faces a freeway overpass.

$$ Riviera Hotel 歐華酒店 – *646 Linsen North Rd.* 林森北路646號. *MRT: Yuanshan.* ✗☏02-2585-3258. www.rivierataipei.com. *112 rooms.* Business travelers frequent this gold-trimmed European-style standby, where guests working out in the rooftop fitness center enjoy mountain views. For art lovers, the Taipei Fine Arts Museum is just down the street; and guests can browse the National Palace Museum's online catalog in the lobby to order souvenirs—perhaps a NT$2,000 replica Jadeite cabbage carving—for hotel delivery within 48 hours. The **Prime Rib Steak House ($$)** serves breakfast, lunch and dinner; while the **Yacht Club ($$)** offers a Chinese and Western menu at dinner only.

$$ Tango Hotel Taipei NanShi 柯旅天閣台北南西 – *3 Nanjing West Rd. 南京西路3號. MRT: Zhongshan.* 📞*02-2567 9999. www.tango-hotels.com. 52 rooms. Breakfast included.* Literally steps from the subway, the intimate Tango Hotel sits in the middle of a bustling shopping area, with the landmark SPOT-Taipei Film House nearby. The hotel's minimalist exterior, moody lobby lighting and electronic soundtrack give way to cleanly designed rooms equipped with flat-screen TVs in the bathrooms.

$$ Y Hotel Taipei 台北青年國際旅館 – *19 Xuchang St. 許昌街19號 MRT: Taipei Main Station.* 📞*02-2311 3201. www.ymcahotel.tw. 84 rooms.* Located in the heart of old Taipei, the Y is convenient to the Taipei train station. Clean, quiet, comfortable rooms are spacious enough that the NT$300 per extra bed attracts groups of students or backpackers looking for a good base of operations. Services are scant here, but rooms are equipped with a mini-fridge and hairdryer, and Internet access is available on computers in the lobby. Cheap eats abound in the surrounding neighborhood.

$$$ Hotel Éclat 怡亨酒店 – *370 Dunhua South Rd., Sec. 1. 敦化南路一段370號. MRT: Da'an.* 📞*02-2784 8888. www.eclathotels.com/taipei. 60 rooms. Breakfast included if room booked through the hotel.* Part hotel, part contemporary art showcase, this nouveau European lodging is opulent to the last detail. The lobby dazzles with Salvador Dalí sculptures and dramatic purple glass fixtures from the Czech Republic. Rooms are equally plush, with automated curtains, Philippe Starck-designed Louis Ghost chairs, Montblanc pens and Bang & Olufsen stereos. Continuing the refined theme, **Ming Yuen ($$$)** restaurant spotlights authentic Cantonese cuisine and **Éclat Lounge ($$$)** serves Mediterranean fare. All this, and Hotel Éclat is just a short walk away from the 24hr Eslite Bookstore in the fashionable Xinyi District.

$$$ Hotel Riverview Taipei 豪景大酒店 – *77 Huanhe South Rd., Sec. 1. 環河南路一段77號. MRT: Ximending.* ✕📞*02-2311 3131. www.hotel-riverview.com. Breakfast included. 195 rooms.* Reasonable prices and fine sunset views across the Danshui River toward Sanchong from the Riverview's higher floors lure guests to this no-frills lodging on the west side of Taipei. Simple rooms, done in white with red carpets, provide a comfy setting for work or play. The Riverview has several eateries, including a buffet-style, all-you-can-eat restaurant, and Internet access is available for a fee. A few blocks away you'll find cinema houses and shopping.

$$$ Landis Taipei Hotel 亞都麗緻大飯店 – *41 Minquan East Rd., Sec. 2. 民權東路二段41號. MRT: Minquan West Rd.* ✕Spa📞*02-2597 1234. www.landishotelsresorts.com. 217 rooms. Breakfast included.* This top-notch Art Deco accommodation caters to well-heeled business travelers with a business center, conference facilities and airport limousine service. Dressed in a top hat and tails, the hotel's doorman can guide you to the rooftop spa or in-house dining options that include the romantic **Paris 1930 ($$$$)**, known throughout the city for delicious multicourse French preparations such as braised snail, pan-fried organic quail and seared foie gras. One wall in the lobby is hung with photos of celebrity guests like producer/director George Lucas and cellist Yo-Yo Ma.

$$$ Les Suites Taipei Ching-cheng Hotel 台北商旅慶城館 – *12 Chingcheng St. 慶城街12號. MRT: Nanjing East Rd.* 📞*02-8712 7688. www.hotelsuitesching-cheng.com. 85 rooms. Breakfast included.* The landscaped gardens, outdoor patio, candlelit nooks lined with art books and gracious staff at this compact Zen-like hotel offer a calm oasis from Taipei's hustle and bustle. Done with clean lines and muted colors, rooms come with local mobile phones and soothing rain showerheads, and the lobby lounge offers snacks and drinks at all hours. The hotel is just steps from the MRT on a busy street full of eateries.

$$$ Royal Biz Taipei 金來商旅 – 71 Jinshan South Rd., Sec. 1. 金山南路一段 71號. MRT: Zhongxiao Xinsheng. ✆02-2397 9399. www.royalbiz.com.tw. 48 rooms. Breakfast included. Large rooms and suites with custom-made furnishings and goose-down comforters couple with deep discounts to make this an attractive nest for both business travelers and tourists to roost. Located close to the Zhongzheng district, CKS Memorial Hall, and a host of good restaurants on Yongkang Street, the hotel runs shuttle buses to the MRT, railway and the Taipei World Trade Convention Center during major conventions. Free Internet access, an on-site gym and conference facility and a buffet breakfast served daily in the lobby lounge are just a few more reasons to stay here.

$$$ San Want Residences Taipei 神旺商務酒店 – 128 Nanjing East Rd., Sec. 1. 南京東路一段128號. MRT: Zhongshan. ✆02-2511 5185. www.swresidences.com. 81 rooms. Breakfast included. The warmly lit Neoclassical lobby, punctuated with works by prominent Taiwanese sculptor Yang Yu-yu and a three-story glass chandelier, hints at this small luxury hotel's elegance. The English-speaking staff is impeccably courteous. Staying connected at the San Want is easy: each room has a fax machine and a local mobile phone. Tastefully appointed rooms include hot-springs-style soaking tubs, clothing steamers and views of Linsen Park. When it's time to eat, sample Western or Shanghainese cuisine on the second floor.

$$$ Taipei Fullerton Hotel (Fu-Xing South) 臺北馥敦飯店復南館 – 41 Fuxing South Rd., Sec. 2. 復興南路二段41號. MRT: Da'an. ✆02-2703 1234. www.taipeifullerton.com.tw. 100 rooms. Breakfast included. This location of the Fullerton group is a mid-price, contemporary hotel sitting within range of the Taipei World Trade Convention Center and Taipei shopping districts. Surprisingly spacious rooms and suites are tastefully decorated in neutral tones. On the 13th floor, you'll find a gym with a sauna and steam room, and both an indoor and outdoor pool. Stop by the lobby for complimentary coffee, tea and homemade cookies.

Far Eastern Plaza Hotel

Mark Caltonhill/Michelin

$$$$ Far Eastern Plaza Hotel 遠東國際大飯店 – 201 Dunhua South Rd., Sec. 2. 敦化南路二段201號. MRT: Liuzhangli. ✆02-2378 8888. www.shangri-la.com. 420 rooms. The tallest hotel in the city, Far Eastern Plaza focuses on facilities—a gym, swimming pool, conference rooms—and service inside its curving structure. Of its five restaurants, **Shang Palace ($$$$)** particularly draws local diners for its elegant atmosphere and Chinese regional cuisine. If you tire of the rooftop pool and state-of-the-art fitness center, there are plenty of designer shops next door at The Mall.

$$$$ Grand Formosa Regent Taipei 台北晶華酒店 – 41 Zhongshan North Rd., Sec. 2. 中山北路二段41號. MRT: Zhongshan. ✆02-2523 8000. www.grandformosa.com.tw/EN. 538 rooms. Breakfast included with select room rates. Situated atop a hill, this monument to luxurious living is arguably without equal in Taipei. The large rooms house memory-foam mattresses and DVD players, and butler service is available to cater to your every whim. Adjacent to the massive property's cavernous atrium are eight restaurants, a full-service spa, a gym with fitness classes, and a rooftop pool. Still have extra cash? Browse the designer stores in the hotel's lower level.

$$$$ Grand Hotel 圓山大飯店 – 1 Zhongshan North Rd. Sec. 4. 中山北路四段1號. MRT: Yuanshan. ✆02-2886 8888. www.grand-hotel.org.

Grand Hotel

© Chris Stowers/Michelin

487 rooms. The Grand's hilltop setting means that many of its rooms enjoy views over the city (note that the cheapest rooms are windowless). The original structure played a role in Taiwan's history; it was built by Chiang Kai-shek as Taipei's first five-star hotel for foreign dignitaries (🕭 *see p.82 and p.139)* The magnificent pagoda-like property, erected on the site of a former Japanese temple, is still a local landmark. Three restaurants offer a range of cuisines, encompassing Western and Chinese fare at the Grand Garden Restaurant, Cantonese-style seafood at the Golden Dragon, and the noodle dishes of northern China at Yuan Yuan.

$$$$ Grand Victoria Hotel 維多麗 亞酒店 – *168 Jingye 4th Rd., Neihu.* 敬業四路168號. *MRT: Jiannan Rd.* ✕ ⬛ ☎ *02-8502 0000. www.grand victoria.com.tw. 96 rooms.* Fusing 19C Victorian architecture with 21C style, the Grand Victoria is a popular choice for wedding receptions and dinners in Taipei's upscale Dazhi Miramar business district. Luxurious rooms display contemporary elements and amenities—such as custom-designed light fixtures and furnishings, electronic blinds on the picture windows and 32-inch LCD TVs—and come with a complimentary fruit basket. Dining options in The East and The West restaurants cover the globe, while **No. 168 Prime Steakhouse ($$$$)** adds classic steaks and chops. After a workout in the fitness center, take a dip in the fourth-floor pool.

$$$$ Howard Plaza 福華大飯店 – *160 Renai Rd., Sec. 3.* 仁愛路三段160號.

MRT: Zhongxiao-Fuxing. ✕ ⬛ ☎ *02-2700 2323. http://taipei.howard-hotels.com. 606 rooms.* Ideally located in one of Taipei's best neighborhoods—midway between the city's old and new centers—the Howard Plaza shows off a tasteful Oriental design. A pool and a fitness facility with a steam room, sauna and aerobics classes will take care of your workout needs. After you've worked up an appetite, six restaurants give you the choice of French and Chinese regional fare. Ample conference rooms can accommodate business meetings.

$$$$ Landis Resort Yangmingshan 陽明山中國麗緻大飯店 – *237 Gezhi Rd.* 格致路237號. *MRT: Jiantan.* ✕ ⬛ ☎ *02- 2861 6661. www.landishotelsresorts.com. 47 rooms.* The only international tourist hotel in Yangmingshan National Park, the Landis is just a 30min drive from downtown Taipei. It's worth the detour to stay at this tranquil place, where views of lush scenery and the Yangming Mountains surround you. Clean lines and soothing tones decorate the rooms, many of which include a custom-built marble bathtub that gets its water from the area's hot springs. Of the resort's three restaurants, **Tien He ($$$$)** serves contemporary fusion cuisine at dinnertime. Guests can soak in the sulfur hot springs or pool filled with heated mountain spring water.

$$$$ Sheraton Taipei 喜來登大 飯店 – *12 Zhongxiao East Rd., Sec.1.* 忠孝東路一段12號. *MRT: Shandao Temple.* ✕ ☎ *02-2321-5511. www.sheraton-taipei.com. 688 rooms.* Sheraton Taipei says luxury in rooms decorated with Chinese pictographs, period reproduction furniture, and soft gold and pale jade tones. Three executive floors add amenities such as lofty city panoramas, the Sheraton's signature Sweet Sleeper bed, and personalized butler service *(fee).* Of the Sheraton's nine restaurants, **The Dragon** (Cantonese), **Momoyama** (Japanese) and the **Antoine Room** (French) have become so popular with locals that diners must book in advance. Location is the only drawback; the city's heart has moved east since the Sheraton was built.

$$$$ Spring City Resort 春天酒店 – *18 Youya Rd., Beitou.* 幽雅路18號. *MRT: Beitou.* ✗ ☎02-2897 5555. *www.springresort.com.tw. 95 rooms. Breakfast included.* Back in Beitou's seedier days, Spring City was one of the few good hotels here. The fact that reservations are still required on weekends shows that this lodging is still held in high regard. Choose from Western- or Japanese-style rooms, all done in creamy tones; some have mountain views. Hot-springs rooms offer private sulfur baths in stone tubs. Outside, nine spring-fed pools provide relaxation. Two on-site restaurants, one Chinese and one Japanese, cater to a range of palates.

$$$$ Grand Hyatt Taipei 君悅大飯店 – *2 Songshou Rd.* 松壽路2號. *MRT: Taipei City Hall.* ✗ ☎02-2720 1234. *www.taipei.grand.hyatt.com. 856 rooms.* Next door to the Taipei World Trade Center and Taipei 101, and a short distance from City Hall, the Hyatt sits in the heart of new Taipei. Contemporary style defines the plush rooms, which come equipped with a work desk, a spacious marble bath, and a robe and slippers. A fitness facility, an outdoor heated pool, a nightclub and meeting rooms add to the amenities. Eight eateries—including **Irodori ($$$$)**, one of Taipei's most popular Japanese restaurants—and five bars offer a wide range of food and beverages.

Grand Hyatt Taipei
Mark Caltonhill/Michelin

$$$$$ The Sherwood Taipei 臺北西華飯店 – *111 Minsheng East Rd., Sec. 3.* 民生東路三段111號. *MRT: Zhongshan Junior High School.* ✗ Spa ☎02-2718 1188. *www.sherwood.com.tw. 343 rooms.* A member of the "Leading Hotels of the World," the Sherwood wraps guests in posh comfort, beginning in the opulent lobby, with its marble floor and crystal chandeliers. A personal safe, mini bar and refrigerator, umbrella and wireless Internet access *(fee)* add to the creature comforts in each room; the hotel's business center offers all the services traveling executives may need. Though set in the business district, this property offers easy access to shopping and Da'an Park. Top-class restaurants (Chinese, Italian, Japanese and international cuisines), a gym, spa and indoor swimming pool are guaranteed to keep you busy.

$$$$$ Villa 32 三二行館 – *32 Zhongshan Rd., Beitou.* 北投區中山路32號. *MRT: Xinbeitou.* ✗ Spa ☎02-6611 8888. *www.villa32.com. 5 rooms. Breakfast included.* Originally a private club, this hot-springs hideaway still feels exclusive. Water, stone and wood blend harmoniously in expansive rooms with private springs and L'Occitane bath products. Choose from Japanese- or European-style rooms, some of which are two stories. If that isn't enough, there's a full-service spa, and private butlers on hand to fulfill requests large and small. For a taste of the good life, you can pay to use the public hot springs for four hours (gender-segregated public bathing is nude), or pamper yourself with a spa treatment. **The Restaurant ($$$$)** at Villa 32 looks to Italy for the inspiration for its well-prepared cuisine.

♀/ EAT

For price categories, ☝ *see Legend on the front cover flap. Restaurants accept credit cards, except where the* ⊐ *symbol is shown. All serve lunch and dinner, unless otherwise indicated.*

$ Alleycat's – *B1 Floor, 6-1 Lishui St.* 麗水街6-1號B1樓. *MRT: Guting.* ☎02-2321 8949. *www.alleycatspizza.com. Eight Taipei locations.* ⊐. This student-friendly pizza place serves up the real deal: stone-oven-baked pies with thin, crispy crusts. Taiwanese-style toppings are nowhere to be found (corn pizza anyone?), just fresh Italian flavors, hearty calzones and plenty of delicious, piping hot cheese—plus an array of beers and ciders to wash it down. **Pizza.**

$ Amis food 二條六 – *Alley 33, 6 Zhongshan N. Rd., Sec. 1,*中山北路一段 33巷6號. *MRT: Zhongshan.* ☎️*02-2521 4333.* If you don't have the time to go to the aboriginal communities, you can try Amis cuisine in this small restaurant with no name. It serves different kinds of mountain vegetables, with grilled fish and some game, such as mountain pig. You might try the rice wine, but be careful, the sweet taste can be overpowering. **Aboriginal.**

$ City Star 京星港式飲茶 – *2nd Floor, 216 Dunhua South Rd., Sec. 1.*敦化南路一段216號2F. *MRT: Zhongxiao-Dunhua.* ☎️*02-2741 2625. www.citystar.com.tw.* 🪧. There are so many Cantonese restaurants in this part of Taipei, that it might be called "Little Hong Kong." Open 24hrs, City Star is the best option for late-night dining. On Friday and Saturday evenings, be prepared for lines that stretch down the stairs and into the street. Tastes of Hong Kong come to the fore in dim sum items like shrimp and pork dumplings, and pineapple and shrimp slices with almond flakes, while polite service exhibits Taipei-style hospitality. (City Star doesn't accept reservations on weekends.) **Cantonese.**

$ Corner 肥前屋 – *13-2 Zhongshan N.Rd., Sec. 1, Alley 121*中山北路一段121巷 13-2號. *MRT: Zhongshan.* ☎️*02-2562 8701. Closes 9pm.* Here, in an appealing atmosphere, you'll taste one of the best *unagi* in the city. The freshwater eel is dipped in a sweet soya sauce, grilled and served on a bed of rice. The place is so popular that you might have to share a table with strangers. Experts recommend the small portions instead of the larger ones; the small are believed to be even tastier. **Japanese.**

$ Haoji Noodle Bar
好級擔仔麵 – *79 Jilin Rd.* 吉林路79號. *MRT: Zhongshan.* ☎️*02-2521 5999. www.hawji.tw. No reservations.* 🪧.

In addition to its claim that "2,000 bowls of shoulder-pole noodles sold every day," Haoji boasts more than 100 classic Taiwanese "small eats" to choose from. There's no menu; patrons just point to the dishes they want. The rough-and-ready environment recalls rural life 50 years ago. **Taiwanese.**

$ Hsiang Yu Cantonese Restaurant 祥鈺港式茶樓 – *65 Huaxin St.* 中和市華新街65號. *Zhonghe City. MRT: Nanshijiao.* ☎️*02-2949 1486. Closes 9pm.* This dim sum restaurant southwest of the city caters to the Cantonese and Southeast Asian immigrant community. Unpretentious, it serves all the classics: steamed ribs, chicken claws, turnip cake and endless pu'er, jasmine and oolong tea. No English menu but English spoken. **Cantonese.** "Burma Street," as **Huaxin** Street is better known, has Burmese, Thai and Yunnanese restaurants catering to more than 10,000 immigrants from mainland China.

$ Longji Restaurant 隆記菜飯– *Lane 101, 1 Yanping S. Rd.* 延平南路101 巷1號 *(opposite Zhongshan Hall). MRT: Ximending.* ☎️*02-2331 5078.* 🪧. *Closes 9pm & third Sun of month.* This authentic, no frills restaurant was established in 1953 by post-civil war immigrants from mainland China. It's popular with "mainlanders," celebrities and increasingly, with tourists. Seafood specialties include freshly fried shrimp (清炒蝦仁). Side dishes of the day are shown in the window. No English menu, but pointing is effective when ordering. **Shanghainese.**

$ Old Wang's 老王記 – *15 Taoyuan St.* 桃源街15號. *MRT: Ximending.* ☎️*0937860050. Closes 9pm (8:30pm weekends & holidays).* Though there's no sign outside, no English name and no English menu, there's no need to worry. Established almost 60 years ago by a civil-war refugee from Hunan and still owned by the family, this restaurant prepares only Chinese beef noodles. Just seven items are available: beef with broth and noodles, broth and noodles, broth and beef, pig knuckle, knuckle with noodles, steamed pork rib pudding, and pickled vegetables. Queues are out the door at lunchtime; evenings are quieter. **Chinese.**

$ Ruo He 若荷 – *Lane 160, 58 Dunhua South Rd., Sec. 1.* 敦化南路一段160巷58號. *MRT: Zhongxiao-Fuxing.* 📞02-2752 0838. www.istea.com.tw. In an elegant traditional Chinese setting, this restaurant offers a vegetarian take on the increasingly popular hot pot–style meal. Customers have a choice of six soup bases of varying spiciness, plus all-you-can-eat vegetables, tofu and meat-like soy items from the buffet. **Vegetarian.**

$ Sababa Pita Bar 沙巴巴 – *Alley 54, Lane 118, 8 Heping East Rd., Sec. 2.* 和平東路二段118巷54弄8號. *MRT: Technology Building.* 📞02-2738 7769. www.sababapita.com. *Four Taipei locations.* 📇. A flavorful alternative when dumpling's just won't do, Sababa is a quick but good spot for fresh Middle Eastern dishes. The hummus is fresh, and the wide selection of pitas, falafel and salads include several vegetarian options. Simple tiled tables and colored-glass lanterns decorate the interior. **Middle Eastern.**

Sababa

Susannah Rosenblatt/Michelin

$ Shan Xi Dao Xiao Mien 山西刀削麵 – *Lane 118, 2 Heping East Rd., Sec. 2.* 和平東路二段118巷2號. *MRT: Technology Building.* 📞02-2378 7890. 📇. This busy, no-frills local haunt offers savory bowls of Taiwan's ubiquitous beef noodle soup filled with chewy, couldn't-be-fresher hand-cut noodles. Juicy stewed tomatoes perfectly complement the tender chunks of beef;

Shan Xi Dao Xiao Mien

Susannah Rosenblatt/Michelin

be sure to top it all off with the rich and spicy house-made chili paste. **Chinese.**

$ Shaoshaoke 勺勺客陝西餐館 – *Lane 41, 15 Ren-ai Rd., Sec. 2.* 仁愛路二段41巷15號. *MRT: Zhongxiao-Xinsheng.* 📞02-2351 7148. www.shaoshaoke.com. *Closed Mon.* Shaoshaoke offers a casual atmosphere in which to enjoy *paomo* 泡饃, a specialty of Shaanxi cuisine. The staff instructs diners to tear up pieces of unleavened flat bread into a bowl. After you add condiments to the bowl, the waiter will pour a fragrant lamb broth over the bread. Once they have soaked up the broth, the tiny pieces of bread take on the texture of pasta. Other northern delicacies include mutton and pig's stomach, and Tibetan-style teas. Comforting hot pots appear on the menu in winter. **Shaanxi.**

$ Sweet Dynasty 糖朝 – *160 Zhongxiao East Rd., Sec. 4.* 忠孝東路四段160號. *MRT: Zhongxiao-Dunhua.* 📞02-2772 2889. www.sweetdynasty.com.tw. Here you'll find all the dim sum and main courses—such as fried turnip pudding in XO sauce, and salt and pepper prawns—that you would expect at a Cantonese restaurant—without the clamor. Savor a relaxing meal in this spacious and refined setting. **Cantonese.**

$ Tang Kung Mongolian Bar-B-Q 唐宮 蒙古烤肉 – *2nd Floor, 283 Songjiang Rd. (entrance around corner off a side street).* 松江路283號2F. *MRT: Zhongshan Junior High*

School or Shuanglian. 📞02-2502 6762. *www.tangkung.htm.tw. Reservations recommended.* A Taipei institution for more than 30 years, this Mongolian restaurant is best enjoyed with a tableful of friends or family. You'll enjoy all-you-can-eat portions of meat, vegetables and spices flame-cooked by chefs with gusto in a huge wok. Not for vegetarians. **Mongolian.**

$ Wistaria Tea House 古蹟茶館 紫藤廬 *–Lane 16, 1 Xinsheng South Rd., Sec. 3.* 新生南路三段16巷1號. *MRT: Gongguan.* 📞02-2363 7375. *www.wistariahouse.com.* This city-designated cultural landmark served as a refuge for the island's literati during the martial-law era. The Japanese colonial building, lined with tatami mats and adorned with freshly arranged flowers, provides a warm environment for savoring the taste and distinctive floral aroma of top-quality Taiwanese

Wistaria Tea House
© Chris Stowers/Apa Publications

oolong tea. The limited menu of seasonal dishes also lists tea snacks like almond cakes, dried mango and pumpkin seeds. **Taiwanese.**

$ Yih-Shiang Yuan 逸鄉園 *– 152 Zhongxiao East Rd., Sec.1.* 忠孝東路一段 152號. *MRT: Shandao Temple.* 📞02-3393 2729. *www.yih-shiangyuan.com. tw.* Despite the explosion of interest in Hakka cuisine over recent years, Yih-Shiang Yuan is one of the few restaurants in Taipei that offers good Hakka dishes. All the classics appear on the menu: bitter gourd with salted egg (苦瓜鹹蛋); pork with dried mustard greens (梅干扣肉); Hakka stir fry (客家小炒); pork intestine with ginger (薑絲大腸); and dozens more. It's a great place to take a group of friends or family (note that there's no English sign). **Hakka.**

$ Yonghe Soy Milk King 永和豆漿 大王 *– 102 Fuxing South Rd., Sec. 2.* 復興南路二段102號. *MRT: Da'an.* 📞02-2703 5051. 🚇. Don't be surprised to see a line snaking out this late-night favorite at the foot of the MRT, where cooks roll, knead, cut and fry dough in a whirl of activity. Sample some of the freshest Chinese breakfast dishes around, like you tiao (light, crispy crullers fresh from the fryer) and dan bing (egg wrapped in a soft crêpe, as greasy as it is delicious). And don't forget the dou jiang—steaming, sweet soy milk. **Chinese.**

$$ AoBa 青葉 *–Lane 105, 10 Zhongshan North Rd., Sec. 1.* 中山北路一段105巷10 號. *MRT: Zhongshan.* 📞02-2571 3859. *www.aoba.com.tw.* Two Taipei locations (see AoBa below). Japanese for "green

Oodles of Noodles, Taiwan-style

One of Taiwan's most famous dishes, **beef noodle soup** (牛肉麵 or *niúroù miàn*) may be simple, but not all beef noodle soup is created equal. So how do you differentiate between a generic bowl of salty stew and something special? You can sample some of the tastiest bowls of *niúroù miàn* in Taipei between Ximen MRT station and the Presidential Office Building, on Taoyuan Street—known for its beef noodle stalls, including **Old Wang's** listed above. Other celebrated shops include **Yong Kang Beef Noodle Soup** (*Lane 31, 17 Jinshan South Rd., Sec. 2* 金山南路二段31巷17號)) and **Lin Dong Fang Beef Noodle Soup** (*274 Bade Rd., Sec. 2* 八德路二段274號). Or check out **Breeze food court** on the second floor of Taipei Main Station. The Taipei City Government holds an **annual beef noodle festival** to find the best noodles in the city.

leaf," AoBa offers upscale versions of local foods (stewed crab with beef noodle curry sauce; stir-fried beef with oyster sauce; radish and egg pancake) served banquet-style in an elegant and quiet space. Catering to the nearby Linsen Road evening entertainment district for more than four decades, AoBa is clearly doing something right. **Taiwanese.**

Din Tai Fung

© Chris Stowers/Apa Publications

$$ Din Tai Fung 鼎泰豊 – *194 Xinyi Rd., Sec. 2.* 信義路二段194號. *MRT: Da'an.* *02-2321 8928. www.dintaifung. com.tw. Four Taipei locations.* There's always a line in front of the original Xinyi District home of world-famous xiao long bao, or soup dumplings. Each hot, juicy bite bursts with flavor (be careful when taking that first bite: it's steaming hot). Even the garlicky greens and wonton soup are memorable at this tourist magnet, where you can watch the chefs hard at work in the downstairs kitchen. **Chinese.**

$$ Flavors Swedish Restaurant 瑞典餐館 – *Alley 26, Lane 300, 13 Ren-ai Rd., Sec. 4.* 仁愛路四段300巷26弄13號. *MRT: Zhongxiao Dunhua or Sun Yat-sen Memorial Hall.* *02-2709 6525. www. flavors.com.tw. Closed Mon. Reservations required for lunch.* A husband-and-wife team runs this little gem, where the focus is on quality. (Note; children under 10 are not permitted for dinner). Located in a buzzing neighborhood of shops and eateries, Flavors' à la carte classics include meatballs with new potatoes, brown sauce and lingonberry jam. Items such as house-smoked salmon and potato-fried halibut are typical of the set menu. Save room for the apple cake. **Swedish.**

$$ Kiki Restaurant – *Lane 280, 47 Guangfu South Rd.* 光復南路280巷47號. *MRT: Sun Yat-sen Memorial Hall.* *02-2781 4250. www.kiki1991.com. Three Taipei locations. Reservations recommended weekends.* Run by singer-actor-celebrity **Lan Hsin-mei** (藍心湄), Kiki draws a young crowd with its lively atmosphere, hip vibe and modern take on Sichuan classics. Popular dishes include sautéed chicken with chili (辣子雞丁) and crispy deep-fried egg tofu (老皮嫩肉). **Sichuan.**

$$ Plum Blossom Room at Brother Hotel 兄弟大飯店梅花廳 – *2nd & 3rd Floors, 255 Nanjing East Rd., Sec. 3.* 南京東路三段255號2-3樓. *MRT: Nanjing East Rd.* *02-2712-3456 ext. 2188. www.brotherhotel.com.tw.* Efficient, friendly waitresses wheel food carts around the room at this spacious restaurant located right outside the subway. An illustrated menu in three languages helps you choose from a variety of tasty dim sum, including favorites like pork and shrimp dumplings; simmered rice noodle rolls stuffed with slightly sweet beef; smoky turnip cakes; and buttery deep-fried sesame balls. Entrées are also available. **Cantonese.**

$$ Shi-yang Culture Restaurant 食養山房 – *Lane 350, 7 Xiwan Rd., Sec. 3, Xizhi City.* 汐止市汐萬路三段350巷7號. *MRT: Nangang; then take a taxi (about NT$350).* *02-2862 0078. www.shi-yang.com.* Make reservations up to six weeks in advance to dine at this contemplative, Zen-inspired space in the woods of Taipei County, just outside the city. Shi-yang attracts local cultural luminaries and those looking for a spiritual as well as gastronomic experience. Set meals, which provide fresh and healthy interpretations of Taiwanese standards, vary with the seasons and arrive at the table immaculately presented. **Taiwanese.**

$$ Shin Yeh Table 蕙花欣葉小廚 – *2nd Floor, 201 Zhongxiao East Rd., Sec. 4.* 忠孝東路四段201號2樓. *MRT: Zhongxiao Dunhua.* *02-2778 8712. www. shinyehtable.com.* In the middle of Taipei's busiest nightlife district, Shin Yeh Table's lively vibe, 80s tunes

Shin Yeh Table

Susannah Rosenblatt/Michelin

and trendy, red-themed decor make the perfect backdrop for a fun night out with friends. The thick illustrated menu in English, Chinese and Japanese guides you through tasty Taiwanese classics like a zippy chicken with tofu and delectable fried oysters wrapped in shiitake mushrooms. **Taiwanese.**

$$ Song Kitchen 宋廚 *–Lane 15, 14 Zhongxiao East Rd., Sec. 5.* 忠孝東路五段15巷14號. *MRT: Taipei City Hall. ☎02-2764 4788.* This unpretentious family-run restaurant has competed successfully for more than a decade with the top hotel restaurants in Taipei's fashionable eastern district. A loyal local clientele keeps coming back for more; they don't seem to mind that they have to reserve their table nearly two months ahead of time *(reservations must be made by the first of the month for dinner anytime during the following month).* **Beijing.**

$$$ AoBa 青葉 *– 116 Anhe Rd., Sec. 1.* 安和路一段116號. *MRT: Da'an. ☎02-2700 0009. www.aoba.com.tw.* Quietly luxurious and dimly lit to create an aura of mystery, AoBa showcases the subtlety of Taiwanese cuisine with expertly conceived seasonal menus. A seafood salad topped with fresh, crispy wontons and sweet tender scallops is memorable, while a stewed chicken braised in soy sauce and ginger melts in your mouth. **Taiwanese.**

$$$$ Mitsui Japanese Cuisine 三井料理 *– 34 Nongan St.* 農安街34號. *MRT: Minquan West Rd. ☎02-2594 3394. www.mitsuitaipei.com.tw. Several Taipei locations.* Preparing exquisite food in a refined setting, Mitsui's meticulous chefs present delicately flavored seasonal seafood, and will customize

dishes to diners' preferences. The omakase (chef's selection) meals are epic, as you make your way through one sweet and tender piece after another of fatty tuna, sweet shrimp and briny uni. Fish is garnished with perfectly proportioned slices of tomato or orange; tea is served in lovely pottery. And you can't get much fresher than crabs plucked straight from the restaurant's giant tank. **Japanese.**

🛒 SHOPPING

VAT Refund
♿*See Shopping p26*

DISTRICTS

North of the Wanhua District, the **Ximending** area is the vibrant heart of the consumerist Taipei. It is the number-one destination for teenagers who want to hang around with friends and shop for cheap goods. In the West, **Xinyi** District, near Taipei 101, provides many international and luxury brand stores. **Zhongshan North Road** is also renowned for designer-brand shops, especially the area in the vicinity of the former US embassy, which has some chic designer boutiques.

Around **Zhongxiao Dunhua** MRT Station, the alleys between Ren-ai Rd., Sec. 3 & 4, Zhongxiao E. Rd. and Civic Blvd. are lined with cafes, teashops and boutiques, and often crowded with young adults, especially at night. If you want a more peaceful atmosphere, head to **Yongkang Street** and **Longquan Street**, north of Taiwan Normal University. For books and Chinese seals, Section 1 of **Chongqing South Road**, also known as Bookstore Street, is the place to go.

For more traditional Chinese merchandise, try **Dihua Street** in Dadaocheng, which has grocery stores, Chinese sweet shops and traditional pharmacies.

DEPARTMENT STORES

Taipei doesn't lack department stores, especially large Japanese chains. **Pacific SOGO** (45 Zhongxiao E. Rd. Sec. 4 忠孝東路四段45號) is a favorite for brand labels.

Shinkong Mitsukoshi, another Japanese chain, is located in the Shin Kong Life Tower (66 Zhongxiao W. Rd., Sec. 1 新光三越, 忠孝西路一段66號), next to Taipei Main Station and in the Xinyi District.

MALLS

Taipei's malls are stocked with international brands. Major malls include:

Breeze Center (39 Fuxing N. Rd. Sec. 1 微風中心, 復興北路一段39號)

Core Pacific City Living Mall (138 Bade Rd., Sec. 4 京華城, 八德路四段 138號)

Taipei City Mall (underground level, above Metro level, Taipei Main Station).

Taipei 101 Mall (45 Shifu Rd. 市府路 45號)

© Chris Stowers/Apa Publications
Breeze Center

SPECIALTY STORES

Most stores below are open daily noon until 9pm or 10pm.

Cang Xi – *Lane 41, 23 Yongkang St.* 藏喜, 永康街41巷23號. *Closed Mon.* ✆02-2322 5437. This store specializes in Tibetan Buddhism artifacts. The incense sold here is made out of 100% natural products. Very welcoming and helping staff.

Earth Tree – *Lane 30, 35-1 Xinsheng S. Rd., Sec. 2* 地球樹, 新生南路二段30巷35-1號. ✆02-2394 9959. *www.earthtree.com.tw.* Fair trade is the motto of this little shop hidden behind trees in a corner between Yongkang Street and Lane 30. It sells clothing, stationery and small items manufactured from different parts of the world.

Booday – *18-1Nanjing W. Rd. , Lane 25* 蘑菇店, 南京西路25巷18-1號. ✆02-2552 5552. *www.booday.com.* This design concept store was created in 2003 during the SARS epidemic. Their motto, "You are not a kind of useful stuff like a mushroom" is illustrated in the simple design of the clothing, bags and other items. On the first floor, a cafe serves drinks and sweets in a cozy ambience. Booday also publishes a magazine.

Lovely Taiwan – *Lane 25, 18-2 Nanjing W. Rd.* 台灣好店, 台北市南京西路25巷 18-2號. ✆02-2558 2616, *www.lovely taiwan.org.* Next door to Booday, this store is run by the Lovely Taiwan Foundation, which promotes Taiwanese goods. You may find some interesting souvenirs and gifts, all crafted by Taiwanese.

Moungar Traces of Books – *1st Floor, Lane 152, 4 Guangzhou St.* 莽葛拾遺, 廣 州街152巷4號1F. *Closes 11pm.* ✆02-2336 2181. *www.rbc.idv.tw.* A second-hand bookstore filled with mountains of books. The store in Yongkang Street is particularly impressive, since it's underground and accessed by a narrow flight of stairs. Moungar also sells second-hand CDs.

Art Space – *1st Floor, National Concert Hall* 好藝術空間, 國家音樂廳. *Open 1pm.* If you want to buy a gift with flair, you'll probably find it in this store located in the basement of the National Concert Hall. Be prepared for higher price tags, since beautiful means expensive here.

SPOT – *18 Zhongshan N. Rd., Sec. 2* 台北 光點, 中山北路二段18號. ✆02-2511 7786. *www.spot.org.tw. Open daily 11am - midnight.* The former US embassy has been transformed in a small exhibition hall for design plus a movie theater. It also houses a coffeeshop, Café Lumière, as well as a store selling all sorts of decorations, stationery and Taiwanese indie music labels.

Eslite – *245 Dunhua S. Rd., Sec. 1* 誠品, 敦化南路一段245號. ✆02-2775 5977. *www.eslite.tw.* One of the largest and trendiest bookstore chains in Taiwan, Eslite sells books in Chinese, Japanese and English as well as magazines and CDs. There's an excellent coffeeshop. The Dunhua store is the historic one

Precious Jade

Jade is a gemstone found in many shades of green, from emerald green to pale green, but it also comes in translucent lavender, red-brown, blue, black and white. Imperial green is the most valued, especially Burmese jade. The generic term "jade" is applied to two kinds of mineral: **jadeite** and **nephrite**, which are difficult to distinguish from each another. Chinese people believe jade has medicinal value and protects against evil. Carvers keep one time-tested rule in mind when working with jade: "choose stone according to its color and carve it according to its shape." Taipei's **Holiday Jade Market** is one of the biggest such markets in Asia, but be aware of fake jade, which is, in fact, mere glass.

(open 24hrs). The flagship store is in the fashionable district of Xinyi.

MARKETS
Antic Market – *Bade & Xinsheng S. Rds.* 八德路與新生南路. *Open weekends only.* The small shops and street stalls of this market are probably the best place to shop for antiques, especially jades, painting scrolls, coins, china (fake or real).

Chinese Handicraft Promotion Center – *1 Xuzhou Rd.* 台灣手工業推廣中心, 徐州路1號 *Open daily 9am–5:30pm.* ℘02-2393 7330. *www.handicraft.org.tw.* Run by the government, this "mall of souvenirs" definitely lacks charm. It is designed for tour groups, but it is efficient. Come here to shop only if you have no time for a more authentic shopping experience.

Holiday Jade Market – *Ren-ai Rd.* 假日玉器市場, 仁愛路. Taipei's Holiday Jade Market is one of the largest such markets in all of Asia, but beware of fake jade, which is, in fact, mere glass.

Jade Market
Florent Bonnefoy/Michelin

ENTERTAINMENT
Consult local newspapers for cultural events, theater productions and concerts or http://eng.taiwan.net.tw for a calendar of monthly events. Also keep an eye on the calendar of programs at the **National Theater** and the **National Concert Hall** (21-1 Zhongshan S. Rd.; ℘02-3393 9888; www.ntch.edu.tw/english/index) as well as **Novel Hall for Performing Arts** (3 Songshou Rd. 新舞堂, 松壽路3號. ℘02-2722 4302; www.novelhall.org.tw). Other popular venues include:

Taipei Eye – *113 Zhongshan N. Rd., Sec. 2* 臺北戲棚, 中山北路二段113號. ℘02-2568 2677. www.taipeieye.com. Accessed from Jinzhou Street, this new venue in Taipei showcases Chinese opera and other Taiwanese performances such as puppet shows and other folk arts. The show is a 90min program tailored to tourists and is an excellent first approach to the traditional Chinese performing arts.

Puppetry Art Centre of Taipei – *2nd–4th Floors, 99 Civic Blvd., Sec. 5* 台北偶戲館, 市民大道五段99號2-4樓. *Open Tue–Sat 10am–5pm. NT$50.* ℘02-2528 9553. www.pact.org.tw. Located at the Living Mall, this venue stages puppet shows from Taiwan but also from other parts of the world. The center also has exhibits that introduce the art of puppetry as well as do-it-yourself classes.

SPOT – *18 Zhongshan N. Rd., Sec. 2* 台北光點, 中山北路二段18號. ℘02-2511 7786. www.spot.org.tw. *Open daily 11am–midnight.* SPOT's Taipei Film House offers one of the best and most diverse programs of cinema in Taipei.

NIGHTLIFE

Many clubs are located in the Xinyi District around Taipei 101. A younger crowd invades the Zhongxiao Dunhua area, while Western expatriates tend to haunt the bars of **Anhe Road**. For a more laid-back environment, try **Shida Road** and its alleys. Taipei's night scene is always changing, so check the local English magazines to find out what's new in town or click on the nightlife tab of www.taiwanfun.com.

Gay-friendly bars are found around **The Red House** in Ximending. For more information access www.fridae.com and www.utopia-asia.com.

Pubs are fairly numerous in Taipei; several are clustered around Normal University's Mandarin Training Center. For a wider sampling, go online to www.taipeipubs.com. At **karaoke** clubs private rooms called **KTVs** are outfitted with big-screen television sets to add music and video-enhancements to your singing. **PartyWorld** (see below) and **Holiday** (www.holiday.com.tw) are two top karaoke venues.

Here are some popular night spots:

People – *Basement level 1, 191 Anhe Rd.* 人間台北, 安和路二段191號B1. *Open daily 11:45am–1am.* 02-2735-2288. The challenge when you get down the stairs to the entrance is how to open the door. Each restaurant of this Shintori restaurant chain has its own sesame. When you finally get the door open, you will discover restaurant space and a bar with a hip vibe and sleek decor. A good place to start the evening.

Blue Note – *4th Floor, 171 Roosevelt Rd., Sec. 3, at Shida Rd.* 羅斯福路三段171號.四樓 *Open daily 7pm–1am.* 02-2362 2333. *Mon–Fri NT$250 (Sat–Sun NT$ 300), including a drink.* If you like jazz, then you won't want to miss this Taipei institution, a fixture in the city's jazz scene. Gigs start at 9:30pm and go on until midnight. You'll enjoy great performances under the gaze of world-famous jazz artists whose photos line the walls.

Carnegie's – *100 Anhe Rd., Sec. 2* 安和路二段100號. 02-2325 4433. This pub was originally opened in Hong Kong. Here in Taipei it serves the usual pub food. The action really gets started around 10pm until late into the night.

Luxy – *5th Floor, 201 Zhongxiao E. Rd., Sec. 4* 忠孝東路四段201號5樓. 02-2772 1000. www.luxy-taipei.com. One of the most crowded clubs in Taipei, Luxy features international DJs and bands. It attracts a young and stylish crowd.

Ziga Zaga – *2 Songshou Rd.* 松壽路2號 *Open 9pm.* 02-2720 1234. Reach the second floor of the Grand Hyatt Taipei and enjoy the posh ambience of this bar, which is filled with a young white-collar crowd.

The Wall Live House – *Basement level 1, 200 Roosevelt Rd., Sec. 4* 羅斯福路四段200號B1樓. 02-2930-0162. www.thewall.com.tw. This premium venue for alternative music is located a few blocks away from the Normal University. Check the website for upcoming programs.

Riverside Live House – *Basement level 1, 200 Roosevelt Rd., Sec. 4* 羅斯福路四段200號B1樓. 02-2369 0103. www.riverside.com.tw. Located in The Red House of the trendy Ximending area, this live-music venue houses concerts by local rock and pop bands.

PartyWorld – *22 Zhongxiao E. Rd., Sec. 4* 錢櫃, 忠孝東路四段22號. 02-40 666 999 (reservation hotline). www.cashboxparty.com. PartyWorld is Taiwan's most popular karaoke chain. Friends gather in private rooms and sing all night long no matter the singing prowess. A buffet is available if you want to eat something to recharge your batteries. Several branches in Taipei.

Carnegie's

Although the Chinese and Western attempts at colonization started in south Taiwan—and that region still has a good claim to being Taiwan's *Hoklo* soul as well as having its top historical sites—the political, economic and cultural center long ago migrated northward. When Taiwan was upgraded to provincial level in China in 1886, there was still some debate as to locating the capital in the south or center, but Taipei was soon chosen even though it had become a walled city only the year before.

Highlights

1 Odd-shaped shoreline rock formations at **Yeliu** (p186)

2 Jinguashi's mining history at **Gold Ecological Park** (p187)

3 Mountain vistas from Yilan's **Forest Recreation Areas** (p197)

4 Riverside park, city moat and museums of **Hsinchu** (p202)

5 Historic theater showing Taiwanese films in **Neiwan** (p209)

The Region's Topography

Northwest Taiwan is essentially a contin-uation of the western plain, with Miaoli and Hsinchu bounded on their east, and Taoyuan and Taipei bounded to their south, by the island's Central Mountains. Keeling, eastern Taipei County and north Yilan are set in high rolling hills. Central Yilan is located on the Lanyang Plain, before more mountains in the south separate it from Hualien. The northern one-quarter of Taiwan proper is home to about 10.5 million Taiwanese (almost half of the total population), with some 6.5 million living in Taipei City and Taipei County alone.

The northern region offers a wide range of natural, cultural, historical, religious and leisure tourist destinations, most of which are accessible as day trips from Taipei. Its scenic coast is its most com-pelling asset, the Pacific Ocean lapping a shore, which at Yeliu, is lined with odd formations of eroded limestone. Shimen boasts popular golf courses. Taiwan's second largest port, Keelung has a lively harbor, a renowned night market and remnants of Qing-era forts. Fulong draws crowds to its golden sand beach for water sports; just south, the famed Caoling Trail leads along coastal cliffs, affording spectacular views. Two Buddhist monasteries here welcome the public. Neighboring villages Jiufen and Jinguashi tout their gold-mining past. The local expression "Hsinchu is windy, Yilan is rainy" sums up the general cli-matic difference between the northwest and northeast. Spring and autumn are the best seasons to visit, but the sum-mers are by no means excessively hot nor the winters too cold.

Lanyang River, Yilan

Mark Caltonhill/Michelin

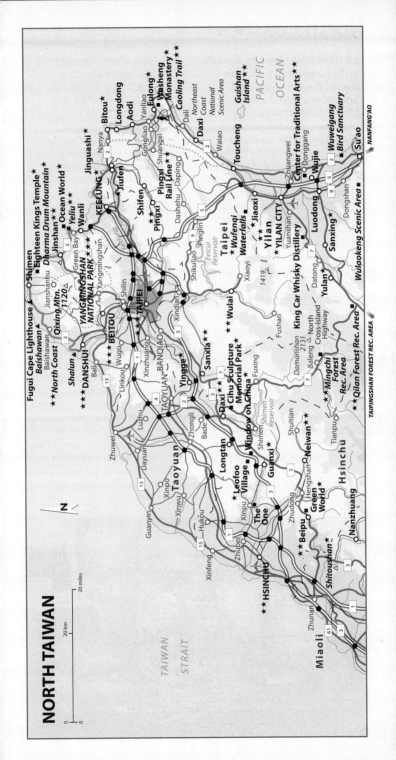

NORTH TAIWAN

N

0   20 km
0   20 miles

TAIWAN
STRAIT

PACIFIC
OCEAN

Fugui Cape Lighthouse ★
Shimen ★
Eighteen Kings Temple ★
Baishawan ✦
★★ North Coast
Baishawan ▲
Qixing Mtn. ▲
Dharma Drum Mountain ★
Ocean World ★★
Jinshan ★
Yeliu ★
Wanli
Green Bay ✦
Jianshanhu
1120 △
YANGMINGSHAN
NATIONAL PARK
Yangmingshan

Shimen ★
Keelung ★★
Bitou ★
Longdong
Aodi
Yanliao
Dali
Northeast
Coast
National
Scenic Area
Waiao
Daxi ★
Nanya
Gongliao
Shuangxi
Daping
Dashehu
Fulong ★
Wusheng
Monastery ★★
Caoling Trail ★★
Guishan
Island ★★

Jiufen ★
Jinguashi ★
Shifen
Pingxi ★
Pingxi
Rail Line ★
Pinglin

NANFANG'AO ➤

Shilin
TAIPEI ★
BEITOU
Shuanghe
Yangmingshan

Shikuijiao
Feicui
Reservoir
1419 △
Xiaoyi

Taipei
Wufenqi
Waterfalls ★
Jiaoxi ★
YILAN CITY
Yuanshan

Toucheng ★
Zhuangwei
Center for Traditional Arts ★★
Wuweigang
Bird Sanctuary ★
Su'ao
Wujie

DANSHUI ★★
Shalun ★
Bali
Linkou
Wugu
Xinzhuang
BANQIAO
TAOYUAN
Xindian
Yilan ★
King Car Whisky Distillery ★
Dongshan
Donggang
Luodong ★
Sanxing
Wulaokeng Scenic Area ■

Zhuwei
Dayuan
Luzhu
Zhongli
Bade
Daxi ●
Cihu Sculpture
Memorial Park ★
Yingge ★
Sanxia ★★
Wulai ★
Fushan
Fuxing
Datong
Yulan ●
Qilan Forest Rec. Area ★

Guanyin
Xinpo
Xinwu
Hukou
Zhubei
Xinpu
Leofoo
Village ★
Longtan
The One ■
Window on China ★
Guanxi
Shimen
Reservoir
Shuitian
Neiwan
Green
World ★
Tianpu
North
Cross-Island
Highway
Damanshan
2131 △
Baleng ●
Mingchi
Forest
Rec. Area ★

Xinfeng
Zhudong
Beipu
Hengshan
Nanzhuang ●
Shitoushan △

HSINCHU ●
Zhunan
Miaoli

TAIPINGSHAN FOREST REC. AREA ➤

North Coast★★

Apart from its southern tip, Taiwan's best beaches lie at the northern crest and the northeast side of the island—within an easy drive of Taipei. Crowds flock here in the summer to exchange frenetic urbanscapes for the sea breezes and relaxing shores of the Pacific Ocean and Taiwan Strait. Surf shops and low-brow amusements as well as hotels and restaurants abound to service the needs and wants of vacationers and tourists who come to slow their pace of life and bask in the sun. Natural sights such as odd rock formations sculpted by ocean waters, as well as man-made attractions, including temples, golf courses and museums, add to the seaside's recreation.

⏱ **Michelin Map:** p177.

ℹ **Info:** North Coast and Guanyinshan National Scenic Area, 33-6 Siayan Valley, Shimen Township. ℘02-8635 5100. www.northguan-nsa.gov.tw.

▶ **Location:** Coastal beaches and villages stretching from Shalun east to Wanli along the No. 2 Highway on Taiwan's north coast.

🕐 **Timing:** Take a half day to drive this coast, but plan to stay overnight if you want to enjoy the swimming beaches and the attractions.

👁 **Don't Miss:** Eighteen Kings Temple in Shimen.

🚗 DRIVING TOUR

48km/25mi from Shalun east to Wanli via Hwy. 2.

Shalun (沙崙) might be the closest beach to Taipei, but it is far too close to the Danshui estuary for swimming.

▶ *Drive east along Hwy. 2 about 10km/6mi.*

Beaches

The beach at **Qianshuiwan** (淺水灣; "Shallow Water Bay) and the beach at **Baishawan** (白沙灣; "White Sand Bay"), some 5km/3mi farther along the coast, are cleaner, but so tightly marshaled by nervous life guards that swimmers are herded into a corral by the shore. Early morning swimmers might have more freedom, but beware of strong currents. Supervision is less vigorous at the beaches of Jinshan and Wanli farther east.

Jinshan's goose-meat snacks

Mark Caltonhill/Michelin

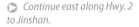

▷ *Continue east along Hwy. 2*

Coffee shops and cheap restaurants line the Hwy. 2. Of cultural interest along the way is Eighteen Kings Temple, of which there are two on the main road. The first, at Kanzaijiao (坎仔腳) just before Fuji Harbor turnoff, is fairly bland, but the second, in Shimen, is worth a stop.

▷ *Continue east along Hwy. 2 to Shimen.*

Shimen Township 石門鄉

Shimen, where the Taiwan Strait meets the Pacific Ocean, is the northernmost township of Taiwan proper. It's popular for its eponymous **stone arch** eroded by sea and wind. Despite having some of the windiest fairways in Taiwan, golfers throng its two **golf courses: North Bay** (北海高爾夫球場; *5 Caobuwei, Caoli Village. 草里村草埔尾5號; ☏02-2638 2930*), and **Ocean** 濱海高爾夫球場; *10 Jianzi Rd., Jianlu Village. 尖子路10號; ☏02-2638 0679*)—the latter, due to having only 15 holes with 3 repeated, is the cheapest golf course near Taipei.

The **Eighteen Kings Temple**★ (十八王公廟) (1-1 Alipang, Qianhua Village. (台北縣石門鄉乾華村阿里磅1-1號) in Shimen is the more interesting of two temples with the same name on Hwy. 2. Look in its tiny basement at the rear. Back upstairs, watch adherents offer ghost money, incense, rice *zongzi* (粽子) and cigarettes to the **18th King**, a dog who survived a nearby shipwreck that killed all 17 Taiwan Strait voyagers, but sacrificed its life out of loyalty to its drowned master.

The specialty of **Shimen** is *zongzi*, bamboo leaves filled with sticky rice, meat and other delicacies. The original shop and still the best place to purchase it is probably **Liu's Zongzi** (劉家肉粽; *30 Zhongyang Rd. 中央路30號; daily 9:30am–10pm; ☏02-2638 1088; www.liujiarice.com.tw. Take-away only shop*).

Fuji Fishing Harbor (富基漁港) sells its live fish fresh from boats, stalls and restaurants. To walk off your lunch, head west along the cliffs past the **Fugui Cape Lighthouse** (富貴角燈塔).

▷ *Continue east along Hwy. 2 to Jinshan.*

Jinshan Township★★ 金山鄉

Most surfers head farther down the east coast, but the long **beach**★ at Jinshan Township is favored by beginners; it rents boards and gear, has instructors and is also popular with stronger swimmers. Jinshan's old street, **Jinbaoli Street** 金包里街, has good snacks, particularly the **goose meat** served in the courtyard of the **Zhangsheng King Temple** (漳聖王廟; *104 Jinbaoli St.*).

Jinshan has two famous residents. Sculptor **Ju Ming** (朱銘) went from being an apprentice temple woodcarver in Miaoli County to international art fame. A large number of his works are on exhibit in the nearby rolling foothills at the **Ju Ming Museum**★★ (朱銘美術館; *2 Xishihu, Xihu Village. 西勢湖2號; ⏱open Tue–Sun 9:30am–5pm; NT$250; ☏02-2498 9940; www.juming.org.tw*).

Higher up the hillside, **Teresa Teng** (鄧麗君) is buried at **Jinbaoshan Cemetery** (金寶山; *18 Xishihu, Xihu Village. 西勢湖18號*). She was born in Yunlin County to civil war immigrants, and became a popular singer throughout the entire Chinese-speaking world before her untimely death in Thailand at age 42. Marked with calligraphy, a life-size statue and huge piano keys that play her songs, Teng's **grave** has become a pilgrimage for her fans.

Dharma Drum Mountain, Jinshan

Mark Caltonhill/Michelin

Dharma Drum Mountain★

No.14-5, Sanjie Village. 三界村七鄰半嶺法鼓山*No.14-5號.* ℘*02-2498 7171. www.dharmadrum.org.*

In the hills overlooking the coast at Jinshan, this sprawling complex is part of the **Dharma Drum Mountain** organization, the largest Buddhist community in northern Taiwan. The scholarly teachings of its late leader Dharma Master **Sheng Yen** (1930-2009) appealed to educated urban workers of nearby Taipei.

Sheng Yen was first known for his academic interpretation of Chan (Zen) Buddhism, and bringing it to the educated middle class (while most Buddhists tended to focus on more religious interpretation to less educated people).

He was later known for his promotion of environmentalism and disaster relief. The complex is formally a Buddhist education center, with a library, meditation halls, conference rooms and accommodations for monastics and visiting scholars, as well as dining halls, landscaped gardens and collections of religious artworks and artifacts.

▷ *Continue east on Hwy. 2 to Wanli.*

Both Jinshan and the next township, **Wanli** (萬里), have **hot springs hotels**, top of the range being the Tien Lai resort (℘*see below*). Wanli has the last large good beaches before Keelung Harbor.

ADDRESSES

🛏 STAY

$$$$ Tien Lai Spring Resort 天籟溫泉會館 – *1-7 Mingliu Rd., Zhonghe Village, Jinshan Township.* 金山鄉重和村名流路1-7號*;* ✕ ▨ Spa ℘*02-2408 0000. www.tienlai.com.tw. 87 rooms.* Located in the cooler Yangmingshan foothills above the coastal plain, Tien Lai is a spacious resort set amid 5ha/12acre grounds with fountains and palm trees. Amenities include a swimming pool, a hot-springs spa and fitness center. Its hotel features European- and Japanese-style rooms; some have balconies. Western-style and Chinese meals are served in its dining facilities. An outdoor barbecue is held under the stars. Breakfast included. Free Internet.

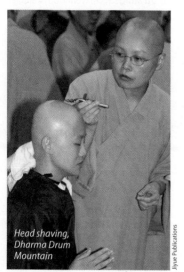

Head shaving, Dharma Drum Mountain

Jiyue Publications

Keelung★

Often neglected in favor of more scenic attractions, the seaport city of Keelung (pronounced *Jilong*; the K comes from an earlier romanization) is of special interest to international visitors because of its long history of contact with foreigners. At various times what is now Taiwan's second largest port was home to Ketagalan plains aborigines, Chinese immigrants, Spanish soldiers and missionaries, Dutch traders, British consular staff, French troops, and Japanese officials and soldiers who landed in 1895 to take possession of Japan's first colony. Most of the gun emplacements seen in Keelung (基隆) today date to the Qing dynasty, and were upgraded during the 1880s. The city's main attractions, however, are its bustling harbor and smaller fishing ports. Keelung's night market is also famous throughout the island. Just half an hour by train northeast of Taipei, the city can be used as a base for exploring nearby Yeliu, Pingxi, Jiufen and Fulong. Swimming and scuba diving are possible near **Waimu Shan fishing port** (外木山) north of Keelung.

▶ **Population:** 390,000
⚸ **Michelin Map:** p177.
🛈 **Info:** Keelung City Government Tourist Office, 1 Yi First Rd. (義一路一號). ℘02-2420 1122. www.klcg.gov.tw.
▷ **Location:** Accessible by Hwys. 1 and 3, Keelung sits northeast of Taipei, at the end of its long, oceanfront harbor. The central core of the city clusters at the south end of the harbor, where the train and bus stations are located, and spills over to its east side, the Zhongzheng District, where Yizheng Park is located.
🕐 **Timing:** Count on spending a full day here. It's a good base to explore the surrounding area (Yeliu, Pingxi, Jinguashi, Fulong).
🅿 **Parking:** Street parking available, or in parking lots such as Dong-an Guangchang (東岸廣場) outside the Cultural Center on Ren 1st Rd. (仁一路)
⌖ **Don't Miss:** Miaokou Night Market.

Keelung harbor

Mark Caltonhill/Michelin

GETTING THERE

BY TRAIN - Trains run several times daily each hour from Taipei Main Station (30 min; NT$43).

BY BUS - Buses travel to Keelung from most towns in northern Taiwan and stop near Keelung's train station (NT$40 from Taipei).

BY CAR - From Taipei, 30km/18mi east by Hwys. nos. 1 and 3 or Provincial Hwy. 5.

BY TWO WHEEL - For those participating in Taiwan's latest cycle craze, most of the 35km/22mi route from Taipei traverses a gently sloped bike path that follows the Keelung River.

GETTING AROUND

BY BUS - Buses depart from Keelung Bus Station on Ren 2nd Rd. (仁二路) every 10-20min to most destinations, including Bus No. 101 to Heping Island, 103 to Badouzi, and 505 to Dawulun. KL Bus (基隆客運) departs from in front of the railway station for outlying destinations, such as Bus No. 1022 to Yeliu.

BY CAR - Island-wide rental companies have no branch offices in Keelung, but they will deliver a car there (🚗 see Hsinchu).

BY TAXI - Taxis are found outside the train station and other transport hubs, or can be flagged down. Sample fares from downtown include Heping Island NT$150, Badouzi NT$200, Yeliu NT$300.

ON FOOT - Walking to the main attractions is possible, but not recommended because of the long distances, except for Story House, the night market and around the harbor terminal.

GENERAL INFORMATION

AREA CODE

The prefix 02, which indicates the area code for Keelung City, has been included in the telephone numbers shown in this chapter, but it is not necessary to dial 02 when making a local call.

For mobile phones the prefix is 09. Some businesses use mobile phone numbers as contact numbers; you must dial the 09 prefix from anywhere in Taiwan to reach a mobile phone.

VISITOR INFORMATION

Keelung City Government Tourist Office: 🚗 See Info above.

ACCOMMODATIONS

Keelung offers a variety of lodgings from major hotels to hostels and homestays. Most are located near the transportation hub (rail, bus, passenger ferry), but more idyllic options can be found in the peripheral fishing harbors. Information from Keelung City Government Tourist Office: www. klcg.gov.tw. *For a selection of lodgings, 🚗 see ADDRESSES.*

A BIT OF HISTORY

Keelung possibly gained its name from a local hill shaped like a "chicken coop" (雞籠; *ji-long*); more plausible is that it derived from an aboriginal name. It was the deposits of gold, copper and coal in these nearby hills that first attracted Chinese and Japanese to the area in the 16C. They were followed in 1626 by Spanish traders and missionaries, who settled on **Heping Island** (separated from the town by a narrow channel) until ousted by the Dutch in 1642. The main Dutch entrepôt continued to be Tainan, but after their defeat there by Koxinga's forces in 1662, the Dutch returned to Keelung before finally ending their occupation of Taiwan in 1668. Due to its naturally deep and protected harbor, as well as its abundant ores, Keelung developed rapidly throughout the Qing dynasty, became a **Treaty Port** following the Second Opium War (1856-60), and had its name changed to the similar-sounding but more auspicious "prosperous base" (基隆) in 1875. French forces occupied Keelung briefly during the **Sino-French War** of 1884-85 *(see sidebar below).*

Keelung's Ghost Festival 中元祭

The seventh lunar month is known as **Ghost Month** throughout the Chinese-speaking world, since popular religious tradition—a unique confluence of both Buddhist and Daoist rituals—maintains that the Gates of Hell open on the first day of this month and close on the last day. During this period spirits of the deceased are free to wander the earth and cause trouble, especially the "hungry ghosts" (餓鬼) more commonly called "good brethren" (好兄弟). Elaborate ceremonies and fabulous feasts are prepared to satiate them.

Grappling with ghosts, Toucheng

Jyue Publications

These celebrations take different forms in different places around Taiwan. Two of the most unusual are the "grappling with ghosts" (搶孤) in Yilan's **Toucheng Township** (頭城), and Keelung's **Badouzi fishing harbor** (八斗子漁港), where lanterns are launched onto the sea.

Floating lanterns, Keelung

Jyue Publications

The main Keelung ceremony takes place on the 14th day of the 7th lunar month, but for the entire month, the city is in party mode. Key activities, starting with ritual opening of the gates of a tower housing funereal urns at **Laodagong Temple** (老大公廟; Lane 76, 37 Le 1st Rd.) are televised and broadcast nationwide. During the evening lanterns, each inscribed with a family name (姓), are paraded through Keelung's streets on decorated floats.

The event originated following a particularly nasty clash between descendents of Quanzhou and Zhangzhou Fujianese immigrants in 1851, in which more than 100 people died. To heal the split community, a lantern festival honoring the dead was devised based on family names, most of which were shared by both groups, rather than based on ethnic division.

The floats make their way along the coast to Badouzi, followed by crowds of citizens. There, shortly before midnight, with fireworks whizzing into the air, the decorated lanterns are carried into the sea by teams of men, and then set adrift until they catch fire and sink. Everyone then heads for home, or back to Keelung's famous **Temple Entrance night market,** which does good business well into the small hours of the morning.

Ninety-five percent of Keelung's topography is hills, and the problem of north Taiwan's main port being cut off from the rest of the island was partially solved when Taiwan's first railway, connecting Keelung and Taipei, was completed in 1891. The harbor continued its growth through the period of Japanese rule. Although it was badly damaged by Allied bombing in WWII, the city re-emerged to become today's second largest **port**. With a 15.5m/51ft-deep main channel and 57 berths, the port handles more than 2 million TEUs of cargo annually, and is home to one of Taiwan's five **Free Trade Zones**. Although Keelung is not a major passenger transportation hub, ferries leave for Okinawa in Japan and Taiwan's outlying islands, and cruise ships dock here routinely.

SIGHTS
Keelung Story House★
基隆故事館
181 Xinyi Rd. 信一路181號. ⏱*Open Mon–Fri 9am–noon & 2pm–5pm, Sat–Sun 9am–5pm.* ☎*02-2420 1885. www.klcg.gov.tw.*
This attraction makes a good place to start your visit. Located next door to the city government building (a short walk along the waterfront from the railway station), the house provides a comprehensive introduction to the area's history, ecology, people, coal

mining—and Steve McQueen. The Hollywood star visited the port in 1966 to film the Oscar-nominated *The Sand Pebbles,* and many locals' claim to fame is having been extras in the movie. The house also has maps and tourist leaflets.

Keelung Harbor Tour★
For an uncommon Taiwanese experience, take a one-hour **boat ride** *(NT$400;* ☎*09 1009 1043)* on the ocean around Keelung Island. Tour boats depart opposite the railway station, or from Bisha Fishing Port (⏱*see below).* The port and small harbors are the main attraction, as well as an opportunity to see Taiwan's coastline from the sea, just as its earliest immigrants saw it.

Historic Forts★
Keelung's historic sights on land consist of several forts and other defensive structures built or renovated in the late Qing dynasty in preparation for the French attack of 1884. **Ershawan Fort** *(二沙灣砲臺; Yizheng Park, Zhongzheng District, 1.5km/1mi east of the harbor; by bus 101/103)* is probably the most worth visiting, though the only vestige of the original outpost is the fortress gate. It can be reached by walking up the hill within **Yizheng Park**. Others forts include **Baimiweng Fort** *(白米甕砲台; Lane 37, Guanghua Rd., Zhongshan District.* 光華路37巷*),* **Dawulun Fort**

Sino-French War (1884-85)
As part of its attempts to wrestle control of northern Vietnam from the Chinese, French forces invaded Keelung in August 1884, and both Keelung and Danshui in October 1884. They failed at Danshui, but occupied Keelung for half a year. Farther advance beyond this bridgehead was stopped by superior Chinese numbers, depletion of French troops from disease, and sound preparation by imperial commissioner **Liu Ming-chuan** (劉銘傳) in the six months of hostilities before the real fighting began. In Keelung the **gun emplacements** are major tourist attractions today, while the **French cemetery**, said to contain the remains of around 600 troops, is of particular interest to Western visitors.

As the French ultimately achieved most of their war aims, they are widely perceived as the victors, but in Taiwan, since Chinese forces performed better there than elsewhere in their 19C confrontations with Western countries and Japan, the war is considered a home victory. The island's elevation to provincial status also derives from this event, and Liu's appointment as its first governor from his successful contribution.

(大武崙砲臺; above Lovers' Lake, Anle District) to the west of town, **Gangziliao Fort** *(槓仔寮砲台; Lane 141, Jiaozhong St., Xinyi District. 教忠街141巷)* to the east, and **Sheliao East Fort** on Heping Island *(see below).*

French Cemetery★ 法國公墓
2.5km/1.6mi east of city center.
2 Zhongbin Section, Zhongzheng District. 中正區中濱段2號
 Open to the public.

Hemmed in by apartment buildings, this small cemetery contains three memorials and the anonymous remains of some 600 soldiers and sailors who died when they tried to invade Taiwan as part of the 1884-85 Sino-French War. Some died of battle-related injuries, but the majority were victims of malaria, cholera, dysentery and other diseases, while some died elsewhere and were moved here at later dates.

Heping Island★ 和平島
This 66ha/163-acre island sitting just off Keelung's north shore on the harbor's east side is connected to the city by a small bridge over a narrow channel. Keelung's laid-back district, the island is popular for seafood, sea breezes and gentle trails. The historic **Sheliao East Fort** *(社寮東砲台; Lane 2, He 1st Rd. 和一*

French Cemetery

路2巷.) was built here in the early years of Japanese rule as a defense against a perceived Russian threat. Getting to it takes you through the village of the Amis people. The nearby government-sponsored **Aboriginal Culture Museum** *(原住民文化會館; 75, Lane 116, Zhengbin Rd. 正濱路116巷75號; open Tue–Sun 9am–5pm; 02-2462 0810; no English information)* introduces the cultures and material artifacts of all Taiwan's indigenous groups. The Amis' small enclave on Heping Island gives visitors an idea of contemporary aboriginal life.

Ruins of Sheliao East Fort, Heping Island

185

EXCURSIONS
Yeliu★★ 野柳

▶ *13km/8mi west of Keelung, along the coast. KL Bus (基隆客運) 1022 from beside Keelung Train Station, or taxi (NT$300) for this scenic trip.*

This small fishing village in Taipei County's Wanli Township (萬里鄉) is typical of those along the north and northeast coast. It's a good place to watch crabbers, see small trawlers come and go, and eat freshly caught seafood at restaurants such as **Sanye Live Seafood Restaurant ($)** (三葉活海鮮; *74-16 Gangdong Rd.* 港東路74號之16; ℘*02-2492 3132*) opposite the harbor. Since the men of this family-run restaurant—started 40-plus years ago as a stall selling snacks—are crabbers and the women do the cooking, the top of the list favorite is **crab** (螃蟹). Other favorites include **sashimi** (生魚片), "fish fin head" (魚翅頭; actually chewy cartilage connecting the fin to the body) and **marine melon seeds** (海瓜子; a species of clam).

Two attractions, plus a renowned festival, make Yeliu one of northern Taiwan's major tourist destinations. Tens of thousands of visitors head here during the **Lantern Festival** (◐ *see Calendar of Events*) two weeks after Lunar New Year to watch local residents leap into the cold harbor waters clutching palanquins bearing statues of the seafarers' deity **Mazu** in the hope of safe voyages and bumper harvests. This custom is followed by a multi-course seafood banquet served to thousands of guests *(tickets available on the day)* and hosted by the county magistrate.

Yeliu Geopark★★ 野柳地質公園
167-1 Gangdong Rd. 港東路167號之1. ◐*Open May–Sept daily 8am–6pm, Oct–Apr daily 8am–5pm. NT$50.* ℘*02-2492 2016. www.ylgeopark.org.tw.*

Other than the festival, a 1.7km/1.1mi-long spit of land jutting into the Pacific from beside the village is a major draw. The **limestone rocks** here have been eroded by wind and sea into curious shapes. In true local fashion they have been given nicknames such as Mushroom, Fairy Shoe, Candle and most famously, Queen's Head. Yeliu is on most mainland tourists' itineraries and gained worldwide attention when a Mr. Zhao from Changzhou carved his name on a park attraction in 2009.

🛉🛉 Ocean World★ 野柳海洋世界
167-3 Gangdong Rd. 台北縣萬里鄉港東路167號之3. ◐*Open Mon–Fri 8:30am–5pm, Sat–Sun 8:30am–5:30pm. NT$350, children under 110cm/43in free,* ℘*02-2492 1111. www.oceanworld.com.tw.*

Next door to the Geopark, this giant aquarium is most suited to a family outing. Performances by dolphins, seals and other sea creatures are regularly staged.

Eroded rocks, Yeliu Geopark

Mark Caltonhill/Michelin

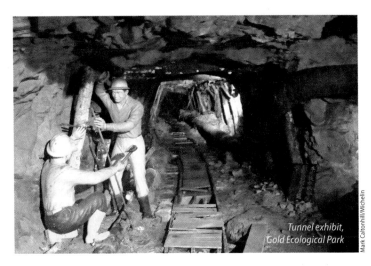

Tunnel exhibit,
Gold Ecological Park

Mark Caltonhill/Michelin

In the **Sea Life Exhibition Hall,** an underwater viewing **tunnel** permits an eye-level look at hundreds of exotic fish and other marine life; there are areas devoted to coral reefs and crustaceans, and a **touch pool** for children.

Jiufen★ 九份 and Jinguashi★ 金瓜石

▶ 13km/8mi southeast of Keelung via Hwy. 102. Buses run to both townships from Keelung (No.1013).

Clinging to the hills above Keelung are the neighboring communities of Jiufen and Jinguashi, known for their gold-, copper- and coal-mining past. Both towns were far beyond their glory when they became major tourist destinations in the last 20 years.

Jiufen's fame came first, having been used as a set location in Hou Hsiao-hsien's (侯孝賢) 1989 film *City of Sadness* (悲情城市). A mining boom town in the 1930s, but a run-down backwater before Hou's film crew arrived in the late 1980s, Jiufen quickly became a popular week-end destination for Taipei residents, with teahouses, snack stalls and crafts shops filling its tiny streets; it is now on the international tour-bus itinerary. Visitors are herded along two main alleyways, but for a taste of life before tourism, head up a side street. Fine **views**★ of the coast are possible from one of several well-positioned teahouses.

The disused mines and buildings of a former gold-mining site developed by the Japanese in Jinguashi, 3km/2mi to the east, were subsequently converted by the county government into the **Gold Ecological Park**★★ (黃金博物園區; 8 Jinguang Rd. 金光路8號; ◷open Tue–Fri 9:30am–5pm, Sat–Sun 9:30–6pm; ℘02-2496 2800; www.gep.tpc.gov.tw). Well-designed, the park has a number of interesting historical and cultural sights and exhibits.

The **Four Joined Japanese-style Residences** were built to house high-level employees of the mining company. One interior re-creates the original Japanese-

Jiufen street

Mark Caltonhill/Michelin

period features. The **Environmental Education Building** introduces local fauna and flora, flourishing again now that mining pollution has been cleared up. The **Crown Prince Chalet** (*access to exterior only*) was built in 1922 for a visit by the Japanese crown prince (later Emperor Hirohito) with a Zen garden in front and mini golf and archery facilities behind; it was never used, since the prince failed to show up.

The **Gold Building** houses the main exhibits, which explain the mining, processing, transportation and applications of gold. Visitors may touch what is reputedly the world's largest (220.3kg/484-pound) block of **gold**.

With life-size models and recorded memories (Chinese only), **Benshan Fifth Tunnel** (*NT$50*) offers a look inside a mine tunnel. Visitors may try their hand at gold-panning (*NT$100*).

Nearby attractions include the ruins of a Japanese **Shinto shrine;** Chinese temples to the **Lord of the Land** (土地公) and **Guandi** (關帝); and the remains of the **Thirteen Levels** spreading downward over the hillside where the precious metals were processed before being smelted. The WWII **Kinkaseki Prisoner of War Camp,** where Allied servicemen captured by Japanese were forced to work, is now marked by a monument.

ADDRESSES

🏨 STAY

$$ Blue Ocean Hotel – *250 Beining Rd., Keelung.* 北寧路250號. ✆02-2469 9552. www.blueoceanhotel.com.tw. *27 rooms.* Down the coast at Bisha Fishing Harbor (碧砂漁港), convenient for boat trips and the Ghost Month Festival, this hotel offers simply furnished, but pleasant rooms. Internet and a breakfast (from McDonald's) included in the rate. Reservations recommended on weekends.

$$ Harbor View Hotel – *200 Xiao 2nd Rd., Keelung.* 孝二路108號. ✆02-2422 3131. http://harborview.hotel.com.tw/eng/. *65 rooms.* Overlooking the water at the western end of the harbor, this hotel offers rooms with an ocean view (at a higher price) and without. Internet and breakfast are included in the rate. Discounts may be available. Reservations advised on weekends and essential during the Ghost Month Festival.

🍽 EAT

$ Miaokou Night Market 廟口夜市; *"Temple Entrance" – Ren 3rd Rd.* 仁三路, *Keelung.* Located about half a mile southeast of the train station, this night market is popular throughout northern Taiwan for an evening visit. It encompasses 72 official stalls (and more around corner) offering up an array of seafood and other snacks and delicacies. Favorite local foods here include **"pot-side noodles"** (鼎邊趖), **oyster omelets** (蚵仔煎) and Taiwan's take on Japanese tempura (天婦羅). **Taiwanese.**

$$ Bisha Fishing Port 碧砂漁港 – *7km/4mi east of Keelung (Bus 103).* For fish, crabs and other seafood bought directly on the wharf and cooked at nearby stands, be sure to head south along the coast road to this popular fishing port. **Seafood.**

Miaokou Night Market

Mark Cattonhill/Michelin

Fulong★

Situated on Taiwan's northeast coast, along Highway 2, Fulong (福隆) sits on the north side of the Cape Sandiao peninsula jutting into the Pacific Ocean. Embraced by verdant mountains, the town borders the broad Shuangsi River, which empties into the marine waters at Fulong's doorstep. A lure for Taipei's relief-seeking crowds in summertime, Fulong's long-time asset has been its golden-sand beach and inviting coastal waters. The popular Caoling Trail, a historic hiking path that provides spectacular views of the shoreline, terminates in Fulong. Occupying the midpoint of one of Taiwan's National Scenic Areas (NSA), Fulong serves as its gateway and home to the NSA administrative center, another tourist draw. Despite Fulong's somewhat rundown hotels and entry fee to access its beach, thousands of vacationers flock to this seaside town each summer for ocean recreation and relaxation. Still, thousands of vacationers flock here each summer for rest and relaxation.

♿ **Michelin Map:** p177.

ℹ **Info:** Northeast and Yilan Coast National Scenic Area Administration visitor center (222 No.36 Xinglong St.; 🕐 open daily 9am–5pm; 📞 02-2499 1210; www.necoast-nsa.gov.tw). Maps of the trails and brochures on the major and minor attractions in the area are free.

▶ **Location:** Off Hwy. 2 on Taiwan's northeast coast, Fulong sits on the north side of Cape Sandiao peninsula. Access to its popular beach is over a bridge onto the sand from the Bellevue Hotel, which charges a beach-entry fee (NT$90).

🕐 **Timing:** Arrive early to see the attractions in the morning and enjoy the beach in the afternoon. Reserve a second day to walk Caoling Trail.

🅿 **Parking:** Beach parking at the visitor center.

😎 **Don't Miss:** Caoling Trail.

A BIT OF HISTORY

Perhaps Fulong's popularity dates to earlier times when there were no private bus companies, and the **Xueshan Tunnel** to Yilan was not even planned. At that time, when Taipei's white-collar workers toiled six days a week, the hour-plus train journey to Fulong was one of few recreational options and the most convenient means of breathing sea air. Today Fulong's reputation as a water-sports magnet remains untarnished; it continues to attract hordes of beach-goers from June to October to swim, surf and windsurf, sunbathe and stroll the shore.

Every July the **Ho-Hai-Yan Rock Festival** draws thousands of music fans here for three days of outdoor concerts (🕐 see Calendar of Events).

Fulong Beach

Mark Caltonhill/Michelin

SIGHTS

Old Caoling Tunnel Bikeway

For bike rentals, ᓑ see Fulong St. below.
Most visitors still arrive by train, though many now bring bikes to explore the 2.2km/1.3mi of disused railway tunnel known as the Old Caoling Tunnel Bikeway (舊草嶺自行車道) and other routes along the coast and into the foothills, rather than bringing swimsuits to play in the waves. The bikeway offers a serene cycle without the danger, or even the sound, of cars.

Fulong Street 福隆街

Bikes can be rented *(NT$100–150/day)* from stores on Fulong Street near the station; surfboards, wind-surfboards and other paraphernalia can be rented at the beach. Fulong Street is also the best place to experience the famous (or infamous) **Fulong lunchbox** (福隆便當) of fatty pork, rice and vegetables, an institution dating back more than half a century to when a local man sold food to passing train travelers.

The recommended place to eat, however, is **Fushi Seafood Restaurant** (ᓑ *see EAT*). It is located in a quiet old fishing community with a small beach *(no entry fee)*, and although swimming is not recommended because of currents, locals do, and there are showers *(NT$20)*. For a wider selection of seafood, head 3km/2mi north of Fulong to **Ao-di** (澳底), the area's culinary center.

Fulong Beach★

⏱*Open mid-May or Jun–Oct daily. NT$90 entry fee.*
The main access to the beach is via the Fulong Bellevue Hotel (ᓑ *see STAY below*). The ocean waters are ideal for swimming as the protected sandbar creates gentle waves and warm temperatures up to 25°C/77°F in the summer, but lifeguards are on duty anyway. Surfboards and other equipment can be rented, changing rooms and showers are available; food must be brought from outside.

Caoling Trail★★ 草嶺古道

8.5km/5.3mi. Allow 3hrs.
🚶The historic Caoling Trail, signed in Chinese and English, starts 2.8km/1.7mi north of town, on the west side of Hwy. 2, and ends at the train station in Dali (大里) farther down the coast. One of Taiwan's prettiest walks accessible by train *(trail head 1km/.6mi from Gongliao* 貢寮 *Station)*, it offers a taste of the wild to walkers of all abilities.

Originally part of a 19C system of pathways linking Danshui with the Yilan plain, the trail includes such historical highlights as a temple, steles erected by government officials who passed by, the **Horse Falling to Death Bridge** and the remains of an old travelers' inn.

The trail earns its stars, however, for its **views**★★ of waterfalls, cow pastures and above all, the sparkling waters of the Pacific Ocean.

Coastal view from Caoling Trail

Jenna Kwiatoski/Michelin

OUTLYING SIGHTS

The rocks at **Longdong** (龍洞), 10km/ 6mi north of Fulong, are popular for climbing and scuba diving. Another 4km/2.5mi back toward Keelung leads to the small fishing village of **Bitou**★ (鼻頭), which has good seafood and a wonderful short walk up onto the cliffs, around its lighthouse, and back past a school nestled into the rocks.

South of Fulong 2km/1.2mi is the turn off to the **Wusheng Monastery**★ (無

生道場; *7-1 Xianglan St., Fulian Village;* ⏰*open Tue–Sun 8am–6pm;* 𝄞*02-2499 1000; www.093ljm.org)* near the top of **Lingjiu Hill** (靈鷲山). Better known for its offshoot, the **Museum of World Religions**★ in Taipei, the monastery is home to the charismatic **Master Xindao** (心道法師) and his growing band of disciples. It is a good place to see an example of Taiwan's typical eclectic mix of religion.

ADDRESSES

🛏 STAY

$ Longmen Park Campsite
龍門河濱公園露營區 – *100 Fulong St.* 福隆街100號. 𝄞*02-2499 1791. http://longmen.cjb.net.* Camping and barbecuing at Longmen Park, just 2km/1.2mi north of Fulong, are popular with youth groups, but the park also takes in passing trade. The entry fee is NT$70, and camping rates are NT$850 for a 4-person tent, and NT$1000 if tent rental is included. Sleeping bags and similar equipment can also be rented. Only gas-powered cooking is allowed, not charcoal. **Hotel rooms ($$)** are also available *(from NT$2300)*.

$$ One House 一間屋 – *1-1 Dongxing St., Fulong Village.* 東興街1之1號. 𝄞*02-2499 2161. http://onehouse.myweb. hinet.net. 9 rooms.* Standing in a cliff hollow about 2 km/1.2mi south of Fulong and hidden from the coast road, this house is indeed the only dwelling around. Run by former residents of Taipei City, One House hosts short-stay guests, mostly weekend visitors also from Taipei. Food is served in its large lobby, where lively intellectual discussions often ensue. Creative moods or quiet contemplation—the atmosphere depends on the disposition of the visitors. Breakfast included.

$$$ Fulong Bellevue Hotel
福隆貝悅酒店 – *40 Fulong St.* 福隆街40號. ✕⛶📶𝄞*02-2499 2381; www.fulongbellevue.com.tw. 54 rooms.* Fulong's luxury option has accommodations ranging from hotel doubles to up to 8-person villas. Guest amenities include a swimming pool, spa, massage room, conference facilities and—since these are the people charging for use of their bridge—free access to the beach for hotel guests. The Bellevue has a decent restaurant.

🍴 EAT

$ Fushi Seafood Restaurant 富士海鮮 – *8 Dongxing St., 東興街8號 Fulong Village, about 1km/.6mi south of town.* 𝄞*02-2499 1001.* Entered through an ornamental archway, Fushi does without a menu since customers simply point to the foods of their choice. Off the tourist radar, the restaurant is well known to locals, and on summer evenings, extra tables spill out onto the square beside the temple in this small fishing community. Fushi serves up fresh seafood according to daily availability. Wash your meal down with Taiwan beer, whisky, *kaoliang* wine or tea. **Taiwanese.**

$ Yilong 宜隆 – *5 Fulong St.* 福隆街5號 . 𝄞*02-2499 1627.* Yilong is one of several takeaway outlets in front of Fulong Train Station claiming descent from the original *bian dang* (lunchbox) seller. Its vegetarian (素食) option, as well as the pork (福隆/排骨) and chicken (雞腿), are as good or better than any in town. **Taiwanese.**

🎭 EVENT

For young people, the highlight of Fulong's year is the three-day summer **Gongliao International Ocean Music Festival** staged on the beach.

Yilan County★★

Long cut off by high hills and steep cliffs, Yilan (宜蘭縣), only formally established in 1813, was one of the last parts of coastal Taiwan to be settled by Han Chinese. Not until 2006, with the opening of the 12.9km/8mi **Xueshan Tunnel** (雪山隧道)—Asia's second-longest road tunnel—did the county's tourism really take off when it became possible to visit anywhere in Yilan as a day trip from Taipei. There has been continued growth in the number of hotel and homestay options for longer visits. But just as Yilan has no real center (Yilan City, although the historic political capital, is not the oldest, largest nor economically most important conurbation), similarly for tourists, there is no obvious choice of base. Yilan has a number of interesting old buildings, Jiaoxi has the Northeast's top hot springs, Luodong is the commercial center, Su'ao has the best harbor, Toucheng has the best surfing, Guishan Island is unique in the whole of Taiwan, and the mountains of Sanxing and Datong townships have their sylvan charms.

Michelin Map: p177.

Info: For tourist information: ☎886-03-925 1592. http://tourism. e-land.gov.tw/EN.

Location: Shaped roughly like a triangle along the northeast coast and inland, Yilan County holds the coastal cities of Toucheng and Su'ao, linked by Hwy. 2. Hot-springs haven Jiaoxi, the historic capital Yilan City, and commercial center Luodong are joined by Hwy. 9. Offshore, Guishan Island requires an advance permit to visit. If you wish to tour more than one area, staying overnight in Yilan, Jiaoxi or Luodong is probably the most convenient.

Timing: Take 3-4 days to explore Yilan County. To visit Guishan Island, apply online in advance (*see below*).

Don't Miss: Center for Traditional Arts, Qilan Forest Recreation Area.

Yilan's southern coastline

Mark Caltonhill/Michelin

Hot Springs Etiquette

Taiwan's hot-springs culture is largely an inheritance of the island's 50 years of colonial rule by Japan; so not surprisingly many Japanese practices are followed too.

Baths may be indoors (室內) or outdoors (戶外), private (個人) or communal (大眾池), and the last usually separated by gender into men's pools (男湯) and women's pools (女湯). Normally 湯 *(tang)* means "hot water" or "soup;" only in Japanese, pronounced *yu*, does it also denote "hot spring." Sometimes the wearing of swimming trunks might be required but, more commonly, will not.

Jiaoxi public hot spring

Mark Caltonhill/Michelin

A small towel may be used for modesty and drying oneself; it might be included as part of the entrance fee, or may be purchased. Lockers are usually provided for one's belongings; jewelry, especially silver, which easily corrodes in spring water, should be removed (and better left in your hotel safe). Bathers should take a "shower" before and after using the hot spring. This shower is usually Japanese style, that is, taken squatting on a wooden stool and using a wooden bucket or ladle rather than a shower head.

Hotels in hot-springs resorts often accord with Japanese custom, and guests are encouraged to wander around the lobby, restaurants and other public areas dressed in a bathrobe and slippers.

Alcohol and hot springs are not a good combination, so many resorts specialize in tea, some adopting the Japanese rather than Chinese ritual tea ceremony.

One's choice of base depends on personal interests, but for those wishing to visit more than one of Yilan County's areas, having accommodations in Yilan, Jiaoxi or Luodong is probably the most convenient (see ADDRESSES below). For travelers with their own transportation (car, hired taxi, scooter or bicycle), a drive along the 120km/75mi **North Cross-Island Highway** (Highway 7) from Yilan west through Qilan, then northwest over the hills to Taoyuan County's Fuxing and **Daxi**★★ townships offers spectacular views and a relatively quiet trip. Be forewarned, however, the road is narrow in some places.

Two forest recreation areas, **Mingchi Forest Recreation Area** ★★ and **Qilan Forest Recreation Area**★★, are passed en route.

A BIT OF GEOGRAPHY

Occupying a large swath of coastal and inland terrain southeast of Taipei, Yilan County encompasses 2,167sq km/837sq mi of mountains, valleys, plains, wetlands, sand dunes, and shoreline. The roughly triangle-shaped county, 63km/39mi wide and 74km/46mi long, is hemmed in by Syueshan Mountain and the Central Mountain Range, and opens onto the Pacific Ocean on its east. The Lanyang River flows 73km/45mi from the mountains to the ocean. Offshore sits volcanic Guishan Island.

The county supports an age-old fishing industry and a more recent aquaculture one. It maintains a prosperous agricultural sector, to which food processing and other light industries have been added, though logging and mining interests have declined.

CENTRAL YILAN

The county's main centers of population, the towns of **Luodong**, **Jiaoxi** and **Yilan City**, are located on the lower sections of the Lanyang Plain. They are connected by the East Coast Rail Line, which extends to Taipei to the north and Hualien and Taitung to the south, as well as by Highway 9. Less busy, Highway 2 to the east runs roughly parallel. Transportation between central Yilan and the rest of the county is quick, convenient and inexpensive.

Sights are ordered geographically from north to south.

Jiaoxi★ 礁溪

▶ *Inland along Hwy. 9.*

Northeast Taiwan's premier **hot-springs** destination, the small town of Jiaoxi has dozens of hotels of all sizes and prices offering hourly or overnight use, as well as associated spa and massage treatments. Most are located less than a mile from the train station. There are a few remaining free hot springs used by the locals, though the most famous is now converted to a feet-only tourist attraction.

Wufengqi Waterfall

Mark Caltonhill/Michelin

There is little else to do in town except eat—visitors can choose from many seafood and Japanese-style restaurants—or browse the innumerable "Yilan renowned produce" (宜蘭名產) shops (⚭ *see sidebar*) to select from an array of snacks. One such specialty is Yilan's **a-hsiew** (鴨賞), or smoked duck, that is unique in Taiwan. Most package tours include a trip to a **duck-smoking house**; independent travelers can go by taxi for about NT$300 round trip *(for details, contact the tourist office: 16 Gong-yuan Rd.; ☎03-987 2403).*

Just 4km/2.5mi west of Jiaoxi, off Wufeng Road, are the **Wufengqi Waterfalls★** (五峰旗瀑布), a picturesque series of three falls cascading, the highest of which is 42m/138ft. A wooded trail leads to the falls, and pavilions are popular for photo opportunities. *Avoid weekends.*

Yilan City★ 宜蘭

▶ *10km/6mi south of Jiaoxi along Hwy. 9.*

This city's main claim to fame is that it once had the most circular city wall in Taiwan. Buildings of the most interest are found on the south and west sections of what is now called **Jiucheng** (舊城路 "Old Wall Road"). The **Yang Shi-fang Memorial Garden★** *(楊士芳 紀念林園; 66 Jiucheng West Rd. 舊城西 路66號; ☎03 935 9748)* was the former home of Yilan's first successful imperial candidate and is now an arts center.

The **official residences★** of the magistrate and general section chief of Yilan Prefecture during Japanese rule are worth a visit *(8 Xianfuyi Lane, Jiucheng South Rd.; ⚭ open Tue–Sun 9am–noon & 1pm–5pm; NT$30; ☎03 935 2545)*; one is now a restaurant *(⚭ see ADDRESSES)*.

The **Yilan Distillery★★** *(宜蘭酒廠 3 Jiucheng W. Rd. 舊城西路3號; ⚭ open daily 8am–5pm; ☎03 932 1517)*, the oldest extant alcohol plant in Taiwan, provides a good bilingual introduction to alcohol-making throughout mainland China as well as Taiwan, and its local evolution from aboriginal production, through the Japanese and KMT eras, to today's free-market conditions. *Free samples and sales outlet; snacks available.*

Center for Traditional Arts and its peaceful lake

Mark Caithness/Michelin

For more alcohol production, head southwest through Yuanshan Township (圓山), whose local delicacy is fish-ball rice noodles (魚丸米粉), and along Highway 7 toward the hills. Another 10km/6mi brings you to the **King Car Whisky Distillery** (金車宜蘭威士忌酒廠; *326, Sec. 2, Yuanshan Rd., Yuanshan. 員山路二段326號;* ◷*open daily 9am–5pm;* ✆*03-922-9000 or 03-922-1104; www.kavalanwhisky.com)*, which offers a free tour (10min) and tasting, followed by the inevitable shopping experience. Those interested in Taiwan's pre-Starbucks take on canned coffee can visit the Mr. Brown factory owned by the same concern and located on the same site.

Luodong 羅東

▶ *Situated 10km/6mi south of Yilan City on Hwy. 9.*

The town of Luodong is connected to Yilan by rail line. For all its economic importance, Luodong has little of cultural interest to attract visitors. Among locals it is proably best known for its landscaped **parks** by day, and more for its **night market** *(羅東夜市; Minsheng Rd. 民生路;* ◷*open 6pm until late)* that attracts diners from all over the county and beyond with what is claimed to be the biggest market in northern Taiwan. It is indeed fairly large. Popular snacks include *bu-rou* (卜肉; deep-fried meat in batter), "dragon and phoenix legs" (龍鳳腿; deep-fried pork paste in pig intestine), and deep-fried onion pancakes (蔥油餅). The latter are called "Yilan onion pancakes" throughout Taiwan. People here queue in long lines at their favorite stalls, some of which are so busy they actually operate a bank-style ticketing system.

On the northeast outskirts of Luodong, off Highway 2 in Wujie Township, the **Center for Traditional Arts**★★ *(國立傳統藝術中心; 201, Sec. 2, Wubin Rd., Wujie Township. 五濱路二段201號;* ◷*open*

Renowned Produce

Many areas of Taiwan include local foods as part of their tourism promotion, but perhaps Yilan County does it more than most. Each of the major towns has dozens of shops selling **Yilan Famous Produce** (宜蘭名產), with many more shops lining the approaches to Highway 5 to Taipei and other major thoroughfares.

Typical items include smoked duck meat, or *a-hsiew* (鴨賞) in a local variation of Taiwanese; peanut candy (花生糖); *yang-geng* (羊羹), a bean-paste flavored gelatin dessert; *mwa-ji* (麻糬), cakes made from rice flour and flavorings; onions (蔥) and onion pancakes (蔥油餅); cow-tongue biscuits (牛舌餅); and *mi-jian* (蜜餞), a wide range of preserved fruit.

Homestays

Promoted by the Tourism Bureau as Taiwan's take on bed and breakfast lodgings, homestays (民宿) vary greatly in style and quality. The best include breakfast and options for other meals, possibly in the company of the owners, who are also a font of local information and may organize transportation to nearby sights. At worst they are simply cheap hotel rooms renamed and re-priced.

daily 9am–6pm; NT$150; ℘03 970 5815; www.ncfta.gov.tw) is part museum, part theater, part DIY workshop and part food market. It focuses on Taiwan's folk culture rather than high culture. The spectrum of arts includes puppetry, opera, architecture, temple sculpture, ceramics, woodcarving and handicrafts. The center is a good place to stock up on souvenirs and gifts.

THE MOUNTAINS

Yilan County is bounded on the north, west and south sides by massifs of the Central Mountain Range that ascend to more than 3,000m/10,000ft. Several forestry recreation areas are open to the public; their accommodations are in great demand during peak seasons.

Sanxing★ 三星

▶20km/12mi west into the hills from Luodong.

Yilan County is famous throughout Taiwan for its scallions, and the town of Sanxing is similarly famed throughout Yilan. Onion pancake (蔥油餅) sellers line the streets, and there is even a **Scallion Cultural Hall** (青蔥文化館; 31 Zhongshan Rd., Yide Village. 義德村中山路31號; ⊙open Mon–Fri 8:30am–5pm, Sat–Sun 9am–6pm; ℘03 989 3170). Really a sales promotion center for the local farmers' association, the hall is worth a look if you're in the area. Information about 40 or so local homestays is also available there.

Yulan★ 玉蘭

▶In Datong Township, just on the other side of the Lanyang River.

About a dozen of the area's homestays are located in Yulan. This small tea-growing and leaf-tea-producing community has transformed itself in recent years, and is now an off-beat tourist destination offering accommodations (⨀see ADDRESSES), food and introductions to the local ecosystems and residents' interactions with them.

Aboriginal mural, Yulan

Mark Caltonhill/Michelin

"Sea of clouds," Taipingshan Forest Recreation Area

Mark Caltonhill/Michelin

Qilan Forest Recreation Area★★ 棲蘭國家森林遊樂區

About 39km /24mi southwest of Yilan City. 6, Sec. 4, Taiya Rd., Datong Township. 大同鄉太 平村泰雅路四段6號. *03 980 9606. www.yeze.com.tw.*

Farther west, up the road from Yulan, and at a higher elevation of about 500m/1,640ft, this recreation area is a former forestry nursery that was visited by **Chiang Kai-shek** in the 1960s (his cottage is maintained as he had equipped it). There is an interesting exhibit about veterans who opened roads and worked in the mountains. Local guided **tours** are offered, and marked forest trails, a **restaurant** (**$$**; open daily 6am–8pm) and wood-hut accommodations (**$$$**) complete the amenities. Almost a dozen "scenery suites" with **views** of the river have been added since a 2008 typhoon damaged the area.

Mingchi Forest Recreation Area★★ 明池山莊

17km/10.5mi northwest of Qilan, along Hwy. 7. 1 Mingchi Mountain Villa, Yingshi Village, Datong Township. 英士村明池山莊1號. *03 989 4106. www.yeze.com.tw.*

Government-owned, this recreation area is managed by the same private

company as Qilan Forest, but it sits at the significantly higher altitude of 1,200m/3,940ft.

Here Taiwanese have a rare opportunity to play in the snow, and rooms (**$$**) in the coldest months are quickly sold out. Attractions include a quaint **lake** (NT$150 entry fee), wooded trails, and the **Sacred Forest** (神木園; guided tours NT$800), where some of the cypress trees are thousands of years old. There's also a restaurant (**$$**; open 6am–8pm) on the premises as well as a hotel and cabins.

Taipingshan Forest Recreation Area★★ 太平山國家森林遊樂區

20km/12mi south of Qilan, across Lanyang Valley. Open summer daily 4am–9pm. Rest of the year daily 6am–8pm. NT$200. *03 980 9619. Entry requires a B-class mountain permit (A-class permit for Cuifeng Lake), obtainable on presentation of passport at Taipingshan inspection post.*

The old logging base at this recreation area is popular for a **view**★★ of the sunrise over the **sea of clouds** filling the valley.

Attractions here include an exhibit of forestry equipment and short rides on a **forestry train** (NT$150), but most enjoyable of all may be a hike on the designated forest **trails** and the splendid **views**★ of the surrounding mountains and valleys.

On-site are a **restaurant** (**$**; *open for breakfast, lunch and dinner until 7:30pm*), and accommodations, for which reservations are required (**$$**; ℘*03 954 8757; http://tps.forest.gov.tw*).

SOUTHERN YILAN

The narrowing southern end of Yilan's triangle consists of the coastal Su'ao and mountainous Nan'ao townships. The mountains form a natural boundary with Hualien County to the south.

Su'ao 蘇澳
▶ *About 17km/10.5mi south of Luodong, at Hwys. 2 and 9.*

City Proper
Located at the southern end of the Yilan Plain, Su'ao is a town whose relatively large port handles overflow from Keelung Harbor, to the north. Su'ao serves as the accommodations center of southern Yilan, but its main attraction is its **mineral baths**. In contrast to Jiaoxi's hot springs, Su'ao has an unusual **cold spring resort** (蘇澳冷泉; *6-4 Lengquan Rd.* 冷泉路6-4號; ◷ *open mid-Jun–Aug daily 8am–10pm, Sep–early Jun daily 9am–6pm; NT$70;* ℘*03 996 0645*) that's popular in Taiwan's hotter months. Locals originally thought the 22°C/72°F waters were poisonous; eventually a Japanese soldier set up a bottling factory in the late 19C to produce naturally fizzy drinks. The resort has a large communal pool, and glass-stoppered bottles of fizzy drinks are once again for sale.

The **Yilan Green Expo** (綠色博覽會) is held annually (*Mar–May*) at Su'ao's **Wulaokeng Scenic Area** (武老坑; *61 Xincheng South Rd.* 新城南路61號; ℘*03 995 2852; www.necoast-nsa.gov.tw*). In the other months this pleasant valley of the Wulaokeng River is available for barbecuing, swimming and camping (*NT$400 including tent rental*). The environmentally themed Expo is a privately organized, government-sponsored day-out for families.

Outlying Sights
A short distance inland lies the village of **Baimi** (白米), a small industrial suburb once famous for producing wooden clogs, which has now reinvented itself as the **Baimi Wooden Clog Village**★ (白米木屐村).

The **Wuweigang Bird Sanctuary** (無尾港水鳥保護區; *www.necoast-nsa.gov. tw*), on the coast north of Su'ao, featuring dunes, lakes, woods and seashore, offers habitats for about 300 species of indigenous and migrant birds. Members

Nanfang'ao harbor

Mark Caltonhill/Michelin

of the local bird-watching clubs are on hand on weekends with telescopes and twitchers' manuals to help beginners. Their pride and joy in recent years has been a resident osprey.

The old fishing harbor of **Nanfang'ao**★★ (南方澳), a couple of miles south of Su'ao, is one of the best places to eat. Tourists compete with locals to buy fish as it is unloaded on the quay. Some of Taiwan's freshest seafood can be consumed in the adjacent buildings, either by choosing from the menu or bringing one's purchases from the market for the restaurant cooks to prepare. The third floor of the **Nantian Gong** (南天宫) **Mazu Temple** *(17 Jaingxia Rd. 南正里江夏路17號)* offers great views across the city's rooftops, masts of anchored fishing boats, distant hillocks and the open ocean, while outside, at street level, a colorful religious parade takes place every weekend. For whiling away an hour on a wet afternoon, visit the **Coral Museum** (珊瑚基金會博物館) on a back street *(220 Nan'an Rd. 南安路220號; Wed–Mon 9am–noon & 1pm–5pm; NT$100)* and the **Fishing History and Culture Exhibition** (漁史文物陳列室) at the Nan'an Junior High School (南安國中– *117 Xuefu Rd. 南建里學府路117號. Thu–Tue 9am–5pm).*

South of Su'ao

For most of the next 100km/60mi south from Su'ao to just before Hualien, there are few habitations. The highlight is the natural landscape.

There is little indication of human activity apart from the road, and the railway which it occasionally intersects. Both pass through steep-sided mountain valleys or cling perilously to the steep cliffs, and it is little wonder that construction of both is legendary, not just in engineering circles, but in Taiwan's popular history.

There are a couple of breaks of interest before crossing the Hualien border. The first is the deserted pebble beach of Fen-niaolin (粉鳥林) at **Dong'ao** (東澳). The second is the village of **Nan'ao** (南澳), which has a few restaurants on the main

Exhibit, Coral Museum

Mark Cattonhill/Michelin

street, a church spire in the distance and a sprawling Atayal aboriginal township in between.

The **Nan'ao Atayal Cultural Museum** (南澳鄉泰雅文化館; *2, Lane 379, Sec. 2, Suhua Rd., Nan'ao Township. 南澳鄉蘇花路二段379巷2號; ℘03 998 4601; Tue–Sun 9am–5pm)* has tools, clothing and other artifacts of the local aborigines and introduces the area's natural sights. These attractions include **Shenmi Lake** (神秘湖), **Aohua Waterfall** (澳花瀑布) and **Siqu Hot Springs** (四區溫泉); outdoor pursuits are being planned that will include family rafting, fishing and in-stream hiking.

NORTHERN YILAN AND GUISHAN ISLAND

Most of northern Yilan is a 20km/12mi-long narrow strip of land between the hills of eastern Taipei County and the ocean, shared by the old coast road and railway. The area lacks the beauty of the Bitou and Sandiao capes to the north, as well as the magnificent cliffs of southern Yilan.

There are a few good beaches. Popular with surfers are **Honeymoon Bay** (蜜月灣) and others near **Daxi** (大溪), which has a train station and is therefore accessible from Taipei. There are also some seafood restaurants, a few tourist farms and a crab museum (螃蟹博物館) near **Gengfang** (梗枋).

"Turtle Back" of Guishan Island

Mark Caltonhill/Michelin

Toucheng 頭城

Yilan's "First Town" has an interesting statue composed of a Chinese-language poem in the shape of a three-sailed boat at **Wushi Fishing Harbor** (烏石漁港), the departure point for Guishan Island. The town's real interest lies in only one night of the year. But what a night it is, with teams of young men competing to climb high up greased tree trunks and bamboo lattices to "grapple with ghosts" (搶孤) and secure a flag that is said to bring safety and good harvests to any boat flying it over the coming year. This contest is Toucheng's unusual take on the 7th lunar month **Ghost Festival**. Yet despite being of major interest to the whole of Taiwan, where it is broadcast live on television, the date of the event is announced only a few days in advance.

Guishan Island★★ 龜山島

▶ 10km/6mi east of Toucheng.
Accessible only by boat from Wushi harbor in Toucheng. The island is open Jun–Aug daily 9am–5pm and Mar–Apr daily 9am–4pm. Advance reservations are required at http://kueishan.necoast-nsa.gov.tw/main.php?id=305&lan=c, which requires Chinese-language skills. International visitors are exempt from the 500 visitors per day limit.
Book the 30min voyage separately at Wushi harbor; local boatmen charge a flat fee of NT$1,200 round-trip.

Toucheng's **Wushi** harbor is the embarking point for Guishan, a whole-day excursion possible from Taipei but best as part of a longer visit to Yilan.
Once a remote fishing settlement, then a military outpost and now an uninhabited natural park, Guishan is unlike anywhere else in Taiwan. The small volcanic island is said to resemble a turtle. The **view**★★ of it is especially fine from **Zhuangwei** (壯圍), south of Toucheng.

Visit

Landing on the pier near the turtle's "tail," a strip of rocks that extends out into the sea and "wags" when moved by ocean currents, visitors may take a bamboo pole to ward off snakes and head east to the island's major summit, **401 Peak** (398m/1,306ft high with a 3m/9.8ft watchtower), or walk south to the gun emplacement and ruined village.
The village was evacuated in 1977, and the military barracks in 2000. Fishermen had settled here from the late 19C, but with little arable land and no protected harbor, life was difficult. Remains of the elementary school; neighborhood chief's house; **Putuoyan Temple** (普陀巖; 1901), later rededicated by the military from the seafarers' deity Mazu (媽祖) to their favored bodhisattva Guanyin (觀音); and the .8km/.5mi tunnels with their out-of-date weaponry are all open to the public.

ADDRESSES

STAY

$ Holiday Hotel 假日大飯店 – *38 Gongzheng Rd., Luodong.* 公正路38號. *03 954 5106. 56 rooms.* Typical of hotels clustered around railways stations, the Holiday dates from 30 to 40 years ago when, newly built, it was the best in the area. Often such establishments are now little more than fleabag hotels, but this one has been renovated over the years and is clean, quiet and inexpensive. A good option for budget travelers for whom the old center is of more interest than the new.

$ Joser Bike Hostel – *112, Sec. 5, Suhua Rd., Su'ao.* 蘇花路5段112號. *03 995 1595. 5 rooms. Reservations recommended on weekends.* This hostel is run by the proprietors of the Giant cycle shop as a budget alternative to camping for other cyclists, especially those doing the popular round-island tour. There's little more than a double bed per room and a view onto the Su'ao River—and late-night chats with fellow bikers. Shared bathroom.

$$ Yi Mei Homestay 泡美茶園 – *12 Luchang Rd., Songluo Village, Datong Township.* 松羅村鹿場路12號. *03 980 2053. http://yimei.ilanbnb.tw. 11 rooms. Breakfast included.* One of several homestays in this village, Yi Mei offers well-appointed rooms and modern fixtures in a converted farmhouse, surrounded by tea fields and ever-higher hills. It's a real chill-out spot, a little over an hour from Taipei by car. The setting and the decor make this lodging a special experience unlike Taiwan and yet essential Taiwan. There's free Internet.

$$$$ Art Spa Hotel 中冠礁溪大飯店 – *6 Deyang Rd., Jiaoxi.* 6號. *03 988 2011. www.art-spa-hotel.com.tw. 64 rooms.* This family-oriented hotel has hot springs for the parents, and pools and slides for the kids. Rooms are spacious, available in Western or Japanese style. Conference facilities, karaoke, a restaurant and free Internet round out the amenities. Day tickets are available for non-guests (NT$250/150).

EAT

$ Lianxin 蓮心素食餐坊 – *429, Sec.3, Zhongshan Rd., Yilan City.* 中山路3段429號. *No English sign.* Lianxin is a most unusual Buddhist-run vegetarian restaurant: a classic Chinese-style "he-cai" (合菜) of Lazy-Susan-style shared meals for groups of diners. Many imitations of banquet dishes such as sweet and sour ribs, three-cups chicken, sizzling-plate king oyster mushroom and "lotus leaf steamed tofu." Also rice and noodle dishes for single diners, as well as a "single person shared meal" (個人合菜; NT$150). **Vegetarian.**

$ Rakuzan 樂山 – *1, Lane 108, Sec. 5, Jiaoxi Rd., Jiaoxi.* 礁溪路5段108巷1號. *03 988 8637. Closed Tue.* Jiaoxi means hot springs, hot springs mean Japanese cuisine, and the budget end of the Japanese-food spectrum is ramen noodles. Rakuzan's boss recommends chicken noodles (雞腿拉麵), but there are a dozen others to choose from, including one vegetarian (蔬食拉麵). Sides include greens, tofu, salads and croquettes (可樂餅). In cold weather, Rakuzan offers tables above a foot bath of Jiaoxi hot spring water. **Japanese.**

$$ Musashibou 武藏坊 – *8 Xianfu Yi Lane, Jiucheng South Rd., Yilan City.* 舊城南路縣府一巷8號. *03 935 8855. www.musashibou.com.tw. Locations in Jiaoxi and Luodong.* This mid-price, good-quality Japanese restaurant is housed in the official residence of a chief official during Japanese rule. It advertises "raw, steamed, boiled, grilled, and fried" preparations, and everything from sashimi and sushi to meat-on-rice to hot pots and grills, as well as desserts, teas and sake. Quiet and elegant. **Japanese.**

$$$ Chateau 夏朵 – *356, Sec.2, Binhai Rd., Toucheng.* 濱海路2段356號. *03 977 1168. www.chateau-villa.com.tw.* Actually a private club (a sign on the door asks tourists not to enter, but in fact they are welcome), the Chateau is a grand Mediterranean-style villa with views of Guishan Island. The dinner menu offers steak, lamb, fish and seafood. Chateau's 11 **rooms ($$$)** are available for overnight stays and include breakfast. **Western.**

Hsinchu★★

Founded in 1733, the oldest city in northern Taiwan boasts many Qing- and Japanese-style buildings in its historic core, and half a dozen museums and galleries—some quite unique in Taiwan. This vibrant community centers on a centuries-old temple and Riverside Park and City Moat. One of the museums is devoted to Hsinchu's (新竹) long association with the glass industry and glass arts. Another introduces life in the city's military dependents' villages, a reminder of the aftermath of the ROC government's arrival in 1949. It is an ultramodern metropolis, hosting several leading high-tech companies, which are based in Hsinchu Technology and Science Park—Taiwan's "Silicon Valley," lying just east of downtown. The city is not lacking in original cuisine; two local specialties are *baozi* (steamed dumplings) and duck-meat snacks. Yet, despite all its assets, Hsinchu City is largely missing from the itineraries of most visitors. And this, for a city just an hour by train from Taipei and with a wide range of hotels available for longer visits, which make it an ideal base for exploring Taiwan's northwest region.

▶ **Population:** 390,000.

⏱ **Michelin Map:** p177.

🏢 **Info:** Hsinchu Foreigner Assistance Center: 107 Zhongyang Rd.中央路107號; ℘03 522 9525; http://foreigner.hccg.gov.tw.

◐ **Location:** This northwest city sits inland 8km/5mi from the coast, but on the coastal railroad route, so access by train is convenient. Easily walkable, the historic city center is located close to the main commercial streets of Zhongzheng and Zhongshan Rds., north of the train station.

👪 **Kids:** Leofoo Village in Guanxi, Window on China in Longtan.

🕐 **Timing:** Spend a day, perhaps during March's "Flower Appreciation Month" (賞花月), September's noodle and meatball festival or December's birthday celebrations for the Lord of Walls and Moats.

⊘ **Don't Miss:** City God Temple's traditional mix of religion and food.

Hsinchu's Riverside Park

Mark Caltonhill/Michelin

GETTING THERE

BY TRAIN - Express train from Taipei 70min/NT$180 (train with stops 105min/NT$116); High Speed Rail 35min/NT$290 to Zhubei 11km/7mi east of city.

BY BUS - A competitive route is served by many companies; 80min/NT$130 from/to the train station.

BY CAR - From Taipei, take Highways 1 and 3 (about 80km/50mi).

GETTING AROUND

BY BUS - Local buses serve the city and townships in Hsinchu County; fares from NT$15.

BY CAR - **Easyrent,** a local branch of an islandwide company: 305 Zhonghua Rd., Sec 1; *℘03-542 7755.* From about NT$2500 per day. Renting a car in Taiwan requires an international or Taiwan driver's license, plus a major credit card or a sizable deposit.

BY TAXI - **Taxis** queue at the station and hover around bus terminals, or can be flagged down throughout the city. Fares are reasonable if calculated by meter, and can be bargained for longer distances, e.g. about NT$120 to National Tsing Hua University and NT$200 to Hsinchu Science Park.

GENERAL INFORMATION
AREA CODE

The area code for Hsinchu is 03. It is not necessary to dial 03 when making local calls, but the area code has been included in the telephone numbers in this chapter.

VISITOR INFORMATION
See Info above.

ACCOMMODATIONS

Hsinchu offers a variety of lodgings from large hotels to hostels and homestays. *For a selection of lodgings, see ADDRESSES below.*

SIGHTS
Riverside Park and City Moat★
Linsen Rd. to Beida Rd.

This long strip of canal bisecting the downtown is the city's most popular gathering place—it's a lovely promenade with a landscaped stream, trees and lengthy grassy area. Lots of restaurants line both banks.

Hsinchu City God Temple
新竹市城隍廟
75 Zhongshan Rd. 中山路75號.
Open daily.

This temple lies at the heart of old Hsinchu. First built in 1748 under governmental authority, it has been rebuilt seven times, lastly in 1924. The main deity is the **City God** (城隍爺), "Lord of Walls and Moats" (*see sidebar below*). Typically, there are numerous altars and statues such as **Old Man under the Moon** (月下老人), who is said to bind lovers together with an invisible red string, and more unusually, the **City God's wife** (城隍夫人) and uniquely in

Hsinchu City God Temple

Mark Caltonhill/Michelin

Taiwan, his two sons (大二少爺). Also atypical is the direct access to the Buddhist temple next door.

The temple is surrounded by food stalls and narrow alleyways—seeing it from the street is difficult.

Hsinchu's Food Specialties

The city has a couple of famous dishes that have spawned numerous imitators. They can be purchased at **Xu's Duck Meat** (鴨肉許; *no English; 212 Zhongzheng Rd.* 中正路; *open daily 11am–3pm;* ☎*03 525 3290)*, which, as its name suggests, sells duck-meat noodles, duck sausages and duck-blood pudding. **Black Cat Baozi** *(*黑貓包, *no English sign, 187 Beimen St.* 北門街; ☎*03 523 3560)* has been located at various venues in the old town for more than 110 years and is now in the fifth generation of the Su (蘇) family. Although there are cheaper **baozi** (包子; a kind of doughy dumpling) stores, the lean ground pork and rich gravy of Black Cat's NT$20 version mean that people still travel here from afar; the current owner claims to sell up to 17,000 per day.

Temple Market

The "temple entrance" market is open day and evening, and sells all the Hsinchu classics, including **meatballs** (貢丸) usually served in thin soup, **rice noodles** (米粉), and pork **meatballs in dough** (肉圓). The presence of the Buddhist temple ensures one or two vegetarian options. If these few dozen stalls are insufficient to sample all Hsinchu has to eat, the city holds an annual noodle and meatball food festival during the last two weeks of September.

City Museums

Hsinchu's many museums include the **Fire Museum** *(*消防博物館; *4 Zhongshan Rd.* 中山路4號; ☎*03 522 2050;* ☎*open Tue–Sun 9am–5pm, Sat until 9pm)*, which features old equipment and educational displays on preventing fires, and the **Image Museum** *(*影像博物館; *65 Zhongzheng Rd.* 中正路65號; ☎*03 528 5849;* ☎*open Wed–Sun 9:30am–noon, 1:30pm–5pm & 6:30pm–9pm; NT$20)* ensconced in a 1930s music hall, and now showing old movies and contemporary art films.

The **Residence of Hsin Chih-ping** *(*辛志平校長故居; *32 Dongmen St.* 東門街32號; ☎*open Wed–Sun 9am–5pm;* ☎*03 524 5965)* has been preserved as a Japanese-era dormitory later used by Mr. Hsin, Taiwan's "sage of education."

The **Art Gallery and Reclamation Hall** *(*美術館暨開拓館; *116 Zhongyang Rd.* 中央路116號; ☎*open Wed–Sun 9am–5pm;* ☎*03 524 7218)* provides an overview of the city's development and showcases a collection of art.

Behind the train station, the **Glass Museum** *(*玻璃工藝博物館; *2 Dongda Rd.* 東大路3號; ☎*open Wed–Sun 9am–5pm; NT$20;* ☎*03 562 6091)* traces the city's long connection with the glass industry and glass arts.

Noodles at Temple Market

Mark Caltonhill/Michelin

Exhibit, Military Dependents' Villages Museum

Mark Caltonhill/Michelin

Most fascinating is the **Military Dependents' Villages Museum**★ *(眷村博物館; 105, Sec. 2, Dongda Rd.* 東大路二段 *105號;* ⏰ *open Wed–Sun 9am–5pm;* ℘*03 533 8442)*, which presents a slice of Taiwan's demographic pie. With the arrival of about one million immigrants from mainland China following the defeat of Chiang Kai-shek's Republican forces by Mao Zedong's Communists, many military dependents' villages were set up throughout Taiwan. **Eleven** such villages still exist in Hsinchu, and this museum depicts the spartan lives of their inhabitants and the culture that blossomed. Try to talk to a member of the staff; many of them grew up in such villages and know more than is explained in the exhibits.

EXCURSIONS
Guanxi★ 關西
▶ *28km/18mi east of Hsinchu via Hwy. 3.*
Nicknamed Long Life Town (長壽鄉), this Hakka farming town on the eastern edge of Hsinchu County is best known for having reasonably priced **golf courses** within driving distance of Taipei. Surrounded by forested hills, Guanxi enjoys a good climate and clear air.
It is home to 🎡**Leofoo Village**★ *(六福村; 60 Gongzigou, Ren'an Neighborhood*新竹縣關西鎮仁安里拱子溝 *60號;* ⏰ *open Jul–Aug daily 9am–9:30pm, rest of the year see website; NT$890, children NT$590/790;* ℘*03 547 5665;*

www.leofoo.com.tw/village). Already a well-established safari park, Leofoo reopened in 1994 as a Disney-style **Wild West** theme park with roller coasters and stunt and cabaret acts. It immediately became Taiwan's No.1 attraction of its genre. Subsequent additions included **South Pacific** and **Arabian Kingdom**, as well as the redesigned **African Safari**. *For those coming from Taipei, shuttle buses on weekends and through summer months from Taipei's Leofoo Hotel* (六福客棧).
South of Guanxi, 17ha/42 acres of forest have been transformed into the **Mautu Discovery Forest**★ *(馬武督探索森林;*

Leofoo Village

Mark Caltonhill/Michelin

The City God

Like many Chinese deities, the Lord of Walls and Moats (城隍爺), better known as the City God, is a position rather than an individual, and sometimes he is both. His status as a representative of heaven's authority on earth requires him to record citizens' moral behavior as well as their birth and death. Worshipers pray for his protection and prosperity, and report births and deaths. But he may also be a commemoration of some local worthy. He's the urban equivalent of the **Lord of the Land** (土地公), having come to the fore during the Tang dynasty (618-907), when China underwent a period of city building.

Many of his subordinate officials are found in his temples, including **Judge Wen** (文判官) for civil matters, **Judge Wu** (武判官) for military affairs, **Lord Ox** (牛爺), **Lord Horse** (馬爺), and **Seventh Lord** (七爺) and **Eighth Lord** (八爺), all of whom help him keep tabs on people's behavior and reward benevolence, or punish wickedness in the courts of hell.

The City God's birthday is celebrated on different days in different cities. In Hsinchu, the City God celebrates three birthdays during the year, but the most important falls on the 29th day of the 11th lunar month.

138-3 Jinshan, Jinshan. 新竹縣關西鎮錦山里12鄰錦山138-3號 🕐 *open Jun–Sept Mon–Fri 8:30am–5:30pm, Sat–Sun 8am–6pm; rest of the year Mon–Fri 9am–5pm, Sat–Sun 8:30am–5:30pm; NT$120; 📞03 547 8645; www.discovery-forest.com.tw).* 🥾 Attractions at Mautu include waterfalls, hiking trails, ecological education, an introduction to **mushroom farming** (for which Guanxi's climate and altitude are well-suited), and at the end of the day, barbecues on open fires. Its popularity really took off, especially with teenagers, after a soap opera starring young actors was filmed here.

Set in even more spectacular countryside to the north—actually in Xinpu Township—**The One** *(南園; 32 Jiuqionghu, Xinpu Township* 新竹縣新埔鎮九芎湖32號; 📞03 589 0011; http://nanyuan.theonestyle.com)* is a palatial hillside complex of classical Chinese buildings tastefully designed as a getaway from city life. A minimalist Zen style pervades the gardens, lakes, and restaurants serving healthy foods (NT$1280 up), guest rooms (NT$3600 per person and up), conference facilities and spa. Opened in 2007, it is the latest addition to The One's integrated-design themed busi-

Longtan's wood-burning furnace

Mark Cattonhill/Michelin

Exhibit, Window on China

Mark Caltonhill/Michelin

nesses, wherein every detail down to the last chopstick is created for the retreat. Everything is for sale too, but not ostentatiously: what The One is selling is a lifestyle. It is open to the public (*daily 9am–5pm; NT$400 fee*).

Longtan 龍潭

▶ *35km/22mi northeast of Hsinchu, but best combined with a visit to Guanxi via Hwy. 3.*

Sitting on the western edge of Taoyuan County, Longtan is worth considering as part of a visit to Guanxi, which lies just 8km/5mi to the southwest. The town is a good place to see **dragon boat racing** in the fifth lunar month (*usually Jun*), and has one of the few remaining **word-burning furnaces** in northern Taiwan. Hakka people, who emphasize learning and knowledge, traditionally did not casually dispose of old paper with written or printed script on it, but brought it to burn in a form of religious offering. Now a protected historical site, the **brick furnace** stands in a small public park.

Another theme park in the Guanxi-Longtan area is **Window on China**★ (*小人國樂園; 60-2 Henggangxia, Gaoyuan Village, Longtan* 桃園縣龍潭鄉高原村橫岡下60-2號; *open Jul–Aug daily 9am–8pm, Sat–Sun until 9pm; rest of the year daily 9am–5pm, Sat–Sun until 6pm; NT$499; 03 471 7211; www.woc.com. tw*). Opened in 1984 Window on China

was one of Taiwan's first amusement parks and has remained consistently in the top 10 in popularity. That record is quite an achievement for what is essentially a collection of **miniature models** of famous landmarks, mainly in Taiwan and mainland China (its Chinese name means "Little People Country," the translation of Lilliput).

A **miniature train** tours the nearby tea fields. Performances include Chinese acrobats. Standard **midway rides** were subsequently added to attract teenagers beyond the park's core audience of families with younger children.

Buses leave for Window on China from Taipei's Zhongxiao-Dunhua Station (and elsewhere) throughout the morning. For more information, call 02 2796 5665.

Neiwan★★ 內灣

▶ *32km/20mi southeast of Hsinchu via Expressway 68 and Provincial Hwy. 3 or train departing regularly from Hsinchu Railway Station.*

Despite its small size and limited sights, Neiwan is one of northern Taiwan's major tourist destinations. Settled in the northern foothills of the Central Mountain Range, this quiet community retains many traditional buildings and offers a range of Hakka cuisine. In addition to its New Year **cherry blossom festival**, Neiwan attracts visitors to see its fireflies (*late Apr–early May*), and its **tung flower**

Vegetarianism

Taiwan is one of the best destinations in the world for vegetarian travelers, largely due to the Chinese interpretation of the Buddhist precept (戒) "do not kill" (不殺生). This precept is taken as meaning "do not kill any sentient being," that is, any member of the animal kingdom, which the religion views as capable of eventual attainment of Buddhahood.

Chinese Buddhism adopted the Hindu **swastika** (卍; *wàn* in Mandarin), which is used for temple decoration; if on a restaurant exterior, the symbol means vegetarian food is served.

Far more common now is 素 (*sù*; originally meaning "simple undyed silk") or more often 素食 (*sù-shí*; "simple food"). Variations on the latter, especially on packaged foods, include 純素 (*chún-sù*; "pure vegetarian," i.e. vegan), 素食可 (*sù-shí-kě*; "ok for vegetarians"), 奶素 (*nǎi-sù*; "dairy vegetarian") and 蛋素 (*dàn-sù*; "egg vegetarian"). Where it is necessary to distinguish, non-vegetarian food is marked 葷 (*hūn*).

The character 齋 (*zhāi*), which visitors may know from elsewhere in Southeast Asia, is not used to indicate vegetarian food in Taiwan. It does occur in terms such as 齋堂 (*zhāi-táng*), the cafeteria at a Buddhist monastery, or 齋戒 (*zhāi-jiè*), to fast.

The areas around temples are good places to look for vegetarian restaurants. Daoists, as well as Buddhists, make vegetarian vows, and although most people do not know it, most vegetarian restaurants are run by members of the Yiguandao (一貫道) religion, which combines Buddhist, Daoist, Confucian and Christian teachings. The only disappointment for Western vegetarians is that Buddhist rules forbid the consumption of the "five pungent foods" (五辛), which are said to incite sexual desires, and so garlic and various onions rarely appear in Taiwan's vegetarian fare.

festival (May–Jun), held later than elsewhere because of the altitude.

Its popularity is also due in part to its location as the terminal station of the **Hsinchu Branch Railway Line**, whose route to Neiwan is especially picturesque. One of few branch lines still operating, it was built to carry camphor and other timber products out of the mountains. From Hsinchu small passenger trains make their way slowly up into the hills; visitors jump out to take photos at the attractive stations along the route.

Neiwan's mountain station

Mark Cattonhill/Michelin

After you visit Neiwan, **Zhudong** is a good stop from which to take a bus or taxi to Beipu, 6km/3.7mi away.

Neiwan's own **wooden train station**, dating from the 1950s, is the first photo opportunity after arrival.

The trains have such a lengthy turnaround time that visitors can even climb the hill on the other side of the tracks to photograph the train, station and wooded hill beyond.

Neiwan also boasts Taiwan's sole remaining wooden Japanese-era **police substation**★ (內灣派出所). Notice the artistically decorated toilet behind it and the cherry trees in front—and imagine the life of a Japanese policeman sent to maintain order on the frontier of this new and still rather wild colony.

On the north side of the railway, the **Liu Xing-qin Cartoon Studio** (劉興欽漫畫暨發明館, *no English*) is housed in the home and workshop of a local artist.

The town's real treat sits at the west end of the old street (*Zhongzheng Rd.*): the historic wooden **Neiwan Theater**★★ (內灣戲院; *227 Zhongzheng Rd.* 中正路227號; ○*open Mon–Fri 9am–5pm, later on weekends;* ℰ*03-584 9260*) has been renovated to its original condition and turned into a restaurant that shows old Taiwanese movies one after another. Memorabilia covers every inch of the walls, and at the entrance, souvenir postcards and posters are sold.

Otherwise unexceptional, the old street offers an opportunity to buy various handicrafts and just about every Hakka snack, such as *cai-bao* (菜包 steamed dumplings), *cao-bo* (菜脯 dried radish), *mei-gan cai* (梅干菜 dried mustard greens), *tang-cong* (糖蔥 "sugar onions," a kind of candy) and *ye-jiang hua* (野薑花 the edible ginger lily flower).

There are also numerous restaurants, but really only one menu: Hakka. Classic dishes include bitter gourd with salted egg (苦瓜鹹蛋), pork with dried mustard greens (梅干扣肉), Hakka stir fry (客家小炒), pork intestine with ginger (薑絲大腸), and because Neiwan is in the mountains, *guo-mao* (過貓; an edible fern).

Pounded Tea

"Pounded tea" with seeds, nuts and grains, *léi-chá* (擂茶) is a Hakka tradition rediscovered for the tourist boom. It's tasty, and is possibly something like the original way tea was drunk in China, being more of a soup-like food than the drink it is today.

Beipu★★ 北埔

⊙ *29km/18mi southeast of Hsinchu via Expressway 68 and Provincial Hwy. 3.*

Because of its buildings of architectural interest, traditional restaurants, and clever marketing to position it as the touristic capital of northern **Hakka** culture, this farming community of some 10,000 residents attracts thousands of visitors every week.

The main sights all lie in and around the town center, within easy walking distance of **Citian Temple**★ (慈天宮; *1 Beipu St.*,北埔鄉北埔街1號; ℰ*03-580-1575*). Built in 1835 this grade-three protected building has been renovated several times. The main deities worshiped here are the bodhisattva **Guanyin** of Buddhism in the center, the **Three Officials** (三官大帝) of the Three Realms: Heaven, Earth and Water) of Daoism on the left, and on the right, the **Three Mountain Kings** (三山國王 from Guandong Province in mainland China), uniquely worshiped by Hakka.

Beipu house

Mark Cattonhill/Michelin

Beipu lane

Mark Caltonhill/Michelin

Jinguangfu Hall★★ (金廣福公館 6 Zhongzheng Rd.,北埔鄉中正路6號 ⌐ not open to public) dating from 1835, was the headquarters of a joint private Hakka-Hoklo venture with Qing-court backing to open up new land for colonization. Its name derived from 金 "gold," an auspicious first character; 廣 Guang[dong], the Hakka homeland; and 福 Fu[jian], the Hoklo homeland. In the face of aboriginal resistance, the organization raised a militia, which later also saw action in the Opium and Sino-French wars. Following damage in the 1935 earthquake, the right side was rebuilt in the Japanese style; the left retains the Qing original. It is the island's only first-class historic site in the Taoyuan-Hsinchu-Miaoli area.

The major Hakka shareholder in Jinguangfu was **Jiang Xiu-luan** (姜秀鑾, 1783-1846), and his descendents still occupy the nearby **Tianshui Hall** (天水堂; 1 Zhongzheng Rd.,北埔鄉中正路1號; ⌐ not open to the public) he built sometime around 1835. Locals call Tianshui Hall "Jiang's Old House," but there is another mansion built by a later head of the family and named after him: **Jiang A-xin's Residence** (姜阿新故宅; 10 Beipu St. 北埔街10號; ⌐ not open to the public). Constructed during Japanese rule, it is designed in accordance with the colonialists' passion for classical Western style.

Other than these, explore the narrow old streets, eat in one of the numerous inexpensive Hakka restaurants in front of the temple.

Popular in summer, **Beipu Cold Spring** (北埔冷泉) is a slightly alkaline river located in the Daping River Valley, 7km/4.5mi southwest of Beipu.

About 5 km/3mi east of central Beipu, the ecology-based theme park **Green World**★ (綠世界; Neighborhood 7, 20 Dahu Village 大湖村7鄰20號; ⏰open daily 8:30am–5:30pm; NT$350; ✆03 580 1000; www.green-world.com.tw) is set on 70ha/173 acres of forested land; it pursues the difficult task of balancing a natural environment with educational and leisure facilities. Food outlets include a restaurant inside a restored Hakka farmhouse.

Cave Monasteries

Buddhist monks are ordained (commonly called "leaving home" 出家) under the auspices of other monastics who claim lineage back centuries, and even millennia, to different schools and sects of the faith. They may then spend the rest of their lives serving in the original monastery, or may leave and form a new community of their own.

New communities are sometimes established after a monk's period of contemplation, which may have taken place in the seclusion of a mountain cave. If he attracts a following of lay supporters who take care of his worldly needs (some of whom may ultimately seek to tonsure and follow his teachings), the new religious community, and sometimes even a new monastery, tends to be established at the site of his meditation.

The Hakka 客家人

Traditional Hakka shop

Meaning "guest people," the term Hakka possibly started as a pejorative word for northern outsiders migrating into mainland China's southern Guandong, Gunagxi and Fujian provinces. Alternatively, it was a title given—along with financial incentives—to immigrants with farming skills needed to repopulate coastal territories evacuated during the prolonged Qing court 17C takeover of Ming territories. Either way, the appellation has long since been adopted with pride by the Hakka people themselves.

Their origins—and even whether they truly represent a subgroup within the **Han Chinese** ethnicity—are not clear. The standard explanation is that social unrest, wars and famine caused waves of migration from northern to southern China from early in the first millennium AD through early in the second millennium.

Indeed, many Hakka kept moving, and today, numbering as many as 100 million, they are prominent in Chinese communities throughout Southeast Asia and farther afield. They were also among the first to arrive in Taiwan, but later found themselves outnumbered by Hoklo-speaking people from Fujian Province, and largely settled in more marginal mountainous regions rather than the fertile plains. Perhaps because of these land limitations, Hakka tended to emphasize education, and succeed in certain occupations, including the police force and railways.

Originally representing about one-quarter of the population, following the influx in 1949 of large numbers of civil-war refugees accompanying Chiang Kai-shek, they now represent just under 15 percent of Taiwan's population. Such figures are inexact because of assimilation, intermarriage and loss of mother-tongue use; nevertheless the Hakka retain their distinctive language (with a number of dialects) and cultural characteristics in cuisine, architecture, religion and attire. One source of pride is that Hakka women traditionally did not bind their feet like many Chinese, probably because they performed more work in agriculture and construction.

Majority Hakka communities are found in Taoyuan, Hsinchu, Miaoli, Kaohsiung and Pingtung counties, with as many as 400,000 residing in Taipei. Their interests are represented by the central-government Council for Hakka Affairs (客家委員會; www.hakka.gov.tw), established in 2001. Taiwan has hosted the **World Hakka Congress** five times, most recently in 2006.

Taiwan's first elected president Lee Teng-hui (李登輝) is Hakka, as were "Founder of the Nation" Dr. Sun Yat-sen (孫逸仙), and Soong Mei-ling (宋美齡), wife of Chiang Kai-shek. Other prominent Hakka include co-founder of the Democratic Progressive Party Hsu Hsin-liang (許信良) and its first female chairperson Tsai Ing-wen (蔡英文), film directors Hou Hsiao-hsien (侯孝賢) and Edward Yang (楊德昌) and Olympic taekwondo gold medalist Chu Mu-yen (朱木炎).

Rich J. Matheson/Michelin

211

Shitoushan★ 獅頭山

🚗 *About 32km/20mi southeast of Hsinchu on Country Rd. 124 via Zhunan.*

By Car: *Head south to Zhunan, then Country Rd. 124 in the direction of Nanzhuang.* **By Bus:** *Buses to Nanzhuang from Hsinchu pass within 1.5km/1mi of the Quanhua Temple; ask the driver where to get off.*

Named for the perceived similarity of its tree-covered spurs and peaks to the head of a lion, Shitoushan, meaning "Lion-Head Mountain," is indeed a magnificent beast. (Chinese imperial artisans were expected to craft the likeness of a lion, an African animal they had never seen—hence the strange-looking beasts outside temples in China and Chinese restaurants in the West.) Straddling 24,221ha/59,851 acres across the Hsinchu-Miaoli county boundary,

492m/1,614ft-high Shitoushan offers a pleasant half-day excursion from Hsinchu. An overnight option is to stay in the guesthouse of the **Quanhua Monastery** (勸化堂) in Nanzhuang Township (🕭 *see ADDRESS below*), and eat monastic vegetarian meals (**$**), including breakfast *(served daily; dinner ends at 6pm)*, with other tourists, not the monks (🕭 *see sidebar "Vegetarianism"*).

In addition to the mountain's natural beauty, there is the semi-natural beauty of "fifth-month snow" (五月雪)—**white-tung tree** (油桐) blossoms falling gently to the ground ("semi-natural" because these trees were introduced as a cash crop during the period of Japanese rule). But the main attraction is the 11 **temples**, most of which started as **cave locations** for ascetic practice (🕭 *see sidebar p210*).

Official "Tribes"

Properly the English word "tribe" means village, but it has also been used in the past to refer to whole ethnic groups. Similarly in Taiwan, both *buluo* (部落; village) and *zu* (族; ethnic group) are frequently translated as "tribe." Regarding the English name "aborigine," although it may not be ideal, this term was selected by Taiwan's indigenous people themselves when they adopted the Chinese term *Yuanzhumin* (原住民; Original Dwelling People) to replace such earlier terms as *Shandiren* (山地人; Mountain Region People) and *Fan* (番; Barbarian).

Hla'lua dance, Namasia
Rich J. Matheson/Michelin

Regarding the 14 officially recognized ethnic groups, since their names were largely derived from Japanese anthropologists' investigations—sometimes by questioning neighboring groups—which were then adopted by Chinese and transliterated into English, many errors are still being sorted out, such as Yami for the Tao people of Orchid Island, and Amis for those of eastern Taiwan who call themselves Banzah.

Of the other mostly assimilated or extinct groups, many lived at lower altitudes and so were referred to as *Pingpu Zu* (平埔族; Plains Peoples). This group is frequently misidentified as a 15th ethnic group, whereas in reality, there were a dozen or more groups, each with their own names, languages and cultures. Their interests are represented by the central-government Council of Indigenous Peoples (原住民族委員會; www.apc.gov.tw), which was established in 1996.

Shitoushan temple entrance

Mark Caltonhill/Michelin

The original caves have been added to so greatly that they are barely dissimilar from urban or rural temples. As long as you don't expect the likes of the sculptures at Luoyang or Datong in mainland China, you will have a pleasant wander. Unfortunately, most of the temples are open to the public only on Sundays, when the hill is at its busiest. Be sure to respect the signs 閉關中勿擾 ("In retreat, do not trouble").

The main **trail**—actually a road for the most part—runs about 4km/2.5mi from the car park below the monastery at the south side, up and across the hill, passing near all the temples, and then down to the **Lion's Head Mountain Visitor Center** (獅頭山旅遊服務中心; 60-8 Liouliao, Qixing Village, Emei Township.峨眉鄉七星村六寮60-8號; ⊙open daily 8:30am–5:30pm; ℘03 580 9296; www.trimt-nsa.gov.tw/cht/subsite.aspx?fname=lion). The center is a good source for maps and leaflets, and has exhibits about the area's ecology and human culture.

There are maps in Chinese along the trail, but it is not easy to get lost: there really is only one route. The most interesting sights, from south to north, include calligraphy carved into the rock face (石壁文字); a stele marking the Miaoli-Hsinchu border; the **Moon-Watching Pavilion** (望月亭) with views across Miaoli; the **Lingxia Cave**★ (靈霞洞), which looks like a Baroque French

church outside but is completely Chinese Buddhist inside, and is one of few temples open every day; the elegant and calm **Jin-gang Temple**★ (金剛寺) with its cave origin still apparent; and the **Wanfo Nunnery** (萬佛庵).

Nanzhuang 南庄鄉

▶40km/25mi southeast of Hsinchu by County Rd. 124 via Zhunan.
By Car: From Hsinchu head south to Zhunan, then take Country Rd. 124.
The rural area of Nanzhuang Township in Miaoli County to the south of Shitoushan is far less developed. Its forests, aboriginal and Hakka communities, and mountain peaks rising to 2,200m/7,218ft

Lingxia Cave

Mark Caltonhill/Michelin

provide an idea of what Taiwan was like in earlier times.

Exploring the area requires your own transportation. Country Road 124 through the west side of the township offers a scenic diversion from Highway 3 heading toward central Taiwan, while Highway 21, which climbs steadily through the eastern side, is more interesting but leads to a dead end.

Your first stop should be the **Nanzhuang Visitor Center** (南庄旅遊服務中心; *151 Zhongzheng Rd., East Village;* 中正路151號; ○ *open daily 8:30am–5:30pm;* ✆ *03 782 4570),* which has maps and leaflets and can help book homestay accommodations *(alternatively www. ioneone.com; Chinese only).*

The area just north of the Nanzhuang Bridge is the commercial center. It is inhabited mostly by Hakka, who made their living from timber and charcoal in earlier times. Aborigines from outlying areas can be seen selling vegetables along the road.

Heading east, then south along Highway 21 brings you to the **Walo Visitor Center** (瓦祿產業文化館; *78 Donghe Village 5 Neighborhood;* 苗栗縣南庄鄉東河村5鄰78號; ○ *open Wed–Mon 9:30am–6pm;* ✆ *03-782 3 050).* This modern wooden building has exhibits introducing the culture of the local **Saisiyat** (賽夏) ethnic group *(*🕯*see sidebar)* and sells handicrafts and local produce.

Most interesting are the **photographs** of tribal life 50-60 years ago. A cafe has drinks and snacks for sale.

A more thorough introduction to this group, one of Taiwan's smallest extant ethnicities, is offered at **Saisiyat Culture Hall** *(*賽夏族文物館; *25 Xiangtianhu, Donghe Village;* 向天湖25號; ○ *open Tue–Sun 9am–5pm;* ✆ *03-782 5024),* a short distance farther down Highway 21, after turning right and crossing the river. With limited displays, the hall, indeed the whole community, is best visited during the biennial **Pas-taai Ceremony** honoring the dwarf people from whom, according to tribal legend, the Saisiyat gained their knowledge and culture. This location, beside the small **Xiangtian Lake** (向天湖), witnesses its cultural climax on the 15th day of the 10th lunar month every even-numbered year, with especially large events every decade (next in 2016).

Back on Highway 21, the higher-altitude area farther up the valley is home to **Atayal** (泰雅族) aborigines, one of Taiwan's most numerous indigenous groups. It has cultural halls elsewhere; here there are a few restaurants and homestays.

Of most interest are the 🚶 **hiking trails** leading to 2,220m/7,283ft-high **Mount Jiali** (加里山) and 1990m/6,529ft-tall **Mount Hakanni** (哈堪尼山).

ADDRESSES

For price categories, 🕯*see Legend on the front cover flap. All hotels in Taiwan are non-smoking. Most hotels, especially the high-end properties, recommend or require reservations; to be safe, book in advance*

🏠 STAY

HSINCHU

$ East City Hotel 東城大旅館 *– Lane 5, 1 Fuhou St., Hsinchu.* 府後街5巷1號 . ✆*03-522 2648. 28 rooms. Breakfast included.* Located right in Hsinchu's cultural heart, where young lovers spoon beside the landscaped stream and diners frequent some of the

trendiest restaurants, the East City targets short-term as well as overnight trade, but avoids the seediness that often characterizes the former. Clean establishment, friendly staff, good value for budget travelers. The same boss has another hotel nearby *(*✆*03-524 3164)* at similar rates should this one fill up.

$$ Wego Boutique Hotel Hsinchu 薇閣精品旅館 *– 137 Zhongzheng Rd., Hsinchu.* 中正路137號. ✆*03-523 8080; www.we-go.com.tw/hsinchu. 72 rooms. Breakfast buffet.* Actually part of a motel chain, Wego is famed throughout Taiwan for its themed rooms aimed at lovers. Choose from 19 designs, with four-poster beds, two-person spa baths and world views from the "windows" including "Monaco at night," "secret garden," "Bali villa." But beware you might get your photo in the newspaper because the paparazzi hang out at the Taipei branch to snap photos of Taiwan's rich and famous getting up to mischief. Free Internet.

$$$$ Howard Plaza Hotel Hsinchu 福華大飯店新竹 – *178 Zhongzheng Rd., Hsinchu.* 中正路178號. *03-528 2323. www.howard-hotels.com. 125 rooms. Breakfast included.* This hotel is the best choice to be close to the historic downtown area of Hsinchu. There are two restaurants (Western buffet and Cantonese) plus a bar, with all the facilities of a Howard at a fraction the cost of Taipei. Free shuttle to Science Park and glass museum, walking distance of other museums and nightlife. A swimming pool and gym are on the premises.

SHITOUSHAN
$ Quanhua Monastery 勸化堂 – *242 Shishan Village, Nanzhuang Township, Miaoli County.* 獅山村17鄰 242號. *03-782 2563; www.1-god. com.tw/lion/; 40 rooms.* For your stay in the Shitoushan area, be sure to get an even-numbered room for a magnificent view past the classically shaped pagoda (actually part of the cemetry) across the valley toward Nanzhuang and central Miaoli. Double or twin option (if you book early) plus a few 4-bed guest rooms.

⊠/EAT

HSINCHU
$ Jia Zhu Ting 家竹亭– *16 Wenhua St., Hsinchu.* 文化街6號. *03-535 9910. Closes 9pm.* 🪑. Authentic Japanese low-end food in authentic Japanese atmosphere, located beside a pleasant park with cooling river. Basic menu includes rice dishes, barbecued meats and fish, and pork cutlets with curry sauce. Just 9 tables on a first-come, first-served basis. Chinese-English-Japanese menu. **Japanese.**

$$ Xinqiao Yinjiucang 新橋隱酒藏 – *18 Wenhua St., Hsinchu.* 文化街8號. *03-534 0828. Dinner only.* Next to Jia

Quanhua Monastery

Mark Caltonhill/Michelin

Zhu Ting (which is equally authentic, but has a different owner and a different style), this is the Xinqiao sake bar (there are other branches in the area focusing on different aspects of Japanese cuisine) selling grilled fish and meat, sushi and sashimi, seafood, but all best washed down with Japanese beer and spirits. Chinese-English-Japanese menu. **Japanese.**

🛒 SHOPPING

In Hsinchu's old town, visit the **puppet store** (國達批霹靂精品; *no English; 109 Beimen St.* 北門街109號; *03-525 0289).* Glove, string and stick-operated puppets have a special place in Taiwanese culture. Many older people remember when there was little entertainment in rural villages, so the arrival of a traveling puppeteer was a treat. Puppetry has changed with the times and now younger people watch puppet shows on television with laser lighting, smoky explosions and swashbuckling storylines.

🍸 NIGHTLIFE

On evenings and weekends Hsinchu's **City Moat and Riverside Park** attracts crowds to its restaurants for an enjoyable evening.
Lane 18, **Guanghua Street** (光華街 18巷) slightly north of the old center, mostly consists of bars and cafes; on warm evenings customers spill out onto the small, pleasant, tree-lined plaza on the lane's north side.

CENTRAL TAIWAN

Central Taiwan is not the most famous or exotic region in Taiwan, but it completely captures the essence of the island. Central Taiwan has the most scenic alpine road in Taiwan—the Central Cross-Island Highway—as well as its tallest peak, Yushan, and top mountain getaway, Alishan Forest Recreation Area. It is home to the widely attended Dajia Mazu Pilgrimage, a 200km/124mi, nine-day religious parade that loops through the region every April. The region's historical attractions include the well-preserved Qing-era town of Lugang and a remarkable narrow-gauge rail line built by the Japanese in 1912. Nor is it short on modern sights: Sun Moon Lake is a favorite island playground with a scenic new cable car, and nearby there's an astonishing monastery, completed in 2001.

Highlights

1   Modern monastic life at **Chung Tai Chan monastery** (p229)

2   Old town of **Lugang** and its magnificent temples (p233)

3   The beauty and tranquility of **Sun Moon Lake** (p239)

4   **Alishan Forest Railway's** thrilling mountain ride (p256)

5   Spectacular mountain sunrise at **Zhushan** (p258)

The Region Today

The area extends north to south from the Dajia River to Chiayi, and from the flat shores of the Taiwan Strait in the west to the alpine peaks of the Central Mountain Range in the east. Its cultural hub is the user-friendly city of Taichung, known for its museums, universities and atmospheric teahouses, and for its fresh seafood and regional Chinese cuisines.

Not everything in the region is scenic. It is the cradle of Taiwan's economic miracle, and much of the central plain is an unsightly sprawl of factories, tile-clad buildings and charmless small towns. Taichung is easy to reach: just two hours from Taipei by car or bus on Freeway 1, and an hour away on the high-speed rail. Lugang lies 45min from Taichung by road, while the drive to Sun Moon Lake takes less than 90min.

Chiayi, the jumping-off point for trips to Alishan and Yushan, is a three-hour road trip from Taipei, or a 90min jaunt on the High Speed Rail. Taichung Airport serves the outlying islands and cities on the east coast.

Temperatures are similar to those in Taipei, but it's drier here. The lowlands and Sun Moon Lake are year-around destinations, although they can be rainy in the spring. The high mountains are at their best from September through November.

Sunset, Chilai Ridge

Brent Hannon/Michelin

216

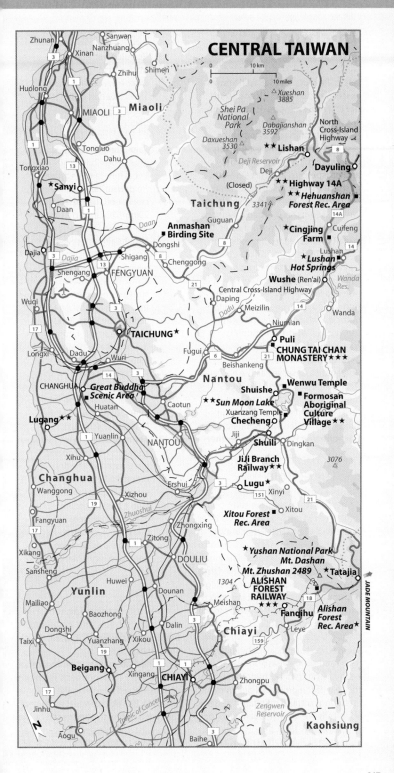

CENTRAL TAIWAN

Zhunan
Sanwan
Nanzhuang
Xinan
Zhihu
Shimen
Huolong
MIAOLI
Miaoli

Tongluo
Dahu
Tongxiao

△ Xueshan 3885

Shei Pa National Park

Dabajianshan 3592 △

North Cross-Island Highway

Daxueshan 3530 △

★★ **Lishan**

Deji Reservoir

Deji

Dayuling

★ **Sanyi**
Daan

(Closed)

★★ **Highway 14A**
★★ **Hehuanshan Forest Rec. Area**

Taichung
3341 △

Dajia
Dajia
Shigang

Anmashan Birding Site
Dongshi

Chenggong

★ **Cingjing Farm**
Cuifeng

Lushan

Shengang
FENGYUAN

★ **Lushan Hot Springs**

Wushe (Ren'ai)
Wanda Res.

Wuqi

Central Cross-Island Highway

Daping
Dadu
Meizilin

Longxi
Dadu
Wuri

TAICHUNG ★

Niumian
Wanda

Fugui
Puli
CHUNG TAI CHAN MONASTERY ★★★

CHANGHUA
Great Buddha Scenic Area

Beishankeng

Nantou

Shuishe
● **Wenwu Temple**

Caotun

★★ *Sun Moon Lake*
Xuanzang Temple
Checheng

● **Formosan Aboriginal Culture Village** ★★

Lugang ★★

Huatan

NANTOU

Jiji
Shuili
Dingkan

Xihu

JiJi Branch Railway ★★

3076 △

Changhua
Wanggong

Ershui

Lugu ★
Xinyi

Xizhou

151

Fangyuan

Zhongxing

Xitou Forest Rec. Area
Xitou

21

Zitong

Zhuoshui

Xikang
Sansheng

DOULIU

★ **Yushan National Park**
Mt. Dashan

Yunlin
Huwei

1304

Mt. Zhushan 2489 ★ **Tatajia**

ALISHAN FOREST RAILWAY ★★★

Mailiao
Baozhong

Dounan

Meishan

Alishan Forest Rec. Area ★

Dalin

Fanqihu

18

Dongshi
Yuanzhang
Xikou

Chiayi

Taixi

159

Leye

Beigang
Xingang

Zhongpu

CHIAYI

Jinhu
Tropic of Cancer

Kaohsiung

Zengwen Reservoir

Aogu
Baihe

N

0   10 km
0   10 miles

JADE MOUNTAIN

Taichung★

Taichung (台中), the third-largest city in Taiwan, is not as well known as its rivals to the north and south, nor is it as developed: it still has no subway system, and until 2004, it had no international airport. Yet residents of Taichung are unlikely to complain. Their city is friendly and prosperous, and has a wealth of space that is evident in its roomy teahouses, abundant park space and vast museums, and broad meridians lined with restaurants and cafes. It is well connected to the rest of the island by high-speed rail, regular train service, and fast highways. Taichung is a working class city, the hub of a large network of factories that fueled the island's economic miracle in the decades following the Second World War. But it is also a city of culture, with a pair of high-quality museums and many universities. It serves as the gateway to Sun Moon Lake and the high-mountain delights of the Central Cross-Island Highway. Drier than Taipei and cooler than Kaohsiung, Taichung also has the best weather in Taiwan.

A BIT OF HISTORY

Plains aborigines were the earliest settlers here; they grew taro, millet and sweet potato, and hunted deer in the fertile plains. It wasn't until the 1700s that Chinese settlers began to move here in large numbers. Taichung's importance surged when the **Qing dynasty,** aware of the city's strategic position as a crossroads between north and south, and a key entry point into the central mountains, built a fort near the current Taichung Park, from which they subdued several rebellions by aboriginal tribes and Ming dynasty loyalists.

Beginning in 1885 Taichung was briefly the seat of the provincial government, attracting cultured mandarins and the educated elite. When the Japanese took over Taiwan in 1895, they modeled Taichung after Kyoto, their own city of

▶ **Population:** 1,006,300.

Michelin Maps: p217, p219.

Info: Travel Information Service Center at the train station. Also at 95 Gan Cheng St. 南屯區干城街 95 號; ◷open Mon–Fri 9am–5pm; ✆0800 422 022; http://english.tccg.gov.tw.

▶ **Location:** Taichung means "middle of Taiwan." The city lies on the west coast 20km/12mi inland from the Taiwan Strait, and about halfway between Taipei and Kaohsiung, each less than 2hrs drive away. The downtown stretches north and west from the train station to include Taichung Park, the Museum of Natural Science, the Museum of Fine Arts and beyond.

Kids: See dinosaur displays at the Museum of Natural Science, and the interactive artwork at the Museum of Fine Arts.

◷ **Timing:** Taichung is known for its year-round good weather; the dry months (Oct–Mar) are especially pleasant.

Don't Miss: Museum of Natural Science, Museum of Fine Arts, a teahouse or two, and perhaps a night market.

culture, establishing Taichung Park, a railroad, schools and government buildings, including City Hall, which still stands.

After the Nationalists took control of Taiwan in 1945, prominent Taichung citizens lobbied for roles in the new government. But like islanders elsewhere, they were ruthlessly suppressed by the Nationalist government of Chiang Kai-shek (see History in the Introduction).

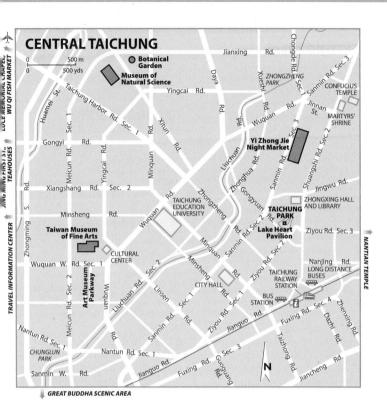

CENTRAL TAICHUNG

Botanical Garden
Museum of Natural Science

Jianxing Rd.
Chongde Rd. Sec. 3
Daya Rd.
Yingcai Rd.
Xueshi Rd.
ZHONGZHENG PARK
Sanmin Rd. Sec. 3
CONFUCIUS TEMPLE
Jinnan St.
MARTYRS' SHRINE
Taichung Harbor Rd. Sec. 1
Huamei St.
Sec. 1
Wuquan Rd.
Gongyi Rd.
Minquan Rd.
Xitun Rd.
Liuchuan Rd.
Zhonghua Rd.
Yi Zhong Jie Night Market
Shuangshi Rd. Sec. 2
Meicun Rd.
Yingcai Rd.
Sec. 2
Zhongzheng Rd.
Gongyuan Rd.
Sanmin Rd. Sec. 3
Jingwu Rd.
Xiangshang Rd.
TAICHUNG EDUCATION UNIVERSITY
ZHONGXING HALL AND LIBRARY
Minsheng Rd.
Wuquan Rd.
TAICHUNG PARK
Lake Heart Pavilion
Ziyou Rd. Sec. 3
Taiwan Museum of Fine Arts
CULTURAL CENTER
Minquan Rd.
Sanmin Rd. Sec. 2
Ziyou Rd. Sec. 2
Nanjing Rd.
LONG DISTANCE BUSES
Wuquan W. Rd. Sec. 1
Zhongming S. Rd.
Art Museum Parkway
Meicun Rd. Sec. 2
Liuchuan Rd. Sec. 2
Minsheng Rd.
CITY HALL
Sanmin Rd. Sec. 1
Ziyou Rd.
TAICHUNG RAILWAY STATION
BUS STATION
Fuxing Rd. Sec. 4
Zhenxing Rd.
Dazhi Rd.
Nantun Rd. Sec. 1
Wuquan Rd.
Linsen Rd.
Ziyou Rd. Sec. 1
Jianguo Rd.
Taizhong Rd.
CHUNGLUN PARK
Nantun Rd. Sec. 1
Jianguo Rd.
Fuxing Rd. Sec. 3
Gloguang Rd.
Jiancheng Rd.
Sanmin W. Rd.

TRAVEL INFORMATION CENTER
LULE MEMORIAL CHAPEL
WU QI FISH MARKET
JING MING FIRST ST.
TEAHOUSES
NANTIAN TEMPLE

N

GREAT BUDDHA SCENIC AREA

Yet Taichung prospered. Riding the crest of Taiwan's economic miracle, it became the center of small and medium-sized factories that helped fuel the island's rapid rise to first-world status. The high tech and aviation industries boomed.

In the 1960s and 70s, the Vietnam war brought a **military airbase** to the area nearby. The city became the bawdy host to the thousands of American and Taiwanese soldiers stationed there, as nightclubs and houses of ill repute pro-

Jing Ming First Street

Brent Hannon/Michelin

GETTING THERE

BY AIR - Taichung International Airport (www.tca.gov.tw/english/introduction.htm) offers domestic flights to Penghu, Kinmen, Hualien and Mazu, but not Kaohsiung or Taipei, which are better served by road and rail. It has a growing overseas network, including flights to Hong Kong, Saigon, and Xiamen in Fujian Province. The airport is 20km/12mi northwest of downtown.

BY TRAIN - Taichung is well-connected to the west coast corridor by rail; Taichung Railway Station is downtown, and both medium and fast trains are available; the fast line connects Taichung to Taipei in about 2.5hrs *(NT$375 round-trip)*. Taiwan **High Speed Rail** is so fast and predictable that it has eliminated air travel on the Taipei and Kaohsiung routes. For schedules, access www.railway.gov.tw/en/index/index.aspx.

As at other stations, a **free shuttle bus** takes High Speed Rail passengers to several downtown Taichung locations.

BY CAR - Cars can be rented at the airport and downtown, using either a Taiwan license or an international driver's license. Four companies rent cars in Taichung, though **Chailease** is more popular because staff speak good English (English service hotline: ℰ886 2 2828 0033; www.rentalcar.com.tw). Other companies include **Formosa Rentals** *(ℰ04 2425 9831; www.dragoncar.com.tw)* and **IWS Rent-a-Car** *(ℰ0800 000 414; www.iws.com.tw)*. Daily rentals start at NT$2200 and average about NT$3200 for a mid-size car.

BY BUS - Buses are an excellent option for Taichung, as they are for the entire west coast. Four main companies serve the city, and key stops are next to the Taichung Railway Station, and Taichung Gang (harbor) road; the trip from Taipei or Kaohsiung takes about 2 hrs. **Free Go Bus Co.** *(ℰ0800 051 519)* sometimes has English speakers. **Kuo-kuang**, or Taiwan Bus *(ℰ0800 010 138)* services the region. Tickets range from NT$100 to NT$300, depending on the type of bus and time of day.

GETTING AROUND

BY BUS - Three local bus companies serve Taichung (though taxis are easier), and stop next to the Taichung Railway Station.

BY CAR - Taichung is easy to negotiate in a rental car *(✆see rental information above)*.

BY TAXI - Taxis are the best way to travel in Taichung. They are cheap and frequent, and the drivers are honest, though few speak English. Five companies offer taxi service in Taichung, including **Fego Radio Taxi** *(ℰ04-2287 8888)*, **Taichung Taxi** *(ℰ04-2246 5555)* and **Yi Mei** *(ℰ04-2437 1000)*.

BY TWO-WHEEL: Officially, scooter rental requires either a Taiwan license or an international driver's license, but in practice, **scooters** can sometimes be rented near the train station, or at the airport, without one.

A deposit is required; expect to pay NT$500 or more per day, depending upon your bargaining skills and the length of rental. **Bicycles** can be rented across from the train station, and are a good option for the brave-of-heart during good weather.

GENERAL INFORMATION

AREA CODE

The prefix 04 is the area code for Taitung County. It is included in the telephone numbers shown in this chapter, but it is not necessary to dial 04 when making a local call. For mobile phones the prefix is 09. To reach a mobile phone, you must dial the 09 prefix from anywhere in Taiwan.

VISITOR INFORMATION

Travel Information Service Center, 95 Gan Cheng St. (南屯區干城街95 號). ⏰Open Mon–Fri 9am–5pm. ℰ0800 422 022. http://english.tccg.gov.tw.

ACCOMMODATIONS

Taichung has a range of lodgings available, from major hotels to bed and breakfast inns. *For a selection of accommodations, ⓘsee ADDRESSES.*

liferated. Gangsters thrived in the new environment, giving Taichung a parallel reputation for lawlessness, which eventually died down in the early 2000s.

Yet the city was also known for its museums and universities (there are **nine universities** today). A local saying that means "city of culture, city of sin" sums up the yin and yang of Taichung, the combination of high culture and lowbrow fun.

Although many factories have decamped to mainland China, Taichung is still an important hub of high-tech manufacturing. The city now has a quieter, more settled atmosphere. The opening of the new Taichung International Airport at Chiang Ching-kuo military base in 2004, and the opening of the Taiwan High Speed Rail in 2007 both helped revitalize the city. As the gateway to Sun Moon Lake, Taichung attracts a large number of mainland travelers.

During the annual **Lantern Festival** *(15th day of the Lunar New Year holiday)*, Taichung Park comes alive with red and yellow glowing lanterns. On the evening of the festival, just before the full moon

rises, firecrackers resound throughout the town, scaring ghosts. At dusk crowds pour into the park, carrying lanterns. This gathering is one of the city's favorite communal events, an ancient tradition that remains alive in the 21C.

DOWNTOWN
Museum of Natural Science★★
國立自然科學博物館

1 Guanqian Rd. 館前路1號 Open Tue–Sun 9am–5pm. Closed Lunar New Year. NT$100 (free Wed before 10am). Cosmo Theater NT$100. 3-D Theater NT$70. Botanical Garden NT$20. Free English audio. Shows in Chinese only. 04-2322-6940. www.nmnsedu.tw.

Taichung in general has a wealth of space, and so it is with this ambitious, hands-on science museum, which has a space theater, 3-D theater, and enormous halls for life science, Chinese science and the global environment. Life-size prehistoric skeletons, moving **dinosaur displays**, a giant mosquito proboscis, African habitats and the first machines ever invented are all here (too much for a single visit). Displays are excellent if slightly dated, but English captions are spotty.

Because of the audio handsets that provide information on command, in three languages, the highlights are the Chinese **Spiritual Life★★** and Chinese

Museum of Natural Science

Brent Hannon/Michelin

Dajia Mazu Pilgrimage

At midnight on a carefully chosen day during the third lunar month—usually in mid-April—surrounded by throngs of people, clusters of devotees, swirls of chaotic ritual and the ear-splitting thunder of fireworks underfoot and overhead, a magnificent icon of the goddess **Mazu** is lifted from her altar at **Zhenlan Temple** in Dajia *(45min north of Taichung)*, and the annual Mazu Pilgrimage begins.

Dajia Mazu pilgrimage, Zhenlan Temple

Brent Hannon/Michelin

For more than 200km/124mi, the statue of Mazu, goddess of the Sea, is carried on a palanquin from the temple south through Taichung, Changhua, Yunlin and Chiayi, and then back again to Zhenlan. Along the way, the goddess will visit more than 80 temples, bringing them good fortune by her very presence.

The pilgrimage, a chaotic procession often more than a kilometer long, is a churning sea of activity that combines vigorous rituals, solemn parades of devotees, clusters of curious onlookers and the colorful costumes, masks and icons of various folk deities. Sometimes, rascals from local temples will try to detain or "steal" the Zhenlan Mazu, and bring the good-luck goddess to their own temples to acquire good karma. Shoving, scuffling and even brawls are not uncommon. Devotees will also try to ignore the roaring firecrackers and duck beneath the palanquin to bring themselves good luck.

Despite the all-encompassing commotion, visitors will be struck by the genuine devotion etched on the faces of the believers, many of whom leave their jobs and follow the goddess for the entire journey. The layers of Taiwanese folk religion run deep, and the Mazu pilgrimage is a pageant that beautifully illustrates this unique aspect of Taiwan.

Science and Technology★★ halls. Visitors learn, for example, that unmarried daughters and the lowest concubines lived in the coldest, most distant corners of traditional Chinese houses.

Adjacent to the museum, the **Botanical Garden**★ harbors nearly 800 species of plants. It is divided into two parts: the **lowland vegetation** of the island, which features plants from the coral atolls, the littoral forests of southern Taiwan, and the plants of Orchid Island, and the central, southern and northern lowlands. The second part, the tropical **rain forest greenhouse,** re-creates the original primal conditions that existed throughout Taiwan before the arrival of large numbers of Chinese settlers.

▲▲ National Taiwan Museum of Fine Arts★★ 國立臺灣美術館. *2, Sec. 1, Wu Chuan W. Rd., Taichung. 五權西路一段2號. ◐Open Tue–Fri 9am–5pm, Sat–Sun 9am–6pm. ◐Closed Chinese New year. English-speaking guides can be arranged in advance; English audios available for permanent exhibits. Some English signage. ✆04-2372 3552. www.ntmofagov.tw.*

Park-like grounds, a spacious interior with uncrowded galleries, combined with carefully curated artwork, make this one of the top museums in Taiwan. The curators place great emphasis on nurturing local artists, and much of the art has a playful quality that is unusual but welcome.

In 2004 it reopened after a long closure due to the 9-21 earthquake damage in 1999. The revamp has resulted in a loftier, more modern space with several new galleries. The original setting in a large grassy park has been retained, and if the outdoor **sculpture park** is included, it is the largest art museum in Asia.

The collection of **abstract paintings** is a highlight, and features mostly mainland Chinese and Taiwanese artists. Themed exhibits *(1st and 2nd floors)*, which rotate once a year, specialize in cutting-edge contemporary art. The third floor houses the permanent collection.

Child-friendly additions include the **Picture Book Area** and **Family Room**, which have books in Chinese and English, along with hands-on exhibits and creative playthings that children will surely enjoy.

Yi Zhong Jie Night Market
一中街夜市
Sanmin Rd., near Taiping Rd. 三民路, 接近太平路.

Taichung has four night markets, all of them similar, but this student favorite is among the most popular. Visitors will find the usual outpouring of cheap handbags, shirts and shoes, because local teens and 20-somethings shop here for bargains. All the time-honored Taiwanese street favorites are here, including grilled squid with chili powder and hoisin sauce, barbecued sweet sausages, soup noodles, oyster omelet, grilled spicy corn, battered squid balls, and many more. Most popular of all, and a Yi Zhong specialty, is a stand called **Fried Chicken Bigger Than Your Head**, where pressed chicken is indeed that big and accompanied by wedge-cut french fries, all for NT$54.

Yi Zhong Jie has the signature hallmarks of a full-throttle Taiwan night market: the crowds, the scooters, the touts, the smell of stinky tofu, and even illegal mobile stands sometimes rattling down the street pursued by leisurely policemen.

Jing Ming First Street
精明一街
Between Dalong Rd. 大隆路 *and Dadun 19th St.* 大墩19街.

This two-block pedestrian lane, twinkling with lights and lined with shops, cafes and outdoor tables, is a creation unknown elsewhere in Taiwan. Visitors flock to its coffeehouses, pubs, bookstores and cobblestone walkways, which sit beneath a profusion of graceful trees that adorn the leafy street.

National Taiwan Museum of Fine Arts

Brent Hannon/Michelin

This street is a kinder, gentler shopping venue and a favorite local hangout, where residents walk dogs, browse bookstores, dine al fresco, and sip coffee and tea.

Taichung Park
台中公園 or 中山公園
Guangyuan Rd. 公園路, *Sanmin Rd.* 三民路 *and Shuang Shi Rd.* 雙十路.
This leafy downtown oasis has been the city's best-loved park since the Japanese built it in 1903. Though since eclipsed by bigger parks, the park has a comfortable vibe and time-honored sense of place that make it a firm favorite among local residents. Many of them have paddled boats on its placid lake, or strolled its quiet lanes. The **Lake Heart Pavilion**, a double pagoda perched gracefully over **Sun Moon Pond**, has been a symbol of the city since it was built more than a century ago. Now a City Historic Site, the twin pagodas underwent a NT$14 million renovation in 2006 that restored their hardwood floors and added a new layer of luster to the ivory-white pillars, wooden slats and balustrades and signature slate-blue roofs.

Art Museum Parkway
Wuquan West 1st, 2nd, 3rd & 4th Sts., south of fine arts museum.
Eating out in Taichung is a pleasure, and the city abounds with options that are as good as those in Taipei, and much more reasonable. Filled with grass and trees and lined with some 30 **restaurants**, this wide meridian makes an excellent place to begin. The parkway consists of four parallel streets, but for dining purposes most of the restaurants are on Wuquan West 3rd and 4th Streets. Here,

a hungry visitor can stroll the strip and select from a trans-global smorgasbord of Italian, Indian, Continental, American, Shanghainese, Taiwanese, Thai, and Taiwan aboriginal cuisine.

TEAHOUSE TOUR
Because of its proximity to top tea-growing areas, and because residents love to sip fine tea, Taichung is the top **teahouse city** in Taiwan. It has lower rents and more space, allowing for large, rambling teahouses filled with cozy nooks, picture windows and outdoor patios where friends can enjoy some of the finest tea in the world. The Chinese believe that tea clears the mind, and promotes good conversation and clear conclusions. Groups of people drinking tea and engaging in conversation, both indoors and out, are a common sight. In Taichung, teahouses are the new pubs.

Wu Wei Tsao Tang★★ 無為草堂
106 Gongyi Rd., Sec. 2公益路二段 106號 Open daily 10am–11pm. Reservations recommended. 04-2329 8321. www.wuwei.com.tw.
This calm oasis in bustling downtown Taichung is a picture-perfect traditional teahouse, a rambling two-story building filled with private alcoves, wooden walkways, unvisited corners and balconies, plants and paper lanterns, waterfalls and ponds filled with lazy colorful carp. Guests sip tea and gaze into the clear pool and watch the fish, white and orange flashes in the sun-dappled ponds, as they swim beneath the walkways and tea rooms.
Tea is said to have mysterious properties that provide gentle exhilaration and mild intoxication, and Wu Wei fully

Making Tea, Wu Wei Style
The servers at Wu Wei are expert tea-makers. First they "wake up" the tea leaves by washing them in boiling water, then empty the pot into a ceramic pitcher, then empty the pitcher over the assorted mugs and cups to scald them. The second pour—the best—is steeped for one minute, then put into the pitcher to stop contact with the leaves. It goes from a smelling cup into a drinking cup, and then the mild flavorful tea is slowly sipped. The tea leaves can be brewed eight times, soaking for an additional 10 seconds each time.

Restaurant Specialties

Displays of uber-fresh fish and crustaceans, some on ice and some swimming in tanks, include snapper, squid, yellow croaker, grouper, prawns and oysters. Unique to the area, the bamboo snail, a 5cm-long shelled isopod that is unlike anything other crustacean, has a chewy texture and a slightly bitter taste.

Restaurant specialties at the fish market are stir-fried oysters with black bean sauce; bamboo shoots with pork, white bean sauce and scallions; fresh steamed fish; and flash-fried peeled shrimp with as much garlic and chili as you like.

The Taiwanese like their seafood mild, fresh and lightly spiced, and lean toward fermented bean, garlic, ginger and scallions as their favorite flavorings. They prefer to "soup," steam or stir-fry fish, rather than grill it.

evokes these properties. The name of the teahouse means "doing more by doing less," or even, "doing everything by doing nothing," a reference to the famous work *Tao Te Ching* by Laozi, and a reference also to the contemplative qualities of good tea. The house specialty is San Lin oolong tea, a close relative to the more famous Dong Ding oolong, but grown at a higher elevation. Wu Wei also serves a selection of food and tea snacks (the smoked camphor duck is a highlight). Visitors can buy tea leaves and tea-making utensils.

Chun Shui Tang Cultural Teahouse★ 春水堂人文茶館
Building 1, 8 Chao Ma 3rd St., Xi Tun District 朝馬三街12號. ⏱*Open daily 10:30am–midnight.* ☎*04-2254 4729.*
A teahouse chain, this flagship branch sports a semi-modern teahouse decor, awash with tea-related souvenirs

such as teapots, tea tongs, and cups, and filled with flower arrangements, wooden tables and chairs, and booths that give it a bright atmosphere. Chun Shui Tang, or spring water hall, offers a broad palette of top Taiwanese teas, including Tie Guan Yin or the Iron Buddha, a dark, heavily fermented oolong with a sweet, smooth and astringent flavor.

Chun Shui Tang is famous as the teahouse that invented **bubble milk tea**, or pearl milk tea 珍珠奶茶—the milk-and-tea drink that subsequently swept the world. The success of bubble milk tea lies in its perfectly balanced sweet-bitter flavor along with its thick "pearls" of gelatin, plus the thick straw to suck them up. Chun Shui Tang carries a number of cold tea drinks, many of them fruit-flavored with the gelatin pearls. Highly recommended is the Oriental Beauty, or **white-tipped oolong**, a unique

Wu Wei Tsao Tang teahouse

Brent Hannon/Michelin

Taiwanese tea that derives some of its earthy, Earl Grey-like flavor from the saliva of a rare and esteemed bug that lives among the tea plants.

Qio Shan Tang
秋山堂精品茶莊

8 Chao Ma 3rd St. 西屯區朝馬三街八號, *two doors from Chun Shui Tang, Xi Tun District.* ⏰*Open daily 10:00am–midnight.* ☎*04-2254 4729. Tea-making lessons NT$400. Tea pottery lessons must be arranged in advance.*

Qio Shan Tang, or autumn moon, is a wood-lined teahouse with a Japanese Zen ambiance. Like a small temple dedicated to the art of tea, this venue is appealing for visitors who wish to learn more about the time-honored drink. After a lesson, visitors may drink the tea they make. Rare and beautiful teapots line the shelves, many of them antiques, and some costing up to NT$10,000. Visitors are encouraged to bring their own tea leaves, and for NT$140, Qio Shan Tang will supply hot water. As in most Taichung teahouses, cakes, nuts, fruit, pickles and other snacks are on hand.

Shuei Wu Zhuan★ 水舞饌
38 Huizhong Rd., Sec. 2 惠中路二段38號 *near Jing Ming pedestrian street.* ⏰*Open daily 10am–midnight.* ☎*04-2255 3678. www.swmall.com.tw.*

This flagship branch of a popular chain features fine semi-fermented oolongs from the nearby mountains. It also caters to students and office workers with a wide selection of cold teas containing ingredients from passion fruit and jasmine to osmanthus, lavender, smoked plum and wolfberry.

The easy sociability of the place is its attraction. The large, shady outdoor patio provides excellent people-watching, while inside are three stories of alcoves, tables and counters for groups of all sizes. The vast menu is a tribute to the sheer versatility of tea, and to the eclectic and experimental tastes of Taichung's tea drinkers.

OUTLYING SIGHTS
Luce Memorial Chapel★
▶ *10km/6mi northwest of downtown, on Donghai University campus, Taichung Harbor Rd.* 東海大學, 台中港路.

This iconic chapel sits in a field on the tree-lined campus of Donghai University. Named after 19C mainland China missionary **Henry Luce**, the 19m/62ft-tall chapel is by far the most famous church in Taiwan.

Conceived in the early 1950s and completed in 1963, it is one of the earliest works by renowned Chinese-American architect **I.M. Pei** (b.1917), most famous, perhaps, for his glass pyramids in front

Luce Memorial Chapel

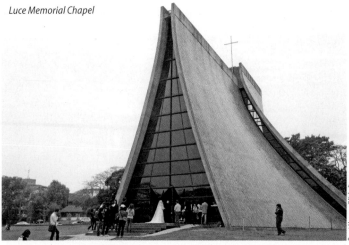

Brent Hannon/Michelin

Great Buddha Scenic Area

Brent Hannon/Michelin

of the Louvre in Paris. Said to resemble hands at prayer, it is the only Pei-designed building in Taiwan. Its slender, elegant shape belies the chapel's strength: it has survived several strong earthquakes.

Wu Qi Fish Market at Taichung Harbor★ 梧棲觀光漁港
❯ *Well signed, at the end of Taichung Harbor Rd. NT$50 entry fee.*
The **fish market** serves two purposes: in the pre-dawn hours, it is a gritty fisherman's wharf, where the night's catch is offloaded and sold at a lively auction. Later it becomes a tourist attraction, as visitors graze through rows of grilled squid, breaded fried crabs, deep fried oysters and other fast-food marine snacks.
Harbor cruises *(1-3hrs; NT$270-$450; irregular departures)* provide a close-up look at the thickly clustered oil refineries, seaside factories, container docks and warehouses along the shoreline that are typical of central Taiwan's concentration of industry. The boat itself dodges container ships, tugboats and other commercial traffic.
A strip (🕐 *open 10am–midnight)* of **seafood restaurants**, housed in a high-ceilinged warehouse, attracts diners. Ignore the ever-present touts, and choose a restaurant that is busy and has fresh seafood: look for clear eyes, shiny scales and firm flesh.

Adjacent to the dining strip, and just as popular, is a retail **seafood market** with tables, buckets and tanks overflowing with just-caught seafood. Since the catch is so fresh, the market is usually crowded with shoppers.

Great Buddha Scenic Area 八卦山大佛風景區
❯ *In Bagua Shan, 20km/12mi south of Taichung via Provincial Hwy. 19 and follow the signs.* 🕐*Open 24hrs. www.trimt-nsa.gov.tw/eng.*
Dominated by a giant golden Buddha that can be seen from afar, this Scenic Area is the most famous attraction in Bagua Shan, or **Eight Trigrams Mountain**. The tree-lined park is graced with winding pathways, fountains and waterfalls.
Among the diverse low-key attractions are a C119 **cargo plane** parked in a far corner; a small **museum** with photos of bird species that live in the area; and a **monument** to the resistance to Japan, in which this area played a key part. Highlights are frequent **views** of the factories and other blue-collar features of Changhua, an industrial city some 10km/6mi south of Taichung; and of course the 22m/72ft seated **statue** of the Buddha, also known as the big Buddha of Changhua.

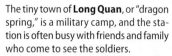

Taiwan's Branch Rail Lines

Jiji Branch Railroad is one of four branch rails in Taiwan. Like the other three (the Pingxi, Alishan, and Neiwan lines), the old railroad is both scenic and historic. It was built in 1921 by the Japanese to haul farm products and hydroelectric gear up and down the scenic **Zhou Shui River Valley**. Jiji, like the other branch lines, is now a passenger and tourist train, ferrying visitors.

EXCURSIONS
Jiji Branch Rail Line★★

▶ *35km/22mi south of Taichung.*
Allow a full day. Departs from Ershui Rail Station in the town of Ershui (take a train from Taichung Railway Station or a taxi to Ershui). Round-trip NT$60.
Along the rail line's 27km/17mi of track, the key attractions are the towns of Shuili, Jiji Town and Checheng.

The Ride

Shuili is home to the **Snake Kiln**, a 40m/131ft-long ceramic kiln that is the longest in the world. It was built 85 years ago to make industrial-size pipes, but because those pipes are now made of concrete, the kiln is used today mostly by artists. It lies on an uphill slope, and viewed from below, its rustic, textured exterior does resemble an enormous snake. **Clay-making exhibits**, guided tours, art studios and snack bars make Shuili a pleasant stop.

Shuili's Snake Kiln

Its textured exterior is like a snake's. Every two months or so the town's 85-year-old kiln is fired up, a whale of a process that means piling wood through the many openings, setting it afire, and then "feeding the snake" with more and more wood. Eventually, after three or four days, the temperature soars to 1,100°C/2,012°F. The intense heat is perfect for making ceramic art.

The tiny town of **Long Quan**, or "dragon spring," is a military camp, and the station is often busy with friends and family who come to see the soldiers.

After Long Quan, the scenery becomes classic central Taiwan: steep foothills nestle near the rails and betel-nut trees cradle the tea fields. Soon the train enters the famous **green tunnel**, where camphor trees grow so thick that they overhang the tracks on all sides. Wild orchids add blazes of color; **butterflies** dance among the branches in shades of red, blue, purple and yellow. The camphor trees are a legacy of the Japanese, who asked everyone in the area to plant two camphors each. Camphor oil was big business in the 19C.

Soon the train pulls into **Jiji Town**, the epicenter of a devastating **earthquake**, which struck the morning of September 21, 1999. The once-famous Jiji train station was destroyed, but has been rebuilt. On weekends musicians cluster near the train station, crowds throng the barbecue vendors, and kids play in a nearby park. Jiji means "to collect"; it was once a market town where the region's produce and timber were gathered.

Checheng, the final stop, is a former logging town dominated by a huge sawmill and an equally huge dormitory, both made from cypress wood. The **sawmill** has been renovated and is now a museum dedicated to the days when the thick trees that carpeted the surrounding slopes were cut down. Checheng also features a selection of shops, restaurants, and souvenir stores; the highlight is Checheng Chateau, a boutique **winery** that turns out 300 bottles of plum wine per day. The handmade wine is brewed from local plums, and has a fruity bouquet and plenty of sweetness. For this reason, the wine is served with salty spicy sausages.

Looming above the town, the **Mingtan Dam** is one of the biggest hydroelectric facilities in Asia. It's responsible for the "tides" of **Sun Moon Lake**: during daytime peak power periods, water spills through the generators and electricity is sent into the island's grid. At night, the water is pumped back into the lake, and the next day the process begins again, making Sun Moon Lake the biggest battery on the island. Mingtan Dam survived the 1999 earthquake intact.

Chung Tai Chan Monastery★★★ 中台禪寺

2 Chung Tai Rd. 中台路2號, in Puli,
▶ *40km/25mi southeast of Taichung via Hwy. 6. Open daily 8am–5:45pm. To see sights above the second floor, arrange English tour in advance. Walk-in visitors see only the first two floors. ☎04-9293 0215. www.ctworld. org. No photography allowed above the second floor. Dress conservatively; no smoking, no using mobile phones, or bringing pets or meat into the monastery.*

Dominating the Puli Basin like a golden exclamation mark, this astonishing monastery opened in 2001. At night it glows like a beacon, and daylight reveals a vast complex that includes a spacious park and botanical garden with hundreds of trees, and a museum filled with rare Buddhist artifacts that span the Chinese, Tibetan and Indian traditions. Also on the grounds are new junior and senior high schools that opened in 2009, and dormitories for the 1,200 shaven-headed resident monks, called **cultivators**.

Visit

The Chung Tai Chan monastery tour begins in the **Hall of the Four Heavenly Kings** *(1st floor)*, featuring 12m/39ft stone statues that bestride the room like a colossus, their scowling faces serving as warnings to would-be iconoclasts. The **Great Majestic Hall**★★ *(2nd floor)* holds a striking statue of the **Shakyamuni Buddha**, the historical Buddha known to ordinary people. Rendered in rose-colored granite, it sits on a pedestal of gray slate, flanked by a pair of amber pedestals. In this hall, the elaborate iconography of the religion is lushly depicted, in golden swirls representing enlightenment, in sandalwood carvings and amber statues, and by saintly arhats and bodhisattvas of all kinds, in rare metals and stones.

The **Great Meditation Hall** *(5th floor)* is a spartan room where 500 monks meditate each morning at 4:30am. At the opposite end lies the **Great Magnificence Hall**★★, where an image of the **Rocana Buddha**, whose white body and golden backdrops manifest themselves only to enlightened disciples, sits surrounded by walls adorned with thousands of icons. Intricate wheels and flowers and patterns based on designs from the Dunhuang caves in mainland China are hand-painted on the ceiling.

In the **Great Enlightenment Hall**★★★ *(9th floor)*, bathed in natural light, is a smooth four-story statue of the seated **Vairocana Buddha**, carved in snow-white marble from Brazil, and symbolizing the pure nature of all beings. The floors are smoky white Egyptian marble, and the ceiling depicts the starry heav-

Chung Tai Chan Monastery
Brent Hannon/Michelin

The Shakyamuni Buddha, Chung Tai Chan Monastery

Brent Hannon/Michelin

enly skies at night, recalling the moment of enlightenment when the Buddha beheld the morning star just before dawn. Vairocana is flanked on one side hall by an elephant, indicating just practice, and on the other by a bodhisattva indicating great wisdom. On this floor the icons and decor are whiter, brighter and smoother, as visitors make a symbolic ascent toward nirvana.

The most impressive chamber is the **Hall of 10,000 Buddhas**★★★ *(16th floor)*. The soaring, cathedral-like interior is dominated by a majestic **seven-story pagoda** of Vietnamese teak, made without nails, and lining the walls are 10,000 images of the **Medicine Buddha**, meticulously hand-cast in copper from Vietnam. Daylight floods the hall through 30m/98ft-high lotus-shaped picture windows, while a balcony *(25th floor)* offers a **view** of the apex of the splendid teakwood pagoda.

At the top of the tower *(37th floor)*, the titanium-coated **Golden Dome**★★ represents the **mani pearl**, symbol of the luminous nature of all sentient beings. Rendered in a kaleidoscope of colors, the exquisite **ceiling** depicts concentric layers of lotus leaves and flowers,

Buddhism in Taiwan

In Taiwan a grand age of cathedral-building is underway, fueled by a powerful renaissance in the ancient religion of Buddhism. Taiwan-style Buddhism isn't the gentle philosophy of self denial and meditation that most people associate with the ancient religion; rather, the island's monasteries have transformed it into a vibrant force that competes vigorously for the hearts and minds of modern believers.

There are four main Buddhist organizations in Taiwan: Foguangshan, Chung Tai Chan, Tzu Chi, and Dharma Drum. Led by charismatic monks, all four are wealthy and have built extravagant temples and founded schools, hospitals, charities and/or meditation centers in many countries. **Tzu Chi** has its base in Hualien, where it has a large temple, while **Foguangshan**, near Kaohsiung, has been attracting tourists, worshipers and disciples to its elaborate grounds for several decades. The latest to open a lavish monastery was **Dharma Drum Mountain**, which inaugurated a massive temple complex just north of Taipei in 2005. By far the most impressive of the four is **Chung Tai Chan** Zen monastery (chan is Chinese for Zen) on the outskirts of Puli.

with the pearl at their center. Gold **wall panels** depict the six parameters of Buddhism, illustrated in exquisite Han dynasty-style works of art. Overlooking the circular room, a priceless Ming dynasty "baby faced" **bronze Buddha** brings an end to the symbolic spiritual evolution, and to the tour itself.

Next door, the **Chung Tai Museum** (⏰ *open daily 9:30am–5:30pm, closed 2nd & 4th Mon each month;* ☏*04-9293 2000; www.ctmuseum.org*) houses a priceless collection of **Buddhist artifacts**, most of them in stone, gilt bronze, and wood, and many of them from the Tang and Song dynasties, although some are even older.

From Puli, you have the option of heading west into the mountains (⏺ see Central Mountains chapter).

Sanyi Township★ 三義鄉

▶ *About 35km/22mi north of Taichung by Fwy. 1 and Provincial Hwy. 13.*
Trains run to Sanyi from Taichung, but no local buses. Taxi from Sanyi Railway Station to the museum costs about NT$130, to Shengxing Station about NT$200. Walking is an option.

The main attraction in Miaoli County (苗栗縣) is Sanyi Township, and just about the only attraction of Sanyi is **woodcarving**. Dozens of shops (as well as a few ceramic, clothing and other handicrafts outlets) sell locally carved and imported articles. Add workshops and a woodcarving museum, and there is more than enough for a half-day visit.

Upon entering the town, the smell of freshly carved wood is everywhere. Most stores are located on the section of Highway 13 called **Shuimei Road** (水美路). (The best restaurants can also be found on Shuimei Road.)

Among the many products made from wood, you'll find furniture, tea-making sets, 3-D landscapes, aboriginal-style decorations, games, masks, incense, bathroom equipment, kitchenware—and statues of a whole pantheon of gods, bodhisattvas and Confucian scholars. Top-notch woods include **camphor**, which is ideally suited to making furni-

ture as its oils repel termites, and various cypresses. Tour buses stop farther up the hill, where shops sell higher-end goods, and shopkeepers are more receptive to bargaining.

A short walk west up Bagu Road (八股路) leads to **Guangsheng St.** (廣勝街), the touristic "woodcarving street."

Sanyi Wood Sculpture Museum★
三義木雕博物館; *88 Guangsheng St.* ⏰*Open Tue–Sun 9am–5pm. NT$80.* ☏*03 787 6009.*

This museum sits at the end of Guangsheng Street. Its exhibits are spread over seven floors of two buildings and include works from different Chinese dynasties and the arts and crafts of Taiwan's aborigines.

Among the displays are temple deities, furniture and selections from architecture and international invitational exhibitions, plus prize-winning selections from the annual **Sanyi Woodcarving Festival** (三義木雕節) held each May. Though the crowds are massive, the festival is the best time to visit Sanyi: sculptors are working outdoors and classes are available to the public.

At other times of the year, sculptors can usually be seen in their side-street studios.

Outlying Sights

South of town 2km/1mi, **West Lake Resortopia** (西湖渡假村; *11 Xihu, Xihu Village;* ⏰*open daily 8:30am–5:30pm; NT$399;* ☏*037-876699)* is a theme park with gardens, lake, woods, restaurants, mini-golf and a roller coaster.

If time allows, walk or cycle along the 5km/3mi of disused railway line from Sanyi to **Shengxing**★ (勝興, *parking NT$50 weekends)*. Although highly commercialized, the Japanese-era, nail-less wooden **railway station**—the highest on the western line before it closed—and the **themed teahouses** and restaurants are worth a visit. The next stretch of track *(3.5km/2mi)* is only slightly less busy, and leads to the dilapidated **Longteng Viaduct** (龍騰斷橋), which dates to 1905 but was destroyed by an earthquake in 1935.

ADDRESSES

🛏 STAY

$$ Chun Feng Leisure Motel – 春風休閒旅館台中館: 市政北一路177號 *177 Shi Zhen North 1st St.* ☏*04 2255 8080. www.we-home.com.tw. 33 rooms.* Taichung has taken the motel concept and pushed it to a new level: guests drive in and park in private garages, and take the stairs to their second-floor rooms. This motel offers large guest rooms with rather extravagant designs. Staff bring breakfast to the room, free of charge, from a nearby KFC. No restaurant on the premises.

$$$ Chateau Boutique Motel – 雲朵精品旅館朝馬二街46號 *46 Chao Ma 2nd St.* ☏*04 2258 7789. 27 rooms.* Another Taichung-style motel, the Chateau offers an abundance of space, with extra-big rooms, many with patios and/or ponds, and all of them wood-paneled and comfortable. It has no on-site restaurant, but a catered Western breakfast is included.

$$$ Hotel One – 亞致大飯店, 西區英才路532號 *532 Ying Cai Rd.* ☏*04 2303 1234. www.taichung-en.hotelone.com.tw. 202 rooms.* This property is the latest venture by well-known Taiwanese hotelier Stanley Yen, whose company also manages the island's Landis hotels. A chic and contemporary tower hotel with a good location, it combines five-star hardware with friendly service. Rooms have high-tech amenities like laser printers and ipod docks. Western breakfast included. **Top of One Restaurant ($$$)** on the 46th floor specializes in American beef and a panorama of the city.

😊 Touring Tip 😊

By law all hotels in Taiwan are non-smoking, but in practice, this means smoke-saturated hotel rooms are all too common, since many managers do not enforce the regulation. Smoky rooms are most prevalent in tourist-class hotels that cater to large groups. Ask to see—and smell—the room before you settle in.

$$ Shen Diao Cun Homestay – 神雕邨三義鄉廣盛村廣聲新城2巷26號 *Lane 2, 26 Guangsheng St., Sanyi.* ☏*037-875858. www.netmotel.com.tw. 10 rooms. Breakfast included.* Located near the Wood Sculpture Museum and above a teahouse selling Hakka food, this well-located family-style hotel has everything within reach. Rooms are quite basic, but come with a TV.

🍴 EAT

$ Lugang Restaurant – 鹿港店台中港梧棲觀光漁市台中縣清水鎮中華路445號 *Wu Qi Fish Market at Taichung Harbor.* ☏*0921 388 781. www.666A.com.tw. Closes 1am.* Like other restaurants in the Wu Qi strip, the Lugang is friendly and inexpensive, and serves superior seafood in a simple setting. Excellent choices are oysters with scallions and black beans, steamed fish and stir-fried bamboo shoots, or fried rice with fresh peeled shrimp and a hint of garlic. **Taiwanese.**

$$ 1924 Shanghai Restaurant – 新月梧桐, 五權西三街95號 *95 Wu Quan West 4th St., near the Museum of Fine Arts.* ☏*04 2378 3181. www.theme.net.tw. Closes 9pm.* This packed, popular restaurant serves up classic Shanghai dishes like Wuxi spare ribs, stewed tofu with crab roe, red-cooked pork belly and lion's head meatballs in an upscale setting. The crab roe arrives in a bubbling flame-heated glass dish, while the tender spare ribs burst with a sweet-salty flavor. **Shanghainese.**

$$ Wu Jiao Chuan Ban – 五角船板, 西屯區府會園道6號 *6 Fu Hui Yuan Dao, Xi Tun District.* ☏*04 2254 5678. www.five-dime.com.tw. Closes 10pm.* This giant restaurant, with hundreds of seats beneath super-high ceilings, is an only-in-Taichung extravaganza. No other city has enough space for such an array of cave-like features, ponds, waterfalls and winding staircases. It is a fine dining spot for a large group. The set menu offers various price ranges. Try the superb sliced pork in miso. **Taiwanese.**

🛒 SHOPPING

Round like the sun, Taichung's **sun cakes** are sweet flaky pastries. Taichung is also a good place to buy a **tea set**.

Lugang★★

The second-oldest city in Taiwan has displayed a chameleon-like ability to adapt to historical change. Initially a trading port, Lugang (鹿港) later became one of the island's most important cities, but fell into decline when its harbor silted over. It later evolved into a center for handicrafts, famous today for its lanterns, woodcarvings, handmade fans, paper lanterns, and other crafts. This busy, chaotic little town has a fine collection of Qing-era architecture, including courtyards, gated mansions, winding alleys and stone arches, and boasts several superb temples, including Longshan Temple, widely regarded as one of the finest in Taiwan.

A BIT OF HISTORY

From 1700 to 1850, Lugang thrived. It was Taiwan's biggest port and second-largest city; only the capital city, Tainan, was larger. Located in a rich plain, with a good harbor that was only a day's sail from mainland China, Lugang was a center of commerce, a seat of learning, a magnet for mainland immigrants. But then the city's fortunes fell. The harbor silted over as a result of typhoons and shifting tides, and better natural

▶ **Population:** 84,100.
◔ **Michelin Map:** p217.
▷ **Location:** A 45min drive southeast of Taichung, Lugang sits inland, off coastal Hwy. 17. The city center flanks major thoroughfare Zhongshan Road, which runs diagonally south to north, lined with temples, shops, restaurants, banks and the bus station. Lugang's major sights are close to one another, and its small size and pedestrian-only lanes make it easy to see on foot.
🕐 **Timing:** Lugang can be visited year-round, but the dry months *(Oct–Mar)* are best.
😊 **Don't Miss:** Longshan Temple, Nine Turns Lane and Old Street.

harbors were found in Keelung and Kaohsiung. In the year 1700, some 36,000 ships called upon Lugang; by 1851, that number had dropped to 7,000 ships per year. Even so, city rulers did not allow modernity to pierce their little fiefdom, and they prevented rail-

Lugang Old Street

Brent Hannon/Michelin

233

GETTING THERE

BY TRAIN - The nearest train station is in Changhua, which is northeast of Lugang, a 20min drive away.
BY CAR - Lugang lies 45min southwest of Taichung. Take Provincial Highway 1 to Changhua, then County Road 142 (*see Taichung for car rental information*).

GETTING AROUND

BY TWO WHEEL - Bike rentals are available at the Folk Art Museum.

GENERAL INFORMATION

AREA CODE: The prefix 04 is included in the telephone numbers shown in this chapter, even though it is not necessary to dial 04 when making a local call.

VISITOR INFORMATION

Lugang Town Office, 168 Minquan Rd. Open Mon–Fri 8am–noon & 1:30pm–5:30pm. *04 777 2006*.

ACCOMMODATIONS

Lugang has only a handful of very basic hotels. Taichung has a better lodging selection *see ADDRESSES in Taichung chapter.*

roads and modern roads from passing through the city. Lugang later slipped into a period of warfare, and as the Qing dynasty crumbled in the late 1800s, clan families fought for control of the town. When the Japanese took over Taiwan in 1895, they re-established order.

Lugang found a new livelihood. The town turned to handicrafts, and in the early 1900s the city blossomed again, as a provider of bamboo and wooden articles, temple sculpture, candles, incense, paintings, lamps, ironware, fans and tinware, produced by Lugang artisans, and sold around the island, and to Japan.

China regained control of Taiwan in 1945, but even as the island prospered, Lugang remained a quiet place: it had no harbor, it wasn't an industrial zone or a capital, and the island's railroads and modern roads still circumvented the city. But that lack of development, as it turned out, safeguarded the visible history of Lugang and turned it into one of the island's top domestic tourist attractions. Because its venerable buildings are so well preserved, Lugang has become a magnet for students of Chinese history and architecture.

⚓ WALKING TOUR

5km/3mi. Allow 4hrs. Major sights are signed in English, commonly with accompanying maps.

▷ *Start at Mo Lu Lane, near the corner of Sanmin and Gong Zheng Sts., in the southwest corner of town.*

Mo Lu Lane 摸乳巷

Mo Lu literally means "breast-touching," and refers to the extreme narrowness of this lane—so narrow that the chests of passing pedestrians touch. It is also called Gentleman's Lane, because any true gentleman, seeing a lady proceeding his way, would wait for her to exit the lane before starting through. The extremely tight fit was a defensive strategy designed to slow down the bandits and warlords who thrived in old Lugang.

▷ *Return to Sanmin St. and proceed east, following the signs to Longshan Temple, a five-minute walk away.*

Longshan Temple★★★ 龍山寺

Longshan St. 龍山街, off Sanmin St. Open daily.
Taiwan has about a dozen world-class temples, all of them rich in folklore, and all with multiple layers of meaning written into their architecture and decor. But even by these standards, this Qing-era masterpiece is exceptional, a graceful compound that is mystical, textured and intriguing. According to the Taiwan Tourism Bureau, it is the best-preserved and most beautiful Qing dynasty building in Taiwan.

Unlike some of the temples in Taiwan, Longshan is finely crafted and rich in delicate features, from the double lotus designs on the pillars and the octagonal window lattices, to the majestic main hall. The materials—stone, fir and bricks—were imported from mainland China, as were the 16C craftsmen who built it. The temple's brown and gray color scheme, natural-colored brick and tile roofs, and simple ornamentation are unique in Taiwan temple architecture.

Visit

The layout unfolds in a series of courtyards and gates, but Longshan exceeds other temples in size and scale, with four courtyards, each more elaborate than the last. The first is a simple **paved courtyard** of rough granite stones, flanked by a pair of banyan trees. Slightly more elaborate, the **second courtyard** lies behind a two-tiered pagoda gate; pine and juniper gardens highlight its enclosed walls.

Five doors lead into the **third courtyard**★, evidence of the temple's status: other large temples have only three doors. As always, the middle door is reserved for the goddess. The shaded corridors on the sides are filled with monks whose chanting resounds from the old granite stones and fir beams. This courtyard also contains the temple's signature feature, a **domed ceiling** called the **spiderweb pagoda**★★★, designed to fool the fire gods into believing that the temple is underwater, and thus fireproof. The domed ceiling is made of countless carved and painted wooden pieces, put together like a multi-colored jigsaw and fitted onto 16 supporting spines. In the center of it sits a **gilded dragon**, a menacing presence that looks like a spider in a web, with the spectator as the fly.

The pagoda heralds the entrance to the **main shrine**★★★ *(flash photography is not allowed inside the main shrine)*, on top of which is a seven-layer pagoda. Exquisitely carved into the granite pillars in front of the main shrine are dragons, phoenixes, *qi lin* (kirin), turtles and cranes, all auspicious icons. During the 9-21 earthquake in 1999, these pillars shifted six inches; the former pillar footprints are visible. After the earthquake, the temple was lightly renovated: bright strips of new fir can be seen in the ceilings, in sharp contrast to the aged beams they help support.

Inside the **third pavilion**, the temple's main deity, the Buddhist goddess of Mercy **Guanyin**, is depicted here with a gentle golden face, and surrounded by purple orchids, fruit, candles and incense left behind by worshipers. She is flanked on the right by **Wei Tuo**, and on the left by **Qie Lan**, her two protectors. Other deities including Guang Gong are housed in this shrine, in lesser positions on the side. These are not jealous gods: in Taiwan different deities and religions co-exist peacefully side by side.

The **fourth courtyard** is an intentional anticlimax, so as not to distract from the main shrine; it has an unadorned rooftop, and it is meant to extend only

Spiderweb pagoda ceiling, Longshan Temple

Brent Hannon/Michelin

the temple grounds and add depth and dignity to the complex.

▷ *Return to Sanmin St., turn right, and proceed a few minutes toward Zhongshan Rd. About 20m/65ft before Zhongshan Rd., turn left (north) into tiny Xing Hua lane, which soon turns into Nine Turns Lane. Walk north.*

Nine Turns Lane 九曲巷

This lane is not a rebuilt tourist street; rather, it is filled with a typical selection of buildings both old and new. Yet much of it is the classic redbrick and stone architecture of old Lugang, notable for its thin gates and narrow passageways that protected it from violence.

▷ *Continue north on Nine Turns Lane.*

Xing An Gong Temple 新安宮
🕐*Open daily.*

This tiny temple is dedicated to **Mazu**, goddess of the Sea. One of the oldest in Lugang, it was built in 1684. Inside, Mazu is flanked by her familiar companions, **Thousand Mile Eyes** (also known as Thousand League Eyes 千里眼) and **Thousand Mile Ears** (or Thousand League Ears 順風耳), who help her locate sailors in distress. Here she is a dark-faced Mazu, which means that she saved a sailor in distress, who erected the temple upon arriving in Lugang.

Nine Turns Lane

Brent Hannon/Michelin

▷ *After the temple, the lane is paved with red bricks. Stay on the red bricks, and admire the architecture, until you reach the first busy street, Minzu Rd. Turn right and walk to Zhongshan Rd.*

On the northwest corner of Minzu and Zhongshan Roads is the **Yu Zhen Zai bakery**, famous for its milk cakes, salt crackers and other traditional Lugang sweets and snacks.

▷ *Walk north on the west side of Zhongshan Rd. for five minutes, until you reach Minquan Rd., and turn left. Continue 100m/328ft until you reach Lugang Old St., which is clearly marked.*

Lugang Old Street★★ 鹿港老街

This winding walk paved with cobblestones is a pleasant pedestrian-only passage that contains many of the top sights in Lugang. A few steps in sits the **Half-sided Well**, where a rich clan family allowed the neighboring peasants to share their water. Near the well is a raised stone platform where intellectuals gathered to engage in the 10 Pursuits of the Wealthy: poetry, flowers, wine, antiques, painting, smoking, tea drinking, books, chess and star-gazing.

A few steps farther rises **Memorial Tower** and the widow's window where a Lugang wife sat waiting for her husband, who had sailed to mainland China. He never returned, and the wife, too, is long gone, but the latticed window and sweeping green **Carambola tree** remain. Notice the slotted door where rich ladies could peer out onto the lane: they were not allowed outdoors on their little bound feet.

The next sight is a streetside **noodle tea shop**, and the key offering here is Lugang noodle tea. This tea is made by adding hot water to a fine flour of sesame, sugar, peanuts, oil and onion, which results in a sort of thick hot shake.

Visitors can buy bags of noodle tea to take home, while other shops sell salted mullet roe and other local treats. There are hand-made lantern shops, tin

Tian Hou Temple

Brent Hannon/Michelin

smiths, incense makers, and food stalls selling grilled squid, grilled sausages, fried doughy octopus balls, and other Taiwan treats. The most famous of these is *oah jien*, or **oyster omelet**, popular all over Taiwan, but the Lugang version is said to be the best.

The omelets are made from oil, oysters, egg, glutinous rice batter, green vegetables and hot sweet sauce, all fried together.

Xin Zu Temple 新祖宮
🕐*Open daily.*

Xin Zu means new Mazu Temple. This busy Daoist shrine was built in 1786 by Qing dynasty officials after they successfully quelled a rebellion in Lugang. The beams inside are black and tarry from the smoke generated by hundreds of years of burning incense and candles. In this temple the Mazu icon has a red

face, signifying her ascension to godly status.

▶ *Proceed in the same direction 10min more, and turn right at the T-intersection, continuing until you reach Tian Hou Temple.*

Tian Hou Temple★★ 天后宮
🕐*Open daily.*

Also dedicated to the Daoist goddess Mazu, this temple is the spiritual and aesthetic opposite of the Longshan Temple. Instead of brown and gray colors, Tian Hou Temple is ablaze in hues of bright red, gold, yellow and green, and its rooftop is capped by a riot of gaudy ceramic ornamentation. A beehive of activity, Tian Hou Temple is filled with people throwing oracle, or diving, blocks, burning incense and paper money, and drawing lots and reading

---

Lugang Architecture

Lugang's thin lanes and narrow stone gates, which open onto streets and neighborhoods throughout the town, were built for protection. In its early days, Lugang was wild and adventurous, as powerful clan lords carved out farming and trading fiefdoms, which they ruled with tyrannical authority. As the local warlords fought for control, residents were forced to contend with invasions, pirate raids, family feuds and pitched battles, many of which took place in the nearby Changhua plain. Bands of robbers also invaded from time to time, and new immigrants from Fujian formed gangs and fought each other. In such a climate, protection was paramount. Each neighborhood built narrow stone gates, often with gun turrets on top, to seal itself off from the violence. The gates, and the narrow twisted alleys, spared the residents from much of the violence, and the unique architecture is one of the hallmarks of Lugang.

Lugang Folk Arts Museum

Brent Hannon/Michelin

their fortunes. It has three **courtyards**; the first is open, the second contains an algal well and a huge urn bristling with incense. The main shrine houses a gold-faced **Mazu** who sits beneath jet black beams. Worshipers jostle and vie to light candles, pray, and burn incense as they ask favors from the goddess.

ADDITIONAL SIGHT
Lugang Folk Arts Museum
鹿港民俗文物館

152 Zhongshan Rd. 彰化縣鹿港鎮中山路152號 ⏰ *Open Tues–Sun 9am–5pm. NT$130.* 📞 *04 777 2019 www.lugangarts.org.tw. Guided tours in Chinese.*

Built in 1919 as a residence for the Koo family, and opened to the public in 1973, this graceful compound offers insight into how the wealthy lived in the early 20C.

Faithful re-creations of early 20C bedrooms, kitchens and parlors are on view. The museum houses many examples of the crafts that are associated with Lugang, including wheat flour **figurines** shaped like turtles, fish and shrimp that were used as offerings to the gods, as well as shadow puppets and elaborately sewn **hand puppets** on intricately carved wooden stages.

ADDRESSES

🍴/EAT
The courtyard in front of **Tian Hou Temple** contains a small army of **shrimp monkey** vendors and oyster **omelet makers**. The shrimp monkeys are legitimately local, and they can be found only in Lugang. If you look at one from the front, it is said to resemble a monkey. The unusual looking little shrimp are deep fried, coated with salt and pepper, and served in large piles. They go well with cold beer or iced oolong tea.

🛒 SHOPPING
Old Street is filled with craft shops offering a variety of hand-made souvenirs such as wood carvings, silk and paper fans, tinware and paper lanterns. The handmade **paper lanterns** are of particular interest since they are one of Lugang's local specialties. These intricate works, rendered in yellow, silver, green, gold, red and other dazzling hues, can take a week or longer to make. The painstaking labor is reflected in the price tag, with some lanterns costing NT$20,000 or more.

Sun Moon Lake★★

With its lofty peaks, mist-shrouded valleys, and hilltop temples and pagodas, Sun Moon Lake (日月潭) resembles a Song-era landscape painting. Such paintings evoke feelings of peace and contentment, and so it is with Taiwan's largest and most famous lake. Cool in summer and pleasant in winter, sitting at an elevation of 748m/2,454ft, and cradled in a natural amphitheater of mountains, Sun Moon Lake is one of the most tranquil places in Taiwan.

Its soul-restoring reputation extends all the way to mainland China, as visitors from the mainland always put this evocative lake high on their list of places to see. Whether the lake can handle a huge influx of tourists is uncertain, and some unsightly buildings have already sprung up along its shores, but for the time being it retains its pastoral calm and restful ambiance.

A boat trip around the lake is highly recommended, especially for first-time visitors. From the water, the views of the mountains that ring the lake are dramatic.

- **Michelin Map:** p217.
- **Info:** Shuishe Visitor Center, 163 Zhongshan Rd., Open daily 9am–5pm. 049-2855-668. www.sunmoonlake.gov.tw.
- **Location:** About 70min from Taichung via Freeway 6. **Shuili,** southwest of the lake area, is the gateway town, lying off Hwy. 16. Provincial Hwys. 21 and 21A ring the lake, around which sit the only two villages: **Shuishe**, the main hub, where the visitor center and bus station are located, on the north shore, and tiny **Itathao**, on the south shore. Tiny **Lalu Island**, in the round lake, is a favorite boating destination.
- **Kids:** The Ropeway, and the amusement rides at the aboriginal village.
- **Timing:** Temperate year-round, but the dry months *(Oct–Apr)* are especially nice.
- **Don't Miss:** The Ropeway, Formosan Aboriginal Culture Village, Ci'en Pagoda, a boat ride on the lake.

Sun Moon Lake

Brent Hannon/Michelin

GETTING THERE

BY CAR - Sun Moon Lake, southeast of Taichung, can be reached in 70min from Taichung via the new Highway 6. The new highway is a pretty drive with views of emerald-green hills, betelnut plantations, high bridges over rocky rivers, and the jagged sawtooth mountains of the Central Mountain Range itself.

BY BUS - Direct buses serve Sun Moon Lake from Taipei and Taichung, and arrive opposite the visitor center in Shuishe. Buses from Taipei leave hourly, and cost NT$420 to NT$500, depending upon the company and the season. Buses from Taichung depart twice a day; more frequently if you are willing to transfer in Puli. *For schedules and contacts, access www.sun moonlake.gov.tw/sun.aspx?Lang=EN.*

GETTING AROUND

BY BUS - A bus circles the lake every hour and stops at all the major sights. Passengers can board and exit as they please; NT$80 for a complete loop, or NT$21 for a single leg. Schedule at *www.sunmoonlake.gov.tw/ EN/02001269.aspx.*

BY CAR - ⬧*see Taichung for information on car rental.* Highway 21 and Provincial Highway 21A circle the lake.

BY TAXI - Taxis can be hired in Shuishe, at 4hrs for NT$1200. Most drivers double as tour guides, although only in Chinese.

BY TWO WHEEL - Bicycles (NT$300 to NT$500) and scooters (NT$500/day and up) can be rented in Shuishe. Some international-class hotels also have bicycles for rent.

BY BOAT - Sun Moon Lake **shuttle boats** depart every 30min from the docks at Itathao, Shuishe, and Xuanguang Temple. Each sector is NT$100, half price for children less than 140cm/55in tall (NT$20 for children under 115cm/45in). **Private boats** also operate from all three docks, and prices are negotiable; expect to pay about NT$200 for a 2hr trip with two stops, usually including Lalu Island.

GENERAL INFORMATION

AREA CODE: The prefix 04—the area code for Nantou County—has been included in the telephone numbers shown in this chapter, but it is not necessary to dial 04 when making a local call.

VISITOR INFORMATION

Shuishe Visitor Center, 163 Zhongshan Rd. 水社遊客中心南投縣魚池鄉中山路163號. ◐Open daily 9am–5pm. ℘049-285-5668. *www.sunmoonlake. gov.tw.*

ACCOMMODATIONS

Sun Moon Lake area offers a range of lodgings from major hotels to bed and breakfast inns. *For a selection, ⬧see ADDRESSES below.*

A BIT OF HISTORY

The emerald-green freshwater lake owes its shape to the Japanese, who made the key engineering change that turned the lake into one of Taiwan's top tourist destinations. In 1937 they dammed the west side of the lake for **hydroelectric power** generation, filling a couple of valleys and providing its signature sun-and-moon shape: the western end looks like a crescent moon; the eastern part is round like the sun.

The lake was home to the **Thao abo-rigines**, who were relocated after the lake was dammed. The smallest tribe in Taiwan, the Thao comprise fewer than 300 families. They are also the newest tribe, having been formally recognized in 2000 as Taiwan's tenth aboriginal group.

The Taiwanese later added the temples, pagodas, docks, gardens and amuse-ment parks that ring the lake and pro-vide its recreation.

Most of the attractions are rather mod-est—the shimmering beauty of the lake itself is the focal point for most visitors.

🚗 DRIVING TOUR

Circular trip of about 32km/20mi. Allow a full day. Tourist attractions are clearly posted in English and Chinese.

▶ Leave Shuishe on Provincial Hwy. 21 and proceed clockwise around the lake.

You will drive alongside mossy **retaining walls** and lush fields of elephant grass, fern, lowland trees and other tropical growth. The road has many twists and turns, and ups and downs, as it hugs the steep shores of the lake.

▶ At the 2km mark, Hwy. 21 becomes Provincial Highway 21A. Stay on Hwy. 21A and drive another 1.8km/1mi to Wen Wu Temple.

Wen Wu Temple 文武廟

🕐 *Open daily. Main gate closes 8pm.*
Most temples in Taiwan are either Buddhist or Daoist, but Wen Wu is a relative rarity: a Confucian temple. Temples dedicated to the sage are solemn and simple, although they spring to hectic life on the philosopher's birthday, September 28. Wen Wu was rebuilt in 1996, and is large and colorful, though somewhat lifeless.

The two bright red **stone lions** in front of the temple were donated by insurance tycoon Wu Huo-shih, whose name means "fire lion." Here, as elsewhere, Sun Moon Lake steals the show, and the hillside temple mostly provides a backdrop for sightseeing and photos.

The view from the temple is partly blocked by the unsightly Ching Sheng Hotel; a former prime minister once asked the owners to remove the hotel, to which they replied, "yes, if you can find an equally good spot for it." So there it sits, because there are few finer locations in all of Taiwan.

▶ Drive another 4.7km/3mi on Hwy. 21A to the Ropeway.

Sun Moon Lake Ropeway★★

🕐 *Open daily 10:30am–4pm. Closed 2nd Wed of month. 7min one way. NT$300 round-trip. www.ropeway.com.tw.*

Sun Moon Lake Ropeway
Brent Hannon/Michelin

This Austrian-built, NT$1 billion **cable-car attraction** opened in early 2010. The super-scenic ride connects the shores of Sun Moon Lake with the Formosan Aboriginal Culture Village. A splendid addition, the 1.9km/1.2mi ropeway seamlessly joins the lakeshore to the aboriginal park, and provides jaw-dropping **views**★★★ along the way. The trip from the lake to the park is scenic enough, but the return trip is flat-out spectacular. From its terminus at the aboriginal park, the brightly painted gondolas, which hold eight passengers each, first glide to the top of a steep 1,044m/3,425ft hill, then soar high above a broad forested valley, offering views of the bamboo, ferns and trees that grow far below, as well as glimpses of the lake itself. This 786m/2,579ft stretch is the longest unsupported section of the ride, and the cable cars dangle 140m/459ft above the forest floor. The ropeway then crests a final hill, before dropping straight down onto the shores of Sun Moon Lake. This final, steep descent, with its **panorama** of the lake, provides a thrilling finale to the aerial ride.

▶ Drive .8km/.5mi to Itathao.

Itathao 伊達邵

South side of lake.

Chiang Lands a Whopper

One of the legends of Sun Moon Lake is the story of Nationalist leader Chiang Kai-shek and the big fish. As the story goes, the day after he retreated to Taiwan in 1949, following the defeat of the Nationalists in the Chinese Civil War, Chiang sought solace on the shores of Sun Moon Lake. As soon as he arrived he went fishing, and supposedly caught a giant two-meter fish, which he took to be an auspicious sign that the Nationalists would reclaim mainland China. But few people around Sun Moon Lake believe the story. Some say the fish was caught for Chiang by Thao aborigines, while others say the entire story is a whopper and that no such two-meter fish ever existed. However fishy the story may be, it is true that Chiang loved Sun Moon Lake, which he visited often, and where he built a lakeside home for himself and the Ci'en Pagoda in honor of his mother.

The Thao tribe was relocated to this hamlet after the lake was dammed in 1937. The tiny community has a pleasant collection of hotels, convenience stores, souvenir stands and restaurants on a small peninsula. Lakeside boardwalks provide excellent **sunset views**. Local charms include abundant street food, aboriginal and Chinese restaurants, and small-town peace and quiet. Itathao is less expensive and more peaceful than the village of Shuishe. Boats connect to several lakeside attractions, so many people choose to overnight here.

◐ *Drive 4km/2.5mi to Xuanzang Temple.*

Xuanzang Temple 玄奘寺
◐*Open daily 5am–6pm.*

View from Ci'en Pagoda

Brent Hannon/Michelin

Xuanzang, or **Tripitaka**, was the legendary Tang dynasty-era monk famous for making an epic 17-year trip to India to acquire Buddhist scripture, as immortalized in the novel *Journey to the West*. Some of the monk's crystal remains (according to Buddhist legend, deceased believers leave crystals when they die; holier believers leave more crystals) are said to be housed in the temple. With its hushed atmosphere, holy relics and waterfront view, Xuanzang is an unparalleled place for quiet meditation.

◐ *From Xuanzang Temple, walk half a mile along Qinglong Mountain Trail (trail clearly marked in English).*

Qinglong Mountain Trail★ and Xuanguang Temple
青龍山步道玄光寺
Temple ◐*Open daily 5am–9pm.*
🚶This gentle 850m/.5mi **trail** leads from Xuanzang Temple down to the lakeside Xuanguang Temple. The picturesque path is planted in an array of flower species that bloom at different times of the year such as magnolias, orchids and jasmine, so visitors have flowers to enjoy year-round.
Xuanguang Temple is a modest shrine where the remains of the monk were first placed in 1955, until Xuanzang Temple was completed in 1965. Xuanguang Temple is known for its excellent tea eggs, cooked in their shells in soy sauce and medicinal herbs, and sold at the **La Mei Shop** just above the lake. Attractive young women in Taiwan are often called

La Mei, or spice girl, and the proprietor of this shop was a legendary beauty in her youth. But that was decades ago, and though she still dishes up top-notch tea eggs, most people now call the shop Ah Mei, which means grandmother.

○ *Drive another 300m/.20mi along Hwy. 21A to Ci'en Pagoda.*

Ci'en Pagoda★ 慈恩塔
○*Open daily 6am–10pm.*
This landmark tower is an old-school classic built by former president Chiang Kai-shek in 1971 to honor his mother. It is recounted that young Chiang was a troublemaker, but his stern mother kept him on the straight and narrow path that led eventually to the presidency of the Republic of China; he forever credited her with his success.

After a long ascent up a stone pathway, and another climb up the circular stairs of the 46m/150ft-tall tower, visitors are rewarded with superlative **views**★★ of the lake. The pagoda sits atop 954m/3,130ft **Shabalan Mountain**, and its apex tops out at exactly 1,000m/3,281ft above sea level.

From this lofty perch, if visitors apply enough imagination, they can "see" a water-drinking dragon, lapping up the blue-green liquid of Sun Moon Lake. Even if the dragon doesn't manifest itself, the views are worth the climb.

○ *Drive another 1.8km/1mi to Xuanguang Temple, then another 8km/5mi to the junction of 21A and 21.*

This stretch of road winds through pastoral groves of Tong trees. Every spring, the Tong blossoms carpet the ground in snowy white petals, in a display the Chinese call "May Snow."

○ *Turn right on Provincial Hwy. 21, and drive the remaining 8.5km/5mi back to Shuishe.*

This section has no major tourist sights, but it is a pretty stretch of road, with scalloped jade-colored inlets, betel-nut and banana plantations, thick forests and lakeside paths all adding to the scenery.

ADDITIONAL SIGHT
👤👤 Formosan Aboriginal Culture Village★★ 九族文化村
○ *3km/1.8mi northeast of Sun Moon Lake by town roads 69 and 67, a 12km/7.5mi drive from Shuishe. 45 Ching Tien Lan, Da Lin Village, Nantou County. NT$700 (includes all rides and shows).* ✕ ✆*049-2895361. Cable car and shuttle buses. www.nine.com.tw.*
Sitting in a scenic forested valley, this combination aboriginal village and amusement park rates as one of the best in Taiwan, especially popular with fam-

Formosan Aboriginal Culture Village

Brent Hannon/Michelin

243

Thao Harvest Festival

The festival is held in Itathao in the eighth month of the lunar calendar (usually Aug). A 3km/2mi Sun Moon Lake Swim from the lakeshore, just below Wenwu Temple, to Itathao dock, is held every year (usually mid-Sept). All would-be swimmers must register by July, and all participants are required to wear life preservers.

ilies and children. Large and spacious and filled with trees, the park attracts visitors to its shows and rides, but the village is also rich in information about Taiwan's native tribes.

Visit

Located at the bottom of the valley, the **amusement park** features rides such as a monorail, a roller coaster, a Jurassic cruise along manmade canals and a gentle Love Boat ride. This area also has a Star Trek Carnival and a mockup of a Mayan village.

Higher up the valley, 10 **tribal villages** have been painstakingly re-created, and in some cases relocated piece by piece. A **cable car** and **shuttle buses** carry visitors to the top of the valley, so they can stroll downhill through the tribal villages, one for each of the tribes, starting with Paiwan, then Ami, Rukai, Tao, Puyuma, Bunun, Thao, Tsou, Atayal and

Saisiyat. Among the villages are three **performance areas**, where tribal rituals and dances are performed at regular intervals *(Chinese only)*.

Inside the stone or wood aboriginal **dwellings**, visitors learn *(information in English)* about class structure, crops and food, marriage rites, sacred objects, head-hunting traditions and more. Displays speak volumes about the now-vanished lifestyles of the "original people," as they are called in Chinese. One has a layout of a Paiwan wedding, with the chief, matchmaker, bridesmaids, best men, unsuccessful suitors, and bride and groom all depicted. Next to the bride are traditional gifts: clay pots, glass beads, rifle, formal clothing and other implements. Authentic **carvings** abound, many of them richly detailed, especially the Paiwan, Bunun and Rukai stone carvings, some of which feature stylized depictions of the highly poisonous Hundred-Pace Viper. Authentic **food** is available: several restaurants and food stands serve baked sweet potatoes, grilled smoked pork, rice cooked in bamboo, millet wine, mountain tubers, and other tribal staples. Pottery and weaving **demonstrations**, aboriginal musical instrument **concerts**, and wood-carving **workshops** are offered, while on-site stores sell millet wine, tribal clothes, carvings, woven mats, aboriginal headgear, and other one-of-a-kind souvenirs.

The Lalu overlooking Sun Moon Lake

Brent Hannon/Michelin

ADDRESSES

🛏 STAY

$$ Cherngyuan – 澄園休閒旅店,
南投縣魚池鄉日月村文化街117號
Near Itathao boat dock. ✆049-2850062.
www.cherngyuan.com.tw. 16 rooms.
Breakfast included. A charming small
hotel in quiet Itathao village, the
Cherngyuan has friendly staff, good
coffee and rooms in a variety of sizes,
many with good views of the lake. The
breakfast nook on the top floor has
exceptional views through large picture
windows, and the sunrise from here is
extraordinary. No restaurant on-site.

$$ Teachers' Hostel – 日月潭教師會館,
南投縣魚池鄉日月潭中興路136號.
136 Zhongxing Rd., near Shuishe. ✕✆049-2855991. *www.t-welfare.com.tw/edumoon.*
103 rooms. Breakfast included. Located
on a leafy peninsula near The Lalu, this
hostel has a natural setting and views
of the lake. The old wing, the Bai Ru
building, is less expensive than the new
wing, the Han Xi building. The biggest
rooms can hold up to five guests.
Restaurant on-site.

$$$ Hotel Del Lago – 日月潭大淶閣,
南投縣魚池鄉日月潭中山路101號
101 Zhongshan Rd., Shuishe. ✕✆049-2856688. *www.dellago.com.tw. 88 rooms.*
Breakfast included. The Del Lago has
a fine location overlooking Shuishe
Pier. The rooms above the lake are
overpriced and a bit shabby, while the
rooms overlooking the city, though
cheaper, are somewhat drab. Stay here
only if other hotels are booked. Fruit
basket, free bicycles and mini-bar are
included in the rate. There's a restaurant
on the premises.

$$$$ Fleur De Chine – 日月潭雲品酒店,
臺灣南投縣魚池鄉日月潭中正路23號.
23 Zhongzheng Rd., about 3km/1.8mi from
Shuishe. ✕✆049-2856788. *www.fleurde*
chinehotel.com. 211 rooms. Perched on
a peninsula between Wenwu Temple
and the Sun Moon Lake Ropeway, the
Fleur De Chine opened in 2008, with
bedrooms that provide fine views of the
lake. All guest quarters have balconies,
and the tariff includes breakfast and
dinner in the on-site restaurants.

$$$$$ The Lalu – 涵碧樓大飯店南
投縣魚池鄉水社村中興路142號. *142*
Zhongxing Rd. Shuishe. ✕ 🛋 ✆049-2856888. *www.thelalu.com.tw. 62 rooms.*
The US$65 million Australian-designed
Lalu is a minimalist masterpiece that
blends beautifully with its surroundings.
All rooms are suites, and the overall
design features spacious atriums,
panoramic windows, polished interiors
and Asian motifs like twinkling lanterns
floating on ponds. Every suite has a
bedroom, living room and balcony,
with views of the lake and mountains.
A Japanese teahouse overlooks the
60m/197ft outdoor pool. A tinkling
piano in the cocktail lounge provides
the only nightlife, but no one is likely
to complain, cocooned as they are in
luxurious indolence. Spa salon and
three restaurants on the premises.

🍴 EAT

$ Du Lu Shi Chang – 瑪蓋旦風味餐廳
– *In Itathao. Closes at 8:30pm.* ✆049-2850523. An easy-to-find restaurant in
Itathao, the Du Lu market restaurant
features aborigine-style cooking, while
people sitting outside can watch, and
hear, an aboriginal song-and-dance
program. Stewed pork knuckle, rice and
millet cooked in bamboo, and steamed
president fish are the house specialties.
Taiwanese.

🛍 SHOPPING

Millet wine, a mild sweet wine made
from rice and millet by the aboriginal
tribes, is a popular souvenir along the
lake. At its best, millet wine has enough
acidity to balance its sugar, but some
bottles can be quite sweet.
Many places will serve samples; expect
to pay about NT$600 for a decent
bottle. **Pineapple cakes**, made from
candied pineapple pulp surrounded by
rich flaky pastry, are common as well.
Thao **tribal handicrafts**, artwork and
clothing are also popular Sun Moon
Lake souvenirs. Itathao is the best place
to buy authentic, hand-sewn items,
made on the shores of the lake. The
Formosan Aboriginal Culture Village
also sells a variety of handmade (as well
as machine-made) tribal souvenirs.

Central Mountains★★

From wet wild woods to sun-soaked alpine meadows, this classic stretch of road traverses the breathtaking scenery of Taiwan's Central Mountain Range. Surrounded by some of the highest peaks in East Asia, the highlands combine rare natural beauty with a rich concentration of bird and animal life. Slopes are mantled in apple and pear orchards and tea plantations farmed by Chinese civil war veterans and their descendants. Adventurous souls can don hiking boots and backpacks and walk into remote wilderness, but the road itself features an abundance of superb views, making this the most accessible high-mountain terrain in all of Taiwan.

A BIT OF GEOGRAPHY

East of Taichung the **Central Cross-Island Highway**, a stretch of road that includes Highways 14, 14A and 8 passes through two distinct regions, each with its own microclimate and a diverse suite of plant and animal life.

Central Foothills

As Highway 14 heads east from Puli into the heart of the Central Mountain Range, it soon becomes a slow and winding road as it skirts eroded landforms that are unique to Taiwan.

The steepness of the **western foothills**, and their deposited alluvial nature, combined with frequent typhoons and heavy thunderstorms, has created a jagged, weathered landscape of small pinnacles and steep valleys.

Many of the small peaks are covered only with grass; some of them are barren, as few plants can cling to such unstable ground.

The foothills of the Central Mountain Range are very wet, as moisture-laden marine air hits the mountains and rises, then cools and condenses into frequent rain and thick fog.

- **Michelin Map:** p217.
- **Info:** Fushoushan Visitor Center, 29 Fushou Rd. 福壽路29號, Lishan. ℘04 2598 9205. www.fushoushan.com.tw. Cingjing Farm Visitor Center, 170 Renhe Rd. 仁和路170號, Tadong Village. ℘049-2802748.
- **Location:** From **Puli**, Provincial Highway 14 heads northeast to Wushe; from there Provincial Highway 14A continues on to **Dayuling**, where Provincial Highway 8 leads to **Lishan**. It's best to have your own transport, since bus service is spotty.
- **Timing:** Allow 2-3 days to visit the mountains. Avoid traveling after heavy rains as the roads may wash out. Best time to visit is April to October. It's advisable to carry some cash since few gas stations and restaurants en route take credit cards.
- **Don't Miss:** Hehuanshan, Lishan, Fushoushan Farm.

Formosan Macaques

Rich J. Matheson/Michelin

Conifers in cloud forest zone

Brent Hannon/Michelin

Cloud Forests

As the road reaches an elevation of about 1,800m/5,900ft, it penetrates this **cloud forest zone**, a wet, mossy, fecund climate belt that teems with plant life. Thick mid-elevation forests dominate the terrain, which features rocky metamorphic outcrops, sheer valleys and occasional steep cliffs. **Broadleaf forests** of Machilus-Castanopsis and Evergreen Oak form thick canopies above the forest floor, and provide food and shelter for Formosan Black Bears, Formosan Macaques, pangolins and other mammals.

Conifers are more common on the higher slopes, especially Taiwan Pine, but **mixed forest** is the norm in both the western and eastern mid-elevation zones.

Many kinds of trees thrive in the moist mountain air, along with lush understories of ferns, grass, bamboo, vine maple and other thick ground cover.

Alpine Meadowlands

As it nears 3,000m/9,842ft, the road breaks free from the clouds and dark forests, and enters a spectacular open landscape of junipers, flowers, white "ghost" trees, mountain streams and wide grassy meadows. The **alpine zone** lies above the clouds and mist, and daytime weather is often sunny, while nights are cold and feature starry skies and fine views of the heavens.

Morning views of the sun rising over the "**sea of clouds**" are especially cherished by the Taiwanese. Extremely rare elsewhere, the combination of cloud forests below and clear weather above generates frequent views of the phenomenon in Taiwan.

Impressive groves of Taiwan Hemlock and Taiwan Fir adorn the mountain flanks, along with thick clusters of Yushan bamboo and stands of juniper and birch. Mountain **rhododendron** and azaleas thrive in the open areas;

Anmashan Birding Site

The mecca of birding in Taiwan, and one of the top sites in Asia, is Anmashan (鞍馬山), near Dongshi, at the junction of Provincial Highways 3 and 8 in Taichung County. The area ranges from 1,000m/3,280ft to 3,000m/9,842ft in elevation, and is thickly covered with temperate broadleaf forest, mixed forest and boreal conifer forest. Much of the forest cover is pristine and undisturbed, making it ideal habitat for the two signature pheasant species. A fortunate visitor can see most of the island's endemics here. Anmashan is a must-visit for international birdwatchers who come to Taiwan.

their pink and white blossoms are a common sight on the higher hillsides. The region is habitat for Taiwan's high-mountain birds, while Reeve's Muntjac, a small shy herbivore also called the bark-ing deer, forages in the meadows. As the highway crests the 3,156m/10,354ft pass and begins to descend eastward, it re-enters the cloud forests on the eastern side of the Central Mountain Range.

Fauna

With its quick changes in altitude and climate zones, occasional undeveloped forests, and huge variety of plant spe-cies that provide shelter and forage, the Central Cross-Island Highway is one of the premier **birding sites** in Taiwan. The wet woods and high mountain slopes harbor almost all of the most sought-after birds in Taiwan— the 15 endemic species that are found nowhere else— along with high concentrations of other species.

The most famous bird in Taiwan is the reclusive male **Mikado Pheasant**, the "king of the mists." The males are strik-ing specimens with ruby-red faces, shimmering feathers of deep blue and black, and snow-white stripes near the tail, while the females are a simpler mot-tled brown. Mikados can be found in the undisturbed rain forest belts between Puli and Wushe, with thicker popula-tions living higher up near Wushe.

Many other endemics live in the cloud forest zone, including Steere's Liocichla, a small perching bird with attractive multicolored plumage, and the **Tai-wan Hill Partridge**, White-eared Sibia, Alishan Bush Warbler, Taiwan Yuhina, Taiwan Yellow Tit and others. The sec-ond most sought-after bird in Taiwan is **Swinhoe's Pheasant**, another timid, agile and hard-to-find customer found in the mid-elevation forests. Similar in color to the Mikado, the male Swinhoe's has the same ruby-red face and deep blue feathers as the Mikado, but with a white tail and a snow-white spot on its back—and it prefers slightly lower elevations.

Mountain-dwelling endemics live in the high alpine meadowlands at the apex of the Cross-Island Highway, including the Taiwan **Laughing Thrush**, Taiwan Firecrest, and Taiwan Bush Warbler. Nature lovers need not concentrate only on endemic species, as the fields and skies are filled with many dozens of bird species, as are the lower eleva-tion forests.

🚗 DRIVING TOUR

110km/68mi from Puli to Lishan. Allow minimum of 1 day. Begin with a full gas tank.

Puli 埔里

Near the crossroads of Hwy. 21 and 14, about 40km/25mi southeast of Taichung, and about 20km/12mi north of Sun Moon Lake.

The Kung Fu of Tea

How do Taiwanese people enjoy tea when they use such small cups and two teapots? It is a puzzle for visitors who are not accustomed to Chinese tea culture. The way Taiwanese people drink tea has been inherited from the people of Fujian Province, which is known in Chinese as *gongfu cha* (kung fu of tea). The best teapots are made of clay, preferably *kaolin* clay from mainland China.

Here's how they make the perfect pot of tea:

1. Warm up the clay brewing pot as well as the cups with boiling water.
2. Put the tea leaves in the warmed teapot and pour in boiling water. Pour the brewing into the pouring pot and then into the tea cups, but do not drink it! The only purpose is to rinse and warm the tea service.
3. Brew some tea again; steep it for 40min. Use a strainer to eliminate small parts of tea leaves when you pour the brewed tea into the pouring pot.
4. Serve the tea from the pouring pot, and enjoy the refreshing taste.

Courtesy Taiwan Tourism Bureau

Sheep grazing, Cingjing Farm

A small town of about 90,000 residents, Puli marks the western edge of the mountain traverse. The town sits in a broad basin at an elevation of 500m/1,640ft, and it has a reputation for clean air and healthy living, a place where "no dust settles on the rice bowl." It is also known for its pristine **mountain water**, a resource that gave rise to its wine and paper-making industries, both of which require clear water. And it is home to the remarkable **Chung Tai Chan Monastery**★★★.

▷ *Take Hwy. 14 northeast to Wushe. The road parallels the Mei River.*

Wushe 霧 社
Northeast of Puli, along Hwy. 14.
Wushe was once a stronghold of the **Atayal** aboriginal tribe, one of the most warlike and fiercest of Taiwan's original people. In 1930 the Atayal rebelled against the Japanese, and several hundred Atayal were killed during what is now called the **Wushe Incident**. A monument to their bravery is one of the town's key attractions. Beyond that, there is little else in Wushe, but hikers who plan on trekking into the high mountains should obtain a police permit here and if necessary, arrange pickup at the end of the ▨ **Chilai Ridge Trail**.

▷ *From Wushe, the Highway becomes Hwy. 14A.*

Lushan Hot Springs★
廬山溫泉
Off a spur road to the right of Hwy. 14A.
A few miles northeast of Wushe, this collection of alkaline hot springs was developed by the Japanese a century ago. The transparent, near-boiling water is rich in sodium carbonate, and is supposed to be good for the skin and respiratory system, and cure rheumatism. Lushan is popular for its hot springs hotels, many of which have indoor and outdoor pools filled with the spring water, and overlook the steep gorge upon which Lushan is precariously perched.

♟♟ Cingjing Farm★ 清境農場
Northeast of Wushe on Hwy. 14A. 170 Renhe Rd., Tadong Village. ℘049-2802748. www.chingjing.gov.tw.
Flourishing on the steep hills and carved from the wilderness is a surprising development: this farm, where orchards of pears, apples, kiwi fruit, and **tea fields** grow in the cool climate at 1,600m/5,249ft to 2,200m/7,218ft. The mountains of Taiwan are dotted with several **veterans' farms**, set up for the Nationalist soldiers who came to the island following the Chinese Civil War. But Cingjing Veteran Farm is unique, because it was settled by ethnic tribes from the mountains of Yunnan Province, many of them members of the Bai minority. After the Nationalists lost the Chinese Civil War, the minority soldiers

fled to Burma, Thailand and Laos, where they continued their resistance for nearly a decade. In October 1960, they were ordered to withdraw and come to Taiwan, and 253 were sent to Cingjing Farm, where they planted peach, pear and apple orchards.

Today Cingjing Farm's thriving **orchard**, although it now grows modern fruits like kiwi and California plum as well as peaches, pears and apples. Sheep graze on grassy fields that have been reclaimed from the wilderness. Tourists come to enjoy the fresh air, mountain trails, **ice cream** made from sheep's milk and the **sheep-shearing shows** that are held on weekends.

▷ *Hwy. 14A continues northeast from Cingjing Farm.*

Hehuanshan Forest Recreation Area★★

The road continues its steep ascent through the mist-shrouded landscapes and past tiny roadside collections of gas stations and convenience stores, perched on steep hills or squeezed into narrow valleys.

About 30km/18.6mi east of Wushe, the road emerges from the damp forests and arrives at the open grasslands of Hehuanshan Forest Recreation Area. The easy accessibility of Hehuanshan makes it the best place in subtropical Taiwan to see **snow**, though visitors also come here in summer to escape the heat, and in the spring to see azaleas and rhododendrons bloom. The area features up-close looks at many of the tallest mountains in Taiwan, including 3,416m/11,207ft **Hehuanshan**, 3,886m/12,749ft **Xueshan**, and 3,605m/11,827ft **Chilai North Peak**, the highest point on the saw-toothed range that dominates the eastern horizon.

🚶 A network of **trails** radiates in all directions from **Songxue Lodge**, the only large building in the recreation area. The landscapes are steep and hilly, and the air is thin at these elevations—the lodge sits at 3,150m/10,225ft—so walking is more taxing than usual. Nonetheless, **day hikes** to the top of Hehuanshan, Hehuanshan East Peak, and Mt. Shimen are popular and not overly strenuous. To the east lies the challenging mountain trail that leads to the top of **Mount Chilai**, and then continues south down Chilai Ridge toward Mt. Nenggao, and eventually exits near the Lushan Hot Springs. This entire area, from near Hehuanshan east to the Pacific Ocean, lies in the protective embrace of Taroko National Park, and much of it is wild and undeveloped.

▷ *Continue northeast along Hwy. 14A.*

Highway 14A, Central Mountains

Rich J. Matheson/Michelin

Mount Hehuan to Dayuling★★ 合歡山 to 大禹嶺

With its green meadowlands, high mountain vistas and unrestricted **views**★★ of the surrounding peaks, this superlative stretch of highway is one of the most rewarding drives in Taiwan. About 4km/2.5mi east of Songxue Lodge, the Hehuanshan Ranger Station (KM 36.5, Provincial Hwy. 14A; ℘04 599 1015) features a scenic **viewpoint** that overlooks a vast expanse of wilderness, and several walking paths. At dawn the viewpoint features fine **views**★★ of the "sea of clouds" that cloaks the lower elevations, while evening sunsets and the starry night skies also shine crisp and clear in the mountain air. The high road continues through similar terrain dotted with Chinese hemlock, weather-bleached snags, juniper and rhododendron, and open grasslands with patches of dwarf bamboo and mountain azalea.

◗ Continue on Hwy. 14A northeast to Dayuling (大禹嶺), at the junction with Provincial Hwy. 8.

The Road to Lishan

After it crosses the meadowlands, Highway 14A arrives in the tiny village of **Dayuling** (大禹嶺), where it hits a 'T' intersection with Provincial Highway 8. To the right, heading east on Highway 8, is the ultra-steep, tunnel- and switchback riddled road that snakes down through the wild, remote sections of **Taroko Gorge**. To the left, or north, the high-mountain Highway 8 makes its way to **Lishan**, a tiny fruit- and tea-producing village about 20km/12mi distant. From Lishan, or Pear Mountain, the landmark North Cross-Island Highway (Hwy. 7A) winds its way down eastward to Yilan, on a route that, while initially steep, flattens steadily as it nears the ocean. Highway 8 continues west from Lishan, starting briefly toward Taichung, before terminating at the foot of Deji Reservoir some 15km/9mi from Lishan. This road has been closed since the September 21, 1999 earthquake, and is not expected to reopen any time soon.

Lishan★★ 梨山

About 5km/3mi west of the junction of Hwys. 7 and 8.

Lishan, or **Pear Mountain**, is a vacation and fruit-growing village nestled at 1,620m/5,315ft. For many years, Lishan was a thriving tourist hub, a mountain retreat cherished for its cool weather, clean air, restful views and fragrant, bountiful fruit orchards. It was one of former president Chiang Kai-shek's favorite vacation spots. One of the island's most famous holiday lodges, the **Lishan Guesthouse**, now closed, was built in the Imperial style with red pillars, sloping slate roofs, hardwood floors and broad balconies. The town's fame was enhanced by nearby **Fushoushan Veterans' Farm** 福壽山農場 (29 Fushou Rd.; ℘04 2598 9205; www.fushoushan.com.tw), where retired Chinese Civil War soldiers settled in 1950 to grow apples, pears, cherries and tea in the temperate climate.

But modern-day Lishan is much, much quieter. The tides of tourism have shifted to newer, easier-to-reach destinations, and the apples and pears farmed on the weather-beaten mountain slopes eventually proved to be expensive and uncompetitive compared with cheaper imported fruit. The unkindest cut of all was the **earthquake** of September 21, 1999, which permanently closed a key stretch of Provincial Highway 8, the fastest route to Taichung and the populous west coast. So there sits Lishan, remote and little visited, waiting for an economic lifeline.

In the meantime, its tourism virtues are intact, and visitors who do make the drive are richly rewarded, and often have the village and the veteran's farm virtually to themselves. Lishan offers enchanting **views**★ of the **Xueshan** (Snow Mountain 雪山) range to the north, separated from Lishan by a near-bottomless chasm. The surrounding slopes are cloaked in fruit orchards, which blossom in the springtime, and yield an annual bounty of fresh fruit: cherries (May–Jun), peaches (Jul–Aug), pears and apples (Aug–Nov) and persimmons (Nov–Dec). In the fall, red maples unveil crimson colors, while in the springtime, the first sweet sprigs of Lishan **oolong tea** emerge from winter dormancy.

Because it is sandwiched between two national parks—Shei Pa to the north, and Taroko to the south—the area is rich in flora and fauna, as **swallowtail butterflies** dance in the clearings, Formosan Striped Squirrels, macaques and black bears populate the lower forests, and many species of bird thrive in the mountain habitats.

Lishan has also found a new livelihood: tea. Some of the fruit orchards, especially those on the higher slopes of nearby **Fushoushan**★★ (福壽山), or Fushou Mountain, have been replaced with tea plantations.

The best and tenderest tea leaves are grown at high mountain elevations, and Fushoushan has the highest **tea slopes** in Taiwan, at up to 2,500m/8,200ft. Growing tea this high is a risky propo-

sition, because the yield is just two harvests per year, and because a sudden frost can wipe out an entire crop. But for the harvests that do survive, the rewards are rich: Lishan **oolong** is the most famous and expensive tea in Taiwan, and it fetches about US$250 for 600 grams.

Aside from sightseeing, the main activity in Lishan is arising before dawn, and driving to the top of Fushoushan as the sun rises, on a smooth blacktop road that glows in the radiant pre-dawn light. The weather at these altitudes is reliably sunny and clear, and the road through Fushoushan is usually bathed in mountain sunlight and dotted with snow-white clouds. The tea plantations, pine trees and surrounding mountains make the 30min **drive** to the 2,548m/8,360ft summit a memorable one.

At the top is a leafy **park** where tourists greet the morning with picnic baskets, tai chi, hot tea and general revelry.

ADDRESSES

🏨 STAY

$$ Hehuanshan Songxue Lodge 松雪樓 – km 32, Provincial Hwy. 14A. ✕ ℘04-9280 2980. Reservations ℘04-2522 9797. **80 rooms.** This modern hotel has replaced the former rustic hostel, and while it is nondescript in character, it has brought a welcome new level of comfort to a remote mountain setting. Some rooms are big enough to hold up to five people. Dinner and breakfast are included, but no alcohol is served on the premises.

$$ Lu Shan Garden Resort 廬山廬山園游泳池大飯店 – 12 Nong Hua Alley, Jing Ying Village, Wushe. 南投縣仁愛鄉精英村榮華巷12號. ✕ ℘04-9280 2369. www.lsg-resort.hotel.com.tw/eng. **200 rooms.** The 87°C/188°F water is piped straight into the rooms of the Lu Shan Garden, although public spa baths are

also available, along with a children's spa and a swimming pool. In keeping with the area's heritage—the Japanese originally developed the area's hot springs—the resort features a selection of Japanese-style tatami rooms. Its outdoor cafe and Chinese restaurant both have sweeping views of the valley.

$-$$$ Fushoushan Farm 福壽山農場 – 29 Fushou Rd., Lishan. 福壽路29號. ℘04-2598 1108. www.fushoushan.com.tw. **91 rooms.** The farm offers a variety of overnight lodging, which is broadly scattered throughout the mountaintop. Choices range from a simple group house for six people with a shared bathroom and no breakfast, to the small **Fushou Hotel** with 15 rooms and breakfast included, to a single two-person hut at Tianchi, at the top of the mountain. Dinner is available if arranged in advance.

Hiking Taiwan

The rugged peaks that dominate two-thirds of Taiwan provide one of its choicest recreations. Thousands of trails beckon the would-be walker, ranging from easy but super-scenic two-hour jaunts, to hair-raising hikes along razor-edged ridges, with heavy backpacks balanced on tired shoulders.

Trail to Chilai Ridge

Brent Hannon/Michelin

🥾 EASY HIKES

Taiwan has hundreds of easy walks, but if you do just one, make it **Baiyang Trail** (白楊步道) in Taroko National Park. The easy two-hour stroll begins with a nearly 400m/1,247ft-long **pedestrian tunnel** carved through a sheer cliff, and continues with fine **views**★★ of the marble canyons of Taroko Gorge and peaceful streams, before reaching Baiyang Falls itself, a long graceful ribbon of water that pulsates in the sun.

Closer to Taipei is **Qixingshan** (七星山) in Yangmingshan National Park, a three-hour walk that makes its way past bubbling fumaroles and through green corridors of bamboo on its way to the 1,120m/3,675ft summit of "Seven Star Mountain." The trail then traverses the ridgeline and threads its way through shining meadows of silvergrass, offering fine views of the Taipei Basin.

🥾 MEDIUM HIKES

Caoling Trail (草嶺古道) a well-marked one-day walk on the northeast coast, combines Qing-era history with dramatic ocean views. This ancient route was pioneered in the 19C, and its rich history is evident in its place names, such as Horse Falling to Death Bridge and Bravely Quelling the Wild Mists Pass. The trail starts in thick lowland forest that is alive with butterflies and birds, and then emerges onto a high ridge that offers expansive **views**★★ of the coast.

Dajianshan (大尖山), the rocky spire that looms above the beaches of **Kenting National Park,** is another fine one-day walk. The hike to the top begins as an easy stroll through lowland meadows, but gets rocky and steep near the summit, which has wonderful **views**★★ of the beaches and jungles.

🥾 HARD HIKES

The rugged Central Mountain Range offers dozens of multi-day backpacking trips, but for superlative natural beauty the best is **Chilai Ridge** (奇萊山), a challenging trek that entails a long upward hike to the 3,200m/10,498ft-elevation ridgeline, followed by a remarkable walk along the crumbling tilted shale of the ridge itself. Scenery-wise this trek is unsurpassed, but its steep cliffs and razor-edged ridges are not for beginners.

For permanent bragging rights, the only peak that really counts is **Yushan**, or **Jade Mountain**, the tallest and most famous peak in Taiwan. The easiest trail is a gentle one-day walk to a rustic hostel, and from there, hikers arise in the pre-dawn darkness to trek the remaining two hours to the 3,950m/12,959ft summit. The trail is not a complete cakewalk, as it gains 1,350m/4,429ft of altitude, and is steep and slippery near the top.

Chiayi

The city of Chiayi (嘉義) is nondescript, and its attractions are modest, but that will not be the case when Taipei's National Palace Museum opens its southern branch in Chiayi in 2013; Taipei's top attraction is likely to draw thousands of visitors here to see rotating exhibits of the most renowned collection of Chinese arts on the planet.

For the time being, visitors will notice the fertility of the surrounding land, which sprouts a rich profusion of crops, including fields of rice, tobacco, sugar cane, pineapple, corn, and taro, stands of papaya and betelnut, and orchards of guava, lychee and oranges. The countryside has fewer factories than is common in western Taiwan, and the lack of industry, combined with a sparse population and plentiful pockets of farmland, lend Chiayi a restful character that is rare on the heavily developed west coast.

Rural character notwithstanding, Chiayi is almost exclusively known as the gateway to Alishan and Yushan, two parallel mountain ranges within the Central Mountains—and two of Taiwan's top mountain getaways. Alishan is a forested mountain range, not a single peak, and its tallest point is Mount Dashan; Alishan is often used to refer to the 1,400ha/3,459acre Forest Recreation Area as well, and to the township at its center. Yushan, or Jade Mountain, is both a peak and a national park. Chiayi is the starting point for rail and road trips to Alishan Forest Recreation Area and the "sea of clouds," and road trips to the base of Jade Mountain, Taiwan's most famous peak and most popular mountain trek.

A BIT OF HISTORY

Like most of western Taiwan, Chiayi was originally home to plains aborigines, who were displaced by Chinese immigrants from Fujian Province who began arriving in the 16C. Chiayi, an inland town, was never as prosperous

▶ **Population:** 274,000.

Michelin Map: p217.

Info: Alishan National Scenic Area, 3-16 Chukou, Chukou Village, Fanzhu Township. ℘05 259 3900. www.ali-nsa.net/english/ 02travel/05main.php. Yushan National Park Headquarters, 515 Songshan Rd. Sec. 1, Shuili Township, Nantou County. ℘049 277 3121. www.ysnp.gov.tw/en.

▶ **Location:** Chiayi sits in southcentral Taiwan, about 30km/18.6mi from the coast. From Chiayi City, take Freeway 3 out of Chiayi, then take Provincial Highway 18 east to **Alishan Forest Recreation Area** on a well-signposted road, although taking the **Alishan Forest Railway** is highly recommended. The forest area has a scattering of hotels and restaurants, most of which lie in a ring around a small public plaza in **Alishan Township**.

Kids: Alishan Forest Railway, Alishan Forest Recreation Area.

Timing: One or two nights at Alishan Forest Recreation Area. Best months to go are mid-March through mid-October, before the weather turns cold. Cherry trees blossom from mid-March to early April, while the "sea of clouds" phenomenon appears most often in autumn. Weekdays are generally less crowded, but make hotel reservations in advance, regardless of what days you plan to stay.

Don't Miss: Alishan Forest Railway, and the sunrise at Zhushan.

as port cities like Lugang, Tainan, and later Taipei. It was a farming village, and the agriculture was bolstered by trade in mountain products like lumber, leopard and deer pelts, medicinal herbs, and other goods.

The Japanese kick-started the economy in 1916, when they opened a railway to Alishan and began to carry thick logs of Yellow Cypress back to the town, fueling a large lumber industry, while agriculture thrived side-by-side with the logging. Taiwan was once a major global producer of pineapples and sugar, and for much of the 20C, Chiayi was a center for trade and processing of those important cash crops, and pineapple canneries and sugar refineries dotted the landscape. But the pineapple and sugar cane industries declined as well, crippled by competition from cheaper, far-flung tropical locations.

Chiayi then found a new lifeline: tourism. The Alishan Forest Recreation Area opened in 1963, and tourism surged, boosted by the popular song Gao Shan Qing, and Alishan became a must-see attraction for most Taiwanese. Overseas visitors came too, some of them steam-engine aficionados, although the steam locomotives were replaced by diesel engines in 1969. Many Japanese also visited, often in spring to see the cherry trees bloom.

Provincial Highway 18 opened in 1982, giving a further boost to Alishan and

Touring Tip

The surge in mainland China tourism to Alishan Forest Recreation Area has been a mixed blessing. The limited accommodations and restaurants at the recreation area cannot support the demand, and more than half the tourists must make one-day trips and return to Chiayi each day, rather than spending the night and watching the sunrise at Zhushan. Reservations are thus absolutely necessary, and weekday visits are highly recommended.

Jade Mountain tourism, while in 2007, the opening of the Taiwan High-Speed Rail, which has a Chiayi station, made it easier and cheaper to travel to Chiayi from Taipei, Taichung, Kaohsiung and other big cities. Then in 2009, Taiwan opened its doors to tourism from mainland China, and the future of Chiayi and Alishan was assured. Among mainland Chinese, Alishan is the second-most popular destination in Taiwan, behind only the National Palace Museum.

EXCURSIONS
Alishan Forest Railway★★★
阿里山森林鐵路
▶ 71km/44mi from Chiayi to Alishan Forest Recreation Area. Departs from Chiayi's Beimen Station 北門站.

Alishan Forest Railway

Brent Hannon/Michelin

NT$400 one-way. 3.5hrs. ℘05 276 8094; Alishan Station: ℘05 267 9833. www1.forest.gov.tw/RA_En_JP/ 0500001/RA_En-02.htm.

Check first with Taiwan Tourism Bureau before making reservations, which are essential. The railway often closes due to typhoons. In mid-2009 Typhoon Morakot washed away sections of track. Repairs were ongoing at the time of publication, with a targeted completion date of early 2011.

This railway is a marvel, a time-honored antique train that rolls up and down a narrow-gauge track between Chiayi and the Alishan Forest Recreation Area, and on to the sunrise viewing platform at **Zhushan**.

The trip starts at an elevation of 30m/98ft and finishes at 2,451m/8,040ft. Along the way, it climbs at a maximum grade of 6 percent, compared with just over 2 percent for modern railroads. It crosses 77 bridges and rolls through 50 tunnels and at one point, makes a 180° turn in just 40m/131ft. The narrow-gauge track—just 76.2cm, compared to 1,067cm/42in for regular rail in Taiwan—was laid down by Japanese engineers beginning in 1912, in a construction feat that defies imagination.

The Ride

The ride begins at **Beimen Station** in Chiayi, and for the first 15km/9mi, the little four-carriage train proceeds placidly through southern Taiwan's fertile **banana belt**, past rows of houses, over country roads and through rich tropical farmlands.

After 45 minutes the farmland gives way to a semi-wilderness of banyan trees, Indian rubber figs, camphor trees and elephant grass.

Soon the leisurely little train (it averages just 20km/12mi per hour) reaches the famous **corkscrew section** to the summit of Mt. Dulishan. The train spirals around the steep peak three times, winding its way up the mountain like a roller coaster, and makes a figure eight near the summit, before entering the track's longest tunnel. Because the engine is at the back, there are no diesel fumes in the carriage, and fresh mountain air fills the passenger cars. At the end of the corkscrew section, the train is 1,000m/3,280ft above sea level.

At 1,500m/4,921ft the train pulls into a tiny whistle stop called **Fanqihu** (奮起湖). Soon after the tracks enter a dark forest filled with evergreen and broadleaf trees. These are the famous

Logging on Alishan

The Japanese began to explore Taiwan after taking it over in 1895, and soon they discovered the magnificent forests of Red and Yellow Cypress that once draped the slopes of Alishan from 1,500m/4,921ft to 2,500m/8,200ft. Eager to harvest the thousand-year-old trees, they built a **narrow gauge railway** to the forest, which they began to chop down in 1916. Trains laden with supersize Yellow Cypress tree trunks (as many as 60 trains daily, each loaded with 10 tons of lumber) were a common sight in old Chiayi, as were sawmills and lumber yards.

The Japanese logged the Alishan range until the early 1940s and after their departure, the Nationalist government logged the slopes just as vigorously. In 1963, with most of the big trees gone, logging in the area was finally halted. The Yellow Cypress, called Hinoki by the Japanese, was coveted for its straight grain and high oil content, which gives the wood a fine fragrance and makes it resistant to decay. The Japanese used it in temple gates and roof beams and other structures requiring long, straight beams.

Today, however, few of these forest giants remain. The Red Cypresses were more fortunate: this species grows with a split trunk and often has a rotted core, a process that produces tangled, hollow trees. This characteristic saved them from the chainsaws, and today, most of the large old trees in Alishan are Red Cypresses.

cloud forests of Taiwan, once home to the island's magnificent Red and Yellow Cypresses. This section of rail abounds in scary tunnels and bridges: the tunnels are tiny tubes in the earth, dark and drippy and barely big enough for the four-carriage train; the bridges are see-through affairs, with just two thin rails and a few concrete slats between the train and 200m/656ft of cliff. On sharply curved bridges, the rail cars hang over the edges, affording eye-popping views★★★ of the green void far below.

In places the train breaks free of the cloud forest—now populated mostly by pine and fir planted by the Japanese—and enters a clearing, offering glimpses of towering **Mount Dashan**. Then, suddenly, in the darkest part of the forest, the train slams to a halt, an experience known as "hitting the wall." Next it reverses course and goes backward for a few hundred meters, before stopping once again. An engineer jumps out and throws a switch, and the train moves forward, with passengers again facing the front.

This is the **zig-zag section**, the most famous part of the railway. Faced with the formidable cliff of Mt. Dashan, the engineers pioneered this zig-zag technique. Mt. Dashan is too wide to corkscrew around, so they switch-backed up the face of it. Minutes later, the train arrives at Alishan Forest Recreation Area, and the remarkable journey is over.

Alishan Forest Recreation Area★ 阿里山國家森林游樂區

◯ 71mi/44mi east of Chiayi via Fwy. 3 then Provincial Hwy. 18. Forest Bureau Office No.17, Shunling Village, Alishan Township. **Recreation Area** ◯ open 24hrs. NT$150, children NT$100. ✆ 05 267 9917. www1.forest.gov.tw or www.ali-nsa.net.

Alishan Forest Recreation Area lies within the larger **Alishan National Scenic Area**, a 40,000ha/98,842acre protected area. The recreation area, a wooded 1,400ha/3,459acre preserve, is filled with boardwalks and broad trails and dotted with modest but pleasant

Gao Shan Qing

Alishan's tremendous fame stems from the song Gao Shan Qing, or **Tall Green Mountains**, with its famous words, "Tall green mountains, deep blue waters, the girls of Alishan are as lovely as the waters, the men of Alishan are as strong as the mountains."

Gao Shan Qing was the theme song of the 1950 film "Happenings in Alishan," the first Mandarin language movie produced in Taiwan. The film's heroine Cheung Sai Sai sang the original, but the song was later popularized by the revered and beloved Taiwanese singer **Teresa Teng**. Today Gao Shan Qing is the anthem of Alishan, and is an irresistible siren song that lures people to Alishan from throughout greater China.

sights like the **Two Sisters Pond**, the **Thousand-Year Cypress**, and the **Village God Temple**. But it is famed for watching the sun rise from a viewing platform on **Zhushan** (Celebration Mountain). There are a pair of **Giant Tree Trails**, each featuring several dozen ancient Red Cypress trees. The Japanese also planted decorative cherry

Alishan Red Cypress

Brent Hannon/Michelin

orchards, and the springtime blooms add splashes of pink and white color to the deep green landscape. But in general the sights are secondary to the overall setting, a magnificent melange of clear blue skies, tall trees, and cool mountain air.

Sunrise Train to Zhushan★★★ 祝山

▶ *6.2km/3.8mi from Alishan Forest Recreation Area to the viewing platform. 30min one-way. NT$100. The sea of clouds is also visible from Tatajia; buses (NT$150 one-way) make the 30min drive from the recreation area to another sunrise viewpoint at Tatajia every night. Most hotels in the forest recreation area keep a supply of thick coats on hand, as the sunrise trip can be chilly; be sure to take one.*

"Will we see the sea of clouds tomorrow morning?" The question ripples through the recreation area every night, because virtually every visitor there will rise long before dawn the following morning and board the Sunrise Train to Zhushan, fervently hoping to see the most famous sight in Taiwan, the **sunrise at Zhushan**. But most will be disappointed, because more often than not, the sea of clouds—when the mountaintops are visible around and above a thick "ocean" of clouds—does not reveal itself, as the weather is either too clear or too cloudy.

Nonetheless, in the pre-dawn darkness, passengers board the Sunrise Train for the 30min ride to the **viewing platform** at Zhushan, on the final leg of the Alishan Forest Railway. At 2,451m/8,041ft the train stops, and passengers walk to a broad platform and watch.

As the eastern sky brightens behind the **Jade Mountain** (*see opposite*) range, a magnificent scene unfolds. The distant dawn silhouettes the surrounding peaks, and the stars blink out one by one. When the glittery sun clears the horizon, the audience cheers, and if they are lucky, it illuminates a cottony blanket of red-tinged clouds—the much-hoped for "**sea of clouds**"—in the valleys far below, while the silent mountains stand tall against the dark blue sky. As the sun rises higher, it reveals a landscape of grassy meadows, groves of evergreen trees and tiny streams.

Most people take the train back to the recreation area, but the optional **two-hour walk**★ down is a pleasant stroll through sun-dappled second-growth forest. Helpful signs point out various trees and plants, such as Alishan Elm, Chinese Yew, mountain rhododendron, as well as many Red Cypresses, and even some of the rare Yellow Cypresses.

Sunrise at Zhushan

Brent Hannon/Michelin

Yushan National Park★
玉山國家公園

▶ *Southeast of Alishan. Accessible via Hwy. 18 from Chiayi. Park headquarters, 515 Zhongshan Rd. Sec. 1, Shuili, southeast of Sun Moon Lake.* 玉山國家公園, *address:* 水里鄉中山路一段515號. *℘04-9277 3121. www.ysnp.gov.tw/en.*

🚶 **Hiking:** *Jade Mountain requires minimum 5-day advance booking, and a park entrance permit (NT$10). Apply online at park website www.ysnp.gov. tw. The process takes about five days. Guides are not required, but hikers will need a sleeping bag, a sturdy pair of boots and some warm clothes, perhaps a stove and fuel, and plenty of food.*

Yushan National Park, which has 30 peaks taller than 3,000m/9,842ft, is the least accessible national park in Taiwan. Yushan became a national park in 1985, and the entire area is exquisitely preserved. It is served by only two roads (*off Hwy.18 and Hwy.20*), which loop into the 1,055sq km/407sq mi park on the north and south. Fortunately, for backpackers and day walkers alike, the **hiking** to the top of Yushan is easy, relatively speaking. Rising within the park, **Yushan** (玉山), or **Jade Mountain★★**, is the tallest (3,950m/12,959ft) and most celebrated peak in Taiwan. Its famous fan-shaped peak graces the NT$1000 note and adorns billboards and logos around the island. But Yushan itself yields its charms only to hikers who are strong enough to climb it.

Situated within the park at the junction of Highways 18 and 21, the hamlet of **Tatajia★** (塔塔加) sits at the top of the pass some 40min from Alishan Forest Recreation Area. Primarily a service center (no gas stations, though), it is the most common destination in the park. Four **trails** radiate out from Tatajia, and the **Tatajia Visitor Center** (🕐 *open daily 9am–4:30pm; ℘04-9270 2200*) has maps of the area's hikes, and can offer advice.

The four walks range from an easy one-hour walk through the grassland just above the visitor center to an all-day hike that penetrates the deep surrounding wilderness.

Jade Mountain
Rich J. Matheson/Michelin

Jade Mountain★★

🚶 *The easiest route to the summit of Jade Mountain itself also begins at Tatajia. It starts on a paved road at 2,610m/8,563ft, and proceeds gently upward through a breathtaking piece of wilderness to* **Baiyun Hostel***, at 3,528m/11,575ft. The rugged peaks and near-vertical valleys shielded these slopes from the chainsaws that decimated the rest of Taiwan, and the trail winds through a landscape that is wild, remote, and filled with climax vegetation.*

The **trail** (*9km/5.5mi; 3-5hrs*) from Tatajia to Baiyun Hostel passes through several climate zones, each with its own vegetation and wildlife. The hostel is basic but comfortable, and most hikers wake up in the middle of the night and race to the summit of Yushan, 422m/1,385ft above the hostel and about two hours away, to watch the sun rise. Afterwards, most trekkers retrace their steps to Tatajia, but another trail leads to Dongpu, 23km/14mi away. Called the **Batongguan Trail** (八通關古道) trail, it passes through a similar terrain, and there is a pretty campsite at Batongguan Meadow, 6km/3.7mi from the summit. Other famous sights include the **Father and Son Cliff**, carved into the face of the rock, and the **Dragon Cloud waterfall**, which plunges 50m/164ft, flows beneath the trail, and then drops another 70m/229ft.

Tea Curing

Harvesting tea

© Chris Stowers/Apa Publications

The tea leaves are first warmed in the sun for a few minutes to soften them, then rolled in large drums to bruise the leaves and bring the juice to the surface. The leaves are then exposed to the mountain air, which oxides them, a process known as fermentation. After three hours, the tea leaves are heated, which stops the fermentation.

The light fermentation of the leaves is the key characteristic of **oolong tea. Green tea** is unfermented, and **black tea** is fully fermented. The leaves are then packed into bags and rolled vigorously, until they become hard pellets the size of popcorn kernels. The pellets are dried, then cooked over a charcoal fire, lending it the slightly smoky aftertaste that is one of the hallmarks of **Dongding oolong**. The result is a superb tea that has hints of fruit and a darker, earthier flavor profile and more acerbic bitterness than the very mild high-mountain oolongs grown in Lishan and Alishan.

Lugu★ 鹿谷

▶ *About 45km/27mi northeast of Chiayi via Fwy. 3, and Provincial Hwy. 3 and County Rd. 151.*

This hamlet is surrounded by hills and mountains filled with tea fields. High above the tiny town, which is dotted with tea sheds and tea-curing warehouses, rises **Dongding** (凍頂), or Frozen Peak, the steep mountain that produces the most famous tea in all of Taiwan.

Tea was first planted in the area 150 years ago, and the rich soil, moist climate, and cool temperatures at around 700m/2,296ft proved ideal for tea growing. Dongding isn't the best tea in Taiwan (that accolade goes to Lishan oolong, grown in the high mountains), but it grows abundantly, and yields large commercial crops of excellent oolong tea.

Tea lovers should visit Lugu in the springtime, ideally during its annual **Spring Tea Festival** (*usually May or Jun*), although tea production continues all summer. Visitors can stroll into the tea sheds and observe the curing process.

Xitou Forest Recreation Area
溪頭風景區

▶ *About 10km/6mi south of Lugu via County Rd. 151. Open 24hrs. NT$200. Vehicles not permitted in the recreation area.*

🚶 This 2,500ha/6,150acre recreation area is a locally famous forest getaway that features abundant stands of **bamboo**, along with cypress and many other kinds of trees. An experimental forest belonging to **Taiwan University**, it features rare trees that are a botanist's delight, including Red Cypress, as well as a rare Gingko forest. The area is laced with walking **trails**, and sits at an altitude starting at 1,150m/3,773ft, making it pleasantly cool in summer, and calm and restful year-around.

Beigang 北港

▶ *On Hwy. 19, some 30km/19mi northwest of Chiayi via Fwy. 1, several county roads lead there from Chiayi.*

Beigang is associated with its **Chao Tian Gong Temple**★★(朝天宮), which is rich in lore and tradition, and is a marvel of fine craftsmanship. Every feature of the temple was created by a famous master, including the carved wooden shrines that surround the goddess Mazu, the ceramic icons that dance along the rooftops, the stone carvings that adorn the altars, and the chamber paintings that grace its walls, doors and ceilings. The "Heaven-Facing Temple" also serves as a repository of Mazu culture, as it has since it was built in 1693. On Mazu's birthday, the 19th day of the third lunar month, the icon of the goddess is paraded through nearby temples accompanied by her avatars and embraced by loud and lively ceremony, similar to the longer and more famous Mazu pilgrimage that begins in Dajia.

ADDRESSES

🏠 STAY

$$ Alishan Gao Feng Hotel 阿里山高峰大飯店 – *41 East Alishan, Chungcheng Village* 阿里山鄉中正村東阿里山41號. ✕ ☎05-267 9411 *or* ☎05-267 9893. *www.alishan.net.tw/html/rooms.php. 42 rooms. Breakfast included.* This bright, modern hotel is just a couple blocks from the center of the recreation area at Alishan Township, where the buses and trains arrive and depart. The rooms, while not exciting, have pine-paneled walls and faux fireplaces that add a touch of mountain atmosphere; its rooftop star-viewing terrace has unbroken views of the mountains. The most spacious rooms can accommodate five people. Chinese dinners are served in the restaurant.

$$$ Alishan House Cabins 阿里山賓館 – *No.16 West Alishan, Alishan Township.* 阿里山鄉香林村16號. ✕ ☎05-267 9811 *or* ☎05-276 5956. www.alishanhouse.com. tw. Breakfast included.* In the hills behind Alishan House are several small cabins that have also been renovated, and while still rustic, are comfortable and roomy enough for up to eight people. They are quieter than Alishan House itself, and would be ideal for groups who don't wish to see the sunrise, an event that wakes up virtually everyone in the larger hotels. Cabin guests have use of the Alishan House facilities.

$$$$ Alishan House 阿里山賓館 – *No.16 West Alishan, Alishan Township.* ✕ ☎05-267 9811 *or* ☎05-276 5956. *www. alishanhouse.com.tw. 35 rooms. Breakfast included.* A 90-year-old former Japanese officers' club, Alishan House is by far the finest lodging in the forest recreation area, and it is comfortably removed from the hubbub of the main square. The hotel has new and old wings, and its breakfast nook and Chinese restaurant have excellent views of distant Mt. Dashan. Tea on the terrace beneath the Red Cypresses is one of the hidden pleasures of a trip to Alishan.

🍴 EAT

Hotpot, a traditional winter dish in Taiwan, is popular throughout the recreation area, as its hot spicy broth helps ward off the high-mountain chill. Several hotpot restaurants line Alishan's central square. Ask for an accompaniment of the mountain wasabi, which will be served Japan-style, with soy sauce. The tiny village of Alishan also has a couple of small Chinese restaurants serving stir-fried meat and vegetables, beef noodles, hot tea, and other standard **Taiwanese** fare.

🛒 SHOPPING

The key souvenir is **mountain wasabi,** a locally grown version of the Japanese radish. The Alishan variety is milder and sweeter than the wasabi in Japan, and the roots are said to be descended from wasabi planted by the Japanese 100 years ago.

Beyond that, Zhou **tribal knick-knacks** and clothing are popular as well, including hats, vests and jewelry, most of which appears to be mass-produced, however.

SOUTH TAIWAN

The South's defining feature and greatest strength is its traditional Chinese-Fujianese culture, best seen in its temples and local festivals. Gods and goddesses are honored at spectacular, well-attended events like the Song Jiang Battle Array, the Beehive Fireworks Festival and the burning of ceremonial boats crammed with offerings. Step into any of Tainan's centuries-old temples and you have a good chance of witnessing petitioners praying, meditating and seeking answers from a supernatural power by rituals such as throwing divining blocks, undergoing exorcism, or even flagellating themselves with bats covered with spikes.

Highlights

1 Remains of 17C fort at Tainan's **Chihkan Tower** (p266)

2 300-year-old **Nankunshen Temple** in Beimen (p279)

3 Winged visitors in Maolin's **Purple Butterfly Valley** (p285)

4 **Taiwan Indigenous Peoples Culture Park**'s dwellings (p286)

5 Disneyesque pagodas of Kaohsiung's **Lotus Pond** (p294)

A Region of Cultural Diversity

The southwest coast was the first part of Taiwan Island to be settled by Han Chinese migrants. Their arrival coincided with that of the Dutch East India Company, which in 1624 established a colony in what is now the Tainan suburb of Anping. Koxinga, the man who threw the Europeans out in 1663, purposely introduced classical Chinese culture to bolster the legitimacy of the Ming pretender in whose name he fought. The Confucian traditions Koxinga fostered here still thrive. After the Qing dynasty took control of Taiwan in 1684, Tainan was the capital until the late 19C.

South Taiwan has a great deal more than the flavors of old China. Han settlers pushing southward and into the interior came up against the island's aboriginal inhabitants. These indigenous tribes maintain their cultures in a few corners of the south that are geographically isolated yet scenically splendid. There are also pockets of Hakka culture, most notably Meinong. Kaohsiung, a major metropolis, has a charm all of its own.

At the southernmost tip of Taiwan, Kenting National Park does a good job of reconciling the needs of two different visitors: the hedonistic beach bum and the peace-and-quiet loving ecotourist. Between October and April the south's dry, sunny weather (afternoon highs range from 20°C/68°F to 30°C/86°F) is ideal for urban or rural exploration, and cycling or hiking in the foothills.

Kaohsiung Harbor

Rich J. Matheson/Michelin

SOUTH TAIWAN

Aogu
Puzi
Yunlin
Lucao
Budai
Shuishang
CHIAYI
Zhongpu
Houbi
Yunshui
Baihe
Chiayi
Zizhong 2609 Tatajia
Leye Tropic of Cancer *Yushan (Jade Mountain)* 3952
Yanshui
Beimen
NANKUNSHEN TEMPLE ★★★
XINYING
Liuying
Guanziling
Zengwen Reservoir
Dapu
Yu Da Mountain 2480
2860 *Yushan National Park*
Meishan
Takanua
Fuxing Guanshan 3666
Zhangshan
★★ 20
Xuejia
Xiaying
Jiali
Jiangjun
17
Madou
Shanhua
Guantian
Nanxi
Danei
Yujing
Beiliao
Tainan
Namasia
21
Xiaolin
Taoyuan
Gaozhong
Qigu
Xinshi
Shanshang
20
Zuozhen
Nanhua
Wulipu
Jiaxian
20
Laonong
Beinanzhushan 3293
★ **Anping Fort** ■
★★★ **TAINAN**
Rende
Guanmiao
Neimen
Shiche
Liugui
Kaohsiung
Mountain Villages ★★
27
Chenzhong
Qishan
Meinong ★★
Duona
Maolin ★★
Alian
Tianliao
Dajin
1
Luzhu
3
Yellow Butterfly Valley ★★
Gaoshu
PURPLE BUTTERFLY VALLEY ★★★
17
Yanchao
Gangshan
10
Lingkou
Ligang
3
Jiuru
Yanpu
185
Wutai
South Cross-Island Highway
Nanzi
Dashu
Zuoying
FOGUANGSHAN MONASTERY ★★★
PINGTUNG
★★ **Sandimen**
24
Taiwan Indigenous Peoples Culture Park ★★
★★ **KAOHSIUNG**
FENGSHAN
Wandan
Qianzhen
Neipu
Taiwu
▲ **Mount Northern Dawu**
Zhiben Forest Rec. Area
Xiaogang
21
27
Chaozhou
Bilu
17
Xinyuan
Taitung
Jinlun
Linyuan
Nanzhou
Wanlong
Qijia
Xiadaxi
Donggang
Qijia
Shaoya
9
Linbian
Pingtung
1704 △
Xiao Liuqiu ★★
Baisha
Fangliao
Chunri
Dawu
Nanshi
Shangwu
Daren
Fengshan
1
Shoujia
SOUTH CHINA SEA
Shizitou
9
1062 △
Shuangliu
Xuhai
Fenggang
Shimen
26
Gangzi
★★ **Kenting Area**
26
Zhonggang
Checheng ■
Laofoshan 674 △
Manzhou
★★★ **MUSEUM OF MARINE BIOLOGY AND AQUARIUM**
Hengchun
Jialeshui
★★ *Kenting Forest Rec. Area*
Kending
Maobitou
Nanwan
★★★ **KENTING NATIONAL PARK**
★★ **Eluanbi Park**

N

MAGONG

0   20 km
0   20 miles

Tainan★★★

If you want to truly experience Taiwan, don't miss its oldest and fourth largest city, a port on the west coast that now lies a few miles inland from the Taiwan Strait. Still called "the Capital City" (府城 fǔchéng), Tainan (台南) was Taiwan's first capital from the late 1600s to the late 1800s. Although large in population (771,000) and size (175.6sq km/67.8sq mi), the city projects a small-town atmosphere in the eyes of the Taiwanese, primarily because of its relaxed pace and hospitality. Tainan embodies the breadth and depth of Taiwanese culture in its monuments, historic buildings, and the island's highest concentration of temples—nearly 300, some dating to the 17C. Walking the alleys and streets of this engaging city is like walking through the pages of a history book. Many of Taiwan's rich religious customs, such as the welcoming Mazu parade and dragon boat racing, originated in Tainan. This eldest of Taiwanese cities remains a great place to see traditional festivals, religious street parades, roadside operas and puppet shows.

▶ **Population:** 771,235

Michelin Maps: p263, p265.

Info: Visitor center outside main exit of Tainan train station on Beimen Rd. Open daily 9am–6pm, holidays 8am–6pm. 06-226 5681 or 0800-611-011 (little English). http://eng.taiwan.net.tw.

Location: Major temples and best-known eateries are between the Ximen and Gongyuan traffic circles. Outside the train station, Zhongshan Road has upscale shopping and dining. Anping, 5km/3mi west of the city, is now Tainan's tourism mecca.

Kids: Museum of Taiwan Literature's children's reading room.

Timing: Temperatures are cooler and skies blue Oct–Mar. Avoid heavy "plum" rains (May–Jun) and wet season (Apr–Sept), usually with typhoons (Jul–Sept).

Don't Miss: Chihkan Tower, Confucius Temple and Anping.

Jungshan and Minzu Roads

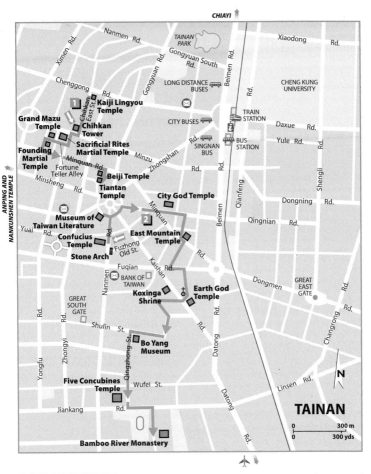

TAINAN PARK

Nanmen Rd.

Ximen Rd.

Xiaodong Rd.

Chenggong Rd.

Gongyuan Rd.

Gongyuan South Rd.

Belmen Rd.

CHENG KUNG UNIVERSITY

LONG DISTANCE BUSES

Chihkan East St.

Kaiji Lingyou Temple

Grand Mazu Temple

Chihkan Tower

CITY BUSES

TRAIN STATION

Daxue Rd.

Founding Martial Temple

Sacrificial Rites Martial Temple

Fortune Teller Alley

Minquan Rd.

Minzu

Zhongshan

Rd.

SINGNAN BUS

BUS STATION

Yule Rd.

Shengli

Minsheng Rd.

Beiji Temple

Tiantan Temple

City God Temple

Minquan

Belmen

Qianfeng

Qingnian Rd.

Dongning Rd.

Museum of Taiwan Literature

Confucius Temple

Stone Arch

Yuai Rd.

Rd.

Fuzhong Old St.

East Mountain Temple

Kaishan Rd.

Rd.

ANPING AND NANKUNSHEN TEMPLE

Fuqian

BANK OF TAIWAN

Koxinga Shrine

Earth God Temple

Dongmen

GREAT EAST GATE

GREAT SOUTH GATE

Nanmen Rd.

Shulin St.

Rd.

Datong

Changrong Rd.

Yongfu

Zhongyi

Qingning St.

Bo Yang Museum

N

Rd.

Five Concubines Temple

Wufei St.

Datong Rd.

Linsen Rd.

Jiankang Rd.

TAINAN

0   300 m
0   300 yds

Bamboo River Monastery

A BIT OF HISTORY

Information about Tainan's earliest aboriginal inhabitants is vague. Tsou aboriginal oral tradition claims Tainan as their ancestral land, but most scholars agree on **Sirayan** aboriginals, with a minority of Han settlers, living here when **Dutch traders** arrived in 1624.

The Dutch claimed the area now called Anping that lies just west of Tainan. At the time, it was a large sand spit delineating a natural harbor.

The indelible influence of the Dutch on Tainan belies their mere 38 years on the island. They built two fortifications, first **Fort Zeelandia**, then **Fort Provintia**, vestiges of which can be viewed today. The 4km/2.5mi of land separating the two strongholds were once engulfed in water. Over centuries, sedimentation filled in what was previously a coastal bay—the reason Fort Zeelandia's remains are so far inland today.

Koxinga, a Ming loyalist fleeing the Qing in China, likely left the greatest historical mark on the city. The artists, artisans, musicians and chefs he brought with him from mainland China passed their expertise on to Tainan's residents. In 1662 Koxinga rid the local populace of the burdensome Dutch colonizers. Although he died after one year of the short 21-year rule of the exiled Ming kingdom in Tainan, monuments and temples here are dedicated to him.

In 1683 Tainan was wrested from Koxinga's grandson by Qing admiral **Shi Lang**, beginning the 212-year rule of the Qing, who were interested in developing Taiwan's economic potential.

GETTING THERE

BY AIR - Tainan Airport (IATA code: TNN) (台南航空站) (𝄞06 260 1017; www.tna.gov.tw) has several flights daily to Penghu and Kinmen islands. There are no flights from Taipei to Tainan.

BY TRAIN - Conventional trains (TRA) stop at Tainan Railway Station (台南火車站 (𝄞06 226 1314), within walking distance of the city's historic heart. Journey times are at least 4hrs from Taipei (one-way on the fastest trains NT$741 up) to 1hr from Kaohsiung (one-way on the fastest trains NT$107).

If arriving by **high-speed railway** (HSR), factor in a slow drive or shuttle bus journey (30min; free) because the station (台南高鐵站) (𝄞06-600 9000) is 14km/8.6mi southeast of downtown. Three services (1hr 40min) daily from Taipei each hour 6:45am–10:27pm (one-way NT$1,350).

BY BUS - Long-distance buses depart 24/7 from stations on Beimen Road, just north of Tainan's train station. Full fare to Taipei (4hrs) varies but costs NT$550 weekends. Arrivals terminate beside Tainan Park where there are always plenty of taxis. For small towns in South Taiwan such as Beimen, Yujing or Qishan, use one of the Singnan Bus Co. (興南客運) stops (𝄞06 265 3121); there is a stop near the train station at 182 Zhongshan Road.

GETTING AROUND

BY BUS - Catch **city buses** around the traffic circle in front of the train station. Services are infrequent and there is little English information, but bus no. 2 is a good way to reach Anping (one-way NT$18). **Free buses** (88 and 99) make the rounds of many tourist sites, beginning at Tainan Park (*on the hour weekdays, on the half hour holidays*), but can be caught at the train station.

BY CAR - Car Plus (8am–8:30pm; 𝄞06 223 5566) has two outlets, one at 115 Beimen Rd., Sec. 2 (*turn right when leaving the TRA station; it's across the road*) and the other in the HSR station.

GENERAL INFORMATION

Tainan Foreigner Assistance Center (臺南地區外國人協助中心) 2F. 6 Yonghua Rd., Sec. 2 (永華路二段6號2 樓). Closed weekends. 𝄞06 298 1000 24hrs. 𝄞0800 024 111 (English). http://foreigner.tncg.gov.tw/en.

At the same time, Tainan began its 203-year reign as Taiwan's **capital city**. In 1886 the island's status was upgraded from prefecture to province and the capital was moved to Taipei; as a result Tainan's political importance gradually diminished.

In the 21C Tainan merged county and city, creating **Greater Tainan**, a more significant political entity, on par with Taipei, Taichung and Kaohsiung.

WALKING TOUR 1

See map. 2km/1.3mi. Allow 1.5hrs.

▷ *Begin at Chihkan Tower on Minzu Rd., 4 blocks west of the train station.*

Chihkan Tower★★★ 赤嵌樓

212 Minzu Rd., Sec.2 (民族路2段212號)
🕐 *Open daily 8:30am–9pm. NT$50.*
𝄞06 220 5647.

This grade-one historic complex contains the scant remains of **Fort Provintia** (👁see Architecture). Built by the Dutch in 1653, the fort was captured by **Koxinga** (👁see History) in 1661. A popular story has the Chinese renaming the fort "red-haired tower" (*chih* means red), since the Dutch were known here as red-haired people. More likely the name is based on the aboriginal term for the area, Sakam. Earthquakes, war and time ravaged the original stronghold and reduced it to a mere foundation. In 1875 a county magistrate proposed the erection of a sea god temple on the fort's foundation. Over a 10-year period, the temple and

Chihkan Tower

Rich J. Matheson/Michelin

a pavilion in the Fujianese style were constructed, as well as buildings for scholars. Also on the premises are the paltry remains of the former **Penghu Academy**, an institution of learning established during the Qing dynasty, when the complex was used as a center of education. The academy was felled by an earthquake in the early 1900s.

In the evening, the buildings and grounds are beautifully lit. Traditional, folk or modern music is usually performed (Wed–Sun 7:30pm, included in admission fee).

Visit

Upon entering the grounds, admire the bronze **statue of Koxinga**, which memorializes his victory over the Dutch, symbolized by a statue of a Westerner with head bowed toward the Ming general. Also notice the nine stone **tablets** carried by stone "tortoises" (actually bisi, mythical offspring of the dragon), erected by order of Emperor Qianlong in 1788 to honor one of his generals for quelling an uprising. Manchu writing, the main language of the Qing dynasty, can be seen on some of them.

The first pavilion was initially the **sea god temple**, but today houses a Chinese language exhibit (first floor) about Chihkan Tower and Koxinga. Ascend (with caution) the rickety wooden steps to the second floor, where there is an exhibit (in Chinese) and model wooden boats.

Between the temple and the second pavilion is a **well** dug by the Dutch; the Taiwanese once thought it was a secret passageway to Fort Zeelandia.

The second pavilion, the **Wenchang Pavilion**, holds a Chinese language exhibit (1st floor) on the civil exam system. On the second floor is a shrine to Kuixing, the god of Literature. Believed to help examinees, "lucky" test boards are full of student petitions for good grades.

Behind Wenchang Pavilion, the ruins of Fort Provintia's northeast bastion were discovered when the Five Scholars Shrine was blown over by a typhoon during Japanese occupation. Stand next to the remains of the fort's brick **enclosure wall** to get a sense of its height; the bricks were reputedly brought by the Dutch from Jakarta, Indonesia. In the northwest corner, a **gate** and a tablet are the only traces of the former Penghu Academy.

▷ *Exit Chihkan and go left along Minzu Rd.; turn north into the brick alley with lanterns strung on both sides.*

Chihkan East Street is pleasant for spending evenings at sidewalk eateries or drinking spots. Near the north end of the street, the clean, bright **Kaiji Lingyou Temple** is a grade-three monument currently under renovation (temple renovations can last tens of years). The principal deity, the Supreme Lord of

Grading System

Taiwan is rich in cultural assets, but it was not until recently that comprehensive laws were introduced to protect them. Historical site inspections began in 1972 and by 1979 a provisional list had been created with 53 grade-one, 84 grade-two and 207 grade-three historical monuments. Since then, the graded assets have grown substantially. The **Cultural Heritage Preservation Law**, drafted in 1982 and implemented in the years 1998-2005, is a robust classification and governing system used to preserve and promote Taiwan's cultural and historical heritage. At most registered sites, a cement pillar indicates their status, such as Grade One Historical Monument (一級古蹟), Grade Two (二級古蹟) or Grade Three (三級古蹟).

the Dark Heavens, is temporarily housed in a tin shack across the lane. Note the black pillars and flags that typify the Supreme Lord's temples.

Backtrack to Chihkan Tower and walk south on Yongfu Rd.

Sacrificial Rites Martial Temple★★★ 祀典武廟
229 Yongfu Rd., Sec.2 (永福路二段229 號) Open daily. ℘06 220 2390.
On the right stretches the iconic 66m/216ft-long vermilion-colored **wall** ★★ of the Martial Temple.
An example of a traditional Minnan-style **horseback wall**, it surrounds the atrium, worship space, main and rear halls, forming a continuous rolling plane said to resemble a horse's back.
The temple's main deity, **Guan Gong**, often called the god of War, is a popu-

Mending, Sacrificial Rites Martial Temple

Rich J. Matheson/Michelin

lar god in Taiwan (*see sidebar*). The Fujianese-style temple was built in the late 17C during the Ming dynasty.

Visit
The main entrance leads into the sprawling and unconventionally asymmetric complex that was originally an extension of the residence of Prince Ningjing (*see Grand Mazu Temple*).
The main doors show off **mending** (literally "door nails"—bowl-shaped pieces of wood or metal attached to the door), and are noteworthy because only temples holding official rites may display mending. (Since 1727 this temple traditionally held official rites bi-annually until they were discontinued in the Japanese era; nowadays, it holds only autumn rites.) The center of the main hall houses a **statue** of Guan Gong, flanked by Chou Chang, his friend and lieutenant, and Guan Pin, his loyal adoptive son. Of the many wooden tablets of repute in the temple, **da zhang fu** (大丈夫) is the most famous; in ancient Chinese it describes Guan Gong's virtues. (In Japanese the same characters translate to male chauvinist.)
Stairs from the open courtyard in the rear lead to **Guanyin Hall**, housing the goddess of Mercy and the 18 **lohan**, or enlightened disciples of Buddha. Farther along are a 300-year-old **plum tree**, a turtle pond and **Liuhe Hall**, where traditional Chinese opera music is performed (*Mon–Tue*).
The open courtyard behind the main hall makes a pleasant place to rest and contemplate the geomantic beauty of architecture.

▷ *Alley 227, or Fortune Teller Alley, where fortune tellers study divination texts and advise clients, runs west from Martial Temple to Grand Mazu Temple.*

Grand Mazu Temple★★★
大天后宮

18 Yongfu Rd., Lane 227, Sec. 2 (永福路 二段227巷18號) Open daily.
06 221 1178.

Mazu, also called goddess of the Sea, is one of the more popular gods of the hundreds of Taiwanese deities, and possibly the most worshiped goddess in the world. Tainan's Grand Mazu Temple is the first officially built Mazu temple, the only one listed historically in the record of rites and one of the largest and oldest temples in Taiwan.

Prince Ningjing, the only remaining heir to Ming rule, originally had the temple built as his residence in 1664. Later he converted his home to a Mazu temple at the urging of his abbot friend before committing suicide upon the fall of the Ming dynasty.

The succeeding Qing emperor Kangxi decreed the residence a Mazu temple, called Tianfei (heavenly princess). In 1684 Mazu was raised to the status of Queen of Heaven by the emperor, and the temple was officially renamed Great Queen of Heaven Temple, the first in Taiwan.

Visit

Mazu is the large gold-faced **statue** with beaded headdress in the center of the main altar. It was a black-faced statue until, in 2004, the head suddenly fell off. The 300-year-old statue was repaired and painted in gold.

The most striking statues in the temple are the two guardian deities flanking Mazu. These were once demon gods who committed evil in the world until Mazu subdued them on Peach Blossom Mountain; since then they have been subservient to her.

The statues **Thousand Mile Eye** (千里眼) and **Thousand Mile Ear** (順風耳), believed to see and hear sailors in distress for thousands of leagues, are crafted of clay.

Mud statue, Thousand League Eyes, Grand Mazu Temple

Rich J. Matheson/Michelin

The temple doors hold 73 **men ding**, as compared to the Martial Temple's 72, in a classic case of temple one-upmanship.

▷ *Go across the front courtyard from Mazu Temple to Xinmei St.*

Xinmei Street was once called Rice Street because of the rice trade that made this street a commercial hub. Today it hosts some authentic old businesses.

▷ *Turn south into the lane.*

Jinchuancheng Tea Shop

Rich J. Matheson/Michelin

On the left is **Zaoxuantang** (昭玄堂), a traditional lantern-painting shop; the fourth-generation artisan paints with a calligraphy brush. Farther into the alley is **Jinchuancheng Tea Shop** (金泉成), whose fourth-generation owner sells tea baked and aged according to tradition dating to 1868. The **Founding Martial Temple** on this street is not as impressive as the Sacrificial Rites Temple, but the divination sticks there are said to be particularly efficacious.

▷ *Turn east up Minquan. Two more blocks uphill reach Tainan's highest point: Beiji Temple.*

Beiji Temple 北極殿

89 Minquan Rd., Sec. 2 (民權路二段89 號) ○*Open daily.* ℘*06 226 8875.*
This recently renovated temple was a hospital during Dutch occupation. In 1661 it was converted into Xuantian Shangdi's temple. The personification of Polaris, **Xuantian Shangdi** was the main god and patron saint of the Ming dynasty. He is commonly portrayed with a black face and beard, and feet resting on the snake and turtle he once subjugated. The frequent use of black and the dragon door gods are distinguishing features.

▷ *Follow the narrow Alley 95 (between the temple and Citibank) to Tiantan Temple.*

Tiantan Temple 天壇

○*Open daily.*
This temple venerates the **Jade Emperor**, believed by many to be the most powerful god in the celestial hierarchy. An important spiritual center, the temple attracts believers year round to pray to the god.

On the ninth day of the first lunar month so much **spirit money** is brought to the temple for burning that it has to be carted to a special area for burning by the Department of Environmental Protection.

Note that the Jade Emperor has a **spirit tablet** but not a statue.

🐾 WALKING TOUR ②

⏱ *See map. 5.6km/3.5m. Allow 3hrs.*

▷ *Begin at Confucius Temple, 5 blocks south of Chihkan Tower, reachable by # 2, city bus 88 from train station.*

Confucius Temple★★★
台南孔子廟

2 Nanmen Rd. (南門路2號) ○*Open daily 8am–5:30pm. Grounds free. Temple courtyard NT$25.* ℘*06 228 9013.*
Of Taiwan's many Confucian temples, Tainan's is the oldest and the most complete. Confucius, one of the world's greatest teachers, thought that education should be available to all, not just to the aristocracy. The tablet hanging above the main entrance, the **East Gate of Great Achievement**, reads "Taiwan's

East Gate of Great Achievement, Confucius Temple

Rich J. Matheson/Michelin

Foremost School" (全臺首學), indicating the temple's status as Taiwan's first official learning institute. Koxinga's son, Cheng Ching, commissioned the temple in 1665, and it remained the most prestigious school until the end of the Qing dynasty (1644-1911).

Like other Confucian temples, its design is elegant and simple, in contrast to Tainan's many ostentatious temples. There have been several reconstructions, but the temple has maintained its original integrity and is believed by many to be the best example of Fujianese-style temple architecture in Tainan (*see Architecture in Introduction*).

Visit

Centuries-old banyan trees, a half-moon shaped pond and aged gates evoke past glories of ancient dynasties.

The layout of the temple and school follows the ritualized spatial organization that characterizes Confucian temples: the school on the right and the temple on the left. Entered by way of the Gate of Virtue *(on the right)*, the **Hall of Edification** once served as the school. Large panel doors in the front spill natural light onto the rear wall's calligraphy: oversize characters on the side walls inscribe moral injunctions, such as loyalty(忠), filial piety(孝) and integrity(節).

In the northeast corner of the complex, the **Wenchang Pavilion** (文昌閣) (*open Sat–Sun 9am–noon & 1:30pm–5:30pm*) honors Lord Wenchang, the god of Education on the second floor and Kuixing, the god of Literature on the third. *Caution: the wooden steps to these floors are steep and narrow.*

Accessed via the **Gate of Great Achievement** (大成門), the **Hall of Great Achievement**★★ (大成殿) is the double-eave structure in the center. The heart of the complex, it holds the heavily gilded **spirit tablet** of Confucius. The **Emperor's Path**, the ramp carved with a dragon leading to the hall, was to be used only by the emperor or by high-scoring imperial examination candidates; small **stone tigers** on the rail symbolize honor and virtue; and **hornless dragons** protruding from the

Hall of Edification, Confucius Temple
Rich J. Matheson/Michelin

four outside corners indicate top exam scores when water spouts from them.

Behind the main hall, the **Shrine of the Great Wise Men** (崇聖祠) pays tribute to ancestors of Confucius, and a **library** (*closed Mon; no English signage)* has a shrine devoted to the five scholar gods. Halls on both sides house spirit tablets, and the rear rooms contain museums describing ceremonial musical instruments, dress and ritual implements used in the Rites of Confucius.

Before leaving, go out the west gate to the Zhongyi Elementary School grounds. The Japanese-style **Tainan Wude Hall** (武德殿), built in 1910, is a rare example of Japanese-style architecture in Taiwan. Once made of wood, this former Japanese training academy for martial arts is now a cement and wood reconstruction used as the school auditorium.

From the East Gate of Great Achievement, walk north 1.5 blocks to the large traffic circle.

Museum of Taiwan Literature★★ 國立台灣文學館

1 Zhongzheng Rd. (中正路1號)
Open Tue–Sun 9am–9pm. 06 221 7201. http://www.nmtl.gov.tw/en. English signage. Free 1.5hr audio tour.
Taiwan's first museum devoted to Taiwanese literature was established in 2003 and housed in a stately, two-story building (1916) designed by Japanese

Museum of Taiwan Literature

Rich J. Matheson/Michelin

architect Matsunosuke. Informative exhibits progress through the island's history by way of the writers and writings of Taiwan's people (☉*see Literature in the Introduction*).

In the Hall of Literary Arts, the first of two permanent exhibits is devoted to the Second Empire-style **museum building**, including its history as the seat of prefecture government and subsequent damage in WWII. Portions of the renovated foundation and reinforced walls are exposed to demonstrate the building's recent restoration.

The second permanent exhibit is an **interactive record** of Taiwan's literary heritage. Even though they have no written history, Taiwan's aboriginal people are not neglected. On display are writings about their lives, past and present; particularly poignant is a lullaby sung in different native tongues.

There's a 👥**children's reading room** (*first floor*), which tailors its literary offerings to works for young people. The adjoining **Center for the Research and Preservation of Cultural Properties** features rotating exhibits.

In the center of the traffic circle is **Tang De Zhang Memorial Park** (湯德章記念公園); be sure to cross the street with caution if visiting the park.

▷ *Continue counterclockwise around the traffic circle; follow the second road (Qingnian Rd.) east.*

City God Temple★★ 城隍廟
133 Qingnian Rd. (青年路133號)
🕐*Open daily 6am–9pm.* ✆*06 223 7316.*
Built in 1669 this temple emits an intentional sinister aura to frighten people into good behavior. Lord Chenghuang (literally "city wall and moat") is worshiped here as protector of the city.

In ancient times people relied on a city's fortifications for protection.

Over time, the physical defenses themselves became objects of worship, personified as a god who safeguards the city. Taiwan's rich pantheon of gods is often likened to a celestial government paralleling human institutions.

Historically, Chenghuang temples were administrative centers, and it is said the Qing dynasty, having minimal control over Taiwan, utilized Chenghuang temples to establish rule on the island. The temples aided the ruler's control through fear of punishment in and by the underworld.

Visit
To the left of the entrance, observe the fierceness of Chenghuang's minions like generals Fan and Liu and on the right Gan and Xie (☉*see sidebar*). Chenghuang uses the **abacus** hung above the main door to tally good and evil, punishing or rewarding people accordingly. The 24 effigies lined on both sides of the **main hall** are Chenghuang's ministers. A room to the left of the main hall displays temple objects (*no English signs*).

Cross Qingnian Rd. and take Alley 132 (next to 7-11 store), which leads to Minquan Rd. The temple is on the left.

East Mountain Temple★
東嶽殿
110 Minquan Rd., Sec. 1 (民權路1段 110號). ℘06 220 2322.

This active temple is even darker and more mysterious than City God Temple. Its main deity is **Yanluo** (閻羅), king of the fifth court of hell but often referred to simply as king of hell. His duty is to punish the wicked and report to the Jade Emperor. Exercise caution in this temple since many worshipers are currying favors for recently deceased friends and relatives. Off to the left are usually Daoist priests chanting, ringing bells, blowing horns and cracking whips in front of elaborate miniature houses made of paper and bamboo. People dressed in white cloth are mourners, and the houses are for the deceased. (A small shop to the right of the temple as you exit makes these paper offerings.)

The main entrance to the temple is very cramped because the temple was shortened when the Japanese widened Minquan Road. Flanking the main altar are two of Yanluo's assistants, **Horse-head** and **Oxface**, who guard the gates of hell. Also notice the gruesome **wall art** depicting punishment in hell.

Across from the temple a narrow residential alley leads to Fuqian Rd. Cross Fuqian and walk left to the first alley. Alley 85 leads past a small Tudigong temple and a park on the left where you will see the cross of Holy Mother Church above the roofs. Jog left when this alley ends at a T-junction and follow the alley that winds around the church to Kaishan Rd. The Earth God Temple is a block down on the left.

Earth God Temple 土地公廟
Kaishan Rd.

The Earth God, or Tudigong, is worshiped for fortune and happiness. Shrines to Tudigong are everywhere, but usually are on a smaller scale than other temples. This unassuming temple still serves as a meeting place for locals, popular for its large, lavish celebrations.

Chinese Holy Mother Chapel
中華聖母堂
195 Kaishan Rd. (開山路195號) ◔Open daily 7am–5:30pm. ℘06 222 9013.

An interesting fusion of East and West, the Chinese palace-style Catholic church (1964) is as uncommon as it is beautiful. It possesses many Taiwanese elements, notably an incense urn in front of the altar and a spirit tablet off to the right so as not to alienate local Taiwanese. The high cathedral roof bathes the sanctuary's tile mosaic of "Our Lady of China holding the Lord" in daylight.

Cross the road to the park complex.

Koxinga Shrine 延平郡王祠
152 Kaishan Rd. (開山路152號) ◔Open daily 8:30am–5:30pm. ℘06 213 5518.

In 1663 locals erected a small shrine commemorating Koxinga; in 1875 it was enlarged and built in the Fujianese style. The Japanese added a Shinto shrine and Tori gate. After much controversy, everything but the gate was demolished in 1961. By 1964 this Northern China palace-style shrine was in its place (℘see also Architecture in Introduction.)

Lords Seven and Eight

Generals Fan and Xie are two of the most recognizable and often seen Taiwanese gods. Popular legends about these two abound. Fan, commonly called **Lord Eight**, is portrayed as a short god with black face and robes (he drowned in an act of devotion to his sworn blood brother Xie). Xie, commonly called **Lord Seven**, is tall and white, often depicted with his tongue hanging out (he hung himself upon seeing the dead Fan). Always seen together, these two subordinates of Lord Cheng Huang are in charge of bringing criminals to the underworld for judgment.

Inside the temple complex are informative panels *(in English)*. The sanctum sanctorum houses a large **seated statue** of the Ming warrior. The gardens and ponds outside are designed according to the principles of fengshui, with three winding bridges, a dragon spouting water and groves of golden stripe bamboo. The **exhibition hall** *(open Tue–Sun 9am–5pm)* hosts interesting exhibits *(no English signs)*.

> *Walk down wooden stairs next to Koxinga Parlor coffee shop. Directly in front is Lane 89, which runs diagonally off Dapu St. and meets Shulin St. Follow Shulin as it passes the University of Tainan (notice the remains of the city south wall on your right). The museum is on the southeast corner of Shulin and Qingzhong Sts.*

Bo Yang Museum 柏楊文物館

33 Shulin St., Sec. 2(樹林街二段33號) Open Tue–Sun 9am–noon & 1:30pm–5:30pm. 06 213 3111 ext 127.
Bo Yang 柏楊 (1920-2008) was a pro-democracy and human rights activist famously jailed on Green Island for his translation of a Popeye comic strip. He authored many books, including *The Ugly Chinaman* (醜陋的中國人), a satirical and highly controversial look at Chinese culture. The museum is signed in Chinese, but his paintings and calligraphy need no translation. The second floor exhibits some of his nearly 300 titles and contains an intimate re-creation of his living room, writing room and Green Island prison cell.

Tainan-style Noodles

Tainan's best food is found in the simple, time-tested restaurants that make one thing and make it well. The most famous food here is Danzai noodles (擔仔麵). "Dan" means to support, and this quintessential Tainan snack was once peddled hanging from a bamboo pole slung over the seller's shoulder.

> *Continue on Qingzhong St. two blocks; the Five Concubines Temple is on the right.*

Five Concubines Temple 五妃廟

201 Wufei St. (五妃街201號) Open daily 8:30am–5:30pm. 06-229 3665.
In 1683, when the last royal of the Ming dynasty realized defeat was at hand, Prince Ningjing hung himself rather than submit to Qing conquerors. In an extreme act of devotion, the prince's five concubines hung themselves in the main hall of what is now Grand Mazu Temple *(see above)*, also called Wufei Temple. The lawn's old trees and botanical gardens are a pleasant place to relax.

> *Continue to the end of Wufei St. and turn left on Jiankang Rd. Walk to the end of the stadium and turn right onto Tiyu Rd. Follow this road downhill, and turn through the large archway before Chuhsi River.*

Bamboo River Monastery 竹溪禪寺

87 Tiyu Rd. (體育路87號) Open daily 4:30am–9pm. 06 215 4957. www.zhuxisi.org.tw.
Possibly constructed in 1661, this large, active Zen Buddhist monastery is reputedly the first temple to house monks and nuns in Taiwan. The oldest structure on the premises today, a **pagoda** for storing bones of the deceased *(to the right of the main hall)*, dates only to the Japanese era. The area is prone to flooding and the structures do not last long. The complex is currently being moved to a location to the east and will be finished in about 10 years.

Underwhelming in appearance, the main building is predominantly designed in the Chinese Palace style. Inside the main gate are statues of generals Xi and Ha (嘻哈二將), often seen guarding entrances to Buddhist monasteries; a **wooden tablet** of great historical value is in the main hall. Listening to the monks and nuns chant in Taiwanese *(daily 4:30am & 5pm)* is an unforgettable experience.

☚☚WALKING TOUR ③
2.km/1.3m. Allow 1.5hrs.

▷ *Begin on Hai'an Rd., 3 blocks west of Chihkan Tower.*

Hai'an Road★ 海安路

This road lies in today's so-called **Five Channels Area**. Now far from Taiwan Strait, the area was once Taiwan's foremost international trading port. Large seagoing vessels docked near present-day Anping, where goods and passengers transferred to smaller boats that plied the channels. During the Japanese era, the canals eventually silted over and became roads. Hai'an Road continued as a commercial area even after the five channels silted over. In the early 1990s, this area was one of the more popular city markets until the government attempted to create an underground shopping center. The problem-plagued project was finally put on hold, and the government is now investing in the area as a historic cultural zone. Chic shops, open-air cafes, and modern and traditional art venues create a retro look. The five blocks between Minzu and Fuqian Roads are the most interesting; early evening hours are the best time to shop and eat, since during the day many stores and eateries are closed.

▷ *Walk south on Hai'an to Minquan Rd.*

Shuisian Temple Market
水仙宮市場

Corner of Hai'an & Minquan Rds.
🕐*Open daily 6am–9pm.*

Taiwan's oldest market once stood advantageously at the terminus of Nan-shih channel, one of the canals giving the area its name. The market is busiest in the morning, selling traditional snacks, fruit, vegetables, meat and more exotic foodstuffs.

The middle aisle leads to **Shuisian Temple**, whose principal deities, five **water fairies**, were especially popular with people who made their living from the sea. Once the glory of Tainan, the temple underwent subsequent renovations that failed to preserve its historical legacy, however; now it is only a grade-three historic monument. Nonetheless, the temple's history and its location in the bustle of the market (stalls crowd right up and on to the temple stairs) lend aspects distinct from other temples in Tainan.

Bounded by Hai'an, Minquan, Guohua and Minzu Roads, the entire area is a large market packed with shoppers morning and evening and ghostly quiet from about 2pm to 5pm. In the northeast corner, **Yongle Market** (永樂市場) has a palpable old Tainan feel and smell (not always pleasant). The second floor is residential and interesting. Becoming disoriented deep in the bowels of this market is easy to do.

Interior, Shuisian Temple

Rich J. Matheson/Michelin

Sedan chairmaker, Shennong Street

Rich J. Matheson/Michelin

Shennong St. begins across the road from the market, between Minquan and Minzu Rds. A large mural by palanquin carver Wang Yongchuan marks the entrance.

Stroll down **Shennong Street**★ (神農街) to experience a living museum of old Tainan. This 130m/426ft stretch of road once had channels behind the houses. The prosperous road was witness to goods coming in from all over the world during much of the 1800s. Around the year 2000, it got a face-lift: the road surface was redone in brick, lights were installed and façades were rejuvenated. The process is still incomplete but the remaining unrefurbished houses give an impression of authenticity. Several retro-style shops, restaurants and museums dot the road. At the beginning of the street stands the **Palanquin Carvers Shop**, where master and apprentices carve delicate sedans for temple festivals. Peek at the ancient (and modern) tools, wooden roof structure, and traditional family altar inside.

The tourist sign at Shennong and Kangle Sts. guides you south for two blocks to the Wind God Temple on the right and Siluo temple on the left.

Wind God Temple★ 風神廟
8 Minquan Rd, Sec. 3, Lane 143 (民權路 三段143巷8號) Open daily.

Originally built in 1739, this unassuming temple is said to be the only one devoted to the Wind god in Taiwan. A receiving hall complex and **Memorial Stone Gate**★ for greeting officials were added later. The Japanese demolished more than half the complex to make room for Minquan Road. Much of what is standing today is a 1924 renovation. The temple received new Qing officials from China, who docked here and passed through the arch. Seafarers expressed their gratitude for favorable winds on arrival, and appealed for a safe trip on departure.

The **stone arch** is considered the finest of Tainan's four famous arches. The temple's English literature includes a delightful story about the **Thunder god** (the statue with beak and hammer) and his wife, the **Lightning goddess** (the statue across from him).

Siluo Temple★ 西羅殿
90 Heping St. (和平街90號)
Open daily.
This temple is the spiritual center for the cult of King Guo, especially venerated by pharmacists and geomancers. In King Guo's mortal life, he was a peasant boy who ascended to heaven around the age of 10. In popular mythology, he has a wife, who is worshiped in an adjoining temple. From the sanctum sanctorum, go left through the small back doorway into a side room, continue through this small kitchen, and the next doorway will take you to a smaller temple on Minquan Road. This temple, the **Shen Wang Ma** Temple, is devoted to King Guo's wife.

To return to Hai'an Rd., walk east on Heping St. along the side of the temple.

WALKING TOUR ④
1.9km/1.2mi. Allow 1hr.
Take a taxi (20min) or free tourist bus 88 or 99 (30min-1hr) from train station to Anping District, about 5km/3mi west of central Tainan.

Begin at Anping Fort, 3km/1.8mi from Gongyuan traffic circle.

Anping Fort★ 安平古堡

82 Guosheng Rd. 國勝路82號 ⏰*Open daily 8:30am–5:30pm. NT$50.* 📞*06 226 7348.*

At the site of the first Dutch stronghold on Taiwan, traces of the 17C fort, coupled with interesting museums and pleasant views, make Anping Fort worth the admission.

In 1634 the Dutch constructed **Fort Zeelandia** (👉*see Architecture in Introduction*) using it as their base until 1662, when Koxinga ousted them. From their castle-like fortress, the Dutch had superior firepower and defenses, but were unable to withstand Koxinga's nine-month siege, as lack of clean water and disease took their toll. In the ensuing Ming and Qing dynasties, the administrative center moved inland and the aging fort was dismantled for its bricks. The Japanese built the raised brick platform and Western-style house that you see today.

Visit

Inside the compound, the only remains of the original fort are the outer **south wall** and a **well**. Two other wall remnants are outside the complex on private land. In 2003 some of the original foundation was excavated. Portions of one excavation, now mostly refilled, are visible; panels explain the digs (*Chinese only*). The **Fort Zeelandia Museum** (*left of the entrance*) tells the history of the fort (*English signage*). Atop the fort

Sword Lions

The people of Anping use sword lions as charms to protect them and bring them peace and luck. One story of their origin is that Koxinga's soldiers hung their shields (which had lion motifs) and swords on their front doors. The residents followed their example and this practice soon became a sort of address or identification. In Anping they are sold as lucky souvenirs.

structure, the **Anping Fort Museum** has Chinese exhibits about the fort. There is good English signage around the grounds.

In front of the fort, you can find traditional Tainan snack foods. **Oyster omelets** here, and throughout Anping, are highly regarded.

▷ *Take the alley next to the fort and follow it east to Gubao St. Turn right at Yanping St.*

Yanping Old Street 延平老街

The Dutch laid out this street in the 17C; its scale remained largely unchanged until it was broadened in 1995. Undoubtedly, some of its charm was lost, but there are still interesting shops selling everything from tourist sword lions (👉*see sidebar*) to traditional crafts. Of note are the 100-year-old shop selling

Altar offerings, Siluo Temple

Rich J. Matheson/Michelin

mijian (蜜餞), a traditional candy of fruit preserved in honey and the **sword lion market** selling local crafts.

▷ *Return to Gubao St., turn right and follow it across Anbei Rd.; circle the school playground to reach the merchant house.*

Old Tait & Company Merchant House★
安平樹屋 英商德記洋行
108 Gubao St. (古堡街108號)
🕐*Open daily 8:30am–5:30pm. NT$50.*
📞*06 391 3901.*

When Western powers were carving up the Far East, Taiwan was opened to foreign trade under the 1858 Tianjin Treaty signed by China after the Opium War. Tait & Company, a British trading firm, was among the companies setting up in Tainan. They built the house with graceful arcade walkways typical of Western-style buildings of the time. In the Japanese era, the lucrative opium and camphor trades became state controlled, and business declined for the foreign trading companies, which were ultimately pressured out. The merchant house became a salt company's building and finally, a museum.

Anping Treehouse★★安平樹屋
The warehouse behind the merchant house was abandoned after WWII; old banyan trees have reclaimed the area. Aerial roots hang from the ceilings of the warehouse and cling to its doors and windows, creating "bars" where roots have found ground and thickened into trunks.

▷ *Continue circling the school on Gubau St. and turn left onto Alley 196, keeping the park and stream on your right. Follow the alley past the Julius Mannich Merchant House where the alley becomes Lane 35.*

Hsi Long Dian 西龍殿
12 Guosheng Rd., Lane 35 (國勝路35巷 12號) 🕐*Open daily 6 am–8 pm.*
Lord Chi (池府千歲), a common plague god, is enshrined as the principal deity in this early 18C temple.

A small statue on the front main altar has a Chinese-style pipe that the temple attendant refills daily with a fresh cigarette. Locals claim the statue smokes one cigarette in 10min. This smoking god is the area's protector, or earth god. Before deification this god was a local man who earned his fortune in the local salt industry; he is attributed with doing much good. **Wang Jishi** (王雞 屎1884-1948) lived in the large house around the corner. It was divined that the Jade Emperor appointed him as the local earth god and today he is worshiped as such.

▷ *Continue down Lane 35 to Anping Rd., turn left, pass the Mazu temple.*

Banyan roots, Anping Treehouse

Rich J. Matheson/Michelin

🚴 CYCLING TOUR

5km/3mi. Allow 45min.

The **tourist office** *(790 Anping Rd. 安平路790號 ⏰ open Tue–Sun 9am–6pm; ☎06 229 0313)* on the left rents bicycles at no charge with ID.

▶ Cycle east on Yunhe Rd. and turning left on Pinshen, cross Anyi Bridge. Pass "Fisherman Wharf" and continue to the intersection of Pingfeng and Anyi Rds.

Cha-ha-mu Aboriginal Park
札哈木原住民公園

472 Anyi Rd. 安億路472號 ⏰ Open Tue–Sun 8:30am–noon & 1:30pm–5:30pm. ☎06 298 2525.

If you plan to visit aboriginal areas in the mountains, you can skip this sight. The large green park hosts aboriginal dances. The **museum** sells aboriginal arts and crafts, and has an **exhibit** *(2nd floor)* of traditional clothing of Taiwan's tribes.

▶ Ride west on Anyi Rd, following the canal. As the road winds to the south, the back of the fort will come into view. Circle around (Fuping then Guangzhou) to get to the main entrance.

Eternal Golden Castle★
億載金城

3 Guangzhou Rd. (光州路3號) ⏰ Open daily 8:30am–5:30pm. NT$50. ☎06 295 1504.

Designed by a Frenchman, this Western-style fortress was built for safety from hungry colonial powers. Once equipped with 13 Armstrong cannon, the square fort has protruding bastions on all four corners and is surrounded by a moat; the brick bridge was initially a drawbridge. The Japanese sold off many cannon to fund their war against Russia, and now only one is original.

Enter through the impressive brick **archway** into the grass field that was formerly the **exercise grounds**. Walk up onto the **walls** to see the cannon and **views** of the area. Under the south wall, structures that were once the barracks and armory were unearthed in 1996. The excavation is now visible, but covered by a glass structure for protection. English signage.

▶ Ride north along Guangzhou and turn right on Anyi Rd. Backtrack to tourist office to return bikes.

EXCURSION

Nankunshen Temple★★★
南鯤鯓代天府

▶ 40km/25mi north of Tainan. Allow 6hrs. **By Car:** *From Tainan, head west on Minsheng Rd. towards Anping. Before reaching the canal, turn right on Provincial Hwy. 17.* **By Bus:** *Buses leave Xingnan bus station daily (6:15am–8:30pm) most every hour (2.5hrs one-way; NT$120). 976 Kunjiang Village, Beimen Township (北門鄉鯤江村976號). ⏰ Open daily 5:30am–9pm. ☎06 786 3711. www.nkstemple.org. tw/2010/indexing.html. Morning hours are recommended for seeing daily Daoist rituals.*

Every year around the fourth lunar month, this temple erupts in a folk-religion extravaganza. For many days, pilgrims by the busload come to pay their respects to the **Great King Li** (李府千歲) and the **Fifth King Fan** (范府千歲). Led into the temple by Daoist priests cracking whips and spirit mediums dripping blood, pilgrims carry incense or a carved statue of a god from a home altar. Processions, one after the other, continue daily for most of the month.

Tucked among the salt flats and fish farms of Beimen Township north of Tainan, this temple is synonymous with the cult of **Wangye** (🕮 *see sidebar*). With more than 300 years of history, Tainan's Heavenly Representative Nankunshen Temple is Taiwan's oldest and largest Wangye Temple.

One evening in the waning years of the Ming dynasty, fishermen saw a three-masted boat accompanied by music sail into Nankunshen harbor. Daybreak revealed a bedraggled junk carrying the Five Kings, the Lord Commander in Chief and a banner reading "Heavenly Patrol." To have navigated the dangerous strait and arrived safely, it was surely a potent

Wangye

One of the more popular gods, Wangye is also one of the more complicated. Wangye are a class of gods in folk religion ranging from Lord Stone to the cult of Koxinga. They are often plague gods that protect against disease, and often historical or mythological people who sacrificed themselves for others; some say Wangye is simply a pronoun for Taiwanese gods. They are often worshiped in groups of five. Nankunshen Temple representatives claim there are 17,395 registered Wangye temples worldwide.

spiritual vessel. A simple thatch hut was erected to house the gods, and thus began the worship of the Five Kings.

Visit

Between the street and the temple, **Dashan Gate** is said to be East Asia's largest wooden five-gated arch. The main altar hall that houses the **Five Kings** is said to be a *xue* (穴 geomantically powerful center) and may not be entered. Called the **money wall**, the back wall of the temple is constructed from blocks of coral that form a pattern of ancient coins. Guanyin, the Buddhist goddess of Mercy is worshiped in a hall behind the five kings. Farther down a covered walkway, a separate **temple** honors Wanshan, the ox herder who fell asleep in the *xue* and became a fairy. The **museum** (⊙ *open daily 8:30am–5:00pm; NT$100*) in a Southern Fujian-style villa on Kanglan Mountain (a hill next to the temple) describes the Wangye faith and temple origins *(Chinese only)*. The gardens, ponds, pagodas and religious curios on the 33ha/81acre grounds take time to explore.

Kanglan Villa (槺榔山莊), a hotel and restaurant designed in the Southern Fujian style, is well worth a wander even if you are not planning to stay or eat there.

Book well in advance if seeking accommodations during festival times.

ADDRESSES

🛏 STAY

$$ Cambridge Hotel 劍橋旅館,民族路二段269號 – 269 Minzu Rd., Sec. 2. ✕ ℘06 221 9966. www.cambridge-hotel.com.tw. 50 rooms. This high-rise hotel's location is great for exploring old Tainan. The decor is somewhat conservative, as befits a hotel that has been in business for decades, but the service is rated highly. Guests enjoy complimentary bicycles, a fitness center and self-service laundry. Restaurant on-site.

$$ Good Ground Hotel 國光大飯店, 尊 王路18號 – 18 Zunwang Rd.; ℘06 222 1105. http://goodground-tainan.hotel.com. 40 rooms. A well-regarded budget hotel in a good central location near Ximen and Fuqian Roads, convenient to shops. No on-site restaurant.

$$Taipung Suites 臺邦商旅, 永華二街199號 – 199 Yonghua 2nd St. ✕ ℘06 293 1888. www.taipungsuites.

com.tw. 103 rooms. Located west of the central core and south of city hall, this strikingly modern hotel lies within walking distance of many restaurants. Guest rooms are appointed with sleek furnishings. A restaurant and bar are on the premises.

$$$ Far Eastern Plaza Hotel 香格里拉台南遠東國際大飯店, 大學路西段89號 – 89 Daxue Rd., West Sec. ✕ Spa ℘06 702 8888. www.shangri-la.com.tw/tainan. 336 rooms. Tainan's newest top-range hotel, a Shangri-La property, is situated just east of the train station and near the university. Spacious rooms have contemporary Asian furnishings and free broadband Internet. Two restaurants, two lounges, a spa and outdoor swimming pool.

$$$ Hotel Tainan 台南大飯店, 成功路1號 – 1 Chenggong Rd. ✕ ℘06 228 9101. www.hotel-tainan.com.tw. 152 rooms. A stone's throw from the railway and bus stations, this city fixture (since 1964) is a convenient base for exploring the Greater Tainan area. Simply furnished rooms come with breakfast. On-site restaurant serves buffet meals. Outdoor swimming pool.

☕EAT

$ Duxioayue Danzai Noodles (度小月擔仔麵) – *16 Zhongzheng Rd.* (中正路16號). ☎*06 223 1744.* Duxioayue has been plying its delectable noodles since 1895. Their fried pork with shallot sauce purportedly bubbled in the same pot until the bottom wore out in its 100th year (and is currently on display). The sauce is served over noodles in a clear shrimp soup and a special "lu" egg and topped with fresh shrimp and coriander. Tiny portions, but only NT$50 per bowl. **Taiwanese.**

$ Fulou (福樓) – *300 Yonghua Rd.* (永華路300號) ☎*06 295 7777.* In Tainan when barbecue (燒烤) is mentioned, Fulou tops the list. Providing a higher class of service and decor than most Tainan restaurants, Fulou attracts actors, athletes and politicians to its modern, dark wood interior. A favorite 10 list with photos makes ordering easy. **Barbecue.**

$ Fuchen Luwei (府城魯味) – *10 Dunning Rd.* (東寧路10號) *Closes 4am.* ☎*06 236 2158. www.tn-luwe.com.tw.* Sitting amid trendy clothing shops near the university, 40-year-old Fuchen Luwei offers an a la carte selection of 60 dishes, from tofu to duck feet and stewed in Fuchen's spicy 40-herb sauce. Try the noodles (肉燥乾麵) (strained) mixed with ground pork, topped with green onions, bean sprouts with a dash of Fuchen's special sauce. **Taiwanese.**

$ Shanghai Huadu Dimsum (上海華都小吃城) – *28 Mingcheng Rd.* (民權路二段28號). ☎*06 221 6268. www.ikl.com.tw.* Decor and service are basic at this well-established restaurant, yet the food is anything but. Order Shaolong soup dumplings (小籠湯包)—steamed tender mincemeat wrapped in a thin flour skin—and fried pineapple shrimp balls (鳳梨蝦球), large, mouth-sized shrimp covered with special paste, fried until crispy and served with sauce and pineapple. **Shanghainese.**

$ Tainan A-hui Fried Eel (台南阿輝炒鱔魚) – *283 Gongyuan S. Rd.* (公園南路283號).* ☎*06 221 8882.* A-hui's new location in Tainan's historic Bei-Fang district is modern and comfortable. The signature fried eel, with its slightly crisp texture and distinctive sweet and sour taste, is one of Tainan's sought-out dishes. Carefully selected fresh eel is stir-fried with onions and scallions and seasoned with a special sauce, pepper powder, rice vinegar and sugar. **Taiwanese.**

🛍SHOPPING

TRADITIONAL CRAFTS

Close to the Martial Temple on Yongfu Road, the **Guangcai Embroidery Shop** (府城光彩繡莊) sells award-winning, traditional Chinese embroidery; workers can often be seen stitching elaborate temple banners. Across from the War God Temple, **Wu Wanchun's Incense Shop** (吳萬春香鋪) has been hand-making incense for more than 100 years.

GENERAL MERCHANDISE

Hai'an and Shennong Roads hold clothing boutiques, curio shops, food stores and coffee shops. Opposite the Taiwan literature museum are **camera shops** on the traffic circle surrounding Tang De Zhang Memorial Park (湯德章記念公園).

Taiwanese embroidery, Yongfu Road

Rich J. Matheson/Michelin

Mountain Villages★★

Inland of the Han-dominated lowlands of Taiwan, east of Tainan and Kaohsiung, a strip of mostly aboriginal settlements presses up against the Central Mountain Range. Home primarily to Bunun, Paiwan, Rukai and Tsou indigenous clans, these mountain communities welcome visitors, making their homes available as lodgings and their handicrafts for sale to the public.

In terms of scenery as well as social organization, this zone is quite unlike the rest of the South. From the waterfalls of multicultural Namasia in the north, through Jiaxian (where carloads of tourists stop for taro-flavored ice cream) down to Maolin's Purple Butterfly Valley and the glass-bead workshops of Sandimen, it offers motorists and motorcyclists some of Taiwan's most enjoyable touring.

A BIT OF GEOGRAPHY

Unless the weather is exceptionally clear, you will not see South Taiwan's mountains when touring Tainan or Kaohsiung. Head inland, however, and within an hour you are among foothills where much higher peaks become visible. The gradients are very steep: Namasia varies in elevation from 430m/1,410ft to 2,481m/8,140ft. Between Jiaxian and Yakou, the midpoint of the typhoon-ravaged **South Cross-Island Highway** (*see sidebar*), the road gains almost 2.5km/1.5mi in altitude. Rivers—attractive creeks during the long dry season—become life-threatening torrents of muddy water during the summer. North-south routes such as Highway 27 and Highway 185 mean those with their own vehicles could, in theory at least, explore all four of the districts detailed in this entry in a single day. The distance from Namasia to Sandimen is only 92km/57mi. The roads are well-maintained and traffic is usually light.

⌚ **Michelin Map:** p263.

ℹ **Info:** Maolin National Scenic Area Administration, 120 Saijia Lane, Saijia Village, Sandimen Township. 三地門鄉賽嘉村賽嘉巷120號; ℘08 799 2221; www.maolin-nsa.gov.tw.

▶ **Location:** A string of villages at the foot of the Central Mountain Range, the south's aboriginal heartlands are 40km-90km/25mi-56mi east of downtown Kaohsiung.

👫 **Kids:** Jiaxian's taro ice cream, Purple Butterfly Valley in Maolin.

🕐 **Timing:** Make it a long day, or better yet two, and be ready to stop at any place that looks intriguing. Avoid visiting in the wet season from May through October.

⊘ **Don't Miss:** Namasia's festivals and waterfalls, Duona's slate houses, Sandimen's glass-bead workshops.

Maolin Village

Rich J. Matheson/Michelin

GETTING THERE

BY BUS - Kaohsiung Bus Co. Station near Kaohsiung Main Railway Station has buses to **Jiaxian** hourly (6:40am–9:40pm; 2hrs 15min; NT$207 one-way). Pingtung Bus Co. Station in Pingtung, a city east of Kaohsiung accessible by train, has several buses per day to **Maolin** and **Sandimen**. The bus station is a few minutes' walk from Pingtung's TRA Railway Station.
Ten buses each day link Pingtung (6:50am–8:45pm; 1hr 15min; NT$101 one-way) with **Dajin** (大津), a tiny village southwest of Maolin, from the Pingtung Bus Co. Station.
Twelve buses a day (6:30am–6pm; 45min; NT$60 one-way) connect Shuimen and Sandi in **Sandimen** Township with Pingtung Bus Co. Station, in Pingtung.

BY CAR - Jiaxian can be reached from Tainan by Hwy. 20 (South Cross-Island Hwy.) Maolin can be reached by Hwy. 27 from the north, Hwy. 185 from the south and Hwy. 28 from the west. From Dajin, at the base of the mountains, Hwy. 132 leads northeast to Maolin and on to Duona.
Gas stations are infrequent in the mountains, so it's best to fill up before you start and refill when you see a gas station en route.

BY ORGANIZED TOUR - Maolin mountain and ecotourism specialists Barking Deer Adventures arrange group and individual tours of Maolin throughout the year. *℘09 3833 7710; www.barking-deer.com.*

GENERAL INFORMATION

VISITOR INFORMATION

Maolin Visitor Center – located in the Farmers' Assn. Building, Maolin Village. Maolin National Scenic Area – *℘08 799 2221; www.maolin-nsa.gov.tw.* Maolin Township Government – www.maolin.gov.tw.

ACCOMMODATIONS

Homestays and bed-and-breakfast lodgings are typically available for overnighting in the mountain areas. *For a selection of accommodations, see ADDRESSES below.*

However, spending a night in an aboriginal village—ideally in a homestay operated by an indigenous family—is highly recommended: as a cultural experience, it will add another dimension to your Taiwan journey.

🚗 DRIVING TOUR

see Map. 184km/114mi. Allow 2 days, with an overnight stay. This driving tour starts from Tainan, heading east to Jiaxian, then to Namasia and back to Jiaxian before going on to Sandimen.

Caution: Because of massive destruction from a 2009 typhoon, the drive from Jiaxian northeast to Namasia is difficult and dangerous. A 4-wheel drive vehicle is strongly advised. Do not attempt the drive during or after heavy rains, as mud slides and washed-out roads are the probable result. It may be best for you to omit this northeast stretch entirely and head south from Jiaxian to Maolin.

▷ *From Tainan drive 55km/34mi east on Hwy. 20. At Yujin, Hwy. 20 joins Hwy. 3 and they split again at Beiliao. Drive east over the foothills of the Alishan Range to Jiaxian.*

Jiaxian甲仙

Considered the gateway to the mountains, this village of 7,527 residents is

Touring Tip

Driving is the only practical way to visit this area since bus services have been severely disrupted by Typhoon Morakot. Driving beyond Xiaolin should not be attempted in heavy rain as the road is prone to washing out, and locals use alternate 4X4 routes over the mountain range.

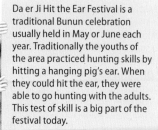

Hit the Ear Festival

Da er Ji Hit the Ear Festival is a traditional Bunun celebration usually held in May or June each year. Traditionally the youths of the area practiced hunting skills by hitting a hanging pig's ear. When they could hit the ear, they were able to go hunting with the adults. This test of skill is a big part of the festival today.

famous for taro. Most people just pass through after sampling Jiaxian's taro delicacies, especially the 🧍🧍 **taro ice cream** (芋頭冰).

▷ *From Jiaxian, drive 14km/8.7mi northeast on provisional Hwy. 21, which follows the Nanzuxian River, to Xiaolin.*

Xiaolin 小林 **and Wulipu** 五里埔

Xiaolin was once a quaint Plains aborigine village until, on Chinese Father's Day in 2009, a huge catastrophic failure in the mountain above dumped an estimated 45 million cubic meters of rock and debris directly onto it. Of the 300 houses, only two remain. More than 400 villagers died in the event. A 3.5km/2.2mi-long scar is clearly visible from **Wulipu**, a village south of Xiaolin. Just down the hill, there is a viewing area and a shrine for the people of Xiaolin. Many of the remaining villagers are being relocated (as of this writing) to Wulipu, to a Red Cross housing complex. In Wulipu a temporary *Gongxie* (公廨) shrine (a traditional Pingpu shrine), a temple to Xuantian Shangdi and a ceremonial bamboo pole have been erected in a makeshift park with the purpose of preserving and promoting the Xiaolin Pingpu culture, which has suffered a massive setback. There is no English language information, but it is an intriguing stop nonetheless.

▷ *A provisional Hwy. 2 continues up Hwy. 21 and over the landslide. Signs indicate a grade of 19 percent for 800m (half a mile). It has proven a very*

dangerous road, especially dropping into the valley on the northern slope. A sharp switchback has already taken five lives at the time of writing. Exercise great caution on this portion of road, use the lowest gear and make sure your brakes are in good working order.

▷ *The asphalt road continues in the riverbed to Holy Mt. Zion just past the 4km marker.*

Holy Mount Zion 錫安山

This place is home to a small community belonging to the New Testament Church. The **rock** seen at the bottom of the commune entrance is a cement reconstruction of the one washed away by Typhoon Morakot. The remnants of the bridge that once spanned 10m/32ft above the Nanzuxian River are now visible at the same height as the riverbed.

▷ *Drive up the steep road.*

At the homestead housing some 300 people, disconcerting posters announcing their millenarian beliefs as well as some highly vitriolic proclamations like "KMT is anti-Christ" belie the peaceful, hard-working disciples. Once heavily persecuted by the Kuomintang, they are now largely left to their own. Under the guidance of Elijah Hong, a pharmacist turned prophet, the group sells organic products and breeds organic rabbits. The educated backgrounds of the followers fostered successful implementation of organic processes to the point that they have become a model organic-farming community.

▷ *Continue north on Hwy. 21 for 1km/.6mi to Namasia.*

Namasia Township 那瑪夏鄉

With a population of 3,484, this township comprises the three villages of Nangisalu, Maya and Takanua. They reside in the valley of the **Nanzuxian River**, which flows between the Yushan Mountain Range and the Alishan Range. Namasia is an aboriginal community whose two major tribes, Tsou and Bunun, have co-existed for hundreds of years. Originally, the **Southern Tsou** lived in the valley until disease wiped out much of the tribe. The **Bunun** came over the mountains and filled the void. Today they still live together, the Bunun being the majority and the Tsou the minority. Also living in the area are Paiwan, Atayal, Hakka and Han Chinese who migrated recently through marriage or work.

The valley is an outdoor paradise with lush green subtropical vegetation and crystal clear river water. During tropical **peach season** *(late Apr–early Jun)*, lowlanders flock to the area to buy the small, sweet mountain-grown variety. Firefly and **butterfly** season *(Apr–May)* also bring tourists, when as many as 89 species of butterfly are on hand, as well as fireflies that light up the night. There is amazing ◨ **hiking** here, but it is underdeveloped. The trails are often unmarked hunting trails, and some of the established trails were damaged in the typhoon. A popular spot for watching the sunrise and sunset over the valley is **Yu Da Mountain** (玉打山).

Maolin village street

Rich J. Matheson/Michelin

◖ *Return to Jiaxian via Hwy. 21 then head east on Hwy. 20 to Laonong. From there, turn south on Hwy. 27 and watch for Hwy. 132. The turnoff to Maolin is clearly marked. Continue up Hwy. 132 to Maolin Village.*

Maolin★★ 茂林

A tiny village with about 700 people, Maolin sits in the valley of the **Zhuokou River**, and in the northeast section of the Maolin National Scenic Area. To Maolin's west runs the **Laonong River**, one of Taiwan's longest rivers, and known for its superb whitewater rafting before the 2009 typhoon. Dotted with pristine creeks and attractive waterfalls, Maolin belongs to the Rukai people, one of Taiwan's smaller aboriginal tribes. Some of their traditional culture and architecture is still evident, and the district is phenomenally rich in birds and butterflies. **Purple Butterfly Valley**★★★ (紫蝶幽谷) like the better-known Monarch Butterfly Valley in Mexico, is a winter destination for millions of migrating butterflies. But while Monarch Valley is associated with just one kind of lepidopteran, Maolin sees massive numbers of at least half a dozen species, including Chocolate Tigers and Striped Blue

South Cross-Island Highway

Until **Typhoon Morakot** struck Taiwan in August 2009, the 209km/130mi-long South Cross-Island Highway (also known as Highway 20) was by far the most scenic way of traveling between Tainan and Taitung. Sadly for tourists, not to mention the aboriginal fruit farmers and others for whom the road was a crucial link with the plains, the high-altitude section of the highway suffered terrible damage in that calamity. After Morakot hit, many of the hot springs along the highway were buried. Warm mineral water came out of the diversion hole that was being drilled through the mountain range. At the time of this writing, the highway was sporadically open but still unsuitable for normal vehicles. If the highway is properly repaired, make every effort to add it to your itinerary, as the alpine scenery is breathtaking. When conditions are good, it is possible to set out from Tainan after breakfast and reach the East Rift Valley before dusk.

Maolin Ecological Park

Rich J. Matheson/Michelin

Crows. Unfortunately, finding these creatures is not easy; they do not always gather in the same places from year to year, and some locations are fenced off for conservation reasons.

If you are short of time or disinclined to walk far, visit **Maolin Ecological Park**★★ (茂林生態公園) (◔*open 24hrs*), in the highest part of Maolin Village. There, butterflies can be seen inside two netted enclosures.

▷ *From Maolin, take Hwy. 132 northeast to the village of Duona, which is 15km/9mi from Maolin.*

Duona Suspension Bridge★★
多納高吊橋

This 232m/759ft-long bridge links Highway 132 with a side road. It makes an excellent place to pause when driving from Maolin to Duona, but do not saunter along the bridge unless you have a good head for heights. The views over the Zhuokou River, 103m/338ft below, are good but dizzying. The bridge was most likely built initially by the Japanese, but has since been upgraded several times.

▷ *From Maolin, follow Hwy. 132 as it winds through the hills to Duona, which sits at the terminus of the road.*

Duona 多納

This hamlet lost its hot springs to Typhoon Morakot. Fortunately, the stacked **slate-stone houses** (◔*see Architecture in the Introduction*) that give this place its distinctive character survived and continue to be inhabited by Rukai farmers and their families.

If you choose to drive just half of this tour, you can return to the freeway system via Qishan (旗山), which is linked to Jiaxian by Hwy. 21 and to Maolin by Hwy. 28. **Neimen** (內門), *on the outskirts of Qishan, is synonymous with the annual* **Songjiang Battle Array**, *an elaborate martial arts dance performed at festivals and in parades.*

▷ *Return to Maolin on Hwy. 132. From Maolin, drive south over Dajin Bridge and turn left onto Hwy. 185. Head south to Hwy. 24 and turn left onto Hwy. 24 to reach Sandimen, which is about 18km/11mi from Maolin.*

Sandimen★★ 三地門

More than 9 out of 10 of Sandimen's nearly 7,400 residents are Paiwan aborigines. The township is widely known for its locally crafted **glass beads**. Other indigenous crafts made in the area include embroidered goods, woven baskets and pottery. The main village, **Sandi** (三地), is a tightly-packed settlement clinging to a hillside that overlooks the southern lowlands. *For lodgings, ◔see ADDRESSES below.*

Sights
Taiwan Indigenous Peoples Culture Park★★
台灣原住民族文化園區

Drive to Shuimen, then follow the signs. ◔*Open Tue–Sun 8:30am–5pm. NT$150, children NT$80.* ✆*08 799 1219. www. tacp.gov.tw. English literature available, and signs in English. Free shuttle buses.*

This government-run, 82ha/202-acre landmark is combination theme park and cultural center showcasing nine of Taiwan's 14 officially recognized aboriginal peoples. Because the park is managed by the government agency responsible for the welfare of Taiwan's indigenous population, there is an emphasis on authenticity.

The life-size **replica dwellings**, artifact displays and cultural performances *(at least one per hour, usually 20min)*

Song Jiang Battle Array

Common in southern Taiwan, this traditional folk performance is a martial arts display usually seen in the region's festivals, parades and competitions. Dressed in matching sweatsuits, members hold weapons, carry banners, and perform choreographed martial arts routines. Often one person will stand in the middle and perform a solo to the sound of beating drums. In the lawless, bandit-infested foothills of early southern Taiwan, communities formed local or family militias to protect themselves. The name of the array derives from a hero in *Water Margin*, a novel set in the Song dynasty, who had 36 companions and led 108 Liangshan braves. Hence 36 and 107 (108 is considered unlucky) are common numbers of performers. Ironically, the real Song Jiang was a bandit who robbed travelers.

The performance traditionally begins with a prayer to their patron god. Then, with weapons held high, the troupe lets out a battle yell. Weapons are farming tools, some modified, some not. Today it is an elaborate, graceful martial-arts dance. The best-known Song Jiang event is the annual Song Jiang Battle Array in **Neimen** village celebrating the birthday of Guanyin, the Buddhist goddess of Mercy. Song Jiang troupes from all over the island come to perform or compete at this week-long extravaganza. The festival takes place around the 19th day of the second lunar month, usually in April. For more info: www.who-ha.com.tw.

are popular with both Taiwanese and Western visitors. Among the dances and songs are ancient marriage rites and harvest celebrations. Indoor display areas feature carved stone furniture and tribal costumes. Two restaurants on the premises serve mainstream Taiwanese and aboriginal food.

Sha Tao's Art Studio 沙滔舞琉璃藝術空間
Lane 37, 7 Zhongzheng Rd., Sec 2中正路二段37巷7號. Open Tue–Sun 8am–6pm. 08 799 4849.
Sandimen's most famous glass-bead workshop is not easy to find: park where

it is legal and convenient and then set off on foot—and ask for directions. Among the items for sale are necklaces, earrings and cell-phone accessories, which vary greatly in size and price. It's worth browsing even if you are not much of a shopper. Peek into the workshop at the back to see how the beads are shaped and colored.

Additional Sight
Mount Northern Dawu 北大武山
Turn east off Hwy. 185 at KM 40 distance post, south of Sandimen. Note: Hikers should be properly equipped and must

Duona Suspension Bridge

Rich J. Matheson/Michelin

obtain permits before they begin their climb from the police station, located on the left 1km/.6mi from Hwy. 185.

▲The most southerly of Taiwan's 200-plus 3,000m/9,842ft mountains, and not as tough a climb as Yushan or Xueshan (but not to be underestimated, though), Mount Northern Dawu makes an excellent two-day/one-night expedition. The majority of hikers spend the night in a rudimentary hut *(free; water available, but bring your own food)*, and then leave before dawn so as to make it to the 3,090m/10,138ft summit in time for the sunrise.

Excursion
Wutai 霧台

Most of Sandimen Township survived Typhoon Morakot undamaged, which sadly, is more than can be said for Wutai, a stunningly beautiful Rukai village farther inland along Highway 24. If the road to Wutai is open—which is unlikely—consider driving eastward. The scenery alone more than justifies the excursion.

▷ *From Sandimen, return to Tainan via Hwy. 24 west and then via Fwy. 3. Kaohsiung, which lies south of Tainan, can also be reached by the same route.*

ADDRESSES

🏠 STAY

$ Den Gorge B&B 得恩谷的民宿 – *Off Hwy. 132, Maolin. From Maolin, turn right after driving 2.5km/1.5mi on Hwy. 132.* ☎*09 8957 9751 or 09 5505 5132 or 07 680 1540. 14 rooms.* Turn down toward the river at the Fire Department building, cross the small bridge and turn left to find this hillside homestay. The Rukai owners, who speak English, are local eco-tourism pioneers. Spacious, slate-floor rooms that sleep up to four are NT$2500.

$$ Sandimen Homestay 三地門民宿, 三地村中正路一段56號 *56 Zhongzheng Rd. Sec 1, Sandimen Village.* ☎*08 752 2953. 4 rooms.* With cool tiled floors, straightforward furnishings, and very large windows that allow you to enjoy the scenery, this B&B has two-, four- and six-person rooms priced from NT$1800 to NT$4500.

JIAXIAN
$ Yongchangsheng Hotel (永長生休閒度假中心) – *10-1 Xinxing Rd., Lane 93 (新興路93巷10-1號)* ☎*07 675 4561. 48 rooms.* Situated on a hill overlooking the river and village, this spartan but clean hotel offers views of the surroundings.

NAMASIA TOWNSHIP
$ Hu Song's Relaxation Farm (呼頌民宿渡假村) – *210 Pinghe Lane 平和巷210號. 6 rooms.* ☎*0933 586 866.*

Advance reservations recommended. Sitting high above the village of Maya and offering great views of the valley, this hostel is run by the former mayor of Namasia. It's a good place to get information about the local culture and sample aboriginal cuisine in the farm's **dining hall ($)** *(by reservation only; NT$350 for wild game barbecue).* Three simple cabins have air conditioning and hot water. There's a barbecue area and a tent site.

🍽 EAT

$ Qiu Yue's Store 秋月的店 – *KM 24, Hwy. 24.* ☎*08 799 1524 (open daily 10am–midnight).* The views are splendid from this open-air restaurant, which is perched between Highway 24 and a precipitous drop down to the Aliao River. Across the valley, you can see the Taiwan Indigenous Culture Park. The menu in this aboriginal-owned establishment includes Taiwanese favorites and Rukai dishes such as stir-fried wild spinach *(NT$150)* and deep-fried bee pupae *(NT$350).* **Taiwanese.**

JIAXIAN
$ Super Spicy Noodles 特辣麵 – *30 Wenhua Rd. (文化路30號). Closes 9:30pm.* ☎*07 675 1991.* This store's specialty is super spicy noodles; if you don't like spicy food, however, the regular noodles are equally tasty. **Taiwanese.**

Kaohsiung★★

Taiwan's largest international port and second-largest metropolis, Kaohsiung (高雄) stretches inland from the Taiwan Strait along the island's southwest coast. The waterfront city centers on its vast harbor, fitted with more than 100 docks and thousands of cargo platforms. A source of recreational boating and cruise tours, the Love River winds 12km/7.5mi through the city before flowing into the harbor. Once beholden to heavy industry, the self-styled ocean capital has made a Houdini-like escape from its gritty past. Few cities have cleaned themselves up and embraced the 21C as successfully as Kaohsiung, but that does not mean everything has been consumed by modernity. Wandering the backstreets of Qihou, or drinking coffee at the hilltop British Former Consular Residence, you will have no difficulty casting your mind back to an era when fishing boats and steamships, not container vessels, filled the harbor.

A BIT OF HISTORY

Imperial armed junks sent to deal with southeast China's perennial pirate problem visited Kaohsiung as early as 1603. The place name they wrote on their

▶ **Population:** 1.52 million (city).

Michelin Maps: p263, p290.

Info: Kaohsiung Main Station (open daily 9am–7pm; ℘07-235 2376) and the airport's international terminal (open daily 9am–12:30am; ℘07 805 7888).

Location: The city's history is concentrated in the southwest and around Lotus Pond in the north. Shoppers and gourmets will find themselves drawn to Wufu and Zhongshan Roads.

Kids: Ride the ferry to Qijin Island and a pedicab through the old streets of Qihou. Alternatively, try the bike routes through the city.

Timing: Allow an entire day to see the old side of this modern city, not including relaxed shopping and eating. Aim for the cooler, dry months between October and March.

Don't Miss: Qijin Island, Former British Consulate Residence, the Love River.

Love River and Kaohsiung skyline

Rich J. Matheson/Michelin

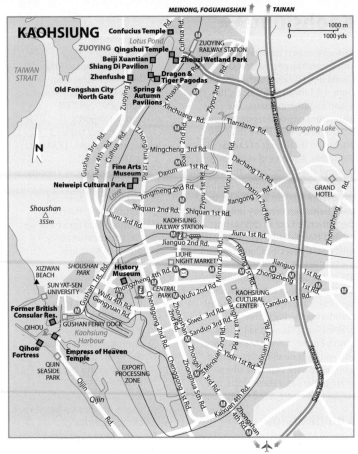

MEINONG, FOGUANGSHAN   TAINAN

KAOHSIUNG

ZUOYING

TAIWAN STRAIT

Confucius Temple
Qingshui Temple
Beiji Xuantian Shiang Di Pavilion
Zhenfushe
Old Fongshan City North Gate
Spring & Autumn Pavilions
Zhouzi Wetland Park
Dragon & Tiger Pagodas
ZUOYING RAILWAY STATION

Lotus Pond

Cuihua Rd.
Huaxia Rd.
Ziyou 3rd Rd.
Xinchuang Rd.
Tianxiang Rd.
Chengqing Lake

Gushan 3rd Rd.
Gushan 4th Rd.
Jiuru 4th Rd.
Cuihua Rd.
Zhonghua 1st Rd.
Mingcheng 3rd Rd.
Boai Rd.
Mingcheng 2nd Rd.
Daxun 1st Rd.
Ziyou 1st Rd.
Minzu 1st Rd.
Dachang 1st Rd.

Fine Arts Museum
Neiweipi Cultural Park
Daxun 1st Rd.
Tongmeng 2nd Rd.
Shiquan 2nd Rd. Shiquan 1st Rd.
Love
Jiuru 3rd Rd.
Jiangong Rd.
Daxun 2nd Rd.

GRAND HOTEL
Zhongzheng Rd.

Shoushan △ 355m

KAOHSIUNG RAILWAY STATION
Jiuru 1st Rd.
Heping 1st Rd.
Jianguo 2nd Rd.
LIUHE NIGHT MARKET
Jianguo 1st Rd.
Zhongzheng 1st Rd.

XIZIWAN BEACH
SHOUSHAN PARK
History Museum
SUN YAT-SEN UNIVERSITY
Zhongzheng 4th Rd.
CENTRAL PARK
Wufu 2nd Rd.
Minzu 2nd Rd.
KAOHSIUNG CULTURAL CENTER
Guanghua 1st Rd.
Sanduo 1st Rd.

Former British Consular Res.
QIHOU
GUSHAN FERRY DOCK
Kaohsiung Harbour
Wufu 4th Rd.
Gongyuan Rd.
Chenggong 2nd Rd.
Zhongshan 2nd Rd.
Siwei 3rd Rd.
Sanduo 3rd Rd.
Guanghua 3rd Rd.
Kaixuan 3rd Rd.
Zhongzheng 1st Rd.

Qihou Fortress
QIJIN SEASIDE PARK
Empress of Heaven Temple
EXPORT PROCESSING ZONE
Qijin
Qijin Rd.
Chenggong 1st Rd.
Zhongshan 3rd Rd.
Minzu 2nd Rd.
Yixin 1st Rd.
Zhonghua 5th Rd.
Kaixuan 4th Rd.
Zhongshan 4th Rd.

Sun Yat-sen Freeway

0   1000 m
0   1000 yds

N

maps, **Takau** (meaning "bamboo forest"), was a corruption of the toponym used by the aboriginal Makatau inhabitants. The Dutch East India Company explored Takau (which the Dutch called

Kaohsiung harbor

Rich J. Matheson/Michelin

Tankoya), but left the region to the Fujianese settlers who began appearing in significant numbers in the 1630s. **Qihou**, the town these migrants established on Qijin Island, remains Kaohsiung's quaintest and most characterful district.

Until the second half of the 19C, Taiwan was a backwater of East Asia, and Takau was a backwater of Taiwan. However, the **foreign merchants** who set up shop here after 1863 made full use of the superb natural harbor. They plugged South Taiwan into the global economy, turning Kaohsiung into the vibrant entrepôt it has been ever since. To meet growing demand for rice, peanuts, sesame and sugar, local farmers and middlemen opened up the hinterland and brought in labor from the Chinese mainland. Channels were cut so

GETTING THERE

BY AIR - Several flights daily from mainland China, Hong Kong, Macau, Japan and other places in Asia to Kaohsiung International Airport (KHH) (高雄國際航空站) (✆*07-805 7631; www.kia.gov.tw*). To reach the airport, take the MRT Red Line to Kaohsiung International Airport Station (R4).

BY TRAIN - Kaohsiung-Zuoying (高雄左營高鐵站) (✆*07-960 5000*) is the southern terminus of the **High Speed Rail** (HSR). Five services (2hrs) daily from Taipei each hour 6:30am–11pm (one-way NT$1,490). Kaohsiung-Zuoying is under the same roof as Xinzuoying Train Station (新左營火車站) and MRT Zuoying Station (R16).

All **conventional trains** (TRA) stop at Kaohsiung Main Station (高雄火車站) (✆*07-236 2710*), at least 4.5hrs south of Taipei (one-way on the fastest trains NT$845). For Lotus Lake and the northern part of the city, Zuoying (左營) and Xinzuoying are more convenient. Direct trains to Taitung (2.5hrs; one-way NT$364).

BY BUS - Long-distance buses arrive and depart 24/7 from stations close to Kaohsiung Main Station. Turn left as you exit the railway or MRT stations. Full fare to Taipei (5hrs) varies but costs NT$520 weekends. Buses to Foguangshan, Meinong, Qishan,

Jiaxian and Kenting depart from Kaohsiung-Zuoying HSR station, or Kaohsiung Bus Co. Station (高雄客運站) (✆*07-237 1230*), 100m/ 300ft east of Kaohsiung Main Station.

GETTING AROUND

BY METRO - The efficient, bilingual, yet underused, Kaohsiung Mass Rapid Transit (MRT) (*www.krtco.com.tw*) has two lines. The Red Line links the HSR station and the airport; the Orange Line serves Xiziwan and the eastern suburbs. Both operate 6am–11pm every 10min or less. Tickets are coin-like plastic tokens sold in vending machines (NT$20–NTD$65 for one ride, NT$200 for day pass). To enter the platform, swipe a token over a sensor. To exit, drop it into a slot.

BY BUS - Local buses are air-conditioned and inexpensive (NT$12 for most rides), but fairly slow. From the city bus hub in front of Kaohsiung Main Station, you can reach Gushan Ferry Dock (bus no. 248), the Cultural Center (no. 50), the Love River and the history museum (no. 12).

BY CAR - At the airport, Car Plus (8:30am–9pm; ✆*07-801 0019*) car-rental office is located between the two terminals. Two car-rental companies located inside Kaohsiung-Zuoying HSR Station keep similar hours.

---

wetlands could be drained; one of these waterways became the **Love River**, which is to modern Kaohsiung what the Seine is to Paris. The population swelled, but in terms of public health and services, Takau was no better than medieval Europe.

After the Japanese took over Taiwan, Takau's European and North American businessmen found themselves squeezed out by Japanese rivals. The colonial regime expanded the harbor, established steel and shipbuilding industries, and linked Kaohsiung to the rest of West Taiwan by railway. In 1920 they changed the written form of

Kaohsiung's name from the uncouth 打狗 (literally "beat the dog") to the far more refined 高雄 ("tall and heroic"). In Japanese, both names are pronounced Takao. When the KMT arrived in 1945, they kept the latter pair of characters but adopted the Mandarin pronunciation: Kaohsiung (*Gaoxiong*).

Post-war life in Kaohsiung was not very different from pre-war conditions. Factories polluted the air and water (the Love River turned black and stayed that way until the 1990s), but the opportunity to earn a steady salary drew migrants from the countryside. The city's inhabitants—who by 1975 numbered more than a mil-

Swinhoe's Discoveries

Among the first wave of foreign arrivals in Kaohsiung were Dr. **Patrick Manson** (1822-1944) and **Robert Swinhoe** (1836-77). The former, a parasitologist from Scotland, is credited with a critical discovery: that malaria could be spread by mosquitoes. For five years he served as the customs office physician in Taiwan. Swinhoe's day job (British consul in Formosa from 1860 to 1873) left him enough free time for extensive travel and some astonishing achievements in the field of natural science. He described dozens of creatures and plants previously unknown to scientists, including **Swinhoe's Pheasant**. His successors lived in Kaohsiung's most famous Western-style building, the Former British Consulate Residence near the harbor's mouth.

lion—like to point out that Kaohsiung has written its share of Taiwanese history. A 1979 riot is considered a turning point in the island's democratization. More recently, it was Kaohsiung, not Taipei, which hosted Taiwan's first-ever international multi-sports event. The 2009 **World Games** epitomizes what has been achieved here. Kaohsiung is now a city for people who love the outdoors and adore sunshine.

QIJIN ISLAND★★ 旗津
Take the 🚶‍♂️🚢 **ferry** *to the village of Qihou* (旗后) *from Gushan Ferry Dock* (鼓山輪渡站) *(departs daily 6am– midnight every 10min; 5min crossing; NT$15 one-way). Disembark in Qihou, at the island's northwest end.*

Acting as a breakwater that protects the harbor, this long, narrow island retains Kaohsiung's oldest settlement, despite being encircled by one of the world's busiest ports. The neighborhood between Miaoqian Road (廟前路) and the hill on which Qihou's lighthouse stands is filled with old houses made of a variety of materials, including wood, granite, brick and coral.

🐾 ISLAND WALKING TOUR
🕐 *See Map. 1.2km/.75mi. Allow 3hrs. Alternatives to walking include renting a bike or taking a pedicab (NT$250 for about 20min; no English spoken). Bike-rental outlets and pedicabs for hire are located near the ferry terminal on Qijin Island.*

▶ *From the ferry terminal, walk straight down the main road leading away from the sea.*

Empress of Heaven Temple★★
旗后天后宫
93 Miaoqian Rd. 廟前路 93號
🕐 *Open daily 5:30am–10pm.*

Distinguished by a square courtyard shaded by scores of red lanterns, the modest exterior and standard layout give no hint as to this temple's age and significance. It is in fact Kaohsiung's oldest shrine, established in 1673. Not surprisingly, given the city's long association with the sea, it is dedicated to Mazu. In addition to ensuring local fishermen made it home safely, the deity is credited with protecting Qijin from the worst of the cholera and malaria epidemics that swept Taiwan in 1946.

In terms of design, the temple features a typical two-chamber, five-door layout. In terms of art, two features inside are most interesting. The **images** of ladies in classical garb and their servants were completed by **Chen Yu-feng** (陳玉峰), an early 20C artist noted for combining painting with clay crafts to produce a three-dimensional effect. Notice also the array of chipped and dented **divining blocks** that worshipers cast on the floor when seeking spiritual advice.

▶ *Take the street that passes right in front of the temple toward the hill at Qijin's northwestern tip.*

Qihou Lighthouse★ 旗后燈塔

🕐 *Open Tue–Sun 9am–4pm.*

At the mouth of the harbor rises the 11m/36ft lighthouse, topping a white-washed 1918 structure that incorporates Western-style features. The tower itself isn't open to the public—this lighthouse is still functioning—but from the grounds there are fine **views**★ of the port, the city and the Former British Consulate Residence.

▷ *Walk southwest (left) from the lighthouse.*

Qihou Fortress★ 旗后砲台

🕐 *Open 24hrs.*

One of several strongholds added to Taiwan's defensive network by a panicky Qing imperial court after the Mudan Incident (⏱ *see History in the Introduction*), this fortress was used as a bunker and observation post by both the Japanese colonialists and the Chinese Nationalists. This end of the hilltop is quite overgrown with vegetation, so take care when exploring, as the cliffs may not be easy to see until you come upon them.

▷ *Reboard the ferry for the return trip to Gushan Ferry Dock.*

DOWNTOWN

⏱ *See Map.*

Former British Consulate Residence★★ 前清英國領事館

20 Lianhai Rd. 🕐 *Open daily 9am–midnight.* 🕐 *Closed 3rd Tue each month.* ✆ *07-525 0271.*

For the last quarter of the 19C, this hilltop compound was home to London's representative in south Taiwan. And a very fine home it was, too—a spacious, single-story mansion with unbeatable views in almost every direction and, in an era when diseases killed many, healthy ventilation and a good distance from crowded neighborhoods near the waterside.

The initial construction (1879) was largely of wood. Natural degradation necessitated restoration in 1900, when the thick arches of brick were added.

After a major typhoon in 1977 wreaked havoc on it, the mansion was rebuilt in 1985 according to the 1900 plan—the appearance of the residence today.

The rectangular structure sports a hipped roof and a wraparound veranda that permits the panoramic **views**★★. A separate building sited at sea level held the consular office. The stone steps linking the residence with the consulate itself still exist. The consulate does not. Several rooms inside the residence house displays: one on 19C international trade, another about amateur natural scientist **Robert Swinhoe** (⏱ *see sidebar*), one of the most distinguished individuals ever to hold the post of HM Consul in Formosa.

Installed within the residence, a **restaurant ($)** offers optional outdoor seating.

Kaohsiung Museum of History★ 高雄市立歷史博物館

272 Zhongzheng 4th Rd. 中正四路272 號. 🕐 *Open Tue–Fri 9am–5pm, Sat–Sun 9am–9pm.* ✆ *07-531 2560.* http://w5.kcg.gov.tw/khm.

Though Asian in overall appearance, this sizable building incorporates decidedly Western features, such as the square towers suggestive of the Italianate style and the porte cochere. It served as city hall in the colonial era. When a new city hall was completed in 1992, the building

Former British Consulate Residence

Rich J. Matheson/Michelin

Zig-zag bridge to Dragon and Tiger Pagodas

Rich J. Matheson/Michelin

was converted to a museum and opened in 1998.

These days, it contains decent bilingual displays about the city's past: permanent exhibits focus on the 2-28 Incident (*see History in the Introduction*) and relics retrived from local temples undergoing renovation. Best of all is the large collection of **photographs**★ of Kaohsiung between the 1920s and 60s.

Love River★★ 愛河

Kaohsiung's defining waterway is now clean and respectable. Ecological engineers have restored a few stretches of riverbank to a semi-natural state, while other parts have been attractively landscaped, with benches, paved paths and street lamps.

The most scenic section is the lower third, around Zhongzheng and Wufu Roads, and the best way to see it is by boat. The half-hour-long **Love Boat Cruise** (愛之船) sets out from a small dock on the east bank just upriver from the Ambassador Hotel (國賓大飯店, *202 Minsheng 2nd Rd.* 民生二路202號 . *daily departures 4pm–11pm every 15min; NT$80, children NT$40*) and takes tourists up and then down the river. The running commentary is in Mandarin, but your enjoyment won't be lessened, especially if you go at dusk when the city's lights start to come on. A solar-powered pleasure craft was added to the fleet in early 2010.

Kaohsiung Museum of Fine Arts★★ 高雄市立美術館

80 Meishuguan Rd. 美術館路80號. *MRT: Aozihdi.* 🕙*Open Tue–Sun 9am–5pm. Fee for special exhibits only.* 📞*07-555 0331. www.kmfa.gov.tw.*

Opened in 1994, Kaohsiung's leading art museum is biased toward post-war works by southern Taiwanese artists and depictions of the South, but often hosts notable touring exhibits such as a recent Auguste Rodin retrospective. Culture vultures should check the website ahead of their visit to find out what is on display.

The four-floor museum boasts 16 exhibit rooms, a sculpture hall, children's museum, classrooms, auditorium, library and restaurant as well as storage space. The permanent collection includes calligraphy, works in traditional ink and wash, oil paintings, sculptures, prints and installation art.

The adjacent **Neiweipi Cultural Park**★★ (內惟埤文化園), where sculptures have been arranged around a restored wetland, is an ideal place to spend the afternoon with a good book or simply daydreaming on a park bench.

LOTUS POND★★ 蓮池潭

👍*See Map.*

Allow 4hrs to visit. 5km/3mi north of Kaohsiung Main Station by Boai Rd. TRA: Zuoying. Bus no. 301 from Kaohsiung Main Station or bus no. Red 51 from MRT Ecological District. Note: Call ahead to arrange a visit to Zhouzi Wetland Park: 📞*07-582 2371.*

A 42ha/104-acre body of water surrounded by fairy-tale statues, elegant pavilions and colorful temples, Lotus Pond makes a splendid half-day outing. Those with a strong pair of legs will have no problem circumnavigating the lake. Despite the name, there are no lotus flowers here, but expect to see ducks and egrets.

In advance of the 2009 World Games, Lotus Pond was drained, cleaned and deepened to serve as the venue for water-skiing and dragon-boat competitions. At the same time, non-native fish and turtle species—many of them released by Buddhists trying to earn merit—were removed (&see p124).

🐾 WALKING TOUR

💬 *Start walking at the southern end by obtaining a map from the **visitor center** (🕐open daily 10am–7pm; 📞07-588 2497).*

💬 *Head to the first of the lakeside attractions.*

Dragon and Tiger Pagodas★★ 龍虎塔

🕐*Open daily 7am–8pm.*

These twin, seven-story pagodas themselves are often overlooked—most visitors walk into the mouth of the dragon at the towers' base, look at the gaudy wall paintings inside, and exit via the mouth of the adjacent tiger.

Leading from the shore to the pagodas, a **zig-zag bridge** is paneled with ceramic squares depicting landscapes and other classical Chinese scenes. Each pagoda is topped with a miniature seven-story pagoda "spire," and ringed by an exterior deck from which to view the lake. Interior **murals**, intended to edify, interpret heaven and hell and depict the 24 Paragons of Filial Piety, sons whose devotion to their parents is celebrated by Chinese society.

💬 *Head up Shengli Rd. (勝利路), away from the water's edge.*

Zuoying (左營)

This area is nowadays a Kaohsiung suburb, but you will find vestiges of the era when it was a county seat and one of Taiwan's four most important towns. The stone-and-coral **Old Fongshan City North Gate**★★ (鳳山縣舊城北門段; 🕐open 24hrs), flanked by carvings of door gods, is just one part of the defensive wall that once encircled Zuoying. It was completed in 1826 to replace a century-old mud barrier.

💬 *Cross Shengli Rd.*

Zhenfushe★★ 鎮福社

⚓ *Closed to the public.*

This exquisitely time-worn temple was founded in the mid-19C, and obviously has not been renovated for a long time. The land-god effigy once venerated in this jail-cell size shrine is now in another temple.

in the alleys located near the **Yuandi Temple**★ (元帝廟; 87 Zuoyingsha Rd.; 🕐open daily 6am–9pm), Zuoying's oldest private residences can be found.

💬 *Return downhill to the pond.*

Qiming Temple★ 啟明堂

🕐*Open daily 5am–9pm.*

Step inside this temple, especially if you find most Taiwanese temples too smoky for your liking. Qiming is pristine inside and out; the effigies—which include a red-faced Guan Gong on the first floor—are enormous and clearly labeled (Chinese only).

Spring and Autumn Pavilions

Rich J. Matheson/Michelin

Cross Liantan Rd. outside Qiming Temple to reach the Spring and Autumn Pavilions.

Spring and Autumn Pavilions★★ 春秋閣

🕐 *Open daily 6am–9pm.*

The name of this pair of pavilions alludes to the period in Chinese history (770-481 BC) when Confucius was alive. The pagodas rises only three and a half stories, but their entrance walkway is dramatic and garish, filled with colorfully painted statues of characters from Chinese legends and a large, sinuous dragon with Guanyin, the goddess of Mercy, standing on its back. Guan Gong, the god of War, crowns a solitary column at the entrance. Lanterns line the walkway and hang from the pavilions.

Proceed to Wuli Pavilion.

Wuli Pavilion 五里亭

This graceful pavilion is the closest you can get to the pond's midpoint without getting your feet wet. The name, which means "five miles," refers to the thick fog that sometimes forms over the lake early in the morning and makes the shore seem far away.

Walk to the lake's north pier.

Beiji Xuantian Shang Di Temple

Rich J. Matheson/Michelin

Beiji Xuantian Shang Di Temple★★ 北極玄天上帝廟

🕐 *Open daily 6am–9pm.*

The most northerly of the piers in Lotus Pond is the grandest. This temple features an elaborate, 22m/71ft-high **statue** of the Daoist god often known as Xuan Wu. The little temple in the base has effigies of the turtle and snake that serve as Xuan Wu's underlings; worshipers leave offerings of eggs for the latter.

Confucius Temple★ 孔廟

400 Liantan Rd. 🕐 *Open Tue–Sun 9am–5pm. ✆07-585 9999.*

At the northern end of Lotus Pond, there is little reason to linger at the Confucius Temple unless you want to read the bilingual panels about the sage, his disciples who are also enshrined here, and **Mencius** (孟子) (372-289 BC), the most important philosopher in Chinese history after Confucius.

Walk to the lake's east side and then southward along the east bank.

Qingshui Temple★★ 清水宮

🕐 *Open daily 5am–9pm.*

The one and only temple on the east side of the lake is sufficiently different from those on the opposite bank to justify a visit. After the glossy oranges of the temples on the west side of the lake, the sea-green roof of Qingshui comes as a refreshing change. The **statue** of Master Qingshui atop the temple was assembled from 387 slabs of stone. Inside, the **ceiling** of the main chamber features a breathtaking amount of intricately carved wood which, unusually, has been left unpainted.

Walk away from Lotus Pond to Liantan Rd.

Zhouzi Wetland Park★★ 洲仔溼地公園

58 Liantan Rd. 🕐 *Open by prior arrangement. ✆07-582 2371. www.chouchaiwetlandpark.tw.*

Ecotourists will find this park to their liking. The restored habitat aims to lure the pheasant-tailed **Jacana** (*Hydrophasianus chirurgus*), a species highly endangered in Taiwan, back to the Kaohsiung area. There are already Mandarin ducks, moorhens and egrets here.

⬤ *Return to the south side of the lake to end the walking tour.*

EXCURSIONS
Foguangshan★★★ 佛光山
⬤ *27km/17mi northeast, in Dashu* (*大樹*). *Allow 1 day to visit.* **By Car**: *Fwy. 10, then follow the signs along Hwy. 21.* **By Bus**: *From Kaohsiung Bus Co. Station daily 6:20am–9:20pm, approx. hourly (1hr; NT$76 one-way).*
Information office ⊙ open daily 7am–8pm; ☏07-656 1921; www.fgs.org.tw. Call 3 days ahead to book English-language guided tour (free, but donations appreciated). Otherwise, report to information office on arrival to see if guide available. Dress modestly.
Do not bring meat or alcohol into the monastery. English signs.

The headquarters of one of Taiwan's highest-profile religious institutions and, it is claimed, the largest Buddhist monastery in Taiwan, Foguangshan was established in 1967 by a Buddhist monk and proselytizer. Foguangshan (meaning "the light of Buddha mountain") comprises various buildings on a hillside west of the Gaoping River.

Among the several hundred outdoor Buddha statues, the most famous one, 36m/118ft-tall **Amitabha**, is central to the Foguangshan emblem. The **Hall of the Great Hero★★★** (⊙ *open daily 7am–7pm*) is a must-see attraction; here, monks, nuns and lay visitors venerate the three imposing Buddhas (*left to right*) of Amitabha, Sakyamuni and Bhasisajyaguru, while surrounded by almost 15,000 wall-mounted Buddha figurines.

A gallery exhibiting Buddhist-inspired art, the **Cultural Exhibition Hall★★** (⊙ *open Tue–Sun 9am–5pm*) features works by mostly Taiwanese artists. Many visitors leave with vivid memories of **Pure Land Cave★★** (⊙ *open Tue–Sun*

Foguangshan

Rich J. Matheson/Michelin

9am–5pm), a three-dimensional imagining of the abode of Buddhas and bodhisattvas, complete with Christmas tree lights, moving statues and other kitschy adornments.

The monastery does not go out of its way to acquire relics, but it does have one of the highest value: a complete **tooth** believed to be from the mouth of the 6C BC founder of Buddhism, **Siddhartha Gautama,** who is worshiped as the Buddha. It was donated with great ceremony to Foguangshan by a Tibetan lama in 1998. Pending completion of the Buddha Memorial Hall (*scheduled for late 2012*), the tooth is currently displayed upstairs in the **Tathagata Hall★★** (⊙ *open Tue–Sun 8:30am–5pm*).

The vegetarian **restaurant** (⊙ *open daily 10am–7:30pm*) serves Taiwanese dishes. Non-monastic guests may stay in air-conditioned rooms in **Pilgrims Lodge ($)** (☏07-656 1921 ext. 6205; 40 *rooms; NT$2000 per night*). Buddhist books (many in English) and other items are sold in the store behind the information office.

MEINONG★★ 美濃
⬤ *40km/25mi northeast.*
Allow 6hrs to visit. **By Car:** *Take Fwy. 1 or Fwy. 3 to Fwy. 10 and follow Fwy. 10 to its northern end near Qishan (1hr). Follow the signs into downtown Meinong.* **By Bus:** *From Kaohsiung Bus Co. Station and Kaohsiung-Zuoying*

Touring Tip

Bike trail maps can be obtained from the **visitor center** on the south shore of **Zhongzheng Lake** (中正湖)*(789 Taian Rd.;* 🕙*open daily 9am–5pm;* 📞*07-681 2433).* Following some or all of the town's seven **bike trails** *(total length 40km/25mi)* will lead you to many of the area's attractions. The light blue route begins at **Guangshan Temple** 廣善堂, west of the downtown, and ends at a 100-year-old hydroelectric power station. To reach the hill country northeast of central Meinong, take the yellow route from Zhongzheng Lake past Meinong's museum, then the green route. Bikes *(NT$100 per day)* can be rented near the bus station.

HSR Station at least hourly 8am–8pm (1.5hrs; NT$147).

Located on a well-watered plain abutting steep hills, the former tobacco-producing town of Meinong is known for its oil-paper **parasols** and Hakka dishes. Its population of almost 50,000 is predominantly Hakka, whose ancestors arrived in the area in the 18C.

Meinong's signature dish is **bantiao** 粄條, thick rice noodles served in soup or stir-fried with small pieces of pork, scallions and slivers of carrot. One portion is enough for a light lunch, but if you're with a small group, order other culinary delights like Hakka-style **cabbage** 高麗菜封 or stewed winter **melon** 冬瓜封 flavored with garlic, soy, sugar and rice wine. Hakka **stir fry** 客家小炒, which combines squid, pork, dried tofu, pepper and various greens, goes well with steamed rice. Several restaurants along Zhongzheng and Zhongshan Roads serve these delicacies.

Sights

Yongan Road★★ 永安路

From the bus station, walk to the main road, turn left and walk 200m (eighth of a mile) south to intersection of Zhongzheng and Yongan Rds.

Stroll down this street to get an idea of how Meinong looked 50 years ago. Many of Meinong's best preserved, most photogenic single-story **courtyard houses** are hidden in the alleyways. The **tailoring shop** at no. 177 is one of just a handful of places where traditonal blue Hakka tunics are still made by hand. At the southeastern end of the road, the old **East Gate** is the only remaining fragment of the wall that kept Meinong safe from bandits in the 18C and 19C.

Meinong Hakka Museum★
美濃客家文物館

民族路49-3號 *49-3 Minzu Rd.*
🕙*Open Tue–Fri 9:30am–4:30pm, Sat–Sun 9:30am–7pm. NT$60, children NT$30;* 📞*07-681 8338. English-language tours available if booked in advance.*

Meinong Hakka Museum

Rich J. Matheson/Michelin

Meinong's Parasols

Few destinations in Taiwan are as closely associated with a single handicraft product as Meinong is with its oil-paper umbrellas. These lightweight, bamboo-framed parasols are effective at blocking both sunshine and rain, although nowadays the vast majority are bought for their decorative rather than practical qualities. And beautiful they are, too. Handmade and hand-painted, most bear classic Chinese images such as majestic dragons, wise sages or swaths of landscape. Souvenir hunters will do well to spend some time at **Yuan Xiang Yuan Cultural Village** (原鄉綠紙傘文化村) *(147 Zhongxing Rd., Sec. 1, beside Hwy. 28;* ◷*open daily 8am–7pm;* ✆*07-681 0888)* on the southern outskirts of Meinong.

Rich J. Matheson/Michelin

This museum is housed in a purpose-built structure whose shape was inspired by Meinong's tobacco-curing barns. Hundreds of these barns still stand in every corner of the township. The museum features displays *(Chinese only)* about the tobacco industry and other aspects of local life. The full-scale, mock **curing chamber** provides an idea of how tobacco was dried immediately after harvesting.

The **photographs** of farm workers carrying huge bundles of leaves make it clear that Meinong's women worked as hard as their menfolk.

👥 Yellow Butterfly Valley★★ 黃蝶翠谷

▶ *5km/3mi northeast of town center, via Hwy. 106.* Follow signs to Shuangxi Tropical Viviparous Forest and continue to the road's end. Note: Carry water and be prepared for afternoon showers.

Nature lovers should allow at least three hours to enjoy this lush, green valley, especially if they come at the right time of year *(mid-May–Jul)*. That's the time when millions of Lemon Migrant butterflies *(catopsilia pomona)* emerge from mid-May to the height of summer. Throughout the year, scores of other butterfly species are out in force, and the bird-watching is just as good. To best experience this place, hike a little farther into the hills.

ADDRESSES

🛏 STAY

$$ T h.o.t.e.l. 大益大飯店, 大同路 – *177 Datong 1st Rd. 177號, MRT Formosa Blvd.;* ✆*07-231 2141. www.t-hotel.com.tw. 42 rooms.* With its central location and English-speaking staff, this hotel is ideal if you want to sample every part of the city within a few days. The decor is clean and neat and the rooms are well-equipped, many with Jacuzzis, computers, CD players and LCD TVs. Free self-service laundromat. Breakfast included.

$$$$ Grand Hi-Lai Hotel 漢來大飯店, 成功 – *266 Chenggong 1st Rd. 路266號; MRT Central Park.* ✆*07-216 1766. www.grand-hilai.com.tw. 540 rooms.* Plush guest rooms located on floors 15 to 39, many with seaward or inland views, and incomparable service make this property one of Kaohsiung's finest hotels. Some rooms have exercise equipment; all are spacious, if conservative in decor. In-house eating options include a lobster bar and a steak house, as well as Japanese, Shanghainese, Cantonese and Taiwanese cuisines. The Hanshin Department Store (third basement level to 8th floor in the same building) has a food court.

Xiao Liuqiu★★

An island made almost entirely of coral, Xiao Liuqiu (小琉球), or Little Liuqiu, sits off the southwest coast due west of Fangliao (枋寮)—and a million miles away in terms of noise and pollution. Despite the island's population of some 12,000 people, crammed into just 6.8sq km/2.6sq mi, the almost total absence of cars and industry means Xiao Liuqiu does not feel at all crowded. Yet there are ample places to stay and eat in Baisha and Dafu, the island's ferry ports and main hubs. There are hotels, homestays and a campground just northwest of Baisha. Most of Xiao Liuqiu's good eateries are situated along Minsheng Road, the main road near Baisha's ferry dock. Daytrippers come to the island for eyefuls of sea; overnighters revel in the skyfuls of stars.

A BIT OF HISTORY

Xiao Liuqiu and its indigeneous inhabitants, the **Lamayan** people, were notorious among Western sailors in the early 1600s. The loss of two Dutch ships near here and the slaughter of the survivors prompted the Dutch East India Co. to

▶ **Population:** 12,716.
⊘ **Michelin Map:** p263.
⊡ **Info:** ⊘ See General Information below.
◗ **Location:** Lying 14km/ 8.6mi off Taiwan's southwest coast, the island can be seen from Kaohsiung on very clear days. The ports of Baisha and Dafu are the main centers.
👪 **Kids:** Mountain Pig Ditch, and wading along the coast if wearing neoprene shoes or strong sandals.
◔ **Timing:** Any time of year is fine for a visit. Arrive by mid-morning to see everything before the last boat leaves. Alternatively, drift over later in the day and spend the night so you can enjoy the sunset and stars.
⊛ **Don't Miss:** Black Ghost Caves, Vase Rock, and fresh seafood.

Xiao Liuqiu's fringing reef

Rich J. Matheson/Michelin

GETTING THERE

BY BOAT - Ferries leave from Donggang (東港), which itself can be reached by bus southeast from Kaohsiung. At least eight boats per day sail to Baisha (白沙) *(depart daily 7am–5:30pm; 30-40min; round-trip NT$410, children NT$210)*, while another five go to Dafu (大福) *(depart daily 8am –5:30pm; 40min; round-trip NT$350, children NT$180)*.

GETTING AROUND

ON FOOT - In the absence of rental cars, taxis and buses, visitors have two options: walking, or riding a rented scooter (*see below*). A 13km/8mi perimeter road encircles the island's outer edge, linking the major sights.

BY BICYCLE - You can bring a bike on the ferry *(extra fee)*, but no bike rentals are available in Donggang or Little Liuqiu.

BY SCOOTER - At the dock in Baisha, 125cc scooters are available for rent *(NT$400/day including gas)*. No deposit or license needed.

GENERAL INFORMATION
VISITOR INFORMATION
Xiao Liuqiu Branch Office, 20-1 Minzu Rd.民族路20號之1, open daily 8:30am–5:30pm. 08-861 4615. Dapeng Bay National Scenic Area: *www.dbnsa.gov.tw*. Liuqiu Township Government: *www.liuchiu.gov.tw*.

invade in 1638. The Lamayans were exterminated; the few who were not killed were taken as slaves to Dutch-controlled Indonesia. Over time, Han Chinese settlers from Fujian discovered that the island's rich **fishing grounds** more than made up for a lack of soil. Apart from the influx of tourists, islanders' lives today have barely changed since the 19C. They continue to sell surplus seafood to "mainland" Taiwan, while importing rice and vegetables. As in Donggang, **boat-burning** events in honor of Wangye deities play a major role in local religious life. Daytrippers should escape from Baisha as soon as they can, not because there is anything dislikable about Xiao Liuqiu's main town (there is not), but because the rest of the island is so much more attractive.

SIGHTS
Ordered clockwise around the island from Baisha.

Zhongao Beach★ 中澳沙灘
800m/.5mi from Baisha.
Close to the island's eastern extremity and within walking distance of Baisha's docks, this strip of clean golden sand lacks shade and facilities, but is the only place where sharp coral doesn't prevent

swimming. Foot protection is advisable anyway, and be mindful of undertow.

Biyun Temple★ 碧雲寺
700m/.4mi inland from Dafu, midpoint on the southeast coast.
If a Xiao Liuqiuer does not live in Baisha, odds are the islander lives in Dafu. The village's main shrine, which is up the hill from the fishing port, bustles on weekends when residents who work or study on Taiwan proper return home. The current structure dates from 1936, yet Guanyin has been venerated at this spot for more than two-and-a-half centuries.

Black Ghost Caves★★ 烏鬼洞
4km/2.5mi past Dafu on the ring road. Open 24hrs daily. NT$120, children NT$80 (charged 8am–5pm).
Xiao Liuqiu's number-one attraction lies on the island's north coast. These caves are so named because they were the scene of a siege that climaxed with the defeat and death of hundreds of dark-skinned Lamayan natives at the hands of the Dutch and their allies, indigenous mercenaries from the Taiwanese mainland. While the cave itself is not exceptional, the site is both atmospheric and scenic.

Vase Rock

Rich J. Matheson/Michelin

👥🧍 Mountain Pig Ditch★★
山豬溝

*800m/0.5mi east of Black Ghost Caves.
NT$120, children NT$80 (charged
8am–5pm).*

There are no pigs to be seen these days,
but the ditch—actually a trail sheltered
by immense chunks of uplifted coral
—is a good spot to get a close look at
Xiao Liuqiu's special geology and the
flora that thrives despite the harsh
conditons.

Beauty Cave★ 美人洞
*1.9km/1.2mi east of Mountain Pig Ditch.
🕐Open 24hrs daily. NT$120, children
NT$80 (charged 8am–5pm).*

This spot, on the island's northeastern
corner, is another monument to the
erosive power of the ocean. Limestone
and coral have been shaped into tidal
platforms, cliffs and grottoes.

Sanlong Temple★ 三隆宮
*49 Zhongshan Rd. 中山路45號.
🕐Open daily 5am–9pm.*

The island's largest temple is set back
from the coast and contains multiple
altars. Pride of place goes to the Jade
Emperor, in the center of the third floor.
Baisha hardly counts as a town, yet there
is a town god, on the left side as you
enter the front of the temple. Wang Ye
spirits are also enshrined here.

Vase Rock★★ 花瓶岩

A tree-shaped outcrop on the top of
which weeds and thistles grow surprisingly well, Vase Rock has been sculpted
by waves eroding the lower half much
faster than wind erodes the top half.

ADDRESSES

🛏STAY

$$ Coconut Grove Resort 椰林渡假
村 – *38-20 Minzu Rd.*民族路38-20 *℘08-
861 4368. www.coco-resort.com.tw.
5 Rooms.* Located a short walk uphill
from Baisha Village, the resort's
comfortable rooms are shaded by
namesake trees and cooled by ocean
breezes.

$$ Dijonghai B&B 地中海渡假民宿–
*161-9 Fuxing Rd. 復興路161-9號. ℘08-
861 1007. www.dijonghai.com. 5 rooms.*
Not a homestay in the true sense, but
rather a purpose-built (but stylish)
building with ocean views, Dijonghai
is decorated in lively Mediterranean
colors. Rooms, sleeping 2 to 8 people,
have balconies facing the sea. Breakfast
included.

$$ Star Sand Homestay 星沙民宿 –
*173-1 Zhongshan Rd.*中山路173-1. *℘08-
861 2101. www.starsand.com.tw. 10 rooms.*
With a super-central location in
Baisha and an owner who speaks
English (a rarity on the island), Star
Sand is understandably popular with
Westerners. Breakfast included.

$$$ 8 Villages Hotel 八村民宿– *161-
10 Fuxing Rd. 復興路161-10號 ℘08-861
1133 www.ueu.com.tw 16 rooms.* Eight
bungalows with vibrant color schemes
and gardens give a tropical atmosphere
to this resort. Pluses are a pool, spa,
game room, restaurant and large front
lawn with 80-degree ocean views.

🍴EAT

$ A-Dui Mian Dian 阿對麵店,民生路
36號– *36 Minsheng Rd. ℘08-861 4290.*
The name implies that this restaurant
on the main road near Baisha's ferry
dock serves up noodles only, but there
are also rice dishes. Try rice fried with
seasoned fish (鬼頭刀炒飯), or fish
cooked with onions and cabbage
(鮪魚蓋飯). **Taiwanese.**

Kenting Area★★

Start with a verdant, hilly peninsula that has never been industrialized nor densely populated. Throw in world-class biodiversity. Add attractive beaches and coves. Steep it in year-round sunshine. Top it off with some of Taiwan's liveliest nightlife and best restaurants—and you have the southern end of the island, sometimes known as the Kenting Area (墾丁), and its namesake national park. To the north, outside the park boundaries, the historic town of Hengchun, a service hub with airline facilities, is a gateway to the park.

KENTING NATIONAL PARK

Established in 1984 and thus Taiwan's oldest national park, Kenting National Park's 18,084ha/44,700 acres encompasses all three sides of the Hengchun Peninsula and a good part of the interior. Within the park the bustling town of Kending, with its many amenities, acts as a service center for park visitors.

A BIT OF HISTORY

Like other lowland indigenous groups, the aborigines who inhabited the Kenting area assimilated or migrated eastward as the Han population grew during the 18C and 19C. The world—and even the Taiwan prefectural government in Tainan—paid scant attention to the

Michelin Maps: p263, p305

Info: Park headquarters, *596 Kenting Rd.* 墾丁路596號; *open daily 8am–5pm;* 08 886 1321; *www.ktnp.gov.tw.*

Location: The most popular beaches are on the southern tip, the Hengchun Peninsula. The main population centers, Checheng and Hengchun, are in the west, but Kenting itself—which is where most tourists stay—lies farther south. Kending is the principal service town within the park. Its main street, Kenting Road, has hotels, restaurants, shops, nightclubs and bars.

Kids: Museum of Marine Biology and Aquarium, Nanwan Beach, Jialeshui.

Timing: Avoid late summer, when typhoons bring heavy rains. Winter weather is unpredictable: it may be cold and blustery one week, beautiful the next.

Don't Miss: Museum of Marine Biology and Aquarium, Kenting Forest Recreation Area, Longpan Park.

Nanwan Beach

Rich J. Matheson/Michelin

GETTING THERE

BY AIR - UNI Airways (☎07 791 1000; www.uniair.com.tw) has three flights per week from Taipei Songshan to **Hengchun Airport** (HCN) (恆春機場) (☎08-89 7120; www.hca.gov.tw; NT$2292 one way). Kaohsiung-Kenting buses stop just outside the airport.

BY BUS - Frequent buses bound for Kenting (3hrs; NT$356) depart the Kaohsiung Bus Co. Station (高雄客運站; ☎07-237 1230) 100m/ 300ft east of Kaohsiung Main Station, and every half hour from Kaohsiung-Zuoying HSR station.

BY TAXI - Outside Kaohsiung-Zuoying HSR Station and Kaohsiung Main Station, taxi drivers will offer to take you to Kenting for about NT$400 per person if they can find four passengers. A **shared taxi** ride is an attractive option for small groups who have heavy luggage and know which hotel they want to stay in.

GETTING AROUND

BY BUS - You can jump on and off Kaohsiung-Kenting buses anywhere along the main road between Hengchun and Eluanbi. Service to other points in the park is spotty.

BY CAR - Renting a car in Hengchun or Kenting is difficult. You're advised to do it in Kaohsiung.

BY SCOOTER - Rental outfits on Kenting Road; from NT$400 per day; international driver's license needed.

GENERAL INFORMATION

VISITOR INFORMATION

Kenting National Park Headquarters: ⓘ see Info above.

An entry permit must be obtained in advance for **Longkeng and Nanrenshan** Ecological Protection Areas. See the national park website for details, or apply in person at park headquarters.

region until the Mudan Incident, which was sparked by the running aground in 1871 of a ship from Japan's Ryukyu Islands. All but 12 of the 66 survivors were massacred by local tribesmen. Tokyo was outraged, but the Qing imperial court rejected demands for compensation, arguing that as the aborigines were beyond their control, they should not be held responsible. Diplomatic exchanges dragged on until, in the spring of 1874, an exasperated Japanese government dispatched a military expedition to press their case. The invaders suffered few casualties when they defeated the aborigines at the Battle of Shimen on May 22, but over the following months more than 500 Japanese soldiers died of disease.

The Kenting area has never been industrialized. However, during the Japanese era, it produced a great amount of sisal, a fiber used to make rope. Today, the economy is dependent on the millions of visitors who flock to the area each year to sun, surf and hike.

SIGHTS

Ordered north to south.

👥👤 Museum of Marine Biology and Aquarium★★★

國立海洋生物博物館

3km/2mi from Checheng by Pingtung County Rd. 153. 2 Houwan Rd., Checheng. Some buses to Kenting stop at the museum (ask before boarding) or take a taxi from Checheng or Hengchun. For buses, access www.nmmba.gov.tw/english/Service/Transportation_Information_/By_Bus_. ⓘ Open daily 9am–5pm (Sat–Sun until 6pm). NT$450, children NT$250. ☎08-882 5001. www.nmmba.gov.tw.

This state-of-the-art compound overlooking the ocean is both a public aquarium and a government research center. One of South Taiwan's best attractions for children, the museum has shows featuring sharks, whales and other sea creatures, plus superbly presented information about maritime topics. Three buildings are devoted to exhibits. The **Coral Kingdom Pavilion** includes an 81m/265ft-long underwater **tunnel**

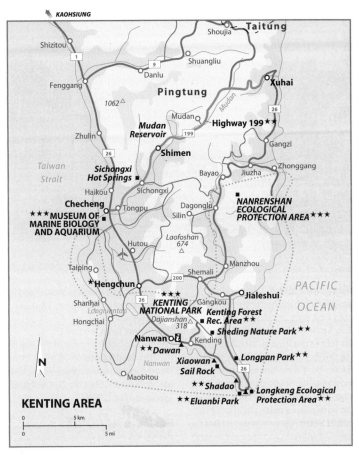

KAOHSIUNG

Taitung

Shoujia

Shizitou

Shuangliu

Danlu

Xuhai

Fenggang

Pingtung

1062 △

Mudan

Zhulin

Mudan Reservoir

Mudan

Highway 199 ★★

Shimen

Gangzi

Haikou

Sichongxi Hot Springs ■

Sichongxi

Bayao

Jiuzha

Zhonggang

Checheng

Tongpu

Dagonglu

NANRENSHAN ECOLOGICAL PROTECTION AREA ★★★

★★★**MUSEUM OF MARINE BIOLOGY AND AQUARIUM**

Silin

Laofoshan 674 △

Hutou

Taiping

Shemali

Manzhou

Longluanta

★Hengchun

Gangkou

★★★ **KENTING NATIONAL PARK**

Jialeshui

PACIFIC OCEAN

Shanhai

Hongchai

Dajianshan 318 △

Kenting Forest Rec. Area ★★

Kending

Nanwan ○ 🛀

Sheding Nature Park ★★

★★**Dawan**

Nanwan

Xiaowan ▲ Sail Rock

Longpan Park ★★

Maobitou

★★ **Shadao**

Longkeng Ecological Protection Area ★★

★★**Eluanbi Park**

KENTING AREA

0   5 km
0   5 mi

N

Museum of Marine Biology and Aquarium

Museum of Marine Biology and Aquarium

that allows visitors to see up close living corals and their inhabitants. An introduction to the island's saltwater and freshwater aquatic environments, the **Waters of Taiwan Pavilion** has a **touch pool**. The section on **oyster farming** will intrigue those who've driven down Taiwan's southwest coast and seen the thousands of oyster beds. **Waters of the World Pavilion** looks back in time to when life emerged from the earth's prehistoric oceans. **Polar Seas** showcases penguins and puffins, always entertaining.

Checcheng 車程

Hwy. 26, at north edge of the national park's western section.

This town is associated with **onions**. Along the main road farmers sell them by the sack. The main reason to come here is to access one of Taiwan's prettiest back roads: Highway 199, which runs diagonally southwest to northeast across the island's tapered southern end.

Old South Gate, Hengchun

Rich J. Matheson/Michelin

Highway 199★★

Begin in Checheng and drive north east. Your first stop should be **Sichongxi Hot Springs** (四重溪溫泉), within the hills of the Paiwan aborigines. During the Japanese occupation, the spa waters here were among the island's most popular. These days, the resort is a bit of a backwater with no outstanding hotels. For a quick dip, try the free **public baths** (🕐*open 24hrs; sections for men and women so no swimsuit needed*) in front of the elementary school. Heading inland, the road becomes more scenic. At **Shimen** (石門), where the valley suddenly narrows, there is a **monument** to the battle fought in 1874 by Paiwan braves against Japanese soldiers (👣*see History above*). At **Mudan Reservoir** (牡丹水庫), the weather-beaten **murals** along the top of the dam include depictions of traditional indigenous activities such as hunting; one man dancing wears a business suit rather than the usual tribal costume. Between Mudan and the east coast, there are more macaques than humans, so make sure you have enough gas to get to **Xuhai** (旭海).

Hengchun★ 恆春

Hwy. 26 at Hwy. 200.
Hengchun is distinguished by its well-preserved defensive **wall**. Constructed

in the 1870s, the wall was more than 90 percent intact as recently as 1950. Surviving sections totaling 2.7km/1.6mi in length have been restored.

The best-known fragment of the wall is the **Old South Gate** (古城門南門). A favorite location for moviemakers, the gate appeared in *Cape No. 7*, a successful Taiwanese film (2008).

KENTING NATIONAL PARK★★★ 墾丁國家公園

The crescent-shaped park can be divided into three sections: a narrow strip of land along the west coast just south of Checheng, the heavily visited south coast around the town of Kending, and the thinly populated hinterland and east portion.

Sights within the national park are ordered west to east.

👤👤Nanwan 南灣

Nanwan Rd., off Hwy. 26, south of Hengchun. 🕐*Open 24hrs.*
Many think Nanwan (which means "south bay") has one of the best beaches. There is another reason to make this nicely sheltered strip of sand your main destination: Nanwan Road's restaurants and watering holes are second only to Kenting Road's.

Yanshui Beehive Fireworks Festival (鹽水蜂炮)

Suddenly all falls quiet—the excitement and fear are palpable. Bearers begin to rock their heavily protected palanquins carrying statues of deities. The first **bottle rockets** shoot out of their "hives" like angry bees and slam into the thrill-seeking festival-goers, who must hop repeatedly to keep from being trampled or hit by the blazing fireworks. Aimed first at the feet, the rocket barrage eventually ends over the heads of the crowds, as each salvo discharges row by row. The noise of hundreds of exploding rockets is deafening. Attracting tens of thousands of spectators, this event is among the world's most dangerous festivals. Ambulances and fire trucks are on hand to deal with emergencies. Between 10-100 attendees end up in hospital each year, either burned or crushed in the mayhem. Village houses regularly catch fire.

Cannon walls are bamboo or metal shelves filled with fused bottle rockets stacked horizontally—like a honeycomb—and aimed at the crowd. They are topped by a vertical pyrotechnic array poised to erupt after the rockets are spent. Large cannon walls are almost two-stories high and eight-meters wide; smaller walls are the size of a sawhorse, but all are loaded with rockets equally capable of inflicting harm. During the festival, rockets ricochet around the town day and night. Personal protection is essential: heavy clothing, helmet, gloves, boots, earplugs, facemask, even a towel for your neck, with all holes taped shut for extra safety.

In the final stage, when fireworks light up the sky, spectators cautiously lift their helmet visors and take a deep breath as the acrid smoke clears. They slap each other on the back, some slaps to congratulate, some to put out lingering fires. Hard-core revelers trudge to the next wall to experience it all again.

What is now a spectacle began as a religious rite to exorcise small towns of disease. When an epidemic plagued the village of **Yanshui** nearly two centuries ago, a statue of **Guan Gong** was carried through the streets on a palanquin accompanied by firecrackers to scare away evil demons associated with the sickness. The epidemic faded after two decades and thereafter, Guan Gong was paraded annually.

For more information, access *http://edu.ocac.gov.tw/local/web/Index.htm (English)*.

Yanshui Beehive Fireworks Festival

Rich J. Matheson/Michelin

Dawan★★ 大灣
Western end of Kenting Rd.
🕐*Open 24hrs.*

Of the controversies involving the park, none have generated as much anger as the decision by Taiwan's Forestry Bureau to lease this beach—easily the nicest in the park—to the Chateau Beach Resort. Under pressure from the park authorities, parts of the 2km/1.2mi-long sandy beach are now open to the public.

Xiaowan 小灣
Eastern end of Kenting Rd.
🕐*Open 24hrs.*

The "little bay" to Dawan's "big bay," Xiaowan is fully open to the public, and often crowded. This nicely sheltered cove has everything from parasols and deck chairs to water-sports equipment for rent.

Kenting Forest Recreation Area★★ 墾丁國家森林遊樂區
Follow signs from west end of Kenting Rd. Allow 3hrs to visit. ♿🕐*Open Dec–Aug daily 8am–5pm. Rest of the year daily 6am–5pm. NT$150, children NT$75. Note: You will need your own transportation to reach the entrance. Wear proper walking shoes.*

As in some other parts of South Taiwan (Xiao Liuqiu, for instance), the land here is mostly uplifted coral reef. The area's consistently warm, wet weather has created one of Taiwan's few monsoon **rain forests**. Barringtonia Asiatica, a small tree with pink-white flowers more usually seen in Southeast Asia, is one of the special species here.

The 150ha/370-acre forest averages 300m/984ft above sea level, offering excellent sea **views**★★.

Sheding Nature Park★★ 社頂自然公園
Turn right when facing entrance to Kenting Forest Recreation Area and head southeast. Allow 1hr to visit.
🕐*Open 24hrs. Parking fee: cars NT$40, motorcycles NT$10. Wear proper walking shoes.*

Despite its popularity this park continues to be a good place to observe birdlife. In addition to avians, there are butterflies to be seen and if you are lucky, a macaque or a **Formosan Sika deer**, a once widespread species that is being reintroduced to the wild after being hunted to near extinction in the 20C.

Sail Rock 船帆石
Taiwanese people say this column of rock, which stands in the next bay east of Xiaowan, is shaped like a yacht's sail. Americans have been known to comment on its resemblance to the late US president Richard M. Nixon. If you come here solely for the rock, you might be disappointed. The beach, however, is an attractive strip of sand and a good fallback if Xiaowan is too crowded.

Sail Rock

Rich J. Matheson/Michelin

Shadao village

Rich J. Matheson/Michelin

Shadao★★ 砂島

On west side of southernmost tip of the peninsula at KM 39 on Hwy. 26.

This stunning 290m/951ft-long beach has, say park authorities, the purest sand in Taiwan in terms of calcium carbonate content (almost 98 percent) from crushed seashells, corals and foraminifera. If you are really into beach debris, visit the **Shell Beach Exhibition Hall** *(224 Shadao Rd. 砂島路224號;* ◷ *open daily 8:30am–5pm;* ✆*08-885 1204).* But do not help yourself to souvenirs from the beach—the removal of sand is now illegal.

Eluanbi Park★★ 鵝鑾鼻公園

◷*Open daily 8am–5pm. NT$40, children NT$20. Parking fee: cars NT$30, motorcycles NT$10.*

This park is centered on Taiwan's southernmost **lighthouse**, a Victorian structure designed not only to make the nearby waters safer for shipping, but also to withstand attacks by the aborigines who then dominated the area. The toponym Eluanbi is a corruption of *Goloan,* this spot's name in the Paiwan aboriginal language.

Longkeng Ecological Protection Area★★ 龍坑生態保護區

1.5km/.9 east of Eluanbi. ◷*Open Wed–Mon 8am–3:30pm. Entry permit must be obtained in advance: see the national park website.*

The park authorities are doing their best to strictly control access to this protected area, which encompasses almost 62ha/153 acres of pristine coast-

Eluanbi Park

Rich J. Matheson/Michelin

Surfing at Jialeshui

Rich J. Matheson/Michelin

line exposed to strong sunshine and unrelenting winds. However, local folk have been known to sneak in to collect edible snails. A 2007 study found 58 species of mollusk, 44 different anthropods (including barnacles) and various other intertidal invertebrates.

Longpan Park★★ 龍磐公園
🕐*Open daily 24hrs. Descending from the highway to the beach is very difficult and dangerous.*

A popular sightseeing spot with motorists and motorcyclists, Longpan is characterized by unceasing winds that blow in from the Pacific, flatten the vegetation and kick up clouds of dusty red-brown soil. This might not sound fun, but the **views**★★★ over the ocean, the slumping cliffs and the rock-strewn coastline are truly impressive.

👥Jialeshui 佳樂水
🕐*Open daily 9am–5pm. NT$50, children NT$30.*

Of the dozen or so places around Taiwan's coastline routinely described as "outdoor geological classrooms," Jialeshui is one of the very best. Originally deep beneath the ocean, the sandstone **outcroppings** here have been carved by the forces of nature and now resemble sea horses, honeycombs and frogs. The admission fee goes toward maintenance of signs and paths and garbage removal.

Nanrenshan Ecological Protection Area★★
南仁山生態保護區
Allow 4hrs to visit. 🕐*Open Wed–Mon 8am–3pm. Entry permit must be obtained in advance.*

Nanrenshan is one of South Taiwan's most important ecotourism and biological research locations. Access is governed by rules similar to those for Longkeng Ecological Protection Area. Within the 5,000ha/12,355acre area, there is a small body of water, **Nanren Lake** (南仁湖). Surrounding it are Taiwan's only remaining patches of lowland primeval forest and para-tropical **rain forest**, where scientists have identified upwards of 1,000 vascular plant species and 100-plus kinds of butterfly.

ADDRESSES

🛏 STAY

$ SummerPoint Hostel – *Hwy. 26, Jialeshui.* 📞*0936 416 006. www.summerpoint.idv.tw. 4 rooms.* Run by a Taiwanese surfer, SummerPoint features rooms with minimalist furnishings in the best sense of the word. There's no unnecessary clutter, yet guests feel comfortable. Because of its location, this place attracts people who value peace. Small dormitory.

$$ Kenting Yoyo Resort Inn 悠遊旅店– *212 Nanwan Rd.* 南灣路212號. 📞*08-888 2627. www.yoyo-resort.idv.tw. 14 rooms.* On the main road and within walking distance of the beach and eateries, Yoyo is comfortable without being ostentatious. The interior has lots of wood on the floors and walls, which gives it an unexpected charm for the reasonable rates. Several rooms have ocean views and small balconies.

$$$ Ocean Paradise Resort 海境渡假民宿 – *No. 2-6 Hongchai Rd., Shanhaili.* 山海里紅柴路2-6號. 📞*08-886 9638. www.oceanparadise.com.tw. 12 rooms.* Located in the western part of the park, along that part of the coast nearest Hengchun, this stylish resort offers homestay-style accommodations in modern structures well away from the busiest part of the Kenting Area.

$$$ Small Path Homestay 小徑民宿
– *Lane 846, 65-1, Chuanfan Rd., Kenting.*
船帆路846巷65-1號. *08-885 1031;*
www.kenting.net.tw; 6 rooms. Bright
colors (the owner favors white and
blue) and a Dali-esque external staircase
make this homestay a feast for the
eyes. Located near Sail Rock. High
season prices from NT$4,200/room for
2 people.

$$$$ Caesar Park Kenting 凱撒大
飯店– *6 Kenting Rd.* 墾丁路6號. *08-
886 1888. http://kenting.caesarpark.
com.tw/en/main.php. 254 rooms.* There
are strong and intentional echoes of Bali
in the decor of the most luxurious of
Kenting's larger hotels. An under-road
walkway provides access to Xiaowan
Beach. Outdoor pool. Weekend room
rates higher than mid-week but usually
include dinner. Breakfast included.

♈ EAT

$ Chez Papa 爸爸花園 – *142 Kenting Rd.*
墾丁路142號 *08-886 1197.* With its
Moroccan-inspired decor that
encourages guests to sprawl out, this
restaurant looks more like a lounge bar;
many people come here solely to drink.
The food (more Italian than French)
wins plaudits for inventiveness and
consistency. **Italian.**

$ Mambo 曼波泰式餐廳 – *46 Kenting Rd.*
墾丁路46號. *08-886 2878.* Said to be
the oldest of Kenting's Thai restaurants,
Mambo is an often-crowded, always-
fun place to be. The menu is extensive,
so groups have no problem satisfying
those who want vegetarian food or
something not spicy. Beer options
include Thai and local brews. **Thai.**

$ Surf Shack – *224 Hengnan Rd.,
Hengchun.* 恆南路224號.; *08-888
1881.* Owned by a Canadian-Taiwanese
couple, the easy-to-find Surf Shack
serves excellent North American
comfort food. One of the cheaper
places to drink in the Kenting area
(beers from NT$80), it also has five
simple **rooms ($)** for one to six people,
with shared bathrooms. **American.**

Mambo

Rich J. Matheson/Michelin

$$ Warung Didi's 迪迪小吃 – *26
Wenhua Lane.* 文化巷26號. *08-886
1835. Dinner only. Closes 1am.* This
extremely popular eatery, which has
both indoor and outdoor seating,
serves Malaysian/Singapore/Thai/
Taiwanese food. Be prepared for spicy
food and to wait to get a table. Despite
its location in the back alleys, it's easy to
find. **Asian.**

⛹ RECREATION
BEACHES
All beaches in the Kenting Area are free,
and equipment, including surf boards,
jet skis, chairs and parasols, is available
for rent. Changing rooms and showers
are located at Nanwan and Xiaowan
beaches. Because of the undertow,
lifeguards may order you to stay close
to the shore.

SNORKELING AND DIVING
The Kenting Area offers visitors
excellent snorkeling and scuba diving.
If you want to rent equipment, hire
a guide or learn from an English-
speaking expert, contact either **U-Dive
Scuba Taiwan Club** (*0913 388 065;
www.udive.com/tw) or **Taiwan Dive**
(*0916 130 288; www.taiwandive.com)
for information and programs.

EAST COAST AND THE ISLANDS

Separated from the rest of the island by two mountain ranges and a few million people, Taiwan's East Coast moves at a more relaxed pace. The region from Hualien south to Taitung is dominated by its wild landscape, not by the sprawling development of Taiwan's West Coast. Here, the Pacific Ocean meets the land on rocky, jagged shores. Inland, the Coastal Mountain Range parallels the Central Mountain Range, sharing the verdant East Rift Valley in their midst. Rather than a region of industry, this is a land of agriculture, a landscape checkered with dazzling green rice paddies and fragrant tea terraces and pineapple plots spiked with spindly betelnut trees—whose tending matches nature's pace.

Highlights

1. Marble canyons of Taroko Gorge in **Taroko National Park** (p317)
2. Dragon-like bridge at **Sanxiantai** on Highway 11 (p328)
3. Neolithic-era slate coffins at Taitung's **Museum of Prehistory** (p333)
4. Highway 9's famous **Chu Lu Ranch** and its dairy cows (p337)
5. Green Island's **Jhaorih Hot Springs** on the ocean (p346)

Taiwan's Slow Lane

Highway 11 traces the stunning, lonely coast. Inland, Highway 9 weaves through pastoral farms. Served by both highways, the two largest cities, Hualien and Taitung, have a laid-back atmosphere, each filled with beautiful parks and seaside bikeways. North of Hualien, it is Taroko Gorge, the jewel of Taroko National Park, that is Taiwan's top tourist destination, a nearly 20km/12mi-long canyon of towering marble walls, bulbous and gnarled in some places, elegantly smooth in others, studded by waterfalls and lush vegetation.

Aboriginals in the largest concentrations live on the East Coast. Indigenous influence remains apparent, from decorative touches on schools and restaurants, to public art and performances, to the people themselves. Various tribes hold festivals throughout the year, continuing to practice ancient rites as Taiwan moves toward a greater respect for its native population.

The islands off the east coast contain some of Taiwan's most distinctive scenery and culture. Green and Orchid islands offer world-class snorkeling and diving just steps from shore. Orchid Island is the isolated home of the Tao tribe, pronounced "Dawu" in Mandarin, and sometimes referred to as the Yami.

The east coast is often pummeled by typhoons between June and October. A tropical/subtropical climate makes it warm and mild, but rainier and more overcast than the west. Winters are drier the farther south you go. Late fall, winter and early spring are good times to visit.

Cingshui Cliffs above the Pacific Ocean

Susannah Rosenblatt/Michelin

EAST COAST

TAROKO NATIONAL PARK

HUALIEN

14
Longjian
Lushan
Wushe (Ren'ai)
Nenggaoshan
3349
Wanda Reservoir
Wanda
Tongmen
Jian
Nanhua
9
Mugua
Liyu Lake
Shoufeng
Farglory
Ocean Park

Nantou

Hualien
East Rift Valley
National Scenic Area
Xikou
2827 △
Linrong
Fenglin
Lintianshan Forestry Park
16
Wanrong
Fangliao
Shanxing
11
Shuilian
◆ Cow Mountain Beach
■ Baci Observation
Platform ★★
◆ Jici Beach

East Coast
National
Scenic Area

PACIFIC
OCEAN

Danda

Dongqundashan
3605 △

△ 3204

Guangfu
■ *Mataian Ecological Park*
★ *Fuyuan Forest Rec. Area*
9
Fuyuan
★ *Highway 9*
Ruisui Hot Springs
Hongye Village
■ Hualien Sugar Factory
Fengbin

Highway 11 ★★

Qimei
■ *Shihtiping*
Changhong Bridge
Jingpu
Ruisui
Dewu
Tropic of Cancer Marker
Sanxian
Wuhe
Dayu

Tropic of Cancer

■ *Tropic of Cancer Marker*
Zhangyuan
Sanjianwu

Xiuguluanshan
3871 △

Dashuiku

Yushan
(Jade Mountain)
3952 △

★ *Yushan National Park*

Kaohsiung

△ 2155
Zhuoxi
Walami Trail
18
Yuli
Zhuhu
Antong
11
Changbin
◆ *Caves of the Eight Immortals* ★

★ *Nanan Waterfall*
7
Nanan
Visitor
Center
Dongli
■ *Antong Hot Springs*

▲ *Sixty Stone Mtn.*
Fuli
Zhongan
Shihyusan
■ *Sanxiantai* ★★

3036 △
20
Lidao
South
Cross-Island
Highway
Xinwu
Wulu
Chishang
○ Chenggong
Taitung Oceanarium
Heping

Guanshan
3666 △

Dalun
Haiduan
23

Guanshan
East Rift Valley
National Scenic Area
9
Ruifeng
Donghe
Amis Folk Center

East Coast

National

Scenic Area

Beinanzhushan
3293 △

Taitung

Luye
Bunun
Leisure Farm
Chu Lu
Binlang
Dulan
Shanyuan Beach
★ *Xiaoyeliu*
11

Pingtung

Luye
Beinan
TAITUNG

24
★ Zhiben
Zhiben Hot Springs

Wutai

N

GREEN ISLAND

0   10 km
0   10 miles

ORCHID ISLAND

CENTRAL MOUNTAIN RANGE

COASTAL MOUNTAIN RANGE

Taroko National Park★★★

Undoubtedly a highlight of Ilha Formosa, spectacular Taroko National Park (太魯閣國家公園) lies north of Hualien City. The 92,000ha/227,337-acre park stretches from the stunning Cingshui Cliffs along Taiwan's east coast inland to encompass snow-capped summits of the Central Mountain Range. The park's most famous views are along the Central Cross-Island Highway (Highway 8) within Taroko Gorge, the park's main attraction. The gorge amazes visitors with its skyscraping marble walls, and the rushing blue-grey waters of the Liwu River that slice through it. Taroko means "magnificent and beautiful" in the indigenous Taroko, or Truku language and was, according to legend, the exclamation of a Truku tribesman upon seeing the gorge against the sea. The description remains apt. Travelers can drive from one lookout to another along Highway 8, a windy, paved road through the gorge, while trekkers can set out on foot to conquer Taroko's many scenic trails.

A BIT OF GEOGRAPHY

The **Liwu River** flows 58km/36mi from the mountains to the Pacific Ocean, carving out Taroko Gorge along the way. The river's changing course over thousands of years formed terraces, including those in the town of Tiensiang and the aboriginal village of Buluowan within the park. Constant river erosion, combined with geological movement and wet weather, make landslides commonplace in Taroko.

The park's dramatic topography is dominated by Taroko's famous 250 million-year-old **marble walls**, formed from pressurized calcium carbonate-rich marine fossils. Weathering by the Liwu River exposed the

Michelin Map: p313.

Info: Visitor centers: at park headquarters near eastern entrance (291 Fushih Village 富世村291號; ✆03-862 1100 ext. 6). In Buluowan (✆03-861 2528) en route to Tiensiang. In Tiensiang (✆03-869 1162).

Location: The park lies off Hwy. 9, some 26km/16mi north of Hualien. It stretches north and south of Taroko Gorge, which itself extends inland west from Hwy. 9; the most-visited portion of the gorge is generally considered to end at the hamlet of **Tiensiang**, where food and accommodations are available. The major sights of the gorge are accessible by Hwy. 8. In addition to Tiensiang, accommodations can be found in **Fushih Village**, which sits along Hwy. 9 southeast of the park entrance, and **Chongde Village**, also on Hwy. 9, but north of the park entrance.

Kids: The nature exhibit in the main visitor center is geared to young ones. Easy, flat trails such as the Tunnel of Nine Turns and Shakadang Trail are suitable for children.

Timing: Late fall, winter and early spring are good times to visit. The park tends to be sunny and warmer earlier in the day, often turning cloudy and cool in the afternoon. Rain can appear suddenly, so bring a jacket or umbrella.

Don't Miss: Tunnel of Nine Turns, Swallow Grotto, Xiangde Temple.

GETTING THERE

BY TRAIN - From Taipei, Tze Chiang express train *(2hrs 45min; NT$445)*; with frequent service, is the fastest way to get to Hualien. Slow trains *(3hrs 30min; NT$343)*.

Alternately, instead of heading all the way south to Hualien, you can disembark from either train earlier at the Xincheng station (☏03-861 1237), just 5km/3mi from park headquarters. From this small station, walk or take a Hualien Bus Co. bus to the park.

BY CAR - From Taipei, take Highway 5 about 60km/37mi from the Nangang area to the Suhua Highway (Hwy. 9) along the coast. Head south 77km/48mi to the park entrance at Highway 8. Turn right *(west)* to enter the park. The drive from Taipei takes about 4hrs 20min.

GETTING AROUND

BY CAR - Car rentals at Hualien's train station. Either an international or Taiwan driver's license is usually required to rent a car.

BY SCOOTER - Scooter rental facilities, many of which require a Taiwan driver's license, are located near the Hualien train station. Scooters average about NT$400/day.

BY BUS - Hualien Bus Co. runs a bus from Hualien Train Station to the park entrance *(1hr)* and on to the village of Tiensiang, within the gorge, four times a day. Some visitors take the bus from Hualien station to its endpoint at Tiensiang *(46km/28.6mi; 1.5hrs; NT$86 one-way)* and hike the 19km/11.8mi back to the entrance, or get dropped off midway at the Tunnel of Nine Turns. Check the schedule, because it is infrequent and may change. Hualien Bus Co. ☏03-833 8146.

BY TAXI - Cabs are usually available at the train station. Hiring a taxi for the day (about NT$2500) is a good way to explore the park at your own pace.

GENERAL INFORMATION

AREA CODE

The prefix 03, the area code for Hualien County, has been included in the telephone numbers shown in this chapter, but it is not necessary to dial 03 when making a local call.

ACCOMMODATIONS

Lodgings can be found in Tiensiang at the west end of the gorge, in Fushih Village (Hwy. 9), southeast of the park entrance and in Chongde Village (Hwy. 9), east of the park entrance.

For a selection of accommodations, ☞*see ADDRESSES below.*

Cihmu Bridge over Liwu River, Taroko Gorge

Susannah Rosenblatt/Michelin

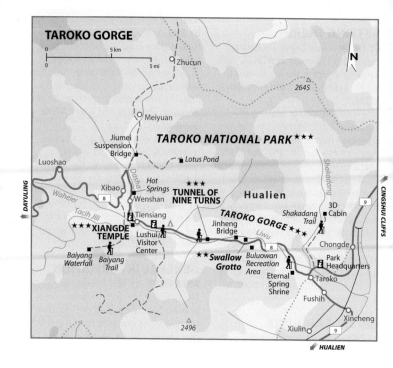

hard marble under the earth's surface, and its forceful waters carved out the deep, narrow U-shaped gorge that attracts visitors today. The continued collision of the Philippines oceanic plate underneath the Eurasian continental plate, which first began 4 million years ago, means the gorge rises upward about .5cm/.2in each year.

The highest peak in the park is **Mount Nanhu**, 3,742m/12,270ft of gneiss, slate, sandstone and limestone. Some 27 mountains in the park tower more than 3,000m/9,843ft.

Flora and Fauna

Taroko's range of elevations, from subtropical to snowy, creates habitats for a wide variety of flora and fauna. The national park is home to one-third of the vascular plant species in Taiwan. The coastal portion of the park is monsoon rain forest, where rare **Chinese juniper** grows. The gorge region features limestone soil and deciduous forests, whose leaves change color come fall. Alpine species such as the **Taiwan Fir** can be found on the park's Mount Hehuan; when Mount Nanhu isn't covered in snow, it explodes with azaleas and wildflowers.

The park hosts half the island's mammal species, and 90 percent of Taiwan's bird species. Several endemic animals thrive in the rain forest, including the green stink bug, Formosan **gem-faced civet** and the Formosan **wild boar**; other notable species include birds such as the **Taiwan bulbul**, common kestrel and **serpent eagle**. Formosan rock macaques, Formosan giant flying squirrels, Chinese lesser civets and birds such as the Japanese white-eye and **bronzed drongo** live here. Migratory **monk gobies**, Taiwan mitten crabs and swamp eels swim in the gorge's rivers.

At middle elevations, squirrels, pheasants, thrushes, weasel-like martens and the Formosan **Reeve's muntjac**—a type of barking deer—run among pine, hemlock and Japanese maple trees. Taroko is also home to black bears, endangered tree frogs, 144 species of bird and more than 300 types of butterfly.

A BIT OF HISTORY

As the ancestral home of several aboriginal tribes, among them the Taroko, or Truku, and the Atayal, some of the park's current trails began as ancient hunting paths. The Truku people, known for weaving, headhunting and ritual facial tattooing, crossed the Central Mountain Range roughly 300 years ago to live in the forests of the Liwu River. "The land is our blood, the mountain forest our home," says Teyra, a Truku man proud to share his people's heritage with guests at his lovely B&B just outside the park. Truku traditionally worshiped ancestral spirits, farmed millet and hunted mountain animals such as wild boar, Formosan Reeve's muntjac, flying squirrels and rabbits. The tribe was officially recognized by the Taiwanese government in 2004. Apart from the Truku culture, archaeologists have unearthed prehistoric artifacts within the park.

For several hundred years, Chinese, Japanese and European fortune seekers would periodically journey to the Liwu River in search of gold rumored to be buried there.

The Truku's first major encounter with outsiders occurred during the Qing dynasty with the construction of the Suhua northern road, as Hualien developed during the late 1800s. Japanese occupiers considered Taroko a scenic tourist locale at the turn of the 19C. In addition to building a road to cross the Central Mountain Range, the colonial government moved to extract marble, hydroelectric power and other natural resources from the area, clashing violently with tribal dwellers. Truku tribe members fought Japanese military for 18 years; many were eventually forced to relocate to Hualien County's foothills in 1917.

Constructed between 1956 and 1960, the twisting **Central Cross-Island Highway** (Highway 8), originally a Truku hunting track, cuts though the middle of the park and connects Taiwan's coasts. The hazardous NT$430 million undertaking was plagued by earthquakes and typhoons, and hundreds of laborers, mostly military veterans, were injured or killed. Many of the thousands of road workers settled nearby, establishing farms. Japanese occupiers' original plans to make Taroko a national park were abandoned during WWII.

One of eight national parks in Taiwan, Taroko was officially designated as such in 1986.

TAROKO GORGE★★★

291 Fushih Village. Park ⏰Open 24hrs daily. Visitor center ✕⏰Open daily 8:30am–4:45pm. ⏰Closed 2nd Mon of month & Chinese New Year Eve; if Monday holiday, closed the next day. ✆03-862 1100 ext. 6. www.taroko. gov.tw.

Maps and brochures, weather conditions, trail closure information available at the visitor center . Additional hikes not listed include overnight backpacking treks requiring a permit.

Begin at the visitor center at park headquarters near eastern entrance. Many of the best and most accessible sights of Taroko Gorge are scattered along Highway 8's first 19km/11.8mi. *Sights below are ordered east to west from park headquarters along Highway 8.*

🚶🏔 Shakadang Trail★
砂卡礑步道

1km/0.6m west of park headquarters.

🔲 Just before Shakadang Bridge, a metal staircase to the right leads to the trailhead. A shady, flat 8.8km/5.5mi round-trip path follows the clear, blue-green **Shakadang River** to the sounds of rushing water and whirring insects. In the early 20C, the Japanese colonial government built the trail to access a hydroelectric power-generating dam. You will pass by indigenous farms of bird's nest ferns along the way. *Hiking past the trail's turnaround point at 3D Cabin requires a permit.*

Eternal Springs Shrine

Susannah Rosenblatt/Michelin

An uphill trail leads to a bell tower and mountain views. *Caution: the steep stairs can be treacherous when wet.*

Swallow Grotto★★ 燕子口
About 9km/5.6mi west of park headquarters.

The pitted limestone cliffs, in varying gradations of gray, were once home to a fluttering colony of swallows.

Squeezed next to the rushing Liwu River, the area is now closed to traffic, so you can take your time searching for birds, springs or the rock resembling a Native American chieftain's profile. Midway down the 1.4km/.9mi path near a snack and souvenir shop is Jinheng Bridge, named for the engineer who died in an earthquake-triggered landslide while inspecting the road in 1957.

Eternal Springs Shrine 長春祠
2.3km/1.4mi west of park headquarters.
⚑ This short 1.4km/.9mi trail, complete with a suspension bridge, spring-fed waterfall, shrine and Zen temple, packs a lot in.

Cross the bridge over the Liwu River to the shrine dedicated to the 212 workers who died and 702 who were injured building the perilous road through the gorge. Landslides have forced three rebuildings of the shrine.

≛≛Tunnel of Nine Turns★★★ 九曲洞
12.5km/7.8mi west of park headquarters.

The marquee destination in a park brimming with wondrous sights, this series of narrow, twisting tunnels has been blasted, incredibly, through the massively thick rock.

The striated marble faces across the river seem close enough to touch. The marble here was formed from 250-million-year-old coral reefs off China's southeastern coast subjected to tectonic plate movement.

Now closed to cars, the tunnels are yours to explore along the entire 1.9km/1.2mi route. Admire the rushing river below and waterfalls above—but keep an eye out for falling rocks. The hard hats provided to visitors might look silly, but they are intended to offer protection from tumbling stones, as the stray piles you see can attest.

Xiangde Temple★★★ 祥德寺
Marking the entrance to Tiensiang, the otherworldly Xiangde Temple sits atop a set of winding, tree-lined stairs, offering commanding views of Taroko's mountains and intersecting Dasha and Tacih Jili rivers. The temple features a golden bodhisattva. Scale the pagoda's

View from Swallow Grotto

Susannah Rosenblatt/Michelin

Bodhisattva guarding Xiangde Temple

Susannah Roser-blatz/Michelin

spiral staircase for an even better vantage point.

The area used to be known as Tapido, a Truku term meaning "sugar palm", named for local vegetation.

Tiensiang 天祥

In this tiny resort village, visitors can eat a pricey meal in the Silks Place hotel or a cheap one at the food stalls clustered there, as well as catch one of the four daily buses to Hualien.

Baiyang Trail 白楊步道

4km/2.4mi round-trip. About 20km/12.4mi west of park headquarters. Note: The trail was recently closed; check on latest conditions before departing. Bring a flashlight.

🥾 A little more than half a mile west of Tiensiang, a 380m/1,247ft-long tunnel leads to this river walk, which passes lovely falls complete with an inviting pavilion. A flashlight helps to navigate the multiple tunnels along the way.

Wenshan Hot Springs
文山溫泉

3km/1.9mi north of Tiensiang.
Now closed due to a fatal rockslide, this naturally warmed, marble-walled pool

down the stairs and across a suspension bridge once soothed hikers with its 48°C/118°F water.

Cingshui Cliffs 清水斷崖

Along Hwy. 9, about 15km/9.3mi north of park headquarters.

🥾 Reachable by car, these magnificent cliffs constitute the only seaside portion of the park. Set against the Pacific's foamy waves, the vertiginous marble and gneiss cliffs rise more than 1,000m/3,281ft.

The 19km/11.8mi coast-hugging drive between Heren and Chongde on the **Su'hua Highway** (Highway 9) is as hair-raising as it is breathtaking, with turquoise sea **views**★★ rivaling those of California's Big Sur. When you take those postcard-perfect snapshots, be sure to pull over, as trucks frequently whip around corners on this narrow and sharply curved road.

A couple of winding **trails** lead from scenic overlooks down to the ocean; a trail just north of the Chongde Tunnel that stretches to Chongde Gravel Beach is a popular spot from which to watch the sunrise.

ADDRESSES

IN THE PARK

$ Heliu 合流 – *At the KM 172 marker on Hwy. 8 within the gorge.* 📞*03-869 1129. 11 campsites.* The lone campsite in the park sits west of the Tunnel of Nine Turns and east of Tiensiang. It's free and has 11 first-come, first-served sites, but you must bring your own tent.

$ Catholic Hostel 天主堂來賓宿舍 – *33 Tiensiang Rd.* 天祥路33號. 📞*03-869 1122. 25 rooms.* 🛏. Utilitarian, clean riverside dorms and private rooms at rock-bottom prices tucked into a tangle of passageways. Both private and shared baths available. Located past the police station up the hill that forks off the main road. Climb the stairs on the left with the red railings.

$ Presbyterian Hostel 德國差會天祥路基督教會招待所 – *19 Tiensiang Rd.* 天祥路19號. 📞*03-869 1203 or 0921 863 206. 11 rooms.* 🛏. A friendly couple keeps this warren of sunny, breezy rooms attached to a church on a hilltop, including 4- and 8-person dorms with roll-up mattresses, and rooms with private bathrooms. The aging common living and kitchen areas overlook the Liwu River. The back dorm overhangs the river with stairs down to the water. Located across the street from the post office, up the hill and to the left behind the Silks Place Taroko.

$$ Tiensiang Youth Activity Center 天祥青年活動中心 – *30 Tiensiang Rd.* 天祥路30號. 📞*03-869 1111. www. cyctsyac.com.tw/index.htm. 63 rooms.* All the bright, tidy rooms and multi-person dorms at this large facility have their own bathrooms, flat screen TVs and refrigerators, plus natural views. Laundry facilities, Wi-Fi, a Western-style cafe, and breakfast included. The white building is up the hill 60m/200ft past the Catholic Hostel at the road's end.

$$$ Leader Village Taroko 立德布洛灣山月村 – *231-1 Fushih Village.* 富世村231-1號. 📞*03-861 0111. www.leaderhotel.com. 73 cabin rooms. Breakfast included. Restaurant with seasonal aboriginal set menus.* In the aboriginal village of Buluowan, situated east of Swallow Grotto, Leader Village

Taroko offers a slightly rustic alternative to the luxury environs of Silks Place. Here, fragrant lemongrass wood cabins blend with peaceful green hills and feature inviting porches to watch the stars come out. Indigenous dance performance every evening and occasional night tours of flying squirrels and fireflies. Hualien pickup provided for a fee.

$$$$ Silks Place Taroko 太魯閣晶英酒店 – 🍴🛁 Spa *18 Tiensiang Rd.* 天祥路18號. 📞*03-869 1155. http://taroko. silksplace.com.tw. 160 rooms.* The former Grand Formosa Taroko has been renamed and renovated in a muted palate of Zen-styled wood paneling. The magical location overlooking the Liwu River is still the main draw. Relax hike-strained muscles at the full-service **Wellspring Spa**, unwind in the outdoor pool or hit balls on the rooftop tennis courts, while the kids run around the basement play area. The site was originally used for diplomatic visits by Chiang Kai-shek. Cantonese/Taiwanese and Western restaurants. Shuttle service from Hualien train station and airport (NT$250/person).

OUTSIDE THE PARK

$$ Crossing the Rainbow B&B 走過虹橋民宿 – *210 Neighborhood #3, Chongde Village.* 崇德村三鄰210號. 📞*03-862 1328 or 0928 570 855. www.teyra.com.tw. 7 rooms.* 🛏. At the foot of the bridge minutes from park headquarters, this B&B was built with environmentally friendly features—like a solar-heated shower—by a retired school principal and member of the Truku tribe. The English-speaking owner leads bicycle tours to Taroko Gorge and proudly teaches guests about his people's rich heritage. Great views, free bikes, high-speed Internet. Breakfast included.

$$ Taroko Hotel 太魯閣飯店 – *258 Fushih Village.* 富世村258號. 📞*03-861 1558. www.taroko-hotel.com.tw. 45 rooms.* This long-established hotel sits only a few hundred meters from Taroko National Park's arched entrance. It has spacious, functional rooms for 2, 4 or 6, and a rooftop terrace overlooking the Liwu River. Free bikes, Internet. Breakfast comes with the rate.

Hualien

Hualien (花蓮) is the largest city on Taiwan's rugged and sparsely populated east coast. Squeezed between the Pacific Ocean to the east and the Coastal Mountain Range to the west, it is the ideal starting point for exploring the region's rocky shores and verdant valleys, particularly the spectacular Taroko National Park, just north. Known for its marble deposits and stone carving, the coastal city has a few minor attractions, but the real draw lies in the scenery, hot springs and aboriginal villages along Highways 9 and 11 to the south. The area is home to Taiwan's largest aborigine population, the Amis, roughly half of whom live in Hualien County.

This modern city has all the usual conveniences, but its smaller size, slower pace and natural splendor provide a calmer alternative to the frenzy of Taipei. Having your own transportation, or a taxi hired for the day, is the best way to take in the sights in Hualien and along Taiwan's east coast. Cycling is growing in popularity on the island, and is a great option for savoring those seaside views.

▶ **Population:** 110,000.
◔ **Michelin Map:** p313.
🛈 **Info:** Visitor center outside the train station at 106 Guolien 1st Rd. 國聯一路 106號. ✆03-836 0634.
◖ **Location:** About 26km/16mi south of Taroko National Park headquarters, Hualien sits on Taiwan's east coast. The airport is north of city center. The train station is northwest of downtown. Major roads Zhongshan and Zhongzheng intersect downtown, which is near the ocean. Just northeast, Hualien County's cultural park holds the Stone Sculpture Museum and other public buildings.
👪 **Kids:** Farglory Ocean Park.
🕐 **Timing:** Skip stormy typhoon season from July through September. Fall and spring, particularly November, December, March and April, are milder and less rainy.
☺ **Don't Miss:** The seaside bike path, Qixingtan Beach and Hualien Stonecrafters Square.

Marble sculptures, Hualien cultural park

Courtesy of Government Information Office

GETTING THERE

BY AIR - Hualien's airport lies 6km/4mi north of the city (*℘03-821 0768; www.hulairport.gov.tw*). TransAsia Airways flies from Taipei to Hualien five times daily. Upon arrival, you can take the **airport bus** to downtown *(about every half hour most of the day; 30min ride; approximately NT$25 one way; runs 8:30am–7:40pm)*, bargain with a taxi driver *(about NT$200 for the 10-15min ride)* or rent a car, with an international driver's license. Cars can be rented at the airport (*see Getting Around, below*).

BY TRAIN - Hualien is easily reachable from Taipei by train (*see Getting There in Taroko Gorge section*). Hualien's train station lies northwest of downtown. *℘03-835 5941.*

BY CAR - From Taipei, take Highway 5 about 60km/37mi from the Nangang area to the Suhua Highway (Highway 9) along the coast. Head south 93km/58mi to Hualien. Driving time is almost 5hrs.

GETTING AROUND

BY BUS - Heading left out of the train station, a large Hualien Bus Co. depot has routes, timetables and fares for destinations around the region posted in Chinese and English (*℘03-833 8146*). For local destinations within Hualien, transportation by bus is not recommended, as service can be infrequent and routes complicated to comprehend for English-only tourists.

BY CAR - Easy Rent is located at the airport (202 Jiali Rd.; *℘03-826 4567*). IWS Rent-A-Car has an office at the Hualien train station *(open 8am-8pm; ℘03-833 8811 or 0800 008 414)*. An international driver's license is required.

BY SCOOTER - Scooters can be rented at Hualien train station for about NT$400 a day.

BY BICYCLE - Free bicycles are available at many hotels and hostels in town, including most of those listed below. If they don't have bikes, they can help arrange rentals.

GENERAL INFORMATION

AREA CODE

The prefix 03, which indicates the area code for Hualien County, has been included in the telephone numbers shown in this chapter, even though It is not necessary to dial 03 when making a local call.

VISITOR INFORMATION

A sensible first stop is the comprehensive **visitor center** *(open daily 8am–10pm; ℘03-836-0634)*, which has literature and English-speaking staff just steps away from the train station *(exit to the right)*. Hualien County's tourist website, http://tour-hualien.hl.gov.tw, also has information.

ACCOMMODATIONS

Lodgings to suit all budgets can be found in Hualien's downtown and near the train station. More expensive hotels line the coast north of downtown. The regional visitor center (*see above*) may be able to help with securing accommodations. *For a selection of places to stay overnight, see ADDRESSES below.*

DOWNTOWN

Easily bikeable, the compact business district has lots of restaurants, lodgings, banks and familiar fast food chains such as McDonald's and Starbucks. The downtown centers on the major streets of Zhongshan, Zhonghua and Zhongzheng Roads, which form a triangle; for serious shoppers, the **Far Eastern Department Store** lies a few blocks beyond. Cake shops along these roads sell Hualien's renowned *mochi*, sticky rice cakes with sweet fillings such as strawberries. The famous Stonecrafters Square lies about five blocks to the southeast. Next door to it is the lively **Nanbin Park Night Market** (*see ADDRESSES*). Northeast of downtown, the Meilun River winds through the city, emptying into the Pacific. Beyond the city center stretch bike paths and the sea; the coast is dotted with high-end hotels.

Hualien Stonecrafters Square
石藝大街
326 Guangdong St. 廣東街326號, near intersection of Chongching Rd. (重慶路) & Boai St. (博愛街) ◷*Open daily 2pm–10:30pm. Free aboriginal dance shows 8:10pm–9:10pm nightly.* ℘*03-835 3730. www.hss.org.tw.*

A stroll through this crafts square, a former railway hospital located close to the water, shows off the "City of Marble's" signature industry with plenty of objets d'art, polished jade and crystals—and loads of marble products—for your choosing. Take home anything from a NT$61,000 giant purple geode to a NT$200 tiger's eye Buddha. Aboriginal crafts, including beaded jewelry, are also for sale.

Temple of Eastern Purity
東淨寺
48 Wuquan St. 五權街48號. ◷*Open daily 5am–3pm.* ℘*03-832-2773.*
Situated about six blocks northeast of Stonecrafters Square, this stunning all-marble monument was built by the Japanese in 1915 on a hilltop among rock terraces, magnolia trees and trickling water.

Stonecrafters Square merchandise
Susannah Rosenblatt/Michelin

The golden Buddha statues inside are worth a look.

ADDITIONAL SIGHTS
Hualien County Stone Sculpture Museum
花蓮石雕博物館
6 Wenfu Rd. 文復路6號. In Hualien County Cultural Center. ✕◷*Open daily 9am–5pm. NT$20.* ℘*03-822 7121. http://stone.hccc.gov.tw. Grounds may be undergoing construction.*
Opened in 2001, this modern museum in Hualien's cultural park near the harbor is

Temple of Eastern Purity
Susannah Rosenblatt/Michelin

one of the most active marble centers in Asia. Here traditional and modern stone art by local and international artists is displayed on a rotating basis.

Hualien is home to many stone artists, and the museum has held an **International Stone Sculptural Festival** in October for several years, attracting sculptors from other countries as well as locally. Attendees watch artists using modern power tools shape large blocks of marble from Hualien's nearby quarries. Many of the works are later exhibited in the museum or placed in parks and other public spaces throughout Hualien. Spacious landscaped **grounds** outside the museum are dotted with a variety of traditionally sculpted statues as well as monumental contemporary pieces. Inside the two-story museum building, traditional works such as religious statues are displayed in one section, while contemporary sculpture is presented separately.

Qixingtan Beach 七星潭

About 6km/4mi northeast of downtown. ⏰*Open daily 8am–6pm.* ☏*03-822 0741. http://gis.hl.gov.tw/website/chisingtan/inside.asp.*

Hualien's 21km/13mi beachfront bike path wends north through three seaside parks, ending at this scenic beach and fishing village near Hualien airport. Known for superb stargazing, the swath of pebbly beach here has stone sculptures and scenic views of the plunging Cingshui Cliffs to the north. Though popular, the beach has signs warning against swimming.

Tzu Chi Still Thoughts Hall 靜思堂

*703 Zhongyang Rd., Sec. 3.*中央路3段 *703號, on Tzu Chi University campus, northwest of downtown.* ⏰*Open daily 8:30am–5pm.* ☏*03-856 1995. http://eng.tcu.edu.tw.*

Hualien is the world headquarters of **Tzu Chi**, a Buddhist relief organization with branches across the globe.
Quiet your mind at this serene building on Tzu Chi's 100ha/247-acre campus. The marble temple has stacked,

Tzu Chi Still Thoughts Hall

Susannah Rosenblatt/Michelin

flying-eave roofs and wide stairs with solid marble banisters leading up to the entrance. The ancient Sanskrit swastika, symbol of harmony in Buddhism and often depicted on the Buddha's chest or soles of his feet, is prominent on the face of the building. The hall shares a campus with the group's hospital and university located near the train station. A video *(26min)* in English and exhibits spotlight the organization's origins. A vegetarian restaurant is on-site.

👪 Farglory Ocean Park 遠雄海洋公園

15km/9mi south of downtown, off Hwy. 11. 189 Fude Rd., Yenliao Village. 鹽寮村 福德路189號. ⏰*Open Jul–Sept daily 9am–6:30pm (Sat–Sun 7:30pm). Rest of the year Mon–Fri 9:30am–5pm, Sat–Sun 9am–5pm. NT$890, children NT$790.* ☏*03-812 3199. www.themeparks.net.tw/eng/park/park23/index.asp.*

This lively marine ecology amusement park above the Pacific is packed with exhibits, rides, shows, acrobatic dolphins and amorous sea lions. Visitors can get up close with aquatic creatures. The 51ha/126-acre park is laid out in themed sections such as a fairy-tale castle, a lagoon, a main street and underwater world. Rides include a Ferris wheel, a water slide and bumper boats. The **aquarium** has underwater viewing tanks as well as interactive programs. Cable cars climb the hill above the park, offering scenic views of the ocean and surroundings.

There's a fancy Victorian hotel with pool, gym and restaurants on-site. *www.farglory-hotel.com.tw.* 👟*See ADDRESSES.*

ADDRESSES

🏠 STAY

$ Amigos Hostel 阿美客國際青年
旅舍 – 68 Guolien 2nd Rd. 國聯二路68號.
📞03-836 2756. www.amigoshostel.tw.
42 beds. 🖶. Breakfast included.
This backpacker heaven offers 8-,
10- and 16-person dorms with shared
bathrooms. Amigos has a laid-back
surfer vibe. The English-speaking
owner doles out local travel tips.
Located in a confusing web of streets a
short walk from the train station. Linens
and Wi-Fi provided.

$$ C'est Jeune Hotel 喜臻藝術精品
飯店 – 122 Zhongfu Rd. 中福路122號.
📞03-833 1388. ww.cj-hotel.com. 42 rooms.
Breakfast included. This boutique hotel's
brick exterior accented with wrought
iron balconies exudes European charm,
while inside the sleek, neutral-toned
lobby features playful contemporary
art. Comfortable, simple rooms and a
helpful staff plus free bicycles; near the
seaside night market in the south of
town.

$$ Classic City Resort 經典假日飯店 –
139 Guolien 5th Rd. 國聯五路139號.
📞03-835 9966. www.classichotel.tw.
79 rooms. Breakfast included. A fresh,
contemporary business hotel with
minimalist decor around the corner
from the train station. Free bicycles,
Wi-Fi, travel assistance.

$$ Ola Hotel 洄瀾客棧 – 11 Haian Rd.
海岸路11號. 📞03-822 7188. www.ola.
com.tw. 113 rooms. Breakfast included.
Chinese and Western restaurant. This
playful oceanfront hotel overlooking
the harbor has a lobby filled with funky
sculptures and provides free bikes and
Internet. Some rooms with sea views;
one block from the Sculpture Museum.

$$ Roseland B&B 玫瑰花園民宿 –
2nd floor, 7 Gongyuan Rd. 公園路7號2樓.
📞03-832 5857 or 0937 532 828.
www.roseland.com.tw/english.html.
21 rooms. 🖶. Breakfast included. This
warm B&B in the heart of downtown
Hualien is run by two sisters who love
decorating. Rooms for 2, 4 or 6 and a
rooftop patio with a sliver of sea view.
Free airport pickup, bikes and help
organizing tours.

$$$ Parkview Hotel 美侖大飯店 –
1-1 Lin Yuan. 林園1-1號. 📞03-822 2111.
www.parkview-hotel.com. 343 rooms.
Western restaurant. This massive
resort north of downtown has all
the trappings to keep the family
entertained, from a huge outdoor pool,
indoor water park and gym to table
tennis, billiards, squash, a climbing wall
and a playground. Some rooms have
ocean or mountain views, and the
16-floor hotel has sculptures
on its grassy grounds.

$$$$ Farglory Hotel 遠雄悅來飯店 –
Off Hwy. 11. 18 Shanling, 山嶺18號
Yenliao Village. 📞03-812 3999.
www.farglory-hotel.com.tw. 391 rooms.
This large Victorian-style hotel is
perfectly sited for visitors to the
adjacent amusement park of the same
name. Rooms comes with free Internet,
in-room safes, slippers and other
amenities. An outdoor pool, a gym
and several restaurants are on-site.

🍽 EAT

$ Bien Chen Restaurant 邊城茶舖 –
10 Lane 26 Mingli Rd. 明禮路26巷10號.
📞03-834 6550. Closes 10pm. http://
038346550.tw.tranews.com. Yunnan
dishes like pepper chicken and hot
and sour shrimp served in a lovely old
Japanese home. **Yunnan.**

$ Nanbin Park Night Market 南濱公園
夜市 – This small, spirited night market
located near the Stonecrafters Square
offers local nibbles like clams steamed
straight from the ocean and warm,
crispy sesame balls, with the rumble of
the waves as a soundtrack. **Taiwanese.**

$ Yixiang Bienshi Dian 液香扁食店 –
42 Xinyi St. 信義街42號. 📞03-832 6761.
Closes 9:30pm. 🖶. Serving up Hualien's
most famous wontons for more than
70 years. Don't let the fluorescently-lit
interior fool you: these steaming bowls
of pillowy wonton and caramelized
onions are surprisingly succulent.
Taiwanese.

$$ Irrawaddy Myanmar Restaurant 伊
江滇緬料理 – 11-1 Minquan Rd. 民權路
11-1號. 📞03-831 0077. irrawaddy.com.tw.
🖶. Closes 9pm. A popular spot for
Burmese cuisine in the north of town
near the water. **Burmese.**

Highway 11★★

This coastal road runs the length of the 168km/104mi East Coast National Scenic Area *(www.eastcoast-nsa.gov.tw)* and spans portions of Hualien and Taitung counties, from Hualien to Xiaoyeliu. Your own set of wheels, whether it's two or four, is the best way to make a leisurely cruise on scenic Highway 11 down Taiwan's wild east coast. This coast is long on incredible scenery and life lived at the slower pace of days gone by. English isn't spoken as widely here, but a few key phrases plus the tendency for locals to be friendly should help you get by.

ABORIGINAL HEARTLAND

Isolated by the mountain ranges that run down Taiwan's spine, this part of the island is home to a large number of aboriginal residents, particularly the Amis tribe. It was the last part of Taiwan to be settled by Han Chinese immigrants, and never developed as much as the densely populated west coast. And that's a good thing.

Leave the tour groups behind and discover the East Coast's aboriginal fishing villages and deserted sea coves, couldn't-be-fresher seafood and an atmosphere of what many term the "real" Taiwan. The sea breeze usually makes for a milder climate than the at

- **Michelin Map:** p313.
- **Info:** Visitor center at 8km marker, south of Hualien, 5 Yen-liao Village. 鹽寮村大坑5號. &03-867 1326. www.eastcoast-nsa.gov.tw. Open daily 8:30am–5pm. 20min film in English, Chinese, Japanese.
- **Location:** Hwy. 11 extends 173km/107mi between Hualien in the north and Taitung in the south. Interesting sights are scattered fairly evenly along the route; while there are plenty of places to stay, restaurants are fewer and farther between, although some attractions have snacks for sale.
- **Kids:** Jici Beach or the tide pools at Shihtiping. Crafts demonstrations at the Amis Folk Center.
- **Timing:** Eastern Taiwan gets more rain than western Taiwan; avoid typhoon season (Jul–Sept).
- **Don't Miss:** The arched bridge and ecological preserve at Sansientai, aboriginal arts at the old Dulan Sugar Factory.

Overlook along Highway 11

Susannah Rosenblatt/Michelin

Arched bridge, Sanxiantai

© JTB/Photoshot

times oppressive heat and humidity of the west coast, but the area is at a greater risk for typhoons and other extreme weather and can quickly grow overcast and rainy.

🚗 DRIVING TOUR

173km/107mi from Hualien City to Taitung via Hwy.11. Allow 1-2 days. Note: It is highly advisable to fill up your car in Hualien before starting out. En route, there are gas stations near the KM24, 50, 86, 130 and 146 markers.

Cow Mountain Beach 牛山灣
KM26 marker.

An isolated short stretch of black sand beach reachable down a narrow, serpentine 1.4km/0.9mi road. There's a small cafe decorated with driftwood carvings that serves Amis food nearby. Be careful not to burn your feet—the sand gets pretty hot.

Between Cow Mountain Beach and Jici Beach to the south, stop at the **Baci Observation Platform** *(芭崎瞭望台; 32km marker)* for coffee and an expansive sea **view**★★, perhaps one of the best along Highway 11.

Jici Beach 磯崎灣
KM38 marker. 🏖♿

Jici is one of two beaches along the East Coast National Scenic Area where swimming is allowed. The curving 3km/1.9mi-long bay off Jici Beach draws swimmers and campers. Tidal movement churns up black sand in winter, gold in summer. Lifeguards are on duty in summer; restrooms, showers and wheelchair ramps are on-site and hiking trails in the nearby hills.

Shihtiping 石梯坪
KM65 marker. Visitor center: 52 Shihtiping, Gangkou Village, Fengbin 豐濱鄉港口村石梯坪52號. 🕗 open daily 8am–5pm. 📞03-878 1452.

Watch erosion in action among the terraced volcanic rocks and 🚹 **tide pools** of Shihtiping, which means "stone steps." Teeming with marine life for more than 1km/.6mi, Shihtiping is great for fishing, exploring and camping (29 campsites, some with covered wooden platforms). A harbor from which whale-watching excursions depart and a small fish market are nearby.

Tropic of Cancer Marker 北迴歸線標誌
Just past the KM70 marker.

A little corny but worth a photo, this obelisk, one of three such markers in Taiwan, identifies the official entrance to the tropics (and the dividing line between Hualien and Taitung counties). It was built to allow visitors to clearly view the sun's northernmost declination on the summer solstice, June 21.

Caves of the Eight Immortals★
八仙洞

Before KM78 marker. 1-4 Shuimuding, Sanjian Village, Changbin. 長濱鄉 三間村水母丁1-4號. ◉*Open daily 8:30am–5pm.* ☎089 881 418.

This well-trafficked attraction is one of Taiwan's most important archaeological sites. More than 10 caves worn from the sea cliffs millions of years ago were forced 150m/492ft upward by tectonic shifts. The site was home to one of Taiwan's earliest known human settlements; archaeologists recovered Paleolithic artifacts including stone tools between 5,000 and 30,000 years old. Now many of the caves, some named for Chinese deities, house brightly colored Buddhist and Taoist shrines connected by wooden walkways. Drinks and aboriginal trinkets are for sale.

Sanxiantai★★ 三仙台

KM111 marker. 72 Jihuei Rd., Sansian Village, Chenggong. 成功鎮三仙里基翬路74號. ◉*Open daily 8:30am–5pm.* ☎089 850 785.

Atop a small volcanic island sit three bluffs thought to resemble a trio of Chinese Taoist deities who stopped there on a journey across the sea. A fanciful, dragon-shaped **arched bridge** 320m/1,050ft long connects the island to the beach. Protected as an ecological reserve, the land mass has rare plants, sea-eroded potholes, a lighthouse, fishing, and reefs for intrepid snorkelers. It takes about 90min to cross the bridge and traverse the island. Food stalls there sell snacks.

Chenggong 成功

KM115 marker. www.changkang.gov.tw. The biggest city between Hualien and Taitung is known for its famous fish market, the busiest on Taiwan's east coast. Be sure to stop in between 3pm and 4pm when fishermen return and auctioneers sell the day's catch in a frenzy of activity. Look for the large white building shaped like a ship's prow. The market area is also home to whale-watching cruises and the **National Taitung Oceanarium** (國立台東海洋生物展覽館), with a touch pool and tanks where jellyfish, rays and sharks swim *(KM119 marker; 21 Harbor Rd.;* 成功鎮港邊路21號; ◉*open mid-Jun–mid-Sept daily 9am-6pm; rest of the year daily 9am–5pm; NT$150;* ☎089 854 702 ext. 3; www.tfrin.gov.tw/TTAR/first/first.htm).

Amis Folk Center
阿美族民俗中心

KM126 marker. 25 Xincun Rd., Xinyi Village, Chenggong. 成功鎮信義里新村路25號. ◉*Open Wed–Mon, 10am–5pm.* ☎089 841 751.

This aborigine center displays traditional crafts and architecture of the area's indigenous people. It is located on the spacious campus of the **East Coast National Scenic Area** headquarters (☎089 841 520 ext. 1800), which has exhibits on local prehistory and culture. The center's wood and thatch-roofed buildings are based on a Japanese ethnographer's observations. Aboriginal dances are performed on weekends.

Dulan Sugar Factory★
都蘭糖廠

KM147 marker. 61 Dulan Village, Donghe 東河鄉都蘭材61號. ☎089 531 702.

Unexpectedly, local artists in this tiny aboriginal village transformed an abandoned industrial building into a creative haven featuring music on Sat-

Dulan Sugar Factory wood carvings

Susannah Rosenblatt/Michelin

GETTING THERE

BY BUS - A couple of buses run between Hualien and Taitung on limited schedules: in Hualien County, Hualien Bus Co. ✆03-833-8146 and in Taitung County, Dingdong Bus coastal line ✆089-333-443.

BY CAR - Car rental available at Hualien's train station. International or Taiwan driver's license usually required. Gas stations near the KM24, 50, 86, 130 and 146 markers.

BY TRAIN - From Taipei, the frequent Tze Chiang express train *(2hr45min; NT$445)* is the fastest way to get to Hualien. There are also slow trains to Hualien *(3hrs 30min; NT$343)*.

GENERAL INFORMATION
AREA CODES

The area code for Hualien is 03 and for Taitung 089. It is not necessary to dial the area code when making a local call. Since non-local calls (for hotel reservations or advance information, for example) and calls made from mobile phones require dialing the area code, it is shown in the telephone numbers in this chapter.

For mobile phones the prefix is 09. Some businesses' contact numbers include mobile phones; you must dial the 09 prefix from anywhere in Taiwan to reach a mobile phone.

VISITOR INFORMATION

There are multiple visitor centers along the route, each with travel information and some with camping facilities. The northernmost **visitor center** (5 Yanliao Village; 鹽寮村大坑5號; open 8:30am–5pm; 20min film in English, Chinese and Japanese; ✆03-867 1326) is south of Hualien at the KM8 marker, inland next to Farglory Ocean Park.

ACCOMMODATIONS

It is possible to **camp** along the coast, but at most sites you need your own tent. The area has plenty of affordable, high quality B&B-style lodgings overlooking the water, and at many places it's possible to drop in without reservations. At the very least, try to call a few hours ahead. *For a selection of lodgings, ⓑsee ADDRESSES below.*

The Amis

Eastern Taiwan is the ancestral home of the Amis people, the island's largest tribe. With more than 170,000 members, Amis make up roughly one-third of Taiwan's aboriginals. Their territory extends from the East Rift Valley, across the coastal mountains to the shore.

In this traditionally matrilineal society, prospective grooms must work in a bride's family home for several years to prove their worth before marriage. Women may reject a husband for being unable to work due to illness or laziness, or failing to help his wife produce a baby girl. Amis society is separated into age-based groups.

The Amis are hunters, gatherers and fishermen. A unique Ami fishing technique, seen at Mataian Ecological Park *(ⓑsee below)*, involves digging a hole topped by a three-layered fish trap. Eels swim into hollowed bamboo tubes on the bottom, crabs and shrimp gather in the sticks in the middle, and fish swim on top. The complex trap becomes a miniature ecosystem before the catch is harvested. Amis celebrate harvest festivals in July and August, after the cultivation of millet. During a village festival, tribe members dance and sing, and shamans summon ancestral spirits. The tribe was briefly in the media when Ami singers sued over use of their original folk song as the theme song for the 1996 Olympics without compensation.

urday nights. The bohemian complex includes an art workshop, a driftwood stage, a homestay, a cafe and a fabulous shop, Good-Buy, selling original work by local artists. Share a cup of tea with the English-speaking proprietor (⏻; ⏱ *shop open daily 10:30am–6pm)*. To the south of town rises **Dulan Mountain** (1,190m/3,904ft), considered sacred by the Puyuma tribe.

Water Running Up 水往上流
KM148 marker. Marked with an English sign.
The water in this irrigation trench appears to flow uphill, defying the laws of gravity at this roadside curiosity.

"Uphill" flowing water

Susannah Rosenblatt/Michelin

Shanyuan Beach 杉原灣
KM154 marker.
A stalled hotel construction site has blocked this 1.5km/0.9mi-long swimming beach for several years. You can still make it down to the golden sand near a temple at the beach's northern end close to White Stone Cow B&B.

Xiaoyeliu 小野柳
KM159 marker. 500 Songjiang Rd., Sec. 1, Taitung City. 台東市松江路一段136號. ⏱ *Open daily 9am–5pm.* ⏿ *089 281 136.*
The weird, imaginatively named formations of sandstone and shale carved by the sea are similar to the more famous

rocks of Yeliu in northern Taiwan. On clear days, you can see Green Island in the distance. There are informative geologic exhibits in English and Chinese as well as camping sites with barbecue pits, restrooms and showers.

Past the KM167 marker, **Taitung** *signals the end of the Highway 11 driving tour, even though the highway continues south to meet Highway 9 near Zhiben Hot Springs.*

ADDRESSES

🏨 STAY

$$ Blue Lagoon B&B 藍色珊瑚礁 – *KM72 marker. 58 Sanfuqiao, Jingpu Village, Fengbin.* 豐濱鄉靜浦村三富橋58號. ⏿ *03 878 1778 or* ⏿ *09 37 622 339. www.bl-hotel.com. 6 rooms.* ⏻. *Breakfast included.* Blue Lagoon is a cream-colored oasis with spacious, contemporary rooms and plentiful views. Accommodating, friendly owner will gladly prepare a reasonably priced dinner of local seafood with advance notice.

$$ Half Moon Bay B&B 半月灣 – *KM36 marker. 98 Jiqi Village, Fengbin.* 豐濱鄉礦碕村98號. ⏿ *09 11 861 731. www.halfmoonbay.com/tw/index_eng.htm. 5 rooms.* ⏻. *Breakfast included. Reservations required.* If this whitewashed, red-roofed B&B were any closer to the ocean, you'd be swimming. Secluded in a rocky sea cove just north of Jici Beach, the sea view rooms have cable, A/C and Internet. One Japanese-style room with tatami mats; two upstairs rooms have a bathroom outside the room. Run by English-speaking retired TV producer.

$$ Moonrise Inn 月昇都蘭景觀民宿 – *KM146.5 marker. Heading south in the village of Dulan, turn right at the second yellow flashing light. Drive 1km to rice paddies. Go uphill and turn left at a y-shaped crossroad. Look for three white rooftops. 30-3 Dulan Village, Donghe.* 東河鄉都蘭村30-3號. ⏿ *089 531 065 or* ⏿ *09 33 519 860. www.moonriseinn.com. 5 rooms.* This eco-friendly inn with solar heating has no TVs or A/C, and the owner requests guests bring their own towels and toothbrushes to conserve resources. Each of five simply decorated rooms has its own color scheme and theme. Wander the landscaped gardens and pond and take in ocean views from the deck.

$$ San Diego Sunrise Mountain Sea View B&B 聖地牙哥山海景日出民宿 – *KM64 marker; turn at the entrance to Shitiwan, the B&B is one of the first buildings along that road. 120 Shitiwan, Fengbin.* 豐濱鄉石梯灣120號. *✆09 32 581 159. www.s1600.com.tw/ocean. 9 rooms. Breakfast included.* Windows seem to wrap all the way around this four-story oceanfront boutique, painted white and ultramarine blue in a color scheme reminiscent of Santorini. Watch the surf crash from crimson couches or your blue tiled bathroom with marble tub. Free bicycles and Wi-Fi.

$$ White Stone Cow B&B 白石牛民宿 – *KM153.5 marker. 30 Shanyuan, Fushan Village, Beinan.* 卑南鄉富山村杉原30號. *✆089 281 688. http://anitahouse. mocoview.com. 8 rooms.* 🍴 *for hotel; credit cards accepted by Western restaurant and bakery on 1st floor. Breakfast included.* Pleasant, plain rooms at this multistory white stucco hotel have large ocean-view balconies with swaying palms beyond. Fresh baked bread and Wi-Fi on 1st floor; stairs down to Shanyuan Beach.

$$-$$$ Hou Hu Garden & Resort 後湖水月– *KM37 marker; heading south, turn right off Hwy. 11 just after the KM37 marker at green sign marked* 後湖19號. *Take this road for 800m/.5mi. Neighborhood 7, 19 Houhu, Jiqi Village, Fengbin.* 豐濱鄉礬碕村7鄰後湖19號. *✆03 871 1295, ✆09 33 799 557. www.houhu.com.tw. 8 rooms. Breakfast included. Western restaurant. Reservations required.* Airy two-story villas look out on a lotus pond, and a unique geometric tent villa has an outdoor soaking tub with ocean views in this valley hideaway. Nap in a hammock among the resort's terraced ponds; pet ducks and dogs wander the private, leafy property near Jici Beach.

🍴 EAT

$ Huting 呼庭 – *KM26.6 marker. Heading south, take the winding road to the left down to the beach. 39-5 Cow Mountain, Shuilian Village, Shoufeng.* 壽豐鄉水璉村牛山39-5號. *✆03 860 1400.* 🍴. *Closes 7pm.* This unusual little spot at Cow Mountain Beach, marked by wooden driftwood signs, is an art studio, cafe and homestay. Pay the NT$50 admission fee (applicable toward a purchase inside), admire the wildly creative sculptures displayed on the hillsides and enjoy a simple **Amis meal** of wild greens, turnip and onion soup, fresh chicken and bamboo shoots while surrounded by wooden carvings. Small **bungalows ($)** are for rent at the former cattle farm; you can also camp and picnic on the grounds for a fee.

$ Marino's Kitchen 馬利諾廚房 – *KM146.2 marker.436-3 Dulan Village, Donghe.* 東河鄉都蘭村463-3號. *✆089 531 848 or ✆09 55 561 722. www.wretch. cc/blog/MRkitchen* 🍴. *Bread and sauces Wed–Fri. Meals Sat noon–7:30pm, Sun noon–5:30pm. Closed Mon–Tue.* A surprising gem, this unassuming corrugated metal cafe on the inland side of Hwy. 11 prepares fresh and flavorful Italian fare on the weekends. American expat couple seasons their pizzas, pastas, soups and homemade sauces with vegetables and herbs they grow nearby, and bake fragrant loaves of cinnamon raisin and pesto olive bread. English menu. **Italian.**

$ Mama Tian's Kitchen 田媽媽廚房 – *KM146.5 marker, on the same turnoff of Hwy. 11 as Moonrise Inn, but close to the highway. 197 Neighborhood 27, Dulan Village, Donghe.* 東河鄉都蘭村27鄰197號. *✆09 55 548 965.* 🍴. *Closed 2pm–5pm & after 8:30pm.* Mama cooks up simple, traditional dishes with whatever ingredients she has that day, whether it's flying fish fried rice or beef fried noodles with savory local mushrooms. **Taiwanese.**

Taitung

One of the largest cities in Eastern Taiwan, Taitung (台東) is bordered by a large forest park to the north and east, the Pacific to the east and is crossed by the Taiping River in the south. Though it doesn't have the star attractions found along Highways 9 and 11, it boasts some important archaeological sites and is a jumping off point for Ludao and Lanyu islands (also known as Green Island and Orchid Island respectively).

VISIT

The city, one of the newest in Taiwan, is situated between the mountains and the sea, and has a relatively mild climate with near-constant sun. With about 110,000 residents, Taitung is sparsely populated compared to other cities in Taiwan, but is a true melting pot of Han Chinese, Taiwanese, Hakka and indigenous cultures.

Tribal decorations on schools and businesses and major festivals in town hint at the large aboriginal population, particularly the Ami tribe. Rather than industry, the region is dominated by lots of farms growing fruit, rice and betelnut trees, among other crops. In terms of food, Taitung offers a mix of Taiwanese fare, aboriginal cooking and international flavors.

▶ **Population:** 110,000
🕐 **Michelin Map:** p313.
📋 **Info:** ☎089 357 131; www.taitung.gov.tw/en. Taitung County Visitors Assn. ☎089 323 987.
📍 **Location:** The main street Zhongshan Road leads diagonally east from the train station and flanking bus stations. The airport lies 1.5km/.9mi northwest.
👪 **Kids:** Prehistoric rhinos at the Museum of Prehistory.
🕐 **Timing:** Allow one day for a visit here.

SIGHTS

Taitung Railway Art Village
台東鐵道藝術村
371 Tiehua Rd., downtown. 鐵花路371號. ☎089 334 999. www.ttrav.org.
Taitung's old train station downtown near Mount Liyu now displays art, hosts theater productions and attracts joggers and walkers.

Taitung Fruit Market 水果市場
A few blocks northeast of the Railway Art Village, downtown.
The city is known for its delicious fruit harvest—particularly creamy, sweet Buddha head fruit—available in color-

Exhibit, Museum of Prehistory

Susannah Rosenblatt/Michelin

GETTING THERE

BY AIR - Regional carriers Mandarin Airlines and Uni Air make a combined five flights daily from Taipei to Taitung Fongnian Airport *(Mandarin Airlines ☎089 362 669. Uni Air ☎089 362 625; both carriers NT$2,238 one way; 50min).* Taitung's airport is also the departure point for Daily Air Corp. flights to Green or Orchid Islands. The airport *(Taitung airport ☎089 361 111; www. tta.gov.tw)* is located about 7km/4mi west of the city center.

You can rent a car or scooter outside Taitung's pleasant airport, which has gift shops, a waterfall and flowering plants.

BY TRAIN - About 14 express or local trains make the 5.5hr to 7.5hr journey between Taipei and Taitung each day *(NT$700-NT$800).* Taitung's train station is located 10min north of city center.

At the train station, car rental offices include Pony Rent-A-Car *(☎089 340 688)* and CarPlus *(☎089 227 979).* In some cases renting a car requires a Taiwanese driver's license.

GETTING AROUND

BY BUS - The Dingdong Bus travels through town and around the region, and stops regularly at the airport and train station *(☎089 333 443).*

BY CAR
🚗See BY TRAIN opposite for car rental companies.

BY TAXI - There are taxis at both Taitung's airport and the train station.

GENERAL INFORMATION

ACCOMMODATIONS

The city offers a variety of lodgings for all budgets. *For a selection of local accommodations, 🚗see ADDRESSES below.*

VISITOR INFORMATION

Visitor centers can be found at the Taitung's airport *(☎089 362 476)*, the new train station *(☎089 238 231)*, and the old train station in the south part of town *(369 Tiehua Rd. 鐵花路369號; ☎089 359 085).* All visitor centers are open daily 9am–5pm.

---

ful piles along Zhengqi Road (正氣路) between Boai (博愛) and Guangming (光明) Roads.

👥 Museum of Prehistory★ 國立臺灣史前文化博物館

1 Museum Rd. 博物館路1號, near the airport. 🕐*Open Tue–Sun 9am–5pm.* 🕐*Closed Chinese New Year's Eve & Day. NT$80, children NT$50. ☎089 381 166. http://en.nmp.gov.tw.*

Don't miss this kid-friendly archaeological museum located near the airport. Ancient relics, including pottery, spearheads, coffins, jade jewelry and tools are on display. Opened in 2002, the museum explains Taiwan's natural history as well as the culture of prehistoric Austronesian peoples and today's indigenous tribes. Workers digging a railway station in 1980 stumbled upon thousands of Neolithic-era slate coffins, human

remains and other artifacts. Construction was halted and excavation began. The museum has colorful exhibits and videos in English and Chinese. Life-size **models**★ of prehistoric elephants and rhinos in the Ice Age area *(2nd floor)* are worth a look. View the short **film** about monkeys shown on the human evolution ramp that goes down the museum's middle. Kids can push buttons to make tectonic plates crash into one another upstairs or assemble shards of "ancient" plastic pottery in the **scientific archaeology gallery** *(basement level).*

A large **garden** out back features a playground, maze and dancing fountain.

Beinan Cultural Park 卑南文化公園

200 Cultural Park Rd. 文化公園路 200號. 🕐*Open Tue–Sun 9am–5pm.* 🕐*Closed Chinese New Year's Eve and Day. NT$30. ☎089 233 466.*

Zhiben hot springs

Susannah Rosenblatt/Michelin

This nearby park, close to Taitung's train station, is connected with the prehistory museum. Taiwan's first archaeological park is an active dig site, the largest to feature slate slab coffins in the Pacific Rim.

Walk among the lawns and lotus pond, and see a view of the city from the observation deck. Anthropological exhibits are in Chinese.

Taitung Forest Park
台東森林公園

North of downtown at the end of Zhongshan Rd. (中山路). Entrance at Mahengheng Ave. (馬亨亨大道).

This natural space on the edge of town spans a forest crisscrossed with bike paths, a lake and a coastal recreation area.

EXCURSION
Zhiben★

◗ *17km/10.6mi southwest of Taitung via Hwy. 11. www.jhihben.com.tw. Dingdong Co. buses run to Zhiben from Taitung, or to drive takes 25-30min.*

Highway 11 ends at Zhiben's famous **hot springs** (知本溫泉區), one of the oldest, and a good place for a soak in spite of overdevelopment and weekend crowds. The resort area is situated in the Zhiben River Valley and bordered by green mountains.

At the turn of the 19C, Zhiben served as a getaway for Japanese military during the country's occupation of Taiwan.

The clear, odorless calcium carbonate water drew bathers then as now for its purported healthful properties. The main drag, **Longquan Road** (龍泉路), runs along the Zhiben River. All of Zhiben's spring water is tapped, available through hotels and public baths; many places allow daytrippers to pay for a soak. Recommended hotels to take a dip include:

Hotel Royal Chihpen 知本老爺大酒店 *– Lane 113, 23 Longquan Rd. 龍泉路113巷23號. ℘089 510 666. www.hotel-royal-chihpen.com.tw.*

This upscale hot springs hotel is perfect for families with young children, as six of 182 rooms are themed for kids. There are also springs-fed soaking tubs, play areas and a pool. Non-guests can use the public springs for NT$350.

Rainbow Resort 泓泉溫泉渡假村 *– Lane 139, 1 Longquan Rd. 龍泉路139巷1號. ℘089 510 150 ext. 9. www.rainbow-hotel.com.tw.*

This hot-springs hotel, with its own underground well, has outdoor pools and a spring-water cooking station.

The area dead-ends at the 110ha/272-acre 🏕 **Zhiben Forest Recreation Area** (知本國家森林遊樂區), with trails, a suspension bridge, a waterfall and giant Banyan trees (*290 Longquan Rd. 龍泉路290號;* ◷ *open daily 7am–5pm; NT$80, weekends NT$100, students with ID NT$50;* ℘089 510 961; http://trail.forest.gov.tw).

ADDRESSES

STAY

$ Taitung Aboriginal Culture Hotel 台東縣原住民文化會館 – *10 Zhongshan Rd.* 中山路10號. ☏*089 340 605. www.tac-hotel.com.tw. 23 rooms.* Across the street from Taitung's Forest Park, this budget hotel has attractive aboriginal decorative touches. You'll find rather spartan rooms for 2, 3, 4, 5 or 10 people.

$ Taitung Hostel for Teachers & Public Workers 台東縣公教會館 – *19 Nanjing Rd.* 南京路19號. ☏*089 310 142. www.ttp-hotel.com.tw. 88 rooms. Breakfast included.* Offering discounts to Taiwan civil servants, this busy, affordable hotel (the "hostel" name is underselling the accommodations) will meet budget travelers' needs. Conveniently located in a cultural plaza near the Railway Art Village and Taitung's fruit market, beds in the seven-story, balcony-lined brick building can fill up. Free bikes, Internet.

$ Taitung Traveler Hotel/Hostel 台東旅行家商務會館 – *42 Anqing St.* 安慶街42號. ☏*089 326 456. www.travelerhotel.com.tw. 51 rooms. Breakfast included.* This plain hotel sitting in downtown Taitung near the fruit market is a good value, with a choice of dormitories, double rooms and single rooms. Guests are provided bikes and other travel assistance.

$$ Apple Hotel 蘋果飯店 – *857 Zhonghua Rd., Sec. 1.* 中華路一段857號. ☏*089 318 928. www.apple-hotel.com.tw. 46 rooms. Breakfast included.* A dash of big-city sophistication on Taiwan's slower paced East Coast, the remodeled Apple Hotel has a crimson-colored lounge and bar and simple, pleasant rooms. Guests are offered free bikes and cycling tours.

$$ Hotel Kindness 康橋商旅 – *Lane 209, 16 Zhongxing Rd. Sec. 1* 中興路一段209巷16號. ☏*089 229 226. www.kindness-hotel.com.tw. 90 rooms. Breakfast included.* A grande dame with a marble-tiled lobby, this classically styled business hotel in the north of the city comes with all the modern conveniences including free bikes, Wi-Fi and a midnight snack.

$$$$ Formosa Naruwan Hotel 娜路彎大酒店 – *66 Lianhang Rd.* 連航路66號. ☏*089 239 666. www.naruwan-hotel.com.tw. 276 rooms. Non-smoking. Breakfast included. Buffet, Chinese restaurant and cafe.* For a more luxurious overnight stay, the Formosa Naruwan Hotel has decor featuring geometric aboriginal motifs. The extensive property has a capacious pool, spa, deluxe rooms with outdoor baths and hosts Amis and Puyuma tribal dance shows nightly at the theater on-site. Yellow signs around town direct you there.

⚊/EAT

$ Beinan Bun 卑南包仔店 – *182 Gengsheng North Rd.* 更生北路182號. ☏*089 231 455. www.backpackerbun.com.tw.* 🚫. *Closes at 5pm.* These steaming pockets of pork, vegetables, taro or cinnamon raisin sell out in the afternoons. Line up to get 'em while they're hot. **Taiwanese.**

$ Lao Dongtai Mitaimu 老東台米台目 – *134 Zhengqi Rd.* 正氣路134號. ☏*089 348 952. Lunch Sat-Sun only.* 🚫. This lively little downtown noodle shop has been doling out savory bowls of steaming rice noodle soup with egg for half a century. **Taiwanese.**

$$ Mibanai 米巴奈 – *470 Chuanguang Rd.* 傳廣路470號. ☏*089 220 336. www.mibanai.com.tw.* An inviting Amis restaurant with an indigenous statue out front. Serves aboriginal specialties such as roast wild boar meat and grilled bamboo shoots and caters to groups. **Taiwanese.**

Apple Hotel lounge

Susannah Rosenblatt/Michelin

Highway 9 ★

Just west of Highway 11's stirring coastal traverse, the parallel Highway 9 traces an inland course through the scenic East Rift Valley, a rural expanse filled with green peaks and greener farms, aboriginal villages and a bounty of natural hot springs. Much of the route is encompassed by the East Rift Valley National Scenic Area, bounded by the Central Mountain Range to the west and the Coastal Mountain Range to the east and stretching from Taitung north to Hualien along the Mugua River. Taiwan's rice basket, the valley is home to fruit, tea and dairy farms. Many farmers growing rice and tea, among other crops, cater to tourists looking for a day in the country. Farmland in the south gives way to forests in the north.

THE REGION

There are several major parks and forest areas along the route that don't receive many visitors, plus concentrations of butterflies, day lilies and rare birds. Three major rivers rushing down from the mountains divide the valley. The island's premier rafting venue is located at Ruisui, positioned roughly midway down the valley, along the Xiuguluan River, where adventurers flock. Paragliding over rolling green farmland is also popular.

Indigenous culture is a major part of the region's identity. The area has large concentrations of Amis, Bunun, Puyuma, Truku, Sakizaya and Sediq people, who call the valley home. Bunun Farm has an aboriginal restaurant and a coffee shop, and many of the hot-springs resorts and hotels have cafes and restaurants.

🚗 DRIVING TOUR

173km/108mi from Taitung north to Hualien via Hwy. 9. Allow 1–2 days.

Note: bring a change of clothes if you plan to white-water raft at Ruisui. Kilometer markers correspond to the full extent of

👍 **Michelin Map:** p313.
👍 *See also www.erv-nsa.gov. tw/images/allmap_en.jpg.*

ℹ **Info:** The southernmost visitor center of the East Rift Valley Scenic Area (花東縱谷國家風景區) is in Luye, 28km/17mi north of Taitung at 46 Gaotai Rd. 鹿野鄉永安村高台路46號 (🕐 *open daily 8:30am–12:30pm & 1:30pm–5:30pm.* 📞 *089-551 637. www.erv-nsa.gov.tw or www.lyee.gov.tw).* Three more visitor centers are along the route. Many sights are signed in English.

▶ **Location:** This inland highway runs between Taitung and Hualien though the East Rift Valley, which is flanked by the Central and Coastal mountain ranges.

👪 **Kids:** Ice Age elephant and rhino at Taitung's Museum of Prehistory. Pony rides at Chu Lu Ranch.

🕐 **Timing:** Rafting season is April to October. The orange day lilies on Sixty Stone Mountain bloom in August and September, overlapping with the Ami tribe's annual Harvest Festival *(Jul–Aug).* Chilly, damp winters when oilseed rape flowers bloom are best for a hot springs soak.

👁 **Don't Miss:** Hiking amid monkeys in Yushan National Park, butterflies and fireflies in Fuyuan Forest Recreation Area, also known as Butterfly Valley Resort.

Highway 9, which runs nearly the length of the island.

👪 **Chu Lu Ranch** 初鹿牧場
18km/11mi northwest of Taitung off Hwy. 9. 1 Muchang, Neighborhood

28, Mingfeng Village, Beinan. 卑南鄉
明峰村28鄰牧場1號. ⏰*Open daily
8am–5pm. NT$100.* 📞*089 571 002.
www.chururanch.com.*
Pastures dotted with grazing black
and white dairy cows set against the
mountains: you're a long way from Taipei. The 70ha/173acre ranch is famous
for its milk. City kids can get a taste of
country life by feeding grass to the cattle or watching the afternoon milking.
Don't miss the ice cream.

Bunun Leisure Farm
布農部落休閒農場

*25km/15.5mi northwest of Taitung.
Neighborhood 11, 191 Taoyuan Village,
Yanping.* 延平鄉桃源村11鄰191號.
⏰*Open daily 7am–10pm. NT$150
($100 of which is applicable toward a
purchase).* 📞*089 561 211 ext. 210.
www.bunun.org.tw.*
Progressive pastor Bai Guang-sheng
envisioned revitalizing a community of
undereducated and low-income indigenous people. Under his leadership, a
Bunun ethnotourism industry, administered by the **Bunun Cultural and Educational Foundation** 布農文教基金
會, developed near Yanping. The tribal
village has transformed into a self-suf-
ficient community, with ethnotourism
boosting the local economy, creating
jobs and promoting culture.

The site holds a theater where regular song and dance performances are
staged, a weaving area and art center,
plus eateries and accommodations.

Luye Tea Highlands
鹿野茶高台

28km/17mi north of Taitung, in Luye.
(🌿*see visitor center information,
opposite, under Info).*
Taiwan is known for its delicate oolong
teas, and the government-sponsored
tea growing area here is a great place
to sample brews. There are plenty of
teahouses in which to sit and enjoy
a leisurely cup of tea, before or after
exploring family-run plantations and
breathing in that heady aroma.
The town of Luye is also known as a scenic launch for paragliders, and boasts
geological oddities such as mud "volcanoes" that burp out natural gas.
From Luye to Guanshan, the highway
parallels the **Beinan River** on its west
side in places.
North of Guanshan, the **South Cross
Island Highway** (Hwy. 20) ends at Highway 9. Completed in the early 1970s, this
highway—a curvy, white-knuckle route
through the mountains—links the East
Coast with the West at Tainan. In 2009
Typhoon Morakot heaped much damage on the road and its surroundings;
some sections may still be closed.

Aboriginal performance, Bunun Leisure Farm

Susannah Rosenblatt/Michelin

GETTING AROUND

BY CAR - Having a car is preferable (or scooter or even a bicycle). You can begin the journey either north in Hualien or south in Taitung, although Hualien is more convenient to Taipei. Rent a car or scooter or even hire a taxi for the day by the Hualien train station. Many car rental companies require an international driver's license (*see car rental information in Hualien, above*).

BY BUS - Dingdong Bus (*089 328 269 or 089 333 023*), Hualien Bus Co. (*03 833 8146; www1.hl.gov.tw/bus*) and Guoguang Motor Transport (*089 343 159, www.kingbus.com.tw*) provide service through the area, but buses don't stop at every village. Yuli Township (玉里鎮), near the entrance to Yushan National Park, is reachable by train and bus.

BY TRAIN - A train runs through the valley and makes many stops, including Yuli; board at Hualien or Taitung.

GENERAL INFORMATION

VISITOR INFORMATION

The East Rift Valley National Scenic Area (花東縱谷國家風景區) has visitor centers scattered along the Highway 9; its website (*www.erv-nsa.gov.tw*) has helpful information. *See Info above for visitor center*. Its headquarters are located at 168 Xinghe Rd., Sec. 2, Neighborhood 17 in Hegang Village, Ruisui. 瑞穗鄉鶴岡村17鄰興鶴路二段168號. Open 8:30am–5:30pm; *03 887 5306.

ACCOMMODATIONS

Like the coast, this mountain area has many affordable, pleasant B&B-style accommodations, more than can be listed here. *For a selection, see ADDRESSES below*.

Sixty Stone Mountain 六十石山
76km/47mi north of Taitung, just north of Fuli 玉里鎮.

In August and September, this hillside explodes with an orange carpet of day-lilies, grown for cooking. Sixty Stone Mountain sits 8km/5mi up the switch-backs of Chanye Road. Flower-themed pavilions with postcard views of farmland dot hilltops.

Butterfly, Fuyuan Forest

Susannah Rosenblatt/Michelin

Antong Hot Springs 安通溫泉
81km/50mi north of Taitung.

Another famous Hualien County hot spring, Antong offers clear, 66°C/150°F waters but the unpleasant smell of hydrogen sulfide is noticeable. The hot springs lie 8km/5mi south of Yuli. Hotels in the area use the potable water to brew coffee.

Just outside Yuli near Highway 9's KM294 marker, head west on **Highway 18**, to Yushan National Park for a hike or a leg stretch.

After 8km/5mi, stop at **Nanan Visitor Center** (南安遊客中心; *open daily 9am–4:30pm; closed 2nd Tue of month, or the following day, if Tue a holiday. *03 888 7560; www.ysnp.gov.tw).

Yushan National Park★ 玉山國家公園
Open year-round daily.

This park is named for **Yushan**, or **Jade Mountain★★**, the highest peak in Taiwan at 3,952m/12,966ft. Another 2km/1.2mi past the Nanan Visitor Center, **Nanan Waterfall★** cas-

Jade Mountain

© Nigel Hicks/NHPA/Photoshots

cades down 50m/164ft; in summer, the pools below are a favored swimming hole. Beyond the falls 4km/2.5mi, the **Walami Trail**, bordered by foliage filled with squirrels and monkeys, stretches 14km/8.8mi to Walami, where a solar-powered cabin can sleep 30 people *(apply for cabin permit at the visitor center)*.

Yuli Township 玉里鎮

This town has several rustic hotels. One option for soaking is the **An-Tong Hot Spring Hotel** 安通溫泉飯店*(36 Wen-quan Rd. 溫泉路36號; ℘03 888 6108; www.an-tong-com.tw)*.

Ruisui 瑞穗

103km/65mi north of Taitung.

Ruisui is the biggest draw in the East Rift Valley. Visitors come seasonally *(Apr–Oct)* to raft the **Xiuguluan River** (秀姑巒溪). In June a rafting race is held. The river is eastern Taiwan's longest, flowing 103km/64mi to the Pacific Ocean from the mountain that shares its name. With more than 20 sets of rapids, the 22.5km/14mi river ride from Ruisui to **Changhong Bridge** *(4hrs)* passes through gorges of the Coastal Mountains and by the aboriginal village of Qimei. Raft trips *(about NT$750)* and camp sites are available from Ruisui Rafting Service Center *(瑞穗泛舟服*

Sixty Stone Mountain

Susannah Rosenblatt/Michelin

務中心; 215 Zhongshan Rd., Sec. 3; 中
山路三段215號; ⏱open Jun–Aug daily
6am–3pm; rest of the year hours vary;
&03 887 5400).

A few miles west of town, the pools of
Ruisui Hot Springs (瑞穗溫泉), tinted
an orangey brown due to iron content,
contain alkaline sodium carbonate.
Just-married couples frequent these
48°C/118°F springs, believing a soak
will help the wife bear a baby boy. The
Japanese first built baths in Ruisui in the
early 20C, and an aging hotel from that
era is still open, the **Ruisui Hot Springs
Villa** (瑞穗溫泉山莊; 23 Hongye Village,
Wanrong;. 萬榮鄉紅葉村23號; &03 887
2170; www.js-hotspring.com.tw).

Fuyuan Forest Recreation
Area★ 富源國家森林游樂區

119km/74mi north of Taitung. 161
Guangdong Rd., Fuyuan. 富源村廣東
路161號. ⏱Open daily 8am–10pm.
NT$100 (NT$60/car). &03 881 2377.
www.bvr.com.tw.

Now privately owned, this forest zone
has been dubbed **Butterfly Valley
Resort**, featuring pricey villas and hot
springs. Filled with camphor trees, the
woods west of Fuyuan Village come alive
with butterflies and fireflies in spring
and summer. Nearly 100 kinds of butterflies appear between March and August.
The 191ha/472-acre site has the largest
camphor forest on the island.

Hualien Sugar Factory
花蓮糖廠

125km/77mi north of Taitung. 19
Tangchang St., Dajin Village, Guangfu.
光復鄉大進村糖廠街19號. ⏱Open
daily 8am–8pm. &03 870 0693.
www.hualiensugar.com.tw.

Established during Japanese occupation, this factory has weathered a colonial government, World War II bombing
and finally, closure in 2002. Japanese-
style employee bungalows made with
Chinese cypress still stand. The factory
now has bike paths and serves deli-
ciously rich ice cream.

Mataian Ecological Park
馬太鞍濕地

Across the road from Hualien
Sugar Factory.

A 12ha/30-acre wetland fed by underground springs and the Fudeng River,
Mataian is home to Amis who have
been fishing here for generations. The
nature preserve at the foot of Mount
Masi is an ecotourism destination with
bike and walking trails. **Shin-Liu Farm**
(欣綠農園) offers local vegetables and
fish prepared the traditional Amis way
in its restaurant; overnight lodgings
available (60 Daquan St., Daquan Village, Guangfu. 光復鄉大全村大全街
60號; &03 870 1861or &09 31 265 898;
www.shin-liu.com).

Mataian Ecological Park

Susannah Rosenblatt/Michelin

Swan boats, Liyu Lake

Susannah Rosenblatt/Michelin

Lintianshan Forestry Park
林田山林業文化園區
136km/85mi north of Taitung, off Hwy. 9 along Hwy. 16. Lane 99, 99 Linsen Rd., Senrong Village, Fenglin 鳳林鎮森榮里林森路99巷99號.
🕐*Open Wed–Mon 9am–5pm.*
📞*03 875 2378.*

Once a booming logging town, the settlement of loggers gradually disappeared over the years. Peek inside a trove of well-preserved historic Japanese buildings and view impressive wood sculpture.

Liyu Lake 鯉魚潭
164km/102mi north of Taitung. 100 Huantan N. Rd., Chinan Village, Shoufeng 壽豐鄉池南村環潭北路100號. 🕐*Open daily 8:30am–5:30pm.*
📞*03 864 1691.*

🚶 Liyu, or Carp, Lake, is a family-friendly locale where daytrippers can walk or bike the 4.4km/2.7mi road ringing the lake or paddle across its calm waters. Hiking trails scale nearby Liyu Mountain; fireflies sparkle in late spring and early summer. There's a commercially run **campground** at the southern end of

Betelnut

Visitors to rural Taiwan are sure to notice fetching young women dressed in short shorts or dresses, sitting in brightly lit glass boxes. These are the betelnut princesses, or *binlang xishi*, named after a legendary beauty from ancient China. The women are selling a product that is entirely legal: a mildly intoxicating nut that is so popular among rural residents that is sometimes called Taiwan chewing gum.

Before it is served, the bittersweet, marble-sized nut is cut, and white lime paste is inserted into the crack. The taste is unique: after a satisfying sharp crunch and some initial grassy notes, the flavor turns sweet, with a hint of licorice and a touch of bitterness. Next the mouth floods with saliva, and a satisfying rosy glow ensues, courtesy of the active agent, arecoline, an alkaloid related to nicotine and caffeine.

Betelnut use is not without controversy. The teeth, gums, and lips of long-term users are stained a deep red, and overuse is associated with mouth and throat cancers. It is also an environmental scourge. As hillsides are cleared of native growth and planted in betelnut, sometimes illegally, they become prone to erosion, due to the dangerous combination of deforested terrain, steep hillsides, and frequent typhoons. Yet *binlang* remains very much a part of local culture, and plantations of the thin, 10m/33ft-tall betelnut palm trees are as much a feature of Taiwan as the glass-boxed beauties themselves.

the lake (*90 Chihnan Rd., Sec. 2, Chinan Village, Shoufeng.* 壽豐鄉池南村池南路二段90號. ☎*03 865 5678; cabins NT$800-NT$1,000).*

▶ *End the driving tour in* **Hualien***, 17km/10.5mi farther.*

ADDRESSES

🛏 STAY

$ Good Friends Homestay 好朋友民宿 – *Lane 161, 5 Zhongshan Rd., Sec. 2, Ruisui.* 瑞穗鄉中山路二段161巷5號. ☎*09 10 522 722 or 09 37 169 880. 4 rooms.* 🍽. *Breakfast included.* Minutes from the rafting center, this multistory B&B has basic, clean rooms with mattresses on the floor. Free bikes; owner leads bicycle tours of the region.

$$ Red Gable Homestay 漱石山居 – *89 Shuiyuan Rd., Fenglin.* 鳳林鎮水源路89號. ☎*03 876 0815 or 09 12 517 236. www.suh.com.tw. 6 rooms. Breakfast included.* Tucked into the mountains and kept by an incredibly gracious hostess, Red Gable is a pleasant base for exploring the northern East Rift Valley. The secluded yard features lotus pond and patios with a loud chorus of frogs.

$$ Wisdom Garden Homestay 智嵐雅居 – *KM289.4 marker. 98-1 Suangan, Dayu Village, Yuli.* 玉里鎮大禹里酸柑98-1號. *www.wisdom-garden.com/index_e.html. 7 rooms. Breakfast included.* Close to Yushan National Park hikes and rafting at Ruisui, this thoughtfully appointed haven is a retreat after the day's adventures. The proprietor was inspired by a pastoral work of Chinese poet Tou Yuan Ming; she also created much of the calligraphy and paintings decorating Wisdom Garden.

$$ Lianji Teahouse 連記民宿 – *100 Gaotai Rd., Yongan Village, Luye.* 鹿野鄉永安村高台路100號. ☎*089 550 707. www.lc550808.com.tw. 5 rooms.* 🍽. *Breakfast included.* This Zen-styled B&B is a relaxing getaway where Taiwan tea reigns supreme. The owner is a tea enthusiast happy to educate guests about tea tradition. Tours provided.

$$$$ Promised Land Resort & Lagoon 理想大地渡假飯店 – *1 Lixiang Rd., Shoufeng.* 壽豐鄉理想路1號. Spa ☎*03 865 6789. www.plcresort. com.tw. 240 rooms. Western and Chinese restaurants.* A Spanish-themed compound with enough to keep the kids entertained for days. Lush landscaping surrounds horseback riding trails, bicycle paths, a boating lagoon, a giant pool with waterslides, a bar and a full-service spa. Finely decorated rooms come with balconies, bathrobes, and dumplings upon arrival.

🍴 EAT

$ Cifadahan Café 紅瓦屋老地方文化美食餐廳 – *16 Lane 62 Daquan St., Daquan Village, Guangfu.* 光復鄉大全村大全街62巷16號. ☎*03 870 4601. www.cifadahan.58168.net. Closes 8pm.* At the Mataian Ecological Park stands a red-roofed Amis restaurant stuffed with aboriginal carvings. An indigenous family prepares local wild vegetables, like edible tree fungus, meats and seafood. **Taiwanese.**

$$ Moonhouse Restaurant 月廬 – *71 Fengwu 1st Rd., Fenglin.* 鳳林鎮鳳鳴一路71號. ☎*03 876 2206. http://moon house.cm-media.com.tw.* 🍽. *Closes 9pm. Follow the blue and white signs off Hwy. 9 at the KM235.5 marker on a nearly 5km/ 3mi scenic drive.* Hakka food served in a beautiful rustic wood-cabin setting; don't miss the succulent duck. **Hakka.**

$$ Elaine's Restaurant 依蓮廳 – *In the Fuyuan Forest Recreation Area. 161 Guangdong Rd., Fuyuan Village, Ruisui.* 瑞穗鄉富源村廣東路161號. ☎*03 881 2377. Closes 9pm.* Elegant Taiwanese and Italian cuisine with live music and dancing during the buffet dinner. Breakfast, lunch and dinner served. **Taiwanese and Italian**.

Green Island★★

Of the two eastern islands, Green Island (綠島)—Ludao in Mandarin—is the more tourist-friendly (and crowded). Its claim to fame is its saltwater hot springs, one of only three in the world. Lying 33km/20.5mi off the main island of Taiwan, Green Island is also known for underwater pursuits: summer crowds descend to snorkel and dive. The warm waters of the Kuroshio Current help cultivate the island's riotously colorful reefs. With an area of only 16sq km/10sq mi, the island finds its shores and tropical rain forests constantly battered by ocean winds, resulting in a dramatic coast ringed with often-deserted beaches.

A BIT OF HISTORY

The first inhabitants of the volcanic isle are believed to have arrived about 4,000 years ago; Han Chinese settlers came by fishing boat in 1803. The island is now home to about 3,000. Green Island was originally known as "Fire-burned Island" because, according to one tale, the hillsides appeared aflame when lit by crimson sunsets. After the end of Japanese occupation, the Taiwanese government dubbed it Green Island. In the 20C Japanese colonial rulers built a fish-processing factory here, and a few decades ago the breeding of Sika deer spiked in popularity.

▶ **Population:** 3,300.

Michelin Map: p313.

Info: Green Island visitor center (綠島遊客中心) is across from the airport. 298 Nanliao Village. 南寮村298號. ☏089 672 026. Open daily 9am–5pm.

Location: 33km/20.5mi east of Taitung, Green Island is compact, just 16.2sq km/10sq mi large. The lone 19km/11.8mi road ringing the island can be bicycled (or even walked) in a day. Near the harbor and the airport, Nanliao Village is the island's busy commercial center; to the north is the calmer Gongguan Village.

Kids: Youngsters might enjoy exploring the Green Island Lighthouse or splashing on one of several swimming beaches.

Timing: In summertime Green Island is packed with vacationers, so opt for spring or fall when it's cooler and less crowded.

Don't Miss: Green Island Human Rights Culture Park, Jhaorih Hot Springs, snorkeling or diving.

Pekingese Dog Rock

Susannah Rosenblatt/Michelin

Green Island Lighthouse

Sesannah Rosenblatt/Michelin

Yet in spite of the cheerful beachcombing vibe, the island's recent history is a troubled one. The isle once served as a political prison where citizens critical of the ruling Kuomintang Party's martial law were sent—and in some cases tortured and executed. Today this jail, dubbed **Oasis Villa**, has been turned into a moving memorial to human rights.

A single 19km/11.8mi road circumnavigates Green Island; it takes about half an hour to circle the entire route by scooter or at least half a day on a bike. **Nanliao Village** (南寮村) is the island's

Oasis Villa

Susannah Rosenblatt/Michelin

commercial hub, lined with hotels and most of the island's restaurants. Besides seafood, ample venison is available, a remnant of the once-thriving deer-breeding industry. The other major village is the quieter **Gongguan Village** (公館村) on the island's north face.

SIGHTS
Sights below are presented clockwise around the island.

🏛️👤 Green Island Lighthouse
綠島燈塔

A natural first stop located just past the airport, this lighthouse is a 33m/108ft tall gift. The US financed the construction of the landmark in 1938 after the US luxury liner *S.S. President Hoover* ran aground on reefs offshore during a storm, and locals bravely dispatched boats to ferry passengers to safety. The lighthouse was later damaged by bombing during World War II and repaired by the KMT in 1948.

Green Island Prison 綠島監獄
Gift shop 🕐*Open daily 8am–5:30pm.*
This squat white building holds an operational, maximum-security prison, completed in 1972, that houses 160 inmates. Oddly, you can visit the prison gift shop to purchase a ceramic coaster or sand art made by those inside.

Green Island Human Rights Culture Park★★
綠島人權文化區
🕐*Open May–Sept daily 8am–6pm, Oct–Apr daily 8:30am–5pm.* 📞*089 671 095. http://gicp.nat.gov.tw.*
This seaside complex includes two former prisons and a **memorial wall** commemorating political dissidents imprisoned during Taiwan's "White Terror" (👀 *see History in the Introduction*). One political prison, ironically called "Oasis Villa" (綠洲山莊), housed thousands of inmates, some of whom were held for decades, tortured or executed. Oasis Villa was operational from 1972 until the end of Taiwan's martial law in 1987. Etched on the monument, first unveiled in 1999, are the words of writer Bo Yang

GETTING THERE

BY AIR - Air service connects Taitung and Green Island. Daily Air Corp. operates three flights a day from Taitung Airport (✆089 362 489; NT$1028 one-way; 12min). Seats in the 19-seat planes fill up in summer, so reserve ahead. Green Island Airport (綠島機場; ✆089 671 261) is located in the northwest corner of the island, about 1km/.6mi north of Nanliao Village.

BY FERRY - Many ferries ply the waters between Fugang Harbor, just north of Taitung, and Green Island's Nanliao Harbor every few hours (one-way about NT$400; 50min). The waters, particularly in winter, can be rough. Many of the ferries continue on to Orchid Island (about 2hrs). Companies in Fugang Harbor include *Kaihsuan Transport* ✆089 281 047; *Star of Green Island* ✆089 280 226; *Super Star* ✆089 280 290; *Venus* ✆089 281 477.

GETTING AROUND

BY BUS - A bus circles the island (daily 8am–5pm). It makes each of 13 stops about every hour or you can wave the driver down; a daily ticket for unlimited rides is NT$100, available at the visitor center.

BY CAR - Automobiles aren't readily available on the island.

BY TWO WHEEL - Scooters are the most common way to get around Green Island and rent for about NT$400 a day; they are in demand in summer. Be sure to fill up at the gas station by the ferry pier. Rental shops for both bikes and scooters are concentrated in Nanliao Village, and the visitor center, or most any lodging, can help you find a ride.

ON FOOT - The island is small enough that you can walk to many destinations.

OTHER TRANSPORT

An established local tour company, Green Island Adventures, rents **cars and golf carts** to non-scooter riders, and offers tour packages for destinations all over Taiwan (✆09 72 065 479; www.greenisland adventures.com).

GENERAL INFORMATION

ACCOMMODATIONS

In summer it's crowded and easy to arrange lodging, meals, scooter rentals and activities, although weekends can fill up so it's best to book in advance during the high season. *For a selection of lodgings, 🛏see ADDRESSES.*

VISITOR INFORMATION

The Green Island **visitor center** is directly across from the airport (綠島遊客中心; ◷open daily 8:30am–5pm; ✆089 672 026). Staff there can help arrange hotels, camping reservations and dive trips.

Many hotels offer rentals and tours, and aquatic adventure shops abound in Nanliao Village. Snorkel tour operators are accustomed to outfitting **snorkelers** in wetsuits and life jackets and guiding them in a group clutching a life-preserver rope. If you're envisioning a more independent swimming excursion, let your tour guide know.

---

who was incarcerated for nine years here. The padded, solitary confinement cells are chilling.

Opened to the public in 2002, the restored Oasis Villa contains poignant art and historical exhibits; a film is also shown (in Chinese). New Life Correctional Center, a hard labor camp for political prisoners open from 1951 to 1965, stands next door.

Guanyin Cave 觀音洞

Around a southerly bend in the island's ring road, this cave is marked with a red and white arch. According to local lore, an unexplained light beaming from the limestone cave guided a fisherman lost at sea to shore. Residents searched for the source of the light, and came upon the cave containing a stalagmite resembling **Guanyin**, the goddess of Mercy

Entrance, Guanyin Cave

Susannah Rosenblatt/Michelin

sitting atop a lotus. The cave, which contains an underground river, remains a holy site today.

A snack stand sells venison fried rice and venison noodle soup, ice cream and sunglasses.

Youzihu 柚子湖

A winding road leads down to the stone ruins of a former aboriginal village, now abandoned and exposed to the elements. Stop by the sea cave.

Pekingese Dog and Sleeping Beauty Rocks★
哈巴狗與睡美人

Here, a 300m/984ft path up from the road, named Little Great Wall (小長城步道) after the slightly longer one on the mainland, leads to a pagoda with **views**★★ of Haishenping Bay and Green Island's extraordinary rock formations. See if you can recognize the romantically named Sleeping Beauty Rock.

🚶 Hiking Trails

Just past the KM11 marker, heading inland from the coastal road, two trails ascend the central hills. The **Cross-Mountain Ancient Trail** (過山古道), an abandoned bridle path, traverses the island's extinct volcano 1.8km/1mi to the west coast's Nanliao Village.

A **Cross-Mountain Trail** (過山步道) starts near the KM13 marker past the hot springs and continues 1.8km/1mi on a similar route northwest to Nanliao Village.

Jhaorih Hot Springs

Susannah Rosenblatt/Michelin

Boat-Burning Festivals

Boat-burning festivals are a tradition born of plagues and other harsh conditions endured by early coastal folk in southeastern China. Desiring to expel an epidemic from their midst, villagers loaded boats with statues of the responsible demons, as well as lavish gifts to coax these gods on board, before sending the vessels out to sea.

Significant numbers of these boats and their pernicious cargo beached on the shores of southwestern Taiwan. There, fearful local recipients built temples to honor the beached gods in hopes of gaining protection from the pestilence—or alternatively, treated them to a feast before the boats were sent to sea again.

Rich J. Matheson/Michelin

Modern medicine has diminished the role of pestilence gods. The once-dreaded ritual has become a much-anticipated festival that culminates in a royal boat being set ablaze. The belief is that disease and disaster will rise to the heavens with the smoke, ensuring peace and prosperity to the faithful. Boat-burnings festivals are held today in Donggang, Penghu Island and elsewhere in Taiwan.

Jhaorih Hot Springs★★
朝日溫泉

167 Gongguan Village. 公館村167號.
Open Oct–Apr daily 7am–midnight, May–Sept 24 hours. NT$200.
℘089 671 133.

This natural phenomenon is one of Green Island's most famous features. Natural saltwater springs as hot as 74°C/165°F warmed by underground lava draw visitors to open-air pools at the ocean's edge, especially for a night-time soak.

Jhaorih is one of only three such saltwater springs in the world; the other two are in Japan and Italy.

Outdoor pools have water of varying temperatures; once you're thoroughly warmed by the chloride-sulfate water you can jump into the waves. An indoor pool, changing rooms and showers are on-site.

Dabaisha Beach and Dive Area★ 大白沙潛水區

On the island's southernmost spit of land, about 1km/.6mi from the hot springs, this beach is known for excellent snorkeling around coral formations and soft sand for relaxing. Just up the west coast are two sea caves worth a look.

ADDRESSES

🛏 STAY

$ PairFar Hotel 雙發渡假飯店 – *146 Nanliao Village.* 南寮村146號. *℘089 672 552 or 09 35 111 649. 18 rooms.*
You can't beat the price at this clean but basic five-story white tiled hotel in the middle of Nanliao Village. All the rooms have ocean views; cable, Wi-Fi and free airport transport.

$$ Mao-Kong Hostel 小猫空民宿 – *1-30 Yugang, Nanliao Village.* 南寮村魚港 *1-30號. ℘089 671 078, ℘09 33 693 779. www.cat-house.idv.tw. 5 rooms.* 🍴. *Breakfast included.* This friendly, family-run hostel sits on a hillside across from Nanliao Harbor. The Tien family grows fruit, serves fresh juice, teaches guests about island plants and offers weekend package deals that include tours and transportation. Look for the black sign with a purple cat on it; climb a steep set of light and dark blue stairs and cross a garden walkway to find the hostel.

$$ Seahome Hotel 海洋之家 – *39 Nanliao Village.* 南寮村39號. *089 672 515. www.ocean-resort.com.tw. 77 rooms. Breakfast included.* This pleasant five-story hotel is convenient to Nanliao Harbor and features spacious rooms for 2, 4 or 6 people. Tour packages are available.

$ Zihping Campground 紫坪露營區 – *089 672 026 ext. 9.* Fall asleep to the sound of the waves at this campground on the island's southern end past Jhaorih Hot Springs. Elevated platforms, water and power are available. Bring insect repellent, however.

$$ Blue Ocean House B&B 綠島藍海奇緣民宿 – *43 Hot Springs, Gongguan Village.* 公館村溫泉43號. *089 672 309 or 09 19 873 586. www.672525. idv.tw. 11 rooms. Breakfast included.* Just minutes from Jhaorih Hot Springs on the island's windswept southeast corner, this B&B has illuminated marine life paintings on the ceilings of some of its rooms. Guest quarters accommodate 4, 8 or 10 people.

$$ Ling Hua Yuan Resort B&B 玲華園 – *95 Chaikou, Gongguan Village.* 公館村柴口95號. *089 672 015 or *0972 028664. www.ludao.com.tw. 20 rooms. Breakfast included.* Located just past Chaikou (柴口) dive area, this four-story orange-painted hotel offers colorful rooms at reasonable rates. A small swimming pool, one of the few on the island, occupies the front yard.

$$ Green Island Bali Resort 綠島峇里島會館 – *2-10 Gongguan Village.* 公館村2-10號. *089 672 799. www.green island-bali.com.tw. 74 rooms. Breakfast included.* A gracious Polynesian style and quiet location on the island's north shore make this resort a slightly upscale overnight option. Overnight options are rooms in the four-story main building or one of the bungalows next door. It's

only a quick walk to the Human Rights Memorial Park. transportation, scooter rental and many local tour packages are available.

♥/EAT

$ Mei&Mei 美而美 – *103-1 Nanliao Village.* 南寮村103-1號. *089 672 915 or *09 35 576 204. Closes 11am.* Get an early start with typical Taiwanese breakfast dishes, from egg pancakes to fried turnip cakes to milk tea, at this chain popular with students crowding onto the second-floor balcony. Just down the street from the PairFar Hotel, if you are headed south. **Taiwanese.**

$ Orange House 橙屋 – *148 Nanliao Village.* 南寮村148號. *089 671 631.* Grab a beer here, or better yet, try the deliciously unusual venison or seaweed soup dumplings. **Taiwanese.**

$$ Chi Tang You Yu 池塘有魚 – *137 Nanliao Village.* 南寮村137號. *089 672 683.* This welcoming seafood eatery is popular among international visitors and has friendly English-speaking servers. Large groups are seated in the space on the first floor, smaller parties at the bistro next door with a cocktail bar. Savor silky tuna sashimi on the deck. **Taiwanese.**

$$ Fisherman Restaurant 钓鱼人餐廳 – *111 Nanliao Village.* 南寮村111號. *089 671 022. http://fish-man.e089. com.tw.* Enjoy fresh meals at this restaurant, including sweet and sour fish, local vegetables and soup on a lively waterfront patio. **Taiwanese.**

⚡RECREATION

DIVE AREAS

The island's coral reefs have been well preserved and teem with hundreds of species of aquatic life. Here are three good diving spots:

Dabaisha Beach (大白沙) on the island's southernmost spit of land.
Chaikou (柴口) near the lighthouse.
Shihlang (石朗) near Nanliao Harbor.

SWIMMING AREAS

Preferred swimming beaches with soft sands are located between Green Island Prison and Oasis Villa on the island's north coast and at Dabaisha Beach in the south.

Orchid Island★★

Larger than its neighbor, Orchid Island (蘭嶼)—or *Lanyu* in Mandarin—lies 62km/39mi off the southeast coast of Taiwan. Orchid Island is geographically and culturally isolated. Less visited than Green Island, Orchid Island lacks major tourist infrastructure; rather than heading to specific attractions, a visitor here is advised to meander the coastal roads and mountain trails, admiring interesting rock formations and observing the island's still-vibrant indigenous culture. The rocky beaches aren't suitable for sunbathing, but diving and snorkeling here are outstanding. Note that Orchid Island is known for a concentration of (harmless) sea snakes.

UNIQUE NATURAL HERITAGE

As for the island's namesake orchids, the flowers have all but disappeared, harvested to near-extinction. There remains an amazing array of animal, plant and insect species, many of them endemic. The volcanic, 45sq km/17sq mi island is largely taken up by two mountains at either end.

▶ **Population:** 4,300.
🖢 **Michelin Map:** p313.
🛈 **Info:** Orchid Island Airport (蘭嶼航空站) visitor counter. 151 Yuren, Hongtou Village. 紅頭村漁人151號. ℘089 732 220. http://lanyu.taitung.gov.tw.
▶ **Location:** This mountainous island lies 62km/39mi southeast of Taitung. It's larger than Green Island, 45sq km/17sq mi in size. Orchid Island's six small villages are scattered along the 37km/23mi road that circles the island. The harbor and airport are north and south of Yeyou Village, respectively; the tourist hub is Hongtou Village, a little farther south. All are on Orchid Island's west coast.
🕐 **Timing:** Most crowded in the summer. Temperatures are mild throughout the year, and rainfall is lower from October to February, after typhoon season ends.
😄 **Don't Miss:** Tao crafts in Dongqing Village.

Traditional Tao boats

Susannah Rosenblatt/Michelin

GETTING THERE

BY AIR - Daily Air Corp. flies from Taitung to Orchid Island six times a day, weather permitting *(NT$1345 one-way; 20min; ℘089 362 489 or ℘089 732 278; www.dailyair.com.tw)*. The airport (蘭嶼航空站; ℘089 732 220) lies several kilometers south of **Yeyou Village** (椰油部落) on the west coast.

BY FERRY - Several ferries *(about NT$900 one way; 3hrs)* depart Fugang Harbor north of Taitung for the island *(☏see telephone numbers in Green Island's Practical Information)*. These boats are known for rocking rides that have made many a passenger seasick. Ferries land at **Kaiyuan Harbor** (開元港) just north of Yeyou Village.

GETTING AROUND

BY BUS - A bus circles the island a few times a day; you can wave it down to board.

BY CAR - A very limited number of cars are available to rent *(NT$1500/day and up)*. It's best to arrange a pickup from the airport or ferry terminal by your hotel beforehand, as it's a long walk to the rental shops in Hongtou Village. The island's lone **gas station** is north of Yeyou.

BY TWO WHEEL - Scooters are the primary mode of transportation *(about NT$500/day)*, and can be rented at many hotels or small shops in Hongtou. Bikes are also available for rent from some of these same small Hongtou shops for about NT$150/day. Inquire at your hotel.

GENERAL INFORMATION
VISITOR INFORMATION

Orchid Island Airport (蘭嶼航空站) has limited visitor information. 151 Yuren, Hongtou Village. 紅頭村漁人151號. ℘089 732 220. http://lanyu.taitung. gov.tw.

The **Pongso No Tao Culture Foundation**, housed in a bright blue and yellow building in Yeyou Village between the harbor and the airport, works to preserve traditions. The CEO speaks English and is happy to educate visitors *(12-1 Yeyou Village 椰油村12-1號; ☾open daily 9am–6pm; ℘089 731 000)*.

ACCOMMODATIONS

Lodging on the island is largely basic and inexpensive. Homestay hosts will often make guests a traditional dinner with advance notice.

Summertime is the busy season so it's recommended that you make hotel and transportation reservations well beforehand.

Lanyu airport

Susannah Rosenblatt/Michelin

Orchid Island goats

Susannah Rosenblatt/Michelin

The vast majority of Orchid Island's 4,000-plus inhabitants are members of the Tao tribe (⟨ *see sidebar*).

Visitors can still catch glimpses of Tao culture; a small number of partially **underground houses** remain, built to withstand damage from typhoons.

Many of Orchid Island's residents continue to fish and farm millet, taro and yams, as well as raise pigs and goats, which graze all over the island.

A 37km/23mi **ring road** circles the island's six villages. Having the most hotels and restaurants, **Hongtou Village** (紅頭部落), located just 2km/1.2mi south of the airport, is the island's commercial center, although nearby Yuren and Yeyou Villages also have meals and lodging. Hongtou means "redheaded," an earlier Chinese name for the island, inspired by red-hued island sunsets. Many hotels, restaurants and shops in Hongtou Village will help visitors arrange snorkeling or scuba diving excursions and equipment rental.

There are three other villages on the island, most on the narrow strip of land between the 552m/1,811ft-tall **Mount Hongtou** (紅頭山) in the north and Mount Dasen in the south.

A twisting 5.7km/3.5mi mountain road connects Hongtou Village on the west coast with **Yeyin Village** (野銀部落) on the east coast.

SIGHTS

Note: Many indigenous people do not want to be photographed. Please ask their permission before taking a snapshot of them, their house or their boat.

Rock Formations★

Several well-known oddly shaped (and oddly named) volcanic rocks are scattered around the island's perimeter, creating bizarre and beautiful natural views during a bike or scooter cruise.

A couple of famous formations you should try to see are **Dragon's Head Rock** (龍頭岩) at the island's southern tip and **Twin Lions Rock** (雙獅岩), which sits to the northeast.

Mount Dasen★ 大森山

🚶 A hiking trail (*allow 3-4hrs round-trip*) south of Hongtou Village leads to a volcanic crater pond atop 480m/1,575ft Mount Dasen.

Yehyin Village

En route to Yehyin Village, also known by its indigenous name, Ivalino, the island's weather station (氣象觀測站) offers a panoramic **view**★★.

Traverse the winding inland road from Hongtou to Yehyin, a community on Orchid Island's east coast where many of the old ways survive. There you'll find a greater concentration of traditional

351

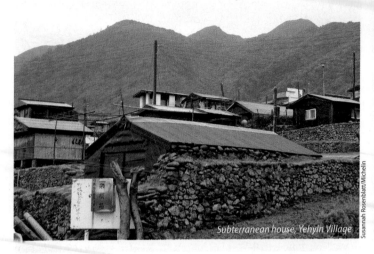

Subterranean house, Yehyin Village

Susannah Rosenblatt/Michelin

subterranean houses made of stone and wood. Residents relax on raised platforms above. Several **carved boats** are usually on shore in the village. Yami boats can also be found in Dongqing and Langdao Villages.

The Tao, A Tribe Across the Sea

The island's Tao [pronounced "Dawu" in Mandarin] inhabitants, also known as the **Yami**, call the island *Pongso no Tao* in their native language—"island of the people." Ancestral Tao hailed from islands north of the Philippines, so contemporary tribe members are more closely related to Austronesian groups than to the Han Chinese who make up the majority of Taiwan's citizens. Because of geographic isolation, the Tao's traditional way of life has been better preserved than that of many of Taiwan's indigenous groups, although in recent years external factors have been eroding Tao culture.

The Tao have had a troubled history with Taiwan's governments. In the early 20C, the occupying Japanese considered the tribe an anthropological wonder and barred public visits to the island. Under KMT rule in the 1970s, the local language was endangered by government-mandated Mandarin education; Taiwanese "mainlanders" were brought over to assimilate locals. The government also pushed the construction of modern concrete houses to replace traditional Yami dwellings built into the ground. During this time Christian missionaries arrived on the island to convert residents; most of the island remains Christian and there are churches in every village. Several decades ago, the government duped Orchid Island's illiterate representative into signing off on a nuclear-waste storage site that was described to him as a "fish cannery." Since discovering the truth, the Tao have fought vocally, with limited success, for the nuclear material to be removed.

Keep an eye out for one of the Tao's famous boats. Prized by locals, the canoe-like vessels are built with 27 pieces of wood—without nails—carved with intricate geometric designs and painted white, black and red. The boats get a workout during the important **flying fish festival** held every spring. During this festival, Tao men, some dressed in traditional loincloths, rattan armor or conical metal helmets made of beaten coins, chant for the flying fish to return and paddle out to sea. If you do see these boats, avoid touching them.

ADDRESSES

🛏 STAY

$ Lan Siang Hostel 籃翔民宿 – *136 Yeyou Village.* 椰油村136號. ☏*089 732 236. 8 rooms.* 🍴. *Restaurant and gift shop.* A family-run hostel located close to the harbor, with access to the airport to the south. One double plus dorms with shared bathrooms.

$ Mercy Home 恩典之家 – *69 Dongqing Village.* 東清村69號. ☏*089 732 885 or* ☏*09 19 127 783. www.mercy-home. idv.tw.* 🍴. *10pm curfew.* Stay in simple surroundings in a local pastor's home and order meals to share with them. Proprietor speaks English and knows island history; shared bathrooms. On the east coast; up a hill, ask for directions.

$$ Clamshell House 五爪貝的家 – *6 Langdao Village.* 朗島村6號. ☏*089 732 127 or* ☏*09 21 207 124. www.kang857. url.tw. 7 rooms.* 🍴. *Breakfast included.* This festive white and blue B&B sits on the island's north coast near the police station at the edge of town. Accommodations sleep groups of 4, 6, or 8; private bathrooms, Wi-Fi, bikes and snorkeling trips.

$$ Lanyu Hotel 蘭嶼別館 – *45 Hongtou, Hongtou Village.* 紅頭村紅頭45號. ☏*089 326 111 ext. 3 or* ☏*089 731 611. www.lanyu. com.tw. 60 rooms.* 🍴. A tour group favorite, this boxy, bare-bones hotel in the middle of the island's main drag has meals available for advance order.

🍴 EAT

$ Bean Sprouts 荳芽菜 – *White beach shack between Yeyou and Yuren villages.* ☏*09 21 486 110.* 🍴. *Open 8:30am–midnight.* This friendly spot serves sandwiches, burgers, cocktails and coffee. Be sure to reserve the deluxe brunch (available 8:30am–11:30am) by 6pm the day before. **American.**

$ The Epicurean Café 無餓不坐 – *77 Yuren Village.* 漁人77號. ☏*089 731 623.* ☏*09 33 840 350. http://epicureanpub. myweb.hinet.net.* 🍴. *Closes 8:30pm, bar open later.* Set meals of Tao cuisine including flying fish and taro, plus curries, brunch and cocktails in a funky

Epicurean Café
Susannah Rosenblatt/Michelin

atmosphere. Postcards and crafts for sale. The cafe is located south of the airport. Free Wi-Fi. **Tao/Thai/International.**

$ Four Seasons Beef Noodles 四季牛肉麵 – *19 Yeyou Village.* 椰油村19號. ☏*089 732 021.* 🍴. This marigold-colored local haunt across the street from La Siang Hostel, marked by a yellow sign with red letters, serves filling, tasty noodles and wontons plus soups, rice, tofu and veggie sides. English menu. **Taiwanese.**

$ Orchid Island Seafood Restaurant 蘭嶼海產店 – *31-7 Hongtou Village.* 紅頭村31-7號. ☏*089 732 599.* 🍴. *Closes 9pm.* This large, no-frills dining room catering to groups prepares set meals of black pepper flying fish and local seaweed, plus Taiwanese dishes made to order. **Taiwanese.**

🛍 SHOPPING

ARTS AND CRAFTS

Orchid Island has many local artists who create driftwood sculptures, beaded jewelry and other crafts. **Dongqing Village** (東清部落) on the east coast has several interesting shops, including **Sikang Chai's** brightly painted wood carving studio at No. 23 之5, on the main road's coastal side (☏*09 89 729 966*). Across the street **Three Sisters Workroom** (三姊妹工作房) is a small space full of handmade jewelry at No. 23 (🕐*open daily 8am–5pm;* ☏*089 732 841*). There's also a bright blue truck parked nearby where an artist sells jewelry, headbands and one-of-a-kind bags (🕐*open daily 8am–5pm;* ☏*09 37 580 541*).

Penghu, Kinmen and Mazu, the three archipelagos in the Taiwan Strait, share little in common beyond their location in the "black ditch" that separates Taiwan from mainland China. All three island chains are served by direct flights from several cities on Taiwan, and Mazu and Penghu are also reachable by boat from Taiwan island.

Highlights

1 The aged beauty of Penghu's **Mazu Tianhou Temple** (p357)

2 Penghu's 300-year-old **Banyan Tree**, with 100 trunks (p359)

3 Night-time **squid fishing** off Penghu Island (p361)

4 Kinmen's granite-carved **Zhaishan Tunnel** (p365)

5 **Dong Yin Island**'s pristine natural beauty (p373)

A Bit of History

Kinmen and Mazu are most alike, because both island chains are near the coast of mainland China, and were once heavily fortified and hotly disputed. As a result each have tunnels, forts and battle sites. Kinmen is mostly flat and featureless, with a few pine trees and some wetlands in the way of natural beauty. The Mazu islands are rocky and scenic, with high granite cliffs that offer inspiring views and dramatic seascapes. Culturally, Kinmen and Mazu are very different. The Mazu islands lie far to the northwest of Taiwan proper, near the mouth of the Min River on the coast of Fujian Province. Mazu's residents speak a rare regional dialect; they have unique architecture and cuisine that tourists find appealing. Kinmen, far south of Mazu, is a few kilometers from Xiamen City in central Fujian Province. Kinmen is culturally and linguistically similar to the rest of Taiwan, though its Qing-era buildings are much better preserved. Penghu lies in the middle of the stormy Taiwan Strait; its strategic location has put it at the crossroads of history.

Over the centuries many countries fought for control of its 64 widely scattered islands. Penghu's rich fishing grounds make it a paradise for seafood lovers. Its long occupation by tough farmers and fearless fishermen have bestowed it with ancient temples, quaint rural villages and honeycombed fields.

The Penghu islands have volcanic topography, and columns of basalt are common throughout the archipelago.

Penghu is best avoided during the stormy winters that begin in early November and end in late March.

Kinmen and Mazu are year-round destinations, though spring and fall are the finest months weather-wise.

Mazu Tianhou Temple, Magong, Penghu

© IMAGEMORE Co., Ltd. / Alamy

Penghu★★

Penghu (澎湖) is a wonderfully quirky archipelago that is nothing like the rest of Taiwan. Unlike Taiwan's other outlying islands, it is a sizable chain, with 64 islands "sprinkled like pearls on the turquoise sea," as the residents say. Dissimilar to the folded limestone of Taiwan proper, the islands are made of volcanic basalt, and the rocky topography, combined with the lashing waves and often fierce winds, lends a weather-beaten appearance to Penghu. Penghu is also a place of rare natural beauty, with dramatic seascapes, sandy beaches and gentle grass-covered hills, and it is famous for its sea birds, nesting sea turtles and other wildlife, including edible fish in abundance. It is historic as well, and its abandoned forts, atmospheric temples, and traditional villages have a patina of well-worn age and a sense of place that are rare in booming, dynamic Taiwan. Seasons matter very much in Penghu. During summer, it is a paradise of clear blue water, white sand beaches, and green rolling hills. But in winter, when the gales howl up the strait, many residents pack up and retreat to the main island of Taiwan, and the population shrinks from 110,000 to fewer than 70,000. Even in summer, just 20 of the 64 islands are inhabited.

A BIT OF HISTORY

People have been living on Penghu since the Stone Age, and prehistoric stone walls and fields attest to its ancient habitation. The archipelago's recorded history began about a thousand years ago, with the arrival of the first **Yuan dynasty** settlers; descendants of those early pioneers are still in Penghu.

The history of Penghu revolves around the sea. Its protected bays and harbors and its mid-strait location made it a safe haven for seafarers and fishermen sailing back and forth between mainland

▶ **Population:** 110,000.
◔ **Michelin Map:** p357.
🚻 **Info:** Tourist Information booth at the airport *(English spoken).* Open daily 8am–8pm. ✆06-922 8115. www.penghu-nsa.gov.tw.
◉ **Location:** Penghu Island, or mainland Penghu, is a collection of four islands joined by bridges, and shaped like a large horseshoe, with the town of **Magong** at one tip of the horseshoe, and **Western Fort** at the other. The four islands are linked by Route 203, and a drive along this road includes many of the top sights on Penghu. Several other islands, notably **Wang'an** and **Qi Mei,** are reachable by ferry.
👥 **Kids:** Shili and Shanshui beaches, Guanyin Ting, Penghu Aquarium.
🕐 **Timing:** Penghu is a summertime destination. Avoid the cold, windy winters of November to late March, when many hotels and restaurants close.
🏵 **Don't Miss:** Tongliang Banyan Tree, Mazu Tianhou Temple.

China and Taiwan; its scattered islands made it a stronghold for pirates. The islands had strategic virtue: at various times the **Qing dynasty**, the Dutch, Portuguese, French and Japanese fought for control of them.

As early as the 12C, the islands were known to mainland Chinese, but were a distant part of the Yuan dynasty. The **Dutch** took over in 1622, before establishing a more permanent base on mainland Taiwan. Later in the 15C, the Qing dynasty took the islands back from the Dutch. In 1884, in the waning days of the Qing, **French** troops tried to take Penghu, but failed. In 1895 **Japan**

GETTING THERE

BY AIR - During summer high season, **Uni Air** (*www.uniair.com.tw*), **TransAsia Airways** (*www.tna.com.tw*; no English) and **Mandarin Airlines** (www.mandarin-airlines.com) operate more than 50 daily flights to Magong from Taipei, Taichung, Tainan, Chiayi and Kaohsiung, with airfares from NT$1,500 to $2400.

BY BOAT - Magong has ferry connections to Kaohsiung (4.5hrs), Tainan (2hrs), and Chiayi (90min). **Tai Hua Shipping** serves the Kaohsiung route; round-trip tickets cost NT$1,080 to NT$2,340, depending on the cabin. Tai Hua contact: Kaohsiung ℘07-551 5823, Penghu *06-926 4087*.

GETTING AROUND

BY CAR - Cars can be rented at the airport or in downtown Magong, starting at NT$1,800 per day for a compact. International or Taiwan license is required.

Taxis can be rented by the hour or by the day, and the drivers often double as tour guides. Expect to pay about NT$400 per hour.

BY FERRY - Magong has boat connections to Wang'an (30km/18mi), Qi Mei (47km/29mi), and several smaller islets. Ferries to Ji Bei (8km/5mi) leave from Baisha island. One-way prices range from NT$230 to Wang'an, to NT$150 to Ji Bei. The

South Sea Tourist Center (℘06-926 4738) in Magong has information and tickets for the islands south of Magong. The **North Sea Tourist Center** (℘06-993 3082) on Baisha Island has information and tickets for Ji Bei and other islands to the north.

BY TWO WHEEL - Scooters and bicycles can be rented at the airport and in Magong; bicycles can be rented at Guanyin Ting and elsewhere in Magong, and through hotels. Scooter rentals range from NT$300–$400/day for 125cc models.

GENERAL INFORMATION
AREA CODE

The prefix 06, which indicates the area code for Penghu Island, has been included in the telephone numbers shown in this chapter, even though It is not necessary to dial 06 when making a local call.

VISITOR INFORMATION

The **Penghu National Scenic Area Administration** (澎湖國家風景區管理處) office is in Magong, at 171 Guanghua Village, 光華里171號; open daily 8am–5pm; ℘06 921 6521. Penghu County Government also provides useful tourism information on its website, at www.penghu.gov.tw.

ACCOMMODATIONS

Lodgings can be found mainly in Magong. ♿ *See ADDRESSES for a selection of places to stay.*

---

seized the archipelago along with the rest of Taiwan, and held the islands until 1945, when China regained control. The legacy of all this warfare is still visible in the scattered ruins and ancient forts that dot the highest points on Penghu. The islands were also known for their fertile fishing grounds. The Portuguese called them the **Pescadores**, or fish islands, and the surrounding deep, cold waters teemed with edible sea life. Life today is not easy on those 64 basalt islands. Among today's signature Penghu sights, its fishing villages hug the cliff-sheltered bays; its farms are criss-crossed by coral-block walls that shield the crops from relentless gales. Life unfolds here in a slow and traditional fashion, as fishermen dry their catches in the courtyards, and farmers tend their melons and sweet potatoes inside the walls. Fishing boats unload their catches on the docks, and multiple restaurants serve fresh seafood.

PENGHU ISLAND★★

Sights are ordered geographically south to north, east to west.

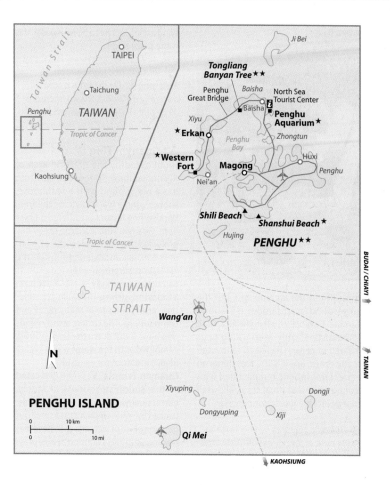

Magong 馬公

West side of mainland Penghu,
4km/2.5mi west of the airport.

Most of the residents of Penghu live in Magong, a tidy little town that combines the old city walls built by the Qing dynasty in 1886, abundant temples and narrow cobblestone streets with convenience stores, traffic lights and other elements of modern Taiwan.

🐾 WALKING TOUR
4km/2.5mi. Allow 2hrs.

▶ *Start at Shuncheng gate 順城門 near Zhongshan and Qingling Rds., the best-preserved section of the old city wall. Head east past tiny Suhu Temple, turn left on Minzu Rd. to find the temple.*

Mazu Tianhou Temple★★
天后宮

19 Zhengyi St. 正義街19號.
🕑*Open daily 5am–8pm.*

Tianhou, or Queen of Heaven, refers to the revered goddess Mazu. This temple isn't the largest or grandest Mazu temple in Taiwan, but it is one of the oldest. Ancient granite thresholds and worn paving stones attest to its venerable age, while a fiery furnace, in which devotees burn paper money as offerings to the goddess, speak to its essential role in the daily lives of Magong residents. The goddess **Mazu**, patron saint and protector of seafarers, is the dominant deity on Penghu. The name Magong itself can mean "Mazu Temple," and shrines to the goddess are scattered

357

Four-Eyed Well

Brent Hannon/Michelin

throughout the archipelago, but the largest and most famous is Tianhou Temple. Originally built in the Fujianese temple style, with interlocking pegs instead of nails, it has been renovated many times. But it is the real thing: an eerie, atmospheric temple filled with iconography and ritual. Its swallowtail roof points are most pronounced,

> *Take the diagonal pedestrian path to the right of the temple entrance, walk past the Well of 10,000 Soldiers (there is a sign in English). After 100m/328ft turn left at a T-intersection. Still on the pedestrian path, walk 30m/98ft to the Four-Eyed Well (its four openings allow four families to use it simultaneously) and turn left, or west, until you reach a small paved road, Hui Min Rd.. Go right, or north, on Hui Min and cross Guangmin St.*

Note the **pigeon coop** on the right: here, as elsewhere in Taiwan, pigeon racing is a passion.

> *Proceed one block.*

Liquid Café
36 Hui Min Rd., 惠民一路36號.
06-926 0361.
This cafe serves as the hub of water sports in Penghu. If you wish to arrange

windsurfing, or have a bowl of pasta, this is the place to go.

> *Turn left, and walk west on Minsheng Rd. On the left is a park with a sculpture of a ship sinking (there are more than 300 known shipwrecks in the Mazu archipelago). Cross Jieshou Rd.*

Guanyin Ting 觀音亭
Highlighted by the graceful arch of Xiying Rainbow Bridge, Guanyin Ting has a playground with a bathhouse, showers and a water park for children. Windsurfing lessons are offered daily at 4pm. Guanyin Ting is a large sandy bay protected by a breakwater, where beginners can sail and windsurf inside the walls, and adrenalin-addicted experts can brave the windy straits. Penghu is a top **windsurfing** and sailing destination, and is the site of many races and competitions. The strong, steady winds that blow south down the Taiwan Strait, combined with the warm water, create ideal conditions for windsurfing.
Guanyin Temple (觀音廟), dedicated to the Buddhist goddess of Mercy, graces Guanyin Ting's shore. The temple, flanked by white elephants, is a small but genuine place of worship, with devotees reading scripture, counting beads, praying and lighting incense.

> *Return to Jieshou Rd. and turn right, or south.*

This shaded, pine tree-lined path proceeds alongside the **old city wall**, complete with banyan roots snaking down the sides of the old structure.

> *After a quarter of a mile, you will see a Y-intersection.*

Red script, painted on a **giant rock**, says 勿忘在莒, or *wu wang zai ju*, a couplet written by Chiang Kai-shek reminding people that Taiwan is not a permanent home, and implying that the mainland will be retaken.

> *Veer left and walk down the lane, still heading south. Notice the flat,*

wind-beaten banyans absorbing an abandoned village. After 250m/820ft, return to Shuncheng gate.

ADDITIONAL SIGHTS
Beaches South of Magong
Shili Beach (蒔裡沙灘) is a beautiful kilometer-long strip of white sand that is popular with backpackers and beachcombers, but has few facilities. On a nearby stretch of seashore, **Shanshui Beach**★, (山水沙灘) is the best and most popular beach in the archipelago. Both beaches are fine places in summer for a picnic and a swim.

Penghu Living Museum 澎湖生活博物館
327 Xinsheng Rd., 馬公市新生路327號. Open daily 9am–5pm. NT$60. 06-921 0405. www.phlm.nat.gov.tw.
This ambitious museum with its signature wave-shaped roof opened in 2009 to illustrate the history, culture and lifestyles of the archipelago. Its state-of-the-art displays include **full-scale boats** that rock and pitch, and large mockups of **Qing-era villages**, stone fish traps, mud villages and fish drying in the sun. Regrettably, it has no English signs.

Prickly Pear Cactus
Prickly pear cactus was brought to the Penghu islands by the Dutch in the 1600s and unexpectedly, it thrived on grassy hillsides in the windy, dry marine climate. The resourceful natives make and sell **prickly pear ice cream** and prickly pear jam. Few visitors leave Penghu without sampling the ice cream and dark purple jam.

Penghu Aquarium★
澎湖水族館
About 12km/7.5mi north of Magong, along Rte. 203. 58 Qitou Village. 白沙鄉歧頭村58號. Open daily 9am–5pm. NT$200. 06-993 3006.
Penghu Aquarium, a modern facility that features audio players and signs in English, provides a close-up look at the wealth of sea life surrounding the archipelago. Exhibits include tanks teeming with coral, lobsters, anemones, clown fish, butterfly fish and various sharks and rays. The **sea turtles** are of special interest—visitors love watching them ply the water with the calm, leisurely strokes of their flippered arms. The **venomous fish** tank is also popular, with its spiny,

Shanshui Beach
© IMAGEMORE Co., Ltd. / Alamy

Tongliang Banyan Tree

Brent Hannon/Michelin

dangerous denizens the lion fish and the scorpion fish, both found in Penghu.

Tongliang Banyan Tree★★
通樑古榕

6km/4mi west of the aquarium, at the junction of County Rd. 203 and Penghu Great Bridge. Courtyard ◷Open daily 4am–8pm.

A vast matrix of branches and leaves suspended above a courtyard, this magnificent banyan, or **ficus**, has been growing for more than three centuries. Banyan trees send soil-seeking roots down from their branches, and for the past 300 years, villagers have cultivated the roots of this particular tree, which have since grown into solid trunks. Over hundreds of years, supported by trellises, the banyan has spread and spread so that, today, this remarkable tree provides a huge canopy of branches that seems almost endless. The growth is ongoing, since the local villagers continue to cultivate new trunks and build new trellises. It now occupies more than 1,000sq m/10,760sq ft and boasts at least 100 trunks.

The tree shades a green, leafy courtyard and overlooks 370-year-old **Bao'an Temple** dedicated to the Daoist god Hei Fu Qian Sui. Both tree and temple have survived countless typhoons, and according to legend, the giant banyan has the power to protect the temple from bad weather. The original trunk,

or "dragon head," is gnarled and twisted, but still alive, at the back of the courtyard. Visitors can enjoy a pot of tea, or a cup of prickly pear ice cream, as they sit in the shade of this remarkable plant.

Erkan Old Houses★ 二崁古厝
Roughly at midpoint of Xiyu Island. ◷Open daily 8am–5pm. NT$30.

The rural charm and traditional lifestyles of Penghu are on display in these old houses, a collection of homes built mostly in the Minnan (southern) style of Fujian Province.

Tourists can stroll through the village and see the famous "veiled ladies," wrapped up to protect themselves from wind and sun. The women work in their "wasp nest" fields—small, honeycombed plots, shielded by coral block walls, that are so much a part of Penghu. The main crops are **peanuts** and different kinds of squash, hardy plants that don't mind the sandy soil and salty marine winds. **Pumpkin** and **loofah** find their way into many dishes in Penghu, while the peanuts are made into snacks.

Mazu has many villages similar to Erkan, but this little village is unique because it is organized to attract visitors as a preservation district. Its 50 households are tourist friendly and display some of the vanishing elements of daily rural life such as urns, Qing-era scales and weights and winnowing machines.

Squid Fishing on Penghu

Life in Penghu revolves around the ocean in general, and fishing in particular, and this is true for tourists and residents alike. The waters teem with edible fish, but the squid and cuttlefish are the prized catches.

Squid fishing is a famous night-time activity that is fun and a tourist favorite. It starts out with a gentle boat ride into the soft green sea, until the captain flicks on the squid lights: 16 bulbs at 2,000 watts each, which light up the ocean with 32,000 watts of incandescent light, including some bulbs dangling in the sea itself. The wild squid are attracted to the bright lights, and once the boat finds a school of squid, the fishing is fast and furious. The tentacled delicacies are cooked and served immediately, usually as a delicious bowl of hot noodle soup with firm white squid meat and chili pepper dip, or sometimes raw, as sashimi. Few visitors come back hungry from these excursions. The squid season runs July through September. Night fishing trips take about three hours (*average cost NT$500/person*); for information contact Qitou Visitor Center: ℘06-993 1527.

Western Fort★ 西台古堡
Southern foot of Xiyu Island near end of Hwy. 203. ⏱Open daily 8:30am–4:30pm. NT$25.

Lying across the Trans-Ocean Bridge, on Xiyu Island, the fort covers 8ha/19acres; many of the ruins and rock walls are held together by a mortar made from sticky rice, in a shallow, crater-like depression surrounded by green fields. An expansive **view** of the sapphire-blue ocean far below is afforded from the fort.

This rocky ruin was built during the Qing dynasty to protect the Taiwan Strait and Penghu itself from pirates and invaders. In 1885 the Qing dynasty defenders of Penghu repelled a French invasion from this outpost, which played a prominent role 10 years later in a battle against Japan.

Nearby, **Xiyu Lighthouse** (西嶼燈塔), permits fine **views**★ from its courtyard (⏱*open Tue–Sun 9am–4pm*).

OUTLYING ISLANDS
Wang'an 望安島
30min ferry ride south from Magong.
Wang'an is famous for its **Green Turtle Tourism and Conservation Center** (⏱*open daily 9am–5pm*). During the spawning season, these rare turtles come to the beaches of Wang'an to lay eggs, although the actual egg-laying is not promoted as a sightseeing activity because the presence of people often disturbs the turtles.

Qi Mei 七美島
1hr ferry ride southwest from Magong harbor.

Two Hearts Stone Weir, Qi Mei

© Videowokart/Dreamstime.com

Qi Mei is chiefly known for its **Two Hearts Stone Weir**, a twin, heart-shaped, stone fishing weir that fills with water at high tide and traps the fish as it recedes. The giant weir has become an iconic symbol of Penghu. Qi Mei, or Seven Beauties, was named for seven women who supposedly threw themselves into a well rather than be ravished by Japanese pirates.

ADDRESSES

🏠 STAY

$$ Er Kan Guesthouse 二崁民宿 – *Xiyu Lane, 20 Erkan Village* 西嶼鄉二崁村20號. ℘*06-998 4406. www.phnet. com.tw/erkan. 10 rooms. Closed in winter.* This guesthouse, built in 2008 in low-rise Erkan-village style, offers wonderful ocean views and plenty of peaceful rural charm. Seafood buffet breakfast is included; no restaurant.

$$ Greek Frontier Villa, 希臘邊境渡假旅店 – *59 Shanshui district* 馬公市山水里59號. ℘*06-995 1926. www.greek-frontier.com. 7 rooms. Closed in winter.* An exceedingly delightful Greek-style guesthouse complete with white paint and blue trim is outfitted with a tiny plunge pool and a pocket-size courtyard garden. It boasts a fine location a couple hundred meters from Shanshui Beach, the best strip of sand in Penghu. Breakfast included, no restaurant.

$$ Ocean Hotel 海洋渡假村 – *3 Lin Hai Rd.* 馬公市臨海路3號. *Magong. 82 rooms.* The Ocean Hotel is a perfectly acceptable accommodation for its reasonable price. The sea-view rooms have quaint tiny balconies, complete with swings, that overlook the peaceful harbor. Breakfast is included and a seafood hot pot dinner is available.

$$$ Hai Yue Hotel 海悅大飯店 – *75 Min Fu Rd.* 馬公市福路75號. *Magong. 79 rooms.* A modern four-star property that opened in 2009, the Hai Yue has a good location in downtown Magong. It lacks character, but its modern amenities and the friendliness and efficiency of its staff make up for the hotel's simple design.

🍽 EAT

$ Jang Jin Restaurant 長進餐廳 – *9 Minzu Rd.* 馬公市民族路九號. *Magong, near Tian Hou Temple.* ℘*06-927 1686, www.jangjin.idv.tw. Closes 9pm.* The plain decor belies the excellent fresh seafood at this local hot spot. Crunchy, salty deep-fried squid and mung-bean noodles with local pumpkin are among the house specialties. Seafood on Penghu tends to be super-fresh, mildly spiced, and lightly cooked. English menu. **Taiwanese Seafood.**

$$ Ching Shin Restaurant 清心飲食店 – *Xiyu Lane, 77 Chidong Village #2,* 西嶼鄉池東村77之2號, *near Erkan Village.* ℘*06-998 1128. www.cs-restaurant.myweb.hinet.net. Closes about 9pm.* Though seemingly simple and rustic, the Qing Xin is a gem of a restaurant. Top Taiwanese officials have dined here and can attest to its excellence. All the seafood is superb, but the deep-fried tempura-style jumbo prawns are exceptional. Every guest gets just one prawn: more than one reduces the pleasure, says the house. **Taiwanese.**

🛍 SHOPPING

MAGONG

Small dried fish in sweet peanut and hot chili coating, salty pastries made of flour and pig fat—like shortbread—and molasses cakes are the most popular snack souvenirs sold in the open-air stalls near Tian Hou Temple.

🎭 EVENT

Each year during Lantern Festival *(15th day of Lunar New Year)*, the **Qi Gui Festival** is held at temples throughout the archipelago. Formerly, turtles were made of glutinous rice or steamed buns. Worshipers threw oracle blocks to "win" the turtles, which they ate, and replaced the following year. These days, the turtles can be 11,000-pound rice and sugar creations, or made from coins or carved gold, and lit up with electric lights; all are appeals for a prosperous new year.

Kinmen★

This 150sq km/58sq mi archipelago is a unique destination that is very different from the rest of Taiwan. Its 15 islands are tucked up against the coast of mainland China, and the closest point is just 2.1km/1.3mi away, while Taiwan itself lies 277km/172mi distant, across the Taiwan Strait. With their signature red soil and ubiquitous pine and eucalyptus trees, these flat islands are not particularly scenic. The bowtie-shaped main island is largely rural, with gentle countryside and fertile brown fields, many blanketed with green and yellow crops of **sorghum**. Traditional lifestyles are well preserved on Kinmen (金門). Old-fashioned farms and Fujianese clan villages are common. Kinmen has some of the best-preserved Qing-era Fujian-style villages in existence, though a few of them are falling into disrepair.

JINCHENG

The little town of **Jincheng** serves as Kinmen's commercial center. In the middle of it is Mofan Street (模範街), with brick archways and souvenir shops, built in 1925 using funds remitted by overseas Chinese, who wished to re-create a Western shopping thoroughfare in their home town.

▶ **Population:** 68,000.

Michelin Map: p357.

Info: Kinmen National Park visitor center. 460 Boyu Rd., Sec. 2, Jinning Village 金門國家公園管理處, 金寧鄉伯玉路二段460號, ✆082 313 100. www.kmnp.gov.tw. The county government also provides tourist information at www.kinmen.gov.tw. Note: 08 is the area code for Kinmen, but it is not necessary to dial it for local calls.

Location: Lying about a mile from mainland China's coast, the largest island, Kinmen, and its western neighbor, Little Kinmen, are the two islands open to tourism. Kinmen's major hub is the southwest town of Jincheng; the town's main street is Mofan Street. Just east of Jincheng, some 4km/2.5mi, is the Kinmen airport.

Don't Miss: Ma Shan Observation Post and the Zhaishan Tunnel.

Mofan Street, Jincheng

Brent Hannon/Michelin

GETTING THERE

BY AIR - **Uni Air** (*www.uniair.com.tw*), **TransAsia**, and **Mandarin Airlines** fly to Kinmen from Taipei, Taichung, Chiayi, Tainan, and Kaohsiung; fares range from NT$2000 to NT$3200, depending on the city. Since mainland Chinese use Kinmen as a transit point into Taiwan, flights are often booked.

GETTING AROUND

BY BUS - Public buses serve the airport, Jincheng, and the villages of Shamei and Shawai, but service is very infrequent.

BY CAR - Cars can be rented at the airport, and in downtown Jincheng, beginning at NT$1,800/day, depending on the model. Kinmen is flat and the main attractions are clearly signposted.

BY FERRY - Ferries run every 30min from Shuitou Harbor in southwest Kinmen to Jiugong Harbor on Little Kinmen. The 15min trip costs NT$20.

BY TWO WHEEL - Scooters can be rented, with an international driver's license or a Taiwan license (or, in the absence of these, by talking the proprietor into renting you one) at the airport, and in Jincheng. Hotels can often help. Bicycles are a fine way to negotiate the island's flat roads, and some of the major tourist sites rent bicycles for NT$150/hr. Bicycles can also be rented in Jincheng.

GENERAL INFORMATION

AREA CODE

The area code 082 has been included in this chapter, but it is not necessary to dial 082 when making a local call.

A BIT OF HISTORY

For most of recorded history, Kinmen was a collection of unremarkable islands near the coast of Fujian Province, where farmers and villagers quietly went about their daily lives. All that changed during the **Chinese Civil War** when the beleaguered Nationalist army of Generalissimo **Chiang Kai-shek** retreated to Kinmen and entrenched itself there. The Chinese Communist army invaded Kinmen in 1949, landing 20,000 troops, but they were defeated at the battle of Guningtou, and Taiwan has occupied 12 of Kinmen's 15 islands ever since.

Following that battle, the Nationalist troops dug in, and built the tunnels, pillboxes and bunkers that give the island its hunkered-down, fortified appearance. Those preparations soon proved their worth, as Kinmen became the target of intense shelling by mainland China for most of the following decade. In one six-week period in 1958, half a million shells rained down on the little islands, and explosives continued to fall on and off for three decades.

After that first decade, the shelling became more ritualistic, and the two sides began shelling each other on pre-arranged days. That gave way to "propaganda" shells containing pamphlets with exaggerations about the virtues of both sides. Shells from China might say, "everyone here owns a bicycle," and Taiwan's shells fired back would say, "so what? everyone here owns a motorcycle." It was literally a war of words.

By the mid-1980s, tensions eased, and many of the soldiers on Kinmen went home. To revive its flagging economy, Kinmen converted 37sq km/14sq mi into a **national park** in 1995, and threw open its doors to tourism. For the following few years, tourists flocked to the islands to see the traditional homes and military sights, drink the famous *gaoliang* liquor, and gaze at nearby mainland China.

Kinmen is now home to about 10,000 soldiers; most are young men serving their mandatory two-year conscription. Tensions between Taiwan and mainland China have eased; fighter jets and cruise missiles have replaced artillery shells. Kinmen, which means "golden gate," faces an uncertain future. If mainland tourism catches on, the gate will open wide once again.

Zhaishan Tunnel

Brent Hannon/Michelin

MILITARY SIGHTS
Sights are arranged clockwise, starting from the southwest.

Zhaishan Tunnel★★ 翟山坑道
South of Jincheng, on southernmost tip of west side of Kinmen. ⏱*Open daily 8:30am–5pm.* ✆*082-313 241.*
The remarkable Zhaishan Tunnel, carved into the tough granite and gneiss bedrock far beneath the red soil and the pine trees, is a signature attraction.
Soldiers labored five years to chip this underground canal from the tough unyielding rock. They eventually achieved a 375m/1,230ft-long underground canal that is 11m/36ft wide, and big enough to hold a fleet of 40 fast combat boats.
As a military site, Zhaishan Tunnel was a failure: the canal constantly clogged with silt. In the end the military stopped dredging the stubborn waterway and eventually abandoned it in 1986. Twelve years later, the national park administration turned it into a tourist site.
Tourists walk on paths alongside the black waterways, in a dim tunnel that smells of damp salty air, and exits at a hidden harbor on a rocky beach.
In-the-know tourists can also visit one of the seaside tunnel exits. Strewn with "danger land mine" signs warning walkers to stay within the fenced boundaries, a **path** to the left of the main entrance leads past a pleasant **sandy beach** and onward to one of the tunnel mouths.

Here visitors can cross a narrow, railless bridge over a yawning chasm high above the sea, and admire the tunnel from the outside.

Qing Dynasty Command Headquarters 清金門鎮總兵署
53 Wujiang St., Jincheng. ⏱*Open daily 10am–10pm.*
Built in 1682 the impressive Command Headquarters housed a command garrison that once governed the archipelago. The headquarters now features a broad, welcoming courtyard surrounded by

Birdwatching
Restrictions on development due to the military presence—no buildings within 500m/1,640ft of the shoreline, and no buildings over three stories high—have proven beneficial to the island's bird life. Lingshui Lake on Little Kinmen, Lake Zu at Guningtou and the wetlands at the mouth of Wujiang Creek—a favorite gathering spot for cormorants—are among the best birding sites. Nearly half the species on Kinmen are migratory and in all, more than 240 species have been recorded in the 12 islands. Kinmen also boasts 45 species of butterfly; some visitors may also be fortunate enough to see the reclusive Eurasian Otter.

Qing Dynasty Command Headquarters

Brent Hannon/Michelin

hallways; dominating the courtyard are two towering 200-year-old banyan trees.

Inside the hallways lies a wealth of information about the early history of Kinmen, along with models of sailing ships, biographies of the 89 people who governed Kinmen during the Qing dynasty, and other items; much of the information is in English.

Guningtou Battle Museum
古寧頭戰史館

Northern coast of west side of Kinmen.
🕐*Open daily 8:30am–5pm. Film (13min) "Battle of Guningtou" shown at 8:40am, 9:30am, 10:30am, 11:30am, 1:30pm, 2:30pm, 3:30pm & 4:30pm.*

This small museum commemorates the ferocious 56-hour battle that took place here in October 1949, when the advancing Chinese Communist army landed more than 20,000 troops and 200 landing craft on Kinmen, in an attempt to

dislodge the Nationalist army of Chiang Kai-shek. The attention of the Western world was focused on this pivotal cold-war conflict, from which the Nationalists emerged victorious.

English signs provide great detail about the battle, a bonus for history buffs. For other visitors, the highlight might be the **film** called "Battle of Guningtou" filled with the deep rumble of artillery and vivid bomb blasts that offer a one-sided portrayal of the battle. The staged, melodramatic battle scenes lend a dated, nostalgic feel to the film *(in Chinese)*, though maps and arrows make the long-ago action easy to follow.

Ma Shan Observation Post★★
馬山觀測所

Northernmost tip of east side of Kinmen.
🕐*Open daily 8:30am–5pm.*

This tunnel perfectly captures the military flavor of the archipelago. Unlike Zhaishan Tunnel, this tunnel is a pedes-

Little Kinmen's Military Sights

A 15min ferry ride west of Kinmen, the smaller island of Little Kinmen (小金門島) largely duplicates the sights found on Kinmen itself, though on a lesser scale. The **Hujingtou War Museum** (湖井頭戰史館), in the northwest corner, offers exhibits and details about a battle that was fought on Little Kinmen; it also has a bunker with views of mainland China. Of greater interest is **Siwei Tunnel** (九宮坑道), often called Jiugong Tunnel because it is adjacent to the Jiugong ferry dock that connects Little Kinmen to Kinmen. Siwei is a sizable seaside tunnel that can dock large ships; herringbone berths are carved into the resistant rock to house small warships. It is less impressive than Zhaishan Tunnel, but it does serve to further highlight the pervasive military history of the archipelago.

trian tunnel meant to protect soldiers and civilians; its narrowness and low ceilings, combined with its great length, make it all the more impressive.

From a deep safe perch beneath the rock, visitors can gaze at the coast of mainland China just 2.1km/1.3mi away. Far from bristling with armaments, mainland China is filled with high rises and smokestacks, and these days, most Taiwanese view it as a place to visit and perhaps do business. Three powerful telescopes arrayed in the tunnel make the mainland seem even nearer. In the old days, Ma Shan Observation Post also broadcast propaganda through 48 high-powered loudspeakers, advertising the relative prosperity of Taiwan.

The bunker also contains some amusing propaganda, including a display rack full of formerly cutting-edge Taiwanese products from the 1960s and 70s, such as tracksuits, sports shoes and lingerie. These were sent aloft on balloons that were meant to drop in mainland China to illustrate the virtues of Taiwan goods. The balloons often went astray, and according to one story, a balloon laden with lingerie flew all the way to Israel, where its load fell into the arms of a startled housewife.

August 23 Artillery Battle Museum 八二三戰史館
Southcentral portion of Kinmen's east side, near Tai Lake. Open daily 8:30am–5pm.

This museum is dedicated to the six weeks of hell that rained down upon Kinmen beginning on August 23, 1958, when more than 50,000 artillery shells exploded on the little island chain in a two-hour period. Bombardment continued until October 3, before easing up.

The museum has a small theater with a powerful **sound-and-light show** of those bygone times, and includes black-and-white **film** of the actual event, taken by military journalists. The pleasant, park-like **grounds** that surround the museum likewise contain a treasure trove of tanks, aircraft, artillery pieces and other weapons, all intact and accurately labeled.

Stoney Guards
"Wind lions" were erected to guard against strong winds and storms, and to coax the sandy soil into greater fertility. Many of these tall statues are located in grassy fields and on country roads—and wear red capes—adding a fairy-tale appearance to Kinmen.

ADDITIONAL SIGHTS
Sights are arranged geographically, west to east.

Jin He Li Steel Knife Factory★ 金合利製刀廠
On the western outskirts of Jincheng. 236 Boyu Rd. 伯玉路一段236號. Open daily 8:30am–6:30pm. *082-323 999. www.5657.com. tw/maestrowu/index.htm.*
The knives made by local entrepreneur Wu Zhongshan are among the most popular souvenirs on Kinmen. Like his father Wu Zengdong, who founded the famous shop, the younger Wu uses spent artillery shells to make kitchen and souvenir knives, with each propaganda shell making about 60 knives, and each explosive shell about 100. He will pay Kinmen farmers NT$700 for each shell they plow up and bring to him.

His knives are widely imitated, so Wu will make a knife in the presence of any tourist who wants one, and emblazon it with his badge of authenticity. The entrepreneur makes an impressive variety of cutlery, ranging from pocket knives to choppers, cleavers, carving knives and other kitchen utensils.

Gaoliang Distillery★ 金門高粱酒廠
East of Jincheng. 1 Taoyuan Rd., Jinning district of Kinmen. 金寧鄉桃園路1號. *Guided tours Mon–Fri 8am–noon & 1:30pm–5:30pm; 1day advance notice preferred: *082-325 628, ext. 129. Shop and tastings* Open daily 8am–noon & 1:30pm–5:30pm (Sat–Sun until 4:30pm). www.kkl.gov.tw.*
Gaoliang liquor, a fiery distilled drink made from fermented sorghum, is by

Folk Culture Village

Brent Hannon/Michelin

far the most famous product of Kinmen. The local climate and soil are perfect for growing sorghum; the tunnels that honeycomb the islands are used for aging the raw liquor. Those attributes, combined with the unique local water and five decades of experience, produces the world's best gaoliang.

The air in the factory is fragrant with the smell of sorghum. The brick red, peppercorn-sized grains are steamed for 2hrs, then fermented 10 days. Next the sour mash is squeezed, and the liquid is distilled into raw liquor. Like olive oil, the first squeeze is the best. The mash is then re-squeezed and made into a lower-grade liquor. Visitors can drink the raw gaoliang straight from the distilling tubes, if they wish, but even at its best, the liquor has a pungent, resinous flavor that is definitely an acquired taste.

Gaoliang has long been a favorite drink in the military ranks, and it is exceedingly popular on Kinmen. The rules for drinking it are simple: the glass can never be empty, and it can never be placed upside down. No sipping is allowed. A drink of cold oolong tea may be used as a chaser, and most importantly, a toast must never be refused, as it would result in a loss of face. *Gan bei.*

Folk Culture Village
金門民俗文化村
Just south of Ma Shan Observation Post 23 ⟡*Open daily 8:30am–5pm.*
Once a thriving township that was built in the early 1900s, this village was rebuilt beginning in the late 1970s.
It is now a well-preserved outdoor museum of buildings that evoke the life of a bygone era.

Fujian Architecture

By limiting commercial development, Kinmen's military presence preserved many of the traditional houses and clan villages, and today the island has some of the finest examples of southern Fujian architecture in existence. The dwellings are neatly aligned on a north-south axis, with the courtyards and most spacious rooms facing south. Red tiles and "swallowtail" rooflines typify the homes of the well to do. Red tiles were exceptionally rare in the 1800s; they required rapid cooling that was hard to control, so the tiles often came out black. These tiles, many of them imported from mainland China and elsewhere, became symbols of the southern Fujian style.

Some of the houses in Kinmen are unique hybrids, as many residents emigrated to Southeast Asia to make their fortunes. Upon returning home with pockets full of foreign currency, they erected large Western-style mansions, or decorated existing homes with Western touches.

Visitors can walk among the old houses, with their finely crafted granite bases, brick walls and tile roofs. Inside are time-honored layouts, with exterior courtyards embraced on three sides by living quarters. The kitchens, filled with sorghum and rice grinders, feature large iron-topped brick stoves that vent to the outside. Simple spare bedrooms are furnished with canopy beds and lean, curved Qing-era wooden chairs.

ADDRESSES

🏨 STAY

$ Hotel Golden King

金帝大飯店 – *107 Minquan Rd.,* 金城鎮民權路107號 *, Jincheng.* ✆*082-323 366. 28 rooms.* A charming boutique hotel located on the outskirts of Jinsheng, the Jin Di, or Golden King, offers clean, bright rooms with balconies, and a welcoming lobby, which are combined with very low prices and good service. A Chinese breakfast of congee, mantou soft bread, fried noodles, pickles, and boiled eggs is included.

$ Hai Fu Hotel & Suites 海福商務飯店
– *85 Minquan Rd.* 金城鎮民權路85號 *, Jincheng.* ✆*082-322 538, www.haifu. com.tw. 67 rooms.* Neat, clean and well-located, the Hai Fu is the best and most reasonable accommodation on Kinmen. It opened in 2009, and boasts a cozy bar and a colorful lobby lounge, along with cheerful staff. Breakfast included.

$$ Chang Hong Hotel

長鴻商務大飯店 –*101 Cihu Rd., Sec. 1,* 金寧鄉慈湖路一段101號 *, Jin Ning Village.* ✕✆*082-328 811. 86 rooms.* The Chang Hong, a group hotel on the outskirts of Jincheng, albeit with comfortable rooms and modern amenities, has one remarkable highlight: its top-floor restaurant, featuring patio dining and restful views of the surrounding villages and sea. Breakfast included.

$$ King Ring Hotel 金瑞大饭店 –
166 Minquan Rd., 金城鎮民權路166號 *, Jincheng.* ✆*082-323 777. 100 rooms.* Low prices and word-of-mouth reputation make King Ring something of an insiders' secret in Jincheng, and it remains highly popular among budget travelers. Though unimpressive from the outside, glass doors open to reveal reasonable accommodation, nice rooms, pleasant atmosphere, and cheerful staff who can speak some English. Breakfast included.

🍴 EAT

$ Qiao Wei Xiang Café 巧味香小吃店
– *39-41 Luguang Rd. Sec. 1,* 金城 鎮莒光路一段 *, 39-41號, Jincheng.* ✆*082-327 652. Closes 7pm.* This busy cafe specializes in oyster noodles, a classic Taiwanese snack that is made from thin vermicelli noodles, topped with small fresh local oysters, fish sauce, a sprinkling of scallions and cilantro, and sometimes a few shreds of chicken and a bit of chili pepper, which float in a bowl of rich fish broth. All noodles at Qiao Wei Xiang are handmade by the owner-operators, and dumplings, meat-broth noodles, fried noodles, and other famous Taiwanese dishes are also on the menu. **Taiwanese.**

$ Xin Da Miao Kou 新大廟口–
Minquan and Guangqian Rds. 西南門 里公所對面 *, Jincheng.* ✆*082-320-753. Dinner only.* Seafood alfresco is served here under the eaves of a temple and beneath a sweeping banyan tree. The "temple mouth" serves Taiwan-style seafood: pick your fish, squid, cuttlefish and crustaceans from an icy tray at the front. Choose a preparation: steam, stir-fry, soup, or deep fry. The "three cup" squid, made with sesame oil, rice wine, soy sauce and basil, is a highlight. **Taiwanese Seafood.**

🛒 SHOPPING

Besides knives and gaoliang liquor, Kinmen is known for its ceramics made from the superior local clay and feldspar. Most of the souvenirs are in the form of wind lions and various containers for gaoliang liquor. Jincheng abounds in shops selling Kinmen souvenirs.

Mazu★

Authentic and uncrowded—and far from Taiwan Island—this group of 18 granite islands and islets (馬祖列島) is more like a well-preserved corner of eastern Fujian Province on mainland China than a real piece of Taiwan. Like Kinmen, a sister island chain that shares a similar history, it came under the control of Taiwan after the Chinese Civil War in 1949. The tiny 28.52sq km/11sq mi archipelago is similarly riddled with tunnels and filled with military fortifications. Lightly populated and seldom visited, this distant corner of Taiwan has some spectacular seascapes, and a collection of military tunnels that surpasses even the more famous ones on Kinmen.

- ▶ **Population:** 7,000.
- ⏱ **Michelin Map:** p357.
- ℹ **Info:** Matsu National Scenic Area 馬祖國家風景區. 95 Ren'ai Village, Nangan 南竿, 仁愛村95號. Open daily 8am–5:30pm. ℘0836 25630. www.matsu-nsa. gov.tw. Nangan Airport also has a visitor information center: ℘0836-26402.
- ▶ **Location:** Located 10km/6mi off mainland China's coast, Beigan and Nangan are Mazu's two largest islands; Nangan township is the main center of the archipelago.
- 👁 **Don't Miss:** Beihai Tunnel, Andong Tunnel.

COASTAL AREA

Beigan and Nangan are the two largest islands, and lie about 10km/6mi apart, some 8km/5mi to 10km/6mi from the coast of mainland China. Nangan township is the political and cultural center of the archipelago. The surrounding oceans play a large role in the lives of the local residents; Mazu is, in fact, named for the Daoist goddess who is the patron saint and protector of seafarers.

A BIT OF HISTORY

Chinese from Fujian Province began settling on Mazu about 1,000 years ago; the influx increased during times of political turmoil on the mainland. Plagued by pirates, and with little arable land, this remote, rugged corner of the empire was scantly populated, and yielded its fish and farm products grudgingly.

The islands got a boost when the Nationalist army retreated to Mazu at the end of the Chinese Civil War in 1950, and for the next 42 years, thousands of soldiers lived on Mazu's islands, where they chipped out tunnels and built fortifications that have become tourist attractions. There

Beigan Island

Courtesy of Government Information Office

GETTING THERE

BY AIR - Beigan Airport is served by direct flights from Taipei. Nangan Airport is connected by air to Taipei and Taichung. Uni Air (*www.uniair.com.tw*) flies both routes; round-trip fares are NT$1850. Flights to Nangan are more frequent.

BY BOAT - The Tai-Ma Ferry leaves Keelung daily at 11pm, and arrives at Dong Yin around 6am; it continues on to Nangan, arriving about 9am. The schedule can be irregular; contact **Shinhwa Ferry** in Keelung, *02 2424 6868* or in Nangan *0836-26511*; www.shinhwa.com.tw. Tickets between Taipei and Nangan range from NT$400 to NT$1200, depending upon the cabin.

GETTING AROUND

BY CAR - Cars can be rented at Beigan and Nangan airports; prices start at NT$1,800/day. An international driver's license or Taiwan license is required. Taxis can be hired by the hour or day, for about NT$400/hr; call the Lienchiang County Taxi Assn. for details, *0836-22705*.

BY FERRY - Lienchiang Ferry connects Nangan to Beigan. The Nangan-Beigan ferries leave Fuao Harbor on the hour daily 7am–5pm; the Beigan-Nangan ferries leave Baisha Harbor on the half hour, daily 7:30am–5:30pm. The 20min trip costs NT$110. Schedules are cut back during the winter.

Lienchiang ferries also intermittently serve the Nangan-Dong Yin route, depending on weather. Contact the company for updated information. Nangan *0836-22193*; Beigan *0836-55614*.

BY TWO WHEEL - Scooters can be rented, sometimes without an international or Taiwan license, from the shops that ring the airports and ferry harbors. Expect to pay NT$300 to $500/day.

---

is still a heavy military presence here, all the more apparent because of the small local population. The occasional crackle of gunfire heard is soldiers only practicing their marksmanship.

Like Kinmen, Mazu faces an uncertain future. Most residents are older, and the bright lights of Taiwan's big cities continue to attract the youth of Mazu. Caught between two cultures, and far from Taiwan Island, the little island chain abides—farming, fishing, and remaining relatively insulated from the world.

NANGAN ISLAND★ 南竿島
Beihai Tunnel★ 北海坑道
◐ *Southern Nangan, east of the Matsu NSA visitor center.* ◑*Open Mon–Fri 9am–5pm.*

Beihai Tunnel is a seaside military tunnel consisting of a series of high-ceilinged corridors, 640m/2,099ft in total length, that are half-filled with seawater and meant for hiding gunboats; the main canal has bays for parking small warships.

Construction of the tunnel began in 1968 and was finished three years later, using hand tools rather than explosives.

A walk through this 700m/2,296ft underground cave delivers the full martial experience of Mazu. Tourists walk alongside the dark water, deep inside the tunnel, until a tiny patch of daylight becomes visible.

Niujiao Village★ 牛角村
◐ *Northeast Nangan Island, northwest of the airport.*

This seaside village, now mostly abandoned, neatly encapsulates the changing fortunes of the residents of Mazu.

In the past it was a thriving fishing village, as residents plied the nearby waters and harvested large numbers of shrimp, clams, eels, crabs, yellow croaker and other fish.

After the fishery declined, the village tried to re-create itself as a tourist attraction; many of the buildings and pathways have been restored to their traditional appearance, but beyond a

Chinese Crested Tern

The boat ride between Nangan and Beigan offers an exceptional opportunity to see one of the world's rarest birds, the Chinese Crested Tern (Thalasseus bernsteini). Once believed to be extinct, it was rediscovered in 1999 on a rocky Mazu islet by a documentary filmmaker. Prior to 1999 there had been only five previous confirmed sightings of this bird, and the revelation that four adult pairs and seven fledglings were alive on Mazu electrified the birding world. Soon thereafter, eight of the tiny islets were established as protected areas for the terns. Visitors cannot set foot on the islands, but they can approach in boats, stop their engines and observe the birds through binoculars. It isn't easy: the Chinese Crested Tern dwells among huge flocks of Greater Crested Terns, and you're looking for a bird with a black beak, not a yellow beak, through shaky binoculars on a rocking boat. Birdwatchers come from around the world to this remote corner of Taiwan just to catch a glimpse of these legendary birds.

restaurant and a nearby outdoor bar, the village is still very quiet.

The houses themselves are designed to protect against the harsh environment: the **roof tiles** are weighted with stones to prevent them from blowing off, and they do not have overhanging eaves, which would also catch the onshore winds. **Stone walls** laid in herringbone patterns provide additional buttressing. To prevent dampness, and to provide views of the sea, most of the dwellings are two stories high.

Iron Fort 鐵堡

❯ Southwest Nangan Island, west of Matsu NSA visitor center.

More than anything else, this small fort sitting atop a granite outcrop that

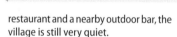
Iron Fort

stretches into a calm bay serves to illuminate the horrors of war.

The fort formerly housed marine amphibious units, and sentry posts, dog kennels, sniper slots and sleeping quarters comprise most of the displays. The dogs were there to warn sleeping soldiers of the approach of the enemy, but many soldiers on both sides were killed during night-time stealth attacks. The name Iron Fort derives from its impregnability, rather than any iron features, since they would definitely not have withstood the salty sea.

BEIGAN ISLAND★ 北竿島

❯ Accessible by ferry from Nangan's Fuao Harbor.

About 5km/3mi north of Nangan (bei means north, nan means south) is its sister island of Beigan, and the two crescent-shaped land masses sit in the sea like a pair of oracle blocks on a temple floor.

Beigan is quieter than Nangan, but it shares the same coastal scenery, military installations and village architecture. The island also features a hillside old-growth forest that makes a pleasant walk to **Qinbi Village** (芹壁村), a series of stone houses lying in parallel rows. Beigan Island, especially Qinbi Village, has some of the world's best-preserved eastern Fujian architecture. The islanders cut their stones from the local granite, using a curved cutting style that is distinct from the square stones used in southern Fujian architecture.

Courtesy of Government Information Office

Perched on a steep green hillside, the **granite houses** have narrow openings that protected the villagers from both strong winds and pirates.

DONG YIN ISLAND★★ 東引島
▶ *Accessible by ferry from Nangan's Fuao Harbor.*

This remote outpost, with its high cliffs of granite and rocky spurs jutting into the surrounding blue waters, is a place of rare natural beauty far off the beaten tourist track. Reachable only by a long boat trip, the third-largest island in Mazu is lightly populated, but has some attractions of interest to tourists.

One of the most intriguing sites is a natural formation called **yi xian tian**, which literally means "strip of sky." This unique natural feature is a thin gap between two giant blocks of granite, with a line of sky visible high above. The sea below is a foaming strip of whitewater, and the sky above looks like a bright blue ribbon framed by the high cliffs of vertical, unyielding rock.

Another Dong Yin attraction is the superb **Andong Tunnel**★★ (安東坑道), a massive tube that was hacked out of the hard granite by the Taiwanese military. Unlike the sea level tunnels on Kinmen and on the other Mazu islands, Andong Tunnel has various lookouts that exit onto high cliff faces that were once used for gun emplacements, but are now tourist sites. These high vistas provide excellent **views**★★ of the granite cliffs, green hills and blue water that comprise the island's spectacular scenery.

Another unspoiled sight is **Dongyong Lighthouse** (東湧燈塔), a snow-white tower originally built by the British to help guide them to the coast of China; it sits serenely above the restless blue sea, providing a restful **view** that is lonely and inspiring. Only a few fortunate tourists make the lengthy boat trip to Dong Yin each year, where they find an island, remote as it is, that is unspoiled and completely natural.

Cuisine

The main ingredients of Eastern Fujian cuisine are seafood, particularly shellfish. The key flavor is that of fermented red rice left over from making *lao jiu* (old wine) from glutinous rice. The lao jiu itself is sweet, smoky, and medicinal. The pork is a highlight; tender pieces of crisp, fried pork, coated in tangy, salty red-rice sauce. Another signature dish is *jiguang* cake. These are simple, donut-shaped pieces of bread, coated with sesame seeds; they look like bagels but are crisper and tastier. Fish ball soup, mussels, fried rice, steamed shrimp, and potato dumpling soup are also common and delicious, and are often "red cooked" with the fermented rice sauce.

ADDRESSES

🛏 STAY

$$ Coast of the Dawn Hotel – 日光海岸海景旅館. *6 Ren'ai Village, Nangan.* 馬祖南竿鄉仁愛村6號. ✈🔋📶 ☎0836-26 666. *www.coasthotel.com.tw/index-2. html. 13 rooms.* This elegant, low-rise hotel combines Zen styling with large French picture windows that display sweeping views of the surrounding seas. A small **restaurant ($$)** with similarly fine views serves dinner and breakfast, and an on-site spa adds to the aura of comfort.

$$ Shen Nong Hotel 神農山莊 – *84-2 Qing Shui Village,* 馬祖南竿鄉清水村84-2號, *Nangan Island.* ☎0836-26 333. The best large hotel in Mazu has a big business-style lobby, a cozy coffee shop that serves breakfast (included) and other meals, plus a karaoke bar and conference room. The rooms come in five price ranges; those on the upper floors offer views of the jungle-clad granite hills and rocky harbors that are so typical of Mazu. The Shen Nong is a bit remote, but Nangan is so small that it doesn't really matter. Like all hotels on Mazu, prices rise on weekends and during holidays. Breakfast included.

INDEX

INDEX

INDEX

INDEX

INDEX

🍴/EAT

INDEX

MAPS AND PLANS

MAP LEGEND

★★★ **Highly recommended**
★★ **Recommended**
★ **Interesting**

Sight symbols

━━●━━━━━━ Recommended itineraries with departure point

✚ ⚑ ⊠ Church, chapel – Synagogue   ▬ Building described

○ Town described   ▭ Other building

B Sight letter reference   ▪ Small building, statue

■ ▲ Other points of interest   ◉ ⁘ Fountain – Ruins

✕ ⌒ Mine – Cave   🛈 Visitor information

🗼 ⚓ Windmill – Lighthouse   ⬭ ⚓ Ship – Shipwreck

☆ ⛪ Fort – Mission   ☀ Ⅶ Panorama – View

Other symbols

═══════ Highway, bridge   ═══════ Major city thoroughfare

▬▬▬▬ Toll highway, interchange   ═══════ City street with median

════════ Divided highway   ◄─── One-way street

━━━━━ Major, minor route   ═══════ Pedestrian Street

↘ 40 ↙ Distance in miles   ⇥⋯⇤ Tunnel

2149 ⟶ Pass, elevation (feet)   ┅┅┅╪ Steps – Gate

△ 6288 Mtn. peak, elevation (feet)   🅿 Parking

✈ ✦ Airport – Airfield   ✉ Main post office

⛴ Ferry: Cars and passengers   ✚ Hospital

⛴ Ferry: Passengers only   🚆 🚍 Train station – Bus station

←⟨←▱ Waterfall – Lock – Dam   ● Subway station

─··─··─ International boundary   ⌂ Observatory

────── State boundary,   ⊞ Cemetery
         provincial boundary
🍇 Winery   ⊠ Swamp

Recreation

■-○-○-○-○-■ Gondola, chairlift   (⊂ ⊃) ▶ Stadium – Golf course

🚂 Tourist or steam railway   ⊕ Park, garden

⛵ ⚓ Harbor, lake cruise – Marina   ◉ Wildlife reserve

🏄 🏄 Surfing – Windsurfing   ◎ Wildlife/Safari park, zoo

🤿 🛶 Diving – Kayaking   ────── Walking path, trail

⛷ ⛷ Ski area – Cross-country skiing   🚶 Hiking trail

**You know
the Green Guide**

**...Do you really
know MICHELIN?**

• Data 31/12/2009

The world No.1 in tires
with 16.3% of the market

A business presence in over **170 countries**

A manufacturing footprint
at the heart of markets

In 2009 **72** industrial sites in **19** countries produced:

- **150** million tires
- **10** million maps and guides

Highly international **teams**

Over **109 200** employees* from all cultures on all continents
including **6 000** people employed in R&D centers
in Europe, the US and Asia.

*102 692 full-time equivalent staff

The Michelin Group
at a glance

Michelin
competes

At the end of 2009

Le Mans 24-hour race
12 consecutive years of victories

Endurance 2009
- 6 victories on 6 stages
in Le Mans Series
- 12 victories on 12 stages
in American Le Mans Series

Paris-Dakar
Since the beginning of the event,
the Michelin group has won
in all categories

Moto endurance
2009 World Champion

Trial
Every World Champion title
since 1981 (except 1992)

Michelin, established close to its customers

○ **72 plants in 19 countries**

- Algeria
- Brazil
- Canada
- China
- Colombia
- France
- Germany

- Hungary
- Italy
- Japan
- Mexico
- Poland
- Romania
- Russia

- Serbia
- Spain
- Thailand
- UK
- USA

● **A Technology Center spread over 3 continents**

- Asia
- Europe
- North America

○ **Natural rubber plantations**

- Brazil

Our mission

To make a sustainable contribution to progress in the mobility of goods and people by enhancing freedom of movement, safety, efficiency and the pleasure of travelling.

Michelin committed to environmental-friendliness

Michelin, world leader in low rolling resistance tires, actively reduces fuel consumption and vehicle gas emission.

For its products, Michelin develops state-of-the-art technologies in order to:
- Reduce fuel consumption, while improving overall tire performance.
- Increase life cycle to reduce the number of tires to be processed at the end of their useful lives;
- Use raw materials which have a low impact on the environment.

Furthermore, at the end of 2008, 99.5% of tire production in volume was carried out in ISO 14001* certified plants.

Michelin is committed to implementing recycling channels for end-of-life tires.

*environmental certification

**Passenger Car
Light Truck**

Truck

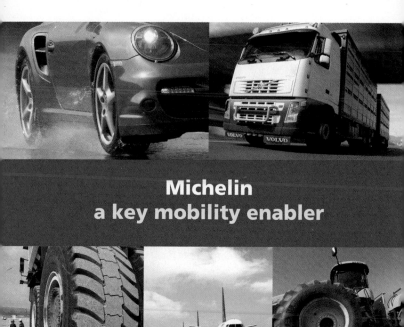

Michelin
a key mobility enabler

Earthmover

Aircraft

Agricultural

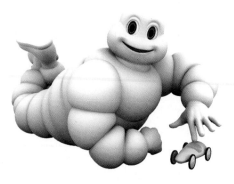

Two-wheel

Distribution

Partnered with vehicle manufacturers, in tune with users,
active in competition and in all the distribution channels,
Michelinis continually innovating to promote mobility today
and to invent that of tomorrow.

**Maps and
Guides**

ViaMichelin,
travel
assistance
services

**Michelin
Lifestyle,**
for your travel
accessories

MICHELIN
plays on balanced performance

- ● **Long tire life**
- ● **Fuel savings**
- ○ **Safety on the road**

... MICHELIN tires provide you with the best performance, without making a single sacrifice.

The MICHELIN tire pure technology

① Tread
A thick layer of rubber provides contact with the ground. It has to channel water away and last as long as possible.

② Crown plies
This double or triple reinforced belt has both vertical flexibility and high lateral rigidity. It provides the steering capacity.

③ Sidewalls
These cover and protect the textile casing whose role is to attach the tire tread to the wheel rim.

④ Bead area for attachment to the rim
Its internal bead wire clamps the tire firmly against the wheel rim.

⑤ Inner liner
This makes the tire almost totally impermeable and maintains the correct inflation pressure.

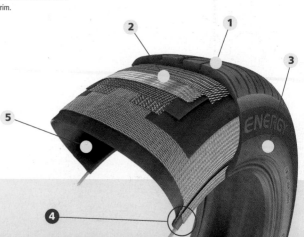

Heed
the MICHELIN Man's advice

To improve safety:

- I drive with the correct tire pressure
- I check the tire pressure every month
- I have my car regularly serviced
- I regularly check the appearance of my tires (wear, deformation)
- I am responsive behind the wheel
- I change my tires according to the season

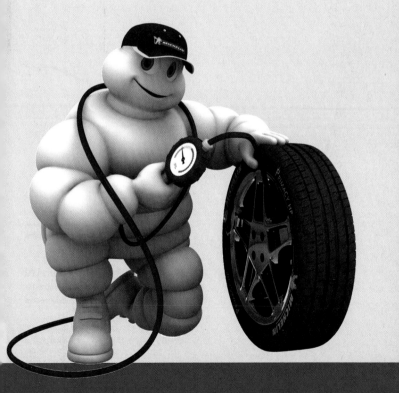

www.michelin.com
www.michelin.(your country extension – e.g. .fr for France)

Michelin Apa Publications Ltd

A joint venture between Michelin and Langenscheidt

58 Borough High Street, London SE1 1XF, United Kingdom

No part of this publication may be reproduced in any form
without the prior permission of the publisher.

© 2011 Michelin Apa Publications Ltd
ISBN 978-1-907099-26-7
Printed: January 2011
Printed and bound in Germany